Numbers, Hypotheses & Conclusions

A course in Statistics for the Social Sciences

Editors:
Colin Tredoux (University of Cape Town)
Kevin Durrheim (University of Natal)

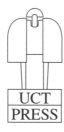

UCT
PRESS

Numbers, Hypotheses & Conclusions: A Course in Statistics for the Social Sciences

© UCT Press, 2002
PO Box 24309
Lansdowne 7779

First published 2002

Revised reprint 2005
Reprinted 2006
Reprinted 2007
Reprinted 2008

ISBN 1-919713-31-X
ISBN 978-1-919713-31-1

Copy editing: Ann Kantey, Cape Town
Proofreading: Alex Potter of FPP Productions, Hermanus
DTP: RHT desktop publishing cc, Durbanville
Cover design: Eugene Badenhorst of The Pumphaus Design Studio cc, Cape Town
Indexing: Jan Schaafsma
Printing and binding: Mills Litho

Set in Palatino and Rotis Semi Sans

The authors and publisher have made every effort to obtain permission for and acknowledge the use of copyright material. Should any infringement of copyright have occurred, please contact the publisher and every effort will be made to rectify omissions or errors, in the event of a reprint or new edition.

Contents

Preface

This book is the core text for a tutorial programme in statistics for social science and humanities students. Although it can be used as a self-sufficient introduction to statistics, we recommend that it be used alongside a structured set of exercises, worked examples, and activities. An excellent collection of support materials is available on a course web page (http://www.uct.ac.za/depts/psychology/plato/numbers/) and on the accompanying CD.

The tutorial programme is aimed at a diverse group of disciplines. Students of Psychology, Sociology, Social Work, Anthropology, Education, and Political Studies – indeed, all students in the social sciences - will be able to use this book. Whatever your area of study, we hope that it will stimulate you, teach you, tease you, and promote you to the rank of inveterate inquirer. The skills we aim to impart are central to any modern knowledge-based enterprise. They are taught all over the world in programmes that are serious about research, and thus provide a universal language for the social sciences. More than that, they underpin successful theory and application in almost every field of enquiry in the social sciences. Indeed, expertise in quantitative methods is one of the strongest transferable skills taught in the social sciences, and many employers demand some level of competence in this area.

Social science students differ in terms of their preparation for courses in quantitative methods. They come from a diversity of disciplines and backgrounds. This means that there will also be differences in their level of mathematics proficiency. We acknowledge this, and see it as a challenge. For this reason, we have included a substantial collection of revision material in the appendices and on the accompanying CD. All students entering a course in quantitative methods will benefit by revising their school mathematics with this material.

Our emphasis in the course, as a whole, is on statistical concepts and techniques. We promote the use of simple mathematical manipulations and calculations to aid understanding. It is important for you to know how to do some basic statistical calculations, and we encourage you to improve your skills no matter what your starting level of proficiency is. In the modern world, however, there are many aids to the error-prone activity of statistical computation, and we specifically show you how to use calculators, spreadsheet programs, and statistical software packages. In the early tutorials, we emphasise calculator and spreadsheet work, and in later tutorials we assume the availability of a statistical package. We have provided material showing you how to use SPSS® for particular statistical analyses, but you could also use a package like STATISTCA, and we have included extensive support material for that package in the accompanying CD.

We have tried to enhance your experience in this text by the extensive preparation of activities, interest boxes, application boxes, graphic material, exercises, worked solutions to problems, and Internet links and resources. You should use these to your advantage. We suggest that you keep a calculator at hand whenever you read the text, and complete the activities and exercises. When you have finished studying the text, we strongly recommend that you spend some time browsing the CD for additional worked examples, exercises, and worked solutions. We also encourage you to use the Internet links, as there are many interactive web sites that demonstrate statistical concepts and techniques in an interactive manner.

Colin Tredoux and Kevin Durrheim, March 2002

Acknowledgements

We would like to acknowledge the following people for support and guidance during the long process of writing and editing the book:

- Diane Gascoigne, Aimée Tredoux, and Aleks Durrheim.
- Solani Ngobeni, Sandie Vahl, Fiona Wakelin and Glenda Younge from University of Cape Town Press.
- Lance Lachenicht, Martin Terre Blanche, David Nunez, Judy Austin, Gillian Finchilescu and Ingrid Palmary, all contributors to this book.

List of Contributors

Judy Austin, Department of Psychology, University of Natal

Kevin Durrheim, Department of Psychology, University of Natal

Gillian Finchilescu, Department of Psychology, University of Cape Town

Lance Lachenicht, Department of Psychology, University of Cape Town

David Nunez, Department of Psychology, University of Cape Town

Ingrid Palmary, Department of Psychology, University of Natal

Martin Terre Blanche, Department of Psychology, University of South Africa

Colin Tredoux, Department of Psychology, University of Cape Town

Glossary of Symbols

α	Alpha (Type I error rate)
β	Beta (Type II error rate)
δ	Delta, a parameter used to determine power of a statistical test
μ	Mu, the population mean
ρ	Rho, the population correlation coefficient
σ	Sigma (lower case), the population standard deviation
Σ	Sigma (upper case), the arithmetic summation operator
χ^2	Chi-square statistic, or Chi-square distribution
η^2	Eta-square, a measure of effect size
ϕ^2	Phi square, the mean square contingency coefficient
σ^2	Sigma square, the population variance
ϕ_c	Cramer's V, a measure of effect size in contingency table analysis
a	The intercept coefficient in regression analysis
b	The slope coefficient in regression analysis
D	Difference between two scores
d	Effect size
E	Expected frequency
F	F distribution, or F ratio
k	Number of groups in a design
MS	Mean Square
N	Population size
n	Sample size
O	Observed frequency
p	Probability
Q	Tukey's Q statistic (studentized range statistic)
R	Multiple regression coefficient
r	The Pearson product moment correlation coefficient
r^2	Square of r; coefficient of determination
R^2	Square of the multiple regression coefficient; degree of linear model fit
r_s	Spearman's rank correlation coefficient
s^2	Sample variance
$S_{\bar{x}}^2$	Standard error of the mean
SS	Sums of squares
t	The t statistic, used to test hypotheses about mean differences; also the t probability distribution
$\bar{x}$	Sample mean
y′	y prime, the predicted score in a regression equation
z	Standard normal deviate

Section 1

Statistics

TUTORIAL

1

Numbers, variables, and measures

Colin Tredoux

> After studying this tutorial, you should be able to:
> - List some of the key functions served by quantitative methods in the social sciences.
> - Distinguish probabilistic and deterministic forms of inductive reasoning.
> - Define a number of basic terms including *variable*, *statistic*, and *parameter*.
> - Distinguish descriptive and inferential statistical methods.
> - Identify some of the arguments against the use of quantitative methods.

As you pick up this text and start to read it, you may be wondering how you managed to get yourself into this predicament. After all, many social science students choose the social sciences to escape the terrors and tribulations of mathematics and numbers. You now find that you are again faced with x and y, Σ and σ, and long strings of numbers. Why do you have to do this? Surely there is no point in trying to measure social phenomena? We all know the social world is inherently slippery, and defies exact representation. Surely this is a mistaken ambition?

You are not alone in this point of view. A number of theorists and writers have put formidable reputations on the line in arguing that quantification and quantitative methods have no place in social science (Hornstein, 1988). Writing over 100 years ago, William

James ridiculed the attempts by psychologists to quantify sensation and perception:

> To introspection, our feeling of pink is surely not a portion of our feeling of scarlet; nor does the light of an electric arc seem to contain that of a tallow candle in itself (cited in Hornstein, 1991, p. 45).

If you sympathise with this point of view, the bad news is that it has lost the battle for sovereignty in the social sciences. Most social sciences make extensive use of quantitative methods, and students in these disciplines typically receive training in these methods from their undergraduate years all the way to doctoral level. A cursory flip through the current periodical holdings of any academic library will convince you of the important place these methods have. Of course, it may indeed be the case that quantification is misguided, and even non-rational (cf. Hornstein, 1991). We cannot defend quantification against these charges, but we would like to persuade you here that there are palpable advantages to quantification. Quantitative methods provide powerful academic and intellectual possibilities, and to jettison them is akin to refusing to use electric lights because no-one has offered a satisfactory theory of electricity.

Most social sciences make extensive use of quantitative methods.

The advantages of quantitative methods

What advantages do quantitative methods confer on us? There are a great many, which we will summarise as *efficiency*, *approximation* (or *modelling)* and *a powerful language.*

Table 1.1 SA Census 1996: Country of birth by population group

	African/Black	Coloured	Indian/Asian	White	Other	TOTAL
South Africa	30 148 148	3 502 353	1 007 865	3 845 099	344 946	38 848 411
SADC countries	413 133	7 792	2 140	2 140	104 480	529 685
Rest of Africa	7 395	329	657	11 358	296	20 035
Europe	4 661	529	783	209 144	2 081	217 198
Asia	405	377	17 888	9 194	691	28 555
North America	362	107	122	4 972	120	5 683
Central and South America	1 772	138	204	6 476	99	8 689
Australia and New Zealand	40	28	34	3 725	60	3 887
Unspecified/Other	74 420	4 522	5 670	55 682	4 162	144 456
TOTAL	30 651 337	3 516 175	1 035 363	4 248 179	355 544	39 806 598

Table reproduced from an Internet page of the South African Statistical Services (http://www.statssa.gov.za/Publications/Census%20summary)

Efficiency

Using numbers to communicate information is often extremely efficient. Every ten years or so, South Africa has a national census, in which information is collected about its inhabitants. Since there are approximately 40 000 000 inhabitants, you will appreciate the enormous amount of work and information that the numerical display in Table 1.1 summarises. (You may also notice how the data implicitly contradicts the notion that South Africa is being swamped by a tide of black immigration from other African countries.)

A non-quantitative approach would have struggled enormously to represent the data in Table 1.1. Not the least of the concerns would have been adequate summary concepts or descriptors. In the case of quantitative research, on the other hand, there is a well-developed theory of summary indicators, and a well-developed technology to support these (e.g. computer software packages).

Activity 1.1

Examine Table 1.1 carefully. Do you see any interesting patterns? Try to describe these without using any summary statistics (e.g. totals or averages), and without using any *symbols* that represent numbers (i.e. you can write 'one', but not '1').

Approximation/modelling

Quantitative techniques are often excellent at representing phenomena in the world, and in that respect they present us with wonderful opportunities for complex study of the phenomena. What dimensions do you think humans use for making similarity judgements of faces?

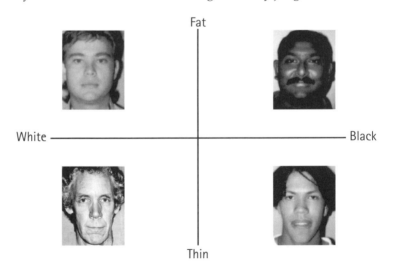

Figure 1.1 A spatial model for understanding human similarity judgements of faces

Simply asking people how they make similarity judgements produces a bewildering variety of responses. However, a quantitative technique called *multidimensional scaling* provides a spatial model in which we can represent each dimension of similarity as an axis, and each face as a point in the intersection space of these axes. Figure 1.1 shows what a two-dimensional example of such a model might look like.

This *modelling* allows us to infer what the important dimensions of similarity judgements of faces are. If we had to sort through a long set of verbal descriptions, it would take us a very long time, and it is doubtful that we would arrive at the *dimensions* as clearly as we can with the quantitative technique in question.

A powerful language

Perhaps the best thing about quantitative techniques is that there is already an established theory and practice. Mathematicians, statisticians, and (latterly) social scientists have spent many hundreds of years developing and refining a powerful quantitative *language*. When we use quantitative techniques we adopt this language, and save ourselves a few centuries of work. This language is powerful, and can make us highly competent in our interactions with the physical world.

Three advantages of quantitative methods:
1. *Efficiency of communication*
2. *Modelling of real-world phenomena*
3. *A powerful and centuries-old language*

Imagine a game of dice on the street corner. Sipho is betting R10 that 5 will come up on the next throw of a single die and Malungisa will pay him R30 if it does. Probability theory tells us that the chance of the 5 coming up on the next throw is 1/6, and that the expected gain in this game for Sipho is –R3.33 per roll of the die. The game of dice can be understood in terms of a 'language of probability', and this allows those who understand it considerable opportunity. Malungisa will be a rich man if he continues to entice players like Sipho into the game.

Consider another everyday situation where quantification is powerful. Activity 1.2 shows a weather forecast map. By looking at it very briefly, you will be able to decide:
1. whether to take an umbrella to college,
2. whether you should nail your roof down, and
3. whether you need to water your vegetable plants tomorrow.

All this information is powerfully and effectively conveyed by numbers, and their position in the two-dimensional diagram.

So, we have seen that quantitative methods are *efficient*, that they provide useful *models* of phenomena, and that they provide us with *a powerful language*. Is this enough to convince us that we should be using them in the social sciences? Perhaps not, but let us reflect for a moment on where we find quantitative methods in the world

Activity 1.2

Inspect the following weather forecast, and see whether you can answer the questions below just from the numbers you see displayed on the map. Assume the forecast is for tomorrow. Justify your answers.

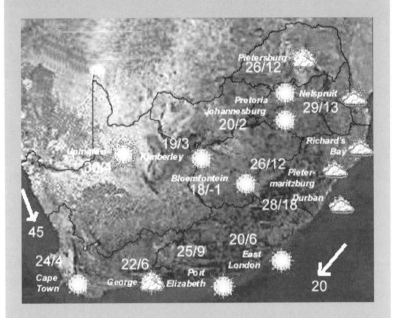

a) Is it likely that you will you need a jersey if you are in Pieter-maritzburg at midday?
b) Would it be a good idea to go kite-flying in Cape Town?
c) Does the pattern shown here suggest summer or winter?
d) If you live in Bloemfontein, should you take precautions against your water pipes bursting?

around us. Clearly, a number of professions depend on them: accountants, actuaries, and engineers make no secret of this, and, less obviously, architects and graphic designers. But there are many other, more apparently non-technical occupations that do so too. Consider the woman who owns the gambling casino down the road. Her livelihood depends on the types of quantitative performance outlined in the example of the game of dice. What about carpenters? Carpentry depends in a fundamental sense on measurement and quantification, and carpenters use quantitative devices ranging from finely graded rules and set squares to sliding angle bevels.

Now think more generally about your everyday life. You probably visit a shop of some kind every day. Shops are highly quantified, and your interaction with them is fundamentally of a quantitative kind: you pay some money to the shop, which has quantified the amount of profit it will take, the amount it will have to pay over to revenue services, and the amount it owes for store rental and salaries. In fact, we are completely embedded in a monetary economy, in which the house we live in, the food we eat, and perhaps even the thoughts that rush ceaselessly in our heads have particular value. This monetary economy brings enormous flexibility to the social exchange that appears to be inherent in human societies.

Still not convinced? Let us try one more argument. Many biologists and physiological psychologists now argue that some kind of quantitative sense is native to the human species. In a recent book entitled *What Counts: How Every Brain is Hard-wired for Math*, Butterworth (1999) summarises evidence suggesting that the human brain has a 'number module' – a specialised circuitry that enables us to categorise objects in terms of numerosity. We recognise and distinguish objects in terms of numerosity (without being taught the meaning of number) in an automatic and involuntary way, just as we automatically and involuntarily see colours. In this way of looking at things, quantification and quantitative thinking is inescapable, and at home in the social sciences as it is in your kitchen.

Functions of quantification

There are a number of ways in which quantitative methods can function within an academic discipline. We saw some of these in the previous section, but it is useful to distinguish at a higher level of abstraction two general kinds of functions that quantification can support.

In the first place, quantification can serve an infrastructural or administrative function. This is the sense in which societies are embedded in a monetary economy, and much of the business of the society has a structure within this economy. It is as if monetary quantification has built a vast set of roads, highways, ramps, and exits, and the society moves backwards and forwards on the roads, just as it does on physical transport roads. As you sit reading this tutorial, for example, the electric light that helps you read is having its output numerically measured (kw/h) by your electricity supplier, and this is in turn being transformed into an amount of money that you will pay over to the supplier. A portion of the money paid over by you may be paid over in turn to the company that produces the electricity at source, say a hydro-electric power station in a foreign country, and at the end of the financial year that company will declare the amount of foreign revenue. This amount will in turn be subsumed into a government report on foreign trade, and will show up again in a number of international-level economic reports. Ultimately, the amount of electricity you consumed reading this paragraph will constitute a (tiny) portion of the index known as global economic growth, which measures by how much the planet's economic activity has increased or decreased. This *infrastructural function* is certainly important, but it is not of central interest to us in this text.

Activity 1.3

Keep a diary or notebook with you for a day, and make a record of instances where you have to deal with numbers as part of your everyday life. Record as many instances as you can. Try to list for each instance what function the quantification serves.

Functions of quantification:
1. *Administrative/ infrastructural (e.g. a monetary economy)*
2. *Aids to argument and reasoning*

Secondly, quantitative methods can function as *evidentiary* aids or systems. In other words, they can provide evidence for an argument, or against it. In addition, they frequently have deductive and inductive devices or mechanisms that can be used to draw conclusions and inferences. It is in this second sense that quantification is of most interest to us in the social sciences. For example, a key issue in health research around HIV is the transmission of HIV between mother and child from breastfeeding. Quantitative research tells us that the risk of transmission is very high, and that anti-retroviral drugs may decrease this risk substantially. In order to draw this conclusion, researchers carefully quantified physiological measures (e.g. T-helper cell responses), and used a research design that allowed them to use inferential statistical methods to determine whether infants administered anti-retroviral treatment showed lower rates of HIV infection than infants not administered anti-retroviral treatment. (Interestingly, a key figure in this research is a South African researcher, Louise Kuhn (Kuhn *et al.*, 2000), who was trained as a social scientist.)

Although quantitative methods are often thought of as the tools of *deterministic* sciences, such as mechanical physics and chemistry, a whole branch of mathematics is devoted to *probabilistic* methods. These methods form the basis for most quantitative inquiry in the social sciences. When we reason probabilistically, we make generalisations and draw conclusions that are supported with probability estimates, as opposed to the law-like statements and predictions we make in deterministic reasoning. For example, we say that we are 95% confident that the average income for social science graduates five years after graduation is between R85 000 and R115 000 per annum. We do not say that we are certain of this, but we express probabilistically defined confidence in it. On the other hand, if we are reasoning deterministically, we say things like 'The force exerted by an object is the product of its mass and its acceleration', and if we have precise estimates of the mass and acceleration, we make a precise prediction.

Sometimes the probabilistic methods available to us can be used to create models so close to the phenomenon that we wish to study that the move from model to phenomenon to conclusion is relatively effortless. Imagine that we are called on to evaluate a police line-up from which an identification has been used as evidence against an accused person. Two out of fifteen witnesses identified the accused person from a line-up that consisted of the suspect and five innocent police officers. One way of reasoning about the rate of identification is to treat the line-up as a die-tossing experiment: the die has six numbered sides (each number corresponds to a member of the parade), and the die is tossed fifteen times (fifteen witnesses). We can use a well-known probability method here (the binomial distribution) to calculate the probability that two of fifteen witnesses who were merely guessing randomly could have identified the suspect. This is worth knowing, as a kind of baseline estimate of the information value of the identifications. The probability turns out to be approximately 0.47. In other words, there is a one in two chance that two (or fewer) witnesses guessing randomly would have chosen the suspect. This is surely not good evidence against the suspect?

Probabilistic methods form the basis for most quantitative inquiry in the social sciences.

Activity 1.4

Read through some back copies of your local newspaper and try to find instances where numbers have been used to support an argument. Try to categorise the ways in which they have been used.

Much of the time, however, the quantitative methods we use do not directly fit the questions we study, and we rely on theorems to justify the application of the methods. When we evaluate the results of a psychotherapy programme, or an AIDS counselling programme, for example, we will often use a theorem called the *Central Limit Theorem*, and a host of its derivatives, to decide whether the treatment is effective.

Some basic concepts

In order to prepare for material in later tutorials, it is useful to introduce some basic concepts.

Variables and constants

The first step in using a quantitative language is to convert objects or entities in the real world into symbols and concepts of the language. Thus, when we measure something like height, we talk about height as being a *variable*, and we typically symbolise it in some way, e.g. x. Since we will collect height measures from a

Variables are measured entities (or attributes of entities) that can take on different values, e.g. height, weight.

number of different people, we can expect these measures to *vary*, that is to take on different values. For this reason, we call height a variable, and we use a subscript or index variable to identify particular scores on that variable. Thus, if we collect 5 measures of height, the first score is x_1, the second is x_2, the third is x_3, etc. Often the subscript is implicit, and we will write x = {1.9, 1.5, 1.7, 1.6, 1.8}, meaning $x_1 = 1.9$, $x_2 = 1.5$, etc.

Constants are quantities that do not change, but always have the same value, e.g. the speed of light.

When we deal with a quantity that does not change, but always has the same value, we refer to it as a *constant*, e.g. the speed of light.

Continuous vs discrete variables/measures

Continuous measures can take any value within the range defined as valid for a particular variable.

Many variables and constants are measured on *continuous* scales, which is to say that they can take any value in a defined range. Measures of height and weight are obvious examples: given a sufficiently accurate scale, and considerable patience, you can measure out 30 grams of Beluga caviar per dinner guest, or 30.1 grams – or any amount again between these points. It is in this sense of covering all possible values within a defined range that the word continuous is used.

Discrete measures can take only certain values within a range, e.g. 1, 2, 3, but not 1.5, 2.5.

Discrete variables, on the other hand, can take only certain values. A variable that records the order in which athletes finish the 100-metre egg-and-spoon race, for instance, can only take the values 1, 2, 3, etc. It is not possible to finish in 3.25th place. Similarly, a variable that records gender by assigning 1 to males and 2 to females excludes all other values – it is not possible to receive a score of 1.5. Discrete variables are also known as *categorical* variables.

Activity 1.5

Decide whether each of the following measures is a *variable* or a *constant*, and whether it is *continuous* or *discrete*:
a) the time taken to complete a marathon race
b) the weight of the moon
c) the troy ounce weight of a kilogram of gold
d) the HIV status (+ or –) of an individual
e) the number of judges in the Cape High Court.

The difference between these two classes of variables or measures is important. For our purposes, recognising whether a measure is continuous or discrete will help us decide which kind of statistical test to use. When we collect data on continuous variables (e.g. birthweight, caloric consumption per day), we will use a set of techniques that exploit this continuous nature (e.g. *t*-tests, ANOVA), and when we collect data on discrete variables (e.g. votes for a political party, choice of spread for a sandwich), we will use a quite different set of techniques (e.g. χ^2, Mann-Whitney). Tests for use on continuous data are usually not appropriate for categorical data, and vice versa.

Nominal, ordinal, interval, and ratio variables

Another way of distinguishing between different kinds of variables is in terms of the mathematical properties of the numbers that the variables can assume. We can use the numbers 1 and 2 to represent males and females, to represent the individuals who came first and second in an exam, or to represent the actual marks the two very weak students got in an exam. In each of these cases, the numbers have different mathematical properties. Mathematically, it is perfectly legitimate to subtract 1 from 2 to get 1 (i.e. $2 - 1 = 1$), but it is absurd to say that subtracting a female (1) from a male (2) results in a female (1). We say that the variables are measured on different *scales of measurement*. It is conventional to distinguish between four scales (or levels) of measurement: nominal, ordinal, interval, and ratio.

Nominal variables indicate only that there is a difference between categories of objects, persons, or characteristics. Numbers are used here as labels to distinguish one category from another. For example, numbers can be used as category labels to distinguish between different categories that make up the variables gender (male and female), religion (Protestant, Catholic, Jewish, Muslim), and psychopathology (schizophrenic, manic-depressive, neurotic). We can label males 1 and females 2, but it would make no difference if we labelled females 1 and males 2, or females 1 and males 0. All the numbers do is distinguish individuals in one group from individuals in another. No mathematical operations $(+, -, \times, \div)$ or mathematical relations (<, less than; >, greater than) may be performed with these numbers because the attributes that are represented by these numbers do not allow such operations. Although we can add or multiply 1 and 2, we cannot add or multiply the attribute Protestant and Catholic.

Ordinal variables indicate categories that are both different from each other, and ranked or ordered in terms of an attribute. When we label developing countries '1', and developed countries '2', not only are we distinguishing between them, but we are also marking the fact that developed countries have more of the attribute 'economic development' than developing countries. The same holds true when we label university grades as A, B, C, D, or when we label opinions as strongly agree, agree, disagree, and strongly disagree. With ordinal measures we may perform mathematical relations (<, >), but not mathematical operations $(+, -, \times, \div)$. Just because $2 = 2 \times 1$, we cannot say that developed countries (2) have twice as much economic development as developing countries (1). We can only say that they have more economic development. The differences between the

*We distinguish between variables in terms of their **scales of measurement**.*

amounts of the attributes that objects have do not correspond with the mathematical differences between the numbers that are used to represent these amounts. When the horses come in 1st, 2nd, and 3rd at the races, the numbers 1, 2, and 3 are measured on an ordinal scale, and do not tell us how far the second horse was behind the first horse (i.e. the distances between the horses). The intervals between the numbers on an ordinal scale are meaningless, and therefore no mathematical operations can be performed on these numbers.

Interval variables are true quantitative measures because in addition to marking difference and rank, the differences or distances between any two numbers on the scale are meaningful. This means that the difference between two scores is an accurate reflection of the difference in the amount of an attribute that the two objects have. Temperature, measured in degrees Celsius, is measured on the interval scale, and a difference between 18 degrees and 20 degrees will be exactly the same as the difference between 25 degrees and 27 degrees. Most measures in the behavioural sciences (e.g. IQ scores, scores on attitude scales, and knowledge tests) are considered interval measures. In addition to performing mathematical relations ($=$, $<$), we may also legitimately perform the mathematical operations of addition and subtraction ($+$, $-$) with these numbers.

Ratio variables have all the properties of interval scales, but because they have a true zero value (which interval scales do not have), the mathematical operations of multiplication and division ($\times$, $\div$) may also be performed on these scales. Since the variable age has a true zero value – i.e. at the moment when an individual is born she or he has zero of the property age – we can say that a 40-year-old person is twice the age of a 20-year-old person. Interval scales do not have a true zero point. Although someone may get 0 out of 100 for an exam, this does not mean that the person has zero of the attribute 'knowledge'. Thus we cannot say that someone who got 80% has twice as much knowledge as someone who got 40%. It is generally only physical properties – e.g. time, length, weight – that have real zero points and are thus measured on ratio scales. However, for most practical purposes in research, variables measured on the interval and ratio scales can be treated similarly.

Since the scale of measurement determines the kind of mathematical operation that may legitimately be performed on a variable, it also determines the kind of statistics that can be used to investigate the scores on the variable. Although the distinction between the four scales of measurement has been subjected to critique, we will use the distinction throughout the book to help you make decisions about how to describe and analyse data.

Independent and dependent variables

Very often we are interested in *relations* between variables, particularly if there is a temporal or logical reason to suspect a causal connection. For example, public health researchers have long been interested in the relation between cigarette smoking and the incidence of lung cancer. There are few people now who do not accept the conclusion that the relation is causal. When we investigate relations of this kind between variables, we refer to the outcome (e.g. incidence of lung cancer) as the *dependent* variable (DV), and the other variable as the *independent* variable (IV). The choice of names derives from the assumption we make that one of the variables is dependent on the other, or a consequence of the other.

In experimental design, the independent variable is usually under the direct control of the experimenter, and is actively manipulated. Imagine that we are investigating the effectiveness of an anti-depressant with a classic randomised experiment. This would involve actively randomising participants into an experimental and control group, administering a dosage to the experimental group, and withholding it from the control group. After the intervention we would measure depression levels. The independent variable in this experiment is Dosage (administered vs not administered), and the dependent variable is Depression.

Independent and dependent variables are also commonly known as *predictor* and *criterion* variables, or as *predictor* and *response* variables.

Independent variables are variables that are presumed to affect or determine other variables.

Dependent variables are variables affected or determined by independent variables.

Activity 1.6

In the following problems, identify the IV, DV, predictor, criterion, and response variables:
a) We measure the amount of red wine consumed in a country, and the rate of heart attacks per 100 000 people.
b) We compare general happiness in those who have pet dogs, and those who do not.
c) We compare the suicide rate among the married to that among the unmarried.

Samples, populations, statistics, and parameters

For many people the word *statistic* implies a calculation that attempts to make a historical record of a quantified phenomenon, e.g. Donald Bradman's batting average in test cricket was 99.4 runs, and the lowest atmospheric pressure ever recorded was 880 mb. The way we use the term statistic in this text is somewhat different. To explain this usage, we make a distinction between *sample* and *population*.

A **population** is an entire collection of objects or entities.

A **sample** is a subset of such a collection.

A *population* is an entire collection of elements or individuals. When we want to know what the average income per capita is in South Africa, we really do want to know what the number is when we sum *every* person's income and divide it by the number of people in the country. This is a very daunting task, and it is in fact extremely rare to attempt a calculation of this sort! This does not stop us from being interested in what the result of the calculation would be.

Since we are usually unable to collect scores from an entire population, we do the next best thing, which is to collect a *sample* of scores. Our reasoning here is to use the sample calculation of the measure we are interested in (e.g. average income) as an *estimate* of the population value. These sample calculations are known as *statistics*. The population value we attempt to estimate is called a *parameter*.

Activity 1.7

In each of the following, decide which is a *parameter* and which is a *statistic*:
a) the average matric History score in the 1937 end-of-year examinations in South Africa
b) the average matric History score at Platbakkies High School in 2001
c) the average matric History score in a collection of 10 Platbakkies High School pupils who happen to be on Clifton 4th beach on 1 January 2001.

Of course, there are many factors that affect whether our sample estimate is accurate. The basic idea is that a *random sample* should be drawn from the population, but there are many complications as to exactly how this is done. By a random sample, we mean a sample that is gathered in such a way that every element in the population has an equal likelihood of selection, and the selection of a particular element is independent of, and does not influence, the selection of any other element.

Statistical interference is the act of generalising from a sample to a population.

The act of generalising from sample data to populations is called *statistical inference*, and is probably the central goal of statistical methods. A great many techniques and methods we will cover in this text are really just variations on this.

Activity 1.8

a) List five ways of drawing a sample that clearly do not satisfy the requirements of randomness.
b) List three ways of drawing a sample that clearly do satisfy these requirements.

It is extremely important to note that although the notion of a *population*, as used in statistical work, frequently corresponds to our ordinary or everyday understanding of the word, it is also used in a more abstract way that can be quite confusing. Thus, we ordinarily assume that a population is a totality of real individuals, as in 'the population of a country', but we also use the term to refer to hypothetical populations. Thus, when we treat an experimental group with anti-retroviral medication, and compare that group to one not treated with the medication, we will say that we are trying to make inferences about *a population* treated with anti-retroviral medication, even though that is only a hypothetical population. Similarly, a population need not be a large collection of entities: we can study small collections of entities that are populations because they are the totality of individuals that satisfy the membership conditions of the group. Imagine trying to study the population of vegetarian Buddhist Free State crocodile skinners, for example …!

In statistics we are often interested in hypothetical populations.

Problems with the quantitative approach

Although we have argued at some length in this chapter in favour of the use of quantitative methods in the social sciences, we also wish to point out that there are grave problems. The key problem is perhaps the way in which the easy rationality of probabilistic inference has become an institutionalised canon, and has usurped other evidentiary forms. Very few research articles will fail to apply some statistical inferential method in support of a claim, and a great many will rely solely on such methods to support conclusions, and to generate questions for further research. This practice is reinforced by journal reviewers and editors who often will not accept articles that have not used some statistical inferential method – and by universities that insist on teaching these methods, year after year, despite strong student opposition!

Many critics have railed against this state of affairs. J. G. Taylor (1958) denounced it as '… a cloak for intellectual sterility', and authors like Bakan (1966), Gonzalez (1994), and a slew of others have called for a change in approach. The criticisms are usually well founded, but there is a danger of discarding the wheat with the chaff. There can be little doubt that probabilistic methods are extremely useful in some social science research; it is just that they are too pervasive, and are treated with singular reverence. Social scientists have equated 'quantitative' and 'probabilistic', and in so doing have overlooked a vast array of quantitative techniques and methodologies. The problem is not quantification, as some argue, but the canons of quantification in the social science tabernacle.

Summary

1. Quantitative methods make up an important part of social science research. They are especially useful to us because they are efficient in communicating information, they allow modelling of real-world phenomena, and they are part of a well worked-out and powerful disciplinary *language*.

2. In the social sciences we are particularly interested in the way of arguing with evidence that quantitative methods make available. We tend to use *probabilistic methods*, rather than the deterministic methods of some sciences. This shows in many of our claims, where it is typical for us to argue that we are 95% confident that an intervention works, or 99% confident that the average birthweight of South African infants is between 2.2 and 3.4 kilograms.

3. Important basic concepts introduced in this chapter include: population, sample, random sample, parameter, statistic, estimate, variable, discrete measure, continuous measure, independent variable, and dependent variable.

Exercises

1. Give three examples of claims or propositions that are *deterministic*.

2. Give three examples of claims or propositions that are *probabilistic*.

3. List three well-known physical constants.

4. Provide an example (real or hypothetical) where what is considered a population in one study is considered a sample in another study.

5. One commonly used method of drawing a random sample from a particular population is to generate a list of random telephone numbers, and to conduct telephone interviews with respondents on this list. Discuss four problems that can potentially render this method invalid, using the definition of randomness offered in this tutorial.

6. List ten continuous variables, and ten discrete variables.

7. Provide examples of potential or real research problems that use designs that lend themselves to description in terms of independent and dependent variables.

8. Identify the scale of measurement of each of the following variables:
    a) Systolic blood pressure, measured in millibars.
    b) IQ, measured with a standard intelligence test.
    c) Customer satisfaction, measured on a 3-point scale – unsatisfied, neutral, satisfied.
    d) The price of petrol, measured in Rands per litre.
    e) Handedness, including the categories left-handed, right-handed, and ambidextrous.

Displaying data

Judy Austin

After studying this tutorial, you should be able to:
- Represent a dataset in tabular form, specifically as a grouped or ungrouped frequency distribution table or cumulative frequency distribution table.
- Represent a dataset graphically in the form of a bar chart, histogram, or box-and-whisker plot.
- Interpret visual displays of data.
- Calculate and understand percentiles and percentile ranks.

The decision to collect information in the form of quantitative measurements or scores usually results from a desire to 'see what is going on' with respect to some aspect of our existence. We collect data on this 'aspect of our existence' in the form of scores on the variable of interest. For instance, we may wish to know which undergraduate courses are the most popular, or how other class members fared in a recent test, or what salaries new graduates are earning. Since raw data is difficult to 'read', it is necessary to process this data in order to inspect and interpret a distribution of scores. Thus, to understand and describe class performance, rather than inspecting a list of test scores of the class, we would first collate the data and represent the scores graphically. This will enable us, quite literally, to *see* what is going on.

Tabular and graphical displays provide us with a compact picture or summary of the dataset from which we can gain an impression of the overall trend in a distribution of scores. Displays provide us with a means to inspect the shape of a distribution and they help us to determine where an individual score lies relative to others in the distribution. In this tutorial you will first learn about different ways of displaying data in tabular and graphical form. You should already be familiar with some of the displays that are used in the media daily, such as in reporting economic indicators or sports results. In the final section of the tutorial, you will learn how to locate individual scores in a distribution of scores.

Graphical and tabular displays of data allow us to 'see' the distribution of scores on a variable.

At the outset, an important distinction needs to be made between types of data that require different kinds of display. We distinguish between variables that can take on few values (usually integers), known as *discrete* variables (e.g. number of students in a class, goals scored in a soccer match), and those for which a theoretically infinite number of values is possible, known as *continuous* variables (e.g. height or mass of humans) (see Tutorial 1). You know you are dealing with a discrete variable when there is a 'gap' between the values that the variable could possibly assume. For instance, shoe sizes occur in halves – you may wear size $5\frac{1}{2}$ or 6, but you cannot buy shoes of size $5\frac{7}{8}$. In contrast, when dealing with a continuous variable such as time, there is an infinite number of values between, say, $5\frac{1}{2}$ and 6 minutes that the variable could assume. We are simply limited by our capacity to measure very small distinctions. The reason for this distinction should be clear to you: in representing discrete data, we need to capture the 'gaps' between values, and we need to represent the continuity between values of continuous data.

Compile a list of ten variables and decide whether each is continuous or discrete.

Activity 2.1

The frequency distribution

The first step in ordering a dataset is to identify the range of scores and establish the *frequency* with which each occurs. An efficient way to summarise this information is to prepare a *frequency distribution* table. To do this we need to list all the values that the variable takes and then count how many times each of those values or scores appears in the dataset, recording the tally or count for each score in an adjacent column. From this table, we can begin to see patterns in the dataset.

Consider the tuberculosis (TB) treatment outcomes that are reported in Table 2.1. These come from records of a local

*The **frequency** of a score refers to the number of times that the given score appears within a dataset.*

*A **frequency distribution** is a tabular or graphical representation of a dataset indicating the set of scores on a variable together with their frequency.*

Community Health Clinic. One of six possible outcomes is reported for each of 50 new patients treated at the clinic during the preceding six months.

Whereas the dataset in Table 2.1 is difficult to interpret, the frequency distribution reported in Table 2.2 shows a clear pattern in the distribution of scores. The 'frequency' column reports the *number* of scores in each category. The majority of patients were either cured or had completed treatment without having the test needed to verify the cure. While very few patients died or failed to respond to treatment, an alarming number of treatments were not completed (patients either interrupted treatment or transferred to another centre). The '% frequency' column reports the *percentage* of observations that fall in each outcome category. The percentage for each category is calculated by dividing the frequency for the category by the total number of subjects (i.e. N). The frequency distribution allows us to describe the health of our 50 patients (i.e. our dataset).

Activity 2.2

Recalculate the percentages in the '% frequency' column of Table 2.2.

Table 2.1 Treatment outcomes for N = 50 patients treated for pulmonary TB

Rx	C	I	C	T	C	Rx	C	C	T
T	C	Rx	D	Rx	I	C	T	Rx	I
C	I	C	Rx	C	C	T	I	D	C
F	T	Rx	C	C	Rx	D	C	I	Rx
I	Rx	C	I	T	C	I	T	C	C

C = Cured; Rx = Treatment completed; F = Treatment failure; T = Transferred out; I = Interrupted; D = Died

Table 2.2 Frequency distribution of TB outcomes

Item	Frequency	% frequency
C	19	38
Rx	10	20
F	1	2
T	8	16
I	9	18
D	3	6

The frequency bar chart

We said that frequency distributions could be tabular or graphical representations of data. We have seen the frequency table, but how do we produce a graph from this data?

Nominal data can readily be displayed by means of the frequency bar chart. Figure 2.1 reports a bar chart for the TB treatment outcome data. Each category is designated by a bar placed on the horizontal axis (*x*-axis). To emphasise the discontinuity or 'gap' between categories, the bars are separated by blank spaces. As we are dealing with nominal data in which categories differ qualitatively, no particular ordering of categories along the horizontal axis can be prescribed. Some authors do however suggest that a modicum of logic be applied, such as arranging categories from highest to lowest frequency. The bars in Figure 2.1 are organised so that the desirable outcomes are placed to the left of the undesirable outcomes.

The frequency (number of cases) of each category is indicated on the vertical axis (*y*-axis). Each bar indicates the same frequency reported in the frequency distribution table, and the sum of the frequencies is equal to the total number of items in the dataset (N = 50). The range of frequencies provided on the vertical axis slightly exceeds the maximum observed frequency of any of the categories. Do you see how much easier it is to 'see what is going on' once we have a concise visual summary of the data?

The ratio of the height to the width of the graph is known as the *aspect ratio*. Changes in this ratio can alter the impression given by the graph. Be sure to carefully examine bar graphs that appear in

*The values or scores of **nominal data** are used for identification (e.g. 1 = female, 2 = male), and do not indicate the amount of an attribute.*

*A **bar chart** is a graphical representation of nominal data in which a vertical bar reflects the frequency of each category on a discrete (or categorical) variable.*

*The **aspect ratio** of a bar chart is the ratio of the height to the width of the 'bars'.*

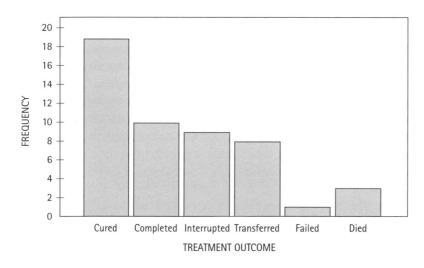

Figure 2.1 Frequency bar chart of TB treatment outcome data

the media, paying particular attention to the y-axis (see Figure 2.2). Differences between the frequencies of each category are enhanced when the y-axis does not begin at zero and the bars are short. Conversely, differences can be minimised when the y-axis does start at zero and the bars are tall. It is legitimate practice to have a break in the vertical axis, hence the onus is on you to interpret the graph correctly – and not be caught napping!

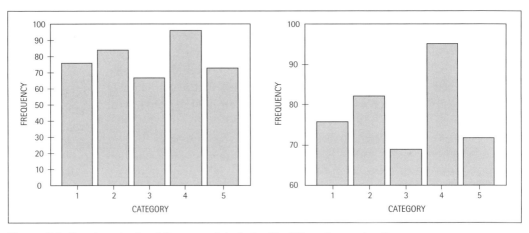

Figure 2.2 Two bar charts of the same data but with different aspect ratios

Grouped frequency distributions

So far we have dealt only with nominal or discrete data. How do we represent ordinal, interval, or ratio data by means of a frequency distribution? Here we want to capture the characteristic that there are no discrete gaps between the data scores.

Consider student test marks, which have a potential range from 0 to 100. By gathering the full set of marks for a class, you can answer questions such as 'Was the test too easy?' (i.e. are most of the scores clustered at the upper end of the range?) or 'How many students failed the test?' (i.e. how many scores are lower than 50%?). Here again, these questions are difficult to answer by inspecting the 'raw' list of scores. It is much easier to make sense of the data once they have been organised into a frequency distribution table. If we were to follow the format used in the ordinal frequency distribution (Table 2.2), where a frequency was computed for every score, we would need 101 rows, to allow for every possible mark from 0 to 100%! If there were only 120 people in the class, we might well end up with very few cases at each mark and we would not be much better off than we were with the raw data. A better way to tabulate the data so that we get a sense of 'what is going on' is to reduce the number of possible values in the left-hand column by collapsing the data into groups, thereby forming a *grouped frequency distribution*.

*A **grouped frequency distribution** is a tabular or graphical representation of ordinal, interval, or ratio data. Scores are grouped into class intervals, for which frequencies are given.*

To prepare a frequency distribution table, we need to consider the size of the dataset, i.e. the number of observed scores, and the range or distance from the lowest to the highest score. This will help us decide how to divide the distribution into groups. For a set of class marks ranging from 0 to 100%, we could use groups of 10% where all scores falling between 1 and 10% are lumped together, all scores between 11 and 20% form the next group, those between 21 and 30% the following group, etc., up to 100%. Categories of scores determined in this manner are referred to as *class intervals*.

The most difficult step in constructing a grouped frequency table is deciding how many class intervals to use. How many categories should data be grouped into? There are no hard and fast rules. Nevertheless some tables are more informative than others. Tabulation of a small dataset across many class intervals will yield little new information. Conversely, the compression of a large dataset into very few class intervals will result in an excessive loss of detail. Guidelines for determining the number and appropriate size of class intervals are given in Box 2.1.

*A **class interval** is a division or category of scores on a grouped frequency distribution.*

Creating class intervals

Box 2.1

There are several methods for creating class intervals. As long ago as 1926, Herbert Sturges derived a formula for this purpose – based on advanced statistical and mathematical techniques – that, despite some criticism, is still widely used today in textbooks and computer packages. For our purposes, however, it will be sufficient to use either of the following procedures.

1. *Use an existing convention*
   There is often an existing convention for dividing the data into groups. For example, matriculation examination marks are graded 'A', 'B', 'C', etc. where an 'A' represents marks of 80% and higher, a 'B' represents marks from 70 to 79%, a 'C' represents marks from 60 to 69%, etc. University marks are normally categorised by a different convention, where '1st' represents marks from 75% upwards, 'upper 2nd' represents marks from 70 to 74%, 'lower 2nd' represents marks from 60 to 69%, '3rd' represents marks from 50 to 59%, etc. Where such a convention exists, it usually makes sense to use it when constructing a grouped frequency distribution.

2. *Use equally spaced 'arbitrary' categories*
   Where no convention exists for breaking the data into categories, arbitrary categories are employed, by dividing the data into equally spaced intervals. The following steps will help you decide on the size and the number of intervals to use.
   a) *Determine the range* of the data by subtracting the lowest value from the highest value and adding 1 to this difference score.

b) Given the range, *consider what number of divisions* of a reasonable length, such as 5, 10, 50, or 100 units, could be accommodated. Do this by dividing the range by the size of the class intervals. It is conventional to have approximately ten class intervals.

c) Given the *sample size*, decide whether the chosen interval range – and hence the number of class intervals – is appropriate by estimating the number of data items that could be expected to fall within each division (bearing in mind that there are likely to be more items in the middle than the outer class intervals). A display with *too many or too few items per class interval is little better than an ordered set of raw data* – it does not help much in our quest to see what is going on in the sample.

d) Determine the *apparent limits* of each class interval. These are the highest and lowest scores that bracket the interval (e.g. 70–79%). Ensure that the extreme values have been provided for.

Which method you use depends on what you want the frequency distribution to show and how you want to use the distribution. Equally spaced intervals are most commonly employed since they give a clear overview of the scores that is easily understood. In contexts where specific categorical conventions are widely used and understood, these should be used.

There is flexibility in constructing the class interval, but the aim should be to produce a table or graph that enhances the readers' ability to describe and interpret the data. Obviously, when data from a large dataset are grouped in this manner, some of the detail is lost and we would need to weigh that up against the advantage of gaining a better idea of the overall shape of the dataset.

Although a given class interval may appear to range from two integer values (e.g. 10 to 19), these 'apparent limits' of the category are not the same as the actual limits that are used to determine whether individual scores fall within the category. Where do we place a score of 19.4? Does it fall within the 10–19 interval or the 20–29 interval? The values 10 and 19 are defined as the *apparent* lower and upper limits respectively of the 10–19 class interval. The true limits of the interval, termed the *real upper limit* (RUL) and *real lower limit* (RLL), actually extend beyond the apparent limits by half of the distance between the limit in question and the apparent limit of the succeeding (or preceding) class interval. Given succeeding class intervals 10–19 and 20–29, the real upper limit of the interval 10–19 would be 19.5, i.e. the midpoint between 19, the

*The **real upper limit** and the **real lower limit** refer to the true boundaries of a class interval. They are found midway between the apparent limits of neighbouring class intervals.*

apparent upper limit of the first interval, and 20, the apparent lower limit of the succeeding interval. Of course, 19.5 is also the real lower limit of the class interval 20–29.

Let us consider an example in which we have results, expressed as percentages, for a class of 80 learners (see Table 2.3). When devising class intervals, wherever possible it is best to choose intervals that have some logical significance. In the present example, groups of 10% correspond with the familiar breakdown used in allocating symbols to marks at school. Also, with a range of 100, class intervals of size 10 would give us an optimal number of 10 intervals. Table 2.4 is a frequency distribution for the test mark data.

> Identify the real upper limits and real lower limits of the class intervals in Table 2.4.

Activity 2.3

Table 2.3 Marks from a class test (N = 80)

56	67	77	51	62	57	69	58	67	71
83	58	46	79	69	53	72	64	63	76
71	73	59	60	48	52	64	70	57	69
64	62	70	58	53	61	58	69	55	65
48	55	62	54	57	69	62	57	73	60
63	72	39	73	61	64	53	68	46	57
62	61	66	60	70	58	75	67	52	66
57	43	72	54	59	81	51	59	54	61

> Using the data in Table 2.3, prepare a frequency distribution table with class intervals representing university grades: First class pass (75%+), Upper second (70–74%), Lower second (60–69%), Third (50–59%), and Fail (< 50%).

Activity 2.4

From the 'Frequency' column of Table 2.4 we can see that the majority of students scored in the 50s and 60s, while relatively few achieved extremely high or low scores. Note that no students scored marks below 30%. When several class intervals at the extremes of a distribution are empty, they may be combined into one class. Thus the distribution in Table 2.4 may be rewritten to begin with a class interval labelled '< 30'.

You will notice that, aside from the columns for frequency and percentage frequency with which we are already familiar, Table 2.4 has additional columns reflecting *cumulative frequency* and *cumula-*

Cumulative frequency refers to the frequency of all data items with a value less than or equal to a specified score.

Table 2.4 Frequency distribution table of test marks

Class interval	Frequency	Cumulative frequency	% frequency	Cumulative % frequency
> 89	–	80	–	100.00
80–89	2	80	2.50	100.00
70–79	15	78	18.75	97.50
60–69	30	63	37.50	78.75
50–59	27	33	33.75	41.25
40–49	5	6	6.25	7.50
30–39	1	1	1.25	1.25
20–29	–	–	–	–
10–19	–	–	–	–
< 10	–	–	–	–

Cumulative percentage frequency refers to the percentage of items within a dataset that have a value less than or equal to a specified score.

tive percentage frequency. Figures in these columns reflect the frequency or percentage frequency of all cases with scores less than the upper limit of the class interval alongside which they appear. Cumulative frequencies and percentage frequencies for each class interval are computed by summing the frequency or percentage frequency for that interval together with the frequencies or percentage frequencies in all lower intervals. Thus, the cumulative frequency for the 40–49 interval is 6 (i.e. 1 + 5) and the cumulative frequency for the 50–59 interval is 33 (i.e. 6 + 27). The cumulative frequency in the highest category should sum to N, and the cumulative percentage frequency should sum to 100%. Can you see why?

Cumulative indices are useful for answering questions such as 'How many students failed?' or 'What percentage of students achieved a grade of less than 50%?' Can you read these values from the table? The class interval 50–59 has a cumulative frequency of 33. This means that 33 students scored 59% or less in the class test. A cumulative percentage frequency of 41.25 is recorded for this class interval. This enables us to speak of the percentage of students with a test mark of 59 or less. We can say that 33 students or 41.25% of the class achieved a test mark of 59 or less.

Activity 2.5

Using the frequency distribution in Table 2.4, calculate the percentage of students who achieved 70% or more. There are two simple methods for doing so. Can you see them?

The histogram

Histograms are used to represent the distribution of interval or ratio data. Histograms look like bar charts, but differ in much the same way that the frequency distribution table for continuous data differed from the nominal data table. Firstly, rather than using bars to represent the frequency of individual data item values (e.g. males and females), the bars represent frequencies of cases within class intervals, which are arranged along the horizontal axis from left to right in order of increasing magnitude. Secondly, no blank spaces are allowed between class intervals as there are no 'gaps' between classes. The test results reported in Table 2.3 are presented in the form of a histogram in Figure 2.3.

Histograms are graphical displays that use bars to represent the frequencies of continuous data that are arranged into class intervals.

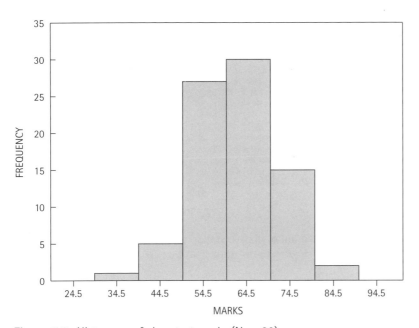

Figure 2.3 Histogram of class test marks (N = 80)

Note that the midpoint of each class interval, i.e. the point midway between the real lower limit and the real upper limit, is indicated on the horizontal axis. Some people like to ensure that the midpoint has an integer value by creating class intervals of which the width is an odd number. The midpoint is obtained by means of the following formula:

$$\text{midpoint of class interval} = \text{RLL} + \left(\frac{\text{RUL} - \text{RLL}}{2} \right)$$

Equation 2.1

As the bulk of the marks are clustered between 50 and 69%, our graph does not provide a great deal of information about the distribution. A more detailed breakdown would be useful. We could therefore choose to have class intervals of five rather than the ten employed previously. Confining ourselves to the range within which data items have been observed, we would have a histogram with class intervals encompassing values from 35 to 85 as shown in Figure 2.4. The decrease in interval size has given us more intervals, and a more detailed breakdown of the distribution.

Activity 2.6

Use Equation 2.1 to compute the midpoints of the class intervals in Table 2.4.

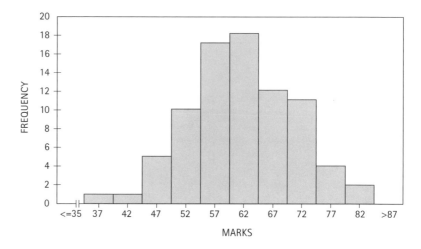

Figure 2.4 Histogram of class test marks (N = 80)

Describing frequency distributions

One of the main reasons why we construct frequency distributions is to describe the distribution of scores on a variable. This is what we mean by 'seeing what is going on' with the data: we describe the distribution stating how the scores are arranged in categories or class intervals.

We should answer two questions when describing the shape of a frequency distribution. Firstly, are most of the scores low, or are the majority of the scores in the middle or upper range of the distribution? Secondly, are the frequencies in some intervals much higher than those in other intervals, or do all the intervals have roughly the same frequency? The first question refers to the *skewness* of the distribution and the second question refers to the *peakedness* or the *kurtosis* of the distribution.

The skewness of a distribution refers to the degree to which it deviates from symmetry. The frequency distributions in Figure 2.5 are roughly symmetrical. A *symmetrical distribution* has its centremost point lying in the middle of the distribution, and the distribution of scores to the left and the right of this centremost point are mirror images of each other. Symmetrical distributions often have the majority of scores lying in the middle categories, and have a single peak (i.e. they are *unimodal*). Class results on tests and examinations are usually distributed symmetrically, with most students scoring in the middle ranges, and with fewer students doing very well or very poorly. Distributions with two peaks are called *bimodal distributions*.

Asymmetrical distributions can either be positively or negatively skewed (see Figure 2.6). Positively skewed distributions have the majority of the sample scoring in the lower range of the variable, whereas negatively skewed distributions have the majority of scores in the upper range of the variable. The skewness and symmetry of a frequency distribution provide useful information about the sample and/or the measurement instrument. A positively skewed distribution of test marks indicates that the sample did poorly on the test and/or that the test was too difficult. On the other hand, a negatively skewed distribution of test marks indicates that the students did well on the test and/or that the test was too easy.

To describe the shape of a frequency distribution, comment on its symmetry, modes, skewness, and kurtosis.

Another way of describing the shape of a frequency distribution is to examine its peakedness, also known as the kurtosis of the distribution. Here we judge the degree to which certain intervals or categories have higher frequencies than others. The two distributions in Figure 2.7 have the same number of subjects. The peaked distribution has some intervals with high frequencies and other intervals with low frequencies. In contrast, the flat distribution has roughly similar frequencies in all intervals.

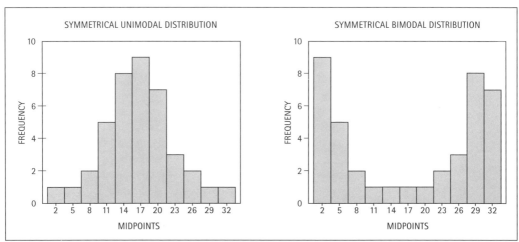

Figure 2.5 Symmetrical unimodal and bimodal frequency distributions

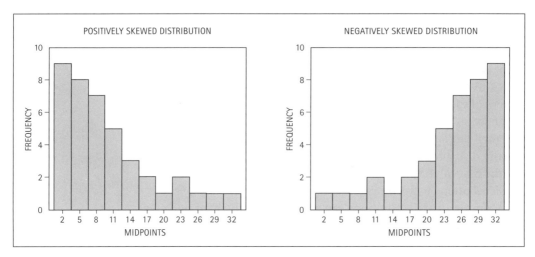

Figure 2.6 Asymmetrical frequency distributions

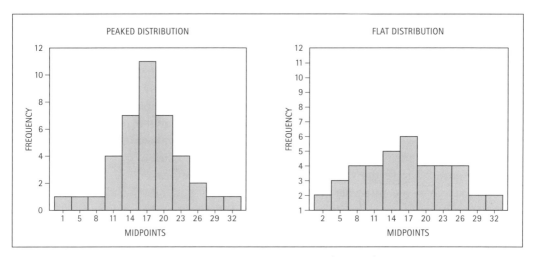

Figure 2.7 Frequency distributions with different peakedness (kurtosis)

For each of the distributions reported in Figures 2.5 to 2.7, determine the following:

a) What is the sample size?

b) What was the range of scores?

c) What are the apparent limits and real upper and lower limits of the first and last categories?

d) What is the highest and lowest class interval frequency?

e) What is the cumulative frequency of the interval with midpoint 17?

f) If the scores are marks on a test out of 35, what does each of them reveal about the class performance and/or the test?

NUMBERS, HYPOTHESES AND CONCLUSIONS

Frequency distributions allow us to describe a set of scores by revealing patterns of symmetry, skewness, and peakedness of the distribution. They also show the modes of the distribution. When interpreting frequency distributions, it is important to ask what the distribution shows about the sample and/or the measure. Imagine that each of the distributions in Figures 2.5, 2.6, and 2.7 represents marks on a class test. What does each of them reveal about the class performance and/or the test?

Remember the difference between the shape of positively and negatively skewed distributions.

Percentile ranks and percentiles

One of the main advantages of producing tables of frequencies and cumulative frequencies is that they allow us to determine where a particular score lies relative to other scores in a distribution. If you scored 65% in a test, how well did you do? The answer depends on how everyone else scored in the test. If the test was easy and 65% was the lowest score, you did not do very well. However, if the test was difficult and 65% was the highest score, you did very well. This illustrates an important kind of statistical reasoning: we judge individual scores in the context of all the other scores in a distribution. The cumulative frequency and cumulative percentage frequency allow us to locate an individual score in the context of the other scores in a distribution. They tell us the number of scores (or the percentage of scores) that fall below a specified score.

Consider first a mark of 50%. You may be relieved to have 'scraped through' with a mark of 50%. Another way to evaluate your performance is to ask: 'How many students scored less than 50%?' After all, 50% may have been the lowest or the highest score on the test. You could also ask how many students did better than you. We can simply read the answers to these questions off the cumulative frequency table. From Table 2.4 we can see that 6 students (7.5%) received marks below 49.5% (the RUL of the 40–49 class interval). If you received a mark of 50% for this test, you did not do very well, because only 7.5% of students performed worse than you. To determine how many students did better than you, simply subtract the number that did worse than you from the total number of students: 74 (i.e. 80 – 6) students scored 50% or more.

*A **percentile rank** indicates the percentage of cases that lie at or below a specified point on the scale on which the data were measured.*

When investigating questions such as these, we are, in fact, referring to a statistic known as the *percentile rank*. Thus, when we stated earlier that 41.25% of the students achieved a test mark of 59 or less, we were saying that a test mark of 59 has a percentile rank of 41.25 (or 41, with rounding). The mark, 59, is referred to as the 41st *percentile*.

*A **percentile** is a point on a scale at and below which a specified percentage of cases in a dataset falls.*

Thus far we have been using easy examples that involved reading off from a frequency table the percentile rank associated with the RUL of a category. But what do we do when we want to compute the percentile rank of a score that falls within an interval? What is the percentile rank of a score of 65? Notice that 65 falls inside the class interval 60–69 in Table 2.4.

To calculate a percentile rank from a cumulative frequency table, we first need to identify the class interval into which the mark or score of interest falls. Clearly, all cases falling into the class intervals below the identified interval also fall below the score whose percentile rank we are trying to determine. Thus the cumulative frequency of the class interval below comprises part of our percentile rank. To that, we need to add the percentage of the identified interval consisting of marks equal to or less than the mark or score of interest. The formula is as follows:

Equation 2.2

$$\text{percentile rank} = \% \text{ below} + \frac{\text{score} - \text{RLL}}{\text{class int. width}} (\text{interval \%})$$

where: % below = cumulative percentage frequency of the class interval below the interval in which the score of interest occurs

score = the score in respect of which we wish to determine the percentile rank

RLL = real lower limit of the interval in which the score of interest occurs

class int. width = the width of the class interval

interval % = the percentage of the distribution that falls within the interval of interest

For example, to return to Table 2.4, the percentile rank of a mark of 65 is calculated as follows:

$$\text{percentile rank} = 41.25 + \frac{65 - 59.5}{10} (37.5)$$

$$= 61.88$$

$$= 62$$

The formula can best be understood with reference to Figure 2.8. The formula uses known information about the placing of a score on a class interval to determine the unknown value for the percentile rank, which is a point on an associated percentage interval. Since we know the interval width and RLL of the class interval, we can determine 'how far' the score lies from the RLL (i.e. 65 – 59.5). From the calculation, you can see that the formula expresses this as a proportion by dividing the distance by the interval width (i.e. 10). The score of 65 lies just over half way from the RLL (i.e. 0.55 of the interval). We now have enough information to compute the percentile rank. We know the width of the percentage interval (i.e. 37.5), and we now know that the percentile rank we are looking

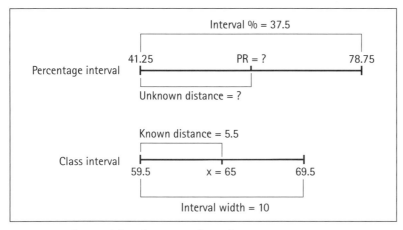

Figure 2.8 Determining the percentile rank

for lies a similar distance (i.e. 0.55) away from the lower limit of this interval. We multiply the 'interval %' by 0.55 to determine that 20.63% of the distribution lies between 59.5 and 65. This is the 'unknown distance' in Figure 2.8. Thus, approximately 62% of the scores (41.25 + 20.63) lie below the value of 65.

To calculate a percentile from a cumulative frequency distribution table, we work the other way round, starting with a cumulative percentage frequency to determine a corresponding score. Once again, the first step is to identify the class interval and corresponding percentage interval within which the percentile rank lies. The formula for this procedure is as follows:

$$\text{score of } p = \text{RLL} + \frac{\text{PR} - \% \text{ below}}{\text{interval } \%} (\text{interval width})$$

Equation 2.3

where: score of P = the score associated with a percentile rank of p

% below = cumulative percentage frequency of the class interval below the interval in which the score of interest occurs

PR = the percentile rank for which we wish to identify a score

RLL = real lower limit of the interval in which the percentage of interest occurs

interval width = the width of the class interval

interval % = the percentage of the distribution that falls within the interval of interest

Thus for our class test marks in Table 2.4, the 75th percentile, i.e. the score at and below which 75% of the students' marks are to be found, would be calculated as follows:

It is important to
distinguish between:
1. the **score** that
an individual
achieved on a test,
2. the **percentile
rank** that this score
represents, and
3. the **percentile,**
which is the point
on the scale
corresponding to
a given percentile
rank.

$$\text{score of } p = 59.5 + \frac{75 - 41.25}{37.5} \quad (10)$$

$$= 68.5$$

Figure 2.9 shows how the formula goes about determining the percentile. It determines 'how far' the percentile rank of 75 lies from the lower limit of 41.25 (i.e. 75 – 41.25 = 33.75), and then expresses this distance as a proportion of the interval % (i.e. 33.75 ÷ 37.5 = .90). The percentile that we want to calculate thus lies .90 of the class interval away from the RLL, and we determine that the 75th percentile is 68.5. The value 68.5 is the *point on the scale* that cuts off the lower three-quarters of the distribution. Note that this is true even though no actual score of 68.5 was observed. The percentile relates to the scale on which the scores were observed and not the actual raw data.

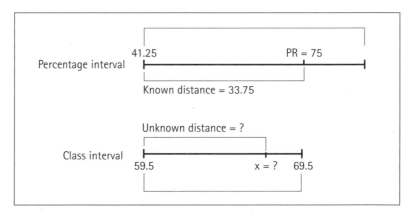

Figure 2.9 Determining the percentile

Thus far we have focused solely on the cumulative frequency, computing the proportion of scores that fall at and below a specified value. However, we can also compute the proportion of cases that scored higher than a specified value, or the proportion of cases that fall between two specified values.

Since we know that the cumulative frequency for all intervals sums to N, and the cumulative percentage frequency sums to 100, we can calculate the *frequency* or *proportion of scores that lie above a specified score* by a simple subtraction:

(frequency > x) = N – (frequency ≤ x)
(% frequency > x) = 100 – (% frequency ≤ x)

Thus, if we know that the cumulative frequency of the score 59.5 is 33 and we know that there are 80 scores in the dataset, we know also that 47 scores (i.e. 80 – 33) are greater than 59.5 (see Table 2.4). Likewise, if the percentile rank of a score of 68.5 is 75, we also know that 25% of the distribution (i.e. 100 – 75) scored higher than 68.5.

It is possible to compute the proportion of a distribution that lies below or above a particular score, or between two scores.

Since we can determine the frequency or proportion of scores that lie below a specified value and we can calculate the frequency or proportion of scores that lie above another specified value, we can calculate the *frequency* or *proportion of scores that lie between the two values*. Here what we do is to subtract from the total number of scores (N) or from the total percentage (100), the frequency or percentage of scores that lie below the lowest specified value (x_l) and the frequency or percentage of scores that lie above the higher value (x_h).

(frequency between x_l and x_h) = N – (frequency $\leq x_l$) – (frequency $\geq x_h$)
(% frequency between x_l and x_h) = 100 – (% frequency $\leq x_l$) – (% frequency $\geq x_h$)

Refer back to Table 2.4. How many scores lie between 39.5 and 59.5? Since we know that the cumulative frequency of 39.5 is 1, and the frequency above 59.5 is 47 (see above), using the formula, we determine that 32 (i.e. 80 – 47 – 1) scores lie between 39.5 and 59.5. Similarly, we can compute the proportion of scores that lie between the value of 65 and the value of 68.5. We have already computed the percentile ranks for these values: 62% of the scores are less than or equal to the value 65, and 25% of the scores are greater than the value 68.5. Thus 13% of the observed scores (i.e. 100 – 62 – 25) lie between 65 and 68.5.

Percentiles can be understood as a way of dividing up a distribution of scores into 100 small intervals – 1st percentile, 2nd percentile, 3rd percentile ... 100th percentile. Dividing a distribution into 100 equal proportions is just one of a number of conventional ways of 'cutting up' a distribution of scores. Distributions are also often divided into halves, quarters, and tenths. The formula for computing percentiles is used to compute the corresponding scores. To divide the distribution in half, compute the 50th percentile (also know as the median). To divide the distribution into quarters, compute the 25th percentile (also known as the 1st quartile), the 50th percentile, and the 75th percentile (also known as the 3rd quartile). The 1st, 2nd, 3rd ... deciles are determined by calculating the 10th, 20th, 30th percentiles.

*The **median** or **50th percentile** is a value that divides a distribution into two halves.*

Activity 2.8

For the data reported in Table 2.4 compute the following:
a) The median, and the 1st and 3rd quartiles.
b) The 1st, 3rd, 6th, and 9th deciles.
c) The proportion of scores above 55.
d) The proportion of scores between 47 and 72.

Worked example

South African meteorological services keep records of average day-time temperatures for different areas of the country. To determine the effects of global warming on daytime temperature in South Africa, a researcher collects the yearly average temperature from the records of 36 weather stations. Data are collected for the year 1960 and compared with data for the same stations for the year 2000 (see Table 2.5).

Table 2.5 Average daytime temperature in South Africa, 1960 and 2000

Station	1	2	3	4	5	6	7	8	9	10	11	12	13	14	15	16	17	18
1960	18.91	11.62	16.45	18.21	17.93	14.36	13.46	14.98	19.50	24.78	20.65	14.43	17.21	22.96	18.84	13.69	16.21	15.10
2000	18.97	12.56	16.40	19.10	17.43	15.21	14.21	15.21	19.53	26.33	19.59	14.65	18.32	23.06	18.06	14.34	16.89	15.21
Station	19	20	21	22	23	24	25	26	27	28	29	30	31	32	33	34	35	36
1960	14.85	15.54	17.01	11.41	15.98	12.70	22.15	17.89	13.02	19.68	14.03	20.71	18.89	17.31	18.34	15.09	13.09	13.03
2000	14.90	16.03	17.39	13.41	16.93	14.09	21.89	17.93	19.56	19.98	14.65	21.00	19.69	18.56	19.24	15.79	14.01	14.38

Tables 2.6 and 2.7 are frequency tables for the two years respectively. Each table divides the data into five equal class intervals, each with an interval width of 2 degrees Celsius. The highest frequencies for both tables are in the lower temperatures, especially the category with a RLL of 12.95 and a RUL of 14.95. It is also apparent that the 2000 temperatures have a narrower range, and there appears to be fewer observations in the lower ranges of temperature. Thus, the per-centile rank of the temperature 14.95 is 36% in 1960, but is only 28% in 2000. Evidence for an increase in temperature is also apparent at the higher values of both distributions: the 97th percentile is higher for the 2000 distribution (97th percentile = 24.95), than the 1960 distribution (97th percentile = 22.95).

To provide a more detailed view of the distributions of scores, the histograms reported in Figure 2.10 have an interval width of 1 degree Celsius. The 1960 distribution is unimodal and slightly positively skewed. The 2000 distribution is bimodal, approximately symmetrical, and appears to have an outlier in the topmost category.

This example illustrates the value of generating tabular and graphical representations of the distribution of scores on a variable. These basic descriptive statistical procedures allow us to see what is going on with the data. On the basis of our displays, we can see that there appears to have been a shift in temperature between 1960 and 2000. Specifically, whereas the 1960 distribution is positively

Table 2.6 Average daytime temperature, 1960

Class interval	Frequency	Cumulative frequency	% frequency	Cumulative % frequency
11.0–12.9	3	3	8	8
13.0–14.9	10	13	28	36
15.0–16.9	6	19	17	53
17.0–18.9	10	29	28	81
19.0–20.9	4	33	11	92
21.0–22.9	2	35	6	97
23.0–24.9	1	36	3	100
25.0–26.9	–	–		

Table 2.7 Average daytime temperature, 2000

Class interval	Frequency	Cumulative frequency	% frequency	Cumulative % frequency
11.0–12.9	1	1	3	3
13.0–14.9	9	10	25	28
15.0–16.9	8	18	22	50
17.0–18.9	7	25	19	69
19.0–20.9	7	32	19	89
21.0–22.9	2	34	6	94
23.0–24.9	1	35	3	97
25.0–26.9	1	36	3	100

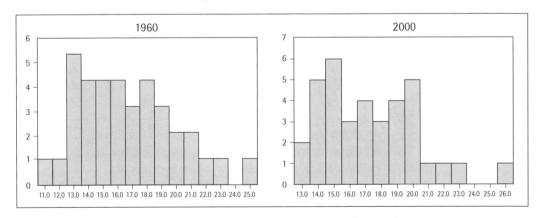

Figure 2.10 Histograms of annual average daytime temperature (N = 36)

skewed, with lower temperatures clustered in the lower regions, the 2000 distribution is symmetrical. There are more observations in the upper regions of temperature, and the middlemost score has moved higher. There also appears to have been a reduction in the range of temperatures, with observations in 2000 clustering more tightly around the median.

Summary

1. Categorical or discrete data are displayed in tables and bar charts, whereas continuous data are displayed in tables, histograms, and boxplots.

2. Tabular displays are interpreted by commenting on the frequencies, percentage frequencies, and cumulative percentage frequencies in different categories. Graphical displays of distributions are interpreted by commenting on their symmetry or their skewness, their modes, and their peakedness.

3. In addition to giving us a feel for the data, frequency displays with cumulative percentage frequencies allow us to compute percentiles and percentile ranks. This enables us to locate particular values relative to other values in a distribution, to determine the proportion of scores higher or lower than a specified value, and to determine the proportion of scores between two values.

Exercises

1. Four political parties nominated candidates to contest the local by-election. In order to assess their relative popularity, a journalist conducted a telephone survey of 40 residents, asking them to identify the party for which they intended to vote. The responses were as follows:

D	Z	M	Z	H	M	D	H	M	H
H	M	D	H	D	M	H	D	Z	D
Z	D	H	M	Z	H	Z	H	Z	H
H	M	Z	Z	H	Z	H	Z	H	M

a) What level of measurement has been employed here?
b) Construct a frequency distribution table for this data.
c) Construct a frequency bar chart for the data.
d) Interpret the distribution of scores.

2. Refer to data for average daytime temperature in 1960 and 2000 reported in Table 2.5. Do the following:

a) Construct a frequency table for the 1960 data with class interval width equal to 1 degree Celsius.
b) Construct a histogram for the 1960 data with class interval width equal to 2 degrees Celsius.
c) Places with annual temperatures greater than or equal to 19.4 are considered 'hot' places. What proportion of observations is 'hot' in each distribution? (*Hint: Compute the percentile rank.*)
d) If we wanted to select the highest and lowest 10% of scores in each distribution, which temperatures would be the cut-off values? (*Hint: Compute the 1st and 9th deciles.*)

3. Sixty aspirant computer programmers underwent a battery of aptitude tests, from which the following IQ scores were extracted:

96	104	102	95	118	116	125	87	99	100
87	88	106	108	98	102	90	119	105	97
100	91	112	91	104	93	98	91	96	111
94	103	94	124	89	92	93	95	110	87
97	101	93	104	100	96	120	107	93	114
85	120	87	107	102	110	131	89	98	103

a) Construct a frequency distribution table for the data. What size class interval did you choose? Why? What are the real upper and lower limits of the class interval that contains the data item '98'?
b) Construct a histogram of the data. Be sure to mark the *midpoint* of each class interval on the graph.
c) Determine the percentile rank of a score of 100. Assuming that the test has been designed to have 100 as the norm, what can you say about this sample?
d) What score is found at the 75th percentile?
e) What proportion of the sample scored between 92 and 107?

Central tendency

Martin Terre Blanche

After studying this tutorial, you should be able to:
- Explain the purpose of measures of central tendency.
- Identify three measures of central tendency.
- Explain the principle on which the mean, median, and mode are based.
- Calculate the mean, median, and mode.
- Explain the advantages and disadvantages of using the mean, median, and mode in different circumstances and in relation to different kinds of data.

We live in an age of information overload and it is only by simplifying and summarising that we are able to make sense of it all. In Tutorial 2 we considered one useful way of summarising numerical information, namely by using graphical displays. In this tutorial we will discuss another approach, collectively known as *measures of central tendency*. Such measures are single numbers that provide a summary of a whole collection of numbers, e.g. the average score of a group of students in a Sociology test or the average number of goals of a soccer team. The average (usually called the *mean* in statistical language) is one of the most useful measures of central tendency; others are the *median* (the middle number when numbers are arranged from largest to smallest) and the *mode* (the most frequently occurring number in a group of numbers). Each of these measures of central tendency (mean, median, and mode) is a single number summarising a group of numbers, but each is calculated in a different way and each is used for different purposes.

The mean

The **mean** is the arithmetic average of a group of numbers.

The mean is simply the arithmetic average of a group of numbers. If you want the mean of scores in a Sociology test, add together all the scores and then divide the result by the number of scores. The formula for this statistic is:

$$\bar{x} = \frac{\Sigma x}{n}$$

Equation 3.1

where: $\bar{x}$ is the mean
          Σ (the Greek letter sigma) indicates summation (or adding up)
          x stands for each score
          n is the number of scores

The mean equals the sum of all the scores divided by the number of scores.

Let us see how we apply this formula to a set of scores. Imagine that we have collected the annual income of five well-known South African arms dealers, and these are (in R100 000s): 8.1, 7.6, 3.2, 12.3, 5.6. Then the calculation will be:

$$\Sigma x = (8.1 + 7.6 + 3.2 + 12.3 + 5.6) = 36.8$$
$$n = 5$$
$$\bar{x} = \frac{\Sigma x}{n} = \frac{36.8}{5} = 7.36$$

This is not complicated, and most of us have been calculating means (or averages as we usually call them) almost since we learnt to add and divide.

The formula above uses the notation for what is called a *sample mean*. When we calculate a *population mean* we use a slightly different notation, but the mechanics of the calculation are identical. The formula for the population mean is:

$$\mu = \frac{\Sigma x}{N}$$

Equation 3.2

where μ = the population mean, and the other symbols are as discussed earlier.

Using a calculator to find x̄

All calculators that label themselves as 'scientific' offer functions that make the work of calculating the arithmetic mean – and, in fact, most calculations involving sigma (Σ) notation – dead easy. Although not all models work in exactly the same way, they generally ask you to turn the calculator into STAT mode, and enter the data points. A great many calculations are then automatically available to you – just pushing the 'Σx' key will give that calculation, the 'x̄' key will give you the mean, the 'S' key gives the sample standard deviation (see Tutorial 4), etc.

Step 1: Put the calculator in the STAT mode. Try pressing the button marked MODE, then the • (point) button.

Step 2: Enter the data. Do this by entering the first data value (e.g. 8.1) and then pressing the data button. Try using the button marked M+. Then enter the second data value (e.g. 7.6) and press the data button. Enter all the data in this way.

Step 3: Find the desired calculations. Statistical functions (e.g. Σx, Σx^2, s, x̄) are often found above the number buttons of the calcultor. Press the SHIFT button first before pressing the statistical function button.

Binet, the French educationist, who developed the first IQ test, administers a test to 40 five-year-old children. The children are required to complete a maze puzzle, and Binet times each child who completes the puzzle. Here are the data (numbers refer to time, measured in seconds, and rounded to the nearest millisecond):

34.56	56.78	32.97	34.23	56.21	43.23	40.0	34.21	30.09	43.67	32.67	47.43	44.44
67.34	59.9	45.34	45.23	38.00	26.56	54.67	34.65	44.54	60.34	34.55	47.33	32.67
32.66	32.54	46.34	41.39	39.23	30.00	34.65	39.56	42.67	52.78	35.32	33.33	50.00
60.00												

Using your calculator, calculate and report the mean of the dataset. Now check this by doing the calculation by hand.

The distinction between a population and sample mean is important, particularly when we do *inferential statistics*. We will discuss this more fully in later tutorials; for the moment all that we need to note is that the sample mean attempts to *estimate* the population mean. When we calculate the mean salary of five arms dealers, as we did above, we intend that the sample statistic (x̄) will give us an estimate of the corresponding population statistic (μ), which is the mean of *all* arms dealers in South Africa.

The mean is by far the most versatile and commonly used measure of central tendency, but there are occasions when it can be quite misleading. Suppose you want to know how long, on average, students at your university spend browsing the Internet per week. You ask 9 students and get the 9 answers as shown in Table 3.1.

The mean can be misleading when there are extreme values in a dataset.

Table 3.1 Time on the Internet

Name	Time	Name	Time
Itumeleng	0 hours	Pravani	0 hours
Mcebesi	1 hour	Johan	1 hour
Stephen	4 hours	Xavier	4 hours
Ingrid	1 hour	Linda	3 hours
Tumelo	31 hours		

If you add up the hours, you will see that together the students spend 45 hours on the Internet per week, or an average of 5 hours each (45 hours divided by 9 students). However, in some ways this is quite misleading, since with one exception all the students spend *less* than 5 hours per week on the Internet. The mean is as high as 5 because of a single atypical person (Tumelo). So if you want to tell somebody how long a typical student spends on the Net, you will have to find a measure of central tendency more appropriate in this instance than the mean.

The trimmed mean

One useful way of reducing the influence of extreme scores (also called *outliers*) is to exclude the highest and lowest scores before calculating the mean. This is known as a *trimmed mean*. To get the trimmed mean for the sample data in Table 3.1, we first discard Itumeleng's and Pravani's scores (the lowest); to balance that we then also exclude the highest score (Tumelo's); and finally we add up the remaining scores and divide by 6 (because we are now only working with 6 of the original 9 scores). Thus the trimmed mean is 2.33 (14 divided by 6), which gives a much better idea of how much time a typical student spends on the Internet than the 'ordinary' mean of 5. But be careful – calculating a trimmed mean involves throwing away some information (in this case Itumeleng, Pravani, and Tumelo's scores), and can be misleading. Suppose you were in charge of the university's computer system and had to determine how much time to make available on the system per student for Internet browsing. For such a purpose the mean of 5 would be a more accurate figure than the trimmed mean of 2.33. Can you see why?

Data entry errors are commonly responsible for outliers in a dataset. A noticeable difference between the 'ordinary' and the trimmed mean can be an indication that such errors have occurred.

Box 3.2

Trimmed means are not used because they include discarding data.

Calculating the mean from grouped data

Percentage	Frequency	Midpoint	Frequency × midpoint
1–10	0	5.5	0
11–20	0	15.5	0
21–30	0	25.5	0
31–40	2	35.5	71
41–50	2	45.5	91
51–60	3	55.5	166.5
61–70	4	65.5	262
71–80	4	75.5	302
81–90	5	85.5	427.5
91–100	0	95.5	0
	N = 20		Σx = 1 320

The best way to find the mean is to add together each individual's score and to divide by the number of individuals. However, sometimes we no longer have the individual scores and need to calculate (approximately) the mean from data that have already been grouped into class intervals.

To calculate the mean from such data, we should first multiply the midpoint of each interval by the frequency (i.e. the number of people in that interval), then add these together, and then divide by the number of people (the total frequency).

Consider the table of marks obtained for a sociology research project, shown above. The necessary calculations to determine the mean are shown in columns alongside the frequency distribution. Since Σx = 1 320, we must divide this by 20 (the total number of students, NOT categories in the distribution), and this gives an approximate mean mark for the project of 66%.

Another problem with the trimmed mean is that it can be difficult to decide when scores are outliers that should be trimmed away. What if there were three people who spent many hours on the Internet? Could you afford to trim them away together with the three lowest scores, leaving only three scores from which to calculate the mean? How could you be sure that those students were really atypical?

A frequency distribution of the data in Activity 3.1 is given below.

Category	Frequency
25.01–30	2
30.01–35	13
35.01–40	5
40.01–45	6

Category	Frequency
45.01–50	6
50.01–55	2
55.01–60	4
60.01–55	1
65.01–70	1

Provide an estimation of the mean of the data, given the methods of Box 3.2.

Calculate the trimmed mean for Binet's data given in Activity 3.1.

Activity 3.3

The median

The median is a useful alternative to the mean. It is simply the middle score when a group of scores are arranged from smallest to largest. Another way of expressing this is to say that the median is the score below which 50% of the scores fall. In the case of our Internet example, Johan, who spends 1 hour per week on the Internet, is right in the middle of the group, so the median is 1. If there were an even number of people in the group (e.g. 10), nobody would have been exactly in the middle of the group, and you would have had to take the average of the person just below and the person just above the middle as the median.

The median is the middle score in a ranked distribution of scores.

More formally, we can say that the median is that score which is to be found in the *median position*, where the median position is defined as the 50th percentile of the distribution of scores. When the number of scores, N, is odd, and the scores are in ranked order, this location is $\frac{N+1}{2}$. When N is even, this formula will give us a fractional number (e.g. 5.5), which is nonsensical, unless we agree that this just implies the average of the scores adjacent to the fractional number (e.g. in the case of 5.5, the scores in positions 5 and 6).

Like the trimmed mean, the median is useful for counteracting the influence of an extreme score that causes the mean to be excessively high or low. In addition, the median is useful where the mean is pulled up or down by more than just one high or low score. Consider, for example, the average income of South Africans. In this country there are a small number of people who earn very high salaries and a large number who earn very low salaries. The high earners' incomes are so large that together they pull up the mean income, giving the impression that the typical working South

The median is not influenced by extreme scores.

Just as the median divides a dataset into two halves, the dataset can also be divided into smaller parts called quartiles (quarters), deciles (tenths), and percentiles (hundredths).

African is not too badly off. In the 1996 Census, the mean income was R2 140 per person per month. However, the median income was only R1 100 per month, that is, 50% of working South Africans earned R1 100 per month or less. Thus a typical South African is far poorer than one would think by looking at mean income only. Income levels in different countries are often reported in terms of medians as well as means, and from this example we can see why.

Activity 3.4

a) Determine the median for Binet's data (see Activity 3.1).
b) What do you think is the 'median category' for the frequency distribution given in Activity 3.2? Can you define the notion of a 'median category'?

*The **median** is often used as a measure of central tendency for very skewed data.*

The median is useful for any measure where there is a sub-group that seems to be pulling the mean up or down. We say that the median is useful for *skewed distributions*. Examples of distributions that are skewed include income (there are many low incomes and a small number of inordinately high incomes), exams where the answers have been 'leaked' (a small number of students with access to the 'leaked' answers do inordinately well), and winnings at a casino (most winners win small amounts, but a lucky few win millions). The median is usually a good measure of central tendency for such scores.

Most collections of scores are symmetrically distributed, that is, high and low scores are more-or-less evenly arranged around the mean. Examples include newborn babies' heartbeats per minute, the number of words in students' essays, and the petrol consumption of different types of cars. The mean is usually a good measure of central tendency for such scores.

The mode

The mode is the score in a dataset that occurs with the greatest frequency. Let us have another look at our table of hours spent on the Internet (Table 3.1 on page 43).

*The **mode** is the most frequently occuring score in a distribution.*

As you can see, 1 hour per week is the most popular number of hours spent on the Internet (3 of the 9 students). The mode is therefore 1, and we could say that the modal number of hours spent by students on the Internet is 1 hour per week. Many datasets have a single mode (they are 'unimodal'), but sometimes two different scores or categories occur with the same top frequency, in which case we would say that the group of scores is 'bimodal'. If, for example, there were another student who spent 4 hours per week on the Internet, we would have two modes – 1 hour and 4 hours –

since there would be 3 students in each category. Bimodal distributions can be an indication that we are dealing with two different populations. In this case we might suspect that there could be two basic types of students – those who use the Internet very little and those who use it almost on a daily basis.

Unimodal distributions have one mode and bimodal distributions have two modes.

Symbols for measures of central tendency

The mean of a *sample* is most commonly represented by a bar over the letter representing the variable, e.g. $\bar{x}$ if the variable is or x. A *population* mean is usually indicated by μ (the Greek letter mu). An all-purpose symbol sometimes used for the mean is M.

The median is usually abbreviated as Md.
The mode is usually abbreviated as Mo.

Box 3.3

The mode can be a useful measure of central tendency for all sorts of data, but is the *only* suitable measure when we are dealing with nominal data, that is, data that consist of a series of labels rather than numbers. For example, Table 3.2 shows political party support by the same students as those in our Internet study.

The central tendency of nominal data is always represented by the mode.

Table 3.2 Student political party support

Itumeleng	NNP	Pravani	ACDP	Ingrid	ANC
Mcebesi	ANC	Johan	APP	Linda	ANC
Stephen	DA	Xavier	NNP	Tumelo	ANC

If data have already been grouped into class intervals, the mode is taken to be the midpoint of the class interval containing the largest number of cases.

The appropriate measure of central tendency for data of this sort is the mode, which in this case is the ANC.

---

a) Determine the mode for Binet's data (see Activity 3.1).
b) What do you think is the 'modal category' for the frequency distribution given in Activity 3.2? Can you define the notion of a 'modal category'?

Activity 3.5

Worked example

In quantitative media studies, a measure that is often used is the amount of space (in column inches, or percentage of total space) given to stories covering particular issues. For example, Edward Herman and Noam Chomsky used this measure in their influential book *Manufacturing Consent* (Herman & Chomsky, 1988) to argue that differential newspaper coverage of the conflicts in East Timor and Cambodia betrayed a conspiracy to safeguard American interests.

Imagine that we have tabulated the amount of space given in a selection of South African publications to the coverage of violent crime, to see whether there is differential coverage. The data are shown in Table 3.3. We want to calculate indices of central tendency.

We start by ranking the data, to prepare for calculating the median and mode. This is shown in Table 3.4.

Table 3.3 Newspaper coverage of violent crime

Publication	% of space	Publication	% of space
The Cape Crimes	3.8	The Dullstroom Magnate	0.2
Soweto Times	2.3	The Natal Witless	7.8
City Blues	1.2	The Beaufort West Globe	1.1
The Pretoria Gnus	4.5	Burger	4.3
The Weekly Wail	6.7	De Wildernis Krokodil	6.8
The Argosy	4.5	Die Bult	5.6
Ulundi Ululator	0.2	Die Afrikana	9.8
Business Whey	9.4	The Sunday Crimes	9.9
The Sunday Dependent	1.8	His Majesty's Voice	0.1
Rapper	5	Pieterseburger	3.2
The Daily Dispute	4.2	The Eastern Cape Herod	2.2

Table 3.4 Ranking of data

Rank	Publication	% of space	Rank	Publication	% of space
1	His Majesty's Voice	0.1	12	Burger	4.3
2	Ulundi Ululator	0.2	13	The Pretoria Gnus	4.5
3	The Dullstroom Magnate	0.2	14	The Argosy	4.5
4	The Beaufort West Globe	1.1	15	Rapper	5
5	City Blues	1.2	16	Die Bult	5.6
6	The Sunday Dependent	1.8	17	The Weekly Wail	6.7
7	The Eastern Cape Herod	2.2	18	De Wildernis Krokodil	6.8
8	Soweto Times	2.3	19	The Natal Witless	7.8
9	Pieterseburger	3.2	20	Business Whey	9.4
10	The Cape Crimes	3.8	21	Die Afrikana	9.8
11	The Daily Dispute	4.2	22	The Sunday Crimes	9.9

Using a calculator

Mean

To calculate this, we use our calculators, following the procedure in Box 3.1. Thus, we put the calculator into STAT mode, and enter each of the data points. Then we press the key for the mean, usually SHIFT + $\bar{x}$, and we see that the answer is 4.3.

Median

We note that there are 22 newspapers in our survey. Noting that this is an even number, we apply the formula for the median position, $\frac{N+1}{2}$, which gives us 11.5 or, following the earlier discussion, the average of the 11th and 12th numbers, i.e. the average of 4.2 and 4.3 = 4.25.

Mode

We use the ranking to find data points with the same value, and we notice that both 0.2 and 4.5 are repeated, once each. The dataset is therefore bimodal, and the modes are 0.2 and 4.5.

We think you will agree that this was relatively easy, but we could have made the task even easier, and more reliable, by using a spreadsheet computer program. On the CD, we introduce you to spreadsheets, so we will show you here how to go about doing the calculations above with the aid of a spreadsheet.

Using a spreadsheet

Start by creating a new worksheet (use the 'File', 'New' command). Then enter the row headings as you see them in the original data table (create two columns only, as in the ranked data). Then enter

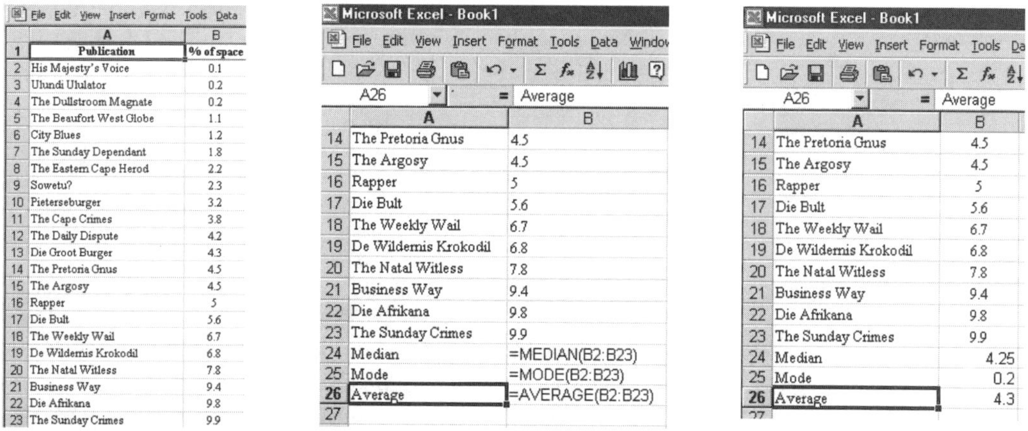

Figure 3.1 Calculating the median, mean (average), and mode in Microsoft® Excel

the data in the spreadsheet. You should now see something similar to that shown in Figure 3.1. You then enter built-in formulas below the data, entering the beginning and ending cell addresses of the data range, as shown in Figure 3.1. Excel automatically calculates the results, and displays them.

Summary

1. Measures of central tendency are shorthand ways of describing large collections of data. They are single numbers summarising a set of numbers.

2. The three most commonly used measures of central tendency are the mean, median, and mode.

3. The mean is the arithmetic average of a group of scores, the median is the middle score when scores are arranged from smallest to largest, and the mode is the most common score.

4. The mean is by far the most commonly used measure of central tendency and in most situations provides a good summary of where the midpoint of the data is. It is sensitive to outliers, though.

5. The median is particularly useful when working with skewed distributions.

6. The mode is particularly useful when working with nominal data.

Exercises

1. Which measure of central tendency – the mode, median, or mean – is the highest for the following group of test scores? Which is the lowest?

    8, 11, 12, 3, 31, 12, 8, 9, 12, 10, 5

2. The management board of a small mental hospital is budgeting to re-plan facilities for patients, and needs to decide on how to apportion funds to fit the needs of various disorders. They find that in the past 6 months they have had the following pattern of admissions: 8 patients with anxiety disorders, 41 with mood disorders, 35 with schizophrenia, 4 with substance-abuse disorders, and 8 with cognitive disorders. What measure of central tendency would you use to identify a 'typical' patient at the hospital?

3. In a study undertaken at the Witwatersrand Technikon on people suffering from a condition called *Moriti wa letswele*, it was

found that in the 11–20-year group there were 7 participants; in the 21–30-year group there were 15 participants; in the 31–40-year group there were 9 participants; and in the 41–50-year group there were 5 participants. What was the typical age of participants in this study?

4. Draw a picture of what central tendency means to you. Can you give your drawing a name?

5. You are interested in the types of non-alcoholic drinks students prefer. What measure would you use to find the most popular type of drink?

6. You are a photographer arranging 7 members of a family for a family photograph. You want to do a fan-like arrangement around the person who occupies the middle position in height. After placing the family in order of height, how would you decide which person should occupy the middle position?

7. A soccer coach wants to encourage more goal-scoring in his club. To motivate players he organises a competition among the 3 teams. They are each to play 10 matches in the season, and the team that has the highest average of goals scored in the season will win a prize. Which statistic would you use to calculate the highest average?

8. In a skewed distribution, which measure (mean, median, or mode) is a better reflection of central tendency?

9. Why would a government report the *median* national income, while reporting the *mean* educational level?

10. In wage negotiations, management often refer to mean salaries, while trade unions refer to median salaries. Why?

TUTORIAL 4

Variability

Martin Terre Blanche

After studying this tutorial, you should be able to:
- Explain the purpose of measures of variability.
- Name four measures of variability and explain how they differ from each other.
- Calculate the range, average deviation, variance, and standard deviation for a population.
- Calculate the variance and standard deviation for a sample.
- Explain and calculate the coefficient of variation.

Measures of central tendency (see Tutorial 3) tell us, in a highly economical fashion, where the midpoint of a group of scores is, but they do not reveal anything about the way the scores are arranged around that midpoint. Measures of variation do exactly that – they tell us how widely dispersed numbers are. There are three commonly used measures of variation – the *range*, the *variance*, and the *standard deviation* – each of which helps us to understand the degree of variability in a dataset in a different way.

Suppose we measured how many seconds it took people in three different rooms to respond to having their name called out, and got the results shown in Figure 4.1. These sets of scores have exactly the same mean (3), but are very different sets of data. The first set shows no variation at all, the second shows some variation, and the third, by comparison, shows a lot of variation.

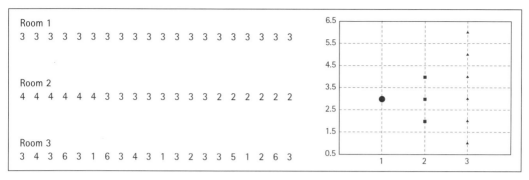

Figure 4.1 Reaction times in seconds, with a plot of the scores

As another demonstration, consider the two bar charts in Figure 4.2, depicting students' scores out of 20 in a Psychology test.

There are about 500 students in each class and in each case the mean, median, and mode are exactly 13. So, on average, the two classes did equally well on the test. As you can see, however, the classes are very different in other respects. In Class 1, many students got low scores (20 cases as low as 7), but many other students got exceptionally high scores. The students in Class 2 are more similar to each other, with almost everybody scoring between 10 and 16. Thus there is less variability in Class 2 than in Class 1. Measures of variability are ways of expressing such differing degrees of variability mathematically.

Of course, the concept 'variability' has wider application and relevance than the prospect of measuring numerical dispersion might suggest. Think about the great interest that 'difference' or 'variation' has in our daily lives. Why are we interested in the practices and beliefs of different cultures? Why are we bored by daily domestic rituals? Think also about the importance of variation to our existence. We wake up 99 mornings out of a 100 feeling more or

Measures of variability *indicate the degree to which the scores are dispersed, or different from each other.*

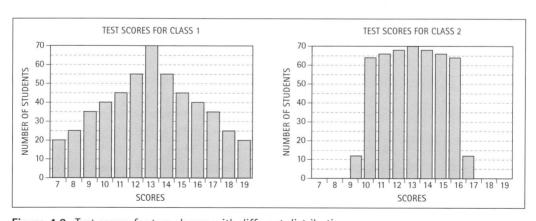

Figure 4.2 Test scores for two classes with different distributions

less the same, but if we should wake with impaired vision and loss of balance, we would be immediately alarmed. On the other hand, we are generally not at all interested in our (near) failure to change height from morning to morning. A strong argument can be made for the epistemological importance of variation or difference in a variety of human enterprises.

The notion of variation is central to many statistical concepts and procedures.

It is thus no accident that the concept of variability is one of the most important and fundamental in statistics. It is vital to have a firm understanding of this concept if we are to progress to an understanding of inferential statistics.

The range

The *range* is the most straightforward measure of variability – it is the difference between the highest and lowest scores in a dataset. So in Class 1 of Figure 4.2 the range is 12 (the highest score, 19, minus the lowest score, 7), while in Class 2 it is only 8 (17 minus 9).

Activity 4.1

Calculate the *extended* and *crude* ranges for the data in each of the sets in Figure 4.1.

*The **range** is the distance between the bottom and top of the dataset, or distribution. The **crude range** is the difference between the maximum and minimum scores. The **extended range** is this difference + 1.*

The range as calculated here is also sometimes referred to as the *crude range*. The *extended range* involves adding one to the crude range. Count the number of bars in the bar graphs for Class 1 and Class 2 and you will see why adding one to the difference between the lowest and highest scores actually gives a more accurate indication of the range of scores obtained. It does not matter much whether you use the crude or extended range, provided it is clear which calculation you used. You should also make it clear whether you are referring to the actual, observed range or the *potential* range of scores. The range in Class 1 is 12, and in Class 2 it is 8, but in both cases the potential crude range is $20 - 0 = 20$. The potential extended range (i.e. the number of possible scores students could have got) is $20 - 0 + 1 = 21$.

Although the range is easy to understand and makes intuitive sense, it is a rough-and-ready indication of variability, as it is based on two numbers only – the highest and lowest scores. Figure 4.3 shows the number of accidents per month at two mines. The range is the same for both mines, namely 7 – i.e. there are between 0 and 7 accidents per month at each mine. However, as you can see, there are from 2 to 4 accidents most months at mine B, whereas there is much more variability at mine A. Thus the range is susceptible to the same problem as the mean – it can give a false impression if there are atypical, extreme scores (outliers).

A range index that tries to avoid the problem of outliers is known as the *interquartile range*, and is similar in some ways to the

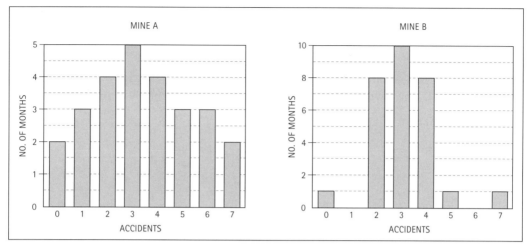

Figure 4.3 Accident rates at two mines

trimmed mean. The interquartile range is the distance between the 25th and 75th percentiles of the dataset. It is the middle 50% of the distribution, and therefore excludes extreme values, which lie at the top or bottom of the distribution.

To see how the range index works, in Table 4.1 we show the frequency distribution of the data from Table 3.1 in Tutorial 3 recording the number of hours a group of students spend on the Internet. Using the methods shown in Tutorial 2, we find that the 25th and 75th percentiles are 1 and 4 respectively. The interquartile range is therefore 3. Notice that this is much smaller and more 'characteristic' than the crude or extended ranges of this dataset, which are 31 and 32 respectively.

*The **interquartile range** is the difference between the 25th and 75th quartiles.*

Calculate the interquartile ranges of the three datasets shown in Figure 4.1.

Activity 4.2

Table 4.1 Frequency distribution of student hours on the Internet

	Frequency	Cumulative frequency	% frequency	Cumulative %
x ≤ 0	2	2	22.2	22.2
0 < x ≤ 10	6	8	66.7	88.9
10 < x ≤ 20	0	8	0	88.9
20 < x ≤ 30	0	8	0	88.9
30 < x ≤ 40	1	9	11.1	100

The average deviation

Table 4.2 Calculating the average deviation

	Courses passed	Difference from mean	Absolute difference
Itumeleng	0	–2	2
Pravani	1	–1	1
Ingrid	1	–1	1
Mcebesi	2	0	0
Johan	2	0	0
Linda	3	1	1
Stephen	3	1	1
Xavier	4	2	2
TOTAL	16	0	8

If at this point you find yourself puzzled by why there is a minus sign before some difference scores, you are probably not familiar with the concept of negative numbers and should seek mathematics instruction. Start with Tutorial 23 in this book.

A more sophisticated way of indicating how much variation there is in a dataset is to calculate, on average, how far each score is from the mean. Table 4.2 shows data for the number of first-year courses passed by a group of students. In total the students have passed 16 courses, and since there are 8 students, the mean number of courses passed is 2 (16 courses divided by 8 students). The table also shows the difference between each student's score and the mean (e.g. Itumeleng passed 0 courses, minus the mean of 2, equals a difference score of –2). Since the mean is by definition exactly at the mid-point of the distribution of scores, the negative differences (scores below the mean) and positive differences (scores above the mean) will cancel each other out. Therefore the total of the difference scores is always 0. (Checking that the total is 0 is a useful way of ensuring that you have not made any errors in calculating the difference scores.)

The last column shows the absolute differences, i.e. how far each score is from the mean, irrespective of whether it is above or below the mean. The absolute differences are just the differences with the negative signs removed. By adding up the absolute differences (which comes to a total of 8) and dividing by the number of students (8), we get the *average deviation*, which in this case is 1 (8 divided by 8). The formula is as follows:

$$AD = \frac{\Sigma \, |x - \mu|}{N}$$

Equation 4.1

where: AD = average deviation
Σ = summate (or add up)
x = each score
μ = the population mean
N = the number of observations

Thus we can say that, on average, students have passed 1 course more (or fewer) than the mean of 2. Suppose now that Pravani actually passed 0 courses rather than 1, and Xavier passed 5 courses rather than 4. In that case the average deviation would have been 1.25 (verify this yourself). Can you see that although the mean remains the same (2), the average deviation has increased slightly? We would then say that on average students have passed 1.25 courses more (or fewer) than the mean.

*The **average deviation** is the average of the absolute distances of individual scores from the mean of the distribution.*

The variance

The most important and commonly used measure of variability in statistics is the *variance*. Like the average deviation, the variance is a more complete measure of variability than the range because it is not derived from the highest and lowest scores only, but from a formula that includes each score in the relevant dataset. Like the average deviation, it also gives an indication of how far, on average, each score is from the mean. It is, however, not quite as easy to calculate or interpret.

If we are dealing with a population of scores, we calculate the variance as follows:

$$\sigma^2 = \frac{\Sigma \, (x - \mu)^2}{N}$$

Equation 4.2

where: σ^2 = the variance of the population
Σ = summate (or add up)
x = each score
μ = the population mean
N = the number of observations

To calculate the (population) variance manually it again helps to draw up a table with columns for the raw scores and for the difference between each raw score and the mean. However, in the last column we will now place the squared difference rather than the absolute difference. Squaring numbers (multiplying them by themselves) has the effect of removing all negative numbers. This time we will use the data from Tutorial 3 on the number of hours students spend on the Internet.

*The **variance** is the average of the squared distances of individual scores from the mean of the distribution.*

Table 4.3 Calculating variance

	Raw score	Difference $(x - \mu)$	Squared difference $(x - \mu)^2$
Itumeleng	0	−5	25
Pravani	0	−5	25
Ingrid	1	−4	16
Mcebesi	1	−4	16
Johan	1	−4	16
Linda	3	−2	4
Stephen	4	−1	1
Xavier	4	−1	1
Tumelo	31	26	676
TOTAL (Σ)	45	0	780

As always, the sum of the differences comes to 0. However, the sum of squared differences is 780. Thus the variance (or average squared difference) is 86.67 (780 divided by 9 students). Suppose we left Tumelo (who had a very extreme score) out of the calculation, then the sum of squared differences would be 104, and the variance would be 13 (verify this calculation yourself). Notice the rather dramatic change.

Calculating the variance in this manner can be quite laborious, especially if you are doing it all by hand. An alternative technique is to use a mathematically equivalent formula, which makes the computation of variance much easier:

Equation 4.3

$$\sigma^2 = \frac{\sum x^2 - \dfrac{(\sum x)^2}{N}}{N}$$

It is best to use this formula with a calculator that has built-in functions for automatically calculating the components Σx^2 and Σx. This is demonstrated in Box 4.1, as are the calculations for some other indices of variation.

Box 4.1

Using a calculator to find σ^2, σ, s^2, and s

Almost all modern scientific calculators offer a mode for entering lists of data, and functions that make it easy to do calculations on the data. Functions that calculate Σx^2 and Σx are very useful shortcuts for working with computational formulae for measures of variation, and there are also functions that will calculate some standard measures of variation in one fell swoop! For the Casio-FX® 280 model, and the data in the example involving courses passed by first-year students (Table 4.2), the steps for calculating the variance with the computational formula (Equation 4.3) are shown below. Your calculator may use different keys to generate output, but most calculator functions are similar to those outlined below. Consult your calculator manual to determine how your calculator works.

Step	Keys
1. Put calculator into STAT mode	You change mode by pressing the 'MODE' key, then selecting STAT mode, e.g. by pressing the · (point) key.
2. Enter data	Enter the first data item, then press the 'DATA' key (M+). Enter the next item and press the 'DATA' key. Continue until all the data is entered.
3. Find Σx^2	You should find the symbol 'Σx^2' above one of your keys. First press 'SHIFT' and then the 'Σx^2' key.
4. Find Σx	You should find the symbol 'Σx' above one of your keys. First press 'SHIFT' and then the 'Σx' key.

To calculate σ^2:

$$\sigma^2 = \frac{\Sigma x^2 - \frac{(\Sigma x)^2}{N}}{N} = \frac{44 - \frac{(16)^2}{8}}{8} = \frac{44 - \frac{256}{8}}{8} = \frac{44 - 32}{8} = \frac{12}{8} = 1.5$$

However, notice that your calculator has the formula for σ (the population standard deviation) built in. So all you have to do to calculate σ^2 is:

1. Put the calculator into STAT mode.
2. Enter the data.
3. Push 'SHIFT' and then the 'σ' key.

This will give you the value of σ. Now, to find σ^2, square the value of σ, using the appropriate function.

> To calculate s^2 (the sample variance) notice that your calculator has the formula for s (the sample standard deviation) built in. Push the 'SHIFT' key and 's' keys after step 2 in the table above, and then square the value.

The variance is not easy to interpret. We can say that the students' average squared difference from the mean was 13, but it is quite hard to visualise what that might mean. The variance is nevertheless a very important statistic, and is very frequently used as part of other statistical calculations. It also forms the basis for the *standard deviation*, another measure of variability, which is easier to interpret.

Activity 4.3	By hand, calculate the average deviance and variance of the data in the worked example of Tutorial 3. Now use your calculator to work out the variance of that dataset, and also of each of the datasets in Figure 4.1 of this tutorial.

The standard deviation

The standard deviation σ, in the case of a population, is the square root of the variance (σ^2), so the formula is the same as for the variance, except that a square root is calculated:

Equation 4.4

$$\sigma = \sqrt{\frac{\Sigma (x - \mu)^2}{N}}$$

Or, more simply:

Equation 4.5

$$\sigma = \sqrt{\sigma^2}$$

Activity 4.4	Calculate the average deviations and standard deviations for each of the datasets in Figure 4.1. Compare them and try to decide which index is more informative.

The computational formula for the population standard deviation is the same as the computational formula for the variance, except that the square root is taken, i.e.

$$\sigma = \sqrt{\frac{\Sigma x^2 - \frac{(\Sigma x)^2}{N}}{N}}$$

Since calculating the square root of a number is the opposite of squaring the number, the standard deviation in a sense undoes the squaring that occurred in the course of calculating the variance and thus brings the result back to the same scale as the original numbers. Thus the (population) standard deviation of the amount of time students spend on the Internet is 9.31 hours (the square root of 86.7). If we left Tumelo out of the dataset the standard deviation would be 3.61 hours (the square root of 13).

Although the standard deviation is not quite as straightforward as the average deviation, it works on a very similar principle and can also be interpreted as the 'average distance' of the cases in a dataset from the mean. As will be evident in a later tutorial, knowing the standard deviation also allows us to compare individuals' scores on different tests, and to predict with some certainty what proportion of individuals scored within a particular range on a test.

*The **standard deviation** is the square root of the average of the squared distances of individual scores from the mean of the distribution.*

Box 4.2

The coefficient of variation

A group of people are employed to clear an area of non-indigenous, invasive trees. Each person is also required to collect the seeds of indigenous trees. The mean number of trees cut down per person on a particular day is 109, with a standard deviation of 4. The mean number of seeds collected per person is 12, with a standard deviation of 2. Thus the standard deviation for cutting down trees is twice as large as that for collecting seeds, and we might be tempted to think that there is more variation in the group with regard to cutting down trees than with regard to collecting seeds. In fact, the group is much more homogenous (similar to each other) in terms of tree-felling than in terms of seed-collecting. A deviation of 4 above and below a large number such as 109 is proportionally much smaller than a deviation of 2 above and below a small number such as 12. This can be mathematically expressed using the coefficient of variation (cv), which is simply the variance divided by the mean. Bearing in mind that the variance is the square of the standard deviation, we find:

*The **coefficient of variation** allows you to compare the variance of samples with different means.*

$$^{cv} \text{tree-felling} = \frac{\sigma^2}{\mu} = \frac{16}{109} = 0.15$$

$$^{cv} \text{seed-collecting} = \frac{\sigma^2}{\mu} = \frac{4}{12} = 0.33$$

Estimating population parameters from sample data

Thus far we have shown how to calculate measures of central tendency and variability of a group where the score of every member of the group is known. Such groups are called populations and can be very large (such as the population of South Africa) or very small (such as those people riding in a particular taxi). Often, though, we do not have information on everybody in a population, but have to estimate population parameters from what we know of a sub-group of this population (a sample). As we saw in Tutorial 3, different symbols are used to indicate whether we are working with a sample statistic or a population parameter. The symbol for the mean of a population is μ while the mean of a sample is usually $\bar{x}$. Similarly, the variance of a population is σ^2 (sigma squared) while the variance of a sample is s^2. The standard deviation of a population is σ and of a sample is s. Finally, it is conventional (but not essential) to use a capital N to indicate the number of cases when dealing with a population, and a small n when dealing with a sample. The definition and computation formulas for sample variance and standard deviation are:

Equation 4.6

$$s^2 = \frac{\Sigma (x - \bar{x})^2}{n - 1} \quad \text{(definition)} \qquad s^2 = \frac{\Sigma x^2 - \dfrac{(\Sigma x)^2}{n}}{n - 1} \quad \text{(computation)}$$

Equation 4.7

$$s = \sqrt{\frac{\Sigma (x - \bar{x})^2}{n - 1}} \quad \text{(definition)} \qquad s = \sqrt{\frac{\Sigma x^2 - \dfrac{(\Sigma x)^2}{n}}{n - 1}} \quad \text{(computation)}$$

Notice, most importantly, that the formulas for calculating the sample variance and standard deviation involve dividing by n – 1 rather than by n. Dividing by n – 1 provides a better, unbiased estimate of the population parameter (σ^2, or σ) than dividing by n. This can be proven both mathematically and empirically, but for the purposes of this course, we will just take it on faith that this is the case.

The boxplot

It is standard practice to start the examination of a dataset with a boxplot.

A *boxplot* or *box-and-whisker plot* is a means of displaying data that emphasises the dispersion of the dataset, rather than the frequency of individual values. Figure 4.4 reports computer-generated boxplots for scores on four variables: a skewed and a symmetrical variable, and variables with a small and a large range. The bold line in the middle of the plots represents the median (the 50th percentile) of each distribution. This is the middlemost score in the distribution. The edges of the box above and below the median are the quartiles (25th percentile below and 75th percentile above). The box represents the middlemost 50% of the distribution. The box has 'whiskers' (i.e. the vertical lines), one below the 1st quartile and one above the 3rd quartile. The whiskers are designed to indicate the lowest and highest values in each distribution: they show the spread of scores of the lower and upper 25% of the distributions. Each boxplot represents the distribution of a full set of scores, indicating the median, and the values that bracket the inner and the outer scores.

A box-and-whisker plot is a graphical representation of the dispersion (or spread) of a dataset.

The plot also indicates *outliers*, which are extreme scores. What the plot does is define values that are deemed to be so extreme or different to the rest that they can be considered outliers. It does this by starting at the median and then defining values that lie 50% (or some other conventional value such as 75%) above and below the median. Any values that lie outside this statistically defined distribution are defined as outliers. The 'Small range' plot in Figure 4.4 contains an outlier. Notice that, besides the single score of 7, the data for this variable includes only values 2, 3, and 4. The value of 7 is deemed to be outside the distribution of scores. Outliers can have a distorting influence on statistical analysis, and should be carefully investigated, and sometimes eliminated from the dataset. Outliers often indicate data entry or measurement errors, which should be corrected before further analysis. On the other hand, outliers can indicate extreme but real observations. In such instances we could either eliminate the outlier or retain it for further analysis. This will depend on the aims of the analysis and the kind of statistical procedures we apply to the data.

Outliers are extreme scores.

Activity 4.5

For each distribution represented in Figure 4.4, determine the value of the median and the first and third quartiles.

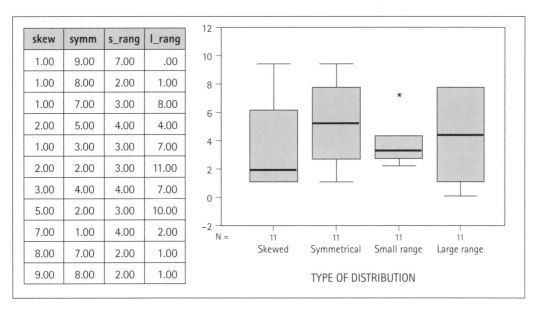

skew	symm	s_rang	l_rang
1.00	9.00	7.00	.00
1.00	8.00	2.00	1.00
1.00	7.00	3.00	8.00
2.00	5.00	4.00	4.00
1.00	3.00	3.00	7.00
2.00	2.00	3.00	11.00
3.00	4.00	4.00	7.00
5.00	2.00	3.00	10.00
7.00	1.00	4.00	2.00
8.00	7.00	2.00	1.00
9.00	8.00	2.00	1.00

Figure 4.4 Boxplots

Boxplots provide a clear representation of the shape of the distribution. The first distribution in Figure 4.4 is positively skewed. We can tell this from the fact that the median is closer to one edge of the box, and there is only an upper whisker. This shows that 50% of the observations lie within the narrow range of 1 and 2, while the upper 50% of observations lie between 2 and 9. The lower categories then have higher frequencies, and hence the distribution is positively skewed. In contrast, the symmetrical distribution has the median in the middle of the box, and has whiskers of equal length. The third distribution has a very low range. This can be seen from the narrow spread of scores represented by the box and the whisker. With the exception of the outlier, the scores tend to be clustered around the median. In contrast, the fourth distribution has a wide spread of scores, it is almost symmetrical, and has no outliers.

Activity 4.6

Use the data in Table 4.4 to calculate the boxplot. Draw the boxplot. Describe the distribution.

Where outliers (i.e. values located beyond the extremes of the whiskers) occur in the dataset, each is represented individually on the graph by means of an asterisk (*).

Worked example

There are a number of practical situations in which variation is an important concept, and in which measures can help you make decisions. One of these faces you when you graduate with a social science degree. What will you do with all the money you are about to earn? If you are considering investing in shares on the stock market, you will want to know how *risky* a particular share is. Although you will no doubt want to invest in a share that gives you a very good return (increases a lot in value), it is also well known that shares that give high returns are also risky – that is, there is a possibility of losing a large amount of money on the share, just as there is of making a large amount! A useful statistic is the standard deviation of the share price over a particular period, which is said to give an index of the *risk* or *volatility* of the share in that period. You can then use that index to rate the riskiness of the share.

In the table below, we have the closing share price over a 20-day period for a well-known South African company listed on the Johannesburg Securities Exchange. We will calculate a number of indices of variation, to demonstrate the concepts developed in this tutorial.

Table 4.4 Share price over a 20-day period (rands)

Day	1	2	3	4	5	6	7	8	9	10
Price	109	103.06	102.75	108	107.56	105.25	107.69	108.63	107	109
Day	11	12	13	14	15	16	17	18	19	20
Price	110	112.75	113.5	114.25	115.25	121.5	126.88	122.5	119	122.5

We start by entering this data into our calculators. This was shown earlier in the tutorial in Box 4.1.

Central tendency

It is useful to know the average price in the period in question. This we get from our calculator as 112.30

Variation

1. *Indices of range*

   We start by rank ordering the data. This tells us that the maximum and minimum values are 126.8 and 102.75, respectively. Therefore the *crude range* = (maximum – minimum) = 126.8 – 102.75 = 24.05, and the *extended range* = *crude range* + 1 = 25.05.

   To find the *interquartile range* we have to find the 25th and 75th percentiles of the frequency distribution of the data. We leave it up to you as an exercise to show that these are 107.625 and 117.125 (see Tutorial 2 for the method). Therefore, the *interquartile range* = (75th percentile – 25th percentile) = (117.125 – 107.625) = 9.5.

2. *Indices of variation*

   We set the data out in calculational format, to show workings, but at the same time advise you to take advantage of your calculator's ability to short-cut this process.

Day	1	2	3	4	5	6	7	8	9	10
Price	109	103.06	102.75	108	107.56	105.25	107.69	108.63	107	109
Day	11	12	13	14	15	16	17	18	19	20
Price	110	112.75	113.5	114.25	115.25	121.5	126.88	122.5	119	122.5
Day	1	2	3	4	5	6	7	8	9	10
Dev.	−3.3	−9.24	−9.55	−4.3	−4.74	−7.05	−4.61	−3.67	−5.3	−3.3
Day	11	12	13	14	15	16	17	18	19	20
Dev.	−2.3	0.45	1.2	1.95	2.95	9.2	14.58	10.2	6.7	10.2
Day	1	2	3	4	5	6	7	8	9	10
Dev²	10.89	85.38	91.20	18.49	22.47	49.70	21.25	13.47	28.09	10.89
Day	11	12	13	14	15	16	17	18	19	20
Dev²	5.29	0.20	1.44	3.80	8.70	84.64	212.58	104.04	44.89	104.04

To calculate the *average deviation*, we simply average the absolute values of the row marked 'Dev.', i.e.

$$\frac{(|-3.3| + |-9.24| + .. + |10.2|)}{20} = 5.74$$

In practice, population formulas are seldom used.

For the *variance* and *standard deviation* we first need to decide whether to use the sample or population formulas. It is seldom that we can make a good case for using the population formula, but in this case we can, since we are only interested in the variation over the 20-day period, and we have all the data for that period. However, we can also make a case for treating the data as sample points, and for the sake of completeness we will calculate sample and population indices.

For all formulas, we will need the following interim results, which can be obtained from our calculators after entering the data in STAT mode: $\Sigma x^2 = 253163$ $\Sigma x = 2246.07$

Then,

$$\text{population variance} = \sigma^2 = \frac{\Sigma x^2 - \frac{(\Sigma x)^2}{N}}{N} = \frac{253163 - \frac{(2246.07)^2}{20}}{20}$$

$$= 46.072$$

and population standard deviation $= \sqrt{\sigma^2} = \sqrt{46.07} = 6.79$.

Similarly,

$$\text{sample variance} = s^2 = \frac{\Sigma x^2 - \frac{(\Sigma x)^2}{n}}{n-1} = \frac{253163 - \frac{(2246.07)^2}{20}}{19} = 48.50,$$

and sample standard deviation $= \sqrt{s^2} = \sqrt{48.5} = 6.96$.

To check our calculations, or as an alternative to the long-winded process we have just gone through, we simply press the 'SHIFT' and 'σ' keys on our calculators to get the population standard deviation. We then square this to get the population variance. Similarly, to get the sample standard deviation, we press the 'SHIFT' and 's' keys, and we square this result to get the sample variance.

As another alternative, if you have started to use spreadsheets for your calculations, here is how to do it in Microsoft Excel:

Start by creating a new worksheet (use the 'File', 'New' command). Then enter the data in the spreadsheet; we show a set-up in Figure 4.5 where the data are entered in columns. You then enter built-in formulas below the data, entering the beginning and ending cell addresses of the data range, as shown in the screenshots (notice the different formulas for populations and samples). Excel automatically calculates the results, and displays them.

Microsoft Excel - B

File Edit View In

C17

	A	B
13	Day	Price
14	1	109
15	2	103.06
16	3	102.75
17	4	108
18	5	107.56
19	6	105.25
20	7	107.69
21	8	108.63
22	9	107
23	10	109
24	11	110
25	12	112.75
26	13	113.5
27	14	114.25
28	15	115.25
29	16	121.5
30	17	126.88
31	18	122.5
32	19	119
33	20	122.5

Formulas:

σ^2	=VARP(B14:B33)
σ	=STDEVP(B14:B33)
s^2	=VAR(B14:B33)
s	=STDEV(B14:B33)
range	=MAX(B14:B33)-MIN(B14:B33)
iq range	=QUARTILE(B14:B33,3)-QUARTILE(B14:B33,1)

Microsoft Excel -

File Edit View

A29

	A	B
18	5	107.56
19	6	105.25
20	7	107.69
21	8	108.63
22	9	107
23	10	109
24	11	110
25	12	112.75
26	13	113.5
27	14	114.25
28	15	115.25
29	16	121.5
30	17	126.88
31	18	122.5
32	19	119
33	20	122.5
34		
35	σ^2	46.07
36	σ	6.79
37	s^2	48.50
38	s	6.96

Data	Formulas	Outcome

Figure 4.5 Calculating measures of variation with Microsoft® Excel

What do these indices of variation mean, in practical terms? The standard deviation in the closing share price is nearly R7, which means that in the 20-day period in question the stock price has on average closed within R7 of the mean share price in the period. One practical way to use this information is to compare this standard deviation to the standard deviations of other share prices calculated in the same way, correcting for differences in scale, or size (see Box 4.2 for an example). Shares that have higher corrected values for the standard deviation are, on average, riskier, and you can use this information to guide your investment strategy.

Summary

1. Measures of variability show how widely dispersed scores in a dataset are.

2. The *crude range* is the highest score minus the lowest score. The *extended range* is the crude range plus one. The range can be unduly affected by extreme scores.

3. The average deviation is the average absolute distance that scores are away from the mean. A large average deviation indicates that scores are widely dispersed. A small average deviation indicates that scores are tightly bunched around the mean.

4. The variance is the average squared distance of scores from the mean. It plays an important role in a number of statistical calculations and advanced procedures.

5. The standard deviation is the square root of the variance. A large standard deviation indicates that scores are widely dispersed. A small standard deviation indicates that scores are tightly bunched around the mean.

6. When the variance or standard deviation of a sample is used to estimate the variance or standard deviation of a population, the formulas involve division by n − 1 rather than by N.

7. The coefficient of variation allows us to compare the variability in two distributions, even though the means of the distributions may be very different. It is calculated by dividing the variance by the mean.

Questions

1. Ten teenagers in a school were given a general knowledge test on AIDS and another ten a test on drug-related behaviour. The scores on the two tests were as follows:

   Knowledge of AIDS: 8, 1, 8, 6, 12, 9, 6, 5, 11, 13
   Knowledge of drugs: 91, 42, 98, 30, 18, 73, 84, 92, 45, 92

   a) Calculate the mean score of the group on each test.
   b) Calculate the variance and standard deviation of the two tests.
   c) On which test is there more variability?
   d) Find the median for each test.
   e) For each test say whether it is positively skewed, negatively skewed, or symmetrical.

2. Two teams of players compete in a computer game. The scores are as follows:

   Team A: 125, 100, 50, 65, 3 000, 90
   Team B: 100, 120, 119, 105, 99, 102

   a) For each team, calculate the range, average deviation, variance, and standard deviation.
   b) Explain why in this case it would not matter much whether you had calculated the crude or the extended range.
   c) Explain why the range is a problematic measure of variability in Team A.
   d) Which team shows more variability?

3. The following represent the number of accidents that occurred at five randomly selected pedestrian crossings in Cape Town in the past year:

3, 7, 2, 3, 5

Estimate the standard deviation of accidents at pedestrian crossings in the whole of Cape Town over the same period.

4. After one month in the country, a group of visiting students from the United Kingdom know the following total number of words in South African languages other than English.

Johnny	22
Fred	12
Mary	14
Bill	12
Jane	14
Susan	14
Michael	17
Sharon	19
Harry	11
Patricia	15
Eric	20

What is the range, average deviation, variance, and standard deviation of the number of words known by these students? For all similar students who visit South Africa, what would be the variance and standard deviation of words known after one month?

Probability and theoretical distributions

Lance Lachenicht

After studying this tutorial, you should be able to:
- Understand probability as a relative frequency.
- Understand the representation of probabilities by numbers.
- Understand the multiplication and addition rules of probability.
- Calculate the probabilities of multiple outcomes.
- Calculate the number of arrangements of multiple events.
- Understand and do simple calculations using the binomial distribution.

Probability as frequency

*The **frequency** view of probability is that the likelihood of an event occurring is its long-term frequency of occurrence (e.g. in a population, or in past history).*

The idea of probability that underlies most of the statistics that you will learn in this tutorial course is that of *frequency* of occurrence. If 50% of coin tosses land as heads, then the chance of getting heads when you toss a coin is 50%. If 95% of 18-month-old children are in the 'one-word-or-later' stage of language learning, then your chance of finding a child of 18 months who is *not* speaking is only 5%, or 1 in 20.

The notion of frequency of occurrence can be expressed in a number of ways. Suppose that 60 out of 150 people report dreaming about a relative every year. We can express this baldly as it stands, but more often we use one of the following expressions: as a simpler fraction by cancelling down, i.e. two-fifths of people report dreaming of a relative (since $^{60}/_{150} = ^{6}/_{15} = ^{2}/_{5}$); as a decimal (0.4 of people report dreaming of a relative); or as a percentage (40% of people report dreaming of a relative). Decimals and percentages represent proportions in a way that lends itself to easy comparison.

Expressing frequencies as percentages and proportions facilitates comparisons.

The notion of probability arising from an underlying frequency is easy to understand but can pose some subtle difficulties when used in arguments. For example, there is a general rule in logic that holds that it is wrong to reason that because 'Every A is B', 'Every B is A'. So if every human is an animal that walks on two legs, it does not follow that every animal that walks on two legs is a human. The same rule holds for frequency-based probabilities. If 90% of cats are black, it does not follow that 90% of black things are cats! This may seem obvious, but consider a parliamentarian who argues against dagga smoking by pointing out that 95% of heroin addicts began as dagga smokers. Presumably this is meant to show how dangerous smoking dagga is. But the argument is fallacious. If 95% of heroin smokers began by smoking dagga, it does not follow that 95% of dagga smokers will become addicted to heroin.

> How good is the following argument? (Defend your answer.) 'More people suffer from mental illness than any other form of serious illness in South Africa. That is clear from the fact that at any time a third of hospital beds are occupied by mentally ill patients, and no other illness approaches that proportion.'

Activity 5.1

If someone says that the probability of a criminal being male is 4 in 5, they are giving a specification of the weight of evidence for or against an assertion (in this case, the assertion that a randomly selected criminal will most likely be male). This kind of probability statement gives a measure of our confidence in the assertion. The higher the probability of a state of affairs, the greater the confidence we are justified in having that it will come about. If the evidence in favour of some event is utterly conclusive, we can assign it the number '1'. On the other hand, if the evidence against some event is utterly conclusive, then we can assign it the number '0'. Between these two points, the stronger the evidence, the greater the number assigned to the probability. So the probability of someone running a mile in 29 seconds is 0, and the probability of a person dying some

The higher the probability of an event occurring, the more confident we are that it will come about.

The value of a probability can vary from 0 to 1.

day is 1. On the other hand, the probability of a human randomly selected from anywhere on earth being Chinese is about 0.2.

Probability and games of chance

Frequency-based probability estimates are based on experience or evidence (e.g. measurements of frequencies). Saying that 'The probability of those who smoke dagga going on to take heroin is about 1 in 100' is an extrapolation from past to future. This probability is based on what has happened before. It could change, so that we could eventually say something like, 'The probability of those who smoke dagga going on to take heroin used to be 1 in 100 but is now 1 in 110'. In either case, we are basing our claim on evidence.

There is a contrast between the kind of claim discussed above, based upon experience, and those involving games of chance such as drawing a card from a pack, or tossing a coin. We also use numbers when estimating chance in such games, e.g. 'The chance of tossing a coin and getting tails is 1 in 2'. Here it is assumed that tossing a coin will approximate very closely to a completely *random* series of two sorts of outcomes called heads and tails (H and T). Statisticians are interested in random series and random selections, and not in actually tossing coins or shuffling real cards. In fact, these activities are close enough to true randomising procedures for mathematical or statistical results to apply. So we ignore the very remote possibility of a coin balancing on its edge, and say that the probability of a coin falling heads upwards is 1 in 2. This implies that the very same 1-in-2 probability applies to the coin falling tails upwards, and that together these two outcomes exhaust all the possibilities when a coin is tossed. Moreover, we assume that the coin will fall randomly so that we cannot predict the outcome of any particular toss, and that we cannot find any pattern in any sequence of throws. Nevertheless, we are certain that in any very long series of throws the number of heads will be very nearly equal to the number of tails.

Box 5.1

Random numbers

It is surprisingly difficult to define what a completely random series of numbers might be. Bennett (1998) provides a good overview of the debate about random numbers, which we summarise here. The statistician Von Mises thought that a random sequence of numbers must be one where it is completely impossible to predict the next element in the sequence. However, every sequence of numbers has to conform to *some* rule or formula (we may simply not know what the rule is ahead of time). Kolmogorov, the famous Russian mathematician, tried to emend Von Mises' definition by suggesting that randomness has to be judged in terms of predictability by a *small* set of simple rules. He thought that the randomness of a series of numbers should be judged by the *length* of the formula required to generate it. A completely random sequence would require a formula nearly as long as the series of numbers itself.

Other thinkers (such as Ian Hacking) suggest that we are wrong to concentrate on the random sequence of numbers, but that we should instead concentrate on *how* the supposed sequence of random numbers is generated. Hacking argues that 'random samples are defined entirely in terms of the sampling device'. But the problem with this approach is that it is entirely possible for a non-random-looking sequence of numbers to be generated by a random process.

The statisticians Kendall and Babington-Smith suggest that it might be better to set aside this debate and concentrate on some tests of the randomness of a sequence of numbers. They propose four tests of the randomness of a sequence of numbers – the frequency test, serial test, poker test, and gap test. Imagine that we have a set of numbers ranging from 1 to 10. The *frequency* test of randomness tests whether each of the ten digits from 1 to 10 will appear an approximately equal number of times, about 1 time in 10. The *serial* test examines each possible two-digit pair of numbers (12, 23, 54, etc.) and determines whether they occur an approximately equal number of times – about 1 time in 100. (This would detect a non-random sequence such as 1 2 3 4 5 6 7 8 9 0 where each digit occurs equally often but where only 5 (12 34 56 78 90) of 100 possible pairs occur.) The *poker* test compares five-digit groups of numbers against the expected occurrence of certain five-card poker hands. The *gap* test examines the number of digits (the gap length) between the occurrences of the digit 0. In the gap test the sequence 043611978500245620 has gap lengths of 9, 0, and 5. The lengths of these gaps are compared with what would be expected of digits selected by chance.

Probabilities are sometimes referred to by small letters such as p and q. If we consider coin tossing, then p might be the probability of throwing a head, and q the probability of throwing a tail. Since $p = 0.5$ (i.e. 50%), and since $q = 0.5$, $p = q$, and $p + q = 1$, or $q = 1 - p$ and $p = 1 - q$.

When an event has more than one possible outcome, we may be particularly interested in one of these possibilities. Perhaps we may bet on that particular outcome. (When we take a ticket in a lottery, we are particularly interested in the probability that *our* ticket is drawn.) Whatever the source of our interest in the outcome, if that outcome comes about we will call it a *success*. The term 'success' is very widely used in statistics irrespective of the intrinsic value of an

The letter 'p' is often used as an abbreviation for probability, e.g. the probability of x is p(x).

outcome or whether any bets have been laid. Our interest may not just be on a single toss of the coin, but on a succession of throws. We might bet that there would be exactly two heads in three successive throws. In that case several possible outcomes would count as a success: HHT, HTH, THH. There are altogether eight possible outcomes of a series of three coin tossings: HHH, HHT, HTH, HTT, THH, THT, TTH, and TTT. Since each of these eight outcomes is equally likely, and three of the eight count as successes, the probability of a success is $^3/_8$, or 37.5%.

The multiplication and addition rules of probability

Probability is defined as p = %ₙ, i.e. the number of 'successes' divided by the total number of events.

Unlike the toss of a coin, a single event may have more than two possible outcomes. If we roll a die, there are six possible outcomes. If we draw a card from a pack of cards, there are 52 possible outcomes. We may bet on such an event in a way that permits several different outcomes to count as successes. For example, we may bet that we will draw a heart from a pack of cards. Since there are 13 different hearts to be drawn from the pack, the probability of a success is $^{13}/_{52}$ or 1 in 4, i.e. 25%. In general we have the following rule:

Equation 5.1

$$p = \frac{a}{n}$$

where: p is the probability of success
n is the total number of equally possible outcomes
a is the number of these that count as successes

The total number of successes can never be more than the number of possible outcomes, so the value of p will always be between 0 and 1.

*Events are said to be **independent** when they do not affect the probability of each other occurring.*

What happens when we bet on the outcome of a series of independent events? Of crucial importance is the notion of *independent events* when thinking about this problem, for the probability of success in a series of independent events is estimated on the basis of the probabilities of the individual events. If the events are not independent, we cannot easily estimate the probability of a series of events taking place. As an illustration of the conceptual difficulties we get into when we base calculations upon non-independent events, consider the explanation a little girl offered a truancy officer for failing to attend school, given on the next page (Gardner, 1978).

Activity 5.2

Suppose a coin is thrown ten times. Below we list two possible outcomes. Many people would argue that the second outcome is more likely than the first. Are they correct? Justify your answer.

a) TTTTTTTTTT   b) HTTTHHTHHT

I sleep 8 hours every day. This means I sleep 8 × 365 or 2920 hours. There are 24 hours in a day so I sleep $^{2920}/_{24}$ or 122 days. The weekend (Saturday and Sunday) does not have school, and this comes to 104 days in a year. The schools have 60 days of holiday every year. I need three hours a day for meals. If you work that out it's 3 × 365 or 1095 hours per year which is about 45 days per year. And I need at least two hours of playtime every day which is 2 × 365 or 730 hours which is about 30 days per year. If you add these up (361 days) you will see I don't have time to go to school.

Can you see the problem with her reasoning? Note that sleep time and weekend time are not independent. She sleeps on weekends.

As already pointed out, the probability of success when we bet on a series of independent events is estimated on the basis of the probabilities of the individual events. There are two cases to consider: the probability of a conjunction (combination) of independent outcomes (i.e. *a* **and** *b*), and the probability of a disjunction (separation) of independent outcomes (i.e. *a* **or** *b*). If we bet on the conjunction of independent outcomes (i.e. two or more things happening together) then we must multiply the probabilities of the outcomes together:

$$p(a \text{ and } b) = p(a) \times p(b)$$

Equation 5.2

For example, the probability of getting heads in two successive tosses of a coin is the probability of getting heads on the first toss multiplied by the probability of getting heads on the second toss (i.e. 0.5 × 0.5 = 0.25). Similarly, the probability of getting heads in three successive tosses will be $(0.5)^3$. In the general case, the probability of getting heads in *n* successive tosses will be $(0.5)^n$.

What is the probability of drawing two successive hearts from a pack of cards? Here we have to ask whether the first card will be replaced after being drawn or not. If it is replaced then the second drawing is independent of the first in the same way that two successive tosses of a coin are independent. If the first card is replaced we can find the probability of drawing two hearts by multiplying together the probabilities of the separate draws, i.e. $p = 0.25 \times 0.25 = 0.0625$. Performing independent trials analogous to this is called *sampling with replacement*. However, if the first card is not replaced, then the second draw takes place under conditions that have been changed by the first and is therefore not independent. Suppose the first card drawn is a heart, and is not replaced. The second draw is therefore not from a pack of 52 cards, but from a pack of 51 cards with only 12 hearts. The chance of drawing

*The **probability law of conjunctions** (the multiplicative law): The probability of two independent events jointly occurring is the product of their individual probabilities, i.e. p(a **and** b) = p(a) × p(b).*

Random sampling without replacement undermines independence of events.

a heart is therefore no longer 1 in 4 but only 12 in 51 (0.235). To get the probability of drawing two hearts when sampling without replacement, we will have to multiply together two different probabilities:

$$p(a \text{ and } b) = p(a) \times p(b) = \frac{13}{52} \times \frac{12}{51} = 0.059$$

When we are betting on the disjunction of two events (i.e. *a* **or** *b*), then the probabilities of the individual outcomes are not multiplied but added together. The formula for this is:

Equation 5.3

$$p(a \text{ or } b) = p(a) + p(b)$$

*The probability law of disjunctions (the additive law): The probability of **either** of two independent events occurring is the sum of their individual probabilities, i.e. p(a or b) = p(a) + p(b).*

For example, we bet that in a single draw from a pack of cards there will be either a diamond or a heart. The probability of a diamond is $^1/_4$, and so is the probability of a heart. The probability of drawing either a diamond or a heart is therefore $^1/_4 + ^1/_4 = ^1/_2$. Likewise the probability of either a head or a tail in a single coin toss is $^1/_2 + ^1/_2$, i.e. a certainty.

The addition rule applies when the outcomes are *mutually exclusive* (no card is both a diamond and a heart, no toss can produce both a head and a tail).

Box 5.2

Coincident birthdays

Most people are surprised to learn that in a random selection of 23 persons there is a 50% chance that at least two of them have the same birthday. The calculation of this result is straightforward. Begin by finding the probability that everyone in the room has a different birthday from everyone else (*x*) and then subtract this fraction from 1 to obtain the probability of at least one common birthday in the group.

Let us start by working out *x*, the probability of no coincident birthdays. Take any particular person in the room. That person has to occupy one of the 365 days. So a second person has a choice of only 364 days if there are to be no coincident birthdays. Similarly a third person has a choice of only 363 days, and the *n*th person has a choice of 366 − *n* days. So the probability of everyone having different birthdays becomes:

For 2 people: $x = 365/365 \times 364/365$.
For 3 people: $x = 365/365 \times 364/365 \times 363/365$.
For *n* people: $x = 365/365 \times 364/365 \times 363/365 \ldots (366 - n)/365 = 365! / [(365 - n)! \times 365]$.

Note that the '!' symbol refers to the factorial operation, e.g. $3! = 3 \times 2 \times 1$; $4! = 4 \times 3 \times 2 \times 1$.

Such large factorials as 365! can only be calculated by a calculator or a computer. At any rate, when $n = 23$ we find that $x = 0.493$. Subtracting from 1 to find p, we get: $p = 1 - x = 1 - 0.493 = 0.507$.

Therefore, there is an even chance of finding two people with the same birthday in a group of 23 people! Obviously, if you were part of that group, it might not be YOUR birthday.

Activity 5.3

Every Saturday, a small principality offers a lottery, in which one of its citizens can win great wealth. The game works as follows. Seven two-digit numbers between '00' and '49' are chosen at random, with great pomp. Gamblers can choose, ahead of time, any set of such numbers, for R2.50. The total available fortune is split between the people who have chosen the winning numbers. If no-one has chosen the winning numbers, the fortune at stake is added to next week's lottery game.
a) For gambler X, who purchases one ticket every Saturday, what is the probability of winning the lottery on any particular Saturday?
b) If gambler X increases his weekly purchase to 25 tickets, what is the probability of winning the lottery?

Probabilities of multiple outcomes

Using a tree diagram can help us calculate the probabilities of different outcomes. Table 5.1 sets out the probability of hearts being thrown in three successive rolls of a four-sided die (i.e. the die is not a cube) marked hearts, clubs, diamonds, and spades. The last column of Table 5.1 sets out all the possible outcomes and their

Table 5.1 Calculating the probability of hearts being thrown in three successive rolls of a four-sided 'card' die

First roll	Second roll	Third roll	Outcome probability
Heart (H) ($1/4$)	H ($1/4$)	H ($1/4$)	HHH $1/64$ = 0.016
		N ($3/4$)	HHN $3/64$ = 0.047
	N ($3/4$)	H ($1/4$)	HNH $3/64$ = 0.047
		N ($3/4$)	HNN $9/64$ = 0.14
	H ($1/4$)	H ($1/4$)	NHH $3/64$ = 0.047
Not heart (N) ($3/4$)		N ($3/4$)	NHN $9/64$ = 0.14
	N($3/4$)	H ($1/4$)	NNH $9/64$ = 0.14
		N ($3/4$)	NNN $27/64$ = 0.42
			$\Sigma = 64/64 = 1$

probabilities calculated by the multiplication rule from the probabilities at each of the three steps. We can then apply the addition rule to work out the probabilities of any given success: for instance, the probability of rolling *exactly* two hearts in three throws is the probability of HHN ($^3/_{64}$) plus that of HNH ($^3/_{64}$) plus that for NHH ($^3/_{64}$). Similarly, the probability of rolling *at least* two hearts is the above probability plus the probability of HHH ($^1/_{64}$) is equal to $^9/_{64} + ^1/_{64} = ^{10}/_{64}$.

The first step in the calculation of these probabilities is to work out the number of possible outcomes that are to count as successes. If a large number of events or trials are in question, it is not possible to do this by enumeration as we did in Table 5.1. For example, if we were considering a run of 10 rolls of the four-sided die, the final column in a diagram such as Table 5.1 would consist of 1024 entries. Fortunately there is a formula for determining how many successful outcomes there will be for any given number of events and given definition of success.

Suppose n is the number of rolls of the die, and suppose that we decide that success is to consist of r events of a particular type. Then we need to know the number of possible *combinations* of r successes from n events. The formula for calculating combinations is as follows:

Equation 5.4

$$\binom{n}{r} = \frac{n!}{r!(n-r)!}$$

Note that the '!' symbol refers to the factorial operation, e.g.

$3! = 3 \times 2 \times 1; 4! = 4 \times 3 \times 2 \times 1$

If we apply this formula to our four-sided die to discover how many possible combinations of two hearts there are in three rolls (substituting 2 for r and 3 for n), we get:

$$\binom{3}{2} = \frac{3!}{2!(3-2)!} = \frac{3 \times 2 \times 1}{(2 \times 1)(1)!} = 3$$

which is what we discovered by listing them. If we want to know how many combinations of five diamonds there are in ten rolls, we apply the formula:

$$\binom{10}{5} = \frac{10}{5!(10-5)!} = \frac{3628800}{14400} = 252$$

In order to work out the probability of a successful outcome, we have to take account of not only the number of combinations but also the probability of each outcome in a single trial. In the case of the four-sided die, for instance, the probability of a heart at each trial (roll) is only 1 in 4. We take this into account by using Equation 5.5.

$$\text{probability of } r \text{ successes in } n \text{ events} = \binom{n}{r} \times p^r \times q^{n-r}$$

Equation 5.5

where: p = probability of success on a single trial (roll)
         $q = (1 - p)$.

Thus the probability of obtaining 2 hearts in 3 rolls of the die is:

$$\binom{3}{2} \times 0.25^2 \times 0.75^{(3-2)} = 3 \times 0.0625 \times 0.75 = 0.141$$

Table 5.1 shows that the probability of each of the three ways of drawing two hearts is 0.047. By the additive rule, the probability of drawing two hearts $= 0.047 + 0.047 + 0.047 = 0.141$.

Activity 5.4

'If an unbiased coin were to be tossed ten times and each time tails came up, could we be certain that an eleventh toss of the coin would show heads?' Discuss, justifying your answer.

The probability of exactly two hearts in six rolls is worked out by the same formula:

$$\binom{6}{2} \times 0.25^2 \times 0.75^4 = 15 \times 0.0625 \times 0.316 = 0.296$$

Where the probability of a success is equal to the probability of a failure at a single trial (as in tossing coins) the calculation is much simpler. This is because when p and q are both equal to 0.5, then $p^r \times q^{n-r}$ is always equal to $\frac{1}{2}^n$ (since $\frac{1}{2}^r \times \frac{1}{2}^{n-r} = \frac{1}{2}^{r+n-r}$). Thus the probability of five heads in ten tosses of coins is:

$$\binom{n}{r} \times \left(\frac{1}{2}\right)^n$$

Equation 5.6

In this formula $n = 10$ and $r = 5$, so the probability is:

$$\binom{10}{5} \times \frac{1^{10}}{2} = \frac{3628800}{120^2} \times \frac{1}{1024} = 0.246$$

The binomial distribution

We could use Equation 5.6 to calculate the probability of each possible successful outcome of ten tosses of a coin, from 0 to 10 heads. The probabilities are set out in Table 5.2.
    We can represent these probabilities on a graph such as Figure 5.1.

Table 5.2 Probability of number of heads in ten coin tosses

No. of heads in ten tosses	Probability
0	0.001
1	0.010
2	0.044
3	0.117
4	0.205
5	0.246
6	0.205
7	0.117
8	0.044
9	0.010
10	0.001

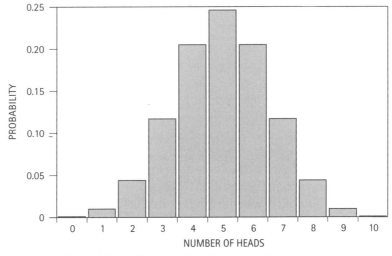

Figure 5.1 Binomial distribution of heads in ten coin tosses

*A categorisation is said to be **exhaustive** when all possible outcomes or states of the phenomenon are represented.*

*Events are said to be **mutually exclusive** when the occurrence of one event makes the occurrence of all the other events impossible.*

The probabilities represented in Table 5.2 are known as *binomial probabilities*. A binomial probability is the probability of 1 out of 2 *mutually exclusive* and jointly *exhaustive* possible outcomes for an event. A graph such as Figure 5.1 gives a binomial distribution, i.e. the distribution of *r* occurrences of successful outcomes of *n* events. The events in question must be independent of each other and each must have only two possible outcomes (either naturally so, as in the case of heads or tails, or because we have so grouped them, as in the case of hearts versus non-hearts). They may have two equally probable outcomes (as in heads versus tails), or two outcomes of unequal probability (as in the case of hearts on a four-sided card die).

The tosses, throws, draws and deals of games of chance provide the paradigm of these binomial events (also known as 'Bernoulli trials', after the mathematician who first studied them). Nevertheless, there are numerous other events that fulfil the definition of a binomial event and that can be studied by means of a binomial distribution. For example, a birth, which may be the birth of a boy or a girl; a personality type, which may be introverted or extraverted; a speech sound, which may be either a vowel or a consonant; an answer to a test item that may be either correct or incorrect, can all be counted as events with two possible outcomes. This means that we can count as a 'success', if we desire, the birth of a girl, the occurrence of a vowel, the personality of an introvert, or the occurrence of a correct answer.

*A **binominal probability** is the probability of one out of two mutually exclusive and jointly exhaustive possible outcomes.*

Activity 5.5

Explain the terms 'independent' and 'mutually exclusive' in relation to probability theory. Give an example to illustrate the application of each of these ideas.

The binomial distribution represented in Figure 5.1 was calculated by applying the formula given by Equation 5.5, above, to particular values of n, r, and p. The 'number of combinations' expression is also known as the 'binomial coefficient' because of this function. But it very quickly becomes tiring to work out binomial distributions in this way. Fortunately, there are tables that give binomial coefficients and binomial probabilities for different values of n and r. Many electronic spreadsheets now include functions that will calculate them. Fortunately for our purposes, you will not have to engage in the regular calculation of binomials once you have grasped the relevant concepts.

Because of the way in which it is calculated, any binomial distribution is completely described by the two parameters p and n, where n is the number of trials (the equivalent of tosses when throwing a coin) and p is probability of a success. The mean of the binomial distribution, i.e. the mean frequency of successes, is $n \times p$. The standard deviation of the distribution is $\sqrt{npq}$, where $q = (1 - p)$. For the number of heads in ten tosses of a coin, $n = 10$ and $p = 0.5$, so that the mean is $10 \times 0.5 = 5$, and the standard deviation is $\sqrt{npq} = \sqrt{10 \times 0.5 \times 0.5} = \sqrt{2.5} = 1.58$.

The binomial distribution of the tossing of coins, as shown in Figure 5.1, is a symmetrical graph. This is because the probability of heads and tails is equal. If we graph the distribution of the number of hearts thrown in five tosses of the four-sided die (or the number of hearts drawn in five draws with replacement from a normal pack of cards), we find a different picture, as shown in Table 5.3. The

A researcher collects opinion poll data in a busy shopping centre on support for 1) public flogging for misdemeanours, and 2) vegetarianism. The data is shown as a cross-tabulation of frequencies, below.

	Support flogging	Oppose flogging
Vegetarian	35	15
Meat eater	15	35

Assuming that this is a representative sample of the South African population, and that the classification is mutually exclusive and exhaustive:

a) What is the probability that a South African vegetarian supports flogging?
b) What is the likelihood that a randomly selected person will be a meat eater, and support flogging?
c) Can you think of any way in which we could use probability calculations to decide whether the variables 'vegetarianism support' and 'flogging support' are independent?

frequency distribution graphed from Table 5.3 is very skew in form. This will be so wherever the probability of success differs from 0.5. If the probability is greater than 0.5, the distribution will be negatively skewed. On the other hand, if (as in Table 5.3) the probability is less than 0.5, the distribution will be positively skewed. (The information in Table 5.3 is graphed in Figure 5.2.)

However, whether the probability of success is equal to or different from 0.5, given a sufficiently large n, the distributions will begin to approach the same form. This form, which is called the *normal distribution*, is of great importance in statistics, and we will briefly consider it now.

Table 5.3 Probability of 0 to 5 hearts being drawn in four draws

No. of hearts in four draws	Probability
0	0.237
1	0.396
2	0.264
3	0.088
4	0.015
5	0.001

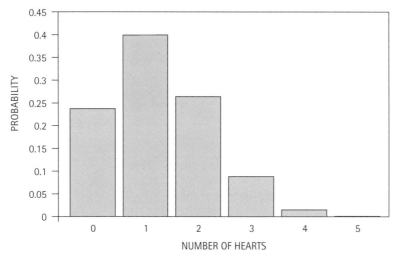

Figure 5.2 Binomial distribution of hearts drawn from a pack of cards

The normal distribution

The normal distribution was developed in the early eighteenth century by the mathematician Abraham de Moivre in his studies of the probabilities of games of chance. He devised it as an approximation to facilitate the calculation of the distribution of chance events. The binomial distribution is a *discrete* distribution. This means that it takes on only whole number values. There can be two or three tosses of a coin, but there cannot be 2.63 tosses of a coin. In place of the stepped histogram, which represents the binomial distribution for a finite number of events, De Moivre developed a smooth *continuous* curve representing the form which the binomial distribution would take for an infinite number of events with equiprobable outcomes. He showed that this normal curve was much easier to calculate than the discrete distribution of the binomial, and that it provided a satisfactory approximation to the binomial distribution, even where the probabilities of the outcomes were not equal, provided that the number of events was relatively large.

The binominal distribution takes the shape of a normal distribution for a very large number of trials.

The graph of a normal distribution is a bell-shaped curve (see Figure 5.3). It is symmetrical and unimodal, so that the mean, the median, and the mode of the distribution all coincide. Its tails extend indefinitely to the right and left, so that it is theoretically possible in normal distributions to obtain values at any distance from the mean. The normal curve, as mathematicians say, asymptotically approaches the zero value on the y-axis.

The normal distribution is symmetrical, unimodal, and bell shaped.

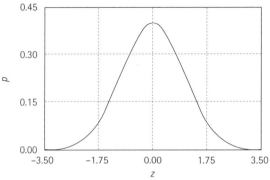

Figure 5.3 Normal distribution

*Many natural
phenomena are
normally distributed.*
The normal distribution has many applications outside the realm of games of chance. Carl Gauss, for instance, discovered that the discrepancies between repeated measurements of astronomical phenomena were distributed according to De Moivre's curve, and he therefore named it 'the normal curve of errors'. But it was soon found that very many natural phenomena, and not just erroneous measurements of them, were distributed normally. Common examples are the heights of human males, the weights of animals of the same species, and the results of IQ tests. Height and weight are continuous variables that can take on any value that the accuracy of measurement permits – hence the need for a continuous curve to represent them. This is one reason why the normal distribution has great importance in the physical and psychological sciences: many of the data that these disciplines collect are themselves values of continuous variables that are normally distributed. But that is not the only reason, as we shall see in Tutorial 7.

The most common form in which you will encounter probability concepts in this tutorial course is in relation to the types of probability distribution we have introduced you to in this chapter. In particular, we will work extensively with the normal distribution in this way. You will need to understand the material introduced in Tutorials 6 and 7 before we can do this properly, but for the moment we give a conceptual account of how this works.

*Like the binomial
distribution, the nor-
mal distribution
allows us to deter-
mine probabilities of
events occurring.*
A commonly used normal distribution in the social sciences is that of the Intelligence Quotient (IQ). IQ tests were developed to exploit the properties of the normal distribution, so we would commonly find that IQ in a homogenous population is normally distributed with a mean $\mu = 100$, and standard deviation $\sigma = 15$. Figure 5.4 shows a plot of this distribution. The typical way of using this distribution is to ask what the probability is of scoring lower than a certain score, or higher than a certain score, or between two scores. Thus, 'What is the probability of scoring an IQ of less than 80 points?' is a typical question.

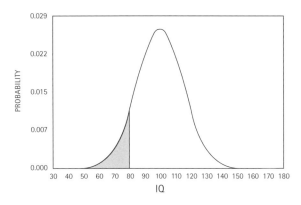

Figure 5.4 Normal probability distribution of IQ

This problem is solved by calculating the area under the curve to the left of the point 80. This is clearly a proportion of the whole area under the curve, and it is more particularly the proportion of scores equal to or less than 80. It is therefore also the *probability in a population* of scoring 80 points, or less than 80 points.

The area under the curve of a normal distribution represents probability.

How do we calculate the area? This used to be a laborious task before the advent of digital computers, involving lengthy and error-prone methods (the integral calculus), and people typically resorted to reasonable approximations, published in table format. (Such a table is included in Appendix 1.) Nowadays, the task is comparatively easy, and normal probability distribution functions are built in as standard parts of spreadsheet programs.

The notion that the size of an area under the curve of a probability distribution can be used to test hypotheses has had profound effects on statistical methods. It is one of the central ideas in all the material that follows in this book.

Worked example

How fair are police line-ups? There are many recorded instances where line-ups have appeared to be unfair, and although some line-ups may be bad enough to dismiss from visual inspection, most are not. For this reason, Doob & Kirshenbaum (1973) devised the 'mock witness technique'. A number of 'mock witnesses' who have never seen the perpetrator are given the verbal description originally made by the eye-witness(es) to the police, and are then shown the line-up and asked to choose the perpetrator. To the extent that mock witnesses choose the suspect as opposed to other members of the line-up, the line-up is considered unfair.

Tredoux (1998) argues for a probability conceptualisation of this task that incorporates the use of the binomial distribution.

Thus, we can think of each mock witness choice as a Bernoulli trial, where the probability of success per trial is $\frac{1}{k}$, where k = the number of people in the line-up. The number of identifications of the suspect will then take the binomial distribution, where we consider identifications to be 'successes' and the total number of mock witnesses the total number of trials.

For example, in the line-up shown as Figure 5.5, the total number of members is six. Malpass *et al.* used 20 African-American mock witnesses to evaluate this line-up (i.e. k = 6, and n = 20). Out of the 20 mock witnesses, 18 chose the suspect (in position 1). Clearly, this appears to be more than if mock witnesses were choosing randomly (i.e. if line-up members were attracting choices equally), since that would be $\frac{1}{k}$ = 0.167. However, we need to know whether this difference could just have occurred by chance – we have only 20 mock witnesses, and we can expect a lot of chance fluctuation with such a small number. One way of testing it is to use the binomial distribution: this will tell us the probability that 18 of 20 witnesses managed to choose the suspect just by chance.

- Late teens, 15–16 years old, no more than 18 years old

- African–American, black male

- Small build, about 120–140 pounds in weight

- Between 5'2 – 5'5 in height

- Long hair in some kind of braids; single row of braids

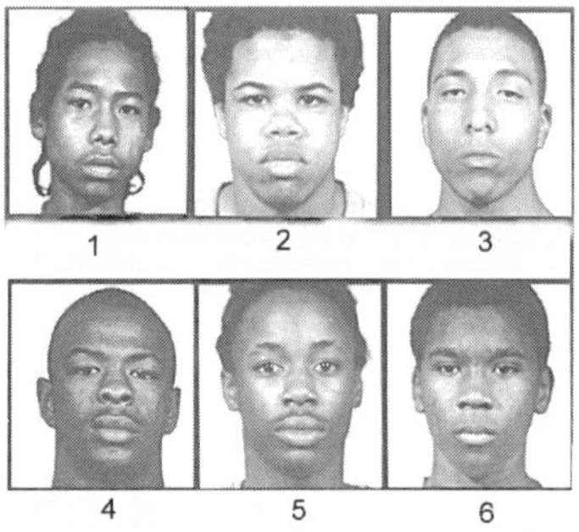

Figure 5.5 A police photo line-up conducted in the USA

However, we need to think a bit more carefully about this calculation. We do not really want to know the probability that exactly 18 out of 20 witnesses choose the suspect; we want to know whether it is unusual that so many witnesses choose the suspect. If it is not unusual, then the probability that more than 18 witnesses choose the suspect should be high. So we calculate this probability (i.e. that more than 18 witnesses choose the suspect), and if this probability is small, then we conclude that it is unusual that 18 out of 20 witnesses choose the suspect.

We can state this as a probability sum, in terms of our problem:

$$\sum_{r+1}^{n} \binom{n}{r} \times p^r \times q^{n-r} = \sum_{r=19}^{20} = \binom{20}{r} \times 0.167^r \times 0.833^{20-r}$$

This calculation will prove difficult to do on a hand calculator, so we use the Microsoft® Excel built-in binomial distribution function, as shown in Figure 5.6. This function takes the following arguments (in order): the number of successes, the number of trials, the probability of a success, and whether the distribution is to be cumulated or not (1 = yes, 2 = no). Notice that the formula in the figure does not use the equation we determined above, but instead calculates 1 – cumulative p (18 out of 20 successes), which is effectively the same calculation. (The cumulative probability is just the sum of probabilities calculated for the number of successes in question, plus all the successes for all numbers of successes below the one in question.)

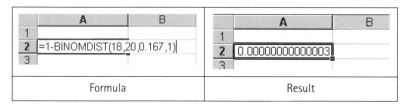

Figure 5.6 Microsoft® Excel formula and result for calculation with the binomial distribution

The result of the calculation is 0.00000000000003, which suggests that such an outcome is extremely unlikely to have occurred by chance alone, and this is very convincing evidence that the line-up was biased against the suspect.

Summary

1. There is no universally accepted definition of 'probability'. A common approach is to define the probability of an event as its long-term frequency of occurrence (the *frequency* approach).

2. Probability is often defined for practical purposes as $p = {}^a/_n$, i.e. the number of 'successes' (a in the equation) divided by the total number of events. It is usually abbreviated as p, and the expression $p(x)$ is thus read to mean 'the probability of x'. As a number, it varies between a minimum of 0 (certainty that an event will not occur) and a maximum of 1 (certainty that an event will occur).

3. Two fundamental probability 'laws' are the *law of conjunctions* (the multiplicative law): $p(a \text{ and } b) = p(a) \times p(b)$; and the *law of disjunctions* (the additive law): $p(a \text{ or } b) = p(a) + p(b)$.

4. Probability calculations with discrete numbers (e.g. the whole numbers) usually involve extensive counting. To simplify this, we make use of counting rules, especially the rule for counting

combinations, and probability distributions. One commonly used discrete probability distribution is the binomial distribution, which we use when an event has two possible outcomes. This allows us to quickly find the probability that n outcomes occurred in r events, e.g. 12 heads in 20 tosses of a coin.

5. We also use probability distributions for continuous numbers (e.g. the real numbers), and our most common method of using these distributions is to calculate areas under a probability distribution curve. These areas represent probabilities, e.g. the probability that a light bulb will burn between 0 and 620 hours without failing. The most commonly used continuous probability distribution in the social sciences is the normal distribution.

Exercises

1. Assume that you have bought a ticket for a lottery and that your sister has bought four tickets. You have just learned that 2 000 tickets have been sold.
   a) What is the probability that you will win the prize?
   b) What is the probability that your sister will win?
   c) What is the probability that you or your sister will win?

2. Assume that you have bought a ticket for a lottery; your brother has bought three tickets; this lottery has two prizes; and only 1 000 tickets have been sold.
   a) Given that you do not win first prize, what is the probability that you will win second prize? (The first-prize-winning ticket is not put back into the draw.)
   b) What is the probability that you will win first prize and that you will win second prize?
   c) What is the probability that you will win first prize and that your brother will win second prize?
   d) What is the probability that between the two of you, you will win first and second prizes?

3. In some homes a mother's behaviour seems to be independent of her baby's behaviour and vice versa. If mother looks at her child for a total of 5 hours each day, and the baby looks at the mother for 6 hours each day, and if they really do behave independently, what is the probability that they will look at each other at the same time?

4. Give an example of a discrete variable and an example of a continuous variable.

5. Explain what is meant by saying that events are *independent*. Illustrate by giving examples where independence is violated and where independence can be safely assumed.

6. In a six-choice task, participants are asked to choose the stimulus that the experimenter has arbitrarily determined to be correct. The 10 participants can guess only on the first trial. Plot the expected distribution of the number of correct choices on trial 1 (i.e. the probability of 0 to 10 participants guessing the correct answer).

7. Refer to problem 6. What would you conclude if 6 of 10 participants were correct on trial 1?

8. In a study of human cognition, we want to look at recall of four different classes of words (nouns, verbs, adjectives, and adverbs). Each subject will see one of each. We are afraid that the order of presentation of the words may affect the results, so we want each participant to have a different order. How many participants will we need to have one participant per order?

9. What two pieces of information would you need to completely describe a binomial distribution?

10. Explain how you might set about determining whether a sequence of numbers was truly random. Could you be absolutely sure of your answer (i.e. that the numbers were completely random)?

11. Find the number of combinations in the word RANDOM, selecting at a time (a) three letters, and (b) five letters.

TUTORIAL

6

The standard normal distribution

Kevin Durrheim

After studying this tutorial, you should be able to:
- Understand key concepts underlying the standard normal distribution.
- Understand what z-scores are.
- Use the z-tables.
- Use the z formula to transform x-scores to z-scores, and transform z-scores to x-scores.

Normal distributions allow us to determine where an individual score lies relative to other scores in a set of scores.

The normal distribution, which was introduced in the previous tutorial, is important since it provides a model of the shape of the frequency distribution of many (but not all) naturally occurring phenomena. We need to know the shape of a frequency distribution if we wish to determine the position of a single score relative to the rest of the distribution. Consequently, since an aim of many statistical operations is to determine where individual cases stand relative to other cases in a distribution of scores (see Tutorial 2), the normal distribution is one of the key concepts you will study in this course.

The notion of the 'relative position' of a case in a distribution has much pragmatic utility. Consider the following question: If your height is 1.6 metres, are you short or tall? The answer to this question depends on whom you are comparing yourself with; it depends on how tall you are relative to other people. If you are a jockey, you may be considered tall, but if you are a professional basketball player, you would be considered short. As you can see from Figure 6.1, the reason why a 1.6-metre jockey would be considered tall is because he or she is taller than most other jockeys. In contrast, a 1.6-metre basketball player is shorter than most other basketball players. In statistics, like in everyday reasoning, we consider individual scores on variables such as height with reference to where these scores fall relative to others on a distribution of scores. The normal distribution provides a powerful way of determining where individuals lie relative to others on many naturally occurring variables, and it is for this reason that it is fundamental to statistical analysis.

Activity 6.1

Think of – and list – ten phenomena that are NOT normally distributed.

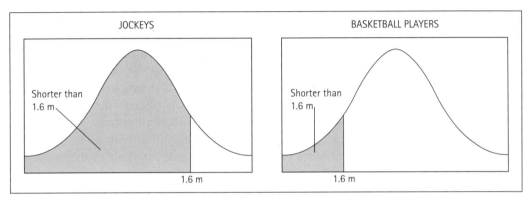

Figure 6.1 Normal curves for heights of jockeys and basketball players

How do we calculate precisely where an individual stands relative to others on a normal distribution? Thus far we have made rather vague claims about an individual jockey or basketball player being taller or shorter than most other individuals in a population. But how much is *most* in each of these cases? A precise science like statistics needs to know *exactly* what proportion of basketball players and jockeys are shorter than 1.6 metres. To answer such questions, we must consider a special type of normal distribution – the *standard normal distribution*.

The standard normal distribution

You will recall that distributions allow us to predict a probability or proportion from an individual score. In order to make such predictions, however, we need to have three pieces of information that define the distribution: the mean, the variance, and the shape. Although the normal distribution defines the shape of the distribution of many naturally occurring phenomena, to determine the distribution for a particular variable (e.g. height, intelligence, physical fitness), we need to know its mean and variance. There are an infinite number of normal distributions, each with a unique mean

A distribution is defined by its shape, mean, and variance.

and variance. There are different normal distributions for the height and weight of males and females, and for the weight, wingspan, and intelligence of pigeons. These normal distributions are different from the distributions of matric results, and the maximum speed of motorcars in South Africa. Although the frequency distributions of all these variables have the same shape (i.e. they are normally distributed), they all differ because they have different means and variances.

The problem that arises from the fact that there are so many different normal distributions is that each of these distributions has a different proportion of cases falling below any particular score. In Figure 6.1, for example, a larger proportion of cases falls below the score of 1.6 metres for jockeys than for basketball players. Each distribution has a unique relationship between scores (i.e. points on the *x*-axis) and proportions (i.e. area under the curve – or to the left of – a particular point on the *x*-axis). To simplify matters, statisticians have defined a single normal distribution that can serve as a measuring standard for all normal distributions. The standard normal distribution is a normal distribution with a mean equal to 0 and a variance equal to 1 (see Figure 6.2). Just as the metre is a standard of length that makes centimetres and kilometres comparable, the standard normal distribution is a standard that is used to make different normal distributions comparable. The standard normal distribution is defined in terms of standard deviation units (i.e. *z*-scores), and since a standard deviation can be calculated for *every* normal distribution, all normal distributions can be related to the standard normal distribution.

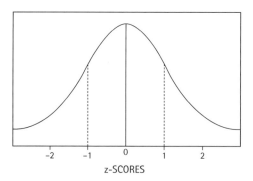

Figure 6.2 The standard normal distribution

As you can see from Figure 6.2, whereas the normal distribution has x-values along the *x*-axis – i.e. individual scores on a particular variable – the standard normal distribution has *z*-values along the *x*-axis. Unlike x-scores, *z*-scores are not individual scores, but are standardised scores. They do not depict the real values that individuals obtained on a variable. Instead they are hypothetical values calculated by statisticians to serve the descriptive function of showing where individual cases lie relative to other cases. These z-scores indicate the number of standard deviation units a score 'lies' above or below the mean. A z-score of 1 lies one standard deviation above the mean, while a z-score of –2 lies two standard deviation units below the mean.

z-scores indicate the number of standard deviation units a score lies above or below the mean.

This standardised distribution is useful because statisticians have calculated the exact proportion of cases that fall above or below any particular z-score on this distribution (see the z-table in Appendix 1). The purpose of developing a standard normal distribution is that if we know the z-score on the x-axis of this distribution, we can simply refer to a table of z-scores and look up the exact proportion of cases that fall above or below this score. The table will tell us, for example, that a proportion of 0.50 (i.e. 50%) of the area under the curve of the standard normal distribution falls above a z-score of 0 (i.e. the mean). This means that 50% of the population of scores that has a frequency distribution exactly the same as the standard normal distribution would be greater than 0. As we will see later, this table of proportions is very useful because we can transform the x-value from any normal distribution into a z-score, and then simply look up on the z-table the proportion of cases that lies above or below the x-value.

The *z-table* tells us what proportion of the area under the curve of a z distribution lies above or below a particular z-score.

Using tables of z–scores

Tables of z-scores contain two pieces of information: z-scores and proportions. The z-scores are printed in the horizontal and vertical margins, and the proportions are printed in the columns and rows of the table (see Appendix 1). When we use the tables we usually aim to associate a single z-score with a single proportion. Figure 6.3 shows a small section of the z-table that appears in Appendix 1.

z	Smaller p	Larger p	Mean to z		z	Smaller p	Larger p	Mean to z
0	0.50000	0.50000	0.00000	...	...	...	...	...
0.01	0.49601	0.50399	0.00399		1.6	0.05480	0.94520	0.44520
0.02	0.49202	0.50798	0.00798		1.61	0.05370	0.94630	0.44630
0.03	0.48803	0.51197	0.01197		1.62	0.05262	0.94738	0.44738
0.04	0.48405	0.51595	0.01595		1.63	0.05155	0.94845	0.44845
0.05	0.48006	0.51994	0.01994		1.64	0.05050	0.94950	0.44950
0.06	0.47608	0.52392	0.02392		1.65	0.04947	0.95053	0.45053
0.07	0.47210	0.52790	0.02790		1.66	0.04846	0.95154	0.45154
0.08	0.46812	0.53188	0.03188		1.67	0.04746	0.95254	0.45254
0.09	0.46414	0.53586	0.03586		1.68	0.04648	0.95352	0.45352
0.1	0.46017	0.53983	0.03983		1.69	0.04551	0.95449	0.45449
0.11	0.45620	0.54380	0.04380		1.7	0.04457	0.95543	0.45543
0.12	0.45224	0.54776	0.04776		1.71	0.04363	0.95637	0.45637

Figure 6.3 A section of the z-table in Appendix 1

The first column, marked 'z', records z-scores. In order to understand the other columns, refer to the diagrammatic representation of the standard normal distribution below (Figure 6.4).

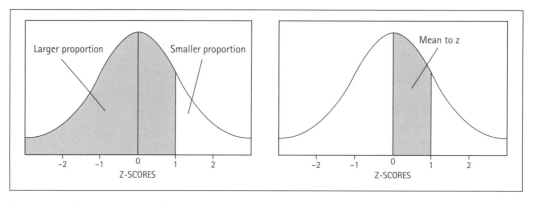

Figure 6.4 Representation of labelled areas assumed by the z-table of Figure 6.3

The z distribution is segmented in Figure 6.4 to create distinct areas. In the first place, we think of a z-score (any z-score, that is) as dividing the distribution into two proportions. Unless $z = 0$, one will be larger, and one will be smaller. This is shown in the left-hand panel. We can also think of a z-score as creating a proportion or segment that extends from the mean (which is always 0), to the score, as is shown in the right-hand panel.

Activity 6.2

a) Find the area 'below' the following z-scores (draw a diagram to assist you – the area could be the 'smaller' or 'larger' proportion):
3.2, 0.45, 1.87, 1.26

b) Find the area 'above' the following z-scores (again, draw a diagram to assist you):
3.1, 0.19, 1.13, 2.54

The z-table assumes this representation, and all quantities reported in the table must be interpreted with this in mind. Thus, the first entry in the table at $z = 0$ yields both 'smaller' and 'larger' proportions of 0.5, and a 'mean to z' proportion of 0. Since the mean z-score is 0, this makes sense – the distance from the mean to a z-score of 0 is 0, and the 'larger' and 'smaller' areas are the left and right 50% of the distribution, as the z distribution is perfectly symmetrical.

On the other hand, to find the areas for a z-score of 1.64, we would run our eyes down the z columns until we find a z-value of 1.64 (highlighted in Figure 6.3), and we read the areas as the entries in the cells alongside 1.64. This gives us a larger proportion of 0.95 (when rounded), a smaller proportion of 0.05, and a mean-to-z proportion of 0.45. In other words, 95% of a z distribution lies below a z-score of 1.64, 5% lies above it, and 45% of the distribution lies between the mean and the z-score. This z-score and its representation is shown in Figure 6.5.

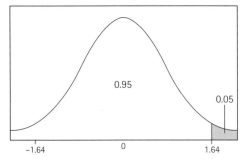

Figure 6.5 A z-score of 1.64 as represented on the standard normal distribution

Since 1 represents unity (or 100% of the area under the curve), we assume that the total area under the curve of the standard normal distribution is equal to 1. Therefore, if we know what proportion of the area lies above a particular z-score, we can also calculate the area that lies below that score. We do this simply by subtracting the area that lies above the z-score from 1. If 0.50 lies above the mean (i.e. z = 0), then 1 – 0.50 = 0.50, the area lying below the mean. If 0.05 lies above a z-score of 1.64, then 0.95 lies below the z-score of 1.64 (see Figure 6.5).

You will note that the z-table only includes positive z-values. This means that it only contains information for the half of the standard

> (Draw diagrams to assist you.)
> Find the area under the standard normal curve to the left of the following z-scores:
> –3.2, 1.45, –1.45

normal distribution that lies above the mean. Since the standard normal distribution is symmetrical (i.e. the half above the mean is a mirror image of the half below the mean), this poses no problem. Any information for a positive z-value applies equally to the negative z-value. Thus, the area that lies *above* a z-score of 1 is exactly the same as the area that lies *below* a z-score of –1. Similarly, if 0.975 of the area lies below a z-score of 1.96, 0.975 lies above a z-score of –1.96.

Occasionally we may want to know the proportion of area lying between two scores. For example, we may want to know the proportion of area between a z-score of 1.96 and a z-score of –1.96. Once you understand that you can subtract and add areas under the curve, such questions become easy to answer. If we know that a proportion of 0.975 lies above a z-score of –1.96, and an area of 0.025

*Although the z-table only gives us proportions lying **above positive z-scores**, 1) because the total area under the curve is 1, we can calculate the proportion below a positive z-score by subtracting the area above the z-score from 1, and 2) because the normal distribution is symmetrical, the proportion lying above a positive z-score is the same as the area below the negative z-score of the same absolute value.*

Activity 6.3

lies above a z-score of 1.96, we can calculate the area between the two z-scores by calculating the difference: 0.975 − 0.025 = 0.95 (see Figure 6.6).

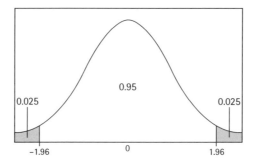

Figure 6.6 The area between two z-scores on the standard normal distribution

Activity 6.4

Calculate the area under the standard normal curve between the following pairs of z-scores:
(−2, 2), (1.2, 2.3), (−0.13, −0.11)

We can also work in the opposite direction with the tables. Instead of determining proportions from z-scores, we can determine z-scores from

The z-table allows us to look up proportions, given z-scores, as well as determine z-scores, given proportions.

proportions. Since we know that a z-score of zero cuts the standard normal distribution exactly in half, we know that a proportion associated with a z-score of zero is equal to 0.50. What then is the z-score that divides the upper 0.20 of the area from the lower 0.80 (see Figure 6.7)? To answer this question, you must first find the proportion of 0.20 in the body of the table, in the '*Smaller p*' column. The closest figure you can find to 0.20 is 0.20045, which has an associated z-score of 0.84. Therefore, the z-score above which 0.20 of the area lies is approximately 0.84.

By way of summary, recall that the z-table for the standard normal distribution allows us to determine the area under the curve

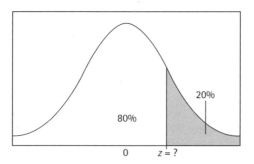

Figure 6.7 Finding z from a known proportion

that lies above or below any z-score, or between any two z-scores. The table also allows us to determine the z-score associated with a certain proportion. Although it can be a lot of fun looking up and calculating values, since the standard normal distribution is a hypothetical distribution (i.e. it is not found in reality, but defined by statisticians), these values are not very interesting in and of themselves. We are usually not interested in merely calculating areas under the curve, but want to calculate the proportion of individuals in a population who score above or below certain values on a variable. What we need to consider now is how to relate everything we know about the statistical world of the standard normal distribution to the real world of individual scores on variables.

Activity 6.5

(Draw diagrams to assist you.)
a) Find the z-scores that 'cut off' the following areas 'below' them: 0.05, 0.91, 0.45
b) Find the z-scores that 'cut off' the following areas 'above' them: 0.05, 0.91, 0.45

Box 6.1

Linear interpolation
If we know that two scales are linearly related to each other, we can use a technique called *linear interpolation* to determine where a score lies on the one scale from our knowledge of where a related score lies on the second scale. Linear interpolation has many applications, but is particularly useful for determining z-scores when we are given proportions that are not represented exactly in the z-tables. Suppose that you are asked to determine the z-score above which 20% of a (normally distributed) population falls. You will note that a proportion of 0.20 is not recorded in the z-table. The closest proportion (rounded) is 0.2005. In fact, 0.20 lies somewhere between 0.2005 and 0.1977. This means that the true z-score lies somewhere between 0.84 (which corresponds to a proportion of 0.2005) and 0.85 (which corresponds to a proportion of 0.1977). We use linear interpolation to determine the exact z-score.

The figure alongside shows graphically how we use linear interpolation to calculate the z-score. We have two scales with a linear relation between them: a scale of proportions ranging from 0.1977 to 0.2005, and a scale of z-scores ranging

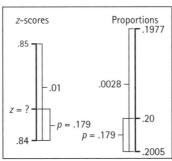

from 0.85 to 0.84. By subtracting 0.1977 from 0.2005 we determine that the length of the proportions scale is 0.0028; and we determine similarly that the length of the *z*-score scale in question is 0.01. The logic now is to determine how far up the proportions scale 0.20 is away from 0.2005 (i.e. 0.20 − 0.2005 = 0.0005), and then determine how much this is as a proportion of the 'Proportions' interval. To do this we divide 0.0005 by 0.0028 to get a proportion of 0.179. We know now that 0.20 lies 0.179 of the way between 0.2005 and 0.1977. To calculate *z* we must find the value that lies 0.179 of the way between 0.84 and 0.85. To do this we multiply the length of the portion of the *z*-scale in question (i.e. 0.01) by the proportion (i.e. 0.179) to obtain a value of 0.0018. By adding 0.0018 to the value of 0.84 we obtain a better estimate of the *z*-value, namely 0.8418.

Two worlds: the statistical world and the real world

The normal distribution is a model that we use to represent many real-world phenomena.

By now you should be aware that the normal distribution provides a model of the distribution of many real-world variables. The height of all South Africans, for example, is a real-world phenomenon, but it can be *represented* in graphical form in the world of statistics by means of a normal distribution with a certain mean and variance. Our earlier discussion of the standard normal distribution was restricted solely to the world of statistics: the questions we were concerned with referred to scores and areas on the hypothetical frequency distribution known as the standard normal distribution.

Since the normal distribution is a statistical model for distributions of scores that appear in the real world, our understanding of this model can be applied to real-world issues. Of great importance is the fact that we can *translate* a proportion of the area under the curve of a statistical distribution into the proportion of a population of cases in the real world.

The area under the curve of a normal distribution, above or below a particular point, can be used to represent a proportion of cases in the real world.

Consider once again the standard normal distribution in Figure 6.2. *Suppose* that this distribution provides an accurate model of the average daily temperature in Iceland. Although the standard normal distribution is a hypothetical distribution, for the purposes of this example *imagine* that the daily temperature in Iceland is normally distributed, and has a mean of 0 and a standard deviation of 1. Since we have assumed that our statistical model (i.e. the standard normal distribution) accurately represents the state of affairs in Iceland, we can translate facts about proportion of area under the curve on this model into information about the daily temperature in Iceland. Since the daily temperature in Iceland is distributed exactly the same as z-scores on the standard normal distribution, we can use the z-tables to answer questions about the number (or proportionate number) of days it is hotter or colder than a particular temperature. This will be the same as the proportion of the area under the curve that lies above or below a particular z-score. What proportion of days in Iceland is colder than –1 degree Celsius? This will be the same as the proportion of area below the z-score of –1. From our z-table we can tell that the area under the curve below a z-score of –1 is 0.1587. Thus, using this distribution as a model for the distribution of temperature in Iceland, we can conclude that the proportion of days colder than –1 is 0.1587. The important point is that *we can translate facts about the statistical world into facts about the real world as long as our statistical models are accurate representations of frequency distributions of real-world phenomena.*

The proportion of the area under the curve of a statistical distribution can tell us two useful pieces of information about real-world phenomena: it can tell us about 1) the *proportion* of a population that scores above or below a particular value, and 2) the *probability* that a randomly selected individual from a population will score above or below a particular value. We have already considered how the area under the curve can be translated into facts about the proportionate number of days in Iceland that the temperature is above or below a particular value. If we assume that the temperature changes randomly every day in Iceland (which it certainly does not), what is the probability that the temperature tomorrow will be below –1 degree Celsius? This is the same as the area below a z-score of –1 on the standard normal distribution, i.e. 0.1587.

The magic of statistical distributions is that they provide models of real-world events, and allow us to use our knowledge of these models to state facts about the real world. We have seen that if a real-world phenomenon is distributed in exactly the same manner as the standard normal distribution, we can use the z-tables to determine proportions and probabilities of events in the real world. *The only problem is that the standard normal distribution is a hypothetical distribution and very few variables in the real world have frequency distributions that are exactly the same as the standard normal distribution.* This is not a big drawback, for, as was stated earlier, the standard normal distribution is a standard that can be used to make the distributions of different real-world phenomena comparable. If we can convert x-scores on real-world variables into z-scores on the standard normal distribution, then we can use the z-table to determine the proportions and probabilities of events relating to these real-world variables.

The area under the curve of a frequency distribution can translate directly into 1) the **proportion** *of a population that scores above or below a particular value, and 2) the* **probability** *that a randomly selected individual from a population will score above or below a particular value.*

Converting x–scores to z–scores

To compare values measured on different scales, we must convert these values to a standard scale.

The standard normal distribution is used as a standard to make different real-world normal distributions comparable. It works much like the metre, which is an internationally accepted standard of length that allows us to compare lengths measured on different scales, by transforming those lengths into metres. Say, for example, that someone asks you which is further, 1 057 miles or 1 860 320 yards? Since we no longer use miles and yards as units of distance, this is quite a difficult question. One way to answer it is to convert both distances to kilometres, a standard measure of distance with which we are all familiar. Once the distances have been converted to a standard, they will be comparable. All we need to know are the formulas by which we can convert miles and yards into kilometres. Since 1 mile = 1.609 kilometres, and 1 yard = 0.0009142 kilometres, by multiplying the 1 057 miles and 1 860 320 yards by these conversion figures we determine that they are both equal to 1 700.7 kilometres, approximately the distance from Cape Town to Durban. When converting scores like this, it is important to remember that although the numbers change, the actual distance from Cape Town to Durban remains the same.

In the same way that we can convert miles and yards to kilometres, we can convert an x-score on any normal distribution, regardless of its mean or variance, into a z-score on a standard normal distribution. The formula for this conversion is as follows:

Equation 6.1

$$z = \frac{x - \mu}{\sigma}$$

*The **z formula** allows us to convert x-scores on a naturally occurring frequency distribution into corresponding z-scores on the standard normal distribution. This conversion allows us to use the z-table to determine the proportion of cases or the probability of events occurring in the real world.*

In this formula, z is the z-score we want to calculate; x is the score in a real-world distribution that we wish to convert into a z-score on the standard normal distribution; μ is the population mean of the real-world distribution; and σ is the population standard deviation of the real-world distribution. Note that Greek letters are used to depict population parameters (i.e. the mean and standard deviation of populations), whereas Roman letters are used to depict sample statistics (i.e. the mean and standard deviation of samples). As long as we know the mean and standard deviation of a variable (i.e. the population parameters) that is normally distributed, we can transform any individual score on this distribution (i.e. an x-score) into a z-score.

Example 1

We know that the height of all professional basketball players in South Africa is normally distributed, with a mean of 1.95 metres and a variance of 0.04 metres. What proportion of professional basketball players is shorter than 1.6 metres?

To calculate a z-score, we need to be sure that the variable is normally distributed, and we need to know the mean and standard deviation of the variable. In this example we are told that the distribution of height in the population of basketball players is normally distributed and we are given the mean and variance of the variable height. We can calculate the standard deviation (see Tutorial 4):

$$\sigma = \sqrt{\sigma^2} = \sqrt{0.04} = 0.2$$

Now that we have all the information required by the z formula, we can compute the z-score that corresponds to an x-score of 1.6 metres simply by substituting the information we have into the formula:

$$z = \frac{x - \mu}{\sigma} = \frac{1.6 - 1.95}{0.20} = -1.75$$

A score of 1.6 metres on the frequency distribution of the height of professional basketball players is thus equivalent to a z-score of −1.75 on the standard normal distribution. What we have done is transform a score on one distribution (i.e. an x-score) into a score on another distribution (i.e. a z-score), much like we would transform a measurement in miles into a measurement in metres. Now we go to the z-table and look up the proportion of the area that lies below a z-score of −1.75. The proportion is equal to 0.0401 (or 4.01%). This proportion under the standard normal distribution is precisely the same as the proportion of professional basketball players who are shorter than 1.6 metres. Although we have converted an x-score of 1.6 into a z-score of −1.75, the proportions below these scores on the two distributions remain exactly the same (see Figure 6.8).

Although we used the z-tables for the standard normal distribution to calculate the area lying under the curve, in effect we have just calculated the proportion of basketball players who are shorter

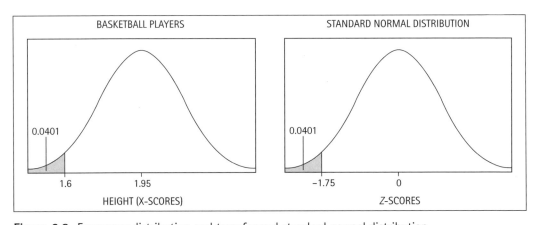

Figure 6.8 Frequency distribution and transformed standard normal distribution

than 1.6 metres. All we needed to know to perform this calculation was: 1) that the height of the population of basketball players was normally distributed 2) it had a mean of 1.95 and 3) it had a variance of 0.04. If we had to randomly select one professional basketball player in South Africa, the probability that this person would be shorter than 1.6 metres is 0.0401. In other words, there would be a 4.01% chance that a randomly selected basketball player is shorter than 1.6 metres.

Activity 6.6

The long-term average for the number of rainy days in Cape Town during the month of April is known to be 9.3, with a standard deviation of 3.6. What is the probability that a visitor to Cape Town in the month of April will experience more than 15 days of rain?

Converting z-scores to x-scores

The standard normal distribution also allows us to work the other way, calculating x-scores from proportions that we know. In such instances, we are given a known proportion or probability and are asked to calculate an x-score.

Example 2

What is the 9th decile of examination results for the research methodology course, given that the results are normally distributed with a mean of 65 and a standard deviation of 9?

Deciles are similar to quartiles (see Tutorial 2), except that quartiles cut a distribution of scores into quarters, and deciles cut a distribution of scores into tenths. Just as 25% of a distribution lies below the 1st quartile and 75% lies below the 3rd quartile, 10% of the distribution lies below the 1st decile, 50% below the 5th decile and 90% below the 9th decile.

In this example, instead of converting an x-score into a z-score, and then going on to determine a proportion, we work in the reverse direction. Since we have been given a proportion, we first go to our z-table to find the z-score that corresponds to the 9th decile. We want to determine the z-score that divides the top 10% of a distribution from the bottom 90%. A proportion of 0.10 of scores lie above the 9th decile, and from the z-tables we can determine that a proportion of 0.10 corresponds with a z-score of 1.28. We now need to calculate an x-score on our distribution of research methodology results that is equivalent to a z-score of 1.28. To do this we need to juggle the z formula around a little, so that it becomes a formula for calculating x-scores from z-scores:

If $z = \dfrac{x - \mu}{\sigma}$, then $z\sigma = x - \mu$, therefore:

Equation 6.2

$$x = z\sigma + \mu$$

By following standard mathematical procedures, we have changed the z formula to enable us to calculate x-scores from z-scores. By substituting the information we have been given into this formula we can calculate the 9th decile (i.e. the x-score below which 90% of scores in the distribution fall):

By basic algebraic manipulation, the z formula for calculating z-scores from x-scores can be transformed into a formula for determining x-scores from z-scores.

$$x = z\sigma + \mu = (1.28 \times 9) + 65 = 76.52$$

The 9th decile for the distribution of research methodology results is thus a score of 76.52. Whereas 90% of the population of students score below this value, 10% of students score above this value (see Figure 6.9).

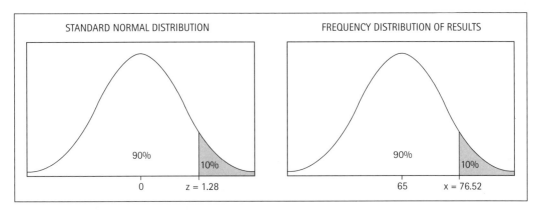

Figure 6.9 Standard normal distribution and frequency distribution of research methodology results

Examples 1 and 2 above illustrate the type of real-world information that can be determined by converting scores on naturally occurring distributions into scores on the standard normal distribution, and vice versa. There are two classes of information that can be derived from using the formula for z-scores:

1. As in Example 1, we can compute z-scores from x-scores that we know. In such cases we aim to determine the proportion of a population falling above or below the x-score, or the probability of a randomly drawn case scoring above or below the x-value.
2. As in Example 2, we can compute an x-score from a z-score. In such cases we are given a proportion or probability, and must first look up the associated z-score, before using the transformed z-score formula to determine the x-score.

Worked example

From the records of the World Health Organisation, we know that the birthweight of babies is normally distributed, with a mean of 2.75 kilograms and a variance of 0.866 kilograms.

1. What is the probability that the next child who is born weighs more than 4 kilograms?
2. What proportion of children has a birthweight of less than 1 kilogram?
3. What weight do the heaviest 15% of infants weigh more than, at birth?
4. Between which weights do 95% of all infants fall at birth?

Solutions

1. $z = \dfrac{x - \mu}{\sigma} = \dfrac{4 - 2.75}{0.931} = 1.34$, thus $p = 0.0901$

2. $z = \dfrac{x - \mu}{\sigma} = \dfrac{1 - 2.75}{0.931} = -1.88$, thus $p = 0.0301$

3. $x = z\sigma + \mu = (1.035 \times 0.931) + 2.75 = 3.714$

4. $x = z\sigma + \mu = (\pm 1.96 \times 0.931) + 2.75$
   $= (2.75 - 1.82, 2.75 + 1.82) = (0.93, 4.57)$

Box 6.2

Using spreadsheets to do z calculations
Spreadsheet software can greatly assist students of statistics, especially at the beginning stages. (You will find a tutorial on using spreadsheets on the CD.) This is certainly true for calculations involving the normal distribution, since spreadsheets can make the use of statistical tables seem antediluvian!

Calculating proportions under the standard normal distribution curve
The easiest way to do this with Microsoft® Excel is to use the built-in function NORMSDIST. Thus, to find the proportion of the standard normal distribution that lies to the left of the z-score 1.25, you enter in a blank cell NORMSDIST (1.25), and Excel returns the answer 0.89435016 to the cell.

Calculating z-scores that correspond to proportions under the standard normal distribution curve
The easiest way to do this with Excel is to use the built-in function NORMSINV. Thus, to find the z-score that cuts off 97.5% of the distribution (i.e. that lies below it, or to the left of it), you enter NORMSINV(0.975).

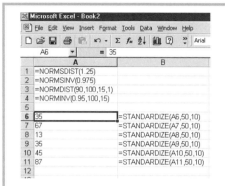

However, and most usefully, Excel can obviate working with the standard normal distribution altogether – it has functions built into it that will do the work necessary to find the proportion (or z-score), based on the value of the mean, the standard deviation and the data point you wish evaluated.

Calculating proportions under any normal distribution curve
Use the built-in function NORMDIST. This function takes a number of arguments, but you can avoid having to memorise these by using the function wizard – '*fx*' on the standard toolbar – or SHIFT + F3 on the keyboard. You will be asked for X, μ, σ, and whether you want the cumulative form of the distribution (which you should choose).

Calculating z-scores under any normal distribution curve
Use the built-in function NORMINV. Again, you will have to specify a number of arguments, namely proportion, μ, and σ.

Calculating z-scores
Excel also has a very useful function called STANDARDIZE, which will return z-scores, and takes as arguments X, μ, σ. This is very useful when you have a large number of z-scores to calculate – you simply copy the formula.

Summary

1. The normal distribution is one of the most important concepts in statistics as it allows researchers to determine where individual scores lie relative to others on many naturally occurring variables.

2. Three pieces of information define any distribution: the mean, the variance, and the shape.

3. The standard normal distribution is a normal distribution with a mean equal to 0 and a variance equal to 1.

4. z-scores depict the number of standard deviation units the score lies above or below the mean.

5. The table of z-values for the standard normal distribution allows us to determine the area under the curve that lies above or below any z-score, or between any two z-scores. The table also allows us to determine the z-score associated with a certain proportion.

6. There are two classes of information that can be derived by using the z formula:
   a) We can compute z-scores from x-scores which are known. In such cases we aim to determine the proportion of a population falling above or below the x-score, or the probability of a randomly drawn case scoring above or below the x-value.
   b) We can compute an x-score from a z-score. In such cases, we are given a proportion or probability, and must first look up the associated z-score, before using the transformed z-formula to determine the x-score.

When transforming x-scores to z-scores or vice versa, visualise the problem by drawing the standard normal distribution and the real-world distribution.

Exercises

1. Use a table of z-scores to determine the following proportions:
   a) below $z = 1.5$
   b) below $z = -0.085$
   c) above $z = 2.8$
   d) above $z = -1.09$
   e) between $z = 1.5$ and $z = 2.8$
   f) between $z = -2.455$ and $z = 1.765$.

2. Use a table of z-scores to determine the following z-values:
   a) the value below which 0.25 of the distribution falls
   b) the value below which 0.85 of the distribution falls
   c) the value above which 0.725 of the distribution falls
   d) the value above which 0.05 of the distribution falls.

3. In a study to examine helping behaviour we ask a confederate (a little old lady) to pretend to collapse in the main road. We count the number of people that walk by before assistance is rendered. We repeat the procedure 2 000 times over a period of one year. The data are normally distributed with a mean of 20 and a standard deviation of 5.
   a) If we assume that this is the data for the population of cases of helping behaviour, what is the probability that at least 35 people will walk past a little old lady who collapses in the main road?
   b) What is the 25th percentile of 'helping behaviour'?

4. The stress of getting engaged has precipitated a neurotic episode and Edward has had to be hospitalised. He is however concerned that this predicament will delay his marriage, which is to happen in 30 days time. He finds out that hospitalisation for neurotic episodes is normally distributed with a mean of 21 days and a variance of 9 days. Edward wants to calculate how long he can expect to be hospitalised. He wants to have 95% confidence in his conclusions.

5. SAFA, the South African Football Association, has been advised by a team of social psychology consultants that crowd disturbances at football matches are much more likely to occur on very hot and very cold days. Apparently, these extreme weather conditions frustrate people, and this frustration easily boils over into crowd disturbances. SAFA decide that they will call off any scheduled soccer match if the temperature is more extreme than it is 98.5% of the time. If the daily temperature in South Africa is normally distributed with a mean of 22 and a standard deviation of 9, at what temperatures will SAFA call off soccer matches?

The sampling distribution of the mean

Kevin Durrheim

After studying this tutorial, you should be able to:
- Develop a conceptual account of the sampling distribution of the mean.
- Understand the significance of the Central Limit Theorem for inferential statistics.
- Calculate standard scores for the sampling distribution of the mean using the z formula.
- Understand the concept 'sampling error' and calculate estimates of standard error.
- Understand the concept 'confidence interval' and calculate confidence intervals around estimates of the mean.

The sampling distribution of the mean is a frequency distribution of sample means, not individual scores.

Thus far we have considered the normal distribution and a special instance of the normal distribution – the standard normal distribution. The normal distribution is a (population) frequency distribution that has a characteristic bell-curved shape, and is defined by its mean and variance. The standard normal distribution has a mean of 0 and a variance of 1. In this tutorial, we will be considering another variant of the normal distribution – the *sampling distribution of the mean*. Outwardly, this distribution looks like any other normal distribution, and it is also defined by its mean and variance. The sampling distribution, however, is a completely different type of normal distribution. It is a (population) frequency distribution of sample means rather than individual scores. Something of a cognitive leap is required to understand the concept of a sampling distribution. This tutorial is designed to help you make this cognitive leap. The sampling distribution is the most important concept you will study in this introductory statistics course, as it is the foundation to all inferential statistics. It is therefore imperative that you develop a thorough understanding of the concept.

One of the main functions of statistics is to make *inferences*. We want to be able to draw conclusions about populations from information we have about samples. For example, we may want to know whether schizophrenics are violent, and are thus a danger to the public. To answer this question we need to know the average level of violence of all schizophrenics. Since there are far too many schizophrenics for a researcher to measure the total population, we need to *estimate* the violence levels of the population of schizophrenics.

Drawing inferences involves estimating properties of populations from information about samples.

Activity 7.1

The collection and use of empirical data to answer research questions is often referred to as an *inductive* approach to knowledge generation, and the wider epistemological tradition as *empiricism*.

Explore some of the philosophical debates about this approach, and its alternatives. Use an academic library, and search for titles in the philosophy of science, or in the philosophy of knowledge. (For a shortcut, consult a dictionary or encyclopaedia of philosophy.)

There are many ways to make such estimates. In day-to-day life, people often make unscientific inferences. They may have heard somewhere that schizophrenics are violent, and then treat this hearsay as fact. A better way of making inferences is to base our conclusions on observation. This is not a sufficient condition, though, as people often draw conclusions after observing a single case. Someone may claim that they know schizophrenics are not violent because their aunt was diagnosed schizophrenic, and she was the sweetest, most harmless little old lady you could ever meet. This is not a very good way of drawing inferences, because single cases may not be representative of the population. The harmless little old lady in the example above may be very different from most other schizophrenics. Scientific inferences are usually based on representative samples. We should collect a random sample of many schizophrenics, measure their levels of violence, and then draw inferences about the violence levels of the population of schizophrenics. If these are higher than the violence levels of non-schizophrenics, only then should we conclude that schizophrenics are more violent that the general population. We may, nevertheless, be wrong. The particular sample that we drew may, purely by

To draw inferences a representative, random sample is required.

chance, not be representative of the population. However, because it is impossible to gain access to the whole population of schizophrenics, this is the best estimate we can make. Statistics is the science of making educated guesses of this kind, i.e. drawing conclusions about populations from samples of cases.

It is because we use samples to draw inferences that we require sampling distributions. The normal distribution, you will recall, is a frequency distribution of single cases. It allows us to estimate where an *individual score* stands in a distribution relative to other individual scores. To draw scientific inferences, however, we need to know where a *sample mean* stands in a distribution relative to other sample means. We need to know, for example, where the mean violence score for our sample of 250 schizophrenics lies in relation to the mean violence scores of other samples we could have drawn from the population. This, as we will see, helps us to determine how accurately our sample mean estimates the population mean.

Sampling means

As you are already aware, the normal distribution is a useful model of the distribution of scores of many real-world phenomena. Imagine that we were awarded an enormous research grant, employed a very large team of researchers, and actually went out and measured the weight of all human beings on earth. As is shown in Figure 7.1, the frequency distribution of these individual scores would be normally distributed. Assume that the mean of all these scores was calculated to be 70 kilograms and their variance was calculated to be 144 kilograms. Using the skills you developed in the previous tutorial, you can now do things like calculate the proportion of people on earth who weigh more than 150 kilograms, or the proportion of people weighing less than 50 kilograms. To do this you need to transform these x-scores into z-scores and look up the proportions in the z-table.

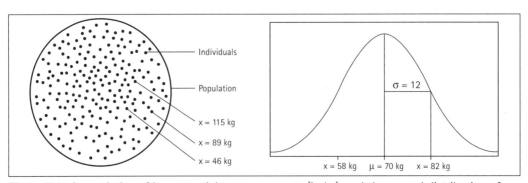

Figure 7.1 A population of human weight measurements (in kg), and the normal distribution of these measurements

Since it is impossible to measure the weight of everyone on the planet, researchers usually rely on drawing samples of cases. *Imagine*, though, that we know that the true mean of the weight of all people on earth is in fact 70 kilograms. If we draw a random sample of 5 people and measure their weight, do you think the mean of this sample will be exactly the same as the mean weight of the population (i.e. 70 kilograms)? This is a most unlikely result. Perhaps, just by chance, we selected a sample of 5 children. Since children, on average, weigh less than adults, the mean of this sample could be as low as 49 kilograms. If we drew a second sample of 5 individuals randomly from the people on earth, do you think this second sample mean would be exactly the same as the first sample mean or the population mean? This is also most unlikely. Suppose that just by chance a very fat person was included in the sample, as well as 3 tall men. Our mean for this sample may well be 88 kilograms. If we continued to draw sample after sample of individuals and calculated their mean weights, we would find variability among these means, just as we find variability among the weight of individuals. If we now took the means of all the possible samples of n = 5 we could draw from the population, and constructed a frequency distribution for these means, we would have a *sampling distribution of the mean* for samples of size 5 (see Figure 7.2).

When we sample repeatedly from the same population, we expect the means of these samples to be different.

Plotting the means of an infinite number of samples of size n, drawn from a population, will give us a sampling distribution of the mean.

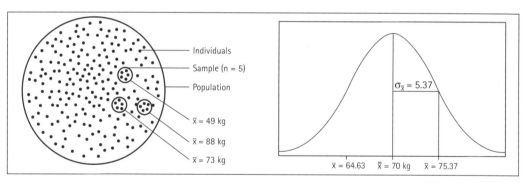

Figure 7.2 Population, sample means, sampling distribution

Activity 7.2

Use a random number generator to draw 20 random samples of size 5 from a uniformly distributed population whose elements vary in weight between 40 kilograms and 120 kilograms. (For how to do this with a spreadsheet, see the tutorial on the CD.) Calculate and tabulate the mean for each sample.

Now repeat the exercise with samples of size 20. Do you see any difference?

At first glance, the distributions in Figures 7.1 and 7.2 seem remarkably alike. They are both normally distributed, and are distinguished by their mean and variance. On closer inspection, you will observe the following differences between these distributions:

1. *Scores.* Whereas the cases marked along the x-axis of Figure 7.1 are x-values, the cases marked along the x-axis of the sampling distribution in Figure 7.2 are $\bar{x}$-values. The sampling distribution of the mean is a frequency distribution of sample means.

2. *Means.* The mean of the distribution in Figure 7.1 is the mean of all the individual scores in the population (i.e. the mean of all x's is $\bar{x}$). If we have calculated the mean of the entire population, then $\bar{x} = \mu$. The mean of the sampling distribution of the mean, in contrast, is the mean of all the sample means (i.e. the mean of all the $\bar{x}$'s).

3. *Variances.* Just as different individuals have different weights, so too, different samples have different means. Where the variance in Figure 7.1 refers to variance between individual x-values, the variance in Figure 7.2 refers to the variance between different sample means, i.e. the variance between $\bar{x}$-values.

The sampling distribution of the mean can therefore be defined as the distribution of sample means for an infinite number of random samples of a particular size drawn from a population. To construct a sampling distribution, we would need to draw as many samples as we could from a population. With large populations, such as all people on earth, this becomes a very large number of samples, approaching infinity. The samples need to be randomly selected to

Box 7.1

The Monte Carlo method
Although many of the models and theorems that statisticians use cannot be tested by empirical measurement, a procedure known as the Monte Carlo method is usually applied to the empirical study of statistical models and theorems. Instead of actual measurements, random number generators are used to generate a large 'population' of data (e.g. 10 000 random numbers between 0 and 100). (This reliance on chance is the origin of the name of the method, referring to the famous gambling casino in the state of Monaco.) The computer can then also be used to select many thousands of samples of a particular size from this artificial population, and can calculate the mean and variance of the samples. The properties of the sampling distribution of the mean can then be investigated by determining the shape of the frequency distribution of these sample means, and by determining the variance and mean of the distribution. For more on Monte Carlo methods, use an Internet search engine to find Internet sites dedicated to Monte Carlo simulations. (See the additional material on the CD for instructions on using the Internet.)

NUMBERS, HYPOTHESES AND CONCLUSIONS

ensure that all the variability between the samples occurs by chance, not because of our biased selection procedures. As we will see later, the variance of the sampling distribution is influenced by the size of the samples selected from the population, hence the need to define sampling distributions in terms of a particular sample size. As you will probably have realised, sampling distributions are not defined empirically (i.e. by measurement). We would not actually draw an infinite number of samples from a population, calculate their means, and then compute a frequency distribution. The task would be impossible, by definition. Instead, the sampling distribution of the mean is defined theoretically by a theorem known as the *Central Limit Theorem*.

*The **sampling distribution of the mean** is the distribution of an infinite number of sample means of a particular size randomly selected from a population.*

The Central Limit Theorem

You will recall that frequency distributions are defined by three things: their shape, mean, and variance. The Central Limit Theorem specifies the shape, mean, and variance of the sampling distribution of the mean, and thus allows us to define completely this sampling distribution without having to draw an infinite number of samples from the parent population. The Central Limit Theorem states that:

*The **Central Limit Theorem** specifies the shape, mean, and variance of the sampling distribution of the mean.*

> Given a population with a mean μ and a variance σ², the sampling distribution of the mean will have a mean equal to μ and a variance σ²/n. The shape of the sampling distribution approaches normal as the sample size (n) increases.

Regardless of the shape of the population distribution, the sampling distribution of the mean will be approximately normally distributed as long as the sample size is not too small.

In other words, the mean of the sampling distribution of the mean is equal to the population mean (i.e. $\mu_{\bar{x}} = \mu$) and the variance of the sampling distribution of the mean is equal to the population variance divided by n (i.e. $\sigma_{\bar{x}}^2 = \frac{\sigma^2}{n}$). Thus, if we knew for a fact that the population of people on earth has a mean weight of 70 kilograms and a variance of 144 kilograms, then the sampling distribution of the mean of samples of size n = 5 will have a mean of 70 kilograms (i.e. $\mu_{\bar{x}} = \mu = 70$ kg), and a variance of 28.8 (i.e. $\sigma_{\bar{x}}^2 = \frac{\sigma^2}{n} = \frac{144}{5} = 28.8$).

Also, regardless of the shape of the population distribution, the sampling distribution of the mean will be approximately normally distributed as long as the sample size is not too small. This is an important property of the sampling distribution of the mean. The normal distribution is a useful model of the frequency distribution of individual cases because many naturally occurring variables are normally distributed. The normal distribution, however, is not appropriate for many other naturally occurring variables that are not normally distributed. Consider infant malnutrition, for example. It is most unlikely that this variable will be normally distributed because most infants in the world are not malnourished. On the other hand, in very poor populations, various degrees of infant malnutrition are prevalent. A likely frequency distribution for the malnourishment index (ranging from 0 to a high of 5) for a population of infants is given in Figure 7.3. Although the normal distribution would be an inappropriate model for this variable, if we selected a large number (e.g. 10 000) of random samples of size 100 each and constructed a frequency distribution of the mean malnourishment score from each sample, this would be approximately normally distributed (see Figure 7.3). If we knew that the population

The two frequency distributions in Figure 7.3 represent the same populations of persons. Do you know why they look so different?

mean malnourishment score was $\mu = 2$, and the population variance was $\sigma^2 = 0.8$, then from the Central Limit Theorem we could conclude that the sampling distribution of the mean for samples of size 100 will have a mean $\mu_{\bar{x}} = 2$ and avariance $\sigma_{\bar{x}}^2 = \frac{0.8}{100} = 0.008$. The standard deviation of the sampling distribution of the mean would be 0.089, the square root of the variance.

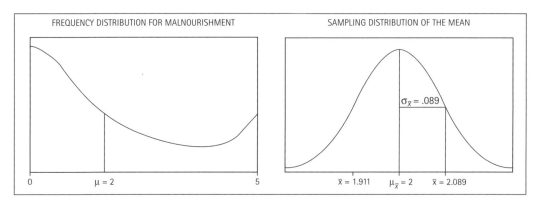

Figure 7.3 Population distribution and sampling distribution of malnutrition variable

Activity 7.3

What would the mean and variance be for each of the following sampling distributions? Draw these distributions.
a) samples of n = 5, μ = 80 kg, and σ = 15 kg
b) samples of n = 10, μ = 80 kg, and σ = 15 kg
c) samples of n = 100, μ = 80 kg, and σ = 15 kg
d) samples of n = 5, μ = 80 kg, and σ = 1.5 kg
e) samples of n = 10, μ = 80 kg, and σ = 1.5 kg
f) samples of n = 100, μ = 80 kg, and σ = 1.5 kg

The sampling distribution and the standard normal distribution

The discussion thus far has explained what the sampling distribution of the mean is. We did this by drawing distinctions between the sampling distribution of the mean and the normal distribution of

NUMBERS, HYPOTHESES AND CONCLUSIONS

individual scores. The Central Limit Theorem defines the properties of the sampling distribution of the mean, given knowledge of the distribution of individual scores. By now you may be wondering what we can do with the sampling distribution of the mean. In fact, you already know how to use the sampling distribution, because this distribution is used in the same way as the normal distribution you considered in previous tutorials: it is used to compute proportion of cases lying above or below a specified value. The only difference is that the type of questions we wish to answer changes because we are now considering the distribution of sample means rather than individual scores. Instead of asking what proportion of individuals score above or below a particular *score*, we could ask what proportion of samples have a *mean* greater or smaller than a particular value. Instead of asking for the probability of a randomly selected individual scoring below a particular value, we ask for the probability of a randomly selected sample having a mean less than a particular value. In other words, the sampling distribution of the mean answers very similar questions to those the normal distribution answers about individual scores.

The sampling distribution of the mean is used to determine the proportion of sample means we expect above or below a specified value.

The calculations and formulas for the sampling distribution of the mean are similar to those you considered in the previous tutorial. Just as we transformed x-scores on the normal distribution into z-scores on the standard normal distribution, we transform x̄-values on the sampling distribution to z-scores on the standard normal distribution. Once the x̄-values have been transformed into z-scores, we can use the table of z-scores to calculate proportions and probabilities.

If you have mastered the exercises in the previous tutorial you should have no problem using the sampling distribution of the mean. You will recall that the z formula is used to transform x-scores into z-scores. To transform x̄-values into z-scores we need to modify the z formula slightly to account for the fact that we are now dealing with a distribution of mean scores rather than a distribution of individual values:

Compare Equation 7.1 and Equation 6.1. Do you see the difference?

$$z = \frac{x - \mu}{\sigma} \text{ becomes } z = \frac{\bar{x} - \mu}{\sigma_{\bar{x}}}$$

Equation 7.1

If you study the formulas carefully, you will note that we have modified the z formula for x-scores into a z formula (Equation 6.1) for x̄-values by substituting $\bar{x}$ for x and $\sigma_{\bar{x}}$ for σ. We must do this because we are now transforming a sampling distribution of x̄-values (with a mean $\mu_{\bar{x}}$ and standard deviation $\sigma_{\bar{x}}$) into the standard normal distribution. We know from the Central Limit Theorem that although the mean of the sampling distribution is equal to the population mean (i.e. $\mu_{\bar{x}} = \mu$), the variance of the sampling distribution is different to the variance of the parent population (i.e. $\sigma_{\bar{x}}^2 = \frac{\sigma^2}{n}$). We must change our z formula accordingly:

Equation 7.2

$$z = \frac{\bar{x} - \mu}{\sigma_{\bar{x}}}; \text{ but } \sigma_{\bar{x}} = \sqrt{\frac{\sigma^2}{n}} = \frac{\sigma}{\sqrt{n}}; \text{ thus } z = \frac{\bar{x} - \mu}{\frac{\sigma}{\sqrt{n}}}$$

This formula allows us to transform $\bar{x}$-values into z-scores, and thus allows us to determine probabilities and proportions relating to sample means.

Example 1

From years of testing, we know that IQ scores for individuals are normally distributed with a mean of 100 and a standard deviation of 15. If we select a random sample of 10 secondary school pupils, what is the probability that their mean is less than 95?

You will note that, unlike the questions in the previous tutorial, here we want to determine the probability that a sample mean, not an individual score, falls below a particular value. Our first step in calculating this probability is to transform our $\bar{x}$-value of 95 into a z-score:

$$z = \frac{\bar{x} - \mu}{\frac{\sigma}{\sqrt{n}}} = \frac{95 - 100}{\frac{15}{\sqrt{10}}} = \frac{-5}{\frac{15}{3.162}} = \frac{-5}{4.744} = -1.054$$

What we have done here is transform a sample mean of 95 from a sampling distribution of the mean with a mean of 100 and a standard deviation of 4.744 into a z-score of –1.054 on the standard normal distribution (see Figure 7.4). In other words, our sample mean of 95 falls just more than one standard deviation unit below the mean of the sampling distribution (i.e. 5 is just bigger than 4.744 in the calculations above). If you now refer to your tables of

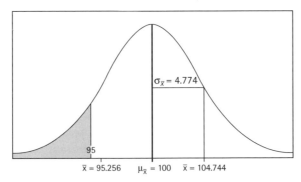

$\sigma_{\bar{x}} = 4.774$

95

$\bar{x} = 95.256$ $\mu_{\bar{x}} = 100$ $\bar{x} = 104.744$

Figure 7.4 Sampling distribution for IQ scores

z-scores, you will see that a proportion of 0.146 lies above a z-score of 1.054. This means that a proportion of 0.146 lies below a z-score of –1.054. Therefore a proportion of 0.146 lies below a score of 95 on our sampling distribution of the mean. This means that the probability that our sample would have a mean lower than 95 is 0.146 (i.e. a 14.6% chance).

The standard error

The Central Limit Theorem shows that *the variance of the sampling distribution can be controlled by the researcher*. Since $\sigma_{\bar{x}}^2 = \sigma^2/n$, as the sample size increases, so the variance of the sampling distribution decreases. This is one of the reasons why researchers usually want large samples: they aim to decrease the variance of the sampling distribution. Decreasing variance in this way helps to increase the accuracy of prediction. If you use a sample mean to predict a population mean, the lower the variance of the sampling distribution, the higher will be the accuracy of prediction. This is why it is more accurate to predict the number of legs that humans have from a sample of 10 individuals, than to predict the average weight of humans from a sample of 10 individuals. Although not all humans have two legs, individuals differ much more in their weight than they do in the number of legs they have. Increasing the sample size, thereby decreasing the variance of the sampling distribution, allows us to use a sample to make more accurate estimates of a population mean. It is for this reason that the standard deviation of the sampling distribution, the square root of the variance (i.e. $\sigma_{\bar{x}}$), is known as the *standard error of the estimate*, or 'standard error' for short.

*The **standard error** is:*
a) the standard deviation of the sampling distribution
b) an estimate of the degree to which the sample means in the sampling distribution are expected to differ from each other
c) an estimate of the degree to which a sample accurately estimates the population mean.

Activity 7.4

> There are two key determinants of the accuracy of sample estimates of the mean – the inherent dispersion of the underlying population distribution (reflected in the variance, σ), and the size of sample (n) drawn from the population. This can be seen from the formula for the standard error, $\sigma_{\bar{x}} = \sigma/\sqrt{n}$.
>
> Substitute values for σ and n to show that greater inherent dispersion or variability requires greater sample sizes for accurate sample estimates of the mean. (*Hint: assume that* $\sigma = 10$, *and try substituting* n = 10, *and* n = 100. *Do this for a variety of values for* n *and* σ, *until you are clear that you understand the relationship.*)

Researchers can increase the accuracy of an estimate of a population mean by increasing the sample size, which in turn reduces the standard error.

The standard error is an estimate of the average degree to which the sample means in the sampling distribution are expected to differ from each other. The standard error serves as an estimate of the degree to which a sample accurately estimates the population mean. Increasing our sample size decreases the standard error and ensures that our sample mean provides a more accurate estimate of our population mean.

Example 2
If we know that the mean weight of all people on earth is 70 kilograms, with a variance of 144, consider the difference in standard error if we draw samples of size n = 5 or n = 50.

As you can see from the calculation below, the standard error is the square root of the variance of the sampling distribution, which we know from the Central Limit Theorem is σ^2/n. For samples of size 5, the standard error is 5.367, i.e.

$$\sigma_{\bar{x}} = \sqrt{\sigma_{\bar{x}}^2} = \sqrt{\frac{\sigma^2}{n}} = \sqrt{\frac{144}{5}} = \sqrt{28.8} = 5.367$$

As you can determine from your tables of z-scores, 68.27% of the area under the normal curve lies between one standard deviation unit above and one standard deviation unit below the mean (i.e. 68.27% lies between the z-scores 1 and –1). This means that 68.27% of the possible samples of size 5 that we could draw from the population of human beings would have means that fall between 64.633 and 75.367 (see Figure 7.5). By using the same calculation procedures, we compute the standard error for samples of size 50 to be 1.697. This means that 68.27% of samples of size 50 that are drawn from the population will have means that fall between 68.303 and 71.697 (see Figure 7.6). The larger samples are more accurate estimates of the population mean than the smaller samples. The middle 68.27% of the sample means lie much closer to the true population mean in Figure 7.6 than they do in Figure 7.5.

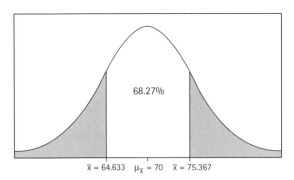

$\bar{x} = 64.633$ $\mu_{\bar{x}} = 70$ $\bar{x} = 75.367$

Figure 7.5 Sampling distribution for mean weight, n = 5

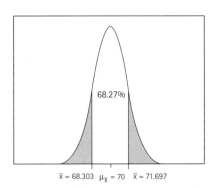

$\bar{x} = 68.303$ $\mu_{\bar{x}} = 70$ $\bar{x} = 71.697$

Figure 7.6 Sampling distribution for mean weight, n = 50

Box 7.2

Using spreadsheets for normal distribution calculations

	A	B
1	μ	100
2	σ	15
3	X	95
4	n	10
5	z	=(B3-B1)/(B2/B4*(SQRT(B4)))
6	p(z)	=NORMSDIST(B5)
7		

	A	B
1	μ	100
2	σ	15
3	X	95
4	n	10
5	z	-1.054092553
6	p(z)	0.145920298
7		

	A	B
1	μ	100
2	σ	15
3	X	95
4	n	10
5	p(x)	=NORMDIST(B3,B1,B2/SQRT(B4),1)
6		
7		

	A	B	C
1	μ	100	
2	σ	15	
3	X	95	
4	n	10	
5	p(x)	0.145920298	
6			

Figure 7.7 A layout in Microsoft® Excel for doing Example 1 (left pane shows formula view, right pane shows the result)

Spreadsheets can be very useful for finding standard (*z*) scores, and for doing precise normal probability calculations (rather than relying on the approximations offered by *z*-tables). Calculations involving sampling distributions of the mean must be treated as for the normal distribution, making the adjustment to σ manually (i.e. $\sigma_{\bar{x}} = \sigma/\sqrt{n}$). In Microsoft Excel, for example, several built-in functions make normal distribution calculations relatively easy.

STANDARDIZE – returns a standard (*z*) score, taking the x-value, μ, and σ as arguments.

NORMDIST – returns cumulative probabilities of the normal distribution, taking x-value, μ, and σ as arguments.

NORMSDIST – returns cumulative probabilities of the standard normal distribution, taking a *z*-value as an argument.

The usefulness of the NORMDIST function is that you do not need to do the standardisation to a *z*-value. A layout in Excel for the calculations involved in Example 1 is shown in Figure 7.7, in two alternate constructions: in the top pane, a layout is shown assuming the calculation of *z*, and in the bottom pane, a layout for bypassing the calculation of *z*.

Example 2 shows how useful the sampling distribution of the mean can be in determining the degree of accuracy with which a sample mean estimates the population mean. The standard deviation of the sampling distribution of the mean, the standard error, should always be reported in surveys that aim to estimate population means from sample means. If we wanted to estimate the average life span of cigarette smokers, for example, we could draw a random sample of say 1 000 smokers who died over the past 10 years, and use the mean age at which they died as an estimate of the population mean. We would then need to calculate the standard error so that we know how accurate the estimate is. Drawing a large sample of 1 000 subjects will usually ensure that the standard error is small, and that the estimate will be reasonably accurate.

What size of sample would we need in each of the following cases to reduce the standard error of the estimate to 0.01?

a) $\sigma = 10$ b) $\sigma = 20$ c) $\sigma = 50$

d) $\sigma = 100$ e) $\sigma = 500$ f) $\sigma = 1\ 000$

Confidence limits and confidence intervals.

Using samples to estimate population parameters always yields uncertain results. Because there is random variance present in the sampling distribution of the mean, we can never be sure that our sample mean is exactly the same as the population parameter we wish to estimate. However, in addition to estimating the population parameter, if we know the variance of the sampling distribution of the mean (or the standard error), we can also estimate how accurate our parameter estimate will be. We use our knowledge of the standard error to set probable limits on an observation. This means that we can define the end points of an interval, that we can say, with a certain known probability, brackets the population mean we wish to estimate. These *probable limits* are also known as *confidence limits*, and the interval that they bracket is known as the *confidence interval*. They are called confidence limits because we can say with a certain confidence that the population parameter we wish to estimate lies somewhere between these two points.

The brackets in Figure 7.8 represent the confidence limits. We calculate confidence limits in order to know how accurate an estimate of a population parameter is. If these were calculated to be the 95% confidence limits for an estimate, we could say with 95% confidence that the population parameter we wish to estimate lies between a value of 105 and 115. The interval between 105 and 115 is known as the 95% confidence interval.

Confidence limits are the end points of an interval that brackets the population mean we wish to estimate with a known probability (i.e. $1 - \alpha$).

A confidence interval is the interval between the confidence limits.

Figure 7.8 Graphical depiction of a confidence interval

Example 3

Assume that we know that the weight of all humans on earth is normally distributed with a variance of 144. To estimate the mean weight of South Africans, we could draw a sample of 100 people, measure their weight, and calculate the mean. If we calculated this mean to be 73 kilograms, we could use this sample mean to estimate the mean weight of all South Africans (i.e. a population parameter). However, we may be wrong. It is unlikely that our sample mean will be exactly the same as the population mean. What we do in such cases is calculate a confidence interval so that we can say, with a certain confidence, that the mean lies between two specified values. Perhaps we could calculate 99% confidence limits, so that we could state with 99% confidence that the real population mean lies between values μ_1 and μ_2. We use our knowledge of the standard normal distribution and the sampling distribution of the mean to calculate confidence limits.

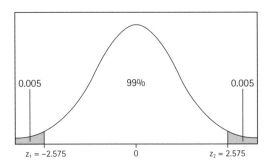

Figure 7.9 99% cut-off points on the distribution (standard normal)

To set probable limits on an observation, we refer in the first place to the standard normal distribution and the z-table. See from Figure 7.9 that we first define z-scores that bracket off 99% of the area under the curve of the standard normal distribution. The z-scores will then be transformed into μ-scores that bracket 99% of all sample means of the sampling distribution. If the total area under the curve is equal to 100%, and 99% of the area lies between the z-scores, then 0.5% lies below z_1, and 0.5% lies above z_2 (99% + 0.5% + 0.5% = 100%). Refer to your table of z-scores and note that the z-score above which 0.5% of the area (i.e. a proportion of 0.005) lies is equal to 2.575. Therefore the z-score below which 0.5% of the area lies is equal to –2.575. What we now need to do is to transform

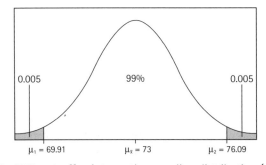

Figure 7.10 99% cut-off points on the sampling distribution (raw scores)

$z_1 = -2.575$ and $z_2 = 2.575$ on the standard normal distribution into μ_1 and μ_2 on the sampling distribution of the mean. We now need to develop an expression for μ in terms of the other variables in the z formula, i.e. we need to manipulate the z formula so that it becomes a μ formula:

$$z = \frac{\bar{x} - \mu}{\frac{\sigma}{\sqrt{n}}}, \text{ thus } z\frac{\sigma}{\sqrt{n}} = \bar{x} - \mu, \text{ thus } z\frac{\sigma}{\sqrt{n}} + \bar{x} = \mu,$$

Equation 7.3
$$\text{thus } \mu = \bar{x} \pm z\frac{\sigma}{\sqrt{n}}$$

We now calculate μ_1 and μ_2 simply by substituting z_1 and z_2 into the formulaas well as the information we have about the sampling distribution:

$$\mu = \bar{x} \pm z\frac{\sigma}{\sqrt{n}} = 73 \pm 2.575 \times \frac{12}{\sqrt{100}}$$

$$= 73 \pm 2.575 \times \frac{12}{10}$$

$$= 73 \pm (2.575 \times 1.2) = 73 \pm 3.09$$

You will notice that the $\pm$ symbol is used in the formula in place of the $+$ sign. This is because one of the z-scores is positive and the other is negative (see Figure 7.9). We can now calculate the values for $\mu_1 = 73 - 3.09 = 69.91$, and $\mu_2 = 73 + 3.09 = 76.09$ (see Figure 7.10). We thus conclude with 99% confidence that the mean weight of South Africans lies between 69.91 kilograms and 76.09 kilograms. The 99% confidence limits are thus 69.91 and 76.09.

Activity 7.6

a) Find the cut-off points on the standard normal distribution that correspond to the:
   i)   90% confidence limits
   ii) 95% confidence limits
   iii) 99% confidence limits.
b) Assuming that $\bar{x} = 100$, $\sigma = 16$, and $n = 100$, find the 90%, 95%, and 99% confidence intervals for the sample estimate of μ.

Worked example

1. The Brief Symptom Inventory (BSI), a measure of psychopathological symptomatology, has been designed in such a way that it is normally distributed, with a mean of 0 and a standard deviation of 18. To examine whether stress affects the psychological well-being of its employees, a large multinational company administers the BSI to a random sample of employees.

NUMBERS, HYPOTHESES AND CONCLUSIONS

a) What statistical information could the researcher use to estimate the psychological wellbeing of the population of employees?
b) If the sample size is 200, what is the standard error?
c) How large would the sample have to be to ensure that the standard error is no larger than 0.8?
d) What is the mean and variance of the sampling distribution of the mean of the BSI for samples of size 200?
e) If the researcher draws a sample of 250 people, what is the probability that the mean for this sample is greater than –1.5?
f) If the researcher draws a sample of 50 people, what is the probability that the mean for this sample is greater than –1.5?
g) Explain why your answers for (e) and (f) above differ.

Solutions

a) The sample mean is an obvious (and easy) statistic for us to calculate, but there are many other possibilities (see Tutorial 3).
b) We write the formula for the standard error, and substitute in the known quantities:

$$\sigma_{\bar{x}} = \frac{\sigma}{\sqrt{n}} = \frac{18}{\sqrt{200}} = 1.273$$

c) We first write the equation for the standard error, and then re-arrange it to solve for n:

$$\sigma_{\bar{x}} = \frac{\sigma}{\sqrt{n}}, \text{ so } \sigma_{\bar{x}}\sqrt{n} = \sigma, \text{ and } \sqrt{n} = \frac{\sigma}{\sigma_{\bar{x}}}$$

$$\text{therefore, } n = \frac{\sigma^2}{\sigma_{\bar{x}}^2} = \frac{18^2}{0.8^2} = 506.25$$

Therefore a sample of 507 would ensure that the standard error was no larger than 0.8.

d) This follows from the Central Limit Theorem, and the formula for the standard error (which we calculated in (b)), i.e.

$$\mu_{\bar{x}} = \mu = 0$$

$$\sigma_{\bar{x}}^2 = 1.273^2 = 1.621$$

e) We need to convert the mean score of –1.5 into a z-score (see Equation 7.1), and then find the area lying above that z-score (i.e. the 'larger p' in the z-table):

$$z = \frac{\bar{x} - \mu}{\frac{\sigma}{\sqrt{n}}} = \frac{-1.5 - 0}{\frac{18}{\sqrt{250}}} = \frac{-1.5}{1.138} = -1.32$$

thus $p = 0.9066$

f) We follow the same procedure as for (e).

$$z = \frac{\bar{x} - \mu}{\frac{\sigma}{\sqrt{n}}} = \frac{-1.5 - 0}{\frac{18}{\sqrt{50}}} = \frac{-1.5}{2.55} = -0.59$$

thus $p = 0.719$

g) There is less variance in the sampling distribution of the mean with a smaller standard error (i.e. a larger n). Therefore, the sample means are more tightly clustered around the population mean, and a greater proportion of samples lie closer to the population mean.

Summary

1. The sampling distribution of the mean is the distribution of sample means for an infinite number of random samples of a particular size drawn from a population.

2. The Central Limit Theorem specifies the shape, mean, and variance of the sampling distribution of the mean, and thus allows us to completely define this sampling distribution.

3. Using samples to estimate population parameters always yields uncertain results. Because there is random variance present in the sampling distribution of the mean, we can never be sure that our sample mean is exactly the same as the population parameter we wish to estimate.

4. The Central Limit Theorem shows that the variance of the sampling distribution can be controlled by the researcher. As the sample size increases, so the variance of the sampling distribution decreases, and the accuracy of prediction increases.

5. The standard error is an estimate of the average degree to which the different sample means in the sampling distribution are expected to differ from each other. It serves as an estimate of the degree to which a sample mean accurately predicts a population mean.

6. Confidence limits are probable limits of an observation. They are the end points of an interval, which we can say with a certain known probability brackets the population mean we wish to estimate. The interval they define is known as the confidence interval.

Exercises

1. Assume that from years of collecting data we know that the weight of all adult South Africans is normally distributed with a standard deviation of 15. A researcher selects a random sample of South Africans.

   a) To estimate the weight of the adult population of South Africans, what information would the researchers require?

   b) If the researcher draws a random sample of 250 adult South Africans, what is the standard error of estimate?

   c) To ensure that the standard error is no smaller than 0.5, how large would the sample have to be?

   d) Let us say that after years of collecting data, the mean weight of the adult South African population is found to be 75 kilograms.

   i) If the researcher selects a random sample of 20 people, what is the probability that their mean weight will be less than 70 kilograms?

   ii) What is the probability that the mean weight of this sample of 20 will fall between a mean weight of 65 kilograms and a mean weight of 80 kilograms?

   iii) If the researcher draws a sample of 50 people, what is the probability that the mean weight for this sample will be greater than 80 kilograms?

   iv) If the researcher draws a sample of only ten people, what is the probability that the mean for this sample will be less than 60 kilograms?

2. A measure of anxiety has been designed in such a way that it is normally distributed with a mean of 0 and a standard deviation of 20. To investigate whether year-end examinations at South African universities are associated with high levels of anxiety among the student population, researchers decide to administer the anxiety questionnaire to a random sample of students.

   a) If the sample size is 200, what is the standard error?

   b) How large does the sample have to be to ensure that the standard error is no smaller than 0.7?

   c) What is the mean and variance of the sampling distribution of the mean for the anxiety questionnaire, for samples of 150 cases?

   d) Knowing the mean and variance of the sampling distribution of the mean for samples of 150 cases, what is the probability that the mean will fall below an anxiety score of –2?

e) If the researcher draws a random sample of 300 students, what is the probability that the mean of this sample will be greater than 1.5?

f) If the researcher draws a random sample of 80 students, what is the probability that the mean of this sample will be less than –1?

3. The records of the World Health Organisation reveal that the birthweight of babies is normally distributed with a mean of 2.75 kilograms and a variance of 0.886 kilograms. Researchers are interested in studying a random sample of 80 babies.

a) What is the mean of the sampling distribution?

b) What is the variance of the sampling distribution?

c) What is the standard error?

d) What is the probability that the mean for the sample of 80 babies will be greater than 3.2 kilograms?

e) What is the probability that the mean for the sample of 80 babies will be less than 1.5 kilograms?

f) If we are going to use a sample mean to predict the population mean, how can we increase the accuracy of the prediction? Substantiate your answer.

8

Hypothesis testing: the z-test

Kevin Durrheim

> After studying this tutorial, you should be able to:
> - Understand the logic of hypothesis testing.
> - Translate research questions into formal statistical hypotheses.
> - Use the z-test to test hypotheses.
> - Understand different kinds of errors that may be involved in hypothesis testing.

The previous tutorial introduced the sampling distribution of the mean. You learned to define this distribution using the Central Limit Theorem, and you learned one of the uses of the sampling distribution, namely to estimate the accuracy with which a sample mean estimates the population mean. Survey researchers, for example, calculate the standard error of the estimate plus confidence intervals to determine how accurate their estimates are.

The sampling distribution of the mean is used to: a) determine the accuracy of an estimate of a population mean b) test hypotheses about a population mean.

In addition to estimating the accuracy of parameter estimates, the sampling distribution of the mean serves a very important function in hypothesis testing. Imagine that someone told you that they had a magic die that was loaded to show 6 when it was thrown. Would you simply believe them and purchase the die for R100? You would surely want to test the die before purchasing it? Specifically, you would want to test the hypothesis that the die is in fact loaded. Researchers often find themselves in similar situations, testing hypotheses, for example, that schizophrenics are violent, or that white South Africans are racist. The whole point of social science is to subject such claims to empirical testing. When we use statistical methods to help assess claims, we call this *hypothesis testing*.

Hypothesis testing

Hypothesis testing is a logical and empirical procedure whereby hypotheses are formally set up and then subjected to empirical test.

A hypothesis is a tentative statement of a relationship between two variables, or as Neuman (1997, p. 108) puts it, hypotheses are educated 'guesses about how the social world works'. Hypothesis testing is a logical and empirical procedure whereby hypotheses are formally set up and subjected to empirical test. In the first stage of hypothesis testing, the researcher states a research question, and poses two hypotheses that refer to the possible outcomes of the empirical investigation. The research question is the question that the researcher wants to answer by doing the research. In our loaded die problem, we would want to test whether the die shows 6 more often than a fair die. This would tell us whether the die was loaded or not. The research question for this investigation would be: 'Does the "magic" die show 6 more often than a fair die?' Answering this question would be the whole point of the research.

Box 8.1

Examples of research questions
All of the following research questions can be investigated with a hypothesis-testing approach:
a) Are individuals less intelligent in crowd situations?
b) Do women and men perform similarly at facial recognition tasks?
c) Have a group of children who were involved in a bus accident suffered mental impairment?
d) Are schizophrenics violent?

Hypotheses tests can be used to compare two means or values.

You will note that all the research questions in Box 8.1 presuppose two conditions or groups, and a comparison between them. We are comparing a fair die with a loaded die; individuals in crowds with the same individuals when they are not in crowds; women and men; and children involved in a bus accident with similar children who were not involved in a bus accident. A comparison group is also implied by the research question 'Are schizophrenics violent?' What we want to know here is whether schizophrenics are more violent than non-schizophrenic people.

*The **null hypothesis** is a statement that maintains that there is no difference between the groups or conditions. It is represented by the symbol H_0.*

The research question in a hypothesis-testing situation typically seeks to determine whether groups are the same or not. Before conducting an empirical investigation to determine this, the research question is first translated into two hypotheses, known as the *null* and *alternative* hypotheses. The null hypothesis is a statement that maintains that there is no difference between the groups or conditions. It is represented by the symbol H_0. From the loaded die research question we would derive the following null hypothesis:

H_0: The loaded die shows 6 with the same probability as a fair die.

Examples of null hypotheses
1. H_0: There is no difference between the intelligence of individuals when they are in crowds and when they are not in crowds.
2. H_0: Men and women perform similarly at facial recognition tasks.
3. H_0: There is no difference in mental functioning between the children who were involved in the bus accident and similar children who have not experienced trauma.
4. H_0: Schizophrenic and non-schizophrenic people display similar levels of violence.

In contrast to the null hypothesis, the alternative hypothesis is a statement that maintains that there are differences between the groups or conditions. This hypothesis makes a conjecture that is diametrically opposed to the null hypothesis. The alternative hypothesis is represented by the symbol H_1. The alternative hypothesis can take two forms, depending on the nature of the research question: it can be either *directional* or *non-directional*. A directional alternative hypothesis anticipates the direction of difference. It states the researcher's expectation regarding whether one group is going to score higher or lower than the other group. A non-directional hypothesis merely states that a difference is expected, without anticipating the direction of the difference. The 'loaded die' research question involves a directional alternative hypothesis because we want to determine whether the loaded die shows heads more often than a fair die:

*The **alternative hypothesis**, H_1, is a statement that maintains that there are differences between the groups or conditions.*

***Directional alternative hypotheses** anticipate the direction of difference whereas **non-directional hypotheses** merely state that a difference is expected.*

H_1: The loaded die shows 6 more often than a fair die.

Examples of alternative hypotheses
1. H_1: Individuals in crowds are *less* intelligent than when they are not in crowds.
2. H_1: Men and women perform *differently* at facial recognition tasks.
3. H_1: The children who were involved in the bus accident show *impaired* mental functioning in comparison with similar children who have not experienced trauma.
4. H_1: Schizophrenics are *more* violent than non-schizophrenics.

Can you identify which of the research questions in Box 8.1 require directional or non-directional alternative hypotheses? Hypotheses 1, 3, and 4 are all directional, whereas 2 is non-directional (see Box 8.3). Can you see why?

Thus far the null hypothesis and alternative hypothesis have been written out in words. However, they are usually written in symbolic format. At the outset of a research project, before engaging in any empirical testing, the researcher should state the research question and hypotheses closely analogous to the following:

1. Research question: Are individuals less intelligent in crowd situations?

$H_0: \mu_1 = \mu_2$

$H_1: \mu_1 < \mu_2$

2. Research question: Do women and men perform the same at facial recognition tasks?

$H_0: \mu_1 = \mu_2$

$H_1: \mu_1 \neq \mu_2$

The research question in the first example implies a directional alternative hypothesis. The words 'less intelligent' in the research question indicate that a 'less than' sign (i.e. $<$) should be used in H_1 to show the researcher's expectation. The research question in the second example is non-directional, and a $\neq$ sign is used in H_1 to indicate the absence of direction.

In hypothesis testing, we are not really interested in whether or not our *sample* means differ. They may differ because of random variation introduced by the sampling process (i.e. error variance – see Tutorial 7). We are interested in whether or not the *population* means differ, therefore the hypotheses are stated in terms of the population parameter (μ) not the sample statistic ($\bar{x}$). The mean of the first population (e.g. individuals in crowds; women) is represented by μ_1, and the mean of the second population (e.g. individuals not in crowds; men) is represented by μ_2. Once the research question and hypotheses have been stated, the researcher may proceed to test the hypotheses empirically. The results of the empirical investigation will indicate whether the null hypothesis or the alternative hypothesis should be rejected.

Activity 8.1

Citizen Joe goes to the local supermarket one Sunday morning, chooses one cucumber, and approaches a checkout till. The till operator swipes the cucumber across the barcode reader and the till declares that Citizen Joe owes R111.78. Citizen Joe refuses to pay, declaring that the automated checkout system has made a mistake. Citizen Joe has just tested and rejected a null hypothesis. What was the null hypothesis? Outline the hypothesis testing procedure that Citizen Joe applied.

There are many different tests that can be used to help us decide which hypothesis to reject. Each test is appropriate only in certain situations. As you will see, doing the calculations is easy – the difficult part is deciding which test is the appropriate one to use! This tutorial will discuss only one test, the z-test. You will consider a second test, the *t*-test, in Tutorial 9.

The *z*-test

Statistical decisions are made on the basis of probability and are always uncertain. Consider, once again, the problem of deciding whether a die is loaded to show 6. Say you throw the die once and it shows 6. Would you be convinced that the die is loaded and purchase it for R100? Surely not? It might have shown 6 even if it is not loaded. If you throw the die a second and a third time, it may well show 6 on each occasion, and although you may now be more convinced that the die is loaded, the three 6s could also have come about by chance (see Tutorial 5). If you throw the die ten times and each time it shows 6, you might decide to purchase the die, convinced that it is in fact loaded. However, you may be wrong – the ten 6s may have been a chance event, and you might not get a single 6 in the next ten throws! However, since it is very unlikely that a fair die would show 6 ten times in a row – i.e. there is a very small probability of this occurring – you might decide to reject the null hypothesis. In hypothesis testing, the researcher must decide how unlikely an event must be before the null hypothesis can be rejected. We need to define a cut-off point that, once reached, allows us to stop throwing the die and make a decision.

Activity 8.2

> Roll a die 100 times, recording the result each time. (If you prefer, simulate this with a spreadsheet program, generating random numbers between 1 and 6.)
>
> Identify sequences of 6s (i.e. when 6 appears two or more times in a row). What are the 'unlikely' sequences? How could you decide what these are?

The z-test helps us to decide whether or not to reject the null hypothesis by estimating how likely it is that the sample mean obtained through research does in fact come from the population defined by the null hypothesis. If only a very small proportion of samples in the sampling distribution of the mean have means the size of our observed mean, we will reject the null hypothesis in favour of the alternative hypothesis.

*The **z-test** allows us to estimate the likelihood that the observed sample mean comes from the population defined by the null hypothesis.*

Example 1
Thousands of studies conducted in all parts of the world over the past 50 years have shown that authoritarianism, measured by the F-scale, is normally distributed and has a mean of 45 and a standard

deviation of 78 (high scores indicate greater authoritarianism). A researcher wants to know whether South Africans are more authoritarian than other people. She selects a random sample of 600 subjects who complete the F-scale. The mean score of this sample is 58. Can the researcher conclude that South Africans are more authoritarian than other groups of people?

As a *first step*, we must state our hypotheses: H_0: $\mu_1 = \mu_2 = 45$, and H_1: $\mu_1 > \mu_2$. The null hypothesis states that the mean authoritarianism score for South Africans is equal to the international mean of 45. The alternative hypothesis is directional, stating that the mean authoritarianism score for South Africans is greater than the international mean.

It is quite clear that the sample mean is different to the population mean. However, this may be attributable purely to error variance. It may have been a random or chance outcome, just like throwing two 6s with two throws of a die is unlikely, but possible nevertheless. We expect means of different samples to vary. What we want to know is whether the sample mean differs so much from the international mean that we can conclude that the two populations, i.e. South Africans and the rest of humanity, do in fact have different means. We make this decision by setting a significance level. The significance level (represented by the Greek symbol alpha, α) is the probability with which we are willing to reject the null hypothesis *when it is correct*. Statistical convention sets this significance level at 0.05 or 0.01. As you can see from Figure 8.1, if our sample mean falls within the region of the sampling distribution that includes the 5% most extreme sample means, we reject the null hypothesis.

*The **significance level** (α) is the probability with which we are willing to reject the null hypothesis when it is correct.*

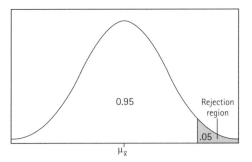

Figure 8.1 Sampling distribution for a one-tailed test ($\alpha = 0.05$)

We may reject the null hypothesis incorrectly. Our sample may be one of those extreme sample means that are legitimately part of the sampling distribution. This can be likened to throwing ten consecutive 6s with a die: it is a possible outcome, so although we reject the null hypothesis and conclude that the die is loaded, we may be wrong. The area within the 5% region is known as the *rejection region* because if our sample mean falls in this area, we reject the null hypothesis.

The ***second step*** in hypothesis testing is to define the significance level. Since the alternate hypothesis in Example 1 is directional, the rejection region lies on only one tail of the sampling distribution. We want to know whether or not our sample mean is greater than the international mean. Thus the rejection region in Figure 8.1 is in the upper tail of the distribution. If our hypothesis were that the sample mean is *lower* than the international mean, we would place the rejection region in the lower tail. If we had a non-directional hypothesis, stating that the sample mean is *different* to the international mean, the rejection region would be placed in both the upper and lower tails (see Figure 8.2). In this case, the area under the curve in each tail would be divided by two so that our overall alpha value remained the same. It is important to state whether the alternative hypothesis is directional or non-directional because this has implications for whether we conduct one-tailed or two-tailed tests of significance. We use one-tailed tests to reach decisions about directional hypotheses, but two-tailed tests to reach decisions about non-directional hypotheses.

*The **rejection region** is the area under the curve of the sampling distribution of the mean that includes sample means that would be observed at probabilities below the significance level. If an observed mean falls in the rejection region, the null hypothesis is rejected.*

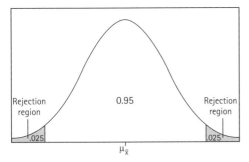

Figure 8.2 Sampling distribution for two-tailed test of significance ($\alpha = 0.05$)

What does it mean if our sample mean falls in the rejection region? (See Figure 8.1.) It could mean one of two things:
1. This sample properly belongs to the sampling distribution of the mean defined by the null hypothesis, and the null hypothesis is correct.
2. The sample mean comes from a sampling distribution with a greater mean, and the null hypothesis should be rejected.

If the alternative hypothesis is directional, use a one-tailed test. If it is non-directional, use a two-tailed test.

In the first case, the sample mean for the population of white South Africans is in reality no different from the international mean, but purely by chance our sample was one of the extreme (i.e. highest 5%

of sample means) but legitimate samples belonging to the sampling distribution defined in the null hypothesis. Another South African sample may be much closer to the international mean (also by chance). In the second case, a sample mean falling in the rejection region would actually come from a population with a higher mean than that defined by the null hypothesis (i.e. some population other than that assumed in the null hypothesis).

Although a sample mean falling in the rejection region could suggest two different things, when this happens we reject the null hypothesis. Of course, the decision to reject the null hypothesis may be incorrect. We may have committed what is termed a *Type I error*, by rejecting the null hypothesis when it in fact is true. We make a Type I error when, for example, we throw ten consecutive 6s with a die, and decide that the die is loaded to show 6 (i.e. we reject the null hypothesis that the die is not loaded), when in fact it is not. The probability of making a Type I error is equal to alpha, α – since 5% of the sample means from the sampling distribution of the international mean fall in the rejection region, the probability of randomly selecting a mean that falls in the rejection region is 0.05.

The solution to this problem may seem at first to be a simple modification of the Type I error rate – we could just set alpha to 0.0001, for example. However, we then open ourselves up to committing a *Type II error*, i.e. not rejecting the null hypothesis when it is false. We are in the same position here as when, after throwing ten consecutive 6s with a die, we decide that the die is not loaded to show 6 (i.e. we do not reject the null hypothesis), but it is in fact loaded. We have to balance the likelihood of these errors against each other – do we prefer to risk the false conclusion that the means differ, or the false conclusion that the means do not differ? In some circumstances we will tend to choose the first (where we want to be sure that we do not miss a research finding), and in others the second (where we do not want to risk an incorrect inference that the groups/conditions in question differ).

Activity 8.3

The following table is often used to cross-classify decisions and the true state of the world. Fill in the missing (?) entries, $\alpha = 0.05$.

Decision	True state of the world	
	H_0 True	H_0 False
Reject H_0	Type ? error $p = ?$	Correct decision $p = 1 - \beta$ = power
Fail to reject H_0	Correct decision $p = ?$	Type ? error $p = \beta$

How do we know whether or not our sample mean falls in the rejection region? We transform our x̄-value into a z-score and decide whether this score falls within the rejection region of the standard normal distribution. To do this, we have to define the rejection region of the standard normal distribution. Thus, the **third step** in hypothesis testing is defining z_{crit} (called the *critical value*). The critical value is the z-score that brackets the rejection region. From your table of z-scores you will see that 5% of the distribution lies above a z-score of 1.645; therefore $z_{crit} = 1.645$ (see Figure 8.3).

*The **critical value** (z_{crit}) is the z-score that brackets the rejection region.*

The **fourth step** in hypothesis testing is calculating z_{calc}. We calculate z_{calc} by transforming our sample mean into a score on the standard normal distribution. Returning to the data in Example 1, we use Equation 7.1 to transform our x̄-value into z_{calc}:

$$z = \frac{\bar{x} - \mu}{\dfrac{\sigma}{\sqrt{n}}} = \frac{58 - 45}{\dfrac{78}{\sqrt{600}}} = \frac{13}{\dfrac{78}{24.495}} = \frac{13}{3.184} = 4.083$$

All we have done in this calculation is substitute the data given to us in Example 1 into the formula to calculate z-scores from x̄-values.

The **fifth step** in hypothesis testing is reaching a decision. We reach a decision by comparing z_{calc} with z_{crit} to determine whether z_{calc} falls in the rejection region. This comparison is best done with the aid of a diagram such as Figure 8.3. As you can see from Figure 8.3, z_{calc} is bigger than z_{crit} and thus falls in the rejection region. We therefore decide to reject the null hypothesis and conclude that South Africans are more authoritarian than other people. We may be wrong (we may have inadvertently made a Type I error), but given the results of our study, this is the best decision we can make.

Decisions about hypotheses are reached by comparing z_{calc} with z_{crit} to determine whether z_{calc} falls in the rejection region.

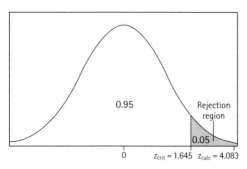

Figure 8.3 Comparing z_{crit} and z_{calc} for the data of Example 1

Box 8.4

The best way to learn the logic and technique of statistical hypothesis testing, in our opinion, is to look at – and attempt – multiple examples. We therefore finish this tutorial with a number of worked examples, and encourage you to try as many of the exercises at the end of the tutorial as you can.

Worked examples

1. We know that the weight of humans is normally distributed with a variance of 144, and a mean of 73 kilograms. To investigate whether the weight of rural South Africans is different from this international mean, we draw a random sample of 100 rural South Africans and calculate their mean weight to be 69 kilograms. Determine whether the weight of rural South Africans is different from the international mean.

Solution
Research question: Is the weight of rural South Africans different from the weight of humans in general?

$H_0: \mu_1 = \mu_2 = 73$

$H_1: \mu_1 \neq \mu_2$

Note that this is a two-tailed test (non-directional). We decide to set $\alpha = 0.01$. This will decrease our chances of making a Type I error but increase our chances of making a Type II error. We decide, however, that for this study, it is more important not to reject a true null hypothesis than it is to accept a null hypothesis that is false.

Since this is a two-tailed test with 1% of the area lying in the rejection region, 0.5% of the area must lie in each tail of the standard normal distribution. To calculate z_{crit}, we must refer to our tables of z-scores and look up the z-score that cuts off an area of 0.5% (i.e. a proportion of 0.005, which is half of 0.01). From our tables we determine that this z-value is equal to 2.575. This means that a z-score of 2.575 cuts off an area of 0.005 in the upper tail, and a z-score of –2.575 cuts off an area of 0.005 in the lower tail. Therefore $z_{crit} = \pm 2.575$ (see Figure 8.4). To determine z_{calc}, we

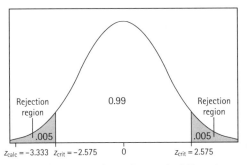

Figure 8.4 Comparing z_{crit} and z_{calc} for worked Exercise 1

substitute the information that we have into the formula to calculate z-scores from $\bar{x}$-values:

$$z = \frac{\bar{x} - \mu}{\frac{\sigma}{\sqrt{n}}} = \frac{69 - 73}{\frac{12}{\sqrt{100}}} = \frac{-4}{\frac{12}{10}} = \frac{-4}{1.2} = -3.333$$

As Figure 8.4 shows, $z_{calc} = -3.333$ is smaller than $z_{crit} = -2.575$ and thus falls in the rejection region. We therefore reject the null hypothesis and conclude that the weight of rural South Africans is lower than the international mean.

Discussion

If you take a look at Example 3 of Tutorial 7, you will note that the sample weight for rural South Africans falls outside the 99% confidence interval. We can use confidence intervals to test hypotheses because both hypothesis testing and confidence intervals rely on the notion that a sample drawn from the sampling distribution has a certain known probability of having a mean greater than or less than a specified value. Confidence limits are values that bracket a certain proportion of means on the sampling distribution. The 99% confidence limits bracket 99% of the means in the sampling distribution. For a sampling distribution with a mean equal to 73 and a variance equal to 144, the 99% confidence limits are 69.91 and 76.09. These confidence limits, once transformed into z-scores, are equal to ±2.575, the critical value for a hypothesis test with $\alpha = 0.01$. Thus a score of 69 falls outside the confidence interval, and its corresponding z-score (i.e. -3.333) falls in the rejection region. Confidence intervals and hypothesis testing are similar ways of using the sampling distribution of the mean to define the probability with which we can expect a particular sample mean to be drawn from a parent population. In hypothesis testing, however, if this probability is very small, we decide to reject the null hypothesis and conclude that the sample mean in fact comes from a different parent population.

2. Research conducted around the world has shown that the Conservatism scale, a measure of conservative ideological beliefs, is normally distributed with a mean of 45 and a variance of 45. To test the theory that conservatism originates in strict parenting, a researcher draws a sample of 45 adults who have had a very strict upbringing. The mean for this sample is 47.

   a) Does the data support the hypothesis that strict upbringing is related to high levels of conservatism (set $\alpha = 0.05$)?

   b) If the mean for the sample was found to be 47, would the data support the hypothesis that there is a *difference* in conservatism between this group of subjects and the international mean (set $\alpha = 0.01$)?

   c) What is the chance of making a Type I error in (b) above?

   d) What is the difference between the chance of making a Type II error in (a) and (b), above?

   e) Between what mean scores would you expect 80% of all randomly selected samples of size 100 to score on the Conservatism scale?

Solutions

a) $H_0: \mu_1 = \mu_2 = 45$; $H_1: \mu_1 > \mu_2$ (or $\mu_1 > 45$); one-tailed z-test; $\alpha = 0.05$; $z_{crit} = 1.645$

$$z = \frac{\bar{x} - \mu}{\frac{\sigma}{\sqrt{n}}} = \frac{47 - 45}{\frac{6.71}{\sqrt{45}}} = \frac{2}{\frac{6.71}{6.71}} = \frac{2}{1} = 2$$

z_{calc} falls in the rejection region (see Figure 8.5). We therefore reject the null hypothesis and conclude that strict upbringing is related to high levels of conservatism.

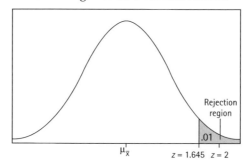

Rejection region

.01

$\mu_{\bar{x}}$ $z = 1.645$ $z = 2$

Figure 8.5 Comparing z_{crit} and z_{calc} in Worked example 2a

b) $H_0: \mu_1 = 45$; $H_1: \mu_1 \neq 45$; two-tailed z-test; $\alpha = 0.01$; $z_{crit} = \pm 2.575$. From 2a), we know that $z_{calc} = 2.0$, therefore z_{calc} does not fall within the rejection region, and we cannot reject the null hypothesis. We conclude that there is no difference in conservatism scores between this group and the international mean (see Figure 8.6).

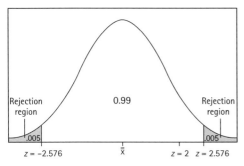

$z = -2.576$ $\bar{x}$ $z = 2$ $z = 2.576$

Figure 8.6 Comparing z_{crit} and z_{calc} in Worked example 2b

c) $\alpha = 0.01$ (remember that the Type I error rate is by definition equal to α).

d) You do not yet have the techniques that would allow you to exactly calculate a Type II error rate. However, note that there is a higher chance of making a Type I error in question (a) than in question (b), and therefore there is a lower chance of making a Type II error in question (a) than in question (b) (given that all other details are identical).

e) $\bar{x} = \mu \pm z \dfrac{\sigma}{\sqrt{n}} = 45 \pm (1.28 \times 1)$ (See Equation 7.3.)

$\therefore \bar{x} = 43.72$ *and* 46.28

Summary

1. Hypothesis testing is a logical and empirical procedure whereby hypotheses are formally set up and then subjected to empirical test.

2. The null hypothesis is a statement that there is no difference between groups or conditions. The alternative hypothesis is a statement that there are differences between groups or conditions. The alternative hypothesis can take two forms depending on the nature of the research question: it can either be directional or non-directional.

3. The z-test helps us to decide whether or not to reject the null hypothesis by estimating how likely it is that the observed sample mean comes from the population defined by the null hypothesis.

4. The significance level (α) is the probability with which we are willing to reject the null hypothesis when it is correct.

5. A Type I error is committed by rejecting the null hypothesis when it in fact is true. A Type II error is committed by not rejecting the null hypothesis when it is false.

6. We reach decisions in hypothesis testing by comparing z_{calc} with z_{crit} to determine whether z_{calc} falls in the rejection region.

7. Statistical hypothesis testing involves the following five steps:
   a) State the hypotheses.
   b) Define the significance level.
   c) Define the critical value.
   d) Calculate the z-score for the sample mean.
   e) Reach a decision.

Exercises

1. State the null and alternative hypotheses for the following research questions. State all hypotheses twice: first in words and then in symbolic form.
   a) Do girls play less roughly than boys?
   b) Are people living in colder climates more susceptible to catching colds and flu than those living in warmer climates?
   c) Do people above the age of 50 have a different metabolism from younger people?
   d) Are men violent?
   e) Do extremely wealthy people have different attitudes towards the poor from people who are less wealthy?
   f) Are women sensitive?

2. A researcher for the Department of Justice conducts a survey to estimate the attitudes of South Africans to the introduction of the death penalty. The researcher measures attitudes on a scale that ranges from strongly opposed (–10) through neutral (0) to strongly in favour (+10). The survey reveals that the scores on the attitude scale were normally distributed with a mean of 5 and a standard deviation of 13. Assume that these are population values. The researcher is also aware that the population in Cape Town appears to be more vocal about the disadvantages of the death penalty than people from other cities. He decides to conduct the very same attitude survey on a random sample of 100 Capetonians, and discovers that the mean score is 1.
   a) Test the hypothesis that Capetonians have a different attitude to other South Africans regarding the introduction of the death penalty ($\alpha = 0.01$).
   b) Are Capetonians more opposed to the death penalty than other South Africans ($\alpha = 0.01$)?
   c) What is the chance of making a Type I error in the above tests?
   d) How would the chance of making a Type I and Type II error change if we changed the significance level to $\alpha = 0.05$?

e) If the researcher conducts the survey on a random sample of 50 Capetonians, would he still find that there is a difference between their attitudes and those of other South Africans ($\alpha = 0.01$)?

3. From the records of the Department of Education, we discover that matric results for the previous five years were normally distributed with a mean of 62% and a variance of 168. The education authorities identified ten schools around the country where they suspected that examination papers had been leaked and decided to test whether students from these schools had performed better at their examinations (i.e. through cheating) than would have been expected. They drew a random sample of 150 pupils from these ten schools and calculated their mean result to be 63.8%.
   a) Did pupils from these ten schools perform better than expected ($\alpha = 0.05$)?
   b) Conduct an analysis on the same data to test the research question of whether the pupils performed differently from expectation ($\alpha = 0.05$).
   c) The two tests result in different conclusions. Explain why.
   d) What is the chance of making a Type I error in the above tests?
   e) How would the chance of making Type I and Type II errors change if we altered the significance level of the tests to $\alpha = 0.01$?

TUTORIAL

9

T-tests

David Nunez

> After studying this tutorial, you should be able to:
> - Compute the standard error of a sample distribution.
> - Check that a dataset does not violate the assumptions required for a *t*-test.
> - Set up a hypothesis test for comparing distributions.
> - Decide on the appropriate *t*-test subtype for a given design.
> - Calculate a *t*-value.
> - Calculate the degrees of freedom for a *t*-calculation.

Research questions in the social sciences are often about group differences. Does an experimental group score differently to a control group? Do men and women differ? If we could access these populations we could simply calculate the means (μs) to identify differences. However, because we seldom have access to populations, we need to decide whether groups differ by inspecting the distribution of sample scores. The *t*-test is used to determine whether the means of two samples are sufficiently different to conclude that they in fact are drawn from two distinct populations, or whether the scores suggest that both samples come from single population.

The difficulty in using sample statistics rather than population parameters is that samples only *estimate* populations. The Central

Limit Theorem tells us that if we draw two samples from a population and calculate the means of these samples, we can expect to get two slightly different scores (see Tutorial 7). In fact, the Central Limit Theorem tells us that we can expect the means of samples to follow a particular distribution – the sampling distribution of the mean. Our sample means are not exact representations of the population mean, but rather differ slightly (on average, by an amount indicated by the standard error – the standard deviation of the sampling distribution of the mean). This variation is the reason why we cannot simply look at the sample means when we want to see how population means differ.

Clearly, we need to overcome the ambiguity imposed by the standard error. How do we do this? The *t*-test provides a mechanism. Basically, the *t*-test scales the difference between the sample means by an estimate of the standard error. This way, we can determine if the difference between the means is large in relation to the standard error. If this is the case, then the difference probably also exists at the level of populations (the level of this probability is determined by the distribution of *t*, which we will explain later).

*The **t-test** is used to compare two (estimated) population means.*

Thinking of the *t*–test graphically

The aim of the *t*-test is to compare distributions that are normally distributed. We can represent such distributions with a bell curve. Imagine we have two distributions, as in Figure 9.1. How can we tell if they actually derive from the same population?

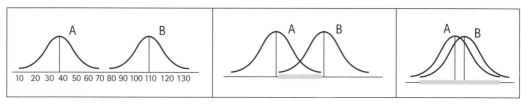

Figure 9.1   Figure 9.2   Figure 9.3

These two distributions are obviously not the same. A covers lower scores (more to the left), and B covers higher scores. We can see that they are not overlapping; this means that scores from A are extremely unlikely to show up in a sample drawn from B. Now consider the situation in Figure 9.2. Here, the distributions overlap. The scores in the region represented by the grey bar are just as likely to belong to either distribution. Although the distributions look quite separate, we might say that they are similar, because they share quite a number of scores. Now consider a final situation – Figure 9.3. Here the distributions are overlapping markedly, and it is beginning to look as if they are definitely the same. The grey bar (common scores) is much larger. This is what the *t*-test does, in essence – it allows us to see how much the two distributions overlap. This overlap is computed by taking into account the distance between the means of the distributions, and also considering the width of the distributions (their variance).

*The **t-test** allows us to determine the degree to which two distributions overlap.*

Activity 9.1

Get some pieces of transparent plastic and an overhead marker pen. Draw a set of four normal curves: two with high variance (very wide), two with low variance (very narrow). Place two of these curves on top of each other to create an image similar to Figure 9.3. Using these curves, investigate the following:
a) To what extent does the *difference (distance)* between the means of the curves affect how much they overlap if both curves have the same or different variances?
b) If both curves have a fixed, known mean, how does the variance affect how much they overlap?

Common concepts behind the *t*-test

There are different types of *t*-tests, and the selection of the correct one depends on the situation you are studying. In this chapter we will first introduce the common concepts at a conceptual level, and then we will look at the specific formulas and calculations involved in performing each of the subtypes.

The general form of the *t*-test equation

The degree to which two distributions overlap is deter-mined by the difference between the means and variance of each sample.

Regardless of the specific type of *t*-test being performed, the *t*-test formula always has the same general form (see Equation 6.1):

$$t = \frac{\text{difference between the means}}{\text{standard error}}$$

This general form should be familiar to you, as it is very similar to the *z*-score transformation:

$$z = \frac{\text{difference between score and population mean}}{\text{standard deviation of the population}} = \frac{x - \mu}{\sigma}$$

The central difference between a *t*-test and the *z*-score transformation is that the population parameters (μ and σ) do not have to be known to perform a *t*-test. This difference is important, because in the large majority of cases the population parameters are unknown. Thus, the *t*-test can be used when we only have information from our sample.

When performing a *t*-test, however, we are still interested in making claims about the population; in other words, we want to make claims of statistical significance. In order to do this with the *z*-test (see Tutorial 7), we had to scale the difference by the population standard deviation. In a *t*-test, we do something similar, but rather than relying on the exact population standard deviation, we make use of a sample-based estimate. It is possible to make this estimate, thanks to the Central Limit Theorem. The theorem specifies the standard error of the sampling distributon of the mean. Recall that:

Unlike a z-test, no population parameters are needed to perform a t-test.

$$\sigma_{\bar{x}} = \frac{\sigma}{\sqrt{n}}$$

The problem with this equation is that we require the population parameter, σ, which we often do not have. The *t*-test allows us to test differences between means using an estimate of the standard error:

*The **standard error** is the standard deviation of the sampling distribution of the mean (the distribution created by taking repeated sample means from a population).*

$$s_{\bar{x}} = \frac{s}{\sqrt{n}}$$

Equation 9.1

The fact that this is not the actual population variance, but rather an estimate is shown by the symbol used (i.e. $s_{\bar{x}}$ not $\sigma_{\bar{x}}$). This estimate is referred to as the *standard error of* $\bar{x}$ (see Tutorial 7). This term lies right at the heart of the *t*-test, and one of the most important issues in this test is ensuring that our approximations are appropriate and correct.

Activity 9.2

Use the standard error formula to calculate the standard error of the following samples:
a) 5, 12, 14, 6, 3, 7
b) 53, 57, 53, 62, 63, 52, 53
c) 12, 14, 10
d) 12, 14, 25

Sadly, calculating the standard error is not always quite as simple as the formulas above suggest. Because in many *t*-tests there are two separate samples, it is important to use the variance of both of these samples to estimate the population standard deviation. How this is done depends on a number of factors, such as the relative sizes of each of the samples and the relative difference in the variance of the samples. Later in this chapter, when we deal with specific subtypes of the *t*-test, we will discuss how to do this for each case.

Interpreting a significant result on a *t*–test

Once you have completed your *t*-test, you will have made a decision to reject (or not reject) H_0. In order to understand what your conclusions means, it is necessary to think back to the meaning of the null hypothesis. The purpose of a *t*-test is to evaluate the difference between two means, so in most cases the null hypothesis states:

$$H_0: \mu_1 = \mu_2$$

Thus, the hypothesis is that the two means are equal. If we reject the null hypothesis, we are saying that it is false. So, if we reject the above hypothesis, we are actually saying that the two means *are not* the same.

'Not the same' can have various meanings. For example, if mean 1 is larger than mean 2, then they are not the same. Also, if mean 1 is smaller than mean 2, they are not the same. Thus, to clear up the confusion of what we mean by 'the means are not the same', we state it, either by means of a directional or non-directional alternative hypothesis.

Assumptions about the data

To analyse your data with a t-test, the data need to comply with the assumptions of normality, homogeneity of variance, and independence.

Only certain datasets are suitable for analysis with *t*-tests. The mechanism of the *t*-test makes certain assumptions about the data, so it is important that you check to see if your data violates any of these assumptions before you begin. If your data is not suitable for this analysis, and you do use it, the results you get will be inaccurate, and your conclusions incorrect. Please note that not all types of *t*-test rely equally heavily on each of the assumptions. When we describe the specific subtypes below, we will mention which are the most important assumptions for each type.

1. *The assumption of normality*
   It is assumed that all the samples you are analysing have been drawn from populations that are normally distributed. To test for normality, you can use formal tests of normality (although these tests are beyond the scope of this chapter). You can get a rough idea if data is normally distributed by drawing a histogram of the data and examining the shape of the distribution. If the histogram has a bell shape, then it is probably normally distributed.

2. *The assumption of homogeneity of variance*
   If your samples have variances that are highly different, then it is difficult to get accurate results from a *t*-test (see the section on coping with heterogeneity of variance later in the tutorial). This can be formally checked for, but is quite complex. We can 'cheat' and say that if the two variances differ by a factor of less than 4, the variance is probably homogenous. This is a rule of thumb, so it is not perfect, but seems to work a lot of the time. Apply the following calculation to check for this:

NUMBERS, HYPOTHESES AND CONCLUSIONS

$$k = \frac{s_1^2}{s_2^2}$$

Equation 9.2

where: k is the ratio of the largest to the smallest variance
and s_1^2 is the *larger* and s_2^2 the *smaller* of the two variances

If, after performing the above calculation, you get a value of 4 or more, your two variances are too different to use a *t*-test. Please note that this is not a fixed rule – it is simply a rule of thumb. Some statisticians insist on ratios of 5 or more; some are willing to go with less.

Activity 9.3

Do the following pairs of datasets show homogeneity of variance? Use the 'times four' method described in the tutorial.
a) $s_1^2 = 21.8994$; $s_2^2 = 15.3448$

b) $s_1^2 = 26.8994$; $s_2^2 = 3.3448$

c) $s_1 = 17.13025$; $s_2 = 8.50541$

3. *The assumption of independence*
The majority of *t*-tests (with the exception of the repeated measures *t*-test) assume that the samples the means were calculated from did not influence each other's scores in any way. For example, if you collect two datasets from the same group of people (as in a pre-test/post-test design), then these two datasets are not independent.

If the same sample of cases is used to generate both distributions of scores, those scores are not independent.

Subtypes of *t*-tests

Now that we have considered the concepts behind *t*-tests in general, we can consider the different specific types of *t*-tests. For each of these tests we will present an example of when it would be useful.

1. One–sample *t*-test

Recall that the z-test was used to determine whether a sample mean differed from a population mean. We could use the z-test because we had the value for the population standard deviation. The one-sample *t*-test uses a similar formula to the z-test, but the standard error is estimated from the sample standard deviation.
The formula for the one-sample *t*-test is as follows:

$$t = \frac{\bar{x} - \mu}{\dfrac{s}{\sqrt{n}}}$$

Equation 9.3

where: $\bar{x}$ is the mean of the sample
μ is the mean of the population
s is the standard deviation of the sample
n is the sample size

Compare Equation 9.3 and Equation 7.2. Notice that the two equations are similar, but that the t formula does not require that we know the population standard deviation.

The same 5-step procedure is used to test hypotheses with the t-test as was used with the z-test (see Box 8.4). There is only one slight complication. Since we used s rather than σ in determining t, the critical value for t has to be adjusted to take into account the fact that we are estimating the standard error from the sample variance. Since this estimate will be more accurate with larger samples, the sample size has an impact on the value of t_{crit}. In statistical terminology, the value of t_{crit} is determined by the degrees of freedom. For the one-sample t-test the degrees of freedom are given by the following formula:

$$df = n - 1$$

where: df stands for the degrees of freedom
           n is the sample size

When looking up critical values on the t-table (see Appendix 1), we need to select the value corresponding to the correct degrees of freedom. Refer to the t-table in Appendix 1. The first column gives the degrees of freedom, and the other columns give t values at different levels of α. If we conduct a t-test with a sample size n = 25, our df = n – 1 = 24. If we are conducting a two-tailed test with α = 0.05, our critical t value is 2.0639.

To sum up, the one-sample t-test is used to determine whether a sample mean differs from a population mean. The following null hypothesis is tested:

$$H_0: \mu = \varepsilon; \text{ where } \varepsilon \text{ is a particular value (e.g. } H_0: \mu = 70).$$

We use the formula for t to compute the observed value, and look up t_{crit} on the t-table, taking the degrees of freedom into account.

Activity 9.4

Identifying the correct type of t-test for a given situation is very important. For practice, go to an academic library and collect 10 journal articles which make use of a two-group design – if possible try to find studies where the data was analysed using a t-test. Turn to the section of each study where the analysis is discussed, and decide on the correct type of t-test to use.

Worked example 1

We are asked to determine if a new meditation technique can help reduce the intensity of panic attacks. We measure the severity of panic attacks by asking participants to rate the intensity of attack on a scale from 1 to 20. From years of using this method, it is known that panic attack sufferers give a mean rating of 14 (i.e. the population mean is 14). We teach the new technique to a group of panic attack sufferers, and ask them to rate their next attack. We collect the following data: 12, 18, 8, 21, 17, 12, 14, 9, 3. We need to calculate t and thus determine if this sample was drawn from the population which has a mean of 14 (i.e. if the meditation has an effect on the panic attack severity). Use $\alpha = 0.05$ and a two-tailed test: H_0: $\mu = 14$, H_1: $\mu \neq 14$.

We begin by calculating the basic descriptive stats:

$$\bar{x} = 12.667; s = 5.567; n = 9$$

We work out the standard error:

$$\frac{s}{\sqrt{n}} = \frac{5.567}{\sqrt{9}} = 1.855$$

Now we are ready to calculate t:

$$t = \frac{\bar{x} - \mu}{\frac{s}{\sqrt{n}}} = \frac{12.667 - 14}{1.855} = -0.719$$

The degrees of freedom for this calculation are $n - 1 = 8$. The critical value for this calculation ($\alpha = 0.05$; two-tailed test) is 2.306. This value is less than our calculated value, so we do not reject the null hypothesis.

Activity 9.5

For the problems below, use a two-tailed test with $\alpha = 0.05$.
a) Calculate t and determine if this sample is drawn from a population with a mean of 12:
    12, 10, 17, 8, 13, 14, 6, 19, 12, 11
b) Calculate t and determine if this sample is drawn from a population with a mean of 135:
    127, 73, 118, 123, 89, 122

2. Independent samples t-test

This test is used to compare two distributions that are independent of each other. The independent samples t-test is suitable in most situations where you have created two separate groups by random assignment. It is not necessary to have equal sample sizes for your samples. It is quite important to ensure that the assumption of homogeneity of variance is not violated for this test, but note that there are corrective formulas if you do violate the assumption.

*The **independent** samples t-test is used to find a difference between the means of two independent samples (e.g. separate groups of subjects).*

The following formula applies to independent samples:

Equation 9.4

$$t = \frac{\overline{x}_1 - \overline{x}_2}{s_{\overline{x}_1 - \overline{x}_2}}$$

where: x_1 is the mean of the first sample
x_2 is the mean of the second sample
$s_{\overline{x}_1 - \overline{x}_2}$ is the estimate of the standard error

Pooled variance

*Use the pooled variance as your standard error estimate unless the sample variances are **not** homogenous.*

Because there are two completely independent samples used for this test, it is problematic to approximate the shared standard error by making use of the variance of one of the samples only, especially if the sample sizes are quite different. To avoid this difficulty, we can find an average variance of the two samples. To ensure that the larger sample does not overwhelm the smaller, we use a weighted average, referred to as the pooled variance, and given by the formula:

Equation 9.5

$$s_p^2 = \frac{(n_1 - 1)\,s_1^2 + (n_2 - 1)\,s_2^2}{n_1 + n_2 - 2}$$

where: n_1 is the sample size of the first sample
n_2 is the sample size of the second sample
s_1^2 is the variance of the first sample
s_2^2 is the variance of the second sample

Use the squared root of the pooled variance as your estimate of the standard error in Equation 9.4. Thus:

Equation 9.6

$$t = \frac{\overline{x}_1 - \overline{x}_2}{\sqrt{s_p^2 \left(\frac{1}{n_1} + \frac{1}{n_2} \right)}}$$

Degrees of freedom

For an independent samples *t*-test use the following formula:

Equation 9.7

$$df = n_1 + n_2 - 2$$

where: n_1 is the sample size of the first sample
n_2 is the sample size of the second sample

Dealing with heterogeneity of variance in the samples

Use separate variance estimates if the variances of your two samples are highly different (i.e. one variance is at least four times as big as the other).

If your data does not have homogeneity of variance, it is still possible to analyse the data by making a few changes to the procedure. These changes will lead to your test being more conservative, however.

There are two changes involved. The first is to *not* pool the variance, but rather use the separate variance estimates formula:

Equation 9.8

$$s_{\bar{x}_1 - \bar{x}_2} = \sqrt{\frac{s_1^2}{n_1} + \frac{s_2^2}{n_2}}$$

where: s_1^2 is the variance of the first sample

s_2^2 is the variance of the second sample

n_1 is the sample size of the first sample

n_2 is the sample size of the second sample

The second change is to use a different formula for degrees of freedom. Rather than using the formula presented above, calculate $n_1 - 1$ and $n_2 - 2$ separately and use the *smaller of these values* as your degrees of freedom.

Worked example 2

We are asked to investigate whether a new technique for teaching mathematics to dyslexic children is effective. To this end, we use the new teaching method on a class of dyslexic children. We prepare a maths test, and administer this test to the class we have taught with the new method, as well as to another dyslexic class in a nearby school, who have been taught with traditional methods.

Because the classes have no common factors between them, we can think of them as independent samples. We name the class taught with traditional methods A and the class taught with the new method B. The results (marks out of 100) for each child are presented in Table 9.1.

Table 9.1 Marks for two remedial mathematics classes

A:	15	23	45	23	43	12	43	27	32	18	19	26	28	23
B:	83	74	85	52	69	46	73	67	85	45	86	34	56	57

Did the new method work? We will need to calculate the value of t for these two datasets. Based on that value, we will decide if the two samples have been drawn from separate populations.

First, we work out the basic descriptive stats for each variable (we will need these later).

A: $\bar{x} = 26.93$ $s^2 = 109.61$ $n = 14$ B: $\bar{x} = 65.14$ $s^2 = 289.67$ $n = 14$

Next, we decide if we should use pooled variance or separate estimates. The ratio of variances ($\frac{289.67}{109.61} = 2.64$) is less than 4, so we decide to use the pooled variance:

$$s_p^2 = \frac{(14 - 1)109.61 + (14 - 1)289.67}{14 + 14 - 2} = \frac{1424.93 + 3765.71}{26} = \frac{5190.63}{26} = 199.64$$

We will need the square root of this number, which is 14.13

Now that we have our standard error estimate, we can calculate t.

$$t = \frac{\bar{x}_1 - \bar{x}_2}{S_{\bar{x}_1 - \bar{x}_2}} = \frac{26.93 - 65.14}{14.13 \sqrt{\left(\frac{1}{14} + \frac{1}{14}\right)}} = \frac{-38.21}{5.34} = -7.16$$

We now need to perform a hypothesis test using this data. As no 'tailness' is given, we will assume a two-tailed test (the most inclusive option). The first step is to determine the null and alternative hypotheses:

$$H_0: \mu_1 = \mu_2$$
$$H_1: \mu_1 \neq \mu_2$$

We need the degrees of freedom.

$$df = n_1 - n_2 - 2 = 14 + 14 - 2 = 26$$

We are not told alpha, so we will assume $\alpha = 0.05$. Using df and α, we consult a table of critical t values. The value given (for a two-tailed test) is 2.056.

Since 2.70 > 2.056, we reject the null hypothesis.

We conclude that the two samples were not drawn from the same population – i.e. we conclude that the children taught with the new method are performing better than those taught with the traditional method. Refer back to Figures 9.1 to 9.3. Which best represents the two samples in this exercise?

Activity 9.6

For each of the following pairs of data, A and B, calculate t and decide if the samples were drawn from the same populations. Assume all tests are one-tailed, $\alpha = 0.05$.

a) A: 12, 13, 15, 18, 11, 9, 12   B: 15, 15, 19, 11, 14, 16
b) A: 102, 97, 57, 106, 12, 15   B: 125, 89, 102, 107, 112, 103
c) A: 5, 3, 6, 7   B: 3, 1, 4, 2, 1, 4

3. Repeated measures t-test

*The **repeated measures** t-test is used to compare means when the samples are not independent. It is also known as the related samples t-test.*

If you cannot ensure independence between your two datasets, you can still compare the means of your data using a repeated measures t-test (provided the other two assumptions have not been violated). For example, if you were conducting a drug trial and wanted to test the number of illness symptoms before and after taking the drug, this would be the test to use (because the same subjects are used for both samples and thus the scores are not independent).

Creating the variable 'D'

To test samples which are related in some way, we create a new variable D, which is the difference between the two measurements:

$$D_i = x_i - y_i$$

where: x_i is the ith observation of the first variable (x)
y_i is the ith observation of the second variable (y)

D is a variable created by subtracting the scores of the first measurement from those of the second measurement for the same subject.

In practical terms, what we do is create a new variable which has the same sample size as the other variable, and then subtract the scores on one variable from those on the other variable to create a score for D. For example, if we had a set of observations for 2 variables (x and y), which are related, we simply subtract y from x for each successive score, as shown in Table 9.2. Be careful to subtract

Table 9.2 Calculating D in the related samples *t*-test

x	10	14	9	13	12	11
y	4	8	12	11	12	4
D	6	6	−3	2	0	7

the correct x from the correct y, as we are interested in the difference exhibited by a subject! Once we have this variable D, we will forget about x and y for the remainder of the analysis – we will need to work out the mean and variance of D, instead. To analyse D, we will compare its mean (the mean difference score) to a hypothetical mean score of zero. In other words, we are testing the hypothesis that the difference between our variables is zero. To work out *t*, we use the following formula:

$$t = \frac{\overline{D}}{\left(\frac{s_D}{\sqrt{n}}\right)}$$

where: $\overline{D}$ is the mean difference score
s_D is the standard deviation of difference scores
n is the number of difference scores

Degrees of freedom
The degrees of freedom for the repeated (or related) measures *t*-test is equal to the number of pairs of observations minus one, i.e. $df = n_D - 1$.

Unequal sample sizes for x *and* y
Usually, there will be the same number of observations for x and for y. However, it may happen (through participant drop-out, for example), that some scores may be missing. Because we need pairs of observations to calculate D, missing data can be a problem. To cope with this, we can use a strategy known as *casewise deletion*, where we simple ignore any subject for whom we do not have a full set of observations (i.e. both an x and a y).

Worked example 3

We are investigating whether a new medication to combat insomnia is effective. We recruit a number of insomniacs, and ask them to record, over a two-month period, how many sleepless nights they experience. Once the two months elapse, we give them the new medication, and ask them to do the same for another two months. Because we are using the same subjects, this is a repeated measures design. We collect the data shown in Table 9.3, and need to calculate t to determine if the improvement was statistically significant. The hypotheses are: $H_0: \mu_1 = \mu_2$, $H_1: \mu_1 < \mu_2$.

Table 9.3 Sleepless nights for insomniacs on medication treatment with difference variable

Before	30	32	27	37	32	26	31	30
After	42	40	26	31	47	23	40	31
D	−12	−8	1	6	−15	3	−9	−1

Firstly, we create D by using D = before − after.

Then we calculate basic descriptive stats of D (we will no longer need the values of *before* or *after*).

$$\overline{D} = -4.375; \ s_D = 7.6333; \ n = 8$$

We calculate the standard error:

$$\frac{s_D}{\sqrt{n}} = \frac{7.6333}{\sqrt{8}} = \frac{7.633}{2.828} = 2.698$$

With these, we can go ahead and calculate t:

$$t = \frac{\overline{D}}{\left(\frac{s_D}{\sqrt{n}}\right)} = \frac{-4.375}{2.828} = -1.6211$$

The degrees of freedom for this calculation are n − 1 (n of the D variable, that is) which is 7. We can then determine if the result is significant as we did in the example above. If the result is significant, it means there is a difference in the distribution of scores before and after the medication. If it is not significant, the two distributions are the same – the medication made no significant difference.

<table><tr><td>
In the following datasets, the variables A and B are related samples. For each, calculate *t* and determine if the results are statistically significant. Assume the tests are one-tailed with $\alpha = 0.05$.

a) A: 10, 8, 15, 3, 10, 11, 12, 8, 15, 12   b) A: 104, 103, 110, 103, 102, 101
    B: 10, 10, 12, 9, 10, 12, 15, 5, 12, 5   B: 106, 110, 109, 124, 123, 104
</td><td>*Activity 9.7*</td></tr></table>

Summary

1. *t*-tests are used to determine the difference between means in situations where we have to estimate the population standard deviation from sample data.

2. Computing *t* involves comparing the difference between the means with the *standard error*, which is the standard deviation of the sampling distribution of the mean.

3. There are three variants of the *t*-test: one-sample *t*-tests, independent samples *t*-tests and repeated measures (within-subjects) *t*-tests.

4. The *t*-test is only appropriate when the data complies with the assumptions of normality, homogeneity of variance, and independence.

Box 9.1

Doing *t*-tests with Microsoft® Excel
Excel works for related samples *t*-tests, and independent samples *t*-tests. It does not provide a function for directly calculating one-sample *t*-tests (although this can be done – see below).

Setting up your data: you can set out your data either in rows or columns. Place each variable (sample) in its own column. Excel will happily deal with unequal sample sizes; it will compensate using the case wise deletion strategy.

Calculating *p*: Once your data is entered, you will use the function TTEST. The arguments are:

    TTEST(first sample, second sample, number of tails, t-test type)

where: *first sample* = the extents of the array (i.e. the cells on the spreadsheet) containing your first sample's data
          second sample = the extents of the array containing your second sample's data
          number of tails = (1 or 2) if this is to be a one- or two-tailed test
          t-test type = (1, 2, or 3) a code representing the type of test to be done (1 = repeated measures, 2 = independent samples with homogeneity of variance, 3 = two samples with unequal variance).

This function returns the *p*-value for the *t*-test on your data (but not the actual *t*-statistic itself).

Calculating t: If you wish to see the actual value of *t*, use the TTEST function above, and then use the TINV function to get the *t*-value. You will need to know the degrees of freedom for the *t*-test (this is not given by the program, so you will have to calculate it manually). The arguments for TINV are:

$$TINV(probability, degrees\ of\ freedom)$$

where: *probability* = the *p*-value as obtained from the TTEST function
degrees of freedom = the df of the calculation.

Calculating p if you know the *t*-value already: In the case of a one-sample *t*-test, you can work out *t* yourself, and then get Excel to show you the *p*-value for that *t*. This function is also useful to get the *p*-value if you do not have a *t*-table, or if you want the exact *p*-value. The function that does this is TDIST. It takes the following arguments:

$$TDIST(t\text{-}value, degrees\ of\ freedom, tails)$$

where: *t-value* = the *t*-value you wish to know the *p* of
degrees of freedom = the degrees of freedom of the calculation
tails = (1 or 2) if the test is one- or two-tailed.

Box 9.2

Doing *t*-tests with SPSS®

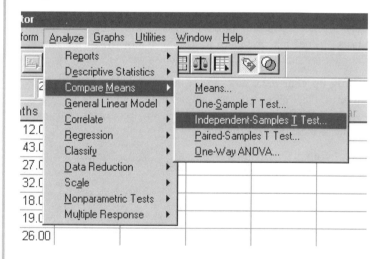

Figure 9.4 Analyze menu entries for *t*-tests in SPSS®

SPSS® will conduct the three *t*-tests discussed in this chapter. All are available off the Analyze menu, as shown in Figure 9.4. The data need to be set up in different ways for the three tests. This is described, along with the dialog boxes, in Figure 9.5.

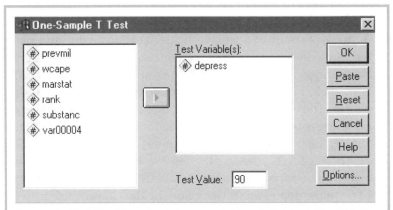

One–sample *t*-test. The data need only be represented in a single column. The dialog box requires you to define the column for the *t*-test, and also requires you to specify the value of ε in the null hypothesis (see earlier discussion).

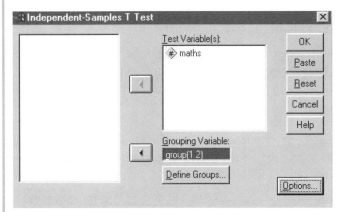

Independent groups *t*-test. The data need to be entered in *two* columns – one containing the group codes, and the other the data on the dependent variable. The dialog box requires you to define the test variable (DV) and the grouping variable.

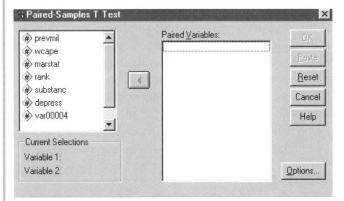

Related sample *t*-test. The data need to be entered in *two* columns – one column for each of the samples, e.g. column 1 for the before data, and column 2 for the after data. The dialog box requires you to select two variables as the related pair.

Figure 9.5 Data layout and dialog boxes for conducting *t*-tests in SPSS®

Exercises

1. A study is conducted to investigate whether living in a place with little sunlight can lead to depression. Researchers recruit two groups of 20 subjects from two locations. One group lives in Springbok, which experiences 8 hours of sunlight daily during winter. The second group is recruited from Moscow, which experiences only 4 hours of sunlight daily during winter. On the winter solstice (the middle of winter), each group has their depression levels measured using the Beck depression inventory, which scores depression on a scale of 1 (no depression) to 10 (extreme depression). The following data are collected:

   Springbok   2, 4, 3, 2, 2, 3, 2, 7, 1, 1, 2, 3, 2, 1, 6, 3, 4, 2, 3, 3
   Moscow   5, 6, 7, 6, 6, 5, 8, 5, 2, 4, 1, 1, 7, 6, 9, 10, 8, 7, 9, 4

   Are the researchers correct in suggesting that living with low levels of sunlight can lead to depression?

2. You are investigating whether psychotic behaviour has a physiological basis. Specifically, you suspect that the *substantia nigra*, a small dense mass of the brain, is reduced in psychotic individuals. It is known that the average diameter for the *substantia nigra* in human adults is 13 millimetres. You obtain the brains of 15 deceased psychotic adults and dissect them to measure the *substantia nigrae* of these brains. Your measurements are as follows (measurements in millimeters):

   Diameter   11, 15, 7, 14, 9, 12, 16, 9, 8, 11, 13, 12, 15, 12, 11

   Determine from these data if the *substantia nigra* of your psychotic sample is indeed reduced.

3. The previous study (from 2 above) is criticised on the basis that the 13-millimetres average used is outdated. To silence these critics, you decide to do a longitudinal study: you will measure the diameter of the *substantia nigra* of recently diagnosed psychotics, and compare them to the diameter after 5 years of having the disorder. This time, you make use of Magnetic Resonance Imaging (MRI) scans of patients to measure the *substantia nigra*. Fifteen patients who have been diagnosed with psychosis less than 1 year ago agree to take part in the study. Your measurements are:

   Measurement 1   13, 12, 16, 14, 13, 15, 17, 13, 14, 16, 13, 16, 13, 19, 12

   After 5 years have elapsed, you contact as many of the patients as you can. Unfortunately, you are only able to contact 9 of them. You again measure (NA in the table means that patient was not available for a second measurement):

Measurement 2   9, 10, NA, NA, 10, NA, 11, 10, NA, 17, 9, 8,
                 NA, 16, NA

Has there been a significant reduction in the size of the *substantia nigra* of these patients?

4. A local basketball team is concerned that the current coach is not training the players well. Specifically, they are concerned that the team scored more points per game under the previous coach than under the current one. You offer to analyse their performance under each coach to settle the question. You are given the number of points scored for each game under the previous coach and under the current one:

Current coach   86, 82, 90, 92, 85, 82, 93, 80
Previous coach   120, 45, 100, 80, 54, 108, 67, 54, 112, 43, 86, 90

Is the team performing any differently under the new coach?

Regression

10

Lance Lachenicht

> After studying this tutorial, you should be able to:
> - Understand and work with paired data.
> - Depict paired data points in a scatterplot.
> - Understand the concept of a best fitting line.
> - Be able to find the coefficients of a best fitting line.
> - Be able to make predictions from a regression equation.
> - Understand the limits of making predictions from a regression equation.
> - Understand that scatter depicts the strength of a relationship between paired data points.

Paired data

Data are usually collected from a sample of things or people. Often the researcher will just take a single measure from each person or item. Sometimes however, data may be collected in *pairs*. Paired data allow us to examine quite different things to what single measures allow. If we have paired data, we may be able to determine the *relationship* between the two measures. To use a simple example, look at Table 10.1, showing 'Per cent ever practising family planning', 'Expenditure on family planning', 'Per cent urbanised', and 'GNP per capita' for 15 countries in 1982. The source (Cliff, 1996,

p. 109) from which this table is taken is not clear about the units, but we can presume that 'Per cent ever practising family planning' and 'Per cent urbanised' are percentages of the country's population. 'Expenditure on family planning' is probably measured in millions of dollars, while 'GNP per capita' is in dollars.

Table 10.1 Selected characteristics for 15 countries

	Expenditure on family planning (x_1)	Per cent urbanised (x_2)	GNP per capita (x_3)	Per cent ever practising family planning (y)
Lesotho	0	4	73	6
Kenya	6	4	108	9
Peru	0	17	367	14
Sri Lanka	12	20	142	22
Indonesia	14	9	61	25
Thailand	20	8	142	36
Colombia	16	47	284	37
Malaysia	18	29	313	38
Guyana	0	20	318	42
Jamaica	23	8	593	44
Jordan	0	53	197	44
Panama	19	50	570	59
Costa Rica	21	18	464	59
Fiji	22	15	321	60
Korea	24	15	188	61

Graphing paired data

Regression analysis may be thought of as a refined way of analysing *scatterplots*. So we need to begin our analysis of the family planning data in Table 10.1 by creating a scatterplot of the data (x_1 and y). This scatterplot is shown in Figure 10.1 on the next page. Is there any pattern in the scatterplot showing a relationship between 'Per cent ever practising family planning' and 'Expenditure on family planning'?

The relationship depicted in Figure 10.1 is actually fairly clear: as expenditure on family planning increases, so does the percentage of the population ever having practised family planning. You should note the possible 'outlier' points associated with countries spending nothing on family planning that seem to deviate from the pattern (i.e. a fairly high proportion of their populations has at some time

Scatterplots can diagnose outlier points.

tried family planning). It is possible that the data from these countries is incorrect or unavailable, or even that these countries may benefit from the family planning expenditure in a neighbouring country.

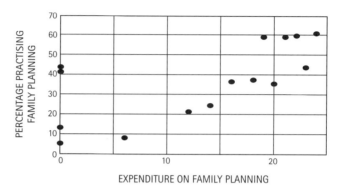

Figure 10.1 Scatterplot of family planning data

*Data for regression is collected in **pairs**, i.e. measurements of two variables are collected on the same person or entity.*

A caveat (or warning) is in order at this stage. The paired data should be collected from *two independent measurements*. This means that, for example, the second datum in each pair should not be created by mathematically manipulating the first datum in each pair in any way, nor should they be two measures of the same thing. If the first datum and the second datum in each pair are not independently derived, you will almost certainly find a strong regression relationship between them, but that relationship may not correspond to any relationship in the real world. Thus, a perfect correlation between daytime temperature in degrees Celsius and degrees Fahrenheit tells us nothing about the weather. It only indicates that the temperatures on the two different scales are mathematically related.

*The x variable, plotted on the horizontal axis, is known as the **predictor** (or independent) variable. The y variable, plotted on the vertical axis, is known as the **criterion** (or dependent) variable.*

In regression analysis, the x variable, plotted on the horizontal axis, is known as the *predictor* (or independent) variable; and the y variable, plotted on the vertical axis, is known as the *criterion* (or dependent) variable. In the dataset of Table 10.1, our predictor variable is 'Expenditure on family planning' and our criterion variable is 'Per cent ever practising family planning'. Note: *You should always plot the predictor on the x-axis and the criterion on the y-axis.*

The best fitting line

The overall shape of points plotted on a scatterplot is called the *trend*. It seems clear that the overall shape or trend in the family planning scatterplot is an upward-sloping one, although this is a vague description upon which we can improve. Imagine drawing a line through the middle of the scatterplot points. If we could find the equation for this line we could move from a vague description to a precise mathematical description. Once the line has been defined in a formal way, it is possible to make predictions about where we think other points might lie. Fitting a line to a scatterplot involves a few graphing ideas that have been explained in earlier tutorials.

The regression line, as it is sometimes called, is the *best fitting line* that can be drawn through the points. However, it is important to realise that not all trends apparent in scatterplots are best fitted with straight lines. Sometimes the trend in a scatterplot shows a curved shape (see Figure 10.8), and for such trends, non-linear regression is required. In the present tutorial we are concerned with fitting straight lines to scatterplots, and for this reason we are dealing with *linear regression*.

The regression line is the best fitting line that can be drawn through the points on a scatterplot.

Finding the regression coefficients for the best fitting line

In order to define a straight line, precisely two pieces of information are required. These are the *slope* of the line and the point on the graph where it crosses the y or vertical axis (known as the *intercept*). Lines that slope from the bottom left to the top right of the scatterplot are said to have a positive slope, i.e. the value of y will increase as the value of x increases (see Figure 10.4). Lines with a negative slope run from the top left to the bottom right, i.e. the value of y will decrease as the value of x increases (see Figure 10.5). These ideas about lines are explained in Tutorial 24. If you are uncertain about them, review this information.

Two pieces of information completely determine a linear regression 'line': the slope coefficient (b), and the intercept coefficient (a).

In the running example, the percentage of people ever having practised family planning is represented on the vertical (y) axis and expenditure on family planning is represented on the horizontal (x) axis. If we are fitting a regression line, the equation to use will have the form:

$$y = a + bx$$

Equation 10.1

where: y represents the percentage of people ever having
practised family planning, the criterion variable
x represents expenditure on family planning, the predictor variable
a and *b* represent the two pieces of information required to fit the
line (i.e. *b* is the slope, and *a* is the intercept)

Most textbooks call *a* and *b* the *regression coefficients*. Try drawing in an imaginary regression line by eye in Figure 10.1. If you do so, it should be easy to read off the value of *a* (the intercept where the line cuts the vertical axis). It is less easy to read the slope from the scatterplot – but remember, the slope of a line is the amount it increases or decreases for each unit it moves from left to right.

Apart from making estimates by eye from scatterplots, there are several other methods of finding the values of a and b. The simplest is to feed your data into a calculator (or computer) and obtain the answers at the press of some buttons. If you have a calculator that will calculate regression, please spend a few minutes entering the paired data from Table 10.1 into your calculator and obtain the values of a and b by pressing the relevant buttons. (If you have never done this before, you will need to spend some time reading the calculator manual in order to understand the necessary steps.) If you do not have a calculator capable of calculating regression, you will find some formulas for manual calculation in the section below.

In the family planning data the slope is positive (+1.3135), reflecting an upward-sloping line. This trend suggests a positive relationship between expenditure on family planning and the percentage of the population ever having used family planning. When the expenditure on family planning increases, the percentage of the population ever having used family planning also rises. If the relationship was negative, expenditure would increase as the percentage of the population ever having used family planning decreased.

The regression line minimises the squared distances of the observed data points from the line.

It is not possible to explain exactly how the best fitting line is determined in this tutorial, as such an explanation requires a knowledge of calculus. Still, it is worth knowing that the best fitting line through a set of points in a scatterplot has an important property – if you take the distances of each point from the line (for an example of these distances, see Figure 10.3), square them and then add the squares together, the sum of the squared distances will be smaller than for any other line you could have chosen. This is why the regression line is sometimes called the *least-squares* line.

Calculating the regression coefficients

Calculating a regression analysis requires that you determine the following statistics:

 n: the number of pairs of values (in our example, n = 15)
 Σx: the sum of the x values
 Σy: the sum of the y values
 Σx^2: the sum of the squares of the x values
 Σxy: the sum of the xy products

These intermediate values are substituted into the following equation to find the covariance, s_{xy}, and following this, the slope, b:

$$S_{xy} = \frac{\sum xy - \frac{\sum x \sum y}{n}}{n-1}$$

Equation 10.2

$$b = \frac{S_{xy}}{s_x^2}$$

Equation 10.3

Having calculated b, we can find the intercept a. The midpoint of all the points on the scattergraph is the middlemost point in the scatter $(\bar{x}, \bar{y})$. An important property of the best fitting line is that it passes through this point. For this reason, we can substitute these mean values into the general equation for a line ($y = a + bx$) and then rearrange to solve for a:

$$a = \bar{y} - b\bar{x}$$

Equation 10.4

The example below uses this method to calculate the regression equation for the family planning data given in Table 10.2:

$$S_{xy} = \frac{\sum xy - \frac{\sum x \sum y}{n}}{n-1} \quad \frac{8820 - \frac{195 \times 556}{15}}{14} = 113.71$$

$$b = \frac{S_{xy}}{s_x^2} \quad \frac{113.71}{86.56} = 1.314$$

Having found the value of b, we can use Equation 10.4 to find a:

$$a = \bar{y} - b\bar{x}$$
$$= 37.067 - 1.314 \times 13 = 19.985$$

So the regression equation is:

$$y' = 19.985 + 1.314\,x$$

The effect of outliers on a regression analysis can be estimated by comparing the equation calculated on all data points with the equation calculated on the data points left after removing outliers.

You may ask, 'What happens to the above regression equation if the possible outlying points of Guyana and Jordan are omitted from the dataset?' Recalculating the regression equation without particular (possibly outlying) points is a way of carrying out *sensitivity* analysis, i.e. investigating the extent to which the regression model depends upon particular, perhaps problematic data points.

Table 10.2 Calculating the regression using data from Table 10.1

Country	Expenditure on family planning (x)	Per cent ever practising family planning (y)	xy
Lesotho	0	6	0
Kenya	6	9	54
Peru	0	14	0
Sri Lanka	12	22	264
Indonesia	14	25	350
Thailand	20	36	720
Colombia	16	37	592
Malaysia	18	38	684
Guyana	0	42	0
Jamaica	23	44	1 012
Jordan	0	44	0
Panama	19	59	1 121
Costa Rica	21	59	1 239
Fiji	22	60	1 320
Korea	24	61	1 464
	$\Sigma x = 195$	$\Sigma y = 556$	$\Sigma xy = 8\ 820$
$n = 15$	$\bar{x} = 13$	$\bar{y} = 37.067$	
	$s_x = 9.304$	$s_y = 18.595$	

A graph of this line over a scatterplot of the data is depicted in Figure 10.2.

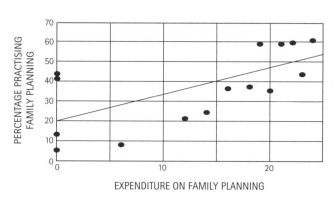

Figure 10.2 Family planning data with regression line

It is worth reflecting on the impact of the scale of the measurements used in the regression analysis. Suppose for example that you wish to calculate a regression line where the chosen variable was 'age'. Would it be legitimate to enter 'age' as years, or would you have to enter it as 'months' or 'days'? The answer here is that ages expressed in years, months, or days are all mathematically related to each other. (You transform the ages from one description to the other by mathematical means.) Any of these units can therefore be used. Using one or the other will not change the shape of the regression line at all, though it will move the line to different positions on the graph.

> As an exercise to test your own understanding, find the regression equation for predicting 'Per cent ever practising family planning' ($\bar{y}$) from 'Per cent urbanised' ($\bar{x}_2$) using the data in Table 10.1.

Activity 10.1

You may ask, 'If the scales of either of the two axes in the scatterplot were changed, would this alter the slope of the regression line?' Actually, changing the scale of either axis may change the slope of the regression line in terms of how steep it looks on the graph, but the actual value for *b* would remain unchanged, so the effect would be purely visual. This means that you should not pay too much attention to how steep the slope looks on the graph, since this will depend on the scales chosen when the graph is plotted.

The slope coefficient, b, is not standardised, and is strongly affected by the relative scales of the x and y variables. Therefore, you should not over-interpret the 'steepness' of the regression line.

Making predictions

The regression equation is essentially a mathematical summary of what we think the relationship between the two variables might be. We can use this mathematical relationship to make predictions, though not without some danger of making a mistake.

Let us recall what the variables x and y are used to represent in the family planning example above. x represents 'Expenditure on family planning' in millions of dollars, and y represents 'Percentage of the country's population ever practising family planning'. So the regression equation above can be written as follows:

average per cent ever practising family planning
= 19.985 + 1.314 × average expenditure on family planning

> Two social scientists develop a measure of general happiness. They each use their measure to collect information about the state of happiness in 35 countries. How should we go about comparing these two different measures of general happiness? What kind of results would lead you to conclude that they are measuring equivalently or differently?

Activity 10.2

What this means is that if the country spends 20 million dollars on family planning, then the predicted percentage of the population practising family planning can be estimated as follows:

predicted per cent of population ever practising family planning
= 19.985 + 1.314 × 20 = 46.265

The scatterplot containing the regression line (Figure 10.2) shows that the data points are widely scattered around the regression line, so our prediction cannot be considered to be very accurate. It would be foolish to report our predictions as '46.265 per cent of the population ever practising family planning' because that suggests a precision quite unwarranted by our scattered data. At best we should report it as 46% and still acknowledge that there is a considerable margin of error in our prediction.

Usually predictions from regression equations are more accurate when they are made about points that fall within the range of points covered by the original dataset (as in our 20-million-dollar example). Such 'within dataset' predictions are called *interpolations*. If we chose not 20 million dollars but 50 million as family planning expenditure, then we would have to *extrapolate* and our prediction would be even less reliable.

Activity 10.3

> As an exercise to test your understanding, use your regression equation for predicting 'Per cent ever practising family planning' (y) from 'Per cent urbanised' (x_2) using the data in Table 10.1 to predict the per cent ever practising family planning in a 70% urbanised country.

The standard error of estimate

How good do you think the fit of the best fitting line has to be for the regression equation to be meaningful? Obviously, if the scatterplot shows a very clear linear pattern, then the best fitting line will be an accurate summary of the relationship in the data. But if the points on the original scatterplot have no clear pattern along with a wide scatter of points, then the line will have very little predictive power and will not be very meaningful.

In Figure 10.3, the hypothetical relationship between fuel consumption and engine size (in motor vehicles) is shown in two ways: in the left-hand panel a line is drawn through $\bar{y}$ (the mean fuel consumption), and in the right-hand panel the predicted regression line is drawn. In both cases, the observed data points are shown, and perpendicular lines are extended from the observed data points to the horizontal or diagonal line (the line of fit). The left-hand panel is actually a representation of the variance in y, since the line is the mean, and the distances from the points to the line are therefore merely the variation around the mean (see Tutorial 4).

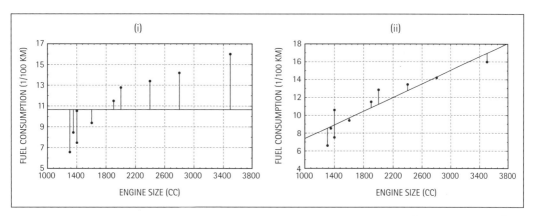

Figure 10.3 Plots depicting distances of points in a regression problem from i) the mean, and ii) the regression line

In the case of the right-hand panel, the distance of each point from the diagonal line is known as a 'residual', i.e. the amount by which the fitted line deviates from that particular data point. If the regression line is a good fit, then the distances in the right-hand panel should be quite small, and – very importantly – they should be a lot smaller than the distances in the left-hand panel, since in the left-hand panel there is no relationship between the variables.

One way of measuring the degree of fit, or the extent to which the regression line is a good 'model' of the relationship in question, is to 'average' the residual distances. However, we cannot simply average the distances, as half of them are positive, and half are negative, and these will simply balance each other out. (This is the same problem we faced when we calculated the standard deviation.) We use a measure that is devised to take account of this difficulty, and is known as the *standard error of estimate*. It is the standard deviation of the residual distances, and is given by the following formula:

*The **standard error of estimate** measures the degree to which the regression line 'fits' the observed data.*

$$\text{S.E. of estimate} = \sqrt{\frac{\Sigma(y - y')^2}{n - 2}}$$

Equation 10.5

where y' = the predicted scores of y, using the regression equation, substituting the observed scores of x

Table 10.3 Layout for calculating the standard error of estimate

Country	x	y	y'	$(y - y')^2$
Lesotho	0	6	19.99	195.72
Kenya	6	9	27.87	356.08
Peru	0	14	19.99	35.88
Sri Lanka	12	22	35.75	189.06
Indonesia	14	25	38.38	179.02
Thailand	20	36	46.26	105.27
Colombia	16	37	41.01	16.08
Malaysia	18	38	43.63	31.70
Guyana	0	42	19.99	484.44
Jamaica	23	44	50.20	38.44
Jordan	0	44	19.99	576.48
Panama	19	59	44.95	197.40
Costa Rica	21	59	47.58	130.42
Fiji	22	60	48.89	123.47
Korea	24	61	51.52	89.87
Σ				2 749.29

A layout for the calculation of the standard error of estimate for the regression calculations reported in (and around) Table 10.2 is shown in Table 10.3. Note that y' is calculated by substituting the observed x scores into the regression equation for Lesotho:

$$y' = 19.985 + 1.314 = 19.99$$

Thus, to calculate the standard error:

$$\text{S.E. of estimate} = \sqrt{\frac{\Sigma(y - y')^2}{n - 2}} = \sqrt{\frac{2749.29}{13}} = \sqrt{211.48} = 14.54$$

A common difficulty with predictions based on regression models

Regression models, when used for prediction, may be controversial not because of the statistical methods involved, but because of the nature of the data used in the model. Our predictions about the use of birth-control methods, for example, are based on data from countries already practising birth control to various degrees. Now it is possible that the family planning budget in these countries simply reflects an awareness of the need for birth control in the government of the country concerned rather than inducing such an awareness **in** the population. Alternatively, consider an example where a regression model was used to predict what proportion of their salaries people saved. Suppose, further, that age was found to be negatively related to high levels of saving (i.e. people save a lower proportion as they get older). It is possible that people become more profligate as they get older. But perhaps it is more likely that as people get older their responsibilities increase and it is not possible for them to save as much as they used to when younger. In this case, a third variable, responsibilities, is mediating the relationship between age and saving. In regression (and correlation) analysis, the temptation to draw causal inferences is always present, and such inferences should always be drawn with great caution.

Causal inferences should only be drawn from regression analyses with great caution.

> Think of an example of two variables where linear regression would be inappropriate because the relationship between the variables is not linear.

Activity 10.4

Scatter and correlation

The regression line is a useful statement of the underlying trend, but it tells us nothing about the strength of the relationship. Correlation is a measure of the strength of linear association between two variables and is the subject matter of our next tutorial. A perfect positive correlation might look like Figure 10.4. In a positive correlation, as one set of scores increases, so does the other set of scores. A regression line fitted to this data should pass through each data point.

The degree of scatter around the straight line is called the 'correlation'.

Correlation is a measure of the strength and direction of the linear association between two variables.

Data that are plotted as in Figure 10.5 would illustrate a perfect negative correlation, an inverse relationship. In a negative or inverse relationship, as the one set of scores increases the other will decrease. A regression line fitted to this data should also pass through each data point.

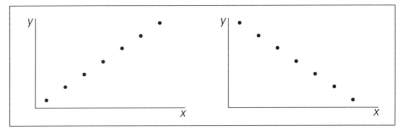

Figure 10.4 Scatterplot showing perfect positive correlation

Figure 10.5 Scatterplot showing perfect negative correlation

In practice, most scatterplots show relationships somewhat between these two extremes. In scatterplots showing zero correlation (see Figure 10.6) all the data points tend to be clumped together in the middle of the plot. A regression line for this data is not very meaningful. As the correlation increases, so the points increasingly take on the form of a line (which may be positively or negatively sloped), and the regression analysis becomes increasingly meaningful and precise. Perfect relationships that are non-linear (see Figure 10.8) are not suitable for regression analysis and may have a zero correlation despite being strongly related.

Figure 10.6 Scatterplot showing zero correlation

Figure 10.7 Scatterplot showing weak negative correlation

Figure 10.8 Scatterplot showing perfect non-linear relation

Worked example

An ubiquitous problem in neuropsychological assessment is how to determine the amount of cognitive damage a person with a head injury has sustained. This enterprise rests on the comparison of cognitive ability after head injury and cognitive ability before head injury (i.e. 'pre-morbid' ability). However, it is rarely possible to directly determine pre-morbid ability. It is usually estimated by gross generalisations about the person's level of education, occupational status, etc. Nelson (1975) explored an interesting alternative, namely the ability to pronounce 'irregular' words. Words like 'drachm' or 'beatify' require specific knowledge of pronunciation – they cannot be pronounced by following rules – and this specific knowledge is unaffected by many types of neurological injury. (A standardised measure of this ability – the National Adult Reading Test (NART) – is available in several countries, including South Africa.) Secondly, this ability is also strongly related to a well-defined and researched cognitive measure, Full Scale IQ (FSIQ), as measured by intelligence tests (e.g. the Wechsler Adult Intelligence Scale). It follows that we should consider using a regression equation that predicts FSIQ from performance on the NART: for neurologically impaired patients, performance on the NART will probably be intact, and if the NART turns out to be strongly correlated to FSIQ, we can use the regression equation relating the NART to FSIQ in a healthy sample to predict the pre-morbid FSIQ of neurologically injured patients.

The data in Table 10.4 reports NART and FSIQ scores for a sample of 40 university students. We will conduct a regression analysis on this data, and make some predictions for three patients, who scored 37, 21, and 48, respectively, on the NART but who now each score a FSIQ less than 80 points.

Table 10.4 NART and FSIQ scores for 40 university students

NART	FSIQ	NART	FSIQ	NART	FSIQ	NART	FSIQ
27	92	44	128	46	122	39	128
27	84	19	99	35	120	30	101
23	113	26	124	25	102	28	110
23	106	17	99	27	123	45	147
27	96	30	113	41	139	42	127
18	103	32	109	28	99	30	119
26	92	20	93	44	131	33	136
15	82	40	130	31	117	39	127
22	75	20	89	44	120	36	127
34	113	38	128	45	123	37	132

Solution

It is good practice to start a regression analysis by constructing a scatterplot, since the plot can provide information on possible departures from important assumptions, e.g. non-linearity of the relationship. Figure 10.9 is a scatterplot of the NART and FSIQ data, and suggests that relationship is linear, and strong.

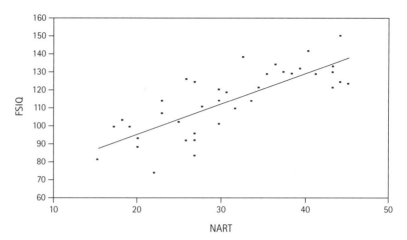

Figure 10.9 Scatterplot of the relation between FSIQ and NART scores in a student sample

It is useful to find the standard error of estimate, since this gives an overall indication of the accuracy of the equation (we do not show the calculation of individual errors of prediction).

$$\text{S.E. of estimate} = \sqrt{\frac{\Sigma(y - y')^2}{n - 2}} = \sqrt{\frac{4382.3}{38}}$$

$$= \sqrt{115.32} = 10.74$$

Although this standard error may seem quite large (it suggests that, on average, our prediction will be 10.74 units in error), it should be judged against the standard deviation of y, which is 17.22. In other words, without our knowledge of NART scores, our predictions would, on average, be 17.22 units in error (since the best we could do is to use $\bar{y}$ as the prediction).

We then calculate interim statistics that we will need later:

$$\Sigma x = 1253, \Sigma y = 4518$$
$$\bar{x} = 31.33, \bar{y} = 112.95$$
$$\Sigma xy = 146229$$
$$s_x = 8.88, s_y = 17.22$$

Then we calculate the covariance:

$$s_{xy} = \frac{\Sigma xy - \dfrac{\Sigma x \Sigma y}{n}}{n - 1}$$

$$= \frac{146229 - \dfrac{1253 \times 4518}{40}}{39} = 120.58$$

Then we calculate b, the slope coefficient:

$$b = \frac{s_{xy}}{s^2_x} = \frac{120.58}{8.88^2} = 1.53$$

Then we calculate a, the intercept coefficient:

$$a = \bar{y} - b\bar{x} = 112.95 - 1.53 \times 31.33$$
$$= 65.07$$

We can therefore write the equation as FSIQ' = 65.07 + 1.53 × NART.

All that remains is the prediction of FSIQ for the patients who scored 37, 21, and 48 on the NART, respectively:

$$\text{FSIQ}' = 65.07 + 1.53 \times 37 = 121.68 \approx 122$$
$$\text{FSIQ}' = 65.07 + 1.53 \times 21 = 97.2 \approx 97$$
$$\text{FSIQ}' = 65.07 + 1.53 \times 48 = 138.51 \approx 139$$

From these predictions, we would suggest that the three patients probably had very different pre-morbid intelligence levels, despite presently having similar and moderately low intelligence scores.

Box 10.1

Doing regression analysis with a spreadsheet program

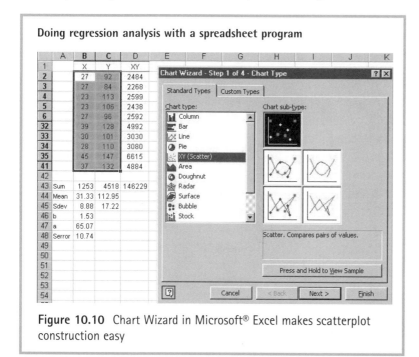

Figure 10.10 Chart Wizard in Microsoft® Excel makes scatterplot construction easy

Although you can use a spreadsheet program to set regression data up for analysis in a manner analogous to that shown in Table 10.2, it is easier to use some of the built-in regression functions that most spreadsheets have. Figure 10.11 shows a layout for use with Excel, incorporating the built-in functions SLOPE, INTERCEPT, and STEYX. (You should be able to work out what these refer to from their names!) These functions work with two cell ranges, representing the y and x data, respectively *(note the order – y before x).* Thus, slope (c2:c41, b2:b41) calculates the slope coefficient for a linear regression with the *y* data in cells c2:c41 and the *x* data in cells b2:b41.

An essential graphic in regression analysis is the scatterplot. It is easy to construct one in Excel: highlight the range of data, and click the Chart Wizard – button 📖 . A 'Wizard' – as shown in Figure 10.10 – will guide you through the rest of the graph's construction.

	A	B	C	D
1		X	Y	XY
2		27	92	=B2*C2
3		27	84	=B3*C3
4		23	113	=B4*C4
5		23	106	=B5*C5
6		27	96	=B6*C6
32		39	128	=B32*C32
33		30	101	=B33*C33
34		28	110	=B34*C34
35		45	147	=B35*C35
41		37	132	=B41*C41
42				
43	Sum	=SUM(B2:B41)	=SUM(C2:C41)	=SUM(D2:D41)
44	Mean	=AVERAGE(B2:B41)	=AVERAGE(C2:C41)	
45	Sdev	=STDEV(B2:B41)	=STDEV(C2:C41)	
46	b	=SLOPE(C2:C41,B2:B41)		
47	a	=INTERCEPT(C2:C41,B2:B41)		
48	Serror	=STEYX(C2:C41,B2:B41)		

	A	B	C	D	E
1		X	Y	XY	
2		27	92	2484	
3		27	84	2268	
4		23	113	2599	
5		23	106	2438	
6		27	96	2592	
32		39	128	4992	
33		30	101	3030	
34		28	110	3080	
35		45	147	6615	
41		37	132	4884	
42					
43	Sum	1253	4518	146229	
44	Mean	31.33	112.95		
45	Sdev	8.88	17.22		
46	b	1.53			
47	a	65.07			
48	Serror	10.74			

Figure 10.11 Layout and calculations for doing regression analysis in Microsoft® Excel; data from worked example at the end of the tutorial

Box 10.2

Doing regression analysis with SPSS®

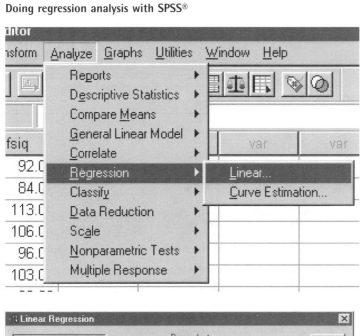

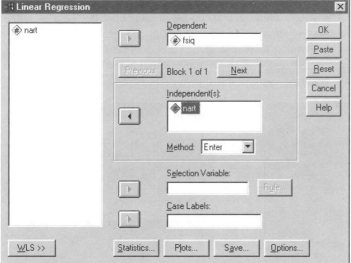

Figure 10.12 SPSS® menu commands for conducting a linear regression

Since SPSS® is one of the major professional statistical packages, it predictably offers extensive support for linear regression analysis. For the types of problem outlined in this tutorial, though, you should stick to the default options. To run a linear regression, select the 'Analyze' menu, and the appropriate sub-menus, as shown in Figure 10.12. Notice that you have to 'move' the predictor (IV) and predicted (DV) variables into the appropriate positions, i.e. from left to right, using the mouse. Abbreviated output for an analysis of the data in the worked example is shown in Figure 10.13.

MODEL SUMMARY

Model	R	R Square	Adjusted R Square	Std. Error of the Estimate
1	.788	.621	.611	10.73877

COEFFICIENTS[a]

Model		Unstandardised Coefficients		Standardised Coefficients		
		B	Std. Error	Beta	t	Sig.
1	(Constant)	65.072	6.298		10.333	.000
	NART	1.528	.194	.788	7.895	.000

a. Dependent Variable: FSIQ

Figure 10.13 Abbreviated output from SPSS® for a linear regression of the data from the worked example

Some of the results reported by SPSS® will make more sense to you when you have studied the multiple regression tutorial (Tutorial 18), but you should be familiar with most of the terms in the output.

The significance test reported here is equivalent to that outlined in the following tutorial on correlation, and can be ignored for the moment. Scatterplots are created very easily in SPSS®, and you should always start your regression analysis with an inspection of one. To construct a scatterplot, you choose 'Scatter' from the 'Graphs' menu, as shown in Figure 10.14. Choose an option (we recommend 'Simple') off the ensuing scatterplot dialog box, and then define the variables for the scatterplot using the SPSS® variable selection dialog control. The resulting scatterplot is shown in the SPSS® output window.

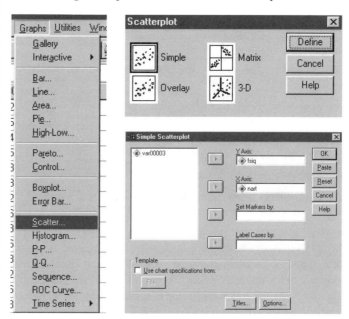

Figure 10.14 Dialog control boxes for constructing a scatterplot in SPSS®

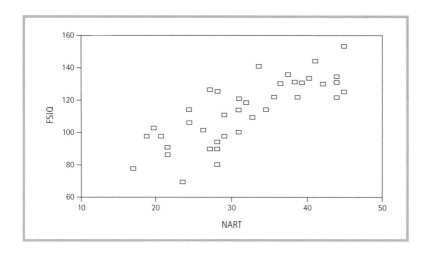

Summary

1. Analysis of independent data pairs can be very fruitful. Graphical analysis of data pairs is typically done with the scatterplot, where the data pairs are represented as points in two dimensional space.

2. The best fitting straight line in a scatterplot of data pairs is referred to as the regression line, and is completely determined by the slope (b) and intercept (a) coefficients. The equation for the straight line takes the general form $y = a + bx$.

3. The equation for a straight line relating x and y can be used as a prediction device, i.e. values of y can be predicted from knowledge of values of x. Predictions are more accurate when they are made about points that fall within the range of points covered by the original data set.

4. The standard error of estimate and correlation coefficient measure the degree to which the regression line 'fits' the observed data.

Exercises

1. Ten pairs of observations on the variables x and y are given below:
   a) Plot a scatter diagram.
   b) Find the values for a and b for the regression line $y = a + bx$.
   c) Draw the regression line on your diagram and mark the point $\bar{x}, \bar{y}$.

x:	2.2	3.2	6.8	7.3	−1.3	−0.8	1.7	9.5	12.3	1.7
y:	1.2	0.5	0.0	−0.8	2.8	3.4	1.7	−1.7	−4.2	1.1

2. Find the regression equation for predicting 'Per cent ever practising family planning' (y) from 'GNP per capita' (x_3) using the data in Table 10.1.

3. Use your regression equation for predicting 'Per cent ever practising family planning' (y) from 'GNP per capita' (x_3) using the data in Table 10.1 (previous exercise) to predict the per cent ever practising family planning in a country with a GNP of 700. How confident are you in your prediction?

4. Below there are figures for a chain of stores linking the number of sales staff to the daily takings in thousands of rands. Plot the relationship between the two sets of scores using a scatterplot. Using Figures 10.4 to 10.8 above as your guides, describe the correlation (if any) between the two sets of test scores.

Shop:	1	2	3	4	5	6	7	8	9	10
Sales staff:	43	25	32	48	10	48	42	36	30	19
Takings (R):	15	11	13	18	3	17	15	14	12	8

5. Find the regression equation for predicting daily takings from the number of sales staff in the table in Question 4.

    If there was an eleventh store in the chain that was omitted from the dataset in the table, and this store had 21 sales staff, what would store 11's daily takings score be?

TUTORIAL
11

Correlation

Lance Lachenicht

After studying this tutorial, you should be able to:
- Understand correlation as a measure of the degree of scatter around a regression line.
- Calculate and interpret Pearson's product–moment correlation, r, and the coefficient of determination, r^2.
- Understand that correlation does not imply causation.
- Understand that correlations measure the strength of linear relations.
- Understand that correlation may be misleading if the underlying populations are not homogenous.

Introduction

The digit span test forms part of many standard intelligence tests. It measures the maximum number of digits a person can retain in short-term memory. The reported average digit spans in speakers of a few languages are set out in Table 11.1.

The data reported in Table 11.1 were collected by several authors in a number of different studies. These studies had their origin in a comparison between the digit spans of Welsh and English speakers (Ellis & Hennelly, 1980). Welsh speakers seem to have a smaller capacity for retaining digit names in short-term memory than their English counterparts. Subsequent studies have reported superior

Table 11.1 Digit span and sound duration in a number of languages

Language	Mean number of syllables per digit name	Digit span	Rapid sound duration (msec/digit)
Welsh	1.1	5.77	385
English 1	1.1	6.55	321
Cantonese	1	9.9	265
English 2	1.1	7.21	256
Spanish	1.625	6.37	287
Hebrew	1.875	6.51	309
Arabic	2.25	5.77	370

Data from Hoosain, 1997, p. 122

performances from Cantonese speakers. Yet, it should be noted that it takes longer to pronounce digit names in Welsh than in English. The speed of pronunciation reported in Table 11.1 is determined by asking participants to pronounce a group of random digits as rapidly as possible and measuring the average time taken for each number. This average time is not entirely a matter of the syllables in each digit name (for example, it takes less time in English to say seven with two syllables than to say six with one), though some languages do seem to have fewer syllables. Perhaps, as some researchers (Ellis & Hennelly, 1980) have argued, it is possible that the differences in digit spans between speakers of the different languages could be accounted for by the different sound durations for numbers in the different languages.

One way of investigating this possibility is to draw a scatterplot of the information in Table 11.1, as shown in Figure 11.1. With the exception of one point (Cantonese), the scatterplot seems to show a clear inverse relationship between average digit span and sound duration. As average sound duration increases, so digit span seems to decrease. The digit span for Cantonese is not completely outside this trend, but it falls fairly far from the other average digit span scores. It is possible that this score is an 'outlier', which means that it is possible that the Cantonese score includes a greater degree of error or measurement imprecision than do the other scores, or even that some other unknown factor has influenced the score. (Of course, it is also possible that the score is correct.)

In Tutorial 10 we showed how we could make the trend shown in Figure 11.1 precise by inserting a regression line into the scatterplot. In this tutorial we will show how we can assign a number to indicate the strength of the inverse relationship visible in Figure 11.1.

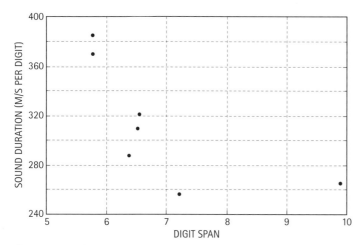

Figure 11.1 Scatterplot of digit span against sound duration

The product–moment correlation coefficient

Although it is useful to gauge the strength of a relationship by looking at a scatterplot (and you should always look at a scatterplot of your data), there are more formal methods based on calculations that give a numerical value for the degree of correlation between two variables. The *product-moment coefficient of correlation*, (also known as *Pearson's correlation coefficient*) is calculated on the basis of how far the points lie from the 'best-fit' regression line. It is symbolised by the small letter *r* (chosen because it is the first letter of 'regression').

*The **product-moment correlation coefficient (r)** is also known as Pearson's correlation coefficient, named after the English mathematician, Karl Pearson.*

The formula for *r*, the (sample) product-moment correlation coefficient, is:

$$r = \frac{s_{xy}}{s_x s_y}$$

Equation 11.1

where: x is the variable on the horizontal axis
y is the variable on the vertical axis
s_x and s_y are the standard deviations of x and y, respectively
s_{xy} is the covariance between x and y

To calculate the covariance between x and y, we use the formula:

$$s_{xy} = \frac{\sum xy - \frac{\sum x \sum y}{n}}{n - 1}$$

Equation 11.2

Certain calculators with statistical functions provide a key (usually marked *r*) for directly calculating the correlation coefficient. If you do not have such a calculator, we give a method for the manual calculation of *r*, below.

The meaning of *r*

s_x = standard deviation of x.

s_y = standard deviation of y.

s_{xy} = covariance of x and y.

The product-moment correlation formula has been concocted in such a way as to ensure that the value of *r* will fall with in the range –1 to +1. An *r* of –1 means a perfect negative correlation (a perfect inverse relationship, where, as the value of x rises, so the value of y falls) and an *r* of +1 means a perfect positive correlation (where the values of x and y rise or fall together). An *r* of 0 means zero correlation, which means that there is no relationship between x and y. Correlation coefficients that fall between 0 and +1, or between 0 and –1, are harder to interpret. Guilford (cited in Sprinthall, 1987) offers informal interpretations for statistically significant Pearson correlations of various sizes, reproduced in Table 11.2.

Table 11.2 Guilford's informal interpretations of the magnitude of *r*

Value of *r* (+ or –)	Informal interpretation
< 0.2	Slight; almost no relationship
0.2 – 0.4	Low correlation; definite but small relationship
0.4 – 0.7	Moderate correlation; substantial relationship
0.7 – 0.9	High correlation; strong relationship
0.9 – 1.0	Very high correlation; very dependable relationship

Calculating Pearson's *r*

r = 0: no relationship

r = +1: perfect positive linear relationship

r = –1: perfect negative linear relationship

It is best, when calculating *r* manually, to use a layout of the kind shown in Table 11.3. Table 11.3 provides you with an efficient, systematic way of calculating s_{XY}, s_X and s_Y, as well as the means of x and y. In Table 11.3 the calculation of *r* is based on the data in Table 11.1, which sets out the data for digit span sets and rapid sound duration as determined in seven studies (i.e. n = 7).

Table 11.3 Calculating the correlation between digit span and sound duration

	x (digit span)	y (sound duration)	xy
Welsh	5.77	385	2 221.45
English 1	6.55	321	2 102.55
Cantonese	9.9	265	2 623.5
English 2	7.21	256	1 845.76
Spanish	6.37	287	1 828.19
Hebrew	6.51	309	2 011.59
Arabic	5.77	370	2 134.9
Σ	48.08	2 193	14 767.94
s	1.43	49.57	

From these results we can calculate r:

$$s_{xy} = \frac{14767.94 - \dfrac{(48.08 \times 2193)}{7}}{6} = -49.14$$

$$r = \frac{-49.14}{1.43 \times 49.57} = -0.6932$$

A value of $r = -0.6932$ shows a substantial inverse relationship between digit span and rapid digit sound duration.

If you complete Activity 11.1 and reflect on the substantial improvement in the correlation that arises from omitting the Cantonese data, you will realise that correlation is not a *robust* measure: it is strongly affected by outlying points. This means that it is important to check data entry very carefully when calculating correlation coefficients, and to carefully investigate any data points that appear to be outliers. Further investigation does suggest that the Cantonese score for digit span may indeed be exceptional because the advantage does not extend to memory for words (word span). Hoosain (1997, p. 123) comments, 'This also weakens the possibility that the digit span difference for Cantonese is due to motivation or inclination of subjects to memorise things'.

Correlation is not a ***robust*** *measure: it is strongly affected by outlying points.*

Activity 11.1

Recalculate the correlation coefficient for the data shown in Table 11.3, omitting the Cantonese data. You should get a value close to –0.9310. This is a much more substantial correlation than we obtained when the Cantonese data was included. Why do you think omitting one data pair causes such a substantial change in the correlation coefficient?

Rank correlation

*An alternative index of correlation is called the **rank coefficient of correlation**, sometimes known as Spearman's coefficient of rank correlation (r_s) after its inventor, Charles Spearman.*

It is not always necessary or possible when investigating correlation to draw upon the sort of measured data reported in Table 11.1. An alternative is to work from rank positions. When gymnastics competitions are judged, for example, the marks that are awarded by the judges may have little deep-rooted meaning, for they are really intended to place the competitors in rank order – first, second, third, etc. In this section we will look at a way of measuring the strength of association between pairs of ranked variables. It would, of course, be possible to use the correlation coefficient r in such cases, but there is an alternative measure that was specially designed for ranked data. It is called the *rank coefficient of correlation* (sometimes known as *Spearman's coefficient of rank correlation* after its inventor, Charles Spearman). We will write the symbol for the Spearman coefficient as r_s. Although it is sometimes referred to as ρ (rho, the Greek letter for r), we will not use this notation, since many authors reserve ρ as the symbol for the population correlation coefficient.

When ranking data, assign the value of 1 to the lowest score.

If your data consists of natural ranks, you may proceed to calculate r_s immediately. However, if your data consists of measures (numbers rather than ranks), you will need to rank your data before you calculate r_s. In Table 11.4 ranks are assigned to the measures reported in Table 11.1. The 'English 2' study reported the lowest digit sound duration (256), so this digit sound duration score is assigned the rank of 1. The Cantonese study reported the second lowest digit sound duration, so the Cantonese digit sound duration score is assigned the rank of 2. We proceed in this manner until all the digit sound duration scores have been assigned ranks. The digit span scores are similarly ranked from lowest to highest. Notice that the lowest digit span score is 5.77, and that speakers of two languages (Welsh and Arabic) share this score. These two languages therefore

Table 11.4 Calculating rank correlation between digit span and sound duration

	x (digit span)	Rank x	y (sound duration)	Rank y	d	d^2
Welsh	5.77	1.5	385	7	−5.5	30.25
English 1	6.55	5	321	5	0	0
Cantonese	9.9	7	265	2	5	25
English 2	7.21	6	256	1	5	25
Spanish	6.37	3	287	3	0	0
Hebrew	6.51	4	309	4	0	0
Arabic	5.77	1.5	370	6	−4.5	20.25
Σ						100.5

share the first two ranks (1 and 2) and each of them receives the average of these two shared ('tied') ranks (i.e. $[1 + 2]/2 = 1.5$). You should be aware that r_s does not give correct correlation values when there are a large number of tied scores in the data – but one or two ties in the data usually makes little difference to r_s.

rs does not give correct correlation values when there are a large number of tied scores in the data – but one or two ties in the data usually makes little difference to rs.

The formula for r_s is based on calculating the differences (d) between each pair of ranks and this is done in the column marked d in Table 11.4. Each of these differences is then squared and summed (see the column marked d^2 in Table 11.4). The formula for r_s is as follows:

$$r_s = 1 - \frac{6\sum d^2}{n(n^2 - 1)}$$

Equation 11.3

where: n is the sample size
 d is the difference between each pair of ranks

Substituting the results from Table 11.4 in the r_s formula we get:

$$r_s = 1 - \frac{6 \times 100.5}{7 \times 48} = -0.7946$$

Notice that the r_s value of –0.7946 is higher than the equivalent r value of -0.6955, calculated earlier. According to Guilford's criteria (Table 11.2) Spearman's r_s yields a high correlation while Pearson's r yields a moderate correlation. This is because methods based on ranks (as opposed to scores) are more robust than methods based on scores – i.e. they will be less influenced by outlying values. Spearman's r_s is therefore useful not only when you have collected naturally ranked data, but also when you suspect that your measured data may contain extreme or outlying scores.

*Spearman's r_s is more **robust** than Pearson's r.*

> Recalculate the correlation coefficient for the data shown in Table 11.4, omitting the Cantonese data. Why do you think omitting one data pair does not cause the substantial change it did in Activity 11.1?

Activity 11.2

If you calculated r_s in Activity 11.2, you should have got $r_s = -0.7286$. This is lower than the equivalent r value of –0.931, calculated previously. It seems that even though rank correlation is more robust than Pearson's correlation, it is also less sensitive when other things such as sample size are equal.

r_s is less sensitive than r, i.e. it has less power.

Box 11.1

Using a spreadsheet to calculate correlations

	A	B	C	D
1		X	Y	XY
2		(digit span)	(sound duration)	
3	Welsh	5.77	385	=B3*C3
4	English 1	6.55	321	=B4*C4
5	Cantonese	9.9	265	=B5*C5
6	English 2	7.21	256	=B6*C6
7	Spanish	6.37	287	=B7*C7
8	Hebrew	6.51	309	=B8*C8
9	Arabic	5.77	370	=B9*C9
10		=SUM(B3:B9)	=SUM(C3:C9)	=SUM(D3:D9)
11	S	=STDEV(B3:B9)	=STDEV(C3:C9)	
12				
13	Covar	=(D10-(B10*C10)/7)/6		
14	r	=B13/(B11*C11)		

	A	B	C	D
1		X	Y	XY
2		(digit span)	(sound duration)	
3	Welsh	5.77	385	2221.5
4	English 1	6.55	321	2102.6
5	Cantonese	9.9	265	2623.5
6	English 2	7.21	256	1845.8
7	Spanish	6.37	287	1828.2
8	Hebrew	6.51	309	2011.6
9	Arabic	5.77	370	2134.9
10		48.08	2193	14768
11	S	1.425861	49.5672	
12				
13	Covar	-49.13952		
14	r	-0.69528		

Figure 11.2 Layout for manual calculation of correlation in Microsoft® Excel

The basic layout for the manual calculation of the correlation coefficient, as shown in Table 11.3, can be constructed with ease in spreadsheet programs. The data are entered just as they are in Table 11.3, and formulas are entered to calculate Σx, Σy, Σxy, s_x, s_y, as well as final calculations involving these components. Figure 11.2, which is a screen snapshot, shows the setup (including the formula notation) and the results, as produced in Microsoft Excel. (An introduction to spreadsheet programs is offered in the additional CD material.)

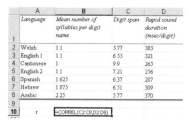

Figure 11.3 Layout for automatic calculation of correlation in Microsoft®Excel

However, Excel also offers very useful shortcut formulas for calculating correlation coefficients. The formula CORREL calculates the product-moment correlation directly, i.e. without all the interim steps! A layout for this method is shown in Figure 11.3.

Box 11.2

Using SPSS® to calculate correlations
Create a new SPSS® data file, and enter the data in two columns, as shown in the accompanying screenshot (Figure 11.4). Name and label the variables if you wish.

Then choose 'Analyze' from the main menu and 'Correlate' then 'Bivariate' from the 'Analyze' sub-menus shown in the screenshot. You will then need to select the variables for the correlation analysis, using the mouse to highlight variable names, and the arrow in the middle of the dialog box to move the variables into the right-hand pane. Notice the options to select particular types of correlation methods, and to calculate significance tests. Click 'OK' when you are done, and you should see the output of Figure 11.5. Notice that the results are represented in the form of a matrix.

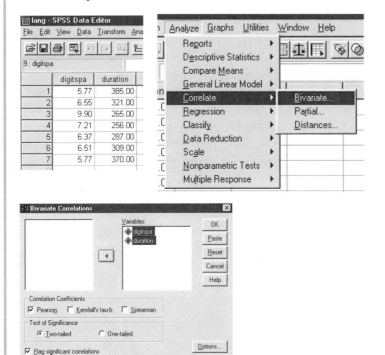

Figure 11.4 Calculation of correlation in SPSS®

Correlations

		DIGITSPA	DURATION
DIGITSPA	Pearson Correlation	1	-.695
	Sig. (2-tailed)	.	.083
	N	7	7
DURATION	Pearson Correlation	-.695	1
	Sig. (2-tailed)	.083	.
	N	7	7

Figure 11.5 Output of correlation analysis in SPSS®

Cause and effect

Correlation does not imply causation.

For many everyday events, the link between cause and effect seems fairly straightforward. Turn on the tap and water comes out; fall to the ground and you will experience pain. But not all relationships are so easy to interpret. If you have persistent back pain and have tried a number of remedies for it, an improvement can be very hard to interpret. It could be because of the hot baths you have been taking, or the exercises you have been doing, or perhaps it is because of the vitamin pills you have been taking, or perhaps it is because of all of these things or none of these things. With many ailments you will get better merely with the passage of time, and it may be impossible to speed the process with attempted cures. As it has been said, 'With proper medication the common cold usually lasts about a week, but left to its own devices it can drag on for seven days'.

Correlations are difficult to interpret in a causal fashion. A strong correlation between two things does not prove that one caused the other.

Correlations are similarly difficult to interpret in a causal fashion. A strong correlation between two things does not prove that the one has caused the other. A strong correlation indicates a statistical relationship, but there may be many reasons for this relationship besides cause and effect. For example, it is known that the number of crimes over time is correlated with the size of the police force. Does this mean that larger police forces cause more crime or (more likely) that greater crime causes police forces to expand? A simpler explanation might be that a larger police force encourages a higher proportion of victims to report crimes. Increases and decreases in crime probably have little to do with the size of the police force and much more to do with changes in the economic and social value system over time.

Activity 11.3

A correlation between two variables, A and B, can arise for one of three reasons: A causes B; B causes A; or A and B are independently related to a third variable, C.

Problems of interpretation frequently arise with the possibility of the two variables being related to an unknown third variable.

Try to find at least two explanations for the following:
a) The number of cigarettes that people smoke is negatively correlated with their income.
b) The average weekly pocket money paid to children in the United States between 1976 and 1990 is strongly correlated with the number of violent crimes over the same period.

A correlation between two variables, A and B, can arise for one of three reasons: A causes B; B causes A; or A and B are independently related to a third variable, C. Problems of interpretation frequently arise with the possibility of the two variables being related to an unknown third variable. For example, for the period covering the last 80 years, the data relating Nelson Mandela's age and the population of the world are positively correlated – not because there is a direct causal relationship but because they are both correlated with a third variable: time.

Some points to ponder

Correlations refer to linear relations between two variables.

Correlations are meaningless if the variables are related in a non-linear manner. Specifically, a lack of correlation between two measures does not imply a lack of association between them if they are non-linearly related. Figure 11.6 illustrates the case of two variables, x and y, that are strongly associated, but in the form of an inverse-U relationship, rather than a linear relationship. Here the correlation between x and y will be close to zero even though the two variables are strongly associated. Because of the possibility of such non-linear relationships, you should always inspect scatterplots of your data rather than simply relying on correlation coefficients.

Correlations are meaningless if the variables are not related in a linear manner.

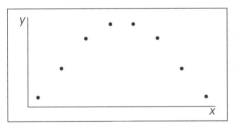

Figure 11.6 Scatterplot showing non-linear relation

Correlation coefficients should not be averaged

Correlation coefficients are not like ordinary numbers and do not obey the normal rules of arithmetic. It is incorrect to average several correlation coefficients by calculating their arithmetic mean. The difference between two Pearson correlations is meaningful, and its statistical significance can be tested, but there is no way of testing the significance of a difference between two Spearman correlations. Calculating the average of several Pearson correlation coefficients involves somewhat complicated methods (the Fisher z transform), beyond the scope of this tutorial, but a set of Spearman rank correlations can be 'averaged' by calculating the median value of the set.

Correlations should not be added, or averaged, without an appropriate transformation.

Correlation coefficients cannot be directly compared

A correlation of 0.8 does not represent an association that is twice as strong as a correlation of 0.4. The correct procedure to compare correlation coefficients is to calculate the square of each of the correlation coefficients (r^2). The square of a correlation coefficient is known as the *coefficient of determination*. Broadly speaking, r^2 is the proportion of variation in one measure that is accounted for statistically by the variation in the other measure. (For a graphical explanation of this notion, see Tutorial 18.) A correlation of 0.8

means that 64% of the variation in one set of scores is accounted for by the variation in the other ($r^2 = 0.8 \times 0.8 = 0.64$). With a correlation of 0.4, one measure accounts for only 16% of the variation in the other measure ($r^2 = 0.4 \times 0.4 = 0.16$). This means that a correlation of 0.8 is really four times greater than a correlation of 0.4 (i.e. compare 64% to 16%). When thinking about what a correlation really means, it is always helpful to calculate r^2. For example, in correlations of the size that Guilford calls slight ($r < 0.2$), one of the measures accounts for less than 4% of the variation in the other measure! In our example, correlating digit span with average digit sound duration, we arrived at a correlation of −0.6955. This means that 48% of the variation in digit span scores can be accounted for by variation in average digit sound duration. However, when we excluded the Cantonese data, we calculated a correlation of −0.931, a value that implies that 87% of the variation in digit span scores can be accounted for by variation in average digit sound duration – a much stronger relationship.

Activity 11.4

Re-calculate the entries in Table 11.2 to reflect values of r^2, rather than r.

Correlations are misleading if the underlying populations are not homogenous

When interpreting a correlation, we assume that the strength of association between two variables applies across the entire range of these variables. This means that we assume that high, middle and low values of one variable are correlated with the other variable – that variable x is affected by variable y in the same way at all levels. When this is true, the underlying population is said to be homogenous.

However, imagine a drug that only affects people at very low or very high dose levels. At low dose levels this drug makes people very silent and at high dose levels it makes people very talkative. It has no effect whatsoever on people at intermediate dose levels. The effect of this drug might be depicted in Figure 11.7, which shows a moderate relationship between drug dosage levels and talkativeness. The danger with the type of correlation depicted in Figure 11.7 is that it implies that there is a general association between increasing dosage of the drug and becoming more talkative. But in fact this association is only true at the extreme ends of the talkativeness spectrum.

A low correlation can also arise if two variables are positively correlated for one part of the population but negatively correlated for another. Consider the introduction of a compulsory training programme for motorcyclists that took place in the UK some years ago. The intention of the training programme was to improve road safety among motorcyclists and it was believed that the longer the training programme (in hours), the more the road safety behaviour of motor-

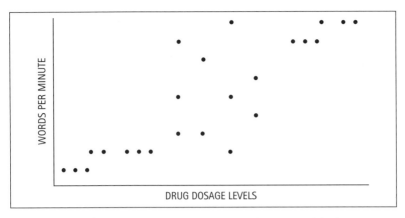

WORDS PER MINUTE

DRUG DOSAGE LEVELS

Figure 11.7 Scatterplot showing two variables that are positively correlated only for extreme values

cyclists would improve (i.e. a positive correlation). In fact no relationship was found between the duration of the training programme and motorcycle road safety habits. When a psychologist was consulted she examined the findings and concluded that the population of motorcyclists was not homogenous. The findings of the study could be depicted as in Figure 11.8, where the two groups are marked using different symbols. Motorcycle enthusiasts loved their motorcycles and rode them for pleasure. This group spent many hours on their motorcycles and were intimate with every detail of the behaviour of their machines. For them the government training programme was insulting because it presumed that they needed basic information about motorcycling. The longer the training programme, the more this group tended to react against the programme and ride dangerously. The other group of motorcyclists, the car enthusiasts, really only rode their machines as a form of transport – they would have preferred to drive cars but could not afford them. This group tended to spend very little time on their cycles and did not know very much about the behaviour of their machines. For this group the government training programme was very helpful because it forced them to spend more time becoming familiar with their motorcycles. The longer the training programme, the more this group benefited.

Correlations are misleading if the underlying populations are not homogenous. Researchers should ensure that sub-groups in the sample do not differ markedly on either of the correlated variables.

Correlations are sensitive to restrictions in the range of variables

The product-moment correlation coefficient can be substantially attenuated by a *restriction of range* in the measured variables, and you should attempt to ensure that this does not occur, or if it does, that you acknowledge the problem when you interpret the correlation coefficient. A clear example of this phenomenon is the relationship between weight and boxing prowess, in the days before boxers and boxing matches were regulated according to weight bands. As you

Correlations are sensitive to restrictions in the range of variables. Researchers should make sure that the correlated variables do not have unrepresentatively small variances.

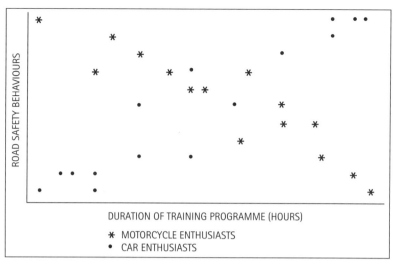

Figure 11.8 Scatterplot showing relation between two variables where the sample is composed of two distinct groups

Life expectancy showed a general tendency to increase during the 19th and 20th centuries as standards of health care and hygiene improved. The higher life expectancy varies between countries, communities, and even families. You come across a graveyard in Scotland and determine the year of death and age of death for 13 males in the Makhatini clan (see Table 11.5). Is there an indication that life expectancy is increasing for this clan? What are the appropriate measures to use in answering this question?

Table 11.5 Ages recorded on gravestones for 13 males in the Makhatini clan

Year	Age	Year	Age	Year	Age	Year	Age	Year	Age
1827	13	1895	34	1918	16	1941	74	1977	83
1828	13	1908	1	1924	68	1965	87		
1884	83	1914	11	1936	77	1965	65		

would expect, when there is no restriction on who can fight whom, there is a strong correlation between the percentage of matches a boxer wins, and his (or her) weight – heavier boxers tend to beat lighter boxers, especially when flyweights are allowed to fight heavyweights! Figure 11.9 shows a scatterplot of this relation (left panel), and what happens to the relationship when the range of weights is restricted (right panel).

As Figure 11.9 shows, restriction of range is a serious threat to the accurate interpretation of correlation coefficients. In order to understand whether a correlation accurately reflects the strength of a relationship, we should ensure that the range of both variables

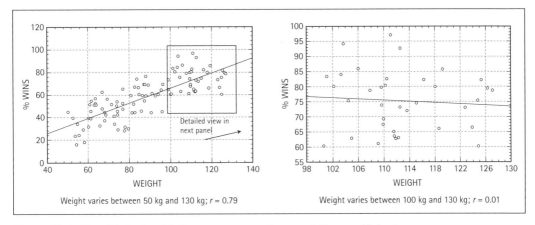

Figure 11.9 The effect of restriction on range on the correlation coefficient

is not restricted. Ideally, we should compare the sample variance in each of our measured variables to the population variance on the same variables. This will often be a very difficult task, since we rarely have information about population variances, but there may well be suitable benchmarks – e.g. the sample variance should not be much less than the variance reported for other samples in the literature.

Significance testing of *r*

Just as we acknowledge that sample means are only estimates of population means, and will exhibit random sampling variation, so we must acknowledge that sample correlation coefficients are only estimates of the population correlation coefficient, ρ (rho), and will also exhibit sampling variation. Thus, the correlation of –0.6932 for the data of Table 11.1 might have turned out to be –0.5, or 0.9, or some other value, had we collected an entirely different sample of languages. Since correlation tests the *strength* of a linear relationship, the critical question is whether the correlation provides evidence of any relationship at all. That is, can we be confident that $\rho \neq 0$, on the basis of the *r* we have calculated?

There are two widely accepted approaches to testing the significance of *r*. The first is the simpler, and involves transforming *r* to a *t*-value. The second involves transforming *r* to a *z*-value, and is too complex to discuss here (see Hays, 1994).

Transforming *r* to *t*
For most purposes, a transformation of *r* to *t* is adequate, assuming that the sample size is not too small (n ≥ 10).

$$t = \frac{r\sqrt{n-2}}{\sqrt{1-r^2}}$$

Equation 11.4

Once we have converted the r-value to t, we proceed as we do for t-tests, i.e. decide whether the calculated t-value exceeds the critical t-value, and accordingly reject or accept H_0.

Thus, for the correlation calculated on the data of Table 11.1:

$$t = \frac{-0.6932\sqrt{7-2}}{\sqrt{1-(-0.6932^2)}} = -2.150$$

If we look up the critical value for t in our t-tables we find that this exceeds the critical t-value ($t = -2.01$) for a one-tailed test, but not for a two-tailed test ($t = \pm 2.57$). A one-tailed test is clearly implied by the wording of the problem, so we reject H_0, and conclude that there is sufficient evidence of a relationship between digit span and sound duration.

Worked example

Nearly all languages in the world include words for the lower cardinal numbers (such as 'one,' 'two', and 'three'). Many languages, however, do not include words for the higher cardinal numbers (such as 'nine', 'ten', a 'hundred', a 'thousand', etc.). One hypothesis to explain this finding is that numeral words originate out of a communicative need for words applicable to collections of things. This hypothesis would hold that lower value number words are invented more readily than higher value number words because they are the ones humans need the most. This amounts to the claim that in human affairs the need to refer to some specific low number n is likely to arise more often than a need to refer to its successor, n + 1. A test of this hypothesis can be found in some data collected by Thorndike and Lorge (1944). They examined 4.5 million words from popular magazines of the time. Table 11.6 sets out the frequency with which the words 'two', 'three', etc. occur in this dataset.

Table 11.6 The frequency of cardinal number words

Words	Rank	Frequency
two	1	5958
three	2	2673
four	3	1637
five	4	1462
six	5	806
seven	6	615
eight	7	657
nine	8	468

Solution

Although we should consider calculating the Pearson correlation coefficient between cardinal number word and frequency, a scatterplot (Figure 11.10) shows that this is not suitable, since the relation is clearly not linear. We therefore decide to calculate the Spearman rank correlation, since ranking the frequencies will counter this problem.

It is easy to rank the cardinal number words in Table 11.6 because they are naturally ordered. Similarly, the frequencies with which the words occur in Thorndike and Lorge (1944) can be readily ranked. Table 11.7 sets out additional information for calculating r_s. There are eight cardinal number words in the dataset, so n = 8.

Table 11.7 Calculating the rank correlation between cardinal numbers and word frequency

Words	Rank	Frequency	Rank y	d	d^2
two	1	5 958	8	-7	49
three	2	2 673	7	-5	25
four	3	1 637	6	-3	9
five	4	1 462	5	-1	1
six	5	806	4	1	1
seven	6	615	2	4	16
eight	7	657	3	4	16
nine	8	468	1	7	49
Σ					166

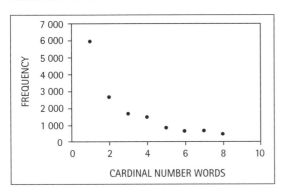

Figure 11.10 Scatterplot of relation between cardinal number words and frequency of usage

From this information, we can work out the Spearman rank correlation:

$$r_s = 1 - \frac{6\sum d^2}{n(n^2 - 1)}$$

$$= 1 - \frac{6 \times 166}{8 \times 63} = -0.9762$$

This is a very high negative correlation, and we conclude that cardinal number words show frequency of usage in inverse relation to their position in the cardinal sequence. Thus, words for earlier numbers (e.g. two, three) are used much more frequently than words for later numbers (e.g. eight, nine).

Summary

1. In this tutorial, we were interested in measures of the strength of linear relationship between two continuous or ranked measures. This type of relationship is called a correlation, and is usually indexed with a correlation coefficient.

2. A useful graphical device in understanding data of this kind is the scatterplot, which is a plot of two variables assigned to the x- and y-axes, respectively. In particular, this plot helps tells us if the relationship is linear and if it is appropriate to calculate a correlation coefficient.

3. The most common correlation coefficient is the product-moment or Pearson coefficient. This is calculated by dividing the covariance of two variables by the product of their standard deviations. The product-moment coefficient is an index of the degree to which the relationship can be described as a straight line (or by a linear equation).

4. The size of (most) correlation coefficients ranges between –1 and +1, where –1 = a perfectly linear negative relationship, 0 = no relationship, and +1 = a perfectly linear positive relationship.

5. In many situations, it is useful to work with ranked data. The Spearman rank correlation coefficient is used for this purpose, although the Pearson coefficient can also be used on ranked data.

6. In correlation problems, one should always beware of interpreting correlations between variables as indicating causal relationships. There might be other reasons for the correlation, most importantly the presence of a 'third variable'.

7. Before interpreting a correlation, one should always make sure that the data does not depart noticeably from linearity, that the underlying population of scores is homogeneous, and that the range of either variable is not restricted.

Exercises

1. The accompanying table shows an IQ score and an English test, for each member of a sample of 10 pupils taken from a mixed ability class. The English test was marked out of 50 and the range of IQ values for the class was 80 to 140.
   a) Estimate the product-moment correlation coefficient for the class.
   b) What does this correlation coefficient measure?

IQ:	110	107	127	100	132	130	98	109	114	124	136	95	102	111
English:	26	31	37	20	35	34	23	38	31	36	42	25	26	27

2. Fill in the blanks in the table below:

Correlation coefficient	Variance shared by two variables
–	100
0.85	–
–	68%
0.79	–
–	40%
–	25%
0.45	–
–	13%
0.22	–
0.19	–
–	0%

3. Fourteen students sat two Statistics tests, one theoretical and one practical. Their marks are shown in the following table:

1	Theory	5	9	7	11	20	4
1	Practical	6	8	9	13	20	9
2	Theory	17	12	10	15	16	14
2	Practical	17	14	8	17	18	18

   a) Draw a scattergraph to represent these data.
   b) Find the product-moment correlation coefficient.
   c) Using evidence from (a) and (b), explain why a straight line regression model is appropriate for these data.

4. Outline and explain the relationship between correlation and regression analysis.

5. Describe an imaginary study measuring the relationship between two variables where the use of correlation coefficients might be misleading because the underlying populations are not homogenous.

6. A cheese expert is blindfolded and asked to taste 10 cheeses and arrange them in order of price. The correct order was A, B, C, D, E, F, G, H, I, J. The order chosen by the expert was A, (B, D), C, G, J, (E, F, H, I). The brackets indicate cheeses to which the expert assigned the same price. Using tied ranks, determine the value of r_s as a measure of the correlation between the expert's opinion and the true order.

Measurements

Gillian Finchilescu

After studying this tutorial, you should be able to:
- Develop a scale to measure a construct or attribute.
- Refine the scale through item analysis.
- Determine the reliability and validity of the scale.

In the social sciences, we often study variables or constructs that are not tangible. Psychologists frequently explore such things as attitudes, abilities, personality traits, perceptions; sociologists pursue such things as social class, delinquency, alienation; political scientists look at political leanings and voting intentions. In order to research these constructs, we need to 'measure' them, i.e. develop an index that allows us to ascertain whether the construct is present, what its magnitude is, or the form in which it exists.

This tutorial discusses psychometric issues and statistical procedures that are used in developing measurement instruments. We will be applying some of the statistical procedures introduced earlier in the text to investigate the 'soundness' of social science measures.

Measuring a construct

Suppose you were interested in investigating people's attitude to a country's new language policy. You could simply ask people a question such as 'Do you think South Africa's language policy is a good thing?', to which they could respond yes or no. However, there are problems with this attitude measure: there is only a two-option answer, for instance, and only one item is used.

The two-option answer, generally referred to as an alternative-choice answer, forces people into one side or the other – pro/anti, agree/disagree. There is no option to express indecision, nor is the strength of the respondent's feelings considered. A respondent who is basically indifferent to the issue might, almost randomly, opt for the negative alternative. This person will be allocated the same score as someone who is fervently opposed to the issue. Thus, this form of response scaling is very imprecise and can be misleading.

In addition, with only one item we have no way of telling how reliable the response is – has the person answered randomly, or are they likely to respond consistently on different occasions? A further problem is that the question is very broad. The language policy includes the stipulations (among others) that there are eleven official languages in South Africa, and that all citizens have the right to receive education in their 'mother-tongue'. It is quite possible that the respondent does not think there should be more than one official language, but completely concurs with the 'education in mother-tongue' stipulation. Thus, one positive or negative answer gives no real information about the respondent's feelings.

A summated scale consists of a series of items that 'sample' the central construct.

Most issues are complex and will require a range of questions to assess them. For this reason it is usually best to create a *summated scale* to measure a construct. A summated scale consists of a series or set of items that 'sample' the construct. The responses to the item ultimately are totalled to produce a single score that is the index or measure of the construct.

Box 12.1

> **Things to beware of when constructing items**
> Once you have decided on the content of the items of the scale or test, and on the type of scaling, the next step is to construct individual items. In doing so it is important to ensure the following:
> 1. The meaning of each item must be clear and not rely on unspecified knowledge or assumptions.
> 2. Items must convey only one idea or question.
> 3. Some of the items in the scale should be phrased so they express a reverse sentiment to that of the other items.
> 4. Try to avoid making the evaluative nature of the item too blatant. Respondents tend to try to present themselves in a positive light, so will frequently endorse socially desirable responses.

Defining the domain

After clearly defining the construct and variable we want to measure, the next step is to specify the domain of the construct. For instance, suppose you wished to construct a scale to measure how people feel about a proposal to privatise a municipal service such as refuse collection. To establish the relevant domain you could do such things as: 1) discover what the proposal involved, 2) read assessments of similar issues in other cities, or 3) establish the range of perceptions held by stakeholders through interviews or focus groups. From this a set of content areas can be formulated.

One means of ensuring that the entire domain is sampled is to set up a grid, with the content areas as columns and the manifestations of these as rows. Then you would devise items to fit each of the cells. Our present example might lead to a grid such as the one in Table 12.1, which gives an example of items that would fit in each cell.

Define the constructs you want to measure clearly, and ensure that the items reflect the 'domain' of the construct.

Table 12.1 The construction of items that sample the domain

Manifestations	Content			
	Labour concerns	**Efficiency**	**Accountability**	**Cost**
Pro-privatisation	Privatisation will lead to workers receiving better salaries	Privatisation will lead to a better service	Privatisation will make the workers more diligent	Privatisation will lead to lower costs for the service
Anti-privatisation	Privatisation will lead to many job losses	In a privatised scheme, efficiency will be measured in terms of cost saving rather than quality of service	Privatisation means that the only concern will be with making a profit, and not with giving householders a good service	Privatisation will lead to an escalation of costs to the householder as the firm will have to show profits

Suggest some other items that fit the cells specified in the domain grid of Table 12.1

Activity 12.1

Response scaling

When you have determined the content of the items, it is then important to decide in what form the respondents will answer the questions. Response scaling refers to methods of associating numbers with responses. Below we discuss four commonly used scaling formats.

Alternative-choice

Alternative-choice format requires participants to respond to an item by marking one of two choices, e.g. 'yes' or 'no', 'true' or 'false', 'agree' or 'disagree'. Each of these options will be associated with a number, e.g. 0 and 1. Although the alternative-choice scale lacks precision, there are instances where it is appropriate, e.g. a lifestyle measure that asks respondents to indicate (yes or no) whether they possess objects such as a cellphone, television, and video recorder.

Multiple-choice

Students are all too familiar with this response format, which is commonly used for achievement and knowledge tests. A number of possible answers are given for each item, and the respondent is usually required to select only one. We could construct a test of the community's knowledge and perceptions of the new municipal policy by using a number of multiple-choice items (see Figure 12.1).

Please answer the following questions by circling the correct answer.

1. According to the new municipal refuse collection policy, how often will refuse be collected?
   a) Daily
   b) Weekly
   c) Monthly
   d) Annually

2. Which of the following statements describes the effect privatisation will have on the cost of refuse collection?
   a) The cost will increase.
   b) The cost will decrease.
   c) The cost will decrease in the short term, but increase in the long term.
   d) The cost will increase in the short term, but decrease in the long term.

Figure 12.1 Instructions and response format for a multiple-choice test

Responses to multiple-choice items are quantified by assigning the value 1 to a correct response and the value 0 to an incorrect response. When the items are not testing knowledge, numbers (e.g. 1–4) or letters (e.g. a–d) are typically assigned to each of the possible responses.

Rating scale

This scale is frequently called the Likert Scale (Likert, 1932), and is especially useful for measuring attitudes and opinions. The item generally consists of a statement to which the respondent must indicate the degree of agreement or disagreement by marking a point on the scale. In this format, a continuum of scale points is presented, anchored by 'Strongly agree' on the one side and 'Strongly disagree' on the other. To quantify the responses to each of the three items of the measure of attitudes towards privatising municipal services (see Figure 12.2), we typically assign numbers to the response items as follows: SD = 0, D = 1, N = 2, A = 3, SA = 4.

Please answer the following questions by indicating your reactions to each statement. Circle the response option, using the following scale, to show the extent to which you agree or disagree with each statement.

SD	if you *strongly disagree* with the statement
D	if you *disagree* with the statement
N	if you are *neutral* about the statement
A	if you *agree* with the statement
SA	if you *strongly agree* with the statement

1. Privatising municipal services will lead to better service delivery.

      SD   D   N   A   SA

2. Privatising municipal services will make workers more productive.

      SD   D   N   A   SA

3. Privatising municipal services will escalate the cost of services.

      SD   D   N   A   SA

Figure 12.2 Instructions and response format for a rating scale

In our measure, we have used a 5-point rating scale response format, but the optimal number of scaling points is a matter of debate. Nunnally (1978) argues that the reliability of the (full summated) scale increases with the number of scaling points used, levelling off at 7 points. Measures with fewer points are easier to complete, but are also less reliable. A further matter of debate is whether we should have the central 'undecided' or 'neutral' point, or whether it is better to have an even number of steps that force the respondent to one side or other. The argument against the midpoint is that it allows respondents to avoid thinking about the item and having to make a decision. On the other hand, respondents who are genuinely undecided or neutral may become frustrated at not being able to express this. Ultimately, the researcher must decide which format best suits the research requirements.

Bipolar adjectives

This scale format is most commonly known as the semantic-differential scale, and was developed by Osgood and his associates (Snider & Osgood, 1969). It is similar to the Likert scale in that a continuum of points is presented, anchored at each end. However, in this type of scaling the anchors consist of adjectives with opposite meanings, such as good–bad, honest–dishonest. Respondents are asked to describe a concept or category of person using this continuum. Thus, marking a number close to one end of the continuum would indicate that the respondent feels that that adjective strongly describes the concept or category, whereas a number towards the centre of the continuum indicates that neither of the adjectives is an accurate representation. An example of such an item would be:

The new municipal refuse collection policy will lead to

Lower efficiency | | | | | | | | Higher efficiency
1 2 3 4 5 6 7

Summing scale scores

The following example will be used to illustrate how to summate the scores and evaluate the scale. A researcher wishes to run a survey on how people feel about the legalisation of marijuana. He develops a questionnaire, which contains 4 knowledge items to establish how much people know about the facts of marijuana, and a 6-item attitude scale to measure the extent to which they would support the legalisation of marijuana. The knowledge questions were designed with multiple-choice responses, and the attitude items responses on a 7-point Likert scale. The questionnaire is shown in Box 12.2.

Box 12.2

Opinions about marijuana (dagga) questionnaire

Thank you for taking part in this study. Your responses to this questionnaire are completely confidential. Your name is not required. When the study is published all participants' scores will be amalgamated, so your particular answers will not be identifiable.

Please complete the following personal questions.

Age: (Please tick the appropriate box)

18–25	26–35	36–50	51+

Sex: Male [ ]   Female [ ]

Please answer these questions by **writing the correct answer in the box next to the questions**:

1. Marijuana (or dagga) is
   A   A synthetic substance
   B   Made from an insect
   C   Made from the leaf and flower tops of a plant
   D   Made from the horn of a rhinoceros   Answer: [ ]

2. Indicate which of the following is NOT another name for marijuana
   A   Crack
   B   Cannabis
   C   Ganja
   D   Grass   Answer: [ ]

3. Which of the following effects are known to occur when a person takes marijuana?
   A Impaired motor skills
   B Impaired sense of time
   C Impaired sight
   D Both A and B   Answer: [   ]

4. The active chemical in marijuana is
   A Ecgonine
   B Tetrahydrocannabinols
   C Phalloidine
   D Tetraiodothyronine   Answer: [   ]

Please read each of the following items and indicate **the degree to which you agree or disagree with the item** by ticking one of the 7 boxes. If you tick

1 – it means you strongly disagree	5 – it means you agree slightly
2 – it means you disagree	6 – it means you agree
3 – it means you disagree slightly	7 – it means you strongly agree
4 – it means you are undecided	

1. Marijuana is not addictive, so it is a mistake to refer to is as a dangerous drug in the same category as heroin or cocaine.
   Strongly [| | | | | |] Strongly
   Disagree   1   2   3   4   5   6   7   Agree

2. Smoking marijuana is less harmful to one's health than drinking alcohol.
   Strongly [| | | | | |] Strongly
   Disagree   1   2   3   4   5   6   7   Agree

3. Smoking marijuana is very likely to lead to the use of more dangerous drugs such as heroine and cocaine.
   Strongly [| | | | | |] Strongly
   Disagree   1   2   3   4   5   6   7   Agree

4. The legalisation of marijuana would lead to lower productivity on the part of the workforce.
   Strongly [| | | | | |] Strongly
   Disagree   1   2   3   4   5   6   7   Agree

5. The many positive medical benefits of marijuana, such as in the alleviation of nausea after chemotherapy and relieving eye-pressure in glaucoma, are a strong argument for its legalisation.
   Strongly [| | | | | |] Strongly
   Disagree   1   2   3   4   5   6   7   Agree

6. The pursuit of people selling marijuana is a waste of the police force's time and energy.
   Strongly [| | | | | |] Strongly
   Disagree   1   2   3   4   5   6   7   Agree

Coding responses

After the questionnaire has been administered to a sample of respondents, the responses to the questions must be coded and stored in a data file. The responses to the marijuana questionnaire are coded into numbers as follows:

- Age: 18–25 = 1; 26–35 = 2; 36–50 = 3; 51+ = 4
- Gender: male = 1; female = 2
- Knowledge items: A = 1; B = 2; C = 3; D = 4
- Attitude items: 1 to 7, as indicated

Figure 12.3 shows the first screen of an Excel spreadsheet holding the coded responses of the representative sample. Notice that each research participant is identified in the first column – P1, P2, P3, … etc. – and that responses to each of the questionnaire items are represented in the columns.

	A	B	C	D	E	F	G	H	I	J	K	L	M
1	ID	AGE	SEX	K1	K2	K3	K4	S1	S2	S3	S4	S5	S6
2	P1	2	2	3	1	4	2	2	7	5	6	3	5
3	P2	3	1	3	2	2	1	1	7		3	6	2
4	P3	1	2	3	2	1	3	4	4	4	4	4	4
5	P4	1	2	1	3	2	4	3	2	5	5	3	5
6	P5	4	1	3	3	4	3	4	7	2	1	7	1
7	P6	2	1	3	1	2	4	5	7	1	1	7	1
8	P7	1	1	3	4	4	1	3	3	1	6	4	2
9	P8	1	2	2	2	4	1	4	4	4	7	2	1
10	P9	2	1	3	3	4	1	4	6	4	2	2	2
11	P10	3	2	4	1	3	2	6	6	4	2	4	4
12	P11	4	2	1	1	3	3		6	4			5
13	P12	4	2	3	1	1	4	3	6	3	3	4	2

Figure 12.3 Microsoft® Excel spreadsheet showing the responses of the first 12 participants

Activity 12.2

Refer to Figure 12.3 and answer the following questions:
a) What is the age and gender of participants P1 and P2?
b) What did participant P3 respond to each of the 4 knowledge items?

Reverse scoring

The researcher has correctly varied the sense of the items such that for some items agreement indicates a positive attitude (e.g. '2. *Smoking marijuana is less harmful to one's health than drinking alcohol*') and for others disagreement indicates a positive attitude (e.g.

'3. Smoking marijuana is very likely to lead to the use of more dangerous drugs such as heroine and cocaine'). This strategy is necessary to ensure that the respondents read each item and do not use a response set in which they consistently mark only one side of the scale. Clearly the scores as they stand could not be summed to give a total score reflecting the stance of the individual. Before summation, you must reverse the scores of the opposite-meaning items (7 for 1, 6 for 2, etc.). You should first decide whether a high score is to indicate a positive or negative attitude. In this case, a high score will indicate a pro-legalisation attitude. A simple method for achieving this reversal is to use the following formula:

$$Y = (K + 1) - X \hspace{4cm} \textbf{Equation 12.1}$$

where: Y = the new score
         K = the number of scaling points used in the
              rating scale or bipolar adjective scale
         X = the number marked by the respondent

For example, in the attitude to marijuana example, a 7-point scale is used. If a respondent has marked 2 on the third item (S3), then the reversed score would be $Y = (7 + 1) - 2 = 8 - 2 = 6$.

Summing the scores

To obtain one score that represents the individual's attitude or opinion, the scores of the items are totalled or, alternatively, the average of the scores can be found. The total is generally considered better as it gives a wider range of scores. However, before doing this, you must consider the missing scores. Missing scores occur when respondents have not answered questions, either accidentally or deliberately. There are a number of options to take in this situation:

After reverse scoring, summed scores for each respondent should be saved in a new spreadsheet variable.

1. *Remove these respondents from the data file.* This is a good option if the sample is sufficiently large for the responses on the answered questions not to be missed. However, if the questions were deliberately missed (e.g. in protest), these respondents may represent a particular viewpoint. Excluding them would then diminish the representativeness of the sample.
2. *Replace the missing number with the average of the respondent's other scores.* The total found in this manner is termed the weighted total (or pro-rated total). The simplest way of calculating this is to (i) find the average of the items for the individual, then (ii) multiply that average by the number of items in the scale. This is the most common method of dealing with missing numbers.

If you replace the missing scores (option 2), it is important to decide on a maximum number of questions a respondent is 'allowed' to miss. A rule of thumb is that every respondent should complete at least 75% of the items. If more than 25% are missing, the respondent should be dropped from the sample. In the above example, respondents were excluded if more than one item was missed.

Activity 12.3

A scale measuring work stress consists of the following five items, each of which was answered using a 6-point Likert scale anchored by 1 = strongly agree and 6 = strongly disagree. The number marked by a respondent (Lindi S.) is given next to each item. It is intended that a total high score on this scale should indicate a high level of stress. Consider the items and decide which require the scores to be reversed. Then calculate Lindi's total score on this scale.

a) I frequently lie awake at night worrying about everything I have to do the next day. (6)
b) I switch off all my work problems the minute I leave the office. (2)
c) I frequently have the experience that my heart seems to start beating faster than normal. (4)
d) I often have a hard time focusing on the task at hand. (3)
e) I take unpleasant events in my stride. (1)

Evaluating a scale or test

Evaluate the psycho-metric properties of a newly developed measure by deter-mining its validity and reliability, and by conducting item analysis.

When a new scale or test has been developed, it is important to check that the scale measures what it claims to measure (its validity), and that it gives consistent scores (is reliable). It is also important to check whether all the items in the scale are valuable and should be retained, through item analysis.

In order to evaluate a scale, it must be tried out on a test sample. Scales are usually constructed for general use, so the test sample should be representative of the population for which the scale is designed. Thus, if a scale is designed to measure the mathematical aptitude of primary school children, the test sample must also consist of primary school children. However, frequently you only wish to evaluate the scale in the context of a particular study. For instance, if in a study a test that has been developed elsewhere is employed, it would still be advisable to check the psychometric properties of scale with the sample used for the study.

In the following section, the concepts of reliability, validity, and item analysis are explained, and procedures for establishing them described. At this point, it may be useful to consider the underlying theory of measurement. This is briefly discussed in Box 12.3.

Reliability

Imagine a ruler made of an elastic material that expands and contracts unsystematically as you make different measurements. This

Box 12.3

Measurement theory and reliability

There are two schools of thought about the underlying theory of measurement – classical measurement theory and generalisability theory.

Classical measurement theory argues that the measure or score produced by a test or scale consists of two components: the stable construct being measured and factors that have nothing to do with the construct. The construct or attribute is the core so its measure does not vary. This is termed the true score, symbolised by T. However, a range of other factors will also be present, and these are what lead to inconsistencies in test scores. This is referred to as measurement error, symbolised by e. Thus, a score (X) measured on any test or instrument can be expressed by the following formula:

$$X = T + e$$

Clearly, the smaller the measurement error, the more accurate the score. Measurement error comes from a number of sources, both unsystematic and systematic. Unsystematic error comes from such things as the choice and expression of items, the way the test is administered, and the test scored. If these procedures are done well, then measurement will be limited. Systematic measurement error arises when the test is not valid, i.e. when it is measuring something other than the true construct.

The reliability of any test hinges on the amount of measurement error relative to that of the true score. Following the basic formula above, the total variability of the scale or test scores in a sample can be expressed as:

$$\sigma_X^2 = \sigma_T^2 + \sigma_e^2$$

where: σ_X^2 = the variability of scores
σ_T^2 = the variability due to the natural distribution of the construct
σ_e^2 = the variability due to measurement error

The reliability coefficient can thus be seen as the ratio of the variability of the true score to that of the observed variability:

$$r_{XX} = \frac{\sigma_T^2}{\sigma_X^2} = \frac{\sigma_T^2}{(\sigma_T^2 + \sigma_e^2)}$$

While classical theory holds that there is a 'true' measure of the trait, behaviour, or sentiment being measured by the test or scale, **generalisability theory** holds that the scale or test is sampling a finite domain of the variable. This locates the measure in a specific context, determined by the particular test, the historical time, the tester, etc. It is hoped to generalise this finite sample of the variable to a wider universe of possible contexts. In this formulation the reliability of the test refers to its generalisability. In practice, this does not differ much from classical theory. The real difference is that it compels the test developer to explicitly define the universe to which the test results are intended to be generalised.

would be an unreliable measurement instrument, as it would give different results when the same object is measured on different occasions. Although you will probably never have to deal with a measuring instrument this unreliable, you should always try to determine the reliability of the instrument you are using. A number of different kinds of reliability indices can be computed for the measurement instruments used by social scientists.

Test-retest reliability

The simplest way to establish reliability is to administer the test or scale to a sample on two different occasions. If the scale is reliable, the scores at the test and retest administration should be strongly correlated. (Note that you would not expect the scores to be identical, as there are bound to be some practice or carry-over effects on the second testing.) There are a number of difficulties inherent in this method of determining reliability, though:

1. What is the optimal length of time that should elapse between the administrations? If it is too soon, the participants may recall their answers from the first administration. If left too long, extraneous events may influence the scores on the scale.
2. How do you maintain participant confidentiality while at the same time asking for their names and addresses so that you can trace them for the second administration of the scale?

The preferred measure of test-retest reliability is the correlation coefficient between the sets of scores collected at the two administrations.

Alternate-forms reliability

Instead of using the same test twice, as in the test-retest method, alternate-forms reliability requires the construction of two equivalent versions of the same test, which have items that are closely matched. Then the two forms are administered to the same set of people either at different times or at the same time. If done at different times, half the sample do version A on the first administration and half do version B. These are then alternated on the second administration. This

Counterbalancing is typically used in assessment of alternative form reliability to control for the extraneous effects brought about as a result of practice with the test, and natural changes over time.

counterbalancing technique controls for carry-over and maturation effects. If the tests or scales are reliable, the scores on the two tests should then not only be strongly correlated but should also produce similar means and standard deviations. This technique removes the problem of participants remembering their first responses.

The alternative forms can also both be administered at the same time. This method is then more a test of internal consistency than of constancy. Alternative forms reliability (in both instances) is the correlation between the scores on the two forms of the test.

A problem with the alternative forms method is that it is both difficult and expensive to produce alternate forms that are sufficiently independent and similar.

Split–half reliability

Split-half reliability is determined by administering the test on a single occasion, then dividing the items of the scale into two equivalent halves. The scores on the two halves are correlated to determine whether they yield similar measures. The logic is that if the scores from the two halves (from a single administration of the scale) are strongly correlated, then administering the whole test on two separate occasions would also lead to strong correlations (i.e. reliability).

The split-half reliability is calculated using the Spearman-Brown formula, rather than the correlation coefficient between the two halves. The correlation coefficient is based on only half the number of items in the scale, so underestimates the reliability of the full scale. The Spearman-Brown formula (r_{sb}) corrects for the loss of scale length:

$$r_{sb} = \frac{2r_{hh}}{1 + r_{hh}}$$

Equation 12.2

where r_{hh} is the correlation coefficient
between the two halves

The problem with the split-half technique is that it is affected by the way in which the scale is split into two. For instance, in ability tests the items are frequently presented in order of difficulty. Thus splitting the test at the middle would give a different reliability coefficient than if alternative items were put into the different halves. Ideally, the scale should be split into halves so that the halves are roughly equivalent in terms of difficulty and coverage.

Internal consistency – coefficient alpha

Cronbach's coefficient alpha is an estimate of consistency of responses to different scale items. The Cronbach alpha can be viewed as the average of the reliability coefficients that would result if all possible split-half analyses were performed. It is, however, strongly affected by the number of items in the scale. The logic here is that high internal consistency within the scale inevitably leads to strong test-retest reliability, since 'the major source of measurement error is because of the sampling of content' (Nunnally, 1978, p. 230).

The Cronbach alpha coefficient formula (r_{α}):

$$r_{\alpha} = \frac{n}{n-1}\left(1 - \frac{\sum \sigma_j^2}{\sigma^2}\right)$$

Equation 12.3

where: $\sum \sigma_j^2$ = sum of the item variances
σ^2 = variance of the total score on the scale
n = number of items

The 5-item stress scale discussed in Activity 12.3 is administered to a large representative sample. The variance of each item and the variance of the total scores on the scale are presented in the table below. Calculate the alpha coefficient for this scale and comment on the scale's reliability.

	Item a	Item b	Item c	Item d	Item e	Total
Variance	2.41	2.16	1.96	2.21	3.36	29.74

Box 12.4

Using SPSS® to compute reliability statistics

In our study, 64 respondents completed the 6-item marijuana attitude scale. The data were analysed using SPSS®. The three figures directly below show you how to conduct reliability analysis with SPSS®. The output for the Cronbach alpha and the split-half reliability coefficients is then given.

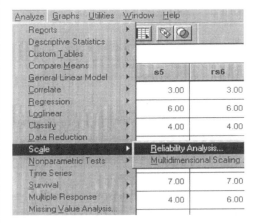

Step 1. Select the 'Reliability analysis' option on the 'Scale' item of the Analyze menu in SPSS®.

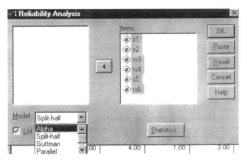

Step 2. (a) Select the scale items, (b) select the kind of reliability analysis you want to conduct, (c) tick the option 'List label items'.

Step 3. Select desired statistical output.

```
                RELIABILITY ANALYSIS- SCALE(ALPHA)

       Mean   Std      Dev       Cases

  1.   S1     3.4194   1.7975    62.0
  2.   S2     5.1935   1.7910    62.0
  3.   RS3    5.2581   1.4365    62.0
  4.   RS4    4.0484   2.1381    62.0
  5.   S5     3.9516   1.9705    62.0
  6.   RS6    5.0484   1.9705    62.0
              N of
```

Statistics for	Mean	Variance	Std Dev	Variables
SCALE	26.9194	61.4196	7.8371	6

Item-total Statistics

	Scale Mean if Item Deleted	Scale Variance if Item Deleted	Item- Total Correl	Corrected Alpha if Item Deleted
S1	23.5000	53.8934	.1627	.8416
S2	21.7258	47.5465	.4318	.7865
RS3	21.6613	47.7031	.5873	.7580
RS4	22.8710	37.3929	.7440	.7062
S5	22.9677	39.0481	.7508	.7072
RS6	21.8710	40.9339	.6585	.7322

Reliability Coefficients
N of Cases = 62.0   N of Items = 6
Alpha = .7928

Step 4. Examine SPSS® output.

Criteria for reliability

The criteria for reliability coefficients vary for the different types of test. Much higher reliability coefficients are found (and demanded) for achievement and ability tests than for personality or attitude scales. However, the purpose of a test or scale is also a factor in deciding whether the level of reliability is adequate. Aiken (1982) argues that if the scale is to be used to compare groups of people, then a reliability of 0.65 is sufficient. However, if an individual's score is to be compared with another, or against a set of norms, then the reliability should be at least 0.85. Nunnally (1978) makes the distinction between scales used for basic research and those for applied (diagnostic) purposes. Reliability coefficients of 0.70 are adequate for research instruments, while coefficients of 0.90 should be the minimum criteria for applied instruments.

There are a number of controllable factors that influence reliability:

1. *The number of items in a test or scale.* In general, the more items in the scale, the higher the reliability it is likely to have. However, this has to be weighed against the problem of participant motivation. You will have more difficulty finding respondents if the task looks very long, and they are likely to tire and give the items less attention.

2. *The variability of the test sample.* In general, the greater the variability in the scale scores, the better the reliability. If a wide range of people is used, as opposed to a small, homogenous group, then a larger standard deviation in scores would be expected. Thus, a better estimate of the reliability of a scale is obtained if the test sample is representative of the wider population.

3. *Limiting extraneous variables.* All the extraneous variables that contaminate ordinary research designs also affect reliability. Badly run testing situations, ambiguous and misleading items, unstandardised testing procedures, perceive-demand effects – all these contribute to increasing the measurement error, thus lowering reliability. Thus, a well-designed scale, with clear instructions, tested under standardised conditions will help limit the measurement error so that it reflects the true content of the scale.

Validity

A reliable scale may or may not be valid, but a scale that is not reliable can never be valid.

A scale or test is valid if it does in fact measure what it claims to measure. This is not an easy judgement to make, as there is no direct measure of validity. In general, this judgement depends on whether the scale or test leads to inferences that are meaningful and useful. There are various aspects to validity, which can be grouped under three main categories: content validity, criterion-related validity, and construct validity.

Content validity

Content validity refers to how well the test or scale items represent the domain of the construct being measured. If a scale measuring stress has items only about the psychological effects of stress and ignores the physical effects, then it will not have good content validity.

There are two ways of ascertaining the content validity of a scale. First, *face validity* can be determined. Face validity refers to the appearance of the test or scale. For example, if respondents were told that the purpose of the previously discussed 'marijuana' questionnaire was to assess how people felt about consumer issues, they would rightly feel they were being deceived. It is important for the test or scale to appear authentic to the participants. While this is not strictly a criterion for validity, it does have an effect on the test scores if the participants have doubts about the test.

Second, the scale items can be evaluated by *expert judges*, who independently examine the items and decide whether each of the items is weakly relevant or strongly relevant to the *content* domain of the construct. This allows us to 'measure' the extent of content validity by calculating the proportion (or percentage) of items that the judges agreed were strongly relevant. This measure ranges from 0 to 1.00 (or 100%).

$$\text{Content validity} = \frac{x}{N}$$

Equation 12.4

where: x = number of items evaluated as strongly
                relevant by both judges
         N = total number of items in the scale

Criterion–related validity

Criterion-related validity refers to how well the scale or test anticipates a criterion behaviour or outcome, either at the present time (*concurrent validity*) or in the future (*predictive validity*). The difficulty with this type of validity lies in selecting the appropriate criterion. The criteria for ability or achievement tests are generally performance in some form of examination. However, determining a criterion for personality and attitude scales is much more difficult. Frequently, other tests that have already been used to test the same construct are used as criteria in evaluating concurrent validity. For example, to evaluate the validity of a new test for depression, you would give the newly developed scale and an established test of depression to the representative sample. A strong correlation between the new and old tests is evidence for concurrent validity. In the case of the 'marijuana' scale, concurrent validity could be established by also getting the sample to complete another scale that measures attitudes to drugs. The scale devised by the Northumbria Drugs Prevention Team in 1995 for use in Whitburn, UK would be one possibility.

Concurrent validity refers to how well the test predicts a criterion behaviour at the present time.

Predictive validity refers to how well the test predicts a criterion behaviour in the future.

A hypothetical measure of the predictive validity of this scale would be a referendum on the legalisation of marijuana. If it was possible to discover whether the individuals in the test sample voted in favour or against the proposition, the predictive validity of the test could be calculated. If the test is valid, the people who scored high on the scale should vote 'yes' to legalisation of marijuana, and those who scored low should vote 'no'. There are numerous statistical tests that could be used to establish whether this relationship exists, e.g. the chi-square test of contingency, or the point-biserial correlation.

Construct validity

This is the most difficult validity to determine, as it attempts to establish whether the scale really does measure the construct it claims to measure. Constructs are intangible and difficult to operationalise. Hence, to establish this validity, an array of methods is used, aimed at discerning behaviour or sentiments that logically emanate from the construct. One method is to find a construct that should theoretically be allied to the one being measured. Thus construct validity would be demonstrated by a strong correlation between a sound measure of hedonism and the scores on our 'marijuana' scale. This is termed *convergent validity*.

Another technique would be to find a construct that would be contrary to the construct being measured. For instance, it could be argued that people who believe in strong policing of the population would be opposed to the legalisation of marijuana. Hence, it could be argued that authoritarianism would be a contrasting construct. We would thus expect a strong negative correlation between the scores on the 'marijuana' scale and an established scale measuring authoritarianism. This is referred to as *discriminant validity*.

Criterion-groups validity is investigated by determining whether groups who would be expected to differ on the construct do in fact score differently on the measure. Thus, in the case of the 'marijuana' scale, the scale could be administered to a group of practising Rastafarians and a group of practising Muslims. It would be expected that the scores of these two groups would be significantly different.

The use of other scales or tests as a check for validity (as in concurrent or convergent validity) does have problems. The criterion scale may itself have dubious validity. Ideally, a behavioural criterion would be advantageous.

Convergent validity ascertains construct validity through comparing the scale with a measure of an allied construct.

Discriminant validity ascertains construct validity through contrasting the scale with a measure of an opposing construct.

Criterion-groups validity ascertains construct validity through comparing groups who logically should respond to the construct antithetically.

Item analysis

Tests of validity and reliability are used to determine the properties of an entire scale. Item analysis is used to determine if an item is 'good'. There are two main criteria for this judgement. Firstly, the item should contribute positively to the scale's reliability, i.e. to its ability to measure the construct. Secondly, the item should differentiate between high and low scorers on the entire scale. The first criterion has been termed 'item facilitation' and the second, 'item discrimination' (Rust & Golombok, 1989).

Item facilitation

In a knowledge test, such as a multiple-choice examination, you would calculate the item-difficulty index. This is the proportion of the test sample that answers the item correctly. If the item difficulty is 0, which occurs when none of the sample gets the item correct, the item is not useful in measuring the knowledge of the sample. There are many reasons why this may occur, ranging from problems in the way the question was presented to inappropriate level of difficulty for the sample. Whatever the reason, the item in question does not add to the value of the test. Similarly, if the whole sample gets the item correct – i.e. the index = 1 – then the item is equally ineffective. In general, items with item-difficulty indices of between 0.3 and 0.7 are acceptable, with 0.5 being optimal.

*The **item-difficulty** index (of a knowledge test item) is the proportion of the test sample that answers the item correctly.*

Consider the four knowledge questions in the 'marijuana' scale. In question 1, the correct answer is C. In our sample of 64 respondents, 58 marked the correct answer and 6 the incorrect answer. The item-difficulty index is: IDI = 58/64 = 0.906

This is too high, indicating the item was too easy. In contrast, consider question 4 on which only 8 people marked the correct response (B). Hence: IDI = 8/64 = 0.125

This is too low, indicating the question was too difficult. Both these questions thus have discriminatory power. On question 2, 43 people selected the correct answer (A), and 20 on question 3 (D) on. The item-difficulty indices on these questions are:

Question 2: IDI = 43/64 = 0.672 Question 3: IDI = 20/64 = 0.313

Both these indices are acceptable.

In other kinds of tests and scales (e.g. attitude measures), where the items are measured on an interval scale, the contribution an item makes to a scale can be discerned using the Cronbach alpha procedure. To examine the items, a series of Cronbach alphas is computed for the measure, removing a different item on each occasion. If the alpha coefficient improves markedly in comparison to when the item is included, this indicates that the item has a detrimental effect and should possibly be excluded from the scale. Note that SPSS® reports this analysis whenever you request a Cronbach alpha.

Reverse scoring should be done before item analysis commences.

Box 12.4 above shows the SPSS® output of a Cronbach alpha analysis done on the 6 attitude items of the 'marijuana' scale. The program provides the alpha coefficients when each of the items is excluded. Consider the furthest column on the right, entitled 'Alpha if deleted'. If item S1 is deleted, the alpha coefficient for the scale will rise from 0.793 to 0.842, a gain of 0.05. No improvement in reliability occurs for any of the other items. The researcher must then decide whether this rise in reliability warrants the removal of the item.

Item discrimination

In a knowledge test, an item-discrimination index (IDsI) can be calculated as follows. The test sample is divided into four sub-samples on the basis of their overall scores. The top 25% and bottom 25% are extracted, and the number within each of these sub-samples that correctly answered the item in question is calculated. The item-discrimination index is then calculated as follows:

Equation 12.5

$$IDsI = \frac{T - B}{N}$$

where: T = number of the top 25% that correctly answered the item
B = number of the bottom 25% that correctly answered the item
N = the total number of people in either the top or bottom 25%

This index can vary from −1 to +1. Clearly, if the index is negative, the item is bad since it means that a larger number of the poor scorers are getting it right than the good scorers. The closer to +1 the index, the better is the item's discrimination power. But very high values are not common. A general rule of thumb is that items with discrimination-indices of 0.20 and above are reasonable.

In the case of items with interval scaling, item discrimination is discerned from the correlation between the scores on the item in question and the total score on the whole scale. (Ideally the total should be calculated without the item score included.) Item analysis programs generally provide this correlation coefficient. Consider the SPSS® output in Box 12.4. The column entitled 'Itm-Ttl Correl.' provides this coefficient. A general rule of thumb is that a correlation coefficient of less than +0.20 indicates a suspect item. In the above example, item S1 has a correlation of 0.16. Thus both the item facility criterion and the item discrimination criterion suggest that S1 is not good, and should be excluded from the scale. A close look at the item *'Marijuana is not addictive, so it is a mistake to refer to it as a dangerous drug in the same category as heroin or cocaine'* suggests that the reason for it being problematic is that it assumes that respondents agree that marijuana is not addictive. Hence, two issues are queried in the item – the addictiveness of marijuana, as well as its degree of danger.

A lecturer constructed a multiple-choice test to evaluate her course at the end of the semester. Below is a table giving the item-difficulty index (IDI) and the item-discrimination index (IDsI) for 8 of the test items. Indicate if any of these items should be excluded from the test bank, giving the reasons for this decision.

Question	IDI	IDsI
1	0.55	0.34
5	0.51	0.54
2	0.62	0.47
6	0.22	0.24
3	0.85	0.60
7	0.40	0.43
4	0.66	0.38
8	0.32	0.14

Standardisation and norms

'Norms' present relatively fixed gradations within the general population that can be used for benchmarking an individual's performance. For example, knowing that an individual's score on the SAWAIS is 70 tells us very little until we know that the average intelligence of the population on this IQ test is 100 with a standard deviation of 15. It then becomes clear that this individual has a low intelligence (the bottom 2.5% of the population). Similarly, we might need to know the level at which people's depression is so bad that it would be advisable to hospitalise them for treatment. In developing such norm-referenced tests, it is important to select a large standardisation samples that are truly representative of the population on which the test will be used. The scores of this sample on the test are then transformed into one of a number of gradation systems:

- *Percentiles and percentile ranks*, in which scores are graded in terms of the percentage of the sample that achieve at levels below the score in question. For example, the score that is marked as the 40th percentile is the score below which 40% of the standardisation sample fall (ranked in terms of scores on the test).
- *Standard scores*, in which the scores are transformed to a standard normal distribution with a mean of 0 and standard deviation of 1, and presented as z-scores (see Tutorial 6).
- *T-scores*, in which the scores are transformed to a normal distribution with a mean of 50 and standard deviation of 10.
- *Stanines*, in which the scores are transformed into a distribution with 9 points. The mean is 5 and standard deviation is 2.

Constructing norms

To illustrate standardisation, the summed scores on the 6-item marijuana attitude scale will be used. Figure 12.4 shows these calculations for a small sub-sample of our sample of 64 respondents. The first step in constructing T-scores and Stanines is to convert the raw scores into z-scores, which requires the mean and standard deviation of the sample's scores. Column Q of the spreadsheet shows the calculated z-scores for some of the data. The Excel instruction on how to get the score for any particular score (i) is shown in cell T3. The T score is found using the formula, $x = (z \times \sigma) + \mu$, substituting $\mu = 50$ and $\sigma = 10$. The Stanines are found in the same way through substituting $\mu = 5$ and $\sigma = 2$. These are illustrated in columns R and S on the spreadsheet. The percentile rank of given score (percentage of the sample that fall below that score) is found from z tables.

	A	P	Q	R	S	T
1	ID	TOTAL	Z	T	Stanine	Excel instructions
2	P1	20	-0.8953	41.047	3.2094	z scores:
3	P2	30	0.3896	53.896	5.7791	=(Pi-26.968)/7.783
4	P3	24	-0.3813	46.187	4.2373	
5	P4	17	-1.2807	37.193	2.4385	T scores:
6	P5	38	1.4174	64.174	7.8349	=(Qi*10)+50
7	P6	40	1.6744	66.744	8.3488	
8	P7	25	-0.2529	47.471	4.4943	Stanines:
9	P8	22	-0.6383	43.617	3.7234	=(Qi*2)+5
65	P64	27	0.0041	50.041	5.0082	
66						
67	Mean	26.968				
68	St. Dev.	7.7833				

Figure 12.4 Microsoft® Excel spreadsheet illustrating calculation of z-scores, T-scores, and Stanines

Use of norms

Norms enable us to interpret an individual's score on a test. By comparing the score to the norms, we can discern whether the individual is 'average' or 'exceptional', and how high or low the score is relative to the population. Further, norms can be associated with a diagnosis so critical norm values can be established for the test user.

Worked example

The following example describes the development of a scale that will measure perceptions of the causes of industrial action. The perception of interest is the degree to which either management or the workers/trade unions are blamed.

Development of the scale items

The researcher starts by considering a range of popular media representations of industrial conflict – in newspapers, magazines, radio, and television. From this a domain of behaviours is outlined. The content of this domain is specified as (i) politics, (ii) management–worker relations, (iii) working conditions, (iv) money, (v) exploitation, (vi) sector interests, and (vii) negative perceptions. As far as possible, the manifestations of these behaviours are expressed as management-blame and union-blame. Table 12.2 presents the grid specifying the content and manifestations of the domain of behaviour sampled.

Table 12.2 The sampling domain for the causes of industrial action scale

	Politics	Worker–management relations	Working conditions	Money	Exploitation	Sector interests	Negative perceptions
Union–blame	The unions' political agendas	The unions failing to foster communication between workers and management.	Workers' failure to acknowledge the benefits of employment	Workers' unrealistic wage expectations	Workers' desire for more money for the minimum amount of work	The union seeking to justify their existence to the workers	Workers' lack of understanding of the broad economic constraints
Management–blame	Management trying to curtail the power of unions	Management's refusal to negotiate with the workers	Workers having real grievances about their working conditions	Management's greed for higher profits	Workers reacting against their exploitation	Management neglecting the interests of workers	Management seeing workers as dispensable and easily replaceable

The scale was designed so that the respondents had to indicate the degree to which they agreed or disagreed that the item was a cause of industrial conflict by marking a box on a 7-point Likert scale, anchored by 1 = strongly disagree and 7 = strongly agree. The full list of items appears on the next page.

Industrial conflict is caused by:

Q1   The unions failing to foster communication between workers and management.
Q2   Workers' failure to acknowledge the benefits of employment.
Q3   Workers having real grievances about their working conditions.
Q4   Management's greed for higher profits.
Q5   The unions' political agendas.
Q6   Workers' unrealistic wage expectations.
Q7   Workers' desire for more money for the minimum amount of work.
Q8   Workers' lack of understanding of the broad economic constraints.
Q9   Management's refusal to negotiate with the workers.
Q10 The union seeking to justify their existence to the workers.
Q11 Management neglecting the interests of workers.
Q12 Management trying to curtail the power of unions.
Q13 Workers reacting against their exploitation.
Q14 Management seeing workers as dispensable and easily replaceable.

The sample

The researcher was interested in the beliefs of people who would be working in management. She thus decided to use as her test sample students studying for degrees in human resource management. Responses from a sample of 415 students were collected. All these responses were quantified, and entered into an Excel spreadsheet, which can be found on the accompanying CD.

Test for reliability and item analysis

The researcher immediately put this data into an item-analysis programme. The results are given in Figure 12.5.

STATISTICA: Reliability and Item Analysis
File Edit View Analysis Graphs Options Window Help

58.03482

Columns Rows

Summary for scale: Mean=63.3557 Std.Dv.=8.26737 Valid N:402

Continue... Cronbach alpha: .559805 Standardized alpha: .557334
Average inter-item corr.: .089020

variable	Mean if deleted	Var. if deleted	StDv. if deleted	Itm-Totl Correl.	Alpha if deleted
Q1	58.03482	61.53610	7.844495	.207924	.542432
Q2	58.00497	64.80594	8.050214	.052471	.571801
Q3	58.32836	61.90213	7.867791	.207625	.542631
Q4	59.47264	57.75174	7.599456	.298558	.522009
Q5	58.14925	63.37075	7.960575	.137840	.555041
Q6	58.91791	64.58778	8.036653	.039671	.577308
Q7	58.96269	61.85184	7.864594	.129135	.560369
Q8	58.38308	63.51992	7.969938	.102028	.563021
Q9	59.89801	58.00203	7.615907	.327126	.517103
Q10	58.66916	61.54974	7.845365	.202823	.543380
Q11	59.66916	56.56467	7.520949	.395527	.502273
Q12	59.10696	59.70746	7.727060	.304315	.524401
Q13	58.78856	59.87818	7.738099	.263152	.531285
Q14	59.23881	55.86337	7.474180	.325843	.513840

Figure 12.5 Item analysis of the industrial action scale, without item reversals

While looking at these results, the researcher noticed that there were a large number of items that had item-total correlations of less than 0.20. She then realised that she had not reversed the items for which a high score (strongly agree) indicated union blame. She reversed these scores using the formula, New score = 8 – Old score, and redid the analysis. Figure 12.6 provides the results.

STATISTICA: Reliability and Item Analysis

File Edit View Analysis Graphs Options Window Help

45.59204

Columns | Rows

Summary for scale: Mean=50.6194 Std.Dv.=10.4374 Valid N:402

Continue... Cronbach alpha: .752479 Standardized alpha: .747985
Average inter-item corr.: .180151

variable	Mean if deleted	Var. if deleted	StDv. if deleted	Itm-Totl Correl.	Alpha if deleted
Q3	45.59204	94.8684	9.74004	.452217	.730522
Q4	46.73632	92.7812	9.63230	.404473	.733937
Q9	47.16169	94.2550	9.70850	.396795	.734890
Q11	46.93283	91.8835	9.58559	.484445	.725625
Q12	46.37065	97.6213	9.88035	.331726	.741477
Q13	46.05224	91.4027	9.56048	.527258	.721685
Q14	46.50249	89.7923	9.47588	.445521	.729029
RQ1	47.94030	117.1755	10.82477	-.342437	.799273
RQ2	47.97015	93.6906	9.67939	.453584	.729506
RQ5	47.82587	96.7757	9.83764	.377311	.737396
RQ6	47.05721	92.4519	9.61519	.442718	.729819
RQ7	47.01244	92.0123	9.59230	.423103	.731790
RQ8	47.59204	93.6594	9.67778	.442044	.730457
RQ10	47.30597	98.3915	9.91925	.288486	.745560

Figure 12.6 Item analysis of the causes of industrial action scale with items reversed

The Cronbach alpha has jumped to a respectable coefficient, $\alpha = 0.75$. However, the reversed score of question 1 (RQ1) appears problematic. Its item-total correlation coefficient is negative, and the alpha coefficient would improve if it were removed. A careful consideration of the item *'The unions failing to foster communication between workers and management'* led to a suggestion as to why it was perceived as problematic by the respondents. It is possible that there was an implicit second question within the item – whether or not it is the responsibility of unions to foster such communication. This differs from the core issue of whether it is the failure of communication that is a cause of industrial action. The researcher consequently decided to remove this question from the scale. The final Cronbach alpha coefficient was $\alpha = 0.80$, with all item-total correlation coefficients being greater than 0.20.

> Use SPSS® to compute the Cronbach alpha coefficient for the scale, with Item 1 removed.

Activity 12.6

Calculating the total scores

Each respondent's score on the scale was calculated by summing their scores on Q3, Q4, Q9, Q11, Q12, Q13, Q14, and the reversed scores RQ2, RQ5, RQ6, RQ7, RQ8, RQ10. However, a number of the respondents (17) had left out at least one question. The researcher decided to replace missing responses with the mean of all other responses (i.e. construct a weighted total), with the stipulation that no more than 3 items can be missing. If a respondent has more than 3 questions unanswered, he or she will be excluded from the data file. These total scores were calculated for each individual.

Test for validity

The researcher had also required the respondents to complete a scale measuring political conservatism, as it would be expected that people who are politically conservative would be more sympathetic to management than to trade unions. On this scale the higher the score, the more conservative the individual. These scores were correlated with the total scores of the developed scale using the Pearson Product-Moment Correlation test. The resultant correlation coefficient was $r(408) = -0.512, p < 0.0001$. This strong negative correlation confirms that the more politically conservative the individual the less blame they attributed to management for industrial action. This test of convergent validity indicates that the scale has construct validity. A final test of construct validity was done using criterion groups. The researcher administered the scale to a group of 12 trade union members and compared their scores to a group of 12 managers. A t-test comparison was statistically significant ($t(22) = 2.351; p < 0.0281$), with the mean of the trade union members being higher than that of the managers. Thus this scale appears to be a good measure of the perceptions of industrial conflict.

Summary

1. The construction of a scale requires a clear definition of the domain of behaviours or sentiments to be sampled. Items or questions are then developed to represent this domain.

2. Item response formats can vary from alternative-choice and multiple-choice options to forms of continuous rating. The most common types of rating are the Likert scale and the bipolar adjectives scale.

3. The phrasing of items is important. Items must contain only one question, and their meaning should be unambiguous. They should also be phrased in ways that limit the likelihood of a socially desirable response. Within the scale, some of the items should approach the question from the opposite sense to prevent the use of response sets.

4. The constructed scale must be evaluated – to check on the quality of the items, and the reliability and validity of the scale. To do this, the scale is administered to a standardisation sample that is representative of the population on which the scale will be used.

5. Norm-referenced tests make it possible to compare the score of an individual on the test with a set of established norms. This is particularly appropriate for diagnostic tests, and achievement and ability tests. Such tests require that the standardisation sample be carefully selected to represent the desired population. Norm-referenced tests generally set the norms in terms of percentiles, z-scores or T-scores.

Exercises

1. Construct a short scale of no more than 10–12 items to measure students' attitudes to sharing accommodation with someone who is known to be HIV positive. Set up a content/manifestation grid to help ensure that the domain is sampled. Think carefully about the type of response scaling you will use.

2. A researcher has constructed a scale with 10 items. The table on the next page gives the results of an analysis providing the Cronbach alpha of this data. The item statistics are also provided. On the basis of this analysis, indicate which items you would suggest dropping from the scale. Give your reasons for this decision.

Summary for scale: Mean = 32.5417   Std. Dv. = 7.70026 Valid N: 72
Cronbach alpha: 0.721950   Standardised alpha: 0.730045
Average inter-item correlation: 0.216908

	Mean if deleted	Var. if deleted	St. dv. if deleted	Item-total correl.	Alpha if deleted
Item1	31.02778	52.08256	7.216825	.359632	.705444
Item2	28.54167	47.30382	6.877777	.412865	.694774
Item3	28.11111	49.07099	7.005069	.366284	.702515
Item4	30.37500	51.56771	7.181066	.403496	.700653
Item5	29.43056	44.52296	6.672553	.562439	.667590
Item6	29.22222	46.64506	6.829719	.481164	.683222
Item7	28.52778	47.94368	6.924137	.498486	.683238
Item8	28.95833	51.45660	7.173326	.216782	.727521
Item9	28.56944	53.05073	7.283593	.124920	.744308
Item10	30.11111	44.59877	6.678231	.477382	.682571

3. a) A class of 360 students took a multiple-choice examination. Each examination item had four possible answers, of which only one was correct. On the first of the items, the following number of people in the class marked the correct answer: Item1 = 62; Item2 = 200; Item3 = 305. Calculate the item-difficulty index for each and comment on the facility of each item.

    b) On the basis of the marks on the whole examination, the class was divided into four. The top and bottom 25% of the class were extracted. The number of each of these sub-samples endorsing each of the answer choices is presented for three items. The answer with the asterisk is the correct answer. Calculate the item discrimination index for the three items and comment on whether the items should be retained or not.

ITEM 15	Alternatives			
	A	B	C*	D
High scorers	38	16	12	24
Low scorers	23	22	30	15

ITEM 22	Alternatives			
	A*	B	C	D
High scorers	50	14	9	17
Low scorers	23	10	42	15

ITEM 15	Alternatives			
	A	B	C	D*
High scorers	6	2	2	80
Low scorers	66	15	9	8

4. A newly developed scale is designed to measure masculinity. The researchers perform a number of evaluative tests on the scale using a large representative sample of men. These are listed below. In each case indicate what psychometric property is evaluated, and what it indicates about the scale.

   a) The sample were given this scale as well as a well-established test that also measures masculinity. The scores on the two tests are correlated.

   b) The sample was given the test twice, three weeks apart. The scores on the test on the two administrations are correlated.

   c) The scale was given to a group of monks and to a group of rugby players, and the scores of the two groups compared.

   d) The sample was given this scale as well as an established scale for androgeny.

   e) The sample's scores on the test were analysed to find the Cronbach alpha coefficient and item-total statistics.

TUTORIAL

13

Statistical power

Lance Lachenicht

After studying this tutorial, you should be able to:
- Understand the analogy between criminal court procedure and statistical test procedure.
- Understand Type I and Type II errors, and relate them to statistical power theory.
- Understand the factors that determine the power of a statistical test.
- Calculate effect size.
- Calculate power for three varieties of the *t*-test.
- Understand the factors that influence the choice of a sample size.

When all is said and done, the essence of science is the requirement that researchers who propose a theory (e.g. the theory that tea-drinking is a source of insomnia) put that theory to empirical test. *Statistical hypothesis testing* is one such 'formal' testing procedure (see Tutorial 8). Its structure is similar to the procedure in a criminal trial (see Kraemer & Thiemann, 1987). In the analogy with a criminal trial, the researchers are the prosecutors, the collection of data is the trial procedure itself, and the statistical test plays the role of the judge deciding the verdict: true or false.

The central principle is that the researchers' theory is considered false until demonstrated beyond 'reasonable' doubt to be true, just as an accused is presumed innocent in law. So, until the evidence demonstrates the dangers of drinking tea, we assume that it is safe to drink tea. All of this is expressed as an assumption of the truth of the *null hypothesis*, which is the contradiction of the researchers' theory (usually expressed in the form of a statement that there is *no difference* between two or more groups) (see Tutorial 8). Thus the null hypothesis in our researchers' theory is that tea-drinking has no effect on sleep patterns. What is considered a 'reasonable doubt' about the truth of the null hypothesis is called a *significance level*. (The significance level is sometimes known as the *alpha level* in a study.) By convention (i.e. simply by common agreement among researchers), a reasonable level of doubt about the truth of a theory is one chance in twenty (5%, or a probability of 0.05) or, occasionally, one chance in a hundred (1%, or a probability of 0.01) that the theory is false.

Significance level and significance testing are *not* the same as practical or theoretical significance. Once again the analogy with a criminal trial can help explain this. Some criminal trials are about important matters (such as murder or other serious crimes) and others are about relatively trivial crimes (such as failure to pay a parking ticket). A prosecution team may prove beyond reasonable doubt that someone failed to pay their parking tickets, but that proof would still not make this a serious crime. However, proving beyond reasonable doubt that someone was a murderer would not only be a successful prosecution but also an important one. Significance in statistical testing is about the trial process – the 'proving beyond reasonable doubt' process – and not about the importance of the issue being tested (e.g. the relative triviality of parking tickets versus the seriousness of murder).

*Significance level and significance testing are **not** the same as practical or theoretical significance.*

Error and statistical tests

Criminal trials may end with erroneous decisions. These are of two kinds: an innocent person may be falsely found guilty, and a guilty person may be falsely found innocent. The system of justice tends to favour the latter error over the former, just as significance testing tends to favour the null hypothesis over the researchers' hypothesis. In significance testing, rejecting the null hypothesis when it is true, which is the error of credulity, the error of taking something seriously that is mere coincidence, is known as a *Type I error*. The alternative error, accepting the null hypothesis when it is false, is the error of scepticism. The error of scepticism, of treating as a matter of luck something that genuinely calls for explanation, is known as a *Type II error*.

The philosopher/mathematician Pascal's famous wager about the existence of God can be seen as a meditation on the difference between Type I and Type II errors. Given the null hypothesis that

Type I error – rejecting the null hypothesis when it is true.
Type II error – failing to reject the null hypothesis when it is false.

You may find it useful to review Activity 8.3 at this stage.

God does not exist, believing that there is a God when there is not, would be a Type I error – if there is no God the null hypothesis is true and the believer errs by being credulous. Failure to believe that there is a God when there is would be a Type II error, for if there is a God, the null hypothesis is false and the atheist errs by being sceptical. Pascal argued that the sceptical error would be more disastrous in its consequences than the credulous error, and therefore drew the conclusion that one should believe in God. Similarly, a statistician may reflect on the consequences of Type I and Type II errors in choosing a significance or *alpha* level, usually with less profound considerations in mind! The situation can be represented in the form of Table 13.1.

Table 13.1 Types of error in hypothesis testing

	H_0 true	H_0 false
H_0 accepted	Correct	Type II error $\{\beta\}$
H_0 rejected	Type I error $\{\alpha\}$	Correct

The probability of making a Type I error is α, and the probability of making a Type II error is β.

The probability of making a Type I error in any particular significance test is *alpha* (α), the significance level. The probability of making a Type II error is *beta* (β). To summarise: Type I errors concern the event of finding a difference that is not there; Type II errors concern the event of not finding a difference that is there. For a variety of reasons, investigators have given much more importance to Type I errors than to Type II errors. The high cost of research and the simple principle that we should plan a research project carefully require that researchers start to pay more attention to Type II errors.

Power is the probability of correctly rejecting a false null hypothesis, i.e. 1 – β.

The *power* of a test is intimately related to Type II errors. *Power* is defined as the probability of correctly rejecting a false null hypothesis, and since the probability of mistakenly accepting a false null hypothesis is β, the inverse or complementary probability (i.e. the probability of correctly rejecting a false null hypothesis) is $1 - \beta$. An experiment with more power has a greater chance of rejecting a false null hypothesis than does an experiment with less power.

When we run statistical significance tests we know the probability of a Type I error (it is the alpha level we have chosen), but the probability of making a Type II error is not known. However, we can often estimate β, the Type II error rate, or power ($1 - \beta$), from other information.

What determines the power of an investigation?

Power is determined by four factors:
1. the probability of a Type I error
2. the true state of affairs guessed at by the alternative hypothesis
3. the sample size
4. the particular test to be employed.

The probability of a Type I error

The way in which the probability of a Type I error affects power is best illustrated graphically. Think about the two distributions in Figure 13.1. The distribution to the left (labelled H_0) represents the sampling distribution of the mean when the null hypothesis is true and μ (the true population mean) equals μ_0. The distribution on the right represents the sampling distribution of the mean that would arise if the null hypothesis were false and μ (the true population mean) equals μ_1. Where the distribution on the right is placed depends on what the value of μ_1 happens to be. Alpha (α), the probability of a Type I error, is represented by the shaded area of the H_0 distribution, assuming that we are using a one-tailed test. (For a two-tailed test, the shaded area would represent $\frac{\alpha}{2}$.) This area contains the sample means that would result in significant values of t, for example.

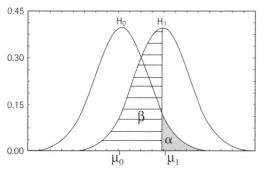

Power diagrams such as Figure 13.1 are conceptual/ hypothetical aids, and not distributions of observed data.

Figure 13.1 An illustration of the sampling distributions of the mean proposed by the null and alternate hypotheses

The second distribution (H_1) represents the sampling distribution of the mean when H_0 is false and the true mean is μ_1. From the figure, it is clear that even when the null hypothesis is false, many of the sample means will fall to the left of the critical value of alpha, causing us to fail to reject the null hypothesis, so making a Type II error. The probability of this error (β) is shown by the striped area of Figure 13.1. However, when the null hypothesis is false and the sample mean falls to the right of the value, we will correctly reject the null hypothesis. The probability of correctly rejecting the null hypothesis is what we mean by *power* and is the unshaded area of the H_1 distribution (remember that the distributions overlap, so the unshaded area includes the area in H_1 which the α portion of H_0 obscures).

Activity 13.1

Consider a two-tailed independent samples t-test ($\alpha = 0.05$) where we find $\bar{x}_1 = 17$, $\bar{x}_2 = 20$, $s_1 = 5$, $s_2 = 6$, $n_1 = n_2 = 16$. Is this difference significant, against H_0: $\mu_1 = \mu_2$?

Assuming that all other values remain constant,
a) What value of $(\bar{x}_1 - \bar{x}_2)$ would make it significant?
b) What values of n_1 and n_2 would make it significant?
c) What value of α would make it significant?
d) What values of s_1 and s_2 would make it significant?
   (*Hint:* For each of (a) to (d), you need to substitute different values for the statistics in question.)

As α increases (becomes less strict), power increases.

Figure 13.1 helps us understand why power is a function of α. If we are willing to increase alpha (from 0.05, to 0.1, for example) the cut-off point will move to the left, thus both decreasing β and increasing the probability of a Type I error. In most real research, the researcher is not willing to increase alpha (and most journals will not publish research with a high alpha), so manipulating alpha is not a practical strategy for increasing the power of a study.

The true state of affairs guessed at by the alternative hypothesis
Power also depends upon the true state of affairs on which the alternative hypothesis speculates. More precisely, power depends upon the difference between the mean under the null hypothesis, μ_0, and the mean under the alternative hypothesis, μ_1 (i.e. $\mu_0 - \mu_1$). This can be seen by comparing Figure 13.1 and Figure 13.2.

In Figure 13.2, the distance between μ_0 and μ_1 has been increased and this has produced a large increase in power (the unshaded area under the H_1 curve). This should not be surprising, since what we are saying is that we have a better chance of finding a difference if that difference is large. If the researchers' hypothesis is that two groups are different but only by a very small amount, the danger of a Type II error is very great. If (to return to our tea-drinking study) tea-drinking does indeed cause insomnia but only by ten minutes a night on average, then, because of the smallness of the difference, it will be *As the true effect* very easy to accept the null hypothesis even though it is in reality *increases in size,* false. However, if tea-drinking causes insomnia by as much as two *power increases.* hours per night, it will be easy to refute the null hypothesis.

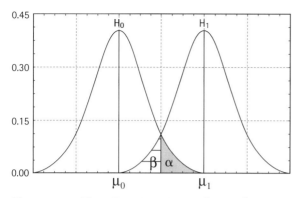

Figure 13.2 The effect that altering $(\mu_0 - \mu_1)$ has on β

The sample size

The relationship between sample size and power is linked to the relationship between the variance of the sampling distribution $(\sigma_{\bar{x}}^2)$ and power. This is because the variance of a sampling distribution will decrease as the sample size increases. Comparing Figure 13.3 with Figure 13.1 illustrates what happens to the two sampling distributions (H_0 and H_1) when we increase n or decrease σ^2. As the variance of the two distributions decreases, so the overlap between them becomes smaller, which means that power increases (the unshaded area under H_1). In terms of our tea-drinking example, our study will have greater power if we study two samples (an experimental and a control group) of 100 participants rather than two samples of 20 participants.

As n increases, so power increases. Of all the factors that affect power, sample size (n) is the easiest to manipulate.

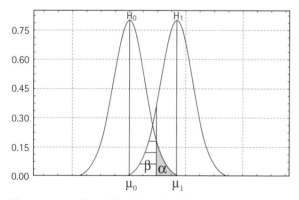

Figure 13.3 The effect that altering sample size has on β

Of all the factors that affect power, sample size (n) is the easiest to manipulate. This means that practical attempts to increase power are generally concerned with the consequences of varying sample size.

A large pharmaceutical company of some impropriety conducts a study in which they administer a daily dose of 5 milligrams of Phlogiston to a sample of obese patients, and a sample of control patients. They find that the average difference after the intervention is 1 kilogram, $s_1 = 50$, and $s_2 = 55$. Since they have already invested a lot of capital in the drug, they must find results that show this difference is statistically significant. They do this by adding more subjects. How many do they need? ($\alpha = 0.05$) What does this tell you about the dependence of significant findings on sample size?

The particular test to be employed

Tests designed for continuous measurements tend to be more powerful than those designed for categorical or ordinal measurements.

The choice of statistical test also affects power. The power of statistical tests is a complex subject beyond the scope of this tutorial. However, you should note that tests designed for continuous measurements tend to be more powerful than tests designed for categorised data. Further, parametric tests, such as *t*-tests and ANOVA, tend to be more powerful than non-parametric tests (such as the Wilcoxon and Mann-Whitney tests: see Tutorial 20), even though they make more assumptions about the data.

Effect size

We have established that power is partly determined by the degree of overlap between sampling distributions under the null and the alternative hypothesis. A widely used measure of the distance between μ_0 and μ_1 (the population means under the null hypothesis and the alternative hypothesis) is called d, the *effect size*. Effect size is defined as follows (when we are dealing with continuous measures):

Equation 13.1

$$d = \frac{\mu_0 - \mu_1}{\sigma}$$

This formula means that d is a measure of the degree to which μ_0 and μ_1 differ in terms of the standard deviation of the parent population. Notice that the formula for d does not include the sample size n, so d can be used in calculations to help us find an appropriate sample size. Notice also that to calculate d we will need either to know the population standard deviation or be able to estimate it. The formula for d is similar to the formula for a z-score (see Tutorial 6). Just as z-scores standardise differently scaled measurements into standard deviation units so that they can be compared, so d standardises research effects into standard deviation units so that they can be compared.

Effect size (d) is a standardised index; in the case of tests on means, it expresses the difference between the means in standard deviation units.

By itself, the formula for d does not tell us how to interpret a particular value of d. Cohen (1988) offers some conventional values of d for small, medium, and large effect sizes, which we have amended slightly in Table 13.2.

The right-hand column of Table 13.2, labelled '% of overlap of distributions', records the degree to which the distributions such as those shown in Figures 13.1, 13.2, and 13.3 overlap. This means that when d = 0.5, the distributions overlap by 67%.

Table 13.2 Notional levels of effect size

Effect size	d	% of overlap of distributions
Very small	< 0.10	> 92
Small	0.20	85
Medium	0.50	67
Large	0.80	53
Very large	> 1	< 45

Source: Adapted from Cohen (1988)

Activity 13.3

In order to 'tie' Cohen's notional levels of effect size to 'real-world' data, collect information about the following group differences, and attempt to calculate the 'degree of overlap', assuming a normal distribution (use your information to estimate μ and σ). All of the information can be found quite easily on the Internet:

a) the average weights for adult rugby players, and adult male ballet dancers
b) the heights of professional jockeys in South Africa, and male basketball players in the USA NBA league
c) the average weight of men who are 6 feet tall, at ages 20 and 40
d) the average fuel consumption for cars that have 1600cc engines, and those that have 1300cc engines.

The 'trial' strategy and power

The fact that statistical tests only control Type I error (this is what they are designed to do) and do not control Type II error at all means that statistical tests can be very misleading. If α is 0.05, and the null hypothesis is true, then a statistical test is defined in such a way that the chance of a Type I error will be, at most, 5%. However, the Type II error is not controlled by a statistical test (it is not part of the statistical testing procedure), and theoretically could be as high as 95%! (See the large Type II error shown in Figure 13.1.) So, if the null hypothesis is false, statistical tests may not reject it with a very high probability. Hunter and Schmidt (1990) offer several (real) case studies where the Type II error rate is as high as 35%, i.e. the theorist's hypothesis is actually true but not reported as 'significant' in 35% of the cases. Just as criminal trials may often find guilty people innocent (and are designed to do so in order to protect the really innocent), so statistical tests are designed to avoid Type I errors and may sacrifice true hypotheses in order to do so.

Statistical tests are designed to avoid Type I errors and may sacrifice uncovering true alternative hypotheses in order to do so.

Researchers ought
to report **confidence
intervals**, as well as
results of statistical
tests.

There are two solutions (that perhaps ought to be carried out in parallel with the significance test) to the problem of uncontrolled Type II error. Firstly, researchers ought to report *confidence intervals* (which were discussed in Tutorial 7), as well as statistical tests. Confidence intervals express statistics (e.g. differences between means) as a range of possible values, and the size of this range is an indicator of the confidence we have in the decision. Secondly, researchers ought to pay great attention to the planning of their studies, making sure that their research plan has sufficient *power* to detect real differences between groups. In the analogy with criminal trials, the prosecution similarly has to plan the case against an accused very carefully if it is to succeed in securing a conviction.

Researchers ought to
pay great attention
to planning their
studies to ensure
adequate **power**.

The researchers, playing the role of the prosecution in the trial of a hypothesis, must first have an adequate case for bringing the theory to trial. Just as it is unreasonable for a prosecutor to bring someone to trial for murder when there is no evidence that the person committed the crime, so it is unreasonable for a researcher to test a hypothesis for which there is no preliminary evidence. Preliminary evidence that researchers commonly consider includes literature reviews of relevant research areas, case histories, pilot studies, theoretical considerations, and the like. Researchers, just like real prosecutors, must decide on the basis of the preliminary evidence whether the case is important enough, or the preliminary evidence convincing enough, to bring the hypothesis to trial, i.e. to test the hypothesis.

Power calculations
should be deter-
mined before data is
collected.

The researchers must also formulate the trial strategy by which they propose to put the hypothesis to the test. They must decide what design to use, which measure of response or which dependent variable to use, the number and timing of measurements per subject, which statistical test to use, and how many subjects to sample. Now it is fairly obvious that all these decisions are going to affect how strong the evidence is likely to be and whether it will be convincing *beyond a reasonable doubt*. The strength of the evidence is called the *power* of the trial (i.e. the probability of correctly rejecting the null hypothesis).

Power calculations
are a central aspect
of good study
design.

In planning a study, it is possible and advisable to determine the necessary *power* of the study if it is to support a hypothesis beyond reasonable doubt. For the computation of power, it is necessary to have developed from the preliminary evidence (pilot studies, research reported in the literature, etc.) a *critical effect size* – a measure of how strong the effect must be to have any practical or theoretical importance. This is the minimum effect size d that the researcher will consider to be of practical importance. In our tea-drinking example, it is possible for tea-drinking to cause a loss of sleep of only a few minutes duration, and it is possible for tea-

The **critical effect
size** is a measure of
how strong the
effect must be to
have any practical
significance.

drinking to cause sleeplessness lasting hours. The researchers must decide what loss of sleeping time is sufficient for the hypothesis to have any importance. Clearly, the choice of a critical effect size has to be based on the researchers' understanding and knowledge of the field, supplemented by any preliminary evidence that is available. It will also reflect the characteristics of the population being studied (e.g. people sleep less as they grow older, so the critical effect size will have to be larger for a sample of older people, and smaller for a sample of younger people). From all of this, it should be obvious that, just as a prosecutor cannot institute a trial without evidence, so it is not possible to plan a powerful study without any background or preliminary information.

Three sources of estimates of effect size (d):
1. Prior research
2. Assessment of practical importance.
3. Cohen's conventions.

Power calculations

Power calculations are important if we are to determine how large our sample should be to prove a hypothesis beyond a reasonable doubt. These must start with an estimate of the critical effect size, d. There are three ways of estimating the critical effect size:

1. *Prior research.* On the basis of previous research we may be able to obtain at least an approximation of d. From such earlier studies we may be able to estimate population means and variances and use these to calculate $\mu_1 - \mu_0$ and σ, and thus calculate d.

2. *Personal assessment of what difference is important.* In many cases a researcher will be able to say something like 'I'm interested in a difference of at least 20 points between μ_0 and μ_1'. Anything less than this is not seen as having practical importance. Suppose a researcher is asked to investigate a procedure that is said to raise the IQs of disadvantaged children. The researcher may decide that anything less than an increase of 10 IQ points is not worthwhile. We already know that the standard deviation of IQ scores is 15, so this researcher is looking for a *d* value of 10/15 or 0.67. We know that $\sigma = 15$, $\mu_1 - \mu_0 = 10$, and we substitute this into the equation for *d*:

$$d = \frac{\mu_1 - \mu_0}{\sigma} = \frac{10}{15} = 0.67$$

3. *Use Cohen's conventions.* The researcher may decide to look for a small, medium, or large effect as defined by Cohen (see Table 13.2). If our IQ researcher had decided to look for a small effect in terms of Cohen's criteria (0.2), this would amount to searching for a difference of 3 IQ points. We know that d = 0.2, and we know $\sigma = 15$, and we substitute this into the equation for d to find $\mu_1 - \mu_0$:

$$0.2 = \frac{\mu_1 - \mu_0}{15}, \text{ so } \mu_1 - \mu_0 = 15 \times 0.2 = 3$$

To calculate power, d is not sufficient on its own. The effect size must be combined with the sample size in order to calculate power. This combination yields a statistic called delta (δ). Delta is calculated differently for each statistical test, so we express it in a generic form as:

$$\delta = d[f(n)]$$

In this formula, $f(n)$ represents some function of the sample size that will differ from one statistical procedure to the next. Once delta has been calculated, it can be used to find power in Table A1.3 of Appendix 1.

We will consider power calculations for the *t*-test below; calculations for the other methods and tests outlined in this text are too complex, and we recommend you to Cohen's (1988) authoritative work for details.

You will need different formulas for each of four possible cases of the *t*-test. Recall from Tutorial 9 three types of *t*-test: single sample, independent means, and matched sample. The fourth case of the *t*-test arises when the independent samples *t*-test has two unequal samples.

Power calculations for the one-sample *t*-test

In the case of a single sample *t*-test, the formulas you will need for power calculations are given in Table 13.3. If you wanted to test the hypothesis that students have a higher IQ than the general population, you would use the one-sample *t*-test. You would need to randomly select a sample of students (say 25) and measure their IQ scores. Let us say that you decide upon a critical effect size of 5 IQ points between the students' average IQ score and that of the general population. So $\mu_1 = 105$, while $\mu_0 = 100$, and $\sigma = 15$ (the known mean and standard deviation of the IQ test). Therefore:

$$d = \frac{\mu_1 - \mu_0}{\sigma} = \frac{105 - 100}{15} = 0.33$$

It is now possible to calculate power, δ:

$$\delta = d \times \sqrt{n}$$

$$= 0.33 \times \sqrt{25} = 0.33 \times 5 = 1.65$$

Table 13.3 Power calculations for the one-sample *t*-test

σ	d	n	δ
Estimate of standard deviation of population	$\dfrac{\mu_1 - \mu_0}{\sigma}$	Size of the single sample	$d \times \sqrt{n}$

Although you expect the students to have higher IQ scores than the general population, you decide to use a two-tailed test at $\alpha = 0.05$ to protect against unexpected events. Using the power table (Appendix 1), you look up $\delta = 1.65$ at $\alpha = 0.05$ and find that power is between 0.36 and 0.4. By linear interpolation (see Box 6.1), power is roughly 0.38. This means that if the null hypothesis (that there is no difference between the IQ of the general population and that of students) is *false*, and the student IQ really is 105, then only 38% of the time will you expect to find a *significant* difference. Turning this around, we can say that 62% of the time you will make a Type II error.

Since you have been far-sighted enough to calculate power before running your experiment, you can take corrective action and increase your sample size. How big should your sample of students be? This will depend upon what level of power you desire. If you decide upon a level of power of 0.8 (i.e. $1 - \beta = 0.8$) you can use the power table in Appendix 1 to find delta (δ), by scanning the table in the reverse direction to the way we used it in the calculation immediately above. We find that for power $= 0.8$, $\delta = 2.8$. We now have enough information to calculate n:

$$\delta = d \times \sqrt{n}, \text{ so } \frac{\delta}{d} = \sqrt{n}, \text{ and } \left(\frac{\delta}{d}\right)^2 = n$$

$$n = \left(\frac{2.8}{0.33}\right)^2$$

$$= 71.9$$

This means that for power $= 0.8$ you will need a sample size of 72 students.

Generally, a power level of 0.8 is reasonable – to obtain higher levels of power requires substantial increases in sample size. To illustrate, consider that for power $= 0.99$ you would need a sample size of 159 subjects, which would considerably increase your costs.

> Generally, a power level of 0.8 is reasonable – to obtain much higher levels of power requires large increases in n.

Power calculations for the two–sample (independent) t-test, $n_1 = n_2$

Here we assume that the two samples have the same standard deviation and that we can find a single value to estimate that standard deviation. The formula for delta is also slightly modified, as shown in Table 13.4

Suppose we are comparing two treatments for depression. We manage to find 50 depressed patients and we have divided them into two equal groups, each receiving a different treatment. We ask our subjects to count the number of times suicidal ideation occurs to them each month. We expect that the difference between the two

Table 13.4 Power calculations for the two-sample *t*-test, $n_1 = n_2$

σ	d	n	δ
Assume $\sigma_1 = \sigma_2 = \sigma$	$\dfrac{\mu_2 - \mu_1}{\sigma}$	Size of each of the (equal) sample sizes	$d \times \sqrt{\dfrac{n}{2}}$

treatments will be 5 suicidal thoughts each month. From previous research we expect a standard deviation of approximately 10 suicidal thoughts each month. From this information:

$$d = \frac{\mu_2 - \mu_1}{\sigma} = \frac{5}{10} = 0.5$$

This is a moderate effect, in terms of Table 13.2. Given that we have 25 observations in each of our two groups, it is now possible to calculate δ:

Equation 13.4

$$\delta = d \times \sqrt{\frac{n}{2}}$$

$$= 0.5 \times \sqrt{\frac{25}{2}} = 0.5 \times 3.54 = 1.77$$

From the power table in Appendix 1, we see that $\delta = 1.77$ with a two-tailed test at $\alpha = 0.05$ will yield a power of approximately 0.43. This means that our attempt to compare the two treatments for depression on a critical effect size of 5 suicidal thoughts a month has a 43% chance of actually rejecting the null hypothesis if it is false (i.e. a 57% chance of making a Type II error).

If you cannot see how to transform the formula for δ into a formula for n, see Tutorial 24.

In this experiment, how many subjects would we need for a power of 0.8? From the power table in Appendix 1 we see that a power of 0.8 will require $\delta = 2.80$. A little algebra will show that the formula for calculating the sample size must be:

$$n = 2\left(\frac{\delta}{d}\right)^2$$

Applying this formula, we get:

$$n = 2\left(\frac{2.8}{0.5}\right)^2 = 2 \times 31.36 = 62.72$$

We will therefore need 63 depressed subjects in each sample. It may be impossible to obtain a sample of 126 depressed people (i.e. 63 in each treatment group), and in this case the researcher may consider lowering alpha to, say, 0.1, though if this is done, it will increase the Type I error rate, and journal editors might be reluctant to publish the findings.

Activity 13.4

What is the practice in your discipline for ensuring adequate levels of statistical power? You may be able to find a review, like that published by Cohen (1962), but if you cannot, pick some *t*-test studies from a few journals, making sure that they report the necessary statistics for calculating power (n, mean and standard deviation will do). Do some power calculations on these, treating the means and variances as estimates of μ and σ.

Power calculations for the two–sample (independent) *t*-test, $n_1 \neq n_2$

Suppose our researcher had to assign depressed subjects to treatment groups on the basis of their hospital locations, and that this resulted in unequal numbers of depressed subjects in each treatment group. In this case we would have to change our power calculations to use the formulas given in Table 13.5.

Table 13.5 Power calculations for the two-sample *t*-test; $n_1 \neq n_2$

σ	d	n	δ
Assume $\sigma_1 = \sigma_2 = \sigma$	$\dfrac{\mu_1 - \mu_2}{\sigma}$	$n_h = \dfrac{2n_1 n_2}{n_1 + n_2}$	$d \times \sqrt{\dfrac{n_h}{2}}$

Notice that the principal change from the equal sample case is that we calculate the harmonic mean (*not* the arithmetic mean) of the two sample sizes and then use this harmonic mean in our calculations. The reasons are beyond the scope of this text.

Consider again our comparison of the effect of two different treatments on monthly suicidal thoughts in depressed patients. In one hospital where treatment A is to be applied we can find 35 depressed patients. In the other hospital we can find only 25 patients. In this case d remains 0.5 as calculated above. But we cannot calculate δ until we calculate the harmonic mean of the two sample sizes.

*The **harmonic mean** is typically used to estimate the average of a number of unequal sample sizes.*

$$n_h = \frac{2n_1 n_2}{n_1 + n_2} = \frac{2 \times 35 \times 25}{35 + 25} = \frac{1750}{60} = 29.167$$

Notice that the harmonic mean is a little lower than the arithmetic mean (30) of the two samples. We can now proceed to calculate δ in the same way as was done previously:

$$\delta = d \times \sqrt{\frac{n}{2}} = 0.5 \times \sqrt{\frac{29.167}{2}} = 0.5 \times 3.82 = 1.91$$

From the power table in Appendix 1, we see that $\delta = 1.91$ with a two-tailed test at $\alpha = 0.05$ will yield a power of approximately 0.48. This is a little better than was the case for the calculation above, assuming equal sample sizes, but is surprising, since we have substantially increased the sample size in one group. We will omit the calculation of the n required to obtain a desired power level of 0.8, since this is somewhat more complex for the harmonic mean: it should normally be adequate to calculate n on the assumption that your research design will contain equal sample sizes.

Activity 13.5

To what extent does the mere presence of an unbalanced design affect power? To understand this, calculate power for the following two-sample t-test parameters:
a) $\mu_1 = 20$, $\mu_2 = 15$; $\sigma = 10$, $n_1 = 35$, $n_2 = 35$
b) $\mu_1 = 20$, $\mu_2 = 15$; $\sigma = 10$, $n_1 = 30$, $n_2 = 40$
c) $\mu_1 = 20$, $\mu_2 = 15$; $\sigma = 10$, $n_1 = 20$, $n_2 = 50$
d) $\mu_1 = 20$, $\mu_2 = 15$; $\sigma = 10$, $n_1 = 60$, $n_2 = 10$

Power calculations for the matched sample t-test

In order to do power calculations for the matched sample t-tests, we need a value for p (rho), the population correlation coefficient.

A different complication arises when we consider the final type of t-test, the matched sample variant. Most of the formulas for a matched sample t-test (given in Table 13.6) are the same as for a single sample t-test. However, our estimate of the standard deviation is different because matched sample t-tests involve calculating difference scores between the two samples. Our estimate of the standard deviation has to be an estimate of the standard deviation of these difference scores. A formula that can be used for this task is given in Table 13.6.

Table 13.6 Power calculations for the matched sample t-tests

σ	d	n	δ
Use $\sigma_{\bar{x}_1 - \bar{x}_2}$ (the standard deviation of the difference scores)	$\dfrac{\mu_1 - \mu_2}{\sigma_{\bar{x}_1 - \bar{x}_2}}$	n (the number of matched pairs)	$d \times \sqrt{n}$

The formula for estimating the standard deviation of the difference scores between the two matched samples requires that we can estimate the correlation between the two populations, and this may be very difficult to do in practice. Assuming that we can obtain this estimate, the rest of the procedure is the same as for the one-sample t-test.

As an example, recall the old naval practice of giving sailors a tot of rum once a day. Suppose we wanted to compare sailors' performance on a vigilance task (using sonar to watch for submarines), before and after receiving their tots of rum. In this task our score will be the number of seconds that pass before the sailors notice a change in the sonar echo. From other research there is reason to believe that this task has a standard deviation of 15. We assume that alcohol will degrade everyone's performance equally, so that the sailors' performance before receiving their tots will correlate highly with their performance after receiving their tots. On the basis of other alcohol research, we estimate a correlation of 0.9. We use this as the population correlation coefficient, ρ, in the calculation below. From this information we can estimate $\sigma_{\bar{x}_1 - \bar{x}_2}$ as follows:

$$\sigma_{\bar{x}_1 - \bar{x}_2} = \sigma \sqrt{2(1 - \rho)} = 15 \sqrt{2(1 - 0.9)} = 15(0.447) = 6.71$$

If we study the before- and after-tots performance of 30 sailors, and obtain a critical effect size of 3, we can now estimate d as follows:

$$d = \frac{\mu_2 - \mu_1}{\sigma_{\bar{x}_1 - \bar{x}_2}} = \frac{3}{6.71} = 0.45$$

Similarly:

$$\delta = d \times \sqrt{n} = 0.45 \times \sqrt{30} = 2.46$$

We look this up in the power table in Appendix 1, which returns a power estimate of 0.7. In other words, we are 70% likely to reject a false null hypothesis, if our assumptions regarding effect size and variance are well founded.

Activity 13.6

Assume the same data as for the 'tots of rum' example in the text, but treat it as if it were an independent sample t-test – i.e. $\mu_1 - \mu_2 = 3$, $\sigma = 15$, $n_1 = n_2 = 30$. Calculate the power of this test. Is it a more powerful or less powerful test than the matched pairs t-test?

Factors that influence choice of sample size

We conclude by briefly considering some factors that influence the choice of an appropriate sample size:
1. The higher the significance level, the greater the necessary sample size in order to attain a certain level of power, i.e. more

subjects are needed for 1% significance level tests than for 5% significance level tests.

Factors that influence choice of n:
- *'tailedness' of the test*
- *desired level of power*

2. Two-tailed tests require larger sample sizes than one-tailed tests for the same level of power.

3. The smaller the critical effect size, the larger the sample size required for the same level of power.

4. The larger the power required, the greater the sample size needed.

5. The smaller the sample size, the lower the power. This means that with small sample sizes there is a greater chance of a non-significant result all other things being equal.

6. Running a study with 20 or fewer subjects in typical social science research designs involves a very high risk of failure unless we are fortunate to have a large critical effect size.

7. The combination of small effect size and great power requires enormous research effort. For example, to achieve 99% power for a critical effect size of 0.01, a researcher must be prepared to find and study more than 150 000 subjects!

Of course, the minimum sample size for a credible study differs from discipline to discipline and from research topic to research topic. Most opinion surveys cannot get away with less than 1 000 respondents, and most sociological and epidemiological studies require many hundreds of subjects. But in some areas of Psychology, sample sizes of 30 to 100 subjects are commonly seen. In some disciplines, where there is little variance in measurements, single subject research may be found.

Worked example

As you may know, one of the greatest threats to national health in South Africa is the HIV virus. In South Africa, the preponderance of evidence suggests that the disease is mostly spread by sexual contact. Social scientists have addressed themselves to this problem by attempting interventions that decrease risky sexual contact, and promote safe-sex practices. A measure that is often used to index these practices in populations at risk is the frequency of unprotected sex outside of monogamous relationships. Since good-quality research is expensive to do in this area, it is important that studies are designed so that they have high levels of statistical power.

Suppose that an intervention costs R73 per subject, and that we know that the preferred dependent measure ('unprotected sex') has a population standard deviation of 5.2. Previous studies have shown that the change in the dependent measure we can expect from interventions like this is approximately 0.23 units. We also know that before and after scores in these interventions tend to be highly correlated: $+ 0.8$ is a reasonable estimate of ρ. If we wish to obtain power $= 0.9$, what sample size will we require? If our budget is R56 000, what level of power will we be able to afford?

Solution
We need to calculate some preliminary statistics that we will need for the final calculations. First, we calculate the standard deviation of the difference scores, $\sigma_{\bar{x}_1 - \bar{x}_2}$

$$\sigma_{\bar{x}_1 - \bar{x}_2} = \sigma \sqrt{2(1 - \rho)} = 5.2 \sqrt{2(1 - 0.8)} = 5.2(0.63) = 3.29$$

Next, we need to establish what the effect size is:

$$d = \frac{\mu_2 - \mu_1}{\sigma_{\bar{x}_1 - \bar{x}_2}} = \frac{0.23}{3.29} = 0.07$$

Now we need the transformation from power $(1 - \beta)$ to n, which we find with some basic algebra:

$$\delta = d \times \sqrt{n}$$

$$\therefore \frac{\delta}{d} = \sqrt{n}$$

$$\therefore n = \left(\frac{\delta}{d}\right)^2$$

We use this result to solve for n. In the present example, we determine δ by looking it up on the power table in Appendix 1. If we look up a power of 0.9 at alpha $= 0.05$ (given in the question), then move across the left-most column (called 'delta'), with linear interpolation, we get a value of $\delta = 3.25$. Therefore,

$$n = \left(\frac{3.25}{0.07}\right)^2 = 2155.61 \approx 2156$$

For the second part of the problem, we need to work out how many participants we can afford, and then calculate the power that they will yield, given our estimates of effect size and σ.

Since we have a total budget of R56 000, and it costs R73 per participant, we can afford R56 000/R73 $= 767$ participants.

To calculate power on the basis of this number, we need to recalculate δ:

$$\delta = d \times \sqrt{n}$$

$$= 0.07 \times \sqrt{767} = 1.94$$

We look up this value of δ in the relevant table, and we see that this is approximately 0.5. In other words, if the assumptions we have made are correct, and we proceed with the intervention, we will only be able to afford a statistical power level of 0.5 within the constraints of our budget.

In short, we will have to re-examine the intervention, since the primary reason for the low power is the small effect size associated with the intervention.

Box 13.1

Statistical software for power calculations

There is a fair amount of statistical software that facilitates power calculations, and the statistical packages we have referred to in this text (SPSS® and STATISTICA) provide support in this respect. However, the support is normally provided in a separate software package, and not as part of the base or regular installation. In our experience, few institutions purchase the add-on package, so this may not be an option for you. You can find a helpful review of statistical software for power calculations at the following Internet address: http://www.zoology.ubc.ca/~krebs/power.html

Luckily, there are several excellent freeware packages, which you can download from the Internet. One of the best of these is GPOWER, written by Franz Faul and Edgar Erdfelder of the University of Dusseldorf. A DOS/Windows version is available at http://www.psycho.uni-duesseldorf.de/aap/projects/gpower/binaries/gpowerdos/ GPOWER2I.EXE

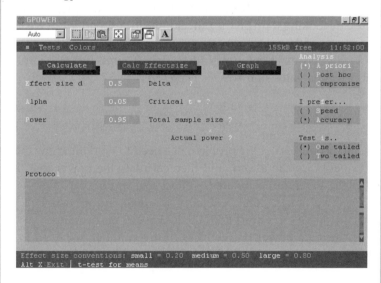

This package is very simple to use. We will demonstrate only one calculation, power of the independent samples *t*-test, assuming the data of Activity 13.6.

To calculate power, select 'Post hoc' under 'Analysis', and complete the data required in the 'Effect size', 'Alpha', n_1 and n_2 cells. You can also select 'one-tailed' or 'two-tailed' in the 'Test is ...' section.

The program then displays the results of the calculation in the 'Delta' and 'Power' tabs.

As you can see, the power of the test in question is very low. If we want to work out what sample size(s) we would need to increase the power to some desired level, say 0.8, then we would select 'A priori' in the 'Analysis' block, and the screen would change to allow the entry of necessary information. Try this yourself, and you will see that the required sample size is 620 in total, or 310 per group. GPOWER also allows you to produce a number of useful graphs, via the 'Graph' button on the main dialog. In Figure 13.4 we have plotted power vs sample size for the 'tot of rum' example.

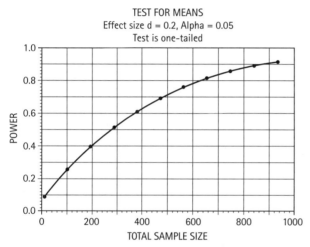

Figure 13.4 GPOWER graph, plotting power as a function of sample size for the 'tot of rum' example

Summary

1. Conducting a statistical test can be likened to running a criminal trial: making a significant finding is a question of correct evidentiary procedure, and does not point to the salience or practical importance of the finding.

2. There are two types of error in statistical hypothesis testing: Type I error (symbolised as α), where we mistakenly reject a true null hypothesis, and Type II error (symbolised as β), where we mistakenly fail to reject a false null hypothesis. The power of a test is the probability of making the correct decision to reject the null hypothesis when it is false – it is the complement of a Type II error, and is therefore symbolised as $1 - \beta$.

3. Five central aspects of a research design determine the power of a statistical hypothesis test: the size of the true difference or effect; the sample size(s); the population variance σ; the α level adopted in the study; and the type of statistical test.

4. Effect size is a measure of the experimental or observed difference, e.g. the difference between two means. The most commonly used index of effect size is Cohen's d, which expresses a mean difference in standard deviation units.

5. Most power calculations require *a priori* information, typically μ and σ. It is usual to estimate this from previous literature, or on the basis of theory.

6. The major aims of power analysis are usually (1) the calculation of $1 - \beta$ (statistical power), or (2) the calculation of the sample size(s) required to obtain a particular value of $1 - \beta$ (statistical power).

Exercises

1. Two graduate students recently completed their dissertations. Each used a *t*-test for two independent groups. One found a significant *t* using 15 subjects per group. The other found a significant *t* of the same magnitude (i.e. the *t*-statistics were the same size) using 55 subjects per group.
   a) Which result impresses you the most? Why?
   b) Draw a diagram of overlapping distributions (analogous to Figure 13.1) to defend your answer.

2. We have just conducted a study comparing cognitive development of low- and normal-birthweight babies who have reached one year of age. Using a scale we devised, we found that the sample means of the two groups were 25 and 30 respectively, with a pooled standard deviation of 8. Assume that we wish to replicate this experiment with 20 subjects in each group. If we assume that the true means and standard deviations have been estimated exactly, what is the *a priori* probability that we will find a significant difference in our replication?

3. A PhD student has the impression that he must find significant results if he wants to defend his dissertation successfully. He wants to show a difference in social awareness, as measured by his own scale, between a normal group and a group of ex-delinquents. He has a problem, however. He has data to suggest that the normal group has a true mean of 38, and he has 50 of those subjects. He has access to either 100 high-school graduates who have been classed as delinquent in the past, or to 25 high-school

dropouts who have a history of delinquency. He suspects that the high-school graduates come from a population with a mean of approximately 35, whereas the dropout group comes from a population with a mean of approximately 30. He can use only one of these groups. Which should he use? (Assume the standard deviation is the same for all groups.)

4. The table below shows sample sizes required for power = 0.80, alpha = 0.05, two-tailed test assumed. Generate a table analogous to that below for power = 0.80, alpha = 0.01, two-tailed.

Effect Size	d	One-sample t	Two-sample t
Small	.20	196	784
Medium	.50	32	126
Large	.80	13	49

5. Generate a table analogous to the one above for power = 0.60, alpha = 0.05, two-tailed test assumed.

6. We want to test a null hypothesis about a single mean at alpha = 0.05, one-tailed test assumed. All necessary assumptions are met. Could there be a case in which we would be more likely to reject a true null hypothesis than a false one? (In other words, can power ever be less than alpha?)

TUTORIAL

14

The logic of analysis of variance

Kevin Durrheim

After studying this tutorial, you should be able to:
- Explain what analysis of variance (ANOVA) is.
- Know the kind of research situations in which it is appropriate to use ANOVA.
- Outline the statistical logic underlying ANOVA.
- Do basic ANOVA calculation with the aid of a calculator.

You have already been introduced to hypothesis testing as the formal process by which we investigate research questions using inferential statistics to reach decisions about the validity of the null and alternative hypotheses. Thus far you have considered the z-test and the t-test. These are inferential tests because they allow us to draw conclusions about populations on the basis of information we gain from observing and measuring samples. The basic difference between *analysis of variance (ANOVA)* and the t-test and z-test is that ANOVA allows us to test the difference between more than two groups of subjects and the influence of more than one independent variable.

Suppose we wanted to test the hypothesis that exposure to violent television programmes makes children aggressive. We could employ the following experimental design:

Recruit 60 fourth grade schoolchildren and randomly assign them into two groups. Show one group a particularly violent movie, and show the other group a non-violent, but otherwise

similar, movie. Immediately after the movie ask each child individually to tell a story about 'a family outing', and measure the
subjects' expressions of aggression in the story-telling task (see
Figure 14.1).

The dependent variable in the experiment is the number of aggressive or violent incidents that the children refer to in their stories.
The null hypothesis is that children exposed to violent television
will be as aggressive as children not exposed to violent television.
The alternative hypothesis is that children exposed to violent television will be more aggressive than children not exposed to violent
television. These hypotheses refer to children in general (i.e. the
population of children), and not merely to the particular group of
children who participated in the experiment. In order to draw
conclusions about the population of children on the basis of our
sample, we need to employ inferential statistics. The appropriate
inferential test to employ in analysing the results of this experiment
is the independent samples *t*-test (see Figure 14.1). This test will tell
us whether the difference between the two groups in our experiment is large enough to conclude that the difference is very unlikely to be a chance event. The t-test is appropriate here because we
have two groups of subjects and only one independent variable.

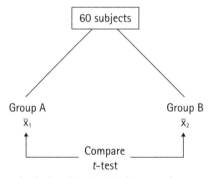

Figure 14.1 Example design for study of aggression

If, in the above study, the researcher wanted to test whether exposure to different types of violence influences aggression, she could
divide her pool of 60 subjects into three groups: a control group that
watches a non-violent movie; an experimental group that watches a
Kung Fu movie; and a second experimental group that watches a
movie depicting domestic violence. In this experiment we have one
independent variable with three groups, and ANOVA is the appropriate statistical procedure to analyse the results (see Figure 14.2),
since the *t*-test cannot be used for a simultaneous test of the differences between the three groups.

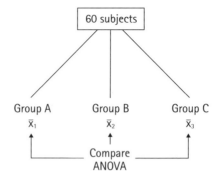

Figure 14.2 Design for three-group study of aggression

There is another type of research design where ANOVA is the appropriate statistical procedure. This is when we have more than one independent variable. Perhaps we hypothesise that males will be more aggressive after watching the Kung Fu movie, but females will be more aggressive after watching the domestic violence movie. This experimental design consists of three groups of male subjects – control plus two experimental groups as in Figure 14.2 – and a similar three groups of female subjects, making six groups of subjects altogether. In this study we have six groups of subjects whose mean scores we want to compare, but we also have two independent variables: gender and movie type. This design can answer questions such as 'Are males more aggressive than females across all movie types?', 'Do the violent movies increase aggression for both male and female subjects?', and 'Are males more aggressive than females after watching the Kung Fu movie, but not the domestic violence movie?' These complex designs with more than one independent variable are known as *factorial ANOVA designs*, and will be considered in a later tutorial. At this stage you should know that ANOVA differs from the *t*-test in that it identifies differences between the means of more than two groups, and can be used in designs with more than one independent variable. In this tutorial we will consider simple ANOVA designs consisting of one independent variable with three groups of subjects.

ANOVA is used to test for differences between the means of more than two groups, and can be used in designs with more than one independent variable.

Activity 14.1

Browse the journal holdings of your institution's library, and try to identify four studies that have used factorial experimental designs in your discipline. Keep a note of how many times you see ANOVA used as a data analysis method.

The rationale for using ANOVA

Although we use the *t*-test and ANOVA for research designs that involve different numbers of groups, both statistical procedures are used to compare group means. In a typical ANOVA problem you have three groups of subjects, whose means you want to compare (see Table 14.1). The null hypothesis for an ANOVA problem is $H_0: \mu_1 = \mu_2 = \mu_3$. (Recall that Greek letters refer to population parameters, thus our null hypothesis refers to population means.) As you can see from Table 14.1, we are no longer talking about a difference between two means as we do for the *t*-test. Here we are dealing with a set of possible differences between means, i.e. differences between:

1. $\bar{x}_1$ and $\bar{x}_2$
2. $\bar{x}_1$ and $\bar{x}_3$
3. $\bar{x}_2$ and $\bar{x}_3$

Table 14.1 Aggression scores for subjects exposed to types of TV violence

Type of television violence		
Non–violent	Kung Fu	Domestic violence
2	3	4
0	6	1
1	4	2
3	6	3
3	1	3
$\bar{x}_1 = 1.8$	$\bar{x}_2 = 4$	$\bar{x}_3 = 2.6$

Analysing this design involves examining all three comparisons simultaneously. Because we are examining a set of possible differences, instead of testing for *a difference* between two means, we test for *an effect*. A significant effect is present in the data when at least one of the possible comparisons between group means is significant.

We could approach the problem by using three different *t*-tests, one for each of the group comparisons outlined above. Although this approach will give you an indication of where the differences lie between the three means, it is an unsatisfactory approach because it leads to an increase in the *familywise error rate*. The familywise error rate is the probability of rejecting at least one null hypothesis when it is true, in a set (family) of comparisons. You will recall that the decisions we reach on the basis of inferential testing are always uncertain. There is always the possibility of making a

*The **familywise error rate** is the probability of rejecting at least one null hypothesis when it is true, in a set (family) of comparisons. The overall Type I error rate (familywise error rate) for a set of comparisons is controlled by ANOVA.*

Type I or Type II error (see Tutorial 13). If we conduct a t-test with $\alpha = 0.05$, then we have a 5% chance of making a Type I error by rejecting the null hypothesis when it is in fact true. If you conduct three different t-tests, as you would need to in a design where you want to compare three group means, the probability of incorrectly rejecting at least one null hypothesis when it is true will be greater than 5%. We calculate the familywise error rate by using the following formula:

Equation 14.1

$$1 - (1 - \alpha)^k$$

where: k = the number of significance tests

Thus, for the present example, the probability of making a Type I error is $1 - (1 - 0.05)^3 = 0.14$. This can have serious consequences. Imagine that you are testing whether a new drug is an effective treatment for cancer, and you make a Type I error. This would lead you to conclude that the drug is effective, whereas in reality it is an ineffective treatment that would bring false hope to millions of people who suffer from cancer.

Activity 14.2

Attempt to estimate the Type I error rate in the following designs ($\alpha = 0.05$):
a) Two groups are compared with a t-test.
b) Five groups are compared to each other with t-tests.
c) Ten groups are compared to each other with t-tests.

ANOVA provides an omnibus test for an effect.

ANOVA helps to deal with the problem of familywise error by countering the increase in alpha that occurs when we compare more than two group means. ANOVA is an 'omnibus' test of significance and as an omnibus test, ANOVA employs a single calculation to test all possible comparisons at once. This is why ANOVA tests for an effect, rather than testing for a difference between means. If the effect is significant, then we know that at least one of the three comparisons is significant.

The logic of ANOVA

Terminology

ANOVA is an acronym for 'analysis of variance'. As the name suggests, the procedure involves analysing variance. You will recall that variance is a measure of the dispersion in a set of scores, and is calculated by determining the 'average distance' of a set of scores from its 'centre' or mean, by the formula:

Equation 14.2

$$s^2 = \frac{\sum(x - \bar{x})^2}{n - 1}$$

The notion of variance and this formula underlies most of ANOVA. Unfortunately we change our terminology slightly here, but the concepts remain exactly the same. In ANOVA terminology, the numerator in the formula – i.e. the top part of the formula, $\Sigma(x - \bar{x})^2$ – is called the *Sums of Squares* (abbreviated to SS). It is easy to see why this is called the Sum of Squares – the numerator estimates the sum (i.e. Σ) of squared differences between each score in a set of scores and the mean of those scores. Instead of talking about variance, in ANOVA terminology we talk about *Mean Squares* (abbreviated to MS). This is essentially what variance is – the mean or average of the sum of squared differences between each score in a set of scores and the mean of those scores. The denominator – i.e. $n - 1$ – we call the *degrees of freedom* (abbreviated to df).

Activity 14.3

Rewrite these expressions (using their definitions) to find which well-known formulae they refer to in 'ANOVA speak':

a) $MS_E = \dfrac{SS_E}{df_E}$

b) $\sqrt{MS_E} = \sqrt{\dfrac{SS_E}{df_E}}$

This change of terminology may appear an unnecessary complication, but in fact it simplifies things. This is because in ANOVA we need to distinguish between, and estimate, two different types of variance – *random* or *error variance*, and *systematic variance*.

Error variance and systematic variance

Error variance should be a familiar concept by now, as you came across it in the discussion of the z-test and t-test. Error variance refers to the random variation between sample means that we find when we randomly select samples from a population. In Figure 14.3, we have randomly selected three samples of size n = 20 from a population that we know has a mean $\mu = 12$ and a variance $\sigma^2 = 9$. As you

Error variance is random or unexplained variance between the means of samples drawn from the same population.

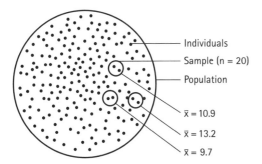

Figure 14.3 Variation in random sample estimates of the population mean

can see, the means of the samples differ from the population mean and from each other. This is expected, because we know from the Central Limit Theorem that sample means from a population will be distributed around the population mean with a certain amount of variance. In other words, a randomly selected sample mean estimates the population mean with some specifiable amount of error. This variance between sample means is unexplained, random variance, and is also commonly known as error variance.

Systematic variance is the variance in a set of scores that we can explain in terms of the independent variable.

The second source of variance of relevance to ANOVA is *systematic variance*. Systematic variance is the variance in a set of scores that we can explain in terms of the independent variable. Say, for example, that we are asked by a cookery school to test their pressure cooker. It is essential that the pressure cooker works correctly at a stable temperature and pressure to ensure that food is never over- or under-cooked. We run the pressure cooker at 20 kilopascals, 40 kilopascals, and 60 kilopascals, and record the temperature at which a liquid boils. We take five temperature readings at each pressure. As you can see from Table 14.2, the five temperature readings at each pressure reading are exactly the same. Our dataset consists of 15 numbers (five 45s, five 75s, and five 92s), and because all the numbers are not exactly the same (i.e. we have 45s, 75s, and 92s in our dataset), we know that there is variance present in this dataset. In this example, however, all the variance is systematic variance, i.e. all the variance can be explained in terms of the independent variable, which in this case is pressure. The variance between the 15 numbers in our dataset can be explained completely by differences in the pressure settings. We know this because there is no variance within each of the groups. All the variance is attributable to differences between the groups.

Table 14.2 Temperature readings at three pressure settings

20 kp	40 kp	60 kp
45	75	92
45	75	92
45	75	92
45	75	92
45	75	92
$\bar{x}_1 = 45$	$\bar{x}_2 = 75$	$\bar{x}_3 = 92$

Comparing variance within and between groups

The whole aim of computing ANOVA is to determine whether there is *systematic variance* present. If there is systematic variance present in a dataset, we have a significant effect. From the above example we know that systematic variance is evident in the differences between the group means. Unfortunately, we never have data like that in Table 14.2. In all real-world research – especially in the social sciences – there is always error variance present in our datasets. Data are composed of some mixture of systematic and error variance. This creates a problem because it means that we can never identify and measure pure systematic variance. The differences between group means will always be influenced by random or error variance in addition to (possible) systematic variance. Systematic variance is not independently measurable. To determine whether or not there is systematic variance present in a dataset, we have to follow a rather indirect path by comparing the variance *within* the groups to the variance *between* the groups.

We have a significant effect when there is systematic variance present.

*Comparing variance within groups with variance between groups identifies **systematic variance.***

Activity 14.4

Invent datasets of 5 cases per group that exhibit the following characteristics:
a) no random or error variation
b) no systematic variation
c) mostly systematic variation, with a little error variation
d) mostly random variation, with a little systematic variation.

Are you uncertain whether you managed to create any of these? If so, why?

Table 14.3 provides an illustration of two different datasets that both have error variance present. We know that there is error variance present in both datasets since, unlike the data in Table 14.2, the scores within each of the cells differ from each other (note that 'cells' in this context is a synonym for 'groups'). However, if you study the pattern of scores in Dataset 1 and Dataset 2 in Table 14.3, you will note that the two datasets are quite different. In Dataset 1, we have a pattern of high variance within groups, but low variance between groups. As you may imagine, it is quite unlikely that there are systematic differences between these groups. Although the group means differ, the differences are small in comparison with the differences between scores within the groups. In other words, it is quite unlikely that a significant effect would be found for this pattern of data, since the difference between group means is small in comparison with the error variance between individual scores within the groups. This is a situation where the null hypothesis, $H_0: \mu_1 = \mu_2 = \mu_3$, is very likely to be true.

Table 14.3 Two datasets for aggression scores in three TV violence conditions

Dataset 1			Dataset 2		
Non-violent	Kung Fu	Domestic violence	Non-violent	Kung Fu	Domestic violence
3	2	7	2	5	9
9	8	4	2	3	7
2	7	1	1	3	9
5	1	9	3	4	8
1	4	3	1	6	5
$\bar{x} = 4$	$\bar{x} = 4.4$	$\bar{x} = 4.8$	$\bar{x} = 1.8$	$\bar{x} = 4.2$	$\bar{x} = 7.6$

If you compare the distribution of scores within the cells of Dataset 2 with the differences between the means, you will note a very different pattern. In this case there is very little variance within the cells (look at the range of scores within each cell), but there are large differences between the cell means. Here it appears as though there may be systematic differences between the groups, since, although there is error variance present, it appears to be relatively small in comparison with the differences between the group means. Although the group means are influenced by the error variance within the cells, the differences between these means appears to be too large to be explained entirely by the within-cell error variance. In other words, it is quite likely that a significant effect would be found for this pattern of data since the difference in group means is large in comparison with the error variance between individual scores within the groups. This is a situation where the null hypothesis, $H_0: \mu_1 = \mu_2 = \mu_3$, is very likely to be false.

*The variance within cells is an estimate of error variance, while the variance between group means is an estimate of error variance plus systematic variance. Comparing **within** and **between** group variance provides an estimate of systematic variance.*

The discussion thus far has been abstract. It has been stated that we can determine the likelihood of there being an effect present in the data – i.e. the presence of systematic variance – by comparing the variation within the groups to the variation between the group means. The reason why this comparison allows us to determine the presence of systematic variance is that the variance *within* the cells is error variance while the variance *between* the cells is made up of a mixture of error variance and systematic variance. As has been noted, it is not possible to measure pure systematic variance because it is always mixed up with error variance. However, if we have one estimate of pure error variance (i.e. the variance within the cells) and one estimate of error variance plus systematic variance (i.e. the variance between the group means), then by comparing the two estimates we can determine the likelihood that there are systematic differences between the groups. If the variance between the group means (error variance + systematic variance) is much greater than the variance within the cells (error variance), then this must be due to the presence of systematic variance.

This comparison can be likened to an old man who, suffering from gout and arthritis along with a number of other ailments specific to old age, wakes up every morning with many aches and pains. One day, however, the old man wakes up with a strong pain in his chest and decides to go to the doctor for a check-up. The decision to go to the doctor is much the same as deciding whether there is systematic variance present in an ANOVA. The daily aches and pains can be likened to error variance. Some days these pains are worse than others, but on the day in question the pain is systematically worse than usual. It is important to note that the daily aches and pains are still there – just because the old man now has a pain in the chest does not mean that the daily aches have disappeared. However, in comparing his health on this particular day to his general aches and pains, he decides that he is feeling significantly worse and consults the doctor. In ANOVA, the variance between the groups contains error variance mixed up with systematic variance, just like the man has a chest pain mixed up with general aches and pains. Just as the old man compares his health on the day in question (a mixture of general pain and new pain) to his daily aches and pains (general pain) to decide if he is systematically worse, in doing ANOVA we compare variance between group means (a mixture of error and systematic variance) with variance within cells (error variance) to determine whether there is a significant effect.

In technical language, the variance within the cells is known as MS_{Error}. As you should realise by now, this is an estimate of error variance. The variance between the groups is known as MS_{Group}, and is an estimate of error variance plus systematic variance. To determine whether an effect is present in an ANOVA, we should estimate mathematically the size of MS_{Group} and MS_{Error}, and then compare them. To the extent that MS_{Group} (error variance + systematic variance) is larger than MS_{Error} (error variance), it is likely that there is a significant effect.

By now you should have a clearer picture of what it means to analyse or partition variance when you are doing ANOVA. The aim is to determine whether there is an effect by teasing out systematic variance (if it is present) from error variance. Comparing MS_{Group} and MS_{Error} does this. What we are doing here is very similar to what we did when calculating t for two independent groups:

MS_{Error} is a measure of variance within cells, and is an estimate of error variance.

MS_{Group} is a measure of variance between group means, and is an estimate of error variance plus systematic variance.

$$t = \frac{\bar{x}_1 - \bar{x}_2}{\sqrt{\dfrac{s_1^2}{n_1} + \dfrac{s_2^2}{n_2}}}$$

Equation 14.3

In the t formula, the numerator $(\bar{x}_1 - \bar{x}_2)$ is a measure of the degree to which the group means differ from each other, similar to MS_{Group}, and the denominator is a measure of error variance, comprised of the variance between scores within each group, similar to MS_{Error}. Dividing the difference between the means by the error variance gives an indication of how much bigger the variance between the means is than the error variance. This increases the value of t and increases the likelihood that we can conclude that there are significant differences between the groups. Although the number of groups is typically greater in ANOVA designs than in t-test designs, and the calculations change, the two statistical procedures are very similar at a conceptual level.

Calculating one–way ANOVA

Although ANOVA calculations can be mathematically demanding, it is important to master the simpler calculations to gain a proper understanding of the basic principles of ANOVA. The simplest case of ANOVA is when we have a research design with one independent variable with three groups of equal sample size. In the remainder of this tutorial, we will see how to determine whether there is a significant effect present in such designs.

It should be clear by now that although we want to identify systematic variance, it is unmeasurable. The question, therefore, is how do we know when systematic variance is present? In practice, we have two sources of measurable variance: MS_{Group}, the variance between group means; and MS_{Error}, the variance within the groups. Doing ANOVA entails calculating MS_{Group} and MS_{Error}, and then comparing them by dividing MS_{Group} by MS_{Error}.

Table 14.4 Aggression scores for subjects exposed to TV violence

Type of television violence		
Non-violent	Kung Fu	Domestic violence
2	3	4
0	6	1
1	4	2
3	6	3
3	1	3
$\bar{x}_1 = 1.8$	$\bar{x}_2 = 4$	$\bar{x}_3 = 2.6$
$s_1^2 = 1.7$	$s_2^2 = 4.5$	$s_3^2 = 1.3$
$n_1 = 5$	$n_2 = 5$	$n_3 = 5$

The *first step* is to determine the intermediate statistics. Below each column in Table 14.4 the intermediate statistics – x̄, s², and n – are recorded. These statistics are easy to calculate using the statistical functions of your calculator (see Tutorials 3 and 4). It is also possible to use a statistical computer package to calculate the intermediate statistics (see Tutorial 25). It is best to calculate these intermediate statistics first, as they are necessary for calculating MS_{Group} and MS_{Error}.

ANOVA step 1: find x̄, s² and n for each subgroup.

The *second step* is to determine MS_{Group} and MS_{Error}. As you will recall from the earlier discussion, MS_{Error} is the variance between scores within the groups. It is calculated simply by finding the average variance within the groups. The formula is reproduced as Equation 14.4, and visual inspection shows that MS_{Error} is calculated by summing the variance within the three groups and dividing by k, the number of groups.

ANOVA step 2: find MS_{Group} and MS_{Error}.

Box 14.1

Using Excel for simple ANOVA calculations

In our introduction to spreadsheet programs on the accompanying CD, we argue that spreadsheets are very useful for forms of statistical analysis where you need – or want – to personally control the analysis. In this respect, they are very handy tools for analysis of uncomplicated one-way 'balanced' ANOVA designs (i.e. equal sample sizes in the groups). Below we show a setup in Excel for the analysis of the data in Table 14.4. We recommend that you try a similar setup for some of the exercises at the end of the tutorial.

	A	B	C	D
1		Type of Television Violence		
		Non-Violent	Kung Fu	Domestic Violence
2				
3		2	3	4
4		0	6	1
5		1	4	2
6		3	6	3
7		3	1	3
8	x̄	=AVERAGE(B3:B7)	=AVERAGE(C3:C7)	=AVERAGE(D3:D7)
9	S²	=VAR(B3:B7)	=VAR(C3:C7)	=VAR(D3:D7)
10	n	=COUNT(B3:B7)	=COUNT(C3:C7)	=COUNT(D3:D7)
11	k	=COUNT(B7:D7)		
12	dfₐ	=B11-1		
13	dfₑ	=B11*(B10-1)		
14	Ave S²	=AVERAGE(B9:D9)		
15	S²x̄	=B10*VAR(B8:D8)		
16	F	=B15/B14		Fₒrit =FINV(0.05,B12,B13)
17	p	=FDIST(B16,B12,B13)		

	A	B	C	D
1		Type of Television Violence		
		Non-Violent	Kung Fu	Domestic Violence
2				
3		2	3	4
4		0	6	1
5		1	4	2
6		3	6	3
7		3	1	3
8	x̄	1.8	4	2.6
9	S²	1.7	4.5	1.3
10	n	5	5	5
11	k	3		
12	dfₐ	2		
13	dfₑ	12		
14	Ave	2.5		
15	S²x̄	6.2		
16	F	2.48	Fₒrit	3.89
17	p	0.1255		

Notice that the setup includes the calculation of a critical value for the F-test, as traditionally used in ANOVA calculations, but also includes an exact probability calculation.

Equation 14.4

$$MS_E = \frac{\Sigma s^2}{k}$$

$$= \frac{s_1^2 + s_2^2 + s_3^2}{k}$$

$$= \frac{1.7 + 4.5 + 1.3}{3}$$

$$= \frac{7.5}{3} = 2.5$$

MS_{Group} is an estimate of the variance between the groups. To calculate MS_{Group}, treat the group means as raw data and calculate the variance between these means. The full calculation of MS_{Group} is shown below to illustrate what is meant by variance between the group means. Each of the group means in Table 14.4, above, is subtracted from the grand mean – i.e. the mean of the group means (2.8) – and this figure is squared to find 'how far' each mean lies away from the grand mean. This figure is then divided by $k - 1$ to determine the average distance the means lie away from their 'centre'. In practice it is much easier to calculate MS_{Group} using the statistical functions on your calculator. All you do is punch in the group means – 1.8, 4, 2.6 – as data, calculate the variance, and then multiply by n. Do this now and you will see that you arrive at the same solution.

Equation 14.5

$$MS_G = n \times s_{\bar{x}}^2$$

$$= n \times \frac{\Sigma(\bar{x} - \bar{\bar{x}})^2}{k - 1}$$

$$= 5 \times \frac{(1.8 - 2.8)^2 + (4 - 2.8)^2 + (2.6 - 2.8)^2}{3 - 1}$$

$$= 5 \times \frac{1 + 1.44 + 0.04}{2}$$

$$= 5 \times \frac{2.48}{2} = 6.2$$

ANOVA step 3: find
$$F = \frac{MS_{Group}}{MS_{Error}}$$

The *third step* is to compare MS_{Group} and MS_{Error}. We compare MS_{Group} and MS_{Error} by dividing MS_{Group} by MS_{Error}. Since MS_{Group} is comprised of error variance and systematic variance while MS_{Error} contains only error variance, as F becomes large, there is a greater probability that there are systematic differences between the groups. If F is 'large enough' we can reject the null hypothesis. F for the data in Table 14.4 is equal to 2.48, as calculated below:

$$F = \frac{MS_G}{MS_E}$$

Equation 14.6

$$= \frac{error + systematic}{error}$$

$$= \frac{6.2}{2.5} = 2.48$$

If you examine the t formula once again, and compare this formula with the F formula, you should note the similarities. Both the F-statistics and t-statistics are calculated by dividing the variation between groups by the variance within cells. However, since the t-test is used for only two groups, the measure of variation between groups is computed by a simple subtraction, whereas MS_{Group} is computed by determining the variance between the group means. The basic logic underlying ANOVA is the same as that underlying t.

The *fourth step* is to compare F_{calc} with F_{crit}. Although the value of F in our example is larger than 1, and leads us to suspect that there may be systematic variance present, this may have been a chance event. The group means may differ from each other purely by chance. As with the t-test, we must define a critical value to determine just how large the F-statistic should be to reject the null hypothesis. We have to define a level of probability with which we are willing to make a Type I error, and then reach a decision regarding our null hypothesis. To make a decision about the null hypothesis, we compare F_{calc} with F_{crit}.

ANOVA step 4: compare F_{calc} to F_{crit}.

The F distribution (for 3, 3 degrees of freedom) is shown in Figure 14.4. Although F is not symmetrical – unlike the z and t distributions – we use the distribution in a very similar manner to reach a decision about the null hypothesis. We define alpha, set at a critical value, and then compare F_{calc} with F_{crit}.

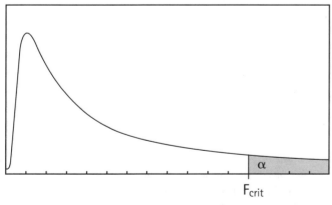

Figure 14.4 The F distribution (for df = 3 and 3)

F_{crit} is defined by two different degrees of freedom: the degrees of freedom for MS_{Group}, and the degrees of freedom for MS_{Error}.

Equation 14.7

$$df_{Group} = k - 1;$$

Equation 14.8

$$df_{Error} = k(n-1)$$

where: k is the number of group means we are comparing
n is the number of scores in each group

In our example, $k = 3$ and $n = 5$, therefore $df_{Group} = 2$ and $df_{Error} = 12$. From our F-tables (see Appendix 1) we read off the F_{crit} value with 2 degrees of freedom for the numerator (i.e. associated with MS_{Group}, which is the numerator in the F formula) and 12 degrees of freedom for the denominator (i.e. associated with MS_{Error}, which is the denominator in the F formula). The value for F is 3.89. Since $F_{calc} = 2.48$ is less than $F_{crit} = 3.89$, we cannot reject the null hypothesis. There are thus no systematic differences in aggression between the three groups of subjects. We conclude that there is no significant effect.

Activity 14.5

Use your calculator to conduct a one-way ANOVA on both datasets in Table 14.3. Were we correct about the relative proportions of random and systematic variation?

The best way to learn the logic of ANOVA, in our opinion, is through examples and exercises. We therefore finish this tutorial with several worked examples, and ask you to attempt the exercises at the end of the tutorial. Remember also that there are many additional problems (with solutions) on the accompanying CD.

Box 14.2

A prayer to accompany ANOVA
Analysis of variance was devised by R. A. Fisher, an English statistician, while working at the Rothamsted agricultural research station in the 1920s (see Fisher, 1937). In a very short space of time it became the dominant analytic technique in experimental design, in a wide variety of disciplines. In fact, its dominance is so overwhelming, it is as if researchers are asked to observe the following creed:

The Design Creed (anonymous)
(To be recited while standing)

I believe in Analysis of Variance, a Gift of the Almighty bestowed upon grateful mankind by Divine Providence through the Inspiration of the venerable Sir R. A. Fisher, Knight of the Realm, and His Disciples.
   I believe in the F Ratio wherein the uppermost Mean Square Between overcomes the lowly Mean Square Within to yield Significant Blessings upon Faithful Researchers.

> I shall continue to maximize Experimental Variance and minimize Error Variance until the last of my Degrees of Freedom be spent and Divine Control shall see fit to lift my soul from this vale of Errors and Confirm my Hypotheses in that Blessed Realm where all Variance be Systematic Variance and Error Variance be Nought.
> Amen

> For a critical look at ANOVA and the impact it had on 20th century social psychology, see Danziger (2000).

Worked examples

1. From years of shop floor experience, a senior trade unionist believes that younger factory workers are more militant than older workers. He decides to test his theory empirically by randomly selecting seven subjects from three groups of workers – young (aged 20–30), middle-aged (35–45), and old (50–60) – at a large metal-processing plant. Each of the workers completes a measure of trade union militancy. The data are reported in the table below. Use a calculator to run a one-way ANOVA on this data ($\alpha = 0.01$). Can the trade unionist conclude that younger factory workers are more militant than older workers?

Young:	75, 86, 33, 62, 41, 68, 56
Middle-aged:	35, 54, 68, 29, 43, 72, 41
Old:	21, 39, 81, 28, 34, 42, 18

Solution

$H_0: \mu_1 = \mu_2 = \mu_3$ $\bar{x}_1 = 60.14$ $s_1^2 = 345.81$ $n = 7$

$H_1: \mu_1 \neq \mu_2 \neq \mu_3$ $\bar{x}_2 = 48.86$ $s_2^2 = 268.48$ $k = 3$

                    $\bar{x}_3 = 37.57$ $s_3^2 = 444.95$

$df_{Group} = k - 1 = 2$
$df_{Error} = k(n - 1) = 18$
Therefore $F_{crit} = 6.01$

MS_G is computed with a calculator. In STATS mode, enter the three group means as data, and calculate the variance. Multiply this value by $n = 7$:

$$n \times s_{\bar{x}}^2 = 7 \times 127.37 = 891.59$$

MS_E is computed with a calculator. Simply average the cell (or group) variances, i.e.

$$\text{average } s^2 = \frac{345.81 + 268.48 + 444.95}{3}$$

$$= 353.08$$

$$F = \frac{MS_G}{MS_E} = \frac{891.59}{353.08} = 2.53$$

Since $F_{calc} = 2.53$ is less than $F_{crit} = 6.01$, we cannot reject the null hypothesis. There are thus no systematic differences in militancy between the three groups of subjects. The trade unionist cannot conclude that younger factory workers are more militant than older workers.

2. A researcher draws a random sample of 12 students and divides the sample randomly into three equally large groups. She then subjects each group to a different level of sleep deprivation and measures the intellectual functioning of each student on a 10-point scale. A high score indicates high intellectual functioning. The data for degree of sleep deprivation are as follows:

Little:	8, 6, 7, 4
Mild:	5, 7, 6, 4
Severe:	7, 4, 7, 5

Does the degree of sleep deprivation appear to effect level of intellectual functioning? Conduct the appropriate analysis and report relevant statistics. Assume $\alpha = 0.05$.

Solution
Do the necessary calculations and draw up the ANOVA summary table.

$H_0: \mu_1 = \mu_2 = \mu_3$ $\bar{x}_1 = 6.25$ $s_1^2 = 2.92$ $n = 4$

$H_0: \mu_1 \neq \mu_2 \neq \mu_3$ $\bar{x}_2 = 5.5$ $s_2^2 = 1.67$ $k = 3$

                       $\bar{x}_3 = 5.75$ $s_3^2 = 2.25$

$df_{Group} = k - 1 = 2$
$df_{Error} = k(n - 1) = 9$
Therefore $F_{crit} = 5.14$

MS_G is calculated with a calculator. Enter the three means as data points, and find the variance. Then multiply by n:

$$nS_{\bar{x}}^2 = 4 \times 0.146 = 0.58$$

MS_{Error} is calculated by averaging the cell variances:

average $S^2 = 2.28$

Thus, $F = \dfrac{MS_{Group}}{MS_{Error}} = \dfrac{0.58}{2.28} = 0.26$

Since $F_{crit} > F_{calc}$ we accept H_0 and conclude that there is no significant difference between the means of the three groups, i.e. we can conclude that mean intellectual functioning does not differ significantly with differing degrees of sleep deprivation.

Summary

1. Analysis of variance (ANOVA) is an inferential statistical procedure that enables one to test for significant differences between the means of more than two groups of subjects, and the influence of more than one independent variable.

2. The familywise error rate is the probability of rejecting at least one null hypothesis when it is true, in a set (family) of comparisons.

3. ANOVA is an omnibus test that protects against an increased familywise error rate by employing a single calculation to test all possible comparisons between means at once. It tests for an effect rather than a difference between means. If the effect is significant, then we know that the means of at least one of the comparisons we are testing are significantly different from each other.

4. In ANOVA terminology, variance is renamed Mean Squares (MS), the numerator in the variance formula is called the Sums of Squares (SS), and the denominator is called the degrees of freedom (df).

5. The aim of computing the ANOVA is to determine whether there is systematic variance present. If there is systematic variance present in our dataset, we have a significant effect. However, we can never identify and measure pure systematic variance. The differences between group means will always be influenced by random (also known as error) variance, in addition to systematic variance.

6. In practice, we find our way around this problem by calculating MS_{Group} (variance between the groups; an estimate of error variance plus systematic variance) and MS_{Error} (variance within cells; an estimate of error variance) and then comparing them (by calculating F). To the extent that MS_{Group} (error variance + systematic variance) is larger than MS_{Error} (error variance), and therefore $F > 1$, it is likely that there is a significant effect.

7. The procedure for calculating one-way ANOVAs (equal sample sizes) by hand is as follows:
   Step 1: Determine the intermediate statistics – $\bar{x}$, s^2, and n.
   Step 2: Determine MS_{Group} and MS_{Error}.
   Step 3: Compare MS_{Group} and MS_{Error} by calculating F.
   Step 4: Compare F_{calc} with F_{crit}.

Exercises

1. Below is a rough description of a number of ANOVA designs. What is specified is k, the number of groups in the design; and n, the number of scores in each group. Use the F-tables to determine F_{crit} values for each design.
   a) k = 3, n = 10, α = 0.05
   b) k = 4, n = 6, α = 0.05
   c) k = 5, n = 5, α = 0.05
   d) k = 3, n = 9, α = 0.01
   e) k = 6, n = 4, α = 0.1

2. Write a short paragraph in which you discuss the similarities and differences between the *t*-test and F-test.

3. A cognitive psychologist tests the hypothesis that memory is influenced by ambient noise. She randomly assigns 30 subjects to three noise conditions, and records the number of words (from a list of 100) the subjects recall after 15 minutes of studying. The data she collected is shown in the table below. Use a calculator to run a one-way ANOVA on this data (α = 0.05). Does ambient noise influence recall?

70 decibels	120 decibels	170 decibels
60, 43, 75, 58, 69, 53, 62, 79, 65, 58	59, 50, 63, 31, 47, 71, 43, 54, 60, 36	49, 65, 53, 59, 40, 61, 47, 53, 60, 55

4. To investigate whether birth order is related to school performance, an educational researcher selects four families with three children, and records the final school results of each of the children. These appear in the table below. Use a calculator to run a one-way ANOVA on this data (α = 0.05). Can the researcher conclude that school performance is related to birth order?

1st born	2nd born	3rd born
41	53	90
47	56	97
43	54	93
45	57	95

TUTORIAL

15

One-way analysis of variance

Kevin Durrheim

> After studying this tutorial, you should be able to:
> - Calculate one-way ANOVAs by hand, and with the help of SPSS®.
> - Explain the concepts 'multiple comparisons' and 'effect size', and calculate them.
> - Construct and interpret an ANOVA summary table.
> - Test that the assumptions underlying the use of ANOVA have not been violated.

In Tutorial 14, we introduced you to *analysis of variance (ANOVA)*, and outlined some simple calculations for a balanced one-way ANOVA design. We will assume in this tutorial that you are familiar with that material.

ANOVA involves a comparison of MS_{Group} and MS_{Error}.

ANOVA (analysis of variance) is a type of statistical analysis that is appropriate for designs having one independent variable consisting of more than two groups (*one-way* ANOVA), or more than one independent variable (*factorial* ANOVA). Because of increased Type I error rates that arise when comparing more than two means, we use ANOVA to detect the presence of a significant effect. Detecting a significant effect involves identifying systematic variation between the group means. However, since systematic variance cannot be measured, ANOVA involves a comparison of the variance between groups (MS_{Group}), an estimate of error variance plus systematic variance, and the variance within groups (MS_{Error}), an estimate of error variance.

Complete the following ANOVA table and decide whether it reports a significant effect – or, if you prefer, use your spreadsheet program to estimate the probability value associated with the F-ratio in the table. (You may need to refresh your understanding of Tutorial 14.)

Source	SS	df	MS	F
Group			0.053	0.63
Error		33		
TOTAL		35		

*If F is significant, and we reject H_0, we must identify **how** the means differ.*

In the worked examples you considered in the previous tutorial, the aim was merely to find out whether or not there was systematic variance present in the dataset. All we set out to do was to determine whether the F-statistic was significant or not. If there is no significant effect present in the datasets, it is appropriate to accept the null hypothesis, and conclude that there are no significant differences between the groups. However, when there is systematic variance present, and we do reject the null hypothesis, further calculation is required to determine the specific pattern of differences between the group means. Does the first mean differ from the second, the second from the third, or are all means significantly different from each other? This is what we will consider in this tutorial. First, however, let us work through an example where there is a significant effect.

Example 1

A Catholic scholar interested in religious matters wants to identify the most devout Catholic order. He thinks that a good way to determine this may be in terms of the number of hours spent praying. He recruits 15 subjects – 5 Jesuits, 5 Benedictines, and 5 Carmelites – and records the average number of hours spent praying per day. He now needs to analyse the data to see if the orders differ on the measured variable.

Step 1: Calculate intermediate statistics. These have been computed with the help of a calculator and are reported in Table 15.1. Already you can note that the variation of scores within each of the groups is quite small, whereas the differences between the group means are quite large. This suggests that there may be a significant effect present in this data (i.e. we may be able to reject the null hypothesis and conclude that there are group differences in the amount of time spent praying).

Step 2: Calculate MS_{Group} and MS_{Error}. MS_{Group} is computed with a calculator, firstly by determining the variance between the group means, $s_{\bar{X}}^2$, and multiplying this by n, the number of subjects within

Table 15.1 Time (hrs) spent praying by three Catholic orders

Jesuit	Benedictine	Carmelite
5	3	11
7	4	9
6	1	12
7	5	8
8	4	10
$\bar{x} = 6.6$	$\bar{x} = 3.4$	$\bar{x} = 10$
$s^2 = 1.3$	$s^2 = 2.3$	$s^2 = 2.5$
$n = 5$	$n = 5$	$n = 5$

each group (as detailed in Tutorial 14). MS_{Error} (denoted as MS_E below) is computed by finding the mean of the variances within all of the three cells in the designs.

$$MS_G = n \times s_{\bar{x}}^2 \qquad \qquad MS_E = \frac{s_1^2 + s_2^2 + s_3^2}{k}$$

$$= 5 \times 10.89 = 54.45 \qquad = \frac{1.3 + 2.3 + 2.5}{3} = 2.033$$

Step 3: Calculate F – i.e. divide MS_{Group} by MS_{Error} – in order to determine the extent to which MS_{Group} (the estimate of error and systematic variance) is greater than MS_{Error} (the estimate of pure error variance).

$$F = \frac{MS_G}{MS_E} = \frac{54.45}{2.033} = 26.78$$

The information we have calculated in the above three steps is usually reported in an ANOVA summary table (see Table 15.2). The first column provides a record of the source of the variance: group, error, and total. The second column reports the degrees of freedom, the third the sums of squares, the fourth the mean squares, and the fifth

Table 15.2 ANOVA summary table for analysis of data in Table 15.1

Source	df	SS	MS	F
Group	2	108.92	54.46	26.78
Error	12	24.4	2.033	
TOTAL	14	133.32		

the F-value. The only values in the table we have not calculated directly so far are the sums of squares. However, since the mean square is equal to the sums of squares divided by the degrees of freedom (see Tutorial 14), we compute the sums of squares simply by multiplying the mean squares by the degrees of freedom. Note that sums of squares are additive, whereas mean squares are not. This means that – as in the case of degrees of freedom – we can add the error and group sums of squares to determine the total sums of squares. As we will see later, this 'additivity' allows us to determine the effect size by calculating the proportion of the total variance associated with differences between group means.

The sums of squares and degrees of freedom are additive.

Activity 15.2

Use a spreadsheet program (or calculator) to conduct a one-way ANOVA on the data below. The data comes from a study comparing the attractiveness of three types of deodorant when worn by rugby players. The ratings were made by fellow players. Remember to estimate effect size.

Deo 1	Deo 2	Deo 3
8.5, 8.7, 9.0, 8.9, 9.1	9.2, 9.5, 9.1, 9.4, 9.3	9.6, 9.7, 9.8, 9.9, 9.8

Step 4: Determine significance. Since MS_{Group} could be greater than MS_{Error} purely by chance, we must refer to statistical tables to determine significance (or use a computer to calculate the exact probability). There are two types of degrees of freedom associated with F: *error degrees of freedom*, and *group degrees of freedom*. If you refer to your F-tables (see Appendix 1), you will see that F_{crit} for 2 and 12 degrees of freedom with alpha set at 0.05 (written as $F_{.05}(2,12)$) is equal to 3.89 (i.e. $F_{.05}(2,12) = 3.89$). We determine significance by comparing F_{calc} and F_{crit}. In this case, F_{calc} is greater than F_{crit}, so we reject the null hypothesis and conclude that there is an effect present in the data. This means that there is at least one significant difference between the means. As an omnibus test, ANOVA only tells us whether *at least* one of the comparisons between means is significant – it does not tell us *which* of the comparisons this is. To determine this, we can conduct multiple comparisons.

Multiple comparisons and effect size

If we reject H_0, then (for the running example) either $\mu_1 \neq \mu_2$, or $\mu_1 \neq \mu_3$, or $\mu_2 \neq \mu_3$, or $\mu_1 \neq \mu_2 \neq \mu_3$. As an omnibus test, ANOVA can only identify a significant effect. It cannot tell us where the differences between the means lie. Post hoc tests – which you can think of as modified *t*-tests that control for familywise error rate – are useful for determining precisely where the differences between the means lie. There are a number of post hoc tests that are commonly used with ANOVA; their relative benefits and rationale are the subject of several book-length discussions (e.g. Rosenthal & Rosnow, 1985). Here we will only consider Tukey's Honestly Significantly Difference test (HSD), since it is the test used most widely in the social sciences.

Post hoc tests are modified t-tests that control Type I error rate.

It is conventional to specify all of the hypotheses in a generic form, i.e.:

$$H_0: \mu_i = \mu_j; \quad H_1: \mu_i \neq \mu_j; \quad (\alpha = 0.05, \text{ for groups labelled i, j, and i} \neq \text{j})$$

The formula to compute the HSD statistic is given below. Although it looks horribly complicated, it is actually quite straightforward. You have already calculated the information that appears under the square root sign (MS_{Error} and n), and this can merely be substituted into the formula. In fact, there is no need to calculate any new data at all, because the value for $Q(k, df_e)$ is determined from the Q-tables (see Appendix 1). In the tables, k refers to the number of means being compared and df_e is the error degrees of freedom. By adjusting for the number of means being compared, the Q-value manages to keep the overall probability of making a Type I error at 0.05 despite the increased number of comparisons. In this case $k = 3$ and $df_e = 12$. The value on the Q-tables that corresponds with $k = 3$ and $df_e = 12$ is 3.77. HSD is thus calculated to be 2.40.

Post hoc tests are used to determine where differences between the means are.

Equation 15.1

$$HSD = Q(k, df_e) \sqrt{\frac{MS_e}{n}}$$

$$= 3.77 \sqrt{\frac{2.033}{5}} = 2.40$$

The HSD statistic is a critical range applied to pairwise comparisons between groups. What this means is that if any of the differences between the group means is greater than this critical range, we can conclude that there are significant differences between these groups. In practice what we do is calculate the differences between all possible pairs of groups and then compare the absolute value of these differences with the critical range:

$$\bar{x}_1 - \bar{x}_2 = 6.6 - 3.4 = 3.2$$
$$\bar{x}_1 - \bar{x}_3 = 6.6 - 10 = -3.4$$
$$\bar{x}_2 - \bar{x}_3 = 3.4 - 10 = -6.6$$

In all three instances, the absolute value of the difference between the group means is greater than the critical range (2.40). We therefore reject the null hypothesis in each case and conclude that all three groups differ from each other. By inspecting the magnitude of each group mean, we conclude that the Carmelites pray the most, followed by Jesuits, and that Benedictines pray the least.

Run multiple comparisons on the three groups in the dataset in Activity 15.2. Would you have run these in the ordinary course of analysing that data? Why?

Effect size is an estimate of the proportion of total variance explained by differences among our treatment means.

The final set of calculations to be performed is to determine the *effect size*. Simply obtaining significant differences between our treatment means does not mean that the differences are large or important. As you will have noted when you studied power (Tutorial 13), a significant result does not necessarily mean that the experimental effect is of practical significance. Effect size is an estimate of the proportion of total variance explained by differences among the treatment means, and is thus an indication of the strength of the effect. The meaning of effect size is evident in the formula to compute eta-squared (η^2), a widely used index of effect size. Although η^2 is a biased estimate of effect size, it is simple to calculate by hand and quite easy to understand:

Equation 15.2

$$\eta^2 = \frac{SS_{group}}{SS_{total}}$$

$$= \frac{108.92}{133.32} = 0.82 \text{ (see Table 15.2)}$$

Eta-squared (η^2) is a biased estimate of effect size.

As you can see from the formula, η^2 is determined by dividing SS_{group} by SS_{total}. Since sums of squares are additive, this is equivalent to calculating the proportion of the total variance that is explained by differences between the group means. For this example, $\eta^2 = 0.82$, meaning that 82% of the total variance between scores is accounted for by differences between the groups. This is an extremely large effect size for an experiment in the social sciences, where significant effect sizes are not infrequently below 0.1.

Using SPSS® to do one–way ANOVA

The examples we have considered thus far involve three groups with an equal number of cases (equal cell sizes). These are called *balanced designs*. The calculations for such balanced designs are straightforward, and have been included to demonstrate the underlying logic of ANOVA. While it is important to have a sound understanding of this underlying logic, ANOVA calculations for more complex designs can be rather complex and are best completed using a computer.

Example 2

An educationist tests the efficacy of a new remedial reading programme on a group of Grade 5 children who have been identified as slow learners. The sample of children is made up of 20 boys and 17 girls, whom she randomly assigns to either an experimental or control group. Fortunately for the researcher, there are no significant differences between the mean reading speeds of the groups before implementation of the programme. The control group attend standard reading lessons while the learners in the experimental condition attend the special remedial reading classes. After 6 months the educationist records the number of words the children read per minute. She must now establish whether there are any significant differences between the groups.

Balanced designs have an equal number of cases per cell.

In this example, we want to test the null hypothesis (H_0: $\mu_1 = \mu_2 = \mu_3 = \mu_4$) that there are no significant differences between the means of the four groups. We can use any standard statistical computer package to perform this one-way ANOVA, but we will demonstrate the use of SPSS®. However, we must first enter the data in appropriate format on the package's datasheet. This requires a different format to that presented in Table 15.3. Instead of having four columns of data, one for each group, we enter the data in three columns (see Figure 15.1). The first column contains subject identification codes; each

Table 15.3 Number of words read per minute – data from Example 2

Female control	Male control	Female experimental	Male experimental
10, 15, 9, 18, 21, 17, 19, 17	17, 11, 23, 8, 12, 18, 11, 14, 16, 10	22, 38, 33, 27, 19, 28, 36, 18, 27	28, 30, 18, 33, 22, 19, 30, 23, 17, 19

Subject	Group	Words	Subject	Group	Words
1	1	10	...	...	...
2	1	15	19	3	22
3	1	9	20	3	38
			21	3	33
...	...	...			
9	2	17	...	...	...
10	2	11	28	4	28
11	2	23	29	4	30
			30	4	18
			...	...	...

Figure 15.1 Data from Table 15.3 in datasheet format

subject is numbered consecutively from 1 to 37. The second column contains an indicator variable that identifies the group identity of the subject. In this example, the female control group is coded 1, the male control group is coded 2, the female experimental group is coded 3, and the male experimental group is coded 4. The third column contains the reading measure for each subject.

Activity 15.4

Set the data from Activity 15.2 up in a form suitable for analysis with SPSS® or another statistical package. Use the computer package to run a one-way ANOVA, with multiple comparisons, to check your answers to the earlier activities in this tutorial.

Once the data are in appropriate worksheet format, the mechanics of running the ANOVA are simple. In this example, the SPSS® one-way ANOVA procedure is used to do the calculations.

Box 15.1

Using SPSS® to conduct one-way ANOVA

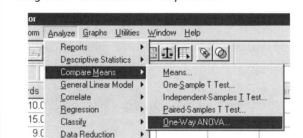

1. Pull down the 'Analyze' menu in SPSS®, select 'Compare Means', and then 'One-Way ANOVA'.

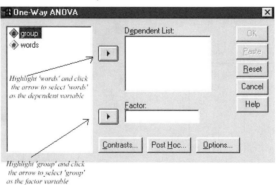

2. The 'One-Way ANOVA' window will now appear on the screen. Now you can define your model, selecting 'words' as your dependent variable, and 'group' as your factor.

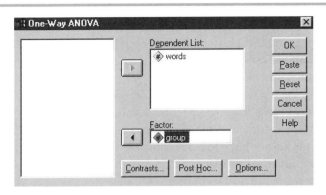

3. You should then see the dialog box above, which confirms your choice of variables. At this stage you can also request multiple comparisons by clicking the 'Post Hoc' button.

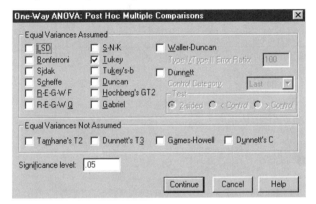

4. The ensuing dialog allows you to choose from a variety of tests. To select Tukey's HSD test, click in the 'Tukey' tick box, and then click 'Continue'. You will return to the dialog in pane 3. Click 'OK' to run the procedure.

The output displayed in Figure 15.2 on the next page was produced by the SPSS® one-way procedure.

You should recognise the top table reported under the heading 'WORDS'. This is the ANOVA summary table, reporting the degrees of freedom, sums of squares, and mean squares for the group and error terms. The table also reports the F-value and p. We use p to determine whether we have a significant effect or not: p is the probability that the null hypothesis is true. If the p-value is less than 0.05, we reject the null hypothesis. In this case $p < 0.0005$, indicating that there is an effect, and that there are significant differences between some of the group means. (Note that the p-value is reported in the column marked 'Sig.', and the value '.000' should not be interpreted to mean that the probability is 0 – it is rounded to 0 at three decimal places, but is better reported as $p < 0.0005$.) We will have to refer to the outcome of the multiple comparison tests to determine the specific pattern of mean differences. You will note that we are using a slightly different procedure for hypothesis testing here than we used earlier in the examples we analysed without the computer. In the earlier worked examples, we compared F_{calc} with F_{crit} to reach a decision. The computer makes life easier for us: we no longer have to look up critical values, because the output reports a close estimate of the exact probability that the null hypothesis is true. All we have to do is compare this probability with the significance level, α, to reach a decision. If the probability is less than α, we reject the null hypothesis.

ANOVA

WORDS

	Sum of squares	df	Mean square	F	Sig.
Between groups	1165.810	3	388.603	12.516	.000
Within groups	1024.622	33	31.048		
Total	2190.432	36			

WORDS

Tukey HSD[a,b]

		Subset for alpha = .05	
Group	N	1	2
2.00	10	14.0000	
1.00	8	15.7500	
4.00	10		23.00000
3.00	9		27.5556
Sig.		.907	.605

Figure 15.2 SPSS® output for one-way ANOVA procedure

Next, the output reports the outcome of the Tukey HSD tests, as well as sample sizes and means for each of the four groups. (The means are the entries in the third and fourth columns.) Clearly, groups 3 and 4 have higher means than groups 1 and 2. The results of the Tukey tests corroborate this impression about the means. The Tukey tests hold the familywise error rate at 0.05 (the entry 'Subset for alpha = .05' in the first row of the subsets table is confirmation). This means that we have a 5% chance of making one Type I error in all of our six individual two-group comparisons. This reduces the Type I error rate (α) for each individual test. As you may well expect, this small probability of making a Type I error is associated with a larger probability of making a Type II error, which may, in certain circumstances, be undesirable. Tukey's is a very conservative test, and in some instances it may be better to specify a familywise error rate of 0.1 rather than 0.05 to reduce the chances of making a Type II error with the individual multiple comparisons.

A conservative test reduces Type I error rate, but at the expense of power.

SPSS® reports the results of the Tukey tests as a number of 'homogenous subsets' – that is, it forms subsets from groups whose means are not significantly different from other groups within the subset, but which are significantly different from groups in other subsets. As the output shows, Groups 1 and 2 form one subset (their means do not differ), and Groups 3 and 4 another subset (their means do not differ from each other, but do differ from the means of both Groups 1 and 2). The final row in the table, labelled 'Sig.' (for 'significance'), reports the probability that the means within the subsets differ, and as we can see these are much higher than α, so we accept that they do not differ.

Overall, the results of the remedial reading experiment are positive. They indicate that both the male and female control groups read more slowly (i.e. fewer words per minute) than the male and female experimental groups. The remedial reading programme appears to work! The final bit of information we could possibly want is to identify how strong this effect is. The one-way ANOVA procedure in SPSS® does not report the effect size (it is available in other SPSS® procedures), but we can calculate it easily by dividing SS_{group} by SS_{total}. In this manner we find $\eta^2 = 0.53$. It would appear not only that there is a significant difference between the experimental and control groups, but that the remedial reading programme has a powerful effect on learners' reading ability, explaining 53% of the total variance in reading speed.

Assumptions underlying ANOVA

As you can see from the worked example above, ANOVA is a wonderfully efficient way of making sense of a dataset. When you first look at the raw data, all you see is a collection of numbers. Once these numbers have been processed and analysed, clear conclusions can be drawn about the outcomes of a research study. However, we need to be careful: ANOVA is based on certain assumptions, which, if violated, can produce misleading results. So before conducting an ANOVA, it is vitally important that you check whether any of the assumptions have been violated.

There are two key assumptions in the case of one-way ANOVA. These are precisely the same assumptions that underlie the t-test for independent samples.

Before performing any inferential statistical procedure, it is vital to check whether any of the assumptions have been violated. If the assumptions are violated, the conclusions may be incorrect.

Normality
The populations from which the data (for each group of the independent variable) are sampled should be normally distributed. Since we have no access to the parent populations, this assumption is tested by examining the distribution of the sample data. In practice,

ANOVA is a robust statistical procedure, and the assumption of normality can be violated with relatively minor effects. As a general rule of thumb, if the populations can be assumed to be either symmetrical or at least of similar shape, ANOVA will produce valid results.

Activity 15.5

Check to see whether the data from Activity 15.2 satisfies the assumptions required by ANOVA.

Homogeneity of variance

ANOVA is a robust statistical procedure, especially in the case of balanced designs.

The populations from which the data are sampled should have the same variance. This assumption can be violated without major effects on the final results. As a general rule of thumb, the largest variance should not be more than four or five times the smallest. However, if you do not have a balanced design (i.e. you have unequal sample sizes), unequal variance can produce misleading results.

To test that the assumptions have been met, we need firstly to examine the shape of the distributions of the data, and secondly to compare the variances of the groups. As you will see in Figure 15.3, a series of boxplots has been used to check the shape of the distributions in the remedial reading example. Since we have very few subjects per group, we cannot expect the distributions to be perfectly normal. The boxplots indicate that the distributions are roughly symmetrical, and we therefore expect the population distributions to be approximately normal. The descriptive statistics for the four experimental groups are reported in Figure 15.2, above.

Note that the scores for each group are similarly dispersed in the boxplots. We can conclude therefore that our data satisfy the requirement of homogeneity of variance. Both assumptions have been satisfied, and we can interpret the results of our significance tests with confidence.

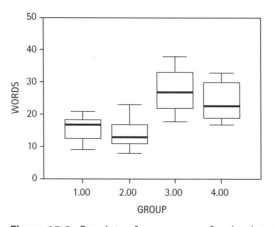

Figure 15.3 Boxplots of group scores for the data from Table 15.3

If assumptions are *seriously* violated, and you suspect that ANOVA will produce misleading results, non-parametric or distribution-free statistical procedures can be used. Although these procedures have less power than parametric tests, they are not based on any assumptions about distributions (hence they are sometimes called *distribution-free tests*). We consider non-parametric alternatives to many parametric tests in Tutorial 19.

If the assumptions of ANOVA are violated, use non-parametric statistics.

Worked example

1. A cognitive scientist is interested in the differential effectiveness of memory-enhancing strategies. She recruits 40 subjects, and assigns them randomly to a control group or one of three experimental conditions. In each experimental condition, subjects are required to learn a list of words using an enhancing strategy particular to their group. All subjects are then tested for their memory of the list of words. The strategies are a *mnemonic strategy* (Group 2), *rehearsal* (Group 3), and a *semantic elaboration strategy* (Group 4). The control group (Group 1) is not trained in any specific strategy. The dependent variable is the number of words recalled correctly. Analyse the data comprehensively to determine which strategy (if any) is effective.

Control	5, 4, 6, 4, 7, 3, 5, 6, 8, 5
Mnemonic	7, 5, 8, 6, 5, 7, 5, 7, 4, 8
Rehearsal	9, 9, 10, 10, 8, 9, 9, 6, 9, 8
Semantic	8, 7, 5, 6, 9, 8, 7, 10, 4, 6

Solution
To analyse the data fully, proceed in three stages:
a) Test assumptions to determine whether or not ANOVA is an appropriate test.
b) Determine significance.
c) If F is significant, conduct post hoc tests and calculate the effect size.

a) *Testing assumptions*
It is useful to calculate descriptive statistics here, and to examine some graphical representations of the datasets. We show the steps for doing this in SPSS®, and the output produced by the program.

Commands

i) Select 'Means' from the 'Compare Means' option.

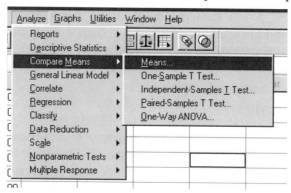

ii) Move the 'group' variable into the independent list, and 'memory' variable into the dependent list, and click 'OK'.

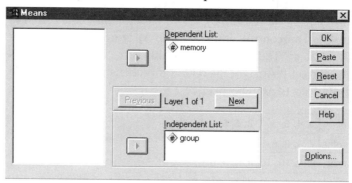

iii) To construct a boxplot, choose 'Graphs', then 'Boxplot', and define the 'Category Axis' and 'Variable' appropriately.

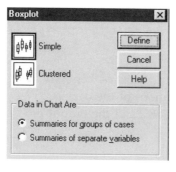

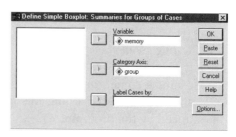

NUMBERS, HYPOTHESES AND CONCLUSIONS

Output

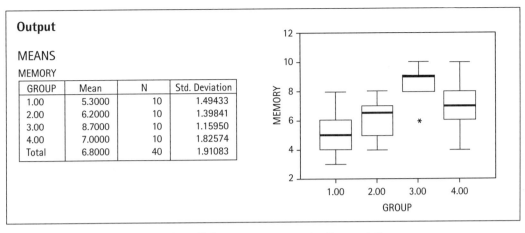

MEANS

MEMORY

GROUP	Mean	N	Std. Deviation
1.00	5.3000	10	1.49433
2.00	6.2000	10	1.39841
3.00	8.7000	10	1.15950
4.00	7.0000	10	1.82574
Total	6.8000	40	1.91083

The standard deviations for all four groups are similar and the 'homogeneity of variance' assumption is thus satisfied. The boxplots show that the data for three of the groups is roughly normal. The data for Group 3 however is very skewed. This could suggest that ANOVA is not appropriate. Since the boxplots are based on small sample sizes and the assumption refers to normality of the parent populations, these plots are not conclusive. Since ANOVA is robust, we proceed with significance testing. Non-parametric tests could also be run to determine whether the same conclusions are reached.

b) *Analysis of variance*

We showed the steps for doing one-way ANOVA in SPSS® earlier, so we will not repeat them here. The output from the one-way procedure is shown below.

ANOVA

MEMORY

	Sum of squares	df	Mean square	F	Sig.
Between groups	62.600	3	20.867	9.414	.000
Within groups	79.800	36	2.217		
Total	142.400	39			

The *p*-value indicates that there is a significant effect and that we can reject the null hypothesis.

c) *Post hoc tests and effect size*

Since the ANOVA produced a significant F-ratio, we conduct multiple comparisons to determine which means are significantly different. We show only the output from SPSS®, not the steps taken to produce it.

Tukey HSD[a,b]

		Subset for alpha = .05	
Group	N	1	2
1.00	10	5.3000	
2.00	10	6.2000	
4.00	10	7.0000	7.0000
3.00	10		8.7000
Sig.		.068	.068

Tukey's HSD tests confirm that the significant differences lie between Groups 1 and 3 and between Groups 2 and 3. This is not that easy to see from the table, but it follows from the fact that Group 3 is in a different subset from Groups 1 and 2. The difficulty is to interpret Group 4 (semantic elaboration), which belongs in both subsets. We are obliged to conclude that although rehearsal (Group 3) achieves better results than the 'control' (Group 1) or 'mnemonic' (Group 2) conditions, there is no evidence that it does any better than the semantic elaboration (Group 4).

It is always useful (and important) to calculate effect sizes, and for the experiment at hand $\eta^2 = 0.44$ (i.e. SS_g/SS_{total}). This is a strong effect size, which indicates that rehearsal can cause substantial improvements in memory.

Summary

1. How to do one-way ANOVA (balanced designs) without the aid of a computer:
   Step 1: Calculate intermediate statistics ($\bar{x}$, s^2, n, k).
   Step 2: Calculate MS_{Group} and MS_{Error}.
   Step 3: Calculate F, and complete the ANOVA summary table.
   Step 4: Look up F_{crit}, and reach a decision.
       – If *not significant*, then STOP.
       – If *significant*, then proceed with Step 5.
   Step 5: Run post hoc tests.
   Step 6: Determine effect size.

2. Post hoc tests are used to determine precisely where the differences between the means lie when we have a significant effect. They are modified *t*-tests that control Type I error rate.

3. Effect size (e.g. eta-squared, η^2) is an estimate of the proportion of total variance explained by differences among the treatment means.

4. The procedure for computing ANOVA with a statistics package is as follows:
   Step 1: Save data in datasheet (worksheet) format.
   Step 2: Test assumptions (boxplots and descriptive statistics).
   Step 3: Run significance test and multiple comparisons.
   Step 4: Determine effect size.

At each stage of analysis, the results reported in the computer output must be interpreted comprehensively.

Exercises

1. Examine and complete the following ANOVA table:

Source	df	SS	MS	F
Drugs	2	?	?	3.75
Error	?	?	8.3	
TOTAL	39	?		

   On the basis of the ANOVA table, attempt to describe the study that generated the results represented by the table. Also, interpret the results of the study as best you can. Indicate what else you would like to know in order to analyse the results more comprehensively.

2. A nurse wants to trace the consequences of premature delivery on later personality development. In particular, the nurse predicts that premature babies will be orally dependent. She examines City Lane Hospital's records and randomly draws three groups of subjects: a group delivered **before** the 7th month of the mother's pregnancy, a group delivered **between** 7 and $8\frac{1}{2}$ months of pregnancy, and a group delivered **after** $8\frac{1}{2}$ months of pregnancy. The nurse contacts each subject's mother and asks her to indicate how old the child was (in weeks) when she stopped breastfeeding. The data are as follows:

Before	Between	After
52 39 67 34 53	35 43 38 50 37	34 38 33 32 47
51 49 63 44 63	45 53 48 40 47	33 49 34 42 57
48 38	35 55	49 39

   Is the nurse's theoretical hunch supported by the data? Analyse the data comprehensively – e.g. run multiple comparisons if necessary, and calculate magnitude of effect size to see how substantial the differences between the groups are.

3. Imagine now that the nurse in question 2, above, only collected information for the first two groups (before 7th month and between 7 and $8\frac{1}{2}$ months). Conduct a one-way ANOVA to establish whether the groups differ. Conduct a t-test and compare the results to those given by the ANOVA. Look closely at the relationship between t and F. What do you observe?

4. Associate-Professor Freud-Detector is browsing through a 1934 education journal and comes across a study authored by the notorious English social scientist, Burtt. The study compares IQ

scores across different socio-economic groups. Burtt reports an analysis of variance and interprets the analysis of variance as supporting the theory that people with higher IQs gravitate towards higher socio-economic groups. Prof. Freud-Detector wants to re-analyse the data and see whether there is any valid statistical support to be found in the data for Burtt's conclusion. Unfortunately, Burtt does not report his raw data (a common practice), but he does report means and standard deviations for the three groups (low, middle, and high socio-economic standing). These are as follows:

Low s.e.s	Mid s.e.s	High s.e.s
$\bar{x} = 87.4$	$\bar{x} = 94.3$	$\bar{x} = 101.4$
$s = 16.4$	$s = 12.4$	$s = 5.6$

Burtt reports the following ANOVA table in his article:

Source	df	SS	MS	F
s.e.s	2	1 256	628	3.75
Error	33	273.9	8.3	
TOTAL	35	1 529.9		

Prof. Freud-Detector smells a rat. Do you?

TUTORIAL

16

Factorial analysis of variance

Kevin Durrheim

After studying this tutorial, you should be able to:
- Understand what a factorial design is, and know when it is appropriate to use factorial designs.
- Understand the underlying logic of factorial ANOVA.
- Use SPSS® to run factorial ANOVA procedures.
- Understand what interactions are, and know how to identify and interpret interactions.
- Conduct and interpret simple effects and multiple comparisons as they apply to factorial ANOVA.

Factorial ANOVA is used for research designs that have more than one independent variable.

The previous two tutorials dealt with one-way ANOVA, a procedure that is used to analyse designs with one independent variable (IV) consisting of more than two groups. ANOVA is also appropriate to analyse designs that have more than one independent variable. These are known as *factorial designs*. Consider a simple study to test whether aggression is caused by the time spent watching TV violence and the type of violence watched. This is an extension of the study we considered in Tutorial 14. We now have two independent variables (type of violence, and time spent watching), and one dependent variable (aggression).

As you can see from Table 16.1, instead of our design having three groups of subjects – one non-violent control group, one Kung Fu group, and one domestic violence group – we now have six groups (compare Table 16.1 below with Table 14.1). To operationalise the amount of TV violence watched, half the subjects are exposed to 2 hours of violence and the other half are exposed to 6 hours of violence.

Table 16.1 Data for TV violence experiment

		Factor B = Type of violence			Marginal means
		Non–violent	Kung Fu	Domestic	
Factor A = Time	2 hours	2, 0, 1, 3, 3 $\bar{x} = 1.8$	3, 6, 4, 6, 1 $\bar{x} = 4$	4, 1, 2, 3, 3 $\bar{x} = 2.6$	2.8
	6 hours	1, 3, 3, 5, 0 $\bar{x} = 2.4$	8, 10, 3, 4, 7 $\bar{x} = 6.4$	9, 6, 8, 10, 7 $\bar{x} = 8$	5.6
Marginal means		2.1	5.2	5.3	Grand mean 4.2

In ANOVA terminology, the independent variables are called *factors*. The design represented in Table 16.1 has two factors: factor A is the time spent watching TV and factor B is the type of violence watched. Each of the factors has a number of *levels*, which are different values of the independent variables. Time has two levels (2 hours and 6 hours) and type has three levels (non-violent, Kung Fu and domestic violence). When the two levels of time are crossed with the three levels of type we obtain a factorial design with six *cells*, or groups of data. The aim of factorial ANOVA is to test differences between the cell means and the marginal (level) means.

Factorial designs are research designs with more than one independent variable, where every level of each variable is paired with every level of all the other variables.

In this tutorial we will be concerned only with factorial designs in which every level of one variable is paired with every level of the other variables. These factorial designs must include data at all combinations of levels of the independent variables. In other words, when the factors are crossed in the form of a table, there should be no empty cells. If we had no non-violent control group in the 6-hour condition in Table 16.1 (i.e. we only had five cells of data), then we would not have a true factorial design.

Since the design in Table 16.1 has two independent variables, it is called a *two-way factorial design*. Another way of describing the design is to specify it as a 2 × 3 (pronounced 'two by three') factorial design, reflecting the number of factors and levels in the design. Factorial designs may have more than two factors: we can design three-way, four-way, five-way, and higher-order factorial experiments. In our TV violence study, imagine adding a further independent variable – the gender of the child. Now we would have three independent variables: type, time, and gender. In this design, instead of having six cells of data as in Table 16.1, we would need 12 cells of data, six for males and six for females. This would be a 2 × 2 × 3 factorial design.

As you can imagine, these designs can become very complex and require a large number of subjects. If we added a fourth independent variable to our study, the age of the child, with four different age groups, we would have a 2 × 2 × 3 × 4 factorial design, which would require 48 cells of data. In this tutorial we will only consider two-way designs.

Activity 16.1

Refer to Table 15.3. Now redraw the table in the form of a 2 × 2 design. Do this by re-arranging the data into rows and columns as we have done in Table 16.1 above. How many factors does the design have? How many levels does each factor have? How many cells are there? What research questions would we be able to answer with this design?

Why use factorial designs?

Factorial designs are preferable to one-way designs for three related reasons:
1. They are realistic, capturing the complexity of social and psychological phenomena.
2. They allow us to analyse interactions between variables.
3. They are economical, allowing many hypotheses to be tested simultaneously.

All social and psychological phenomena have multiple interacting causes. What are the causes of violence, for example? These include psychological states such as frustration and learned aggression, as well as sociological phenomena such as poverty and deprivation, to name but a few. To investigate such phenomena, it makes sense to design experiments that include more than one independent variable. This will give the researcher greater leeway to generalise the results of the research to real-world situations, since such experiments are designed to reflect the complexity of the real world. If a researcher designed an experiment to investigate the impact of frustration on violence, the study would ignore contexts of poverty that often underlie aggression and frustration in real-world situations.

The factors that should be included in a study are those that are related either theoretically or empirically to the dependent variable. Simply including arbitrary factors in an experiment will increase the complexity, cost, and error in the experiment with no additional benefit.

The second important advantage of using factorial designs is that they allow us to analyse data in much more detail. In Example 2 of Tutorial 15 we analysed the data for the remedial reading experiment in the form of a one-way ANOVA. In Activity 16.1 you saw

Factorial designs are generally better than multiple one-way analyses of the same data.

Main effects are the effects for one variable, ignoring all other variables. These are tests of differences between marginal means.

An interaction is a situation in a factorial design in which the effects of one independent variable depend upon the level of another independent variable.

Factorial designs capture the complexity of reality by estimating the effects of multiple, interacting causes.

that the data could be arranged as a two-way design. Now, instead of asking whether there are differences between the mean scores of the four groups (as we did in the one-way design), we can analyse the data in much more detail. We can determine whether males differ from females, and we can determine whether there is a significant difference between the means of the control and experimental groups. The effects for the factors are called *main effects*. In addition, we can investigate interactions between the independent variables. An *interaction* is a situation in a factorial design in which the effects of one independent variable depend upon the level of another independent variable. This would occur if the experiment turned out differently for males and females. If the mean scores for the female experimental and control groups differed significantly, but those for the male groups did not differ significantly, we would have an interaction between our two factors: the programme improved the reading of females but not males. Rather than simply determining whether the reading programme is effective, interactions allow us to determine whether the programme is effective for both males and females. It is preferable to analyse the data by means of factorial ANOVA because, instead of asking whether there is a single effect, we can determine the significance of three different effects. In this study, there are two main effects (gender and group), and an interaction effect (between gender and group).

Factorial designs allow us to investigate the influence of many independent variables, as well as interactions between them. This is a major advantage, because real-world phenomena have multiple determinants, many of which interact with each other. For example, medical research has shown that females lack an enzyme to break down alcohol, and that females therefore become intoxicated more quickly than males. There is an interaction between gender and intoxication after alcohol consumption.

Finally, factorial designs are economical in terms of subjects. As the discussion of the remedial reading experiment has shown, a two-way design with the same number of subjects as a one-way design allows us to investigate the influence of two independent variables with more sensitivity.

Activity 16.2

Think of your performance in exams over the past few years. List eight variables that you believe have influenced your exam performance in different subjects. Imagine that you are designing an experiment to determine two factors – subject difficulty and amount of time spent studying – have an impact on exam performance (the DV). In your experience, is there an interaction between subject difficulty and time spent studying? *(Hint: does five hours of studying have the same effect on exam performance for easy and difficult subjects?)*

The logic of factorial ANOVA

Recall that ANOVA is an acronym for 'analysis of variance'. With factorial designs, the full implications of what it means to analyse variance becomes evident. When we analysed the one-way ANOVA, we partitioned (split up) the total sums of squares (SS_{Total}) into variance between groups (SS_{Groups}) and variance within groups (SS_{Error}). In the two-way ANOVA we begin by doing the same thing: we partition SS_{Total} into error variance and the variance between groups. The groups in factorial designs are arranged in cells, and SS_{Total} is partitioned, at a first stage, into SS_{Error} and SS_{Cells}. The SS_{Cells} term is not very interesting in itself because it only tells us that at least one of the cell means differs from the rest. We are more interested in the pattern of differences between the cells. Are there significant differences between the factor levels, and is there an interaction between the variables? At a second stage of analysis, therefore, we partition SS_{Cells} into sums of squares terms for each of the factors and for the interaction. For the data in Table 16.1, we partition SS_{Cells} into variance due to time (SS_{Time}), variance due to type (SS_{Type}), and variance due to the interaction between time and type (SS_{T*t}) (see Figure 16.1).

Interactions are normally denoted by a multiplication sign, or an asterisk in computerese – e.g. A × B or A*B.

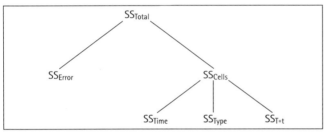

Figure 16.1 Partitioning of variance for the two-way ANOVA

Figure 16.1 can also be rewritten in the form of a simple equation:

$$SS_{Total} = SS_{Time} + SS_{Type} + SS_{T*t} + SS_{Error}$$

Equation 16.1

This equation is a simple model (called the *score model*) of how the variation in the data (or scores) is broken into sections when the data is analysed by ANOVA. It is particularly useful to specify the model in this way because it helps to identify exactly what the ANOVA procedure is doing. It also shows the relation between ANOVA and other statistical techniques such as regression, and many computer packages require you to use a regression model when analysing data.

Although the calculations for two-way ANOVA proceed via the two stages depicted in Figure 16.1, the logic underlying the analysis

*The **score model** shows how variation between the scores is partitioned.*

is very similar to that underlying one-way ANOVA. The computations are also similar to the one-way case. SS_{Total}, SS_{Error}, and SS_{Cells} are calculated in the same way as SS_{Total}, SS_{Error}, and SS_{Groups} in the one-way ANOVA. SS_{Cells} is a measure of the variance between the cell means. However, unlike the one-way case, the variance between the cell means has three possible causes, and it is these causes that we are interested in. The cell means in Table 16.1 may differ because of 1) a difference between the 2-hour and the 6-hour condition, 2) a difference between groups of subjects exposed to the three types of violence, or 3) an interaction between time and type. The ANOVA summary table for two-way ANOVA reports these effects rather than the cells effect.

Assumptions of factorial ANOVA

Factorial ANOVA has the same assumptions as one-way ANOVA.
1. *Normality.* The populations represented by the data should be normally distributed, making the mean an appropriate measure of central tendency. As in the one-way case, we must estimate the distribution of the parent populations from the data at hand. When we have small cell numbers, therefore, we should tolerate deviations from normality, appreciating that our estimates are unreliable. In addition, ANOVA is a robust statistical procedure: the assumption of normality can be violated with relatively minor effects. Nevertheless, ANOVA is inappropriate in situations where you have unequal cell sizes and distributions skewed in different directions.

When cell sizes are unequal, violations of the assumptions can produce misleading results.

2. *Homogeneity of variance.* The populations from which the data are sampled should have the same variance. With balanced designs (i.e. equal numbers of subjects per cell) this assumption can be violated without major effects on the final results.

It is essential to check that these assumptions apply to the data before interpreting the outcomes of the analysis. If the assumptions are not satisfied, you should consider using non-parametric statistics.

Box 16.1

Using SPSS® to run a factorial ANOVA
The procedure for running a two-way ANOVA with a computer package is very similar to running a one-way ANOVA. First, the data must be in appropriate spreadsheet format (see Table 16.2). For a two-way ANOVA, this requires two columns of identifying variables for each of the independent variables. The data in Table 16.1 is recoded into four columns as reported in Table 16.2. The two levels of time are represented in the table by using 1s to indicate subjects who watched 2 hours of violence, and 2s for subjects who watched

6 hours of violence. The 'Type' column contains 1s identifying the control group, 2s for the Kung Fu group, and 3s for the domestic violence group. Note that each of the six cells is thus identified by a different combination of indicator variables, and is thus uniquely defined by the two columns.

Once the data is in appropriate worksheet format, the mechanics of running the ANOVA are simple:

1. *Pull down the 'Analyze' menu.*
2. *Select the 'General Linear Model' option.* General linear model provides general statistical procedures for computing a number of different ANOVA designs. For our purposes, we will only be using the 'Univariate' procedure.
3. *Select the 'Univariate' option.* The 'Univariate' dialog box will now appear on the screen (see Figure 16.2).
4. *Select variables.* The dependent variable is aggression. Select this variable by clicking on 'aggress' in the dialog box, and then click on the arrow to shift the variable into the 'Dependent Variable' box. By the same procedure, shift the independent variables into the 'Fixed Factor(s)' box. The remainder of the boxes allow you to perform analyses that we will not be covering in this tutorial, so they can be ignored.

Table 16.2 Data for the TV violence experiment

Subject	Time	Type	Aggress
1	1	1	2
2	1	1	0
3	1	1	1
4	1	1	3
5	1	1	3
6	1	2	3
7	1	2	6
8	1	2	4
9	1	2	6
10	1	2	1
11	1	3	4
12	1	3	1
13	1	3	2
14	1	3	3
15	1	3	3
16	2	1	1
17	2	1	3
18	2	1	3
19	2	1	5
20	2	1	0
21	2	2	8
22	2	2	10
23	2	2	3
24	2	2	4
25	2	2	7
26	2	3	9
27	2	3	6
28	2	3	8
29	2	3	10
30	2	3	7

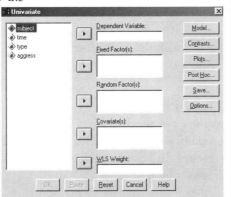

Figure 16.2 SPSS® 'Univariate' dialog box

5. *Specify plots.* The 'Plots' key allows you to generate a graph of the cell means, which will be useful when interpreting the outcome of the analysis. Specify the plot by entering the variable Type into the 'Horizontal Axis' box, and selecting Time into the 'Separate Lines' box. Click on the 'Add' button, and then click 'Continue'.

6. *Select post hoc tests.* Click the 'Post Hoc' button to open the 'Post Hoc' dialog box (compare with Box 15.1). A number of different options are provided. First select the variables for which you want tests conducted, and then select the type of test. For our data, the variable 'time' has only two levels, whose means are interpretable without post hoc comparisons. We thus conduct Tukey's tests on 'type'.

7. *Select 'Options'.* SPSS® provides a number of useful optional analyses. In the 'Options' dialog box, select the following options:

a) *'Estimates of Effect Size'* provides an estimate of effect size (η^2) for the main effects and interactions.

b) *'Homogeneity Tests'* allow us to test whether the assumption of homogeneity of variance is met. Levene's test is used to determine whether the parent populations represented by the data have statistically similar variances.

8. *Run the procedure.* Once the analysis has been specified as set out above, click 'OK' on the 'Univariate' dialog box to run the procedure.

Analysing factorial ANOVA designs

The computations for factorial ANOVA are best done using statistical software. Whichever stats package you use, it will have an option for analysing factorial designs. The data must be entered in spreadsheet format, and then the analysis must be specified. We interpret the output in stages: first, confirm that the assumptions have not been violated; then examine the ANOVA summary table; and finally interpret the main effects and interactions.

Activity 16.3

Construct boxplots and run a factorial ANOVA for the TV violence experiment (see Table 16.1) by following the steps outlined in Box 16.1.

1. Testing assumptions

It is always a good idea to run descriptive analyses before conducting inferential tests.

Boxplots are used to help us decide whether the assumptions of normality and homogeneity of variance have been met. The boxplots in Figure 16.3 were generated using the 'Boxplot' option of the 'Graphs' menu of SPSS®.

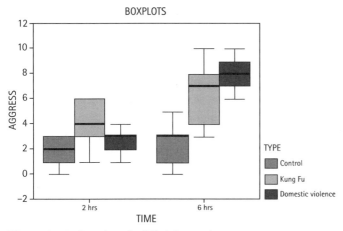

Figure 16.3 Boxplots for TV violence data

Since we have only 5 subjects per cell, we can expect that the box-plots will not be very reliable indicators of population properties. If we randomly selected another 5 respondents from the same population, we would expect these new boxplots to have different means and variances. (If you do not know why, refer to the discussion of sampling distributions in Tutorial 7.)

The boxplots indicate a similar spread of scores for each of the groups, suggesting that the condition of homogeneity of variance has been satisfied. We can confirm this conclusion by inspecting the outcome of Levene's test of homogeneity of variance in the SPSS® output (Table 16.3). The F-value is not significant, suggesting that we cannot reject the null hypothesis of equality of variance.

Table 16.3 Levene's test

Dependent variable: AGGRESS

F	df1	df2	Sig.
1.553	5	24	.211

Tests the null hypothesis that the error variance of the dependent variable is equal across groups.

In the boxplots of Figure 16.3, with the exception of the middle two skewed plots, the distributions have similar shapes, reflecting scores that are roughly normally distributed.

Our exploratory analysis suggests that the population distributions represented by the cell data are roughly normal and have similar variance. As is often the case with real-world research, the evidence for normality and homogeneity of variance is somewhat

When sample sizes are small, boxplots do not provide reliable visualisation of population distributions.

ambiguous. The boxplots do not show perfectly normally distributed data. Nor are the cell variances equal. Given our small cell sizes, we cannot expect this of the data. At the same time, ANOVA is a relatively robust statistical procedure. On balance, then, it appears that ANOVA is an appropriate method for analysing the data.

2. Examining the main effects and interactions

Recall that ANOVA involves partitioning the variation between scores (i.e. on a dependent measure). The ANOVA summary table shows how the total sums of squares for our TV violence experiment ($SS_{Total} = 772$) is partitioned (see Table 16.4). In addition to the estimate of error variance, sums of squares are reported for three effects, namely Time, Type, and Time*Type. Notice that the SPSS® output also reports the sums of squares for the model. The model sum of squares is the SS_{Cells} term in Figure 16.1, and it represents the variation between the cell means. As you can see from Figure 16.1, the model sum of squares is then partitioned into two main effects (Time and Type), and the interaction effect (Time*Type). Thus, if you add together the sums of squares for Time (58.8), Type (66.2), and Time*Type (29.4), you will obtain the value for the model sum of squares (154.4).

The sums of squares for the effects add up to the model sums of squares.

The effects for Time and Type are called main effects because each effect is concerned with the effect of one variable at a time, ignoring the effect of the other variable. If the main effects were analysed by separate one-way ANOVAs, their mean squares, sums of squares and degrees of freedom would be identical to the values reported in the two-way summary table. However, the F-value for each effect would be different, because MS_{Error} in a one-way analysis

Table 16.4 ANOVA summary table

Dependent variable: AGGRESS

Source	Type III sum of squares	df	Mean square	F	Sig.	Eta squared
Corrected model	154.400[a]	5	30.880	8.384	.000	.636
Intercept	529.200	1	529.200	143.674	.000	.857
TIME	58.800	1	58.800	15.964	.001	.399
TYPE	66.200	2	33.10	8.99	.001	
TIME*TYPE	29.400	2	14.700	3.991	.032	.250
Error	88.400	24	3.683			
TOTAL	772.000	30				
Corrected TOTAL	242.800	29				

is greater than MS_{Error} in a two-way analysis. The factorial analysis reduces MS_{Error} in accounting for (or explaining) the variance due to more than one main effect and the interaction. This reduced MS_{Error}, divided into the same MS_{Groups} (see Tutorial 14 for the F formula), increases the value of F. This makes the factorial ANOVA more sensitive than the one-way design, detecting effects that the one-way design might miss.

The SPSS® output provides information that enables us to reach statistical decisions regarding our null hypotheses. The F-values for both main effects are significant at the level $p < 0.001$, and the interaction is significant at the level $p < 0.032$. The eta-squared values indicate the proportion of total variability attributable to a factor. All effects, especially the main effects, are strong. The model – main effects and interaction – accounts for 63.6% of the total variance.

You can confirm this by dividing the sum of squares for the model (154.4) by the corrected total sum of squares (242.8) as per Equation 15.2. Note, however, that SPSS® computes the eta-squared values for the main and interaction effects as a proportion of the model eta-square. This is an inflated estimate and you should rely on Equation 15.2 instead.

The significant main effects indicate that there are differences between the marginal means of the different levels of each factor. The '2-hour' mean is significantly different from the '6-hour' mean, and there is at least one significant difference among the types of violence means. The significant interaction effect reflects differences between the cell means. It indicates that the pattern of differences in aggression scores of the three 2-hour groups (non-violent, Kung Fu, domestic violence) is not the same as the pattern of mean differences among the three 6-hour groups.

Activity 16.4

Use a calculator and F-tables to check the results of the SPSS® ANOVA summary table (Table 16.4). Do the following:
a) Recalculate the mean squares and F-values for all effects, using the reported sums of squares and degrees of freedom.
b) Use the F-tables to determine critical F-values for the effects ($\alpha = 0.05$).

If you have difficulty with this exercise, you should revise Tutorials 14 and 15, and then attempt the questions again.

3. Interpreting main effects

Since the Time*Type interaction is significant, we should exercise caution in interpreting our main effects. The interaction effect indicates that the pattern of differences between the types of violence will be different for subjects in the 2-hour and 6-hour conditions. Interpreting marginal means in this situation can produce mislead-

*Use **multiple comparisons** to interpret main effects.*

Be very cautious in interpreting main effects when the interaction effect is significant.

ing conclusions. Thus, some authors argue that we should ignore the main effects when we have a significant interaction, and proceed directly with an analysis of the interaction effect. This is an overly conservative approach, and there are situations in which we are interested in the difference of marginal means in their own right, regardless of interactions. Cautious interpretation of the main effects is warranted when we have a particular (theoretical) interest in them, and/or when the main effects are strong in comparison with the interaction effect (as is the case with our data).

Because Time has only two levels, we can interpret this effect directly by inspecting the group means (see Table 16.1). The F-value indicates that the 6-hour group ($\bar{x} = 5.6$) scored significantly higher on aggression than the 2-hour group ($\bar{x} = 2.8$).

The 'Multiple comparisons' output reports the results of Tukey's HSD test for Type (see Table 16.5). The first set of comparisons – in the first two lines of the table – shows that the mean for level 1 of Type (i.e. the control group) differed significantly from the means of both the Kung Fu group – level 2 of Type ($p = 0.004$) – and the domestic violence group – level 3 of Type ($p = 0.003$). This conclusion is confirmed by inspecting the confidence intervals (see Tutorial 7) for the difference between the groups. Since the interval between the upper and lower bound scores does not include the value 0, we conclude that the difference between the two means must be greater than 0. An inspection of the means shows that the non-violent group expressed less aggression than the other two groups. The second Tukey's comparison shows that the mean score for level 2 of Type differs from the mean for level 1 (which we already know), but does not differ from the mean for level 3. Thus we conclude that subjects in the two experimental groups express a similar level of aggression, which is significantly higher than that of subjects in the non-violent control group.

Table 16.5 Multiple comparisons

Tukey HSD

(I) TYPE	(J) TYPE	Mean difference (I–J)	Std. error	Sig.	95% confidence interval Lower bound	95% confidence interval Upper bound
1.00	2.00	−3.1000*	.8583	.004	−5.2434	−.9566
	3.00	−3.2000*	.8583	.003	−5.3434	−1.0566
2.00	1.00	3.1000*	.8583	.004	.9566	5.2434
	3.00	−1.0000E−01	.8583	.993	−2.2434	2.0434
3.00	1.00	3.2000*	.8583	.003	1.0566	5.3434
	2.00	1.000E−01	.8583	.993	−2.0434	2.2434

4. Interpreting interactions

Significant interaction effects are often the most interesting findings of factorial designs. They suggest that the experimental factors (the IVs) interact with each other in determining responses (scores on the DV). The approach that we adopt in interpreting interaction effects is to consider mean differences between the levels of one IV separately for each level of the other IV. Whereas interpreting main effects involves investigating differences among marginal means, we interpret interactions by investigating differences among cell means.

Study interactions by inspecting the pattern of differences between cell means.

Consider the data for our TV violence experiment once again (see Table 16.1). To interpret the interaction, we consider the cell means for the 2-hour condition separately from the cell means for the 6-hour condition. How does the pattern of mean scores for the 2-hour condition differ from the pattern of mean scores for the 6-hour condition? Two statistical procedures can be used to help us answer these questions: *cell mean plots* and *simple effect analysis*.

Cell mean plots. The cell mean plot that we specified when we ran the SPSS® 'Univariate' procedure helps us to visualise the interaction (see Figure 16.4). You can now see what it means when we define an interaction as a situation where the effect for one independent variable depends on the level of another independent variable. The plot shows that the effect that type of violence has on aggression depends on the length of time of exposure. There is no single effect for exposure to violence. The graph shows that the 6-hour group is more aggressive than the 2-hour group after watching the Kung Fu movie. A strange thing happens to the groups that watched the domestic violence movie. The 6-hour group is even more aggressive than the subjects that watched the Kung Fu movies, but the group who watched 2 hours of domestic violence was less aggressive than the group that watched 2 hours of Kung Fu. This is a classic interaction: the different types of TV violence have different effects on aggression, depending on the length of time people are exposed to the violence. Domestic violence appears to have a very strong impact on aggression, but only when watched for extended periods of time.

Use plots of cell means and simple effect analysis to interpret interactions.

This example illustrates why we should be wary of interpreting main effects when we have a significant interaction. The marginal means for level 2 and level 3 of the variable Type (i.e. Kung Fu and domestic violence) are almost identical, whereas there are big differences between the Kung Fu and domestic violence cell means for the 2-hour and the 6-hour groups.

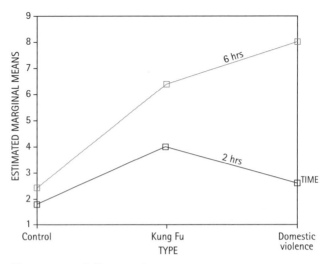

Figure 16.4 Cell mean plots

*A **simple effect** is the effect of an independent variable at one level of a second independent variable.*

Simple effects. Whereas cell mean plots depict the pattern of differences between the cell means, they do not tell us which set of differences are statistically significant. Simple effects analyses are inferential tests of cell mean differences. Running simple effects involves testing for the effect of one independent variable at each level of a second independent variable. We do this by running one-way ANOVAs.

Consider the cell mean plot for the TV violence data. We conduct simple effects for this data by running two one-way ANOVAs, one for the top line (6-hour group) and one for the bottom line (2-hour group). However, the one-way ANOVAs we use here are modified. The estimate of MS_{Error} we employ to calculate F is the error term for the overall factorial analysis. This one-way ANOVA differs from the one-way ANOVAs we considered in Tutorials 14 and 15. Previously, error variance was estimated by the variation in the three cells of the one-way design. With simple effects, we estimate error variance from all the (six) cells of data we have at hand (remember that we tested the assumption that the cells have equal variance), not just from the variance within the (three) cells of data in the comparison. This provides a more reliable estimate of the population variance and it makes for a more powerful inferential test.

Use modified one-way ANOVAs to run simple effects.

Two-way designs allow us to analyse two different sets of simple effects. We can investigate the effect of the first factor for each level of the second factor; or in reverse, we can investigate the effects of the second factor for each level of the first factor. Thus, in addition to conducting two one-way ANOVAs for the lines in the cell mean plot, we can also conduct three one-way ANOVAs for the differences between the two Time groups at each level of Type.

(Although we are comparing two means, the F-test results in the same conclusions as the *t*-test.)

Box 16.2

Computing simple effects with SPSS®

A syntax file must be employed to run simple effects analyses with SPSS®. Fortunately, the procedure and the syntax are simple and intuitive.

Procedure
1. Open the 'Syntax Editor' window. Do this by selecting: 'File' > 'New' > 'Syntax'.
2. Type in the syntax exactly as illustrated below.
3. Run the procedure. Do this by pulling down the 'Run' menu on the 'Syntax Editor' window, and selecting the 'All' option.

Syntax
For each set of simple effects write the following command:
```
Manova
DV BY Factor_A(1, x) Factor_B(1, y)/error = w
/design Factor_A within Factor_B(1) Factor_A within
    Factor_B(2) ... Factor_A within Factor_B(y).
```

This syntax employs the MANOVA procedure, using one DV and two IVs (Factor A, with x levels, and Factor B with y levels). The third and fourth lines specify the effects for Factor A in each of the levels for Factor B.

Example
The syntax for the TV violence experiment is as follows. Note that the syntax is provided to test two different sets of simple effects.

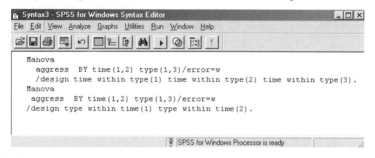

The outcome of the simple effect analysis is reported in Table 16.6. Notice that the estimate of error variance is derived from the full two-way ANOVA summary table. The 'WITHIN CELLS' sums of squares, mean squares, and degrees of freedom are the same as those reported earlier.

Activity 16.5

Use SPSS® to run simple effects analysis for the TV violence data. Follow the procedure and syntax provided in Box 16.2.

Table 16.6 Simple effects

Tests of significance for AGGRESS using UNIQUE sums of squares					
Source of variation	SS	df	MS	F	Sig. of F
WITHIN CELLS	88.40	24	3.68		
TIME WITHIN TYPE(1)	.90	1	.90	.24	.626
TIME WITHIN TYPE(2)	14.40	1	14.40	3.91	.060
TIME WITHIN TYPE(3)	72.90	1	72.90	19.79	.000

Tests of significance for AGGRESS using UNIQUE sums of squares					
Source of variation	SS	df	MS	F	Sig. of F
WITHIN CELLS	88.40	24	3.68		
TYPE WITHIN TIME(1)	12.40	2	6.20	1.68	.207
TYPE WITHIN TIME(2)	83.20	2	41.60	11.29	.000

Once you have successfully run simple effects, save the syntax window. It can be used for later analyses, simply by changing the variable names and levels.

Two sets of simple effects were conducted. The first set reports significance tests for the difference between the two Time means at each of the levels of Type. There are significant differences between the two Time groups only for those in the domestic violence experimental condition. The second set of simple effects pertains to the differences between the three levels of Type separately for the 2-hour and 6-hour conditions. This analysis suggests that exposure to 2 hours of violence (domestic or Kung Fu) has no significant effect on aggression, whereas exposure to 6 hours of violence does increase levels of aggression. The results of the first set of simple effects, as well as the cell mean plot, suggest that long periods of exposure to domestic violence increase aggression.

There is no single correct way of interpreting interactions. Plotting cell means and then interpreting the plot are essential first steps in the analysis. This should provide an overall picture of how the means differ. Emerging explanations of the interaction should then be further investigated by conducting one or two sets of simple effects.

Types of interactions

It is conventional to distinguish between ordinal and disordinal interactions. *Ordinal interactions* have simple effects that are in the same direction, whereas *disordinal interactions* have simple effects that are in opposite directions. We can judge whether an interaction is ordinal or disordinal from the cell mean plots.

Figure 16.5 provides examples of six different patterns of cell means. Each of the graphs represents the cell means for a 2 × 3 factorial design. The three levels of the one variable are marked on the x-axis of the graphs and the two levels of the second variable are represented by the two lines. The top three graphs report the cell means for situations where the interactions are not significant (i.e. there is no interaction). As a general rule, if the cell means plot yields parallel lines, the interaction is not significant. In these instances, the effects of the one variable are exactly the same for both levels of the other variable.

The bottom three graphs represent significant interaction effects. Note that the lines are not parallel. These graphs illustrate, once again, the definition of an interaction. The effect for the one factor differs according to the levels of the second factor. In the graph on the left, the three means are equal for the top line, while the means for the bottom line decrease from level 1 to level 3. The next two graphs illustrate two different types of interaction effect. The middle graph depicts a disordinal interaction. The lines cross, meaning that they represent opposing effects. One of the lines represents increasing means, while the other line represents decreasing means. In these kinds of situations it is especially dangerous to interpret main effects, because they hide important underlying differences. The graph on the bottom right represents an ordinal interaction. Although the lines are not parallel, they do not cross. The two simple effects are in the same direction (both lines

If the lines connecting the cell means are parallel, there is no interaction effect.

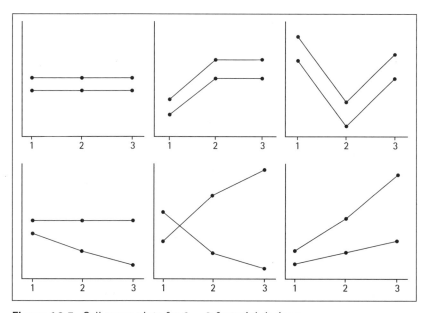

Figure 16.5 Cell mean plots for 2 × 3 factorial designs

represent increasing means). There is a significant interaction because the top line is steeper than the bottom line. The sharper increase of the top line indicates that the factor on the x-axis has a stronger impact on the DV for this level of the y-factor than the level represented by the bottom line.

Activity 16.6

Activity 16.1 required you to represent the data from Table 15.3 in a 2 × 2 table.
a) Analyse this data, following the method outlined above.
b) Interpret the SPSS® output thoroughly. To check whether you have specified the procedure correctly in SPSS®, compare your results with the ANOVA summary table below.

Tests of between–subjects effects

Dependent variable: WORDS

Source	Type III sum of squares	df	Mean square	F	Sig.	Eta-squared
Corrected model	1165.810[a]	3	388.603	12.516	.000	.532
Intercept	15120.785	1	15120.785	486.995	.000	.937
GENDER	67.001	1	67.001	2.158	.151	.061
GROUP	1080.301	1	1080.301	3479	.000	.513
GENDER*GROUP	8.326	1	8.326	.268	.608	.008
Error	1024.622	33	31.049			
TOTAL	17515.000	37				
Corrected TOTAL	2190.432	36				

Conclusion

In the introduction, we argued that factorial designs are valuable tools for social and psychological research. After studying this chapter, you should understand what factorial ANOVA allows you to do.

The discussion in this tutorial is limited to two-way factorial designs, and thus to two-way interactions. These are the simplest factorial designs and are relatively easy to interpret because they can be clearly represented by means of simple mean plots. In most research, more complicated factorial designs are used. Firstly, the effects of more than two factors are often investigated. In designs with more independent variables, it is possible to obtain higher-order interactions (most commonly three-way and four-way inter-actions). As you can imagine, higher-order interactions are more difficult to interpret. Secondly, the effects of repeated measures (within-subjects) factors are often investigated in designs alongside effects for between-subjects factors. These will be considered in Tutorial 17.

The analysis and interpretation of complex factorial designs is beyond the scope of this tutorial. Nevertheless, you should be able to understand the reports of complex factorial analyses in the results sections of scientific journal articles.

Activity 16.7

Stephan and Rosenfield (1978) conducted a naturalistic field experiment to determine whether previous inter-racial contact and actual desegregation affected the race attitudes of American schoolchildren. They selected black and white children living in a Southern American city who had been to either racially segregated or integrated elementary schools (i.e. those who had had previous inter-racial contact and those who had not). They conducted two surveys of these children, one prior to the scrapping of racial segregation laws in the USA, and one after the laws had been scrapped. They wanted to determine the effect that the two variables had on subjects' attitudes towards three ethnic groups (whites, blacks, and Mexican Americans). Each subject completed a questionnaire where they reported their attitudes towards the three ethnic groups. Here is an extract from the 'Results' section of the paper.

'The data was analysed with a 2 × 2 × 3, two-between, one-within analysis of variance. The between factors were pre- versus post-desegregation and whether the students had attended segregated or integrated elementary schools. The within factor consisted of the three ethnic groups being evaluated [whites, blacks and Mexican Americans].

The results for the white students indicated that there was a main effect for ethnic group being evaluated, $F(2, 1008) = 68.03$, $p < 0.001$. Whites evaluated their own group more positively than the other two groups. There was also a significant Type of Background (segregated or integrated) × Pre/Post-Desegregation interaction, $F(1,504) = 6.34$, $p < 0.02$. Follow-up contrasts indicated that whites from segregated backgrounds developed more negative attitudes towards all ethnic groups after desegregation, $F(1,504) = 11.75$, $p < 0.001$; whereas those from integrated backgrounds did not change their attitudes as a result of desegregation ($F < 1$).

For blacks there was a significant ethnic group main effect, $F(2,552) = 53.97$, $p < .001$. As was the case with the whites, blacks evaluated their own group more positively. Again, like the whites, the blacks also showed a tendency toward a Type of Background × Pre/Post-Desegregation interaction, $F(1,276) = 2.77$, $p < 0.10$. Contrasts indicated that blacks from segregated backgrounds developed more negative attitudes towards all the ethnic groups after desegregation, $F(1,276) = 7.46$, $p < 0.02$; whereas blacks from integrated backgrounds did not.'

To test whether you understand the report, answer the following:
a) Was the black sample bigger than the white sample?
b) Why is ethnic group a within-subjects (i.e. repeated measures) factor?

c) Although we do not know the marginal or the cell means, the main effects and interactions are described for us. Draw rough cell mean plots that represent the main effects and interactions for the black and the white subjects.

d) Do you think there is an interaction between ethnic group of the respondent (black, white subject) and the within-subjects ethnic group factor?

Summary

1. Two-way factorial designs are defined as research designs with two independent variables, where every level of one variable is paired with every level of the other variable.

2. Factorial designs are preferable to one-way designs for three related reasons: 1) they are realistic in relation to social-psychological phenomena, 2) they allow us to analyse interactions, and 3) they are economical.

3. An interaction is a situation in a factorial design in which the effects of one independent variable depend upon the level of another independent variable.

The procedure for computing a two-way ANOVA using SPSS®

Step 1: Make an SPSS® worksheet, including columns for each of the independent variables.

Step 2: Test assumptions. Use boxplots to determine the shape of the distributions and Levene's test to determine homogeneity of variance.

Step 3: Conduct significance tests on all effects, and generate a table of cell and variable means. Calculate effect sizes of all significant effects.

Step 4: Is the interaction significant? If so, interpret the main effects cautiously and analyse the interaction by means of 1) cell mean plots, and 2) simple effects.

Step 5: Are the main effects significant? If the interaction is not significant, but the main effects are, use multiple comparisons to interpret the differences between the marginal means.

Exercises

1. There has been some debate about the effect of aging on the human sex drive. Some writers believe that the sex drive peaks in late adolescence and then drops off as the person grows older.

Others believe that the sex drive increases steadily until it peaks during a person's 40s. To investigate this, a researcher measures the sex drive of 1 000 people (500 males and 500 females). These subjects fell into three age groups: 19 to 28 years, 29 to 38 years, and 39 to 48 years.

a) Why are the following analyses inappropriate?
- Conducting a one-way ANOVA for all the data to identify differences between the mean sex drive scores for the three age groups.
- Conducting two one-way ANOVAs (one for males and the other for females) to determine whether different age groups differ in sex drive.

b) Draw cell mean plots representing four different possible outcomes. Interpret each plot in words.

2. To test whether speech style influences the perceived guilt or innocence of a suspected criminal, a forensic researcher conducts an experiment in which English-speaking subjects listen to a tape-recorded interview between an English-speaking male interrogator and a male suspect accused of theft. There are three different versions of the taped interview. In one version the suspect speaks only English (convergent condition); in the second interview the suspect speaks mainly English, but lapses into Afrikaans (partially divergent condition); and in the third interview the suspect speaks only Afrikaans (divergent condition). In addition, half the subjects are informed that the crime is a blue-collar crime (theft of some cash) and the other half of the subjects are informed that the crime is a white-collar crime (fraud). Subjects are randomly assigned to one of the six conditions. After listening to the taped interview they are asked to rate the guilt of the suspect on a ten-point scale. The data are reported in the table below. Write out the score model for the data, and then analyse the data thoroughly using SPSS®.

		Crime type	
		Blue collar	White collar
Speech style	Convergent	9, 5, 5, 7, 6, 5, 10, 6, 6, 8	9, 5, 6, 8, 7, 3, 4, 6, 5, 4
	Part divergent	5, 7, 3, 4, 8, 2, 6, 5, 6, 3	5, 6, 1, 3, 8, 7, 6, 2, 2, 3
	Divergent	9, 10, 6, 8, 7, 9, 4, 10, 2, 4	3, 2, 5, 4, 9, 4, 10, 5, 4, 2

3. To investigate the psychological effects of taxi violence, a researcher surveyed people passing through two taxi ranks. The 'peaceful' taxi rank had no history of violence, whereas the 'violent' taxi rank had a history of violent conflict, including

shootings. Half the subjects were taxi passengers and half the subjects were pedestrians passing through the taxi rank. Subjects responded to a seven-item measure of anxiety. The data are reported below. What conclusions can the researcher draw?

	Violent	Peaceful
Passengers	16, 18, 21, 13, 12, 17, 10, 21, 15, 9, 12, 16	12, 21, 17, 19, 16, 11, 19, 20, 16, 18
Pedestrians	17, 14, 20, 16, 13, 15, 11, 16, 17, 19, 13, 18	16, 7, 13, 14, 9, 15, 13, 17, 9, 11, 7, 8

(Note: high scores on the anxiety measure indicate high levels of anxiety.)

TUTORIAL

17

Repeated measures analysis of variance

Colin Tredoux

> After studying this tutorial, you should be able to:
> - Explain how analysis of variance partitions or decomposes variance.
> - Understand and interpret repeated measures ANOVA tables.
> - Distinguish multivariate and univariate approaches to setting out ANOVA designs.
> - Identify and discuss some statistical assumptions underlying repeated measures ANOVA.
> - Conduct one- and two-way repeated measures ANOVAs with the aid of SPSS®.

Introduction

Earlier in this text you were introduced to ANOVA (see Tutorials 14 to 16). The present chapter extends the discussion to the case of research designs that employ multiple measurements. The best known of this type of design is the classic before-after study: a measurement is made, an intervention is administered, and a second measurement is taken. You were introduced to the analysis of this kind of design in Tutorial 9, namely as a repeated measures t-test, also known as a dependent measures t-test, or a within-subjects t-test. Repeated measures tests are widely used in quantitative social science, especially experimental designs. This is because they confer particular advantages, which have to do with the reduction of error variance. In short, repeated measures designs offer good statistical power, and are more economical than between-subjects designs, but make stronger assumptions, and are more likely to violate these assumptions.

The approach in this tutorial will be to introduce you to relatively simple examples of repeated measures analysis of variance. (For more detailed treatments, see Howell, 1997, and Rosenthal & Rosnow, 1985.) We will show you how to conduct one-way repeated measures ANOVA and two-way repeated measures ANOVA, using SPSS®, and how to interpret graphical and tabular output from that program. Repeated measures ANOVA is typically conducted in one of two ways, often referred to as the 'univariate' and 'multivariate' setups, and we will deal with both. Finally, we will discuss the assumptions underlying repeated measures ANOVA, and show you how to test these.

Decomposition of variance

The key concept underlying ANOVA is that of analysis or decomposition of variance.

The key concept underlying ANOVA is that of analysis or *decomposition* of variance. We start with a dataset, calculate the total variance within this set, and identify sources of variance that make up the total. It is useful to review how this works for one-way between-subjects ANOVA and for two-way between-subjects ANOVA. As an example, consider the dataset in Table 17.1, which represents the kilogram masses of 20 crocodiles on the farm Crocodile Leap.

Table 17.1 Kilogram masses of 20 crocodiles

1	2	3	4	5	6	7	8	9	10	11	12	13	14	15	16	17	18	19	20
231	317	256	287	241	265	304	276	254	239	278	287	311	229	248	295	281	249	259	230

The total amount of variance in this dataset is simply the variance of the scores around the mean. This is simple to calculate, and can be expressed in descriptive statistics notation or in ANOVA notation.

$$s^2 = \frac{\sum (x - \bar{x})^2}{n - 1} = 757.82 \qquad \text{descriptive statistics}$$

$$SS_{Total} = \sum (x - \bar{x})^2 = 14398.55 \qquad \text{ANOVA notation}$$

$$MS_{Total} = \frac{SS_{Total}}{df_{Total}} = \frac{\sum (x - \bar{x})^2}{n - 1} = 757.82 \qquad \text{ANOVA notation}$$

The total variance in the dataset is thus 757.82, or 14 398.55 in terms of sums of squares, which is how we prefer to express it in ANOVA. Now, let us add some information to the set of data scores, by revealing that there are two species of crocodile in the set: the Nile crocodile (*crocodylus niloticus*), and the Zambezi crocodile (*crocodylus chilobicus*).

Table 17.2 Kilogram masses of 20 crocodiles of two different species

Species:	N	Z	N	Z	Z	N	Z	Z	N	N	N	Z	Z	N	Z	Z	N	Z	Z	N
Mass:	231	317	256	287	241	265	304	276	254	239	278	287	311	229	248	295	281	249	259	230

Note: N = Nile, Z = Zambezi

Table 17.3 One-way ANOVA table: variation of kilogram mass across crocodile species

Source	SS	df	MS	F	p
Species	3 883.60	1	3 883.60	6.65	0.019
Error/Residual	10 514.95	18	584.16		
TOTAL	14 398.55	19	757.82		

Do you know how to conduct a one-way ANOVA? If not, revise Tutorial 15.

Table 17.3 has in effect analysed the total variation (SS_{Total} = 14 398.55) into separate components. Thus, the factor 'Species' accounts for 3 883.6 of the total sum of squares, and the error (or unexplained) component accounts for 10 514.95. You will notice that these amounts sum to the total, 14 398.55. It is in this sense that ANOVA 'decomposes' or analyses variance.

In the case of two-way analysis of variance, this principle is extended and becomes a very powerful tool. Let us add some more information to the

Activity 17.1

To refresh your knowledge of ANOVA calculations, use SPSS® to conduct a one-way ANOVA on the data of Table 17.2.

crocodile dataset in order to show this. We discover that the crocodile farmer on Crocodile Leap has been serving the crocodiles three different kinds of diet, in order to see which produces crocodiles with the greatest mass (he grows crocodiles for the export handbag industry): CrocEpol cubes (cu), chopped chicken liver (li), and tournedos Rossini (tr). The data are shown in Table 17.4.

A two-way analysis of variance for this data is shown in Table 17.5. This table shows in a very clear way how analysis of variance works to decompose variance. If you examine the value for error sums of squares in the table, you will notice that it is 2 578.94. In the one-way

Table 17.4 Kilogram masses of 20 crocodiles of two different species, on three different diets

Feed:	cu	tr	li	tr	cu	li	tr	cu	li	cu	tr	li	tr	cu	li	tr	li	cu	li	cu
Species:	N	Z	N	Z	Z	N	Z	Z	N	N	N	Z	Z	N	Z	Z	N	Z	Z	N
Mass:	231	317	256	287	241	265	304	276	254	239	278	287	311	229	248	295	281	249	259	230

Activity 17.2

To refresh your knowledge of ANOVA calculations, use SPSS® to conduct a two-way ANOVA on the data of Table 17.4.

Decomposing variance allows us to 'understand' or 'explain' the variation of scores (on a dependent variable) in terms of the experimental factors (IVs).

Table 17.5 Two-way ANOVA table: variation of kilogram mass across crocodile species and diet

Source	df	SS	MS	F	p
Diet	2	4 987.5	2 493.75	13.54	0.0005
Species	1	995.96	995.96	5.41	0.036
Diet*Species	2	542.72	271.36	1.47	0.26
Error/Residual	14	2 578.94	184.21		
TOTAL	19	14 398.58	757.82		

table, the corresponding value is 10 514.95 – in other words, by adding information about diet, we have considerably reduced the error for the sums of squares (from 10 514.95 to 2 578.94). Since all significance tests of effects in the ANOVA table take the general form $F = {}^{MS_{Effect}}/_{MS_{Error}}$, it should be clear to you that this reduction of error variation is not trivial – it leads to better estimates of effects, and to substantial increases in statistical power.

Analysis of variance is all about analysing and partitioning variance. This is as true of repeated measures designs as it is of other ANOVA designs, as we shall presently see.

Repeated measures designs and reduction/decomposition of variance

Consider the following example of a simple one-way repeated measures ANOVA design.

Thirteen depressed adolescent children in a substance-abuse centre are identified for depression treatment in a cognitive behavioural programme called 'Stop-Think-Don't-Drink' (STDD).

They are measured on the Beck depression inventory before treatment, then admitted into the six-week programme, and finally measured again on the depression inventory. The data for this study are shown below, in Table 17.6.

Do you know how to conduct a two-way ANOVA? If not, revise Tutorial 16.

Table 17.6 Depression scores of adolescents before and after cognitive behavioural intervention

Subject:	1	2	3	4	5	6	7	8	9	10	11	12	13
Before:	16	17	12	14	16	15	17	14	19	18	17	14	16
After:	15	16	11	14	15	15	16	12	18	14	17	14	15

The analysis of this data proceeds as if the design were a two-way analysis of variance, with time (before vs after) and subjects (1 ... 13) as factors. (It may seem unusual to treat subjects as a factor, but this is a well-planned strategy.) We compute the sums of squares, mean squares, and F-ratios just as we would for a two-way ANOVA, but with one very important qualification: the interaction *is* the error term in this model, and all the effects in the ANOVA table must be constructed on this basis. Table 17.7 shows results of calculations and the final ANOVA table.

A one-way repeated measures ANOVA proceeds as if the design were a two-way analysis of variance, with individual subjects (participants) treated as levels of a factor.

Table 17.7 ANOVA on depression scores of adolescents before and after cognitive behavioural intervention

Source	SS	df	MS	F	p
Subjects	79.61	12	6.63		
Time	6.5	1	6.5	11.14	0.006
Time*Subjects (Error/Residual)	7.0	12	0.58		
TOTAL	93.11	25	3.72		

By convention, the table for repeated measures ANOVA does not report an F-ratio for the subjects factor, since it is of no substantive interest in repeated measures designs (nor would it be statistically acceptable – a different MS_{Error} would have to be used for such a test). It is clear, nevertheless, that including 'Subjects' as a factor considerably reduces the amount of error variation: in the ANOVA table, the total SS accounted for by 'Subjects' is 79.61 – if we had not included 'Subjects' as a factor, the error SS would have been 93.11 – 6.5 = 86.61, and the error/residual MS term would have been $^{86.61}/_{24}$ = 3.60, instead of 0.58. In order to see this point clearly, imagine that the data shown in Table 17.6 comes from a two-group experiment, rather than from a repeated measures experiment (i.e. we used two different groups of depressed adolescents, the control group receiving no intervention, and the experimental group receiving the behavioural intervention), as in Table 17.8.

Activity 17.3

See whether you can reproduce the analysis shown in Table 17.7, using the methods you learned in Tutorial 16 for the analysis of two-way ANOVA designs.

Table 17.8 Depression scores of two groups of adolescents in a cognitive behavioural study

Control:	16	17	12	14	16	15	17	14	19	18	17	14	16
Experimental:	15	16	11	14	15	15	16	12	18	14	17	14	15

The key advantage of repeated measures ANOVA is that variation in scores due to differences between individuals is removed from the error variance, thus increasing the power of the significance test(s).

If you conduct a one-way ANOVA on this data, you will arrive at the ANOVA table shown in Table 17.9. The table clearly shows that the difference between the two groups is not statistically significant, even though the means of the two groups are identical to the before and after means in the repeated measures design! The repeated measures analysis produced a statistically significant result, because it was able to massively reduce the amount of error variance. Another way of putting this is that a great amount of the variation in the scores was due to differences between individuals, and the repeated measures analysis factored this into the calculations.

Table 17.9 One-way ANOVA on depression scores of two group of adolescents in a cognitive behavioural intervention study

Source	SS	df	MS	F	p
Group	6.5	1	6.5	1.80	0.19
Error/Residual	86.62	24	3.61		
TOTAL	93.12	25	757.82		

One-way repeated measures ANOVA with SPSS®

Most statistical packages provide modules for computing repeated measures analysis of variance. Let us look at how to use SPSS® to conduct a one-way repeated measures ANOVA.

One-way repeated measures analysis of variance is available in several forms in the SPSS® package, but the best method for entry-level users is to use the 'General Linear Model' procedure.

For most SPSS® modules (and indeed most modern statistical packages), the data needs to be set up in what is called a *multivariate data design*. The data are arranged in columns, without a 'grouping variable', as is common in between-subjects layouts. Thus, for the data in Table 17.6, above, the corresponding multivariate and between-subjects layouts in an SPSS® spreadsheet are shown in Figure 17.1.

To do repeated measures with SPSS®, the data must be arranged in what is known as a ***multivariate data design****.*

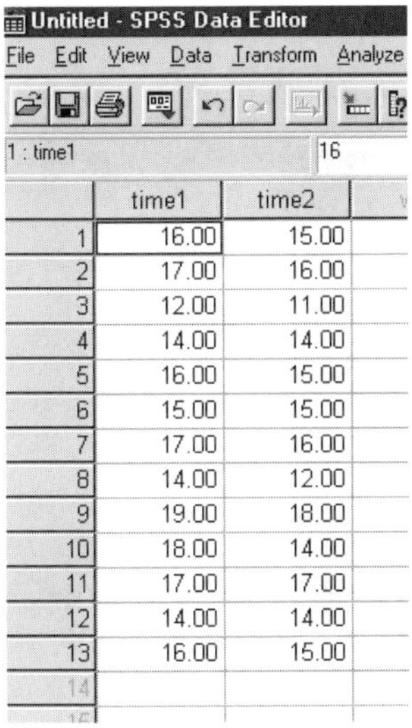

	time1	time2
1	16.00	15.00
2	17.00	16.00
3	12.00	11.00
4	14.00	14.00
5	16.00	15.00
6	15.00	15.00
7	17.00	16.00
8	14.00	12.00
9	19.00	18.00
10	18.00	14.00
11	17.00	17.00
12	14.00	14.00
13	16.00	15.00
14		

MULTIVARIATE LAYOUT

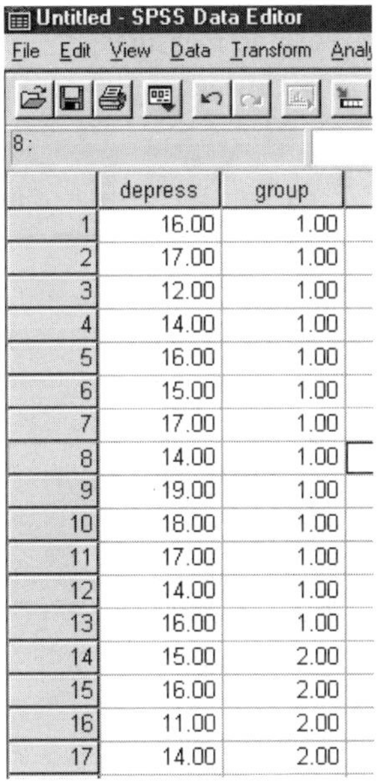

	depress	group
1	16.00	1.00
2	17.00	1.00
3	12.00	1.00
4	14.00	1.00
5	16.00	1.00
6	15.00	1.00
7	17.00	1.00
8	14.00	1.00
9	19.00	1.00
10	18.00	1.00
11	17.00	1.00
12	14.00	1.00
13	16.00	1.00
14	15.00	2.00
15	16.00	2.00
16	11.00	2.00
17	14.00	2.00

BETWEEN-SUBJECTS LAYOUT

Figure 17.1 Multivariate and between-subjects data layouts

After the data have been set up in the multivariate layout, we need to start an appropriate SPSS® procedure to analyse the data. Thus, we select the 'Analyze' menu, choose 'General Linear Model', and then 'Repeated Measures' (see Figure 17.2).

Repeated measures ANOVA designs are anaysed in SPSS® with the General Linear Model command.

The first dialog box that appears after selecting 'Repeated Measures' is shown in Figure 17.3. Here we specify the name of the within-subjects (repeated measures) factor by naming the factor and indicating how many levels it has. For this example, we name the factor 'Time' and indicate that it has '2' levels. Clicking 'Add' inserts the repeated measures factor into the window pane as indicated in Figure 17.3. When you click the 'Define' key, the 'Repeated Measures' dialog box will open (see Figure 17.4).

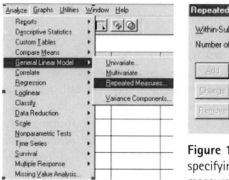

Figure 17.2 SPSS® menu for choosing the repeated measures command

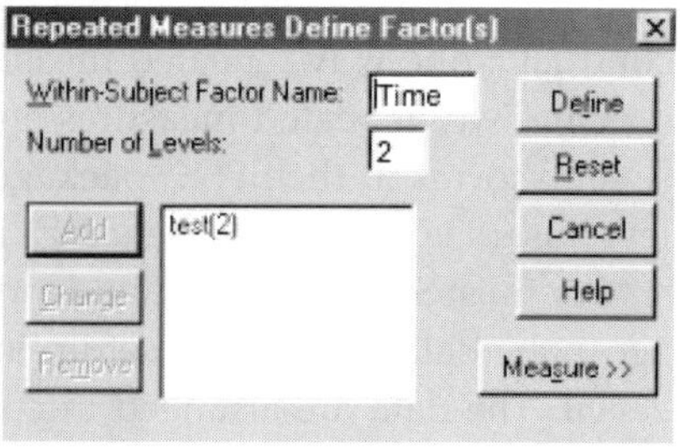

Figure 17.3 Initial dialog box for specifying the levels of a repeated measures factor

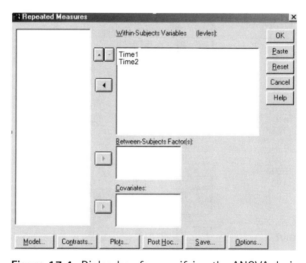

Figure 17.4 Dialog box for specifying the ANOVA design

Be careful to select the repeated measures variables in the correct order in the SPSS® dialog box.

On the 'Repeated Measures' dialog box we select the variables (from the spreadsheet) that make up our within-subjects factor. Since we defined the factor Time as having two levels, this dialog box allows you to select the two variables that make up the factor. The order of selection is important. To reflect the chronological order of measurement, we select 'Time1' first and 'Time2' second. We do this using the dialog box shown in Figure 17.4.

We now run the analysis (by clicking 'OK' on the main dialog box), and SPSS® generates a fair volume of output in the results window. Much of this is of little interest to us in the present case, so we look specifically at the section containing the relevant ANOVA table. This is shown in Figure 17.5, as a slightly modified version of the classic ANOVA table.

Source	TIME	Type III Sum of Squares	df	Mean Square	F	Sig.	Eta Squared
TIME	Linear	6.500	1	6.500	11.143	.006	.481
Error (TIME)	Linear	7.000	12	.583			

Figure 17.5 ANOVA table produced by SPSS®

Figure 17.5 shows that there is a significant effect for the repeated measure Time. This is perhaps all we need to know about the present design, given that it is relatively simple. However, if we wanted to compute post hoc tests of differences between specific means, or to examine whether our data satisfies standard ANOVA assumptions, we could do so. Although it is not really appropriate to conduct post hoc tests for the present design, we will do so here in order to show the method of specifying and interpreting these tests in SPSS®. To conduct post hoc tests, we click the button 'Post Hoc' in Figure 17.4, and use the resulting dialog box in Figure 17.6 to choose the type of test we wish to use. We select the factor we wish to apply this test to in the dialog box of Figure 17.6, and the output is generated as shown in Figure 17.7 (having selected the 'Tukey' test – which is actually the Tukey HSD test).

The output scrollsheet (Figure 17.7) does not present the post-hoc test in an obvious manner. The comparisons are read from the scrollsheet by taking the combinations of levels of the independent variable, as shown in the extreme left-hand column. Thus, the first row of the table below the heading line reports Time1 vs Time2, and the mean difference is reported in the next cell as 1.000, along with the standard error of the mean (next cell), and the significance test probability (0.006 in the present example). A 95% confidence interval is also reported. From these results, it is clear that there is a significant difference between the levels of the independent variable. The second row of the table under the heading line repeats these results (reversing the direction of the comparison), in order to complete the 'cycling' of the levels of the independent variable.

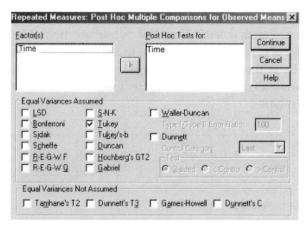

Figure 17.6 Dialog box in SPSS® for specifying post hoc comparison tests

(I) TIME	(J) TIME	Mean Difference (I-J)	Std. Error	Sig.[a]	95% Confidence Interval for Difference[a]	
					Lower Bound	Upper Bound
1	2	1.000*	.300	.006	.347	1.653
2	1	−1.000*	.300	.006	−1.653	−.347

Figure 17.7 Results of the Tukey post hoc analysis

Two-way repeated measures ANOVA

Fully repeated designs include only within-subject factors.

We have looked at the simplest type of repeated measures ANOVA design, namely one-way repeated measures ANOVA. Repeated measures ANOVA designs can involve a great many factors, but the statistical and interpretive problems increase greatly when we use these designs. In this tutorial we will look only at two-way repeated measures ANOVA designs.

Mixed designs include within- and between-subjects factors.

It is necessary to differentiate two types of two-way repeated measures ANOVA designs. In the first we have repeated measures on both factors (*fully repeated designs*), and in the second we have repeated measures on only one factor (*mixed designs*).

Fully repeated designs

Fully repeated designs run all subjects in each of the design cells.

These designs use all research participants at all levels of each of two factors. Imagine that we want to examine the effects of 1) emotional states, and 2) adopted facial expressions, on the physiological measure of skin resistance. Twelve research participants are recruited, and are hooked up to a polygraph while they relive emotional episodes (anger, fear, surprise, happiness, disgust, and sadness), or adopt emotional facial expressions (anger, fear, surprise, happiness, disgust, and sadness) (see Ekman, *et al.*, 1983). In other words, each research participant relives each of these six emotions, and adopts each of these six emotional facial expressions, while a polygraph records their skin resistance.

Mixed designs run subjects in (at least) two independent groups, and on (at least) one repeated measures factor.

As you will remember from the earlier discussion, ANOVA is a variance-partitioning procedure. In repeated measures designs, the partitioning can be quite intricate, since variation due to repeated participation is often conflated with variation due to interventions (or groups). Generally, the partitioning works as shown in Figure 17.8.

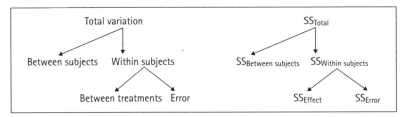

Figure 17.8 General nature of the variance partitioning in repeated measures ANOVA designs

The total variance is broken down at the first level of analysis to that arising from differences 'between subjects' and that arising from differences 'within subjects'. On the ANOVA table, this corresponds to breaking down the total sums of squares (SS_{Total}) into two components ($SS_{Between}$ and SS_{Within}, which sum to SS_{Total}). The variance within subjects is then decomposed into a quantity due to differences between treatments, and a residual or error quantity. On the ANOVA table, this corresponds to breaking down SS_{Within} into SS_{Effect} and SS_{Error}. Sometimes ANOVA tables are constructed to reflect this hierarchical breakdown of variance, as shown in Table 17.10.

It is a good idea to construct variance partitioning diagrams when conducting ANOVAs, since they visualise the central goal of the analysis.

Table 17.10 ANOVA table constructed as a hierarchical partitioning of variance (data from Figure 17.1)

Source	SS	df	MS	F	p
Between subjects					
Time	6.5	1	6.5	11.14	0.006
Within subjects					
Subjects	79.61	12	6.63		
Swg (Error/Residual)	7.0	12	0.58		
TOTAL Ws	86.61	24			
TOTAL	93.11	25	3.72		

Note: Swg = subjects within groups; Ws = within subjects

The partitioning becomes more intricate when we have repeated measurements on more than one of the variables in question. Thus, in the present case (two-way repeated measures, fully repeated), we have the partitioning in Figure 17.9

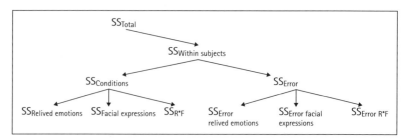

Figure 17.9 Variance partitioning in a two-way fully repeated measures ANOVA design

It is not necessary to understand the partitioning shown here, except to note that there is no computation for between-subjects effects, since all effects are 'wrapped up' within subjects – there are no groups. Notice that there are three separate error terms, one for each of the independent variables, and one for the interaction of the variables.

There is also no need to set the formulas or the calculations out for this design. We enter the data into SPSS® in the format shown in Figure 17.10. Notice how the data are organised into two sets of measures, each repeated for each of the 12 research participants. In SPSS® we have to specify the organisation of measures to form the variables. This involves using the dialog boxes shown in Figures 17.11 and 17.12. The first of these is straightforward, but the second must be used carefully to define the two repeated measures factors. The first step is to define the Emotion factor, which has six levels, and a Condition factor, which has two levels and refers to the type of task (relived emotion or facial expression). The second step is to select each of the variables that make up all combinations of the two factors. Notice that the pane on the right of Figure 17.12 contains 12 spaces in which to enter variable names. It is essential that we enter the variables correctly. The numbers in brackets indicate which variable should be entered first, second, third, etc. At the top of the dialog box, the order of variables is given in the same order that you defined them in the previous dialog box (i.e. Emotion, condition). Define the levels of Emotion as follows: anger = 1, fear = 2, surprise = 3, happiness = 4, disgust = 5, and sadness = 6. Define the Condition factor as follows: relived emotion = 1 and facial expression = 2. We then enter the variables in the following order: the first variable (1,1) is anger_r, the second variable (1,2) is anger_f, the third variable (2,1) is fear _r, etc. Can you enter the remainder of the variables correctly? Once all the variables are entered, click 'OK' to run the procedure.

	anger_	fear_r	surpr_r	happ_r	disgus_r	sad_r	anger_f	fear_f	surpr_f	happ_f	disgus_f	sad_f
1	2.84	2.52	3.22	2.47	86	1.61	3.66	3.32	3.44	3.31	2.69	1.19
2	1.75	.54	3.79	28	1.02	1.29	2.87	2.49	4.05	2.51	1.39	.77
3	2.34	1.50	3.87	2.87	80	1.35	1.69	2.54	1.79	1.50	2.05	1.16
4	4.29	2.83	2.20	2.19	2.76	2.04	4.04	1.05	2.10	1.71	67	.83
5	.94	1.08	2.57	57	61	1.94	2.03	1.47	36	1.35	1.94	.29
6	2.28	1.71	3.75	1.98	3.03	1.38	3.44	1.96	2.19	1.53	2.21	1.59
7	4.50	2.01	2.17	84	2.34	79	4.14	2.96	1.25	1.39	1.11	96
8	4.30	2.95	1.34	1.23	1.10	77	4.39	2.88	1.78	2.73	1.74	1.60
9	2.59	3.77	3.47	19	3.03	95	1.30	2.68	1.31	32	2.26	58
10	4.69	.72	3.34	3.27	84	1.06	1.91	3.36	3.63	1.45	2.39	2.22
11	3.13	1.63	2.12	3.01	06	1.63	3.84	1.27	3.20	2.77	1.64	94
12	3.48	2.73	3.34	1.47	1.37	80	3.10	2.82	2.66	1.24	2.11	1.61

Figure 17.10 Data spreadsheet for two-way repeated measures ANOVA

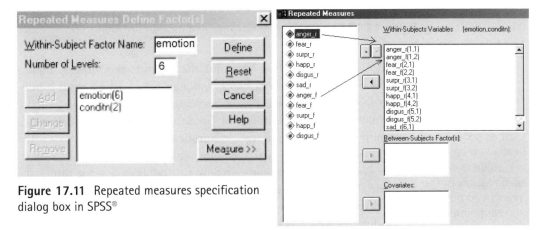

Figure 17.11 Repeated measures specification dialog box in SPSS®

Figure 17.12 Variable selection dialog box in the SPSS® repeated measures analysis

Having specified the design, SPSS® produces the result output shown in Figure 17.13.

The summary table is a little unusual – at this stage you may not understand the terms 'Sphericity', 'Greenhouse-Geisser', etc. It is enough for the moment to note that the standard ANOVA test is the one labelled 'Sphericity Assumed'. Figure 17.13 shows that only the main effect for the Emotion factor is statistically significant, and neither the main effect for Condition, nor the interaction effect, is significant. This means that there are differences in skin resistance readings among the six emotions – in some, the resistance is higher (or lower) than in others. It makes no difference whether the emotions were relived emotions or adopted facial expressions.

Source		Type III Sum of Squares	df	Mean Square	F	Sig.
EMOTION	Sphericity Assumed	54.851	5	10.970	12.156	.000
	Greenhouse-Geisser	54.851	2.867	19.133	12.156	.000
	Huynh-Feldt	54.851	3.984	13.768	12.156	.000
	Lower-bound	54.851	1.000	54.851	12.156	.005
Error (EMOTION)	Sphericity Assumed	49.636	55	.902		
	Greenhouse-Geisser	49.636	31.535	1.574		
	Huynh-Feldt	49.636	43.823	1.133		
	Lower-bound	49.636	11.000	4.512		
CONDTN	Sphericity Assumed	2.669E-03	1	2.669E-03	.003	.960
	Greenhouse-Geisser	2.669E-03	1.000	2.669E-03	.003	.960
	Huynh-Feldt	2.669E-03	1.000	2.669E-03	.003	.960
	Lower-bound	2.669E-03	1.000	2.669E-03	.003	.960
Error (CONDTN)	Sphericity Assumed	11.269	11	1.024		
	Greenhouse-Geisser	11.269	11.000	1.024		
	Huynh-Feldt	11.269	11.000	1.024		
	Lower-bound	11.269	11.000	1.024		
EMOTION * CONDTN	Sphericity Assumed	4.308	5	.862	1.488	.209
	Greenhouse-Geisser	4.308	3.342	1.289	1.488	.231
	Huynh-Feldt	4.308	4.976	.866	1.488	.209
	Lower-bound	4.308	1.000	4.308	1.488	.248
Error (EMOTION * CONDTN)	Sphericity Assumed	31.858	55	.579		
	Greenhouse-Geisser	31.858	36.763	.867		
	Huynh-Feldt	31.858	54.736	.582		
	Lower-bound	31.858	11.000	2.896		

Figure 17.13 Results for two-way repeated measures ANOVA

Just as a significant F-ratio in a between-subjects ANOVA often requires further analysis so a significant F-ratio in a repeated measures ANOVA may require further analysis (e.g. with simple effect analysis or multiple comparisons).

ANOVA is an omnibus test, and the F-ratios reported in Figure 17.13 are calculations for *complex null hypotheses* – the F for the emotion factor could be significant because of an unusually high score on just one of the emotions, or because of a systematic difference among all of the emotions. A significant F-ratio simply tests the hypothesis that there is at least one significant difference in a set (it also keeps a check, to some extent, on the Type 1 error rate – see Tutorial 15). For this reason, we typically run follow-up tests when we do analysis of variance. In the case of factorial ANOVA, we can conduct tests of *simple effects*, or we can do *pairwise comparisons* (see Tutorial 16 for an explanation of these terms). In the present case, only one main effect is significant, so there is no need to analyse simple effects. We can proceed with pairwise comparisons between the levels of the emotion factor, i.e. we will compare anger with each of the other five emotions, sadness with the other five emotions, etc. These are easily specified in SPSS® (see the earlier discussion of the one-way design and Figure 17.6), and the resulting output for Tukey HSD tests is shown in Figure 17.14.

This complex table reveals a number of significant differences among individual levels of the emotion factor. A detailed interpretation would be a formidable task, but it is sufficient to note that a number of the emotions produced different states of GSR activation – which, in this particular case, was all that was at issue. For purposes of clarifying the actual output of the table, note that the first 'block' of the table reports the results of pairwise comparisons between emotion 1 (anger) and each of the other five emotions (labelled 2–6 in the table). Likewise, the second block reports comparisons of emotion 2 (fear) with each of the other five emotions. Notice that the mean difference, the standard error of the difference, the probability returned by the significance test (labelled 'Sig.') and the 95% confidence interval are reported for each test.

We could do a great deal more investigating here, but it is probably adequate for our purposes to end the analysis with the recommendation that you always calculate the effect sizes of significant effects when running ANOVAs (see Tutorial 15). It is preferable to do this with statistical software (SPSS® offers effect sizes as optional statistics), but you can calculate η^2 easily enough by hand (see Tutorial 15).

(I) EMOTION	(J) EMOTION	Mean Difference (I-J)	Std. Error	Sig.	95% Confidence Interval for Difference	
					Lower Bound	Upper Bound
1	2	.865*	.287	.012	.233	1.496
	3	.442	.395	.287	−.427	1.310
	4	1.307*	.284	.001	.683	1.931
	5	1.397*	.330	.001	.670	2.124
	6	1.841*	.270	.000	1.247	2.436
2	1	−.865*	.287	.012	−1.496	−.233
	3	−.423	.309	.198	−1.102	.256
	4	.442	.321	.195	−.264	1.148
	5	.532*	.169	.009	.159	.905
	6	.977*	.220	.001	.493	1.460
3	1	−.442	.395	.287	−1.310	.427
	2	.423	.309	.198	−.256	1.102
	4	.865*	.260	.007	.294	1.436
	5	.955*	.270	.005	.361	1.549
	6	1.400*	.211	.000	.935	1.864
4	1	−1.307*	.284	.001	−1.931	−.683
	2	−.442	.321	.195	−1.148	.264
	3	−.865*	.260	.007	−1.436	−.294
	5	9.000E-02	.325	.787	−.625	.805
	6	.535*	.179	.012	.141	.928
5	1	−1.397*	.330	.001	−2.124	−.670
	2	−.532*	.169	.009	−.905	−.159
	3	−.955*	.270	.005	−1.549	−.361
	4	−9.000E-02	.325	.787	−.805	.625
	6	.445*	.174	.027	6.102E-02	.828
6	1	−1.841*	.270	.000	−2.436	−1.247
	2	−.977*	.220	.001	−1.460	−.493
	3	−1.400*	.211	.000	−1.864	−.935
	4	−.535*	.179	.012	−.928	−.141
	5	−.445*	.174	.027	−.828	−6.102E-02

Based on estimated marginal means
*. The mean difference is significant at the .05 level.

Figure 17.14 Results for post hoc tests in a two-way repeated measures ANOVA design

Activity 17.4

Look at the ANOVA table for the analysis of the data in Table 17.6, and decide whether it is appropriate to conduct multiple comparisons. If so, conduct multiple comparisons by hand, or with the aid of statistical software. Interpret your results.

Mixed designs

The term 'mixed design' is used to describe an experiment or study where one of the factors is a between-subjects factor, and the other is a repeated measures or within-subjects factor. This design is commonly used in experimental research.

Consider a study reported by Schuckit (1985). Schuckit measured the amount of body sway (in cm) in 34 drinking, non-alcoholic 21- to 25-year-old males who had a first-degree alcoholic relative, and compared the results to those of 34 controls. The controls were matched on demographic characteristics and drinking histories, but did not have an alcoholic close relative. Each participant was tested on three occasions, during which they drank 0.75 ml/kg or 1.1 ml/kg of ethanol or a placebo.

Activity 17.5

Using your institution's library resources, find five journal articles in your discipline that use repeated measures designs with ANOVA. Identify whether the designs in question are *mixed* or *fully repeated*.

The level of body sway was measured 230 minutes after consumption by asking participants to stand as still as possible for one minute with their eyes open, feet together, and hands at their sides. The design is shown in Figure 17.15, as well as hypothetical data for 20 participants, as entered into SPSS®.

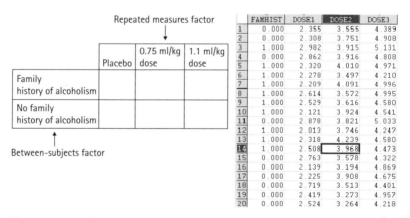

Figure 17.15 Two-way mixed ANOVA design in alcohol study, and data layout

Clearly, family history serves as a grouping variable, and since research participants complete all three of the Dosage conditions, it serves as a repeated measures factor. The partitioning diagram for this design is shown as Figure 17.16.

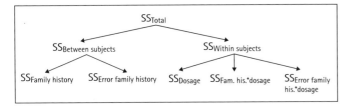

Figure 17.16 Partitioning diagram for mixed model ANOVA (one between-subjects factor, one repeated measures factor)

There is no need to show details regarding the ANOVA computations, since it is unlikely that you will be doing the calculations by hand. We enter this design in the repeated measures module of SPSS® by choosing one independent variable (Family history) and three dependent variables (dose1, dose2, and dose3). We then use the repeated measures dialog box to define our factors. The dialog boxes for doing this, and a selection of the resulting output, are shown in Figure 17.17.

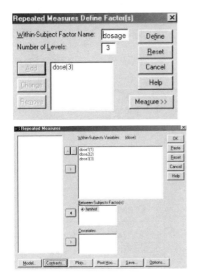

TESTS OF WITHIN-SUBJECTS EFFECTS

Source		Type III Sum of Squares	df	Mean Square	F	Sig.
DOSE	Sphericity Assumed	49.224	2	24.612	397.608	.000
	Greenhouse-Geisser	49.224	1.996	24.663	397.608	.000
	Huynh-Feldt	49.224	2.000	24.612	397.608	.000
	Lower-bound	49.224	1.000	49.224	397.608	.000
DOSE * FAMHIST	Sphericity Assumed	.433	2	.217	3.498	.041
	Greenhouse-Geisser	.433	1.996	.217	3.498	.041
	Huynh-Feldt	.433	2.000	.217	3.498	.041
	Lower-bound	.433	1.000	.433	3.498	.078
Error (DOSE)	Sphericity Assumed	2.228	36	6.190E-02		
	Greenhouse-Geisser	2.228	35.926	6.203E-02		
	Huynh-Feldt	2.228	36.000	6.190E-02		
	Lower-bound	2.228	18.000	.124		

TESTS OF BETWEEN-SUBJECTS EFFECTS

Source	Type III Sum of Squares	df	Mean Square	F	Sig.
Intercept	260.970	1	260.970	6720.659	.000
FAMHIST	1.509E-02	1	1.509E-02	.389	.541
Error	.699	18	3.883E-02		

Figure 17.17 Dialog boxes and selected output for analysis of the data in Figure 17.15

Since there is a significant interaction between Family history and Dosage, it is best to explore the nature of the interaction before deciding on post hoc test strategies. A good way to do this is to request a graph of the interaction, by clicking the 'Plots' option in the main ANOVA menu dialog box (see Figure 17.17). The resulting graph is shown in Figure 17.18, and it is clear from the figure that the interaction is ordinal (see Tutorial 16) and that the Dosage effect is much stronger than the Family history effect. The effect for Family history appears to lie at level 2 of the Dosage factor. It would

Interaction plots (also known as cell mean plots) are very useful for the interpretation of interactions in all types of ANOVA designs.

be appropriate to conduct multiple comparisons on the significant main effect of Dosage, and multiple comparisons on the Family history factor at each level of dosage – i.e. we wish to compare the means of each of the Dosage levels with each other, and we wish to compare the group with a family history of alcoholism to that without such a history, at each Dosage level. To understand this latter comparison, think of it as comparing the alcoholic-family group to the non-alcoholic-family group on body sway when 1) both groups are given a placebo, 2) both groups are given the 0.75 dosage, and 3) both groups are given the 1.1 dosage. The latter analysis is tantamount to a simple effects analysis of the Dosage factor. However, in this particular type of design, the analysis of simple effects over the within-subject factor is very controversial, and many authors recommend against it (e.g. Winer, 1971). For the present data, where there are just two levels on the Family history factor, one can instead consider conducting a t-test at each dosage level. Figure 17.18 shows the results for these t-tests, and the results for the multiple comparisons on the Dosage main effect.

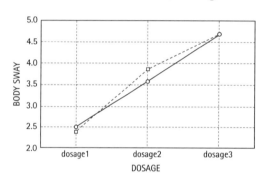
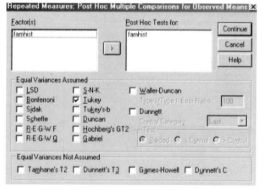

PAIRWISE COMPARISONS

(I) DOSE	(J) DOSE	Mean Difference (I–J)	Std. Error	Sig.	95% Confidence Interval for Difference[a] Lower Bound	Upper Bound
1	2	−1.263*	.078	.000	−1.428	−1.099
	3	−2.211*	.080	.000	−2.380	−2.042
2	1	1.263*	.078	.000	1.099	1.428
	3	−.948*	.077	.000	−1.110	−.785
3	1	2.211*	.080	.000	2.042	2.380
	2	.948*	.077	.000	.785	1.110

Based on estimated marginal means
* The mean difference is significant at the .05 level.

GROUP STATISTICS

	FAMHIST	N	Mean
DOSE3	0	10	4.6580
	1	10	4.6724
DOSE1	0	10	2.5190
	1	10	2.3891
DOSE2	0	10	3.5774
	1	10	3.8577

INDEPENDENT SAMPLES TEST

	t-test for Equality of Means		
	t	df	Sig. (2-tailed)
DOSE3	−.102	18	.920
	−.102	17.831	.920
DOSE1	1.056	18	.305
	1.056	17.980	.305
DOSE2	−2.446	18	.025
	−2.446	17.780	.025

Figure 17.18 Analysis of the effects reported in Figure 17.17

These results support the interpretation obtained from simple visual inspection of the interaction chart (the cell means plot), namely that 1) different dosages of alcohol produce clearly different amounts of body sway, whether you have alcoholic family members or not, and 2) when participants are given a moderate dose of alcohol, those with a family history of alcoholism show greater body sway than those without a family history of alcoholism. However, note that the *t*-tests reported in Figure 17.18 are not corrected in any way for the likely increase in the Type 1 error rate, and corrections should be effected manually. A commonly used statistic is the Bonferroni correction, where the assumed alpha value, usually 0.05, is divided by the number of comparisons. Thus, if you conduct three significance tests, divide alpha by three, and only conclude that there is a significant difference for a particular comparison if the obtained probability is less than 0.017 (i.e. 0.05/3).

*The **Bonferroni correction** is used to reduce the overall Type I error rate in a set (family) of comparisons. However, it is a conservative test.*

Activity 17.6

It is a good idea to practise specifying repeated measures designs in SPSS® (or any other package you might be using). Try doing so for the following (invent appropriate data if it makes it easier):
a) a fully repeated design with 3 levels in factor A and 2 levels in factor B (we call this a 3 × 2 design)
b) a mixed 4 × 6 design (where A is repeated)
c) a fully repeated 3 × 3 × 3 design.

Assumptions underlying repeated measures ANOVA

We make a number of assumptions when we use ANOVA to analyse repeated measures designs. Repeated measures analysis of variance relies on the standard distributional assumptions of all forms of analysis of variance: the assumption of normality, and the assumption of homogeneity of variance. These assumptions are usually not difficult to meet, and the F-test is highly robust with respect to violations of either. The assumption of homogeneity of variance in ANOVA is really a simpler form of an assumption known as *compound symmetry*. This assumption specifies that the matrix of variances and covariances (the *variance-covariance matrix*) associated with the data in question satisfies certain conditions. For example, consider the matrix shown as Figure 17.19, which is the variance-covariance matrix for the data in Table 17.6, a one-way repeated measures design. Variances of variables are reported in cells on the main diagonal of the matrix (top left and bottom right cells), and covariances of variables are reported in cells off the main diagonal (bottom left and top right cells).

*The **variance – covariance matrix** is a matrix that reports variable variances in the cells on the main diagonal, and covariances of variables in the off-diagonal cells.*

Figure 17.19 Variance-covariance matrix for the data in Table 17.6

The assumption of compound symmetry is that 1) the variances are equal, and 2) the covariances are equal. In balanced between-subjects ANOVA designs, however, the independent variables are truly independent, and the covariances of these variables are thus all equal to zero. Only the assumption of equal variance needs to be satisfied. However, in repeated measures designs, the covariances between independent variables are typically not zero, and we have to satisfy the requirement that they are equal. In the case of the data in Figure 17.19, it is obvious that we satisfy these assumptions, but when the matrix is a lot larger, we will not necessarily satisfy the assumptions. In fact, we quite frequently will not satisfy this condition, and unfortunately, the F-statistic is sensitive to such departures, and the computed F-statistic is likely to be biased. There are a number of solutions to this problem, most of which involve adjusting the degrees of freedom. We will not investigate them here, except to say that most computer programs accommodate these solutions. Indeed, that is why the SPSS® output (shown in several earlier tables and figures) contains multiple lines, marked 'Sphericity Assumed', 'Greenhouse Geisser', etc. – the line labelled 'Sphericity Assumed' is the standard ANOVA test, and the other lines report tests that make corrections to accommodate the problems.

Although the F-statistic is usually quite robust, it is sensitive to departures from compound symmetry.

Activity 17.7

If the assumption or compound symmetry is violated, interpret the Greenhouse Geisser (or similar) inferential test.

a) Identify and discuss three situations in which a repeated measures design would be more appropriate than an independent groups design.
b) Identify and discuss three situations in which a repeated measures design would be statistically useful, but methodologically suspect.

There are some circumstances, though, in which the corrections are of little assistance, and in which the use of repeated measures ANOVA is not recommended. Repeated measures designs with unequal cell sizes, and which do not satisfy the requirement of compound symmetry, are especially sensitive, and should not be submitted to ANOVA. Similarly, in all repeated measure ANOVAs, simple effects and linear contrasts are sensitive to departures from compound symmetry, and to use these you usually need to consult a specialised volume on ANOVA (e.g. Winer, 1971).

One way to deal with this problem is to conduct Mauchly's test of sphericity, which is produced by SPSS® as default output from its GLM repeated measures procedure. This test is applicable for designs where the repeated measures factor has more than two levels, and yields a statistic that can be interpreted as a χ^2 deviate. If the probability value for the χ^2 is not less than the alpha level (e.g. 0.05), one can assume that the assumption of sphericity holds. However, Mauchly's test is very sensitive, and if the χ^2 value is significant, it might be a mistake to assume that the assumption of sphericity has been broken.

Use the Mauchly test of sphericity to examine whether the assumption of compound symmetry has been violated.

Clearly, the use of repeated measures analysis of variance involves dodging a number of problems, all related to the assumption of *compound symmetry*. For this reason, a number of authors recommend against it altogether (e.g. Hays, 1994), and propose instead the use of MANOVA (multivariate analysis of variance). MANOVA does not assume compound symmetry, and so escapes many of the problems that beset repeated measures ANOVA. However, research designs that are conceptualised in an ANOVA framework need to be re-conceptualised in a MANOVA framework, and this can be quite tricky with complex factorial designs. A detailed and relatively uncomplicated treatment of MANOVA can be found in Tabachnik and Fidell (1989).

*The most important and exacting assumption of repeated measures ANOVA is that of **compound symmetry**. Unbalanced repeated measures designs are particularly likely to break this assumption, and are not recommended.*

Worked example

Information we receive after an event may often interfere with our memory of the original event. This appears to be true in laboratory settings as well as in natural, 'real-life' settings. Elizabeth Loftus of the University of Washington has done a great deal of research on this phenomenon, known as the *postevent information effect* (e.g. Loftus *et al.*, 1978; Loftus, 1983). The classic experimental design Loftus used in most of her studies is a mixed model, repeated measures variant, which can be reduced diagrammatically to what is shown in Figure 17.20.

Group	OEI	Test A	PEI	Test B
Experimental	X	X	X	X
Control	X	X	–	X

OEI = original event information
PEI = postevent information

Figure 17.20 Classic mixed design used in postevent information experiments

In her experiments, participants are usually randomly assigned to an experimental or a control group, shown a film (or slide show, or real event), and then tested on their recall of some of the information in the showing. The experimental group is subsequently misled about some of the original information (e.g. they might be misled to believe that a person had a moustache), but the control group is not. Both groups are subsequently tested on their recall of the original information, either with the original test, or with a 'parallel' version of it.

Loftus and other researchers have run many variations on this basic design. Figure 17.21 shows data in an SPSS® spreadsheet for a design where there was a third group, which received consistent (rather than misleading) postevent information, and where memory for the original information was measured as the number of items correctly scored on a final test. We need to analyse these data.

	condition	test1	test2
1	Control	3.00	2.00
2	Control	2.00	3.00
3	Control	4.00	3.00
4	Control	3.00	2.00
5	Control	4.00	4.00
6	Misled	3.00	2.00
7	Misled	3.00	2.00
8	Misled	4.00	2.00
9	Misled	2.00	1.00
10	Misled	3.00	2.00
11	Consist	4.00	4.00
12	Consist	3.00	3.00
13	Consist	4.00	4.00
14	Consist	3.00	3.00
15	Consist	2.00	3.00
16			

Figure 17.21 Data for a PEI study

Solution

This design is a 3 × 2 factorial design with one repeated measures factor (two levels: test A and test B), and one between-subjects factor (three levels: control, misled, and consistent). Although it has a very small sample size (only five per condition), there are equal numbers per cell, so the design is balanced.

A boxplot shows that both the pre- and post-tests are a little asymmetrical (see Figure 17.22), but there are no outliers, and there is no clear reason to suspect that ANOVA is inappropriate with this data. We could conduct more formal tests on the data to assess the reasonableness of the sphericity assumption (SPSS® offers a test of sphericity known as 'Mauchly's test of sphericity'), but we will not do that here.

We use the dialog boxes shown in Figure 17.23 to specify the design and run the analysis. Inspection of the ANOVA table shows that there is a significant interaction effect and a significant effect for

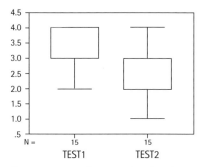

Figure 17.22 Boxplot for the data of Figure 17.21

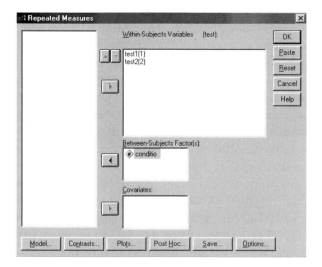

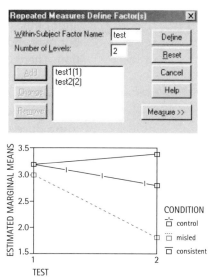

TESTS OF WITHIN–SUBJECTS EFFECTS

Source		Type III Sum of Squares	df	Mean Square	F	Sig.
TEST	Sphericity Assumed	1.633	1	1.633	8.167	.014
	Greenhouse–Geisser	1.633	1.000	1.633	8.167	.014
	Huynh–Feldt	1.633	1.000	1.633	8.167	.014
	Lower-bound	1.633	1.000	1.633	8.167	.014
TEST * CONDITION	Sphericity Assumed	2.467	2	1.233	6.167	.014
	Greenhouse–Geisser	2.467	2.000	1.233	6.167	.014
	Huynh–Feldt	2.467	2.000	1.233	6.167	.014
	Lower-bound	2.467	2.000	1.233	6.167	.014
Error (TEST)	Sphericity Assumed	2.400	12	.200		
	Greenhouse–Geisser	2.400	12.000	.200		
	Huynh–Feldt	2.400	12.000	.200		
	Lower-bound	2.400	12.000	.200		

TESTS OF BETWEEN–SUBJECTS EFFECTS

Source	Type III Sum of Squares	df	Mean Square	F	Sig.
Intercept	126.150	1	126.150	302.760	.000
CONDITION	2.100	2	1.050	2.520	.122
Error	5.000	12	.417		

Figure 17.23 Dialog boxes and resulting output for repeated measures analysis of data in Figure 17.21

Test (the repeated measures factor), but no significant effect for the between-subjects factor, Condition (experimental vs control). The next step is to request an interaction plot via the initial dialog box, and to inspect it. This plot suggests that control participants do more poorly on a recognition test after the passage of some time, whereas misled participants do much more poorly on the same recognition test, and participants who have been reminded of critical details do much better.

The question now is which formal significance tests we need to run in order to formally test our interpretation of the interaction plot. There is no point in performing tests of the differences between the means of the Condition factor on their own, since the logic of the design is to assume that they are identical to begin with, but may end up different as a result of the experimental manipulation. There is no point, either, in comparing means across the Time factor, since the overall F-test for this effect was not significant. In fact, we should go straight to the comparison of the three groups on the second test, i.e. Time2, since the entire logic of the experiment is to produce differences there. This is equivalent to doing a simple effect analysis on the Condition factor, i.e. comparing across Condition means at each level of Test. However, as discussed earlier, most statisticians warn against doing a simple effect analysis over a mixed model repeated-measures factor, so we will instead conduct two one-way ANOVAs on the data, evaluating the effect of Condition at each level of Test. Since you are already familiar with how to do this, using SPSS®, we simply report the overall F-tests, and associated statistics, in Figure 17.24.

At Time1	At Time2	Pairwise comparisons		
F = 0.11	F = 8.17	Condition at Time2		
df = 2,12	df = 2,12		Diff.	Sig.
MS_{Error} = 0.42	MS_{Error} = 0.42	1 vs 2	1	0.04
$p \leq 0.90$	$p \leq 0.006$	1 vs 3	−0.6	0.22
		2 vs 3	−1.6	0.0009

Figure 17.24 Summary results for follow-up analysis of data in Figure 17.21

The significant F-ratio for the test across Time2 tells us that we should conduct multiple comparisons between these three means, and summary results are also shown in Figure 17.24. These results show that the group given misleading information (group 2) performs more poorly at Time2 than either the control group (group 1) or the group given consistent information (group 3). However, the group given consistent information does not perform any better on the final test than the control group.

Summary

1. The key concept in analysis of variance is that variance in a dataset can be decomposed into components. In repeated measures ANOVA, variance is decomposed into that which arises from between-subjects sources, that which arises from within-subjects sources, and that which arises from an unidentified source (the residual or error variance). Variance across the repeated measurements can be partly attributed to variation between the entities or individuals, and the error or residual variance in the ANOVA model can often be reduced substantially.

2. Data from one-way repeated measures ANOVA designs can be analysed just as if they arose from a two-way factorial ANOVA design. A factor coding subject identity is treated as a second factor, and the interaction between this factor and the treatment (or grouping) factor provides the information required for the error term in the ANOVA model.

3. Factorial ANOVA designs that include one or more repeated measures factors are generally either fully repeated (all the factors are repeated) or mixed (some factors are repeated). There are many complexities in the calculation of factorial repeated measures ANOVAs (e.g. appropriate error terms), and we generally entrust the calculations to software packages like SPSS®.

4. Underlying mathematical and statistical assumptions are more important in repeated measures ANOVA than in between-subjects ANOVA. The most important of these is compound symmetry – breaches of this assumption can be serious, especially if the design is unbalanced.

Exercises

1. An educational researcher wants to know how susceptible a widely used reading test is to practice effects. The researcher administers the test to eight school children three times over a period of six weeks (once every two weeks). The data are as follows (the dependent variable is score on the reading test where 1 = poor, 12 = good):

Session 1:	5	6	3	8	5	3	7	6
Session 2:	6	4	7	5	6	4	8	6
Session 3:	8	4	6	6	7	6	5	7

a) What conclusions can the researcher draw? *(Hint: perform a repeated measures ANOVA.)*

b) Calculate the correlation coefficients between the sessions.

c) Modify the data so as to increase the correlation coefficients between the sessions and repeat your earlier analysis (in question a). Report any changes that you might observe.

2. Identify and discuss three situations in which a repeated measures design would be more appropriate than an independent groups design.

3. A sports scientist wants to compare three different methods of fitness training (methods A, B, and C). She wants to use heart rate (in beats per minute) as an indicator of fitness (i.e. as the dependent variable), but she knows that physiological measures show inherent high variability. She decides to control for the high variability by using a repeated measures design and recruits 25 subjects to serve in the study. Their baseline heart rates are determined. For three months they are trained with method A. Their heart rates are then measured, and they are taken off the fitness training regimen for two months. When the two months have lapsed, they are trained for three months with method B, and their heart rates are assessed at the end of this period. The same is done for method C. Data are shown below, as well as output from the SPSS® program. Interpret the output.

Subject:	1	2	3	4	5	6	7	8	9	10	11	12	13	14	15	16	17	18	19	20	21	22	23	24	25
Method A:	67	81	73	69	68	79	78	67	67	69	78	75	81	68	76	69	65	71	66	65	77	81	78	75	76
Method B:	63	77	75	65	67	70	75	67	71	70	72	76	66	73	72	71	66	71	70	63	68	72	76	75	73
Method C:	64	72	73	73	70	74	73	64	70	64	68	63	63	69	72	76	69	67	64	72	65	61	72	63	73

TESTS OF WITHIN-SUBJECTS EFFECTS

Source		Type III Sum of Squares	df	Mean Square	F	Sig.
METHOD	Sphericity Assumed	220.667	2	110.333	6.376	.004
	Greenhouse-Geisser	220.667	1.625	135.836	6.376	.007
	Huynh-Feldt	220.667	1.726	127.873	6.376	.006
	Lower-bound	220.667	1.000	220.667	6.376	.019
Error (METHOD)	Sphericity Assumed	830.667	48	17.306		
	Greenhouse-Geisser	830.667	38.988	21.306		
	Huynh-Feldt	830.667	41.416	20.057		
	Lower-bound	830.667	24.000	34.611		

TESTS OF BETWEEN-SUBJECTS EFFECTS

Source	Type III Sum of Squares	df	Mean Square	F	Sig.
Intercept	374109.453	1	374109.453	11779.677	.000
Error	762.213	24	31.759		

(I) METHOD	(J) METHOD	Mean Difference (I–J)	Std. Error	Sig.
1	2	2.200*	.950	.029
	3	4.200*	1.422	.007
2	1	–2.200*	.950	.029
	3	2.200*	1.108	.084
3	1	–4.200*	1.422	.007
	2	2.000*	1.108	.084

4. Consider the following well-known example from Winer (1971). An experiment is conducted in which six subjects are divided into two groups according to the method of calibrating dials ('Method'). There are four shapes of dials ('Shapes'), and each subject gets four accuracy scores – one for each shape. This is a two-way ANOVA with repeated measures on one factor – the Shapes factor. Conduct the appropriate ANOVA analysis. Interpret your results.

	Shape 1	Shape 2	Shape 3	Shape 4
Method 1	0	0	5	3
	3	1	5	4
	4	3	6	2

	Shape 1	Shape 2	Shape 3	Shape 4
Method 2	4	2	7	8
	5	4	6	6
	7	5	8	9

TUTORIAL

18

Multiple regression

Colin Tredoux

> After studying this tutorial, you should be able to:
> - Give the two central uses to which social scientists put multiple regression analysis.
> - Grasp the key concepts underlying multiple regression analysis.
> - Interpret computer-generated multiple regression analyses.
> - Identify and take precautions against the problem of multicollinearity.
> - Identify non-linear relations and influential outliers.

In Tutorial 10, you were introduced to linear regression, and shown how this technique can be used to describe and analyse simple bivariate relationships. It may have struck you that the social world is not (typically) composed of simple bivariate relationships, and that a method that examines only bivariate relationships probably overlooks the complexity of social and behavioural problems. Indeed, the social world is enormously complex, and behavioural and social phenomena are determined by a great many factors, working in multiple, interacting patterns. We can make the argument that most phenomena in the social and behavioural sciences are inherently complex, and that we will only understand relationships involving these phenomena if we use analytic techniques that enable us to examine multiple, intricate relationships.

There are a number of multivariate procedures that are useful for purposes of 'modelling' complex phenomena and relationships. The most important of these is *multiple linear regression*, since most other multivariate procedures are derived from it, and are easier to understand in relation to it. Multiple linear regression follows in a natural way from simple linear regression, and we will assume in this chapter that you have a sound knowledge of the material covered in Tutorial 10.

Multiple regression is used to model multi-variate relationships.

Multiple regression allows us to find a (linear) combination of independent variables that maximally predicts (or 'explains') a dependent variable. From this, we can gauge the relative contribution of variables in the combination, and we can use the combination (or equation) as a predictive device to predict a value on the dependent variable for particular configurations of data on the independent variables.

An example may make the basic idea clear. Criminologists often use multiple regression analysis to identify predictors of violent behaviour amongst prisoners, and to build predictive models that will allow them to estimate the likelihood that a particular prisoner will commit a violent offense if released from prison. Thus, in the IOWA system (see Duckitt, 1988), the variables *prior violence score, current offense score, street time score, criminal history score, current escape score,* and *substance abuse score* were identified as statistically important predictors of violence risk. These variables are used in a linear combination – i.e. weighted, and added together – to generate predictions of violence risk. This model can be expressed as a regression equation (compare Equation 10.1), that looks something like the following:

$$risk = 0.3*(\text{current offense score}) + 0.09*(\text{street time score}) +$$
$$0.11*(\text{substance abuse score}) + 0.13*(\text{criminal history score}) +$$
$$0.21*(\text{current escape score}) + 0.32*(\text{prior violence score})$$

Let us imagine that John E. Rotten presents himself for early parole. We take measurements on the variables in question, and we enter these values into the equation, and the result it generates (after some modifications) is 4. We can now use the estimate that this equation generates to assist our decision in respect of John E. Rotten's parole application. The IOWA system has conveniently noted that a total score of 4 is high risk, and we will have to factor this prediction into our decision, alongside any other considerations, e.g. John E.'s legendary sense of humour.

Multiple regression is at one level really as simple as this example suggests. A multiple regression equation is just an equation consisting of multiple coefficients and multiple variables. However, it is comparatively rare in the social sciences to use multiple regression analysis in this way (i.e. as an equation generator), and most of the time social researchers are interested in questions that are subsidiary to the generation of the equation itself.

Multiple regression finds a linear combination of independent variables that predicts a dependent variable.

The most common usages of multiple regression in the social sciences are akin to the two examples below:

1. We do not know what the correlates or predictors of post-natal depression are, and suspect that they may include a host of variables, including the mother's previous history of depression, her resources for social support, her socio-economic status, etc. Multiple regression is very useful at identifying such predictors, and their combinatory effects.

2. We know that post-natal depression is correlated with socio-economic status and social support. However, since socio-economic status and social support are strongly negatively correlated, we do not know whether social support offers any unique understanding of post-natal depression, over and above socio-economic status. Multiple regression provides several very effective ways of 'partialling' the contributions of other independent variables out of multiple-way relationships, and is thus an invaluable tool for much social science research.

Although multiple regression is a useful and powerful statistical method, it is also greatly abused in the social (and natural) sciences. This usually happens in the context of situations like (1), above, where researchers use powerful computers to build models of phenomena on the flimsiest of grounds: a computer algorithm is used to identify a set of predictive variables that optimally 'predicts' a dependent variable, regardless of whether the selected set makes theoretical sense.

Activity 18.1

Identify five key social problems that affect people in the area where you live. Now next to each, list all the variables that you think are related to or cause the problems. Do you think these variables are independent, or are some of them related to each other?

This tutorial can do little more than introduce you to multiple regression. For those who wish to study the method in greater detail, the texts by Cohen & Cohen (1975), Pedhazur (1982), and Draper & Smith (1981) are excellent sources.

An example

Imagine that we are interested in predictors of depression in a sample of SANDF soldiers (see Mangxolo, 2000). We have information about a number of psychological and social/demographic characteristics, including their rank, age, race, level of education, and previous military experience. Table 18.1 shows the data for a sample of 40 soldiers. If we postulate a relationship between military Rank (x), an independent variable, and Depression (y), the dependent variable, we can write the regression equation describing the relationship as:

$$y = a + bx$$

Equation 18.1

> where: y is the predicted variable
> b is the regression (or slope) coefficient
> a is the intercept term

We can use the methods set out in Tutorial 10 to determine the values of a and b, which will give us an equation into which we simply need to substitute values of x in order to arrive at predictions of y. With a little additional computation, we can also obtain the standard error of estimate, which will tell us, on average, how far our prediction will differ from the real or true value of the dependent variable. Many other regression statistics are also easily computed, and – as demonstrated in Tutorial 10 – are important aids to the interpretation of the regression equation.

The standard error of the estimate tells us how much, on average, regression predictions differ from observed values.

Useful as this is, we will not be able to proceed beyond the consideration of just one predictor of depression at a time. It does not take great insight to see that this is limiting – many things are likely to affect depression among soldiers, and we need a method that will allow us to simultaneously examine multiple predictors of depression.

Imagine that we wish to examine the joint or simultaneous relationship of Rank and Substance use with Depression. If we agree to assign the notation x_1 to Rank, and x_2 to Substance use, then we can write the (multiple regression) equation relating the combination of x_1 and x_2 to y as:

$$y = a + b_1x_1 + b_2x_2$$

Equation 18.2

> where: b_1 is the regression or slope coefficient associated with x_1
> b_2 is the regression or slope coefficient associated with x_2
> a is the intercept term.

Table 18.1 Data for several variables on SANDF soldiers

S	Rank	Substance use	Depression	S	Rank	Substance use	Depression	S	Rank	Substance use	Depression
1	1	1	2.05	15	3	1	2.11	29	2	2	2.24
2	1	1	0.9	16	3	1	2.1	30	2	2	2.56
3	1	1	1.72	17	3	1	1.44	2	2	2	2.34
4	1	1	1.12	18	3	1	1.58	32	2	2	2.55
5	1	1	1.97	19	3	1	2.4	33	2	2	2.23
6	1	1	1.15	20	3	1	2.95	34	2	2	2.81
7	1	1	2.17	21	1	2	1.3	35	3	2	2.55
8	2	1	2.3	22	1	2	2.85	36	3	2	3.07
9	2	1	0.65	23	1	2	1.69	37	3	2	2.57
10	2	1	1.62	24	1	2	3.04	38	3	2	3.8
11	2	1	0.72	25	1	2	3.16	39	3	2	2.55
12	2	1	2.34	26	1	2	2.85	40	3	2	2.67
13	2	1	1.6	27	1	2	1.21				
14	3	1	1.63	28	2	2	1.91				

S: soldier number; Rank: an ordinal variable lower numbers are lower ranks (lance-corporal = 1, corporal = 2, officer = 3); Substance use: a dichotomous variable (1 = uses substances); Depression = scale score from the Symptom Check List, higher scores = greater depression (max. = 4).

We can solve for a, b_1, and b_2 using well-known mathematical methods, but this is somewhat laborious, especially if we have more than two independent variables. In practice, almost all the computation for multiple regression is done with the aid of statistical software, and the statistical packages reviewed in this text have good multiple regression modules. For the data in Table 18.1, the output given by SPSS® is shown in Figure 18.1 on the next page.

Activity 18.2

In order to refresh your memory of the techniques and methods of simple linear regression, enter the data in Table 18.1 into an SPSS® or STATISTICA datasheet, and do the following:
1. Compute the correlation between rank and depression, and find the regression equation relating the variables (treating depression as a dependent variable).
2. Calculate the standard error of the estimate in this equation and interpret this quantity.
3. Decide on the basis of a scatterplot of the variables if it was sensible to compute a correlation coefficient.

There is much in this Figure (Figure 18.1) that may not be familiar to you. For the moment, concentrate on the column labelled 'B' (we will return to the other columns later in the chapter). The regression coefficients are given here, as well as the value of the intercept

MODEL SUMMARY

Model	R	R Square	Adjusted R Square	Std. Error of the Estimate
1	.612	.375	.341	.58620

COEFFICIENTS

Model		Unstandardised Coefficients		Standardised Coefficients	t	Sig.
		B	Std. Error	Beta		
1	(Constant)	.444	.373		1.188	.242
	RANK	.250	.113	.288	2.213	.033
	SUBSTANC	.782	.185	.549	4.219	.000

ANOVA

Model		Sum of Squares	df	Mean Square	F	Sig.
1	Regression	7.613	2	3.806	11.077	.000ᵃ
	Residual	12.714	37	.344		
	Total	20.327	39			

Figure 18.1 SPSS® output for regression of Rank and Substance use on depression in a sample of soldiers

(labelled 'constant'). By substituting the information in column 'B' into Equation 18.2, we can write the equation relating Depression to Substance use and Rank as:

$$\text{Depression} = 0.444 + (0.25 \times \text{rank}) + (0.782 \times \text{substance use})$$

In other words, for every 1 unit change in Rank, we can expect Depression to increase by 0.25 units, and for every 1 unit change in substance use (in this case there are only two values for Substance use), the Depression score increases by 0.782 units. In other words, higher ranks tend to have higher levels of depression, and those who use substances tend to have higher levels of depression.

We can use this equation to obtain a predicted value of depression for specific sets of values for Rank and Substance use. For example, if a soldier of officer rank indicated abuse of substances, the equation would be written as follows, substituting the value 3 for Rank and 1 for Substance abuse (see codes in Table 18.1):

$$\text{Depression} = 0.444 + (0.25 \times 3) + (0.782 \times 1) = 0.444 + 0.75 + 0.782 = 1.976$$

The predicted level of depression for an officer who abuses substances is therefore 1.976.

Regression coefficients

The values of the coefficients b_1 and b_2 in the equation above are 0.25 and 0.782. These coefficients have much the same meaning as the coefficient in a simple (one predictor) regression equation, with one important difference. They are *partial* gradient or slope coefficients:

for each change of one unit in x_1, y' changes 0.25 units, *provided x_2 is kept constant (does not change)*. The same interpretation holds for x_2: for each change of one unit in x_2, y' changes 0.782 units, *provided x_1 is kept constant*. Another way of saying this is that the regression coefficient of each variable represents the *unique* contribution of that variable to the prediction equation, or the contribution of the variable after 'partialling out' the contributions of all other independent variables.

Consider the one-predictor regression equation relating Rank to Depression:

$$y = a + bx$$
$$\text{Depression} = 1.646 + 0.235 \times \text{rank}$$

Notice how the coefficient of Rank (0.235) changes from that in the multiple regression equation (0.25) – the coefficient of Rank in the multiple regression equation has been corrected according to the amount of variance it shares with Substance use.

Partial correlation and multicollinearity

Perhaps the best way to understand regression coefficients in multiple regression is through the notions of 'partial' and 'shared' variance and correlation.

An example may make this clear. Imagine that we are trying to understand the factors that contribute to a car's fuel consumption. It is fairly clear on common-sense grounds that heavier cars will use more fuel. In other words, the mass of a car (in kilograms) will be a good predictor of fuel consumption. It is also clear that the size of the engine will be a good predictor. However, these two variables are themselves likely to be correlated: you are likely to find bigger engines in heavier cars. This correlation will not be perfect – you will find small, lightweight cars with enormous engines (think of sport cars like Ferraris, Porsches, and Corvettes) – but it will be moderately strong. Table 18.2 is a hypothetical example of a matrix containing the intercorrelations of these variables. In this example, it is very useful for us to know just how much each variable

Table 18.2 Correlation matrix for relations between three motorcar variables

	Fuel consumption	Engine size	Body mass
Fuel consumption	1.0	0.6	0.8
Engine size	0.6	1.0	0.4
Body mass	0.8	0.4	1.0

contributes uniquely to explaining fuel consumption. An index of this unique contribution is the partial correlation (and its square). Figure 18.2 provides a graphic metaphor for the multiple regression analysis in which we try to model Fuel consumption (F) from Engine size (S) and Body mass (M). Each oval represents the total variance of that variable. Any overlap between the ovals represents shared variance, that is co-variance, or the amount of variance in one variable that is attributable to, or explicable from, the variance in the other variable (e.g. the union of the areas marked 'a' and 'b' is the variance shared by S and F). The joint overlap between all three variables (marked 'b') represents the shared contribution of S and M to F, and it can clearly be seen that this total area is the intersection of two non-independent areas (a + b intersecting with c + b). If we consider the unique contribution of S to F, it is the portion marked 'a', and is a visual analog for the squared *partial correlation* of S and F, that is, the proportion $\frac{a}{a+d}$. A quantitity known as the (square of the) *semi-partial correlation* would be the proportion $\frac{a}{a+b+c+d}$.

*The **partial correlation** of x, and y is the correlation between x and y **after** removing a third variable (e.g. x_2) and all its shared variance from both x, and y.*

*The **semi-partial correlation** of x, with y is the correlation between x, and y **after** removing a third variable (e.g. x_2) and its shared variance from x_1.*

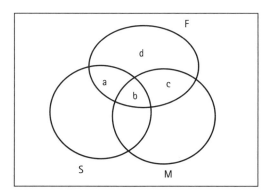

Figure 18.2 Venn diagram illustrating notions of 'partial' and 'shared' variances

In a multiple regression equation, the regression coefficients (*b*) are corrected for the influence of other variables in the equation in the same manner that partial correlations are corrected for their inter-correlation with other variables. However, it is not a good thing to have substantial intercorrelations between independent variables in a multiple regression equation. If the intercorrelations are high, the computational procedure is made vulnerable, and estimates of regression coefficients may in particular be inaccurate. Technical discussions of the reasons for this can be found in Hays (1994), and Draper & Smith (1981). This problem is known as *multicollinearity* and is very common in the social sciences. Although there are a number of ways of dealing with the problem, the best remedy is usually to reduce the predictor set by discarding 'redundant' vari-

***Multicollinearity** occurs when predictor variables are strongly inter-correlated. This should be avoided.*

ables – if two (or more) predictor variables in a particular dataset are highly intercorrelated, the researcher should choose one only, and reject the other(s).

Standardised regression coefficients

One of the problems with regression coefficients – in simple as well as in multiple regression – is that they are expressed in terms of their original measurement scale. Thus, if you develop a regression equation for the relationship that dosage of a drug (usually in milligrams) and body weight (usually in kilograms) have with depression, you may obtain regression coefficients that are based on average dosages of 10 milligrams, and average weights of 70 kilograms. You will probably end up with a set of coefficients like 2.4 and 17.8, and it will not be possible to compare them to each other, since their size depends not only on the strength of their relationship with the dependent variable, but also on the measurement scale you used. Worse, if you were to use a different scale for dosage (say kilograms), then the b coefficient would change radically. *The size of the b coefficients does not indicate the relative importance of variables in a multiple regression equation.*

One way to make regression coefficients comparable is by standardising the variables in the multiple regression equation. Standardisation in this respect is no different from what you were introduced to in the context of z-scores and standard normal distributions (see Tutorial 6) – the means of variables in the equation are set to 0 and the standard deviations to 1. All variables in the equation are thus transformed to the same unit of measure and are (roughly) comparable. The regression coefficients based on standardised variables are called beta coefficients and are denoted by the Greek letter β (beta). When a regression equation is transformed into its standardised form, the intercept term becomes 0, and thus falls away. For the multiple regression equation that relates Rank and Substance use to Depression in soldiers, from the SPSS® output shown as Figure 12.1, we can write the standardised form as:

$$\text{Depression} = 0.288 \times \text{Substance use} + 0.549 \times \text{Rank}$$

The relative size of the coefficients of Substance use and Rank suggests that Substance use is a more 'important' predictor of Depression in soldiers than Rank.

The multiple correlation coefficient (R) and the standard error of estimate

In simple linear regression, there are several measures that express the adequacy or 'tightness' of the fit, i.e. the extent to which the predicted scores deviate from the observed scores. The best known of these is the Pearson correlation coefficient (r), which is usually squared (r^2) for the sake of making the measure interpretable in terms of the *amount of variance* in the dependent variable (y) that is 'explained' by the independent variable (x). The greater r (and therefore r^2) is, the stronger the relationship, and the 'better' the regression equation.

Using a spreadsheet or calculator, and the data from Table 18.1, calculate:
a) the correlation between depression and substance use, partialling out rank
b) the b and β weights for the simple linear regression predicting depression from substance use.

One such measure of the adequacy of the multiple regression equation is the analog to r, known as the *multiple correlation coefficient*, and denoted as R. The multiple correlation coefficient is the correlation between the observed dependent variable (y) and the predicted variable (y'), i.e. the correlation between the actual scores that the sample obtained, and the score each individual would be given on the basis of the regression equation. In the example concerning the prediction of Depression among soldiers from Substance use and Rank, the multiple correlation is 0.612 (see Figure 18.1, 'MODEL SUMMARY'). This value can be interpreted in the same manner that we interpret ordinary correlation coefficients: it varies between –1 and 1, with the relationship becoming stronger the closer it gets to either –1 or 1 (0 = no relationship). The square of R (i.e. R^2) gives the amount of variance in the dependent variable explained by the combination of independent variables in the regression equation. In the case of the equation predicting depression, R^2 is 0.375 – in other words, 37.5% of the variation in depression scores is predicted by the (combined) variation in rank and substance use scores.

'R' is known as the multiple correlation coefficient and is the correlation (r) between y and y'.

Most computer programs will produce a statistic known as adjusted R^2, and denoted by R^2_{adj}. This statistic ostensibly corrects for the degrees of freedom in some of the terms involved in the estimation of R^2, but many statisticians do not place much faith in the adjusted estimator, R^2_{adj} (see Draper & Smith, 1981, for example).

*R^2 and the **standard error of the estimate** are two useful indices of the explanatory power of a regression model.*

Another measure of the adequacy of the regression equation is the standard error of the estimate. This can be thought of as the (corrected) average distance of the observed values from the predicted values. The closer this average distance is to 0, the better the prediction. The closer it gets to $\bar{y}$, the worse the prediction (since just guessing the mean of the dependent variable is the worst we could do, in the absence of any information about predictors). It has the same meaning in simple and multiple regression.

Testing statistical significance in multiple regression

There is always a pair of degrees of freedom values for an F test of a regression model – df model and df residual. Where there are 2 df for model and 100 df for residual, we would write df = (2, 100).

How confident are we that the regression equation we calculated on the data in Table 18.1, above, represents anything more than mere chance, or random sampling variation? Is it any more accurate than if we had just used $\bar{y}$ for each prediction? This is an important question, and we tend to conduct two distinct types of significance test in order to answer it.

The signficance of R², using the F distribution

Here we test whether the particular combination of independent variables represented by the regression equation is better than we could have achieved just by chance, or just by using $\bar{y}$. The test we use is in fact derived from analysis of variance, which is introduced in Tutorial 14. For our sample data, the F-test for R^2 is indicated in Figure 12.1 as 11.077, with a p-value < 0.0005, and degrees of freedom $= 2,37$. Since $p < 0.05$ we can conclude that Rank and Substance use *together* account for a statistically significant proportion of the variation in Depression scores amongst soldiers. (Note that SPSS® rounds the p-values to three places by default, and reports the misleading p-value 0.000 in Figure 18.1 – you should always round these up to the next logical decimal place.)

Activity 18.4

Using a spreadsheet or calculator, and the data from Table 18.1, calculate:
a) R^2 for the relationship between Rank and Depression.
b) the standard error of estimate for the relationship between Rank and Depression. Do this both from the formula (see Tutorial 10), and from the definition above (divide by $n - 1$, rather than n, for the correction).

The signficance of individual variables in the regression equation

Here we test each variable in the equation for statistical significance (in fact, we test whether the value of each regression coefficient is greater than 0). Some computer programs report t-values for this test, and others report F-values – they amount to the same thing. The results for our sample data are reported in Figure 18.1.

The t-tests for the regression coefficients are indicated in the fifth column. For Rank $t = 2.213$, with $p < 0.03$. For Substance use $t = 4.22$, with $p < 0.0005$. From this we can conclude that the (partialled) effect of Substance use on depression is statistically significant, as is the (partialled) effect of Rank on Depression.

Which variables? Methods of model building

One way of thinking about a multiple regression equation is to think of it as a *model*. A number of variables are selected from a potentially large collection, and combined in a linear sum. Each variable is weighted within the combination by its regression coefficient. This weighted combination 'models' the dependent variable, in that it attempts to account for all values of the dependent variable. R^2 can then be thought of as an index of the degree of 'model fit', i.e. how much the predicted values depart from the observed values.

Multiple regression analysis builds models of the dependent variable.

A key problem in this way of thinking about a regression equation is how to select variables for inclusion in the model. In some situations there are theoretical grounds for including variables, but this is (too) rarely the case in social science research. In most situations, we have a large collection of independent variables and little idea of how to choose from this collection. There are a number of solutions to this, ranging from informal inspection of the zero-order correlations between the independent variables and dependent variable, to a method of selecting the regression model that accounts for the maximum possible amount of variation within the set of independent variables ('all possible subsets regression'). By far the most common technique is that known as *stepwise regression*, and we will examine this in some detail a little later.

*The most common 'model-building' in regression is through the use of **stepwise algorithms**.*

Inspection of descriptive data and zero–order correlations

The first step in model-building should be careful inspection of descriptive measures of the independent and dependent variables, the (zero order) correlations of the independent variables with the dependent variable, and the inter-correlations between the independent variables. This inspection will reveal any anomalies in the

The first step in model-building should be careful inspection of descriptive measures of variables.

Activity 18.5

Rank each of the following matrices of intercorrelations in terms of their potential multicollinearity (one of them is deliberately incomplete).

(a)

	y	x_1	x_2
y	1	.4	.7
x_1	.4	1	.1
x_2	.7	.3	1

(b)

	y	x_1	x_2
y	1	.9	.8
x_1	.9	1	
x_2	.8		1

(c)

	y	x_1	x_2	x_3
y	1	.2	.3	.5
x_1	.2	1	.2	.1
x_2	.1	.2	1	.2
x_3	.2	.1	.2	1

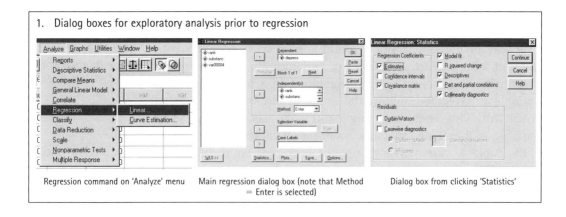

1. Dialog boxes for exploratory analysis prior to regression

Regression command on 'Analyze' menu   Main regression dialog box (note that Method   Dialog box from clicking 'Statistics'
                                         = Enter is selected)

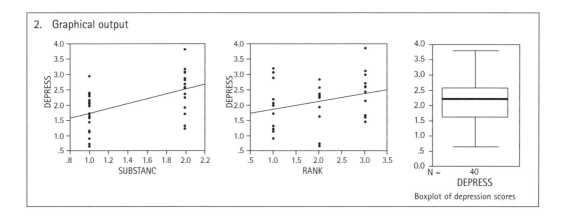

2. Graphical output

Boxplot of depression scores

3. Descriptive statistics and correlations

	MEAN	STD. DEVIATION	N
DEPRESS	2.1110	.72194	40
RANK	1.9750	.83166	40
SUBSTANC	1.5000	.50637	40

		DEPRESS	RANK	SUBSTANC
Pearson Correlation	DEPRESS	1.000	.271	.540
	RANK	.271	1.000	-.030
	SUBSTANC	.540	-.030	1.000
Sig. (1-tailed)	DEPRESS		.045	.000
	RANK	.045		.426
	SUBSTANC	.000	.426	
N	DEPRESS	40	40	40
	RANK	40	40	40
	SUBSTANC	40	40	40

Figure 18.3 SPSS® dialog boxes, boxplot, descriptive statistics, and correlation matrix produced in SPSS® for examining SANDF data prior to regression

data (e.g. outliers, coding mistakes), as well as possible problems for the regression, such as multicollinearity and non-linearity. This is easily done with most statistical packages, including SPSS®. Earlier in this tutorial we looked at a regression equation that attempted to predict soldiers' depression from knowledge of their rank and substance use. Two of the variables we used in the equation are measured at a nominal or ordinal level of measurement, and it is not possible to gain much insight into the data from descriptive measures of these variables. However, it is useful to look at descriptive measures of the dependent variable, and also at the matrix of correlations involving all the variables in the model. Figure 18.3 shows a boxplot for the depression variable, a scatterplot, inter-correlations, and descriptive statistics, as well as the dialog boxes in SPSS® used to produce the latter two.

Scatterplots should always be constructed for all combinations of predictor variables with the dependent variable. This helps detect non-linearity and the presence of outliers.

It is clear from the boxplot that Depression has no obvious outliers, and appears reasonably symmetrical. The matrix of inter-correlations indicates moderately strong correlations between the two predictor variables (Rank and Substance usage) and the dependent variable (Depression), but also shows that the correlation between Rank and Substance usage is negligible (−0.03), which means that multicollinearity is not a threat to the regression analysis.

The sequential F–test

Most *a posteriori* methods of building regression models – i.e. those in which the selection criteria are based on statistical rather than theoretical criteria – rely on a test known as the *sequential F-test*, and it is useful to understand this test before we look at stepwise regression.

The sequential F-test tests whether the addition of a variable to the model significantly improves the fit to the data.

Consider the situation where we have a model that relates one predictor variable to the dependent variable, and this model provides a significant fit to data, given the results of the standard F-test. We now wish to introduce a second predictor variable into the model, but we will want to know whether doing this improves the fit we achieved with just one predictor variable. The sequential (or partial) F-test does exactly this. It compares the F-statistic obtained with the single-predictor model to the F-statistic obtained with the two-predictor model, taking into account the necessary loss of a degree of freedom. This simple test is extraordinarily useful in statistical model-building.

Another equivalent way of thinking about this test is in terms of the change in R^2 that occurs when we add a variable (or variables) to an equation. Referring back to an earlier example, imagine that we are predicting Fuel consumption from Engine size. Then R^2 would be analogous to the union of areas 'a' and 'b' in Figure 18.2.

If we then add car mass as a second variable, we will obtain an R^2 analogous to the union of areas 'a', 'b', and 'c'. The change in R^2 is in effect the area 'c', and the sequential significance test is set up to determine whether the change is statistically significant.

Activity 18.6

What are some other ways to build regression models, apart from stepwise algorithms? Use the resources in your institution's library to find examples of regression model-building that do not rely on stepwise methods.

Stepwise multiple regression

This is overwhelmingly the most popular model-building algorithm amongst social science researchers who use multiple regression. The key idea is to build a model by increasing the number of variables in the regression equation one at a time, testing whether each additional variable increases the F-statistic over the value obtained without the additional variable. The first variable to be included in the model is that which has the highest correlation with the dependent variable. The semi-partial correlations of all other independent variables with the dependent variable are then computed (see the earlier discussion of partial and semi-partial correlation). The independent variable with the highest semi-partial correlation with the dependent variable is then selected, and added to the regression equation. If the sequential F-test shows that this addition is statistically significant, the variable is kept in the equation. This procedure continues until all of the variables have either been accepted into the equation, or rejected. Figure 18.4 shows this algorithm as a flowchart. (This model can also be built by decreasing the number of variables in the regression equation one at a time.)

The sequence of models tested by the SPSS® stepwise procedure is shown in footnotes to the model summary table of the SPSS® output.

Most statistical packages have a good stepwise regression module/procedure, and will produce a summary of the step-by-step selection and rejection of variables. You do not need to do any of the calculations depicted in Figure 18.4 by hand.

For the running example concerning the prediction of depression in soldiers, we added three additional variables – the marital status of the soldier (single vs with partner), whether the soldier lives in the same province as he is stationed in (same province vs different province), and the type of previous military organisation the soldier belonged to, before the integration of the SANDF (statutory vs non-statutory forces). These are abbreviated MARSTAT, WCAPE, and PREVMIL, respectively. Thus, five variables were entered in total, and SPSS® was instructed to use stepwise regression

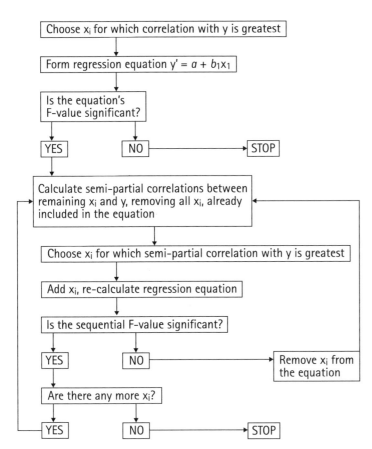

Figure 18.4 Flowchart of the (forward) stepwise multiple regression algorithm

to select and test the best model. The dialog boxes necessary to run the regression are shown in Figure 18.3 (but note that on the main regression dialog box you need to select method = stepwise to run a stepwise regression). Figure 18.5 reports the stepwise summary for the analysis, as well as the ANOVA summary table for each step (called 'Model' in the SPSS® output).

Notice that the model summary table details the amount of change in R^2 for each step, as well as the sequential F-test. The ANOVA and 'COEFFICIENTS' tables treat each step as a separate model, and provide the coefficients and ANOVA analysis of the model at that step. For the running example, the stepwise analysis selected three variables for inclusion in the final model, namely Rank, Substance abuse, and Marital status. It rejected the remaining two variables. The final model ('3' in the table) has an R^2 of 0.45, and its associated F-ratio is significant at $p < 0.0005$.

Model	R	R Square	Adjusted R Square	Std. Error of the Estimate	Change Statistics				
					R Square Change	F Change	df1	df2	Sig. F Change
1	.540[a]	.292	.273	.61554	.292	15.648	1	38	.000
2	.612[b]	.375	.341	.58620	.083	4.900	1	37	.033
3	.671[c]	.450	.405	.55705	.076	4.974	1	36	.032

[a.] Predictors: (Constant), SUBSTANC
[b.] Predictors: (Constant), SUBSTANC, RANK
[c.] Predictors: (Constant), SUBSTANC, RANK, MARSTAT

ANOVA[d]

Model		Sum of Squares	df	Mean Square	F	Sig.
1	Regression	5.929	1	5.929	15.648	.000[a]
	Residual	14.398	38	.379		
	Total	20.327	39			
2	Regression	7.613	2	3.806	11.077	.000[b]
	Residual	12.714	37	.344		
	Total	20.327	39			
3	Regression	9.156	3	3.052	9.836	.000[c]
	Residual	11.171	36	.310		
	Total	20.327	39			

[a.] Predictors: (Constant), SUBSTANC
[b.] Predictors: (Constant), SUBSTANC, RANK
[c.] Predictors: (Constant), SUBSTANC, RANK, MARSTAT
[d.] Dependent Variable: DEPRESS

COEFFICIENTS[a]

Model		Unstandardised Coefficients		Standardised Coefficients	t	Sig.
		B	Std. Error	Beta		
1	(Constant)	.956	.308		3.106	.004
	SUBSTANC	.770	.195	.540	3.956	.000
2	(Constant)	.444	.373		1.188	.242
	SUBSTANC	.782	.185	.549	4.219	.000
	RANK	.250	.113	.288	2.213	.033
3	(Constant)	.990	.431		2.296	.028
	SUBSTANC	.822	.177	.576	4.639	.000
	RANK	.243	.107	.280	2.267	.029
	MARSTAT	-.395	.177	-.277	-2.230	.032

[a.] Dependent Variable: DEPRESS

Figure 18.5 SPSS® summary output of stepwise regression for modelling depression in SANDF soldiers

Hierarchical multiple regression

Hierarchical regression is a form of model-building in which the order of entry is explicitly controlled, usually for reasons of theoretical coherence.

You will frequently find this term used in research reports and journal articles. It describes a form of regression model-building in which the variable selection is explicitly controlled, and variables are entered in a fixed sequence. This is particularly useful if the variables have a logical order, or temporal priority. We do not have the space to discuss this variant here, but refer interested readers to Cohen & Cohen (1975) for a comprehensive discussion.

Activity 18.7

Look carefully at the change in the size of the coefficients of the *x* variables in the regression 'MODEL SUMMARY' section of Figure 18.5. Does this indicate relatively high or relatively low intercorrelations of the predictor variables? Check your answer against the intercorrelations reported in Figure 18.3.

Cross-validation

The key quantitative method that regression assumes is known as *least squares*. This method guarantees an optimally predictive set of regression weights, *but only for the particular data from which they are derived*. If we re-compute the regression on a different set of data, the original regression weights will no longer be optimal. Sometimes the amount of change in the weights can be substantial. This is one of the most notorious features of multiple regression, and one that makes it somewhat problematic as a general purpose research tool.

A method for dealing with the problem is to estimate how 'valid' the weights are for different sets of data. There will be shrinkage in the value of R^2 if the weights estimated on one set of data are used on a second set of data, and the amount of shrinkage can tell us how bad the cross-validation problem is. The simplest way of doing this is to randomly divide the research sample into two, compute a regression model for each half, and compare the regression weights of the two models. More sophisticated methods are discussed in specialised volumes (e.g. Cohen & Cohen, 1975).

*A simple method of **cross validating** a regression analysis is to randomly divide the research sample into two, and compute a regression model for each half.*

Assumptions and limitations

Like most statistical procedures discussed in this text, regression analysis makes a number of assumptions that should be observed in practice. The most important of these is the assumption of *linearity*: it is assumed that the relationship between each of the predictor variables and the dependent variable is linear. If this assumption is not met in practice, it is possible to draw conclusions that are completely mistaken. We should therefore always investigate the linearity assumption – examination of scatterplots is often adequate for this purpose. Although there are ways to remedy non-linearity of relationships, the methods are beyond the scope of this text.

A second assumption is that *residuals* – the amount by which the fitted line deviates from the data points – are distributed normally. The F-test is fairly robust with respect to minor violations of this assumption, so only major violations warrant attention.

'Residuals' are the individual amounts by which the fitted line deviates from the observed data points (see Figure 10.3).

Apart from these assumptions, there are a number of practical limitations and possible hindrances that must be taken into account when conducting multiple regression analysis. One of these is the critical way in which sample size can affect multiple regression results (especially R^2 values). It is possible to obtain very high R^2 results when running multiple regression on small samples – indeed, when there are exactly as many cases (subjects) as there are variables, R^2 will reach its maximum!

*The greatest threats to a successful regression analysis are **departures from linearity**, and the presence of **outliers**.*

For this reason, it is a good idea to have many more cases than variables. Although some authors suggest 10 cases per variable (i.e. if you have 10 variables, you should have 100 cases), statistical opinion is divided on the desirable ratio. The second practical limitation is the sensitivity of regression analysis to *outliers*. These are scores that are 'unusual' in the sense that they have a much higher or lower value than most of the other scores in the dataset (they were discussed in Tutorials 10 and 11). They tend to exert enormous influence on regression results.

Figure 18.6 shows two scatterplots with fitted least-squares lines, which differ only in the presence of a single outlier. We can clearly see from this how much influence outliers can exert on a regression analysis, and for this reason we should make a major effort to ensure that they are either excluded from datasets, or if left in, that they do not exert major influence on the regression results. There are advanced techniques for dealing with outliers, but that is beyond the scope of the present tutorial.

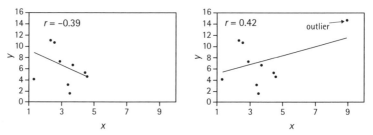

Figure 18.6 The effect of an outlier on a regression line and regression analysis

Worked example

There are a number of jobs that require a certain amount of strength to be able to render good performance (e.g. construction-site workers, lumberjacks, motor mechanics). A specific problem is how to select the best candidates for these kinds of jobs. One solution is to develop an easily administrable measure of physical ability, which does not risk injury, and is related to job performance. A study by Blakley *et al.* (1994) examined the predictive ability of such a measure. Some of the data (50 cases) from that study are presented in Table 18.3. These data were collected from individuals working in physically demanding jobs. Two measures of strength – grip and arm strength – were gathered from each participant, using the Jackson Evaluation System. Two separate measures of job performance were taken. First, the supervisors of the study participants were asked to rate how well

Table 18.3 Predictors of ability in physically demanding jobs

Subject	Grip	Arm	Ratings	Simulations
1	105.5	80.5	31.8	1.18
2	106.58	93	39.8	0.94
3	94	81	46.8	0.84
4	90.5	33.5	52.2	−2.45
5	92	96.5	38.6	−1.17
6	138	84.5	49	1.84
7	91.5	64	28	−0.62
8	189	122	49.266	4.87
9	115	101.5	45.6	0.77
10	121	84	52.6	2.97
11	128.5	93.5	46.4	3.16
12	128	84	46	0.27
13	82	39	31.3	−3.88
14	128.5	88	57	0.91
15	118	70.5	26.4	0.91
16	104.5	69.5	38.2	−0.94
17	120.5	95	48.4	3.09
18	77	29	43.6	−3.38
19	130	84	50.4	1.85
20	86.5	60	35.8	−0.4
21	142	115	26.6	2.69
22	71	66	38	0.2
23	95.5	89	41.4	−1.1
24	136.5	90	36.5	2.13
25	94.5	62.5	56.6	−1.59
26	90.5	64.5	47.8	−2.79
27	111.5	95.5	33	1.53
28	111	101	51.602	0.94
29	119	82.5	31.4	1.21
30	119.5	90.5	48.4	3.04
31	134	103.5	46	3.51
32	134	89	48.4	1.62
33	132.5	83.5	37	−0.62
34	121.5	89	45.4	−0.89
35	91.5	73	33.6	−0.82
36	173.5	117	54.2	0.68
37	128.5	80	56	1.43
38	104	68.5	35.6	−0.92
39	141	113	35.5	4.95
40	84.5	83	30.6	−1.09
41	123	66.5	48.8	0.32
42	133.5	87.5	40	0.21
43	132.5	99	47.4	1.64
44	82.5	57.5	44.8	−0.25
45	131	86	37	1.03
46	147	71	57.2	0.53
47	109.5	86.5	43	2.89
48	54	67.5	41.7	−1.38
49	126	63.5	37	1.33
50	94	38	37.3	−1.53

their employee(s) performed, using a 60-point scale (higher scores indicate better performance). Secondly, a work simulation was developed (higher scores indicate better performance).

Solution

Let us see whether we can predict job performance based on grip and/or arm strength. The first step is to inspect the descriptive statistics from the study to ensure that we do not have outliers, or seriously compromise the assumptions underlying the significance tests. Figure 18.7 displays the output generated by the SPSS® program, as the first step in its regression analysis.

DESCRIPTIVE STATISTICS

	MEAN	STD. DEVIATION	N
SIM	.5932	1.93558	50
GRIP	114.3100	25.34031	50
ARM	80.6400	20.33747	50
RATINGS	42.4994	8.34703	50

CORRELATIONS

		SIM	GRIP	ARM	RATINGS
Pearson Correlation	SIM	1.000	.688	.747	.137
	GRIP	.688	1.000	.682	.294
	ARM	.747	.682	1.000	.105
	RATINGS	.137	.294	.105	1.000
Sig. (1-tailed)	SIM	–	.000	.000	.341
	GRIP	.000	–	.000	.038
	ARM	.000	.000	–	.470
	RATINGS	.341	.038	.470	–
N	SIM	50	50	50	50
	GRIP	50	50	50	50
	ARM	50	50	50	50
	RATINGS	50	50	50	50

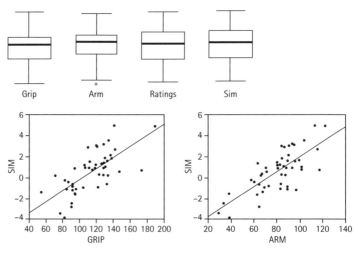

Figure 18.7 Descriptive statistics, correlations, boxplots, and scatterplots for the data in Table 18.3

These data suggest that the variables are reasonably symmetrical, and do not appear to exhibit any patterns that suggest against using tests of statistical significance. The scatterplots do not reveal any outliers or suggest non-linearity, which are potentially grave threats to regression analysis. However, the correlation between Grip strength and Arm strength is high, and we probably have multicollinearity. The low correlation between Supervisor ratings and the Work simulation test is also cause for concern. For simplification, we will assume that the Work simulation test is more accurate than the supervisor's rating, since supervisors are undoubtedly influenced by employee attributes other than physical strength, and we wish to focus only on aspects of the job that require physical strength.

We have one dependent variable – i.e. Work simulation score – and two independent variables, Grip strength and Arm strength. The best way to build a model here is probably to enter the variable that has the highest correlation with the dependent variable, and then force the remaining variable into the equation. The sequential F-test will tell us whether it is worth keeping the second variable. We can obtain all the information we need for this problem by examining the record of a stepwise regression in SPSS®, which is shown in Figure 18.8.

It is clear from this analysis that arm strength is a useful predictor of the simulation score, and it is also clear that grip strength adds something to our prediction over and above that given by arm

MODEL SUMMARY

Model	R	R Square	Adjusted R Square	Std. Error of the Estimate	Change Statistics				
					R Square Change	F Change	df1	df2	Sig. F Change
1	.747[a]	.558	.548	1.30071	.558	60.507	1	48	.000
2	.786[b]	.617	.601	1.22263	.060	7.327	1	47	.009

a. Predictors: (Constant), ARM
b. Predictors: (Constant), ARM, GRIP

COEFFICIENTS[a]

Model	Unstandardized Coefficients		Standardized Coefficients	t	Sig.
	B	Std. Error	Beta		
1 (Constant)	-5.138	.759		-6.766	.000
ARM	0.071	.009	.747	7.779	.000
2 (Constant)	-6.305	.834		-7.560	.000
ARM	0.049	.012	.519	4.202	.000
GRIP	0.026	.009	.334	2.707	.009

a. Dependent Variable: SIM

ANOVA[c]

Model	Sum of Squares	df	Mean Square	F	Sig.
1 Regression	102.368	1	102.368	60.507	.000[a]
Residual	81.209	48	1.692		
Total	183.577	48			
2 Regression	113.320	2	56.660	37.904	.000[b]
Residual	70.257	47	1.495		
Total	183.577	49			

a. Predictors: (Constant), ARM
b. Predictors: (Constant), ARM, GRIP
c. Dependent Variable: SIM

Figure 18.8 Summary of stepwise regression analysis of strength simulation on arm and grip stength

strength (the sequential F-test is significant at $p < 0.01$, even though this variable only adds 6% to the explained variance). The combined model produces an R^2 coefficient of 0.62, which is high for this kind of application. The specific results for Model 2 show us that the overall model is statistically significant, and that it has a standard error of the estimate of 1.22 (predictions of the simulation score will on average be in error to an amount of 1.22). If we wish to write the formal predictive model, in order to use it as an actuarial device, it is

$$\text{simulation score} = -6.31 + 0.026 \times \text{Grip strength} + 0.049 \times \text{Arm strength}$$

Summary

1. Multiple regression is a widely used quantitative method for the analysis of multivariate data. It allows us to find a (linear) combination of independent variables that maximally predicts (or 'explains') a dependent variable. From this, we can gauge the relative contribution of variables in the combination, and we can use the combination (or equation) as a predictive equation. Multiple regression also provides several very effective ways of 'partialling' variables out of multiple-way relationships, allowing us to determine the proportions and sources of variance that are *shared* and that are *unique*.

2. The basic form of a multiple regression equation is $y' = a + b_1x_1 + \ldots + b_ix_i + \ldots b_kx_k$, where y' = the predicted variable, a = the intercept (or constant), and the b_i are the partial regression coefficients. The b_i expresses the unit change in y for the associated x_i, correcting (or partialling) for all other x_i in the equation.

3. A potential danger to regression analysis is the presence of multicollinearity, i.e. when some of the predictor variables are highly intercorrelated. This can make regression coefficients very unstable, and the analysis difficult to interpret.

4. Two useful indices of the explanatory power of a regression model are R^2 and the standard error of the estimate.

5. A common way of building regression models is to use software-based stepwise algorithms, but researchers should be wary of the capitalisation on chance that these algorithms are based on. It is important to cross-validate regression models, and to test them for theoretical coherence.

6. Two potentially grave threats to a regression analysis are breaches of the assumption of linearity, and the presence of data outliers. These should always be explored with scatterplots prior to analysis, and corrected, if possible.

Exercises

Note: Additional exercises are on the accompanying CD.

1. Examine the following results from a statistical package, and answer the questions.

Predictor	Coeff	Stdev
Constant	20	10
Var1	-1	0.25
Var2	12	8
Var3	-15	5

Source	SS	df	MS	F
Regression	7500	3	?	?
Error	?	18	?	
TOTAL	10000	21		

a) Complete the ANOVA table.
b) Test the overall regression model for significance.
c) Test the individual regression coefficients for significance using a *t*-test where $t = \dfrac{\text{coeff}}{\text{stdev}}$, with n – (k + 1) degrees of freedom.

2. A sociologist investigated predictors of amount of money families spend on food. He discovered that the most important predictors were annual income and number of people in the family. The regression equation was:

Food amount = 500 + 0.023*(Annual income) + 252*(No. of persons)

a) How much does amount spent on food increase per family member?
b) If a family earned R1 000 more per year, by how much would the amount spent on food increase?
c) What would a five-person family with an annual income of R20 000 spend on food?

3. Baron and Strauss (1989) report data from the United States for rape statistics per state, as well as additional data that can be argued to be causally important. Use these data, as reported in the table on the following pages to construct a regression model that predicts rape rate on the basis of the listed independent variables.

Rape rate and other sociological variables, per US state

State	Rapes/ 100 000 level	% below poverty	% un– employ	% women/ % men admin.	Md income females/Md income males	Violent TV
1	30	17.9	7.5	51.1	56.8	186
2	62.5	10.1	9.8	64.4	63.9	–
3	45.2	12.4	6.2	58.2	58.8	109
4	26.7	18.7	6.9	45.8	61.6	173
5	58.2	11.3	6.6	57.3	61.2	118
6	52.5	10.2	5	53.1	60.1	153
7	21.6	8.7	4.7	37.7	59	132
8	24.2	11.9	6.3	41.6	58.30	158
9	56.9	13	5.1	55.7	60.50	154
10	44.3	16.4	5.9	49	52.00	208
11	34.7	10	4.7	59.4	59.20	115
12	22.4	12.7	8	57.6	58.9	179
13	26.9	11.5	7.2	46.6	56.6	170
14	33.1	9.8	7.8	45.2	55.6	163
15	14.3	9.4	5	56.9	58.5	153
16	31.5	10.2	4	43.6	59.9	160
17	19.2	18.4	8.5	58.2	57.1	185
18	44.5	18.9	6	49.6	53.2	223
19	12.9	12.9	7.65	52.3	63.5	149
20	40.1	9.9	5.8	50.6	61.9	171
21	27.3	9.8	5.1	44.8	62.5	116
22	46.6	11.1	11	47.6	56.7	153
23	23.2	9.3	5.4	50	58.4	152
24	24.6	24.5	7.2	49.7	60.1	185
25	32.6	12.4	6.9	57.1	57.6	160
26	21	12.4	8.3	60	55.7	200
27	23.2	10.4	3.7	43.1	58.6	135
28	67.2	8.5	5.9	70.6	61.6	125
29	17.3	8.7	4.8	42.5	59.3	–
30	30.7	9.7	6.7	47	57.5	–
31	43.4	17.4	7.1	61.3	58.3	162
32	30.9	13.7	7.1	44.2	64.3	139
33	22.7	14.6	5.5	37.7	66	206
34	9.5	12.8	5.3	43.8	57	155
35	34.3	10.5	8	48.5	56.5	169
36	36.3	13.3	4.1	56.9	58.4	166
37	41.5	11.3	8.3	64.7	58.5	133
38	23	10.5	7.4	44.6	58.3	139
39	17.1	10.3	7	37.7	59.5	108
40	37.5	59.9	6.1	52.1	64.6	226
41	12.5	16.1	4.9	47.1	61.7	165
42	37.4	17	7.4	52.1	59.3	199

Rape rate continued

State	Rapes/ 100 000 level	% below poverty	% un- employ	% women/ % men admin.	Md income females/Md income males	Violent TV
43	47.3	14.9	4	54.7	57.7	167
44	27.7	10.7	5.5	47	54.2	159
45	29.1	11.4	6.3	50.6	64.4	146
46	27.4	11.5	5	52.2	62.2	163
47	52.7	10.2	7.4	60	57.3	131
48	15.8	14.5	8.5	50.3	51.4	189
49	14.9	8.5	6.6	49.1	58.6	164
50	28.6	8	4.1	51.5	50.2	179

Source: Data from Baron & Strauss (1989)

TUTORIAL

19

Chi-square test

Lance Lachenicht

After studying this tutorial, you should be able to:
- Decide whether counted data can be properly arranged into contingency tables.
- Calculate the chi-square test for a contingency table, and determine the degrees of freedom for the table, as well as look up the significance of the chi-square value in a table.
- Find the strength of categorical associations in a contingency table using a variety of measures including Cramer's V, and the odds ratio.
- Find the source of the association in contingency tables greater than 2 × 2 using the method of adjusted standardised residuals.
- Understand the assumptions of the chi-square test, and determine whether these hold.
- Carry out the above procedures using the computer statistics package SPSS®.

In previous tutorials, you have studied significance tests that apply to comparisons between two groups where the data consist of scores (i.e. measurements taken on interval or ratio scales). In the present tutorial, we will study a significance test used where the data consist of *counts* rather than scores.

Classifications

It is possible to classify the members of a population in many different ways. People may be classified into married and single, children and adults, politically active and politically indifferent, etc. These are all examples of *dichotomous* classifications. *Multiple* classifications are also possible, for example, Sheldon's classification of body types as ectomorphic (thin), mesomorphic (muscular), and endomorphic (fat). Classifications are of interest to a researcher mainly when they are *exhaustive* (sufficient categories are provided to 'exhaust' or encompass all members of the population) and *mutually exclusive* (each member of the population can be assigned to one and only one classification).

An **exhaustive classification** leaves no member of a population unclassified.

In a **mutually exclusive classification**, each member of the population can be assigned to one and only one category.

Activity 19.1

Which of the following classification are either **not** exhaustive, or **not** mutually exclusive?

a) We draw cards randomly from a deck of 54 playing cards (i.e. with two jokers) and classify them as hearts, diamonds, spades, or clubs.

b) We randomly sample a group of students and classify individuals as either male or female.

c) A hospital for treating TB looks at its records over the last ten years, and notes that it has data for 389 of 412 patients who underwent treatment. It classifies patients as relapsed or cured.

Classifications are a form of measurement (nominal measurement), but they constitute *qualitative* rather than *quantitative* data. For example, say that a person is classified as a mesomorph, and that the same person is weighed. The person's weight in kilograms is quantitative data but the person's classification as a mesomorph is qualitative data. The same person may be classified and measured in other ways – for example, we may ask whether that person is left- or right-handed *(additional classification)*, and also what that person's IQ score is *(additional quantitative measurement)*.

Contingency tables

When data are classified with respect to two or more qualitative variables, the data form what is known as a *contingency table*. For example, Table 19.1 shows a sample of 300 books classified in two different ways: how the books were bound (three different methods) and whether or not the binding remained intact after five years of use. (Notice that the categories in the table are both exhaustive and mutually exclusive.)

Table 19.1 A contingency table showing cross-classifi-
cation of books by two binding variables

	Sleeve, stitched	Hard cover, glue	Paper cover, glue	TOTAL
Not intact	41	27	22	90
Intact	79	53	78	210
TOTAL	120	80	100	300

A table such as this is known as a contingency table, and this is a 2×3 example, since the sample has been categorised in three ways in terms of binding type (sleeve, stitched; hard cover, glue; paper cover, glue), and categorised in two ways *(dichotomised)* in terms of binding condition (intact, not intact). The simplest contingency table is a 2×2 table (i.e. the data is dichotomised in two different ways).

*A contingency table is also commonly known as a **crosstabulation** (crosstab for short).*

The 'Sleeve, stitched' and 'Not intact' classifications intersect in the above table in what is known as a *cell* of the contingency table, the cell that contains the number 41. The number in each of the cells of the table is a *frequency*, or a *count*. This number may be transformed into a percentage or a proportion, but it must be remembered that this number was originally a count rather than a continuous measurement. Continuous data, such as age, can be broken into discrete form and reported as counts (e.g. by classifying people into age groups), and in this form, continuous data are suitable for analysis in contingency tables.

*A **contingency table** is typically referred to as an **r** × **c** table (e.g. 3 × 2 table), where **r** = the number of rows, **c** = the number of columns, and **r** × **c** = the total number of cells in the table.*

Tables such as our book-binding/durability table above have two classifications of the data and are therefore called *two-dimensional* tables. It is possible to have three-dimensional (and higher) contingency tables, though they are beyond the scope of the present tutorial.

The χ^2 significance test

A test that is appropriate for the analysis of counts is the χ^2 test (spelt 'chi-square test', where the 'ch' is pronounced as 'k'). Since the χ^2 test is a significance test with a very wide and general application, we will devote some time to explaining its method of operation.

A χ^2 test is typically used to test for association between two categorical variables.

When used as a significance test, the χ^2 test can be used as a *goodness of fit* test (i.e. does the existing data fit a theoretical distribution, such as a normal distribution?). More frequently it is used to test the *association* between two or more sets of categories (e.g. is left-handedness associated with unusual prowess at tennis?). The null hypothesis would be that no association exists between the sets of categories (e.g. left-handedness is **not** associated with unusual prowess at tennis). The methods of calculating χ^2 do not differ much between these two kinds of uses, but the material in the present tutorial is exclusively concerned with hypotheses about associations between categories.

The calculation of a χ^2 test is best explained through an example. Imagine that through interviews and advertisements we have found 100 subjects who sleep fewer than five hours every night (and wish to sleep more), and another 100 subjects who sleep eight or more hours every night. Each of these subjects has informed us whether they drink more than three cups of tea a day, three or fewer cups a day, or no tea at all. This information allows us to classify our subjects into long sleepers and short sleepers, and into heavy tea-drinkers, moderate tea-drinkers, and tea abstainers. From all this information we can set up a contingency table (Table 19.2).

The contingency table shows that there are similarities and differences between the two samples. On first inspection, moderate tea-drinkers seem to be long sleepers much more often than are heavy tea-drinkers, and more tea abstainers seem to be short sleepers than long sleepers. However, heavy tea-drinkers seem to be evenly divided between long and short sleepers. How are we to know whether these differences between long and short sleepers are due to sampling or chance variation, or reflect real differences?

*The values in the cells of a contingency table must be absolute frequencies and **not** proportions or percentages. Always retain the original frequencies even if you calculate percentages from your data.*

We can apply the χ^2 test to test the hypothesis that the two samples (long and short sleepers) come from the same population with respect to tea drinking (i.e. that there is no association between the two categorisations).

The values in the cells of a contingency table must be absolute frequencies and **not** proportions or percentages. Always retain the original frequencies even if you calculate percentages from your data.

The key concept in this test is the notion of an *expected frequency*. In a test of association between variables, this boils down to the question of what we would expect if only chance variation were operating across the categories of interest, and the category frequencies were in fact equal in the population. For example, let us say that we select 200 tea-drinkers at random, and there is no population difference between the categories heavy, moderate, and abstainer. We have the categories shown in Table 19.3, and we need to know with what to replace the question marks. You should intuitively see that this will be $^{200}/_3 \approx 66.67$. We call this the expected frequency – the frequency we would obtain if we drew an infinite number of samples of 200 tea-drinkers from the population and randomly classified them according to the agreed categorisation.

Expected frequency is a hypothetical frequency calculated either according to i) a theoretical model of a categorical association ('goodness of fit'), or ii) chance expectation (the classic two dimensional χ^2 test of association).

Table 19.2 Contingency table representing data for insomnia study

	Heavy tea-drinkers	Moderate tea-drinkers	Tea abstainers	TOTAL
Short sleepers	28	32	40	100
Long sleepers	27	52	21	100
TOTAL	55	84	61	200

Table 19.3 Tea-drinkers and expected frequencies

Heavy	Moderate	Abstainer	TOTAL
?	?	?	200

It is not difficult to calculate expected frequencies for the tea-drinker data. The population as a whole contains 84 moderate tea-drinkers. If the sample of long sleepers and the sample of short sleepers were from the same population, we would expect the moderate tea-drinkers to be distributed in proportion to the number of people in each sample. Since the two samples actually contain the same number of people, we would expect the same number of moderate tea-drinkers in both the long and short sleepers, i.e. 42 people. We can work out the other columns in a similar fashion. The general principle for working out the expected frequency in each cell of a contingency table is:

Equation 19.1

$$\text{expected frequency} = \frac{\text{total of cell rows} \times \text{total of cell columns}}{\text{grand total of all subjects}}$$

Activity 19.2

In Tutorial 5, you were introduced to probability calculations. Some of these principles can be applied to contingency tables.

For the contingency table of the 'tea-drinker' data (Table 19.3), for example, what is the probability that you are a heavy tea drinker and a short sleeper? (*Hint: this is a joint or conjunction probability.*) In order to find the *expected number* of heavy tea-drinkers who are also short sleepers, you need to multiply this probability by the grand total n. Show that this set of 'probability calculations' is equivalent to the formula for calculating expected values.

In the case of the expected frequency for moderate tea-drinkers among the long sleepers, using the formula we get $(100 \times 84) \div 200 = 42$. We can set out the expected frequencies for our contingency table in the same form as the original contingency table.

Table 19.4 Contingency table representing expected frequencies for insomnia study

	Heavy tea-drinkers	Moderate tea-drinkers	Tea abstainers	TOTAL
Short sleepers	27.5	42	30.5	100
Long sleepers	27.5	42	30.5	100
TOTAL	55	84	61	200

In this case, the calculation was very easy because the samples are of equal size – this will not always be the case!

Once we have expected and observed values for each cell, we are in a position to calculate the χ^2 statistic. To calculate χ^2, we apply the formula below. The resulting total is the χ^2 value, and we can look up its significance in the χ^2 tables. Obviously, it will always have a positive value because of the squaring of the differences.

$$\chi^2 = \Sigma \frac{(O - E)^2}{E}$$

Equation 19.2

where: O = observed frequency for a cell
E = expected frequency for a cell

Since the formula for χ^2 is a sum of squared numbers, χ^2 is always a positive number (i.e. $\chi^2 \geq 0$).

If you take the square root of this formula, you can see its relation to the t-test $\left(t = \dfrac{\overline{x} - \mu}{\sqrt{\dfrac{s^2}{n}}} \right)$, which you have studied already (see Tutorial 9). Taking the square root you will get: $\dfrac{O - E}{\sqrt{E}}$, where the divisor, the square root of the expected frequency, is equivalent to the standard error in the t-test $\left(\sqrt{\dfrac{s^2}{n}} \right)$, and the difference between O and E corresponds to the difference between means in the t-test $(\overline{x} - \mu)$.

For the data in the tables above we can set out the calculation in the following way, starting at the top left cell and working column by column.

Table 19.5 Table showing calculation of χ^2 for insomnia study

O	E	O – E	(O – E)²	$\dfrac{(O - E)^2}{E}$
28	27.5	0.5	0.25	0.01
27	27.5	−0.5	0.25	0.01
32	42	−10	100	2.38

Table 19.5 continued

0	E	O – E	(O – E)²	$\frac{(O - E)^2}{E}$
52	42	10	100	2.38
40	30.5	9.5	90.25	2.95
21	30.5	–9.5	90.25	2.95
			χ^2 =	10.68

Activity 19.3

Assume that we want to conduct a test of independence of the two dimensions constituting Table 19.1, and calculate the expected values.

Note that the form of the χ^2 significance test is conceptually similar to other significance tests you have encountered, i.e. $\chi^2 \approx$ observed difference ÷ sampling error of expectation.

Thus the χ^2 statistic for the distribution of the three kinds of tea-drinkers in our two samples is 10.68. The final stage of the significance test is to evaluate the probability of obtaining a χ^2 value of this size. If we had carried out the χ^2 test on a computer statistics program, such as SPSS®, the program would have calculated this probability for us, but as we are calculating it by hand at the moment, we will need to consult a table.

The significance of a χ^2 value depends on the degrees of freedom associated with the contingency table. You have already come across the notion of degrees of freedom in this text, so we simply show the formula for determining the degrees of freedom in a χ^2 test. If the table has r rows and c columns (an $r \times c$ contingency table) then the df are:

Equation 19.3

$$df = (r - 1) \times (c - 1)$$

where: r = number of rows in the table
c = number of columns in the table
but if $r = 1$, or $c = 1$, then df = $(c - 1)$, or df = $(r - 1)$

The degrees of freedom for a two-dimensional χ^2 are always $(r - 1) \times (c - 1)$, where r = number of rows in the table, and c = number of columns in the table.

The contingency table containing our tea-drinking data has two rows and three columns. For a 2 × 3 contingency table, the size of the table containing our tea-drinking data, the probability of obtaining a χ^2 value equal to or larger than the tabulated value is shown in Table 19.6.

Table 19.6 Selected χ^2 distribution

χ^2 value	Probability
1.386	0.60
4.605	0.10
5.991	0.05
9.210	0.01

In evaluating the probability of a χ^2 statistic from a contingency table, enter the χ^2 table (see Appendix 1) at the row corresponding to the df for the contingency table. Then move along the row until you reach the value of χ^2 corresponding to the level of significance you have determined. If the χ^2 derived from the contingency table is greater than this, then the null hypothesis of no association is rejected. For our insomnia study, df = 2 and χ^2_{crit} = 5.9915 (α = 0.05). Since our obtained χ^2 (10.68) is greater than the critical value, we reject the null hypothesis and conclude that insomnia and tea drinking are associated.

Measures of association in tables based on the χ^2 statistic

In earlier tutorials (especially Tutorial 13) we introduced the notion of effect size, and argued that it is important to measure effect size(s) when conducting a statistical hypothesis test, and not simply rely on the significance test.

The χ^2 value is not a good measure of effect size.

Activity 19.4

Find the critical χ^2 values for the following tables at α = 0.05 and α = 0.01:
a) 8 × 4
b) 2 × 2
c) 3 × 2
d) 5 × 5
e) 5 × 1

Some measures of association for contingency tables:
1. ϕ^2 *(contingency coefficient)*
2. ϕ_c *(Cramer's V)*
3. *Odds ratio*

In the case of contingency tables, effect sizes are really measures of how *strong* the association is between the two sets of categories that define the table (hence they are usually called *measures of association for contingency tables*). In the study of tea-drinking we introduced earlier, the effect size is how strongly tea-drinking is associated with insomnia. The χ^2 value derived from a contingency table is not a good measure of effect size, even if it is the appropriate measure to be used for testing significance. One reason for not using χ^2 as a measure of effect size is that it rises in proportion to the size of the sample, confounding sample size and effect size. For this reason, the simplest measure of effect size, the *mean square contingency coefficient* (usually denoted by ϕ^2) simply divides χ^2 by the size of the sample:

$$\phi^2 = \frac{\chi^2}{n}$$

Equation 19.4

In the case of our tea-drinking study, $\phi^2 = \chi^2/n = 10.68/200 = 0.0534$, which indicates a very small effect – perhaps too small to stop people drinking tea! ϕ^2 is, however, not considered a good measure of association, largely because it does not generate scores that fall between 0 and 1 in the same way as a correlation does. (Nevertheless ϕ^2 is used, with some modifications, in meta-analytic studies.) A measure of association in contingency tables with somewhat better properties is *Cramer's V*, usually denoted by ϕ_c:

Equation 19.5

$$\phi_c = \sqrt{\frac{\chi^2}{n(k-1)}}$$

where: n is the sample size

k is defined as the smaller of r (the number of rows) or c (the number of columns)

Unlike ϕ^2, the maximum value of Cramer's V is always 1 and the minimum value 0. In our tea and insomnia example,

$$\phi_c = \sqrt{\frac{\chi^2}{n(k-1)}} = \sqrt{\frac{10.68}{200 \times 1}} = \sqrt{0.0534} = 0.2311.$$

Activity 18.5

Calculate Cramer's V and the mean square contingency coefficient for the book data in Table 19.1. Change the cell frequencies to produce increasing sizes of the coefficients. Do the coefficients attain a maximum size? (We suggest you use a spreadsheet program to assist you.)

Still, even Cramer's V can be difficult to interpret. There are no published rules of thumb for how large Cramer's V has to be to have a large, medium or small effect, and it cannot be interpreted probabilistically. It is not directly comparable to any other measure of correlation, such as Pearson's r. Further, although Cramer's V equals 0 when there is no relation between the variables, there may not be perfect association between the variables when Cramer's V equals 1. For these reasons, even though most computer programs calculate Cramer's V, and even though Cramer's V is very widely used, you may wish to use other measures of association that can be interpreted probabilistically in terms of the data in the table.

The odds ratio is very useful for interpreting 2 × 2 tables, especially in medical or epidemiological studies.

Another widely used measure of association is the *odds ratio*. Odds ratios are very often used in medical studies to show the relative risks of various treatments for illnesses. They have a very definite advantage in being unaffected by sample size or by unequal row or column totals.

To illustrate odds ratios using our tea-drinking and insomnia data, we will need to collapse over one of the categories to generate a 2 × 2 table. Collapsing over categories is in general not a good idea because it can (sometimes) alter the meaning of the data, either obscuring or exaggerating the association between the categories. Nevertheless, for the purposes of illustration, we collapse the categories of moderate and heavy tea-drinkers into one category, 'tea-drinkers'. In medical studies it is usual to arrange the disease in the columns, and the treatment, or factor affecting the disease, in the rows. After such rearrangement, our data will appear as in Table 19.7.

Table 19.7 Re-arrangement of data from Table 19.4

	Short sleep	Long sleep
Tea	60	79
No tea	40	21

The risk (or *odds*) of 'short sleep' if you drink tea can be expressed as the ratio of those who sleep little and drink tea to those who sleep long and drink tea, i.e. $60/79 = 0.76$. It seems that tea-drinking helps one sleep longer, for the ratio is less than 1. Similarly, the odds of 'short sleep' if you do not drink tea can be expressed as the ratio of those who sleep little and do not drink tea to those who sleep long and do not drink tea, i.e. $40/21 = 1.9$. It seems that not drinking tea is a risk factor in insomnia because the ratio is greater than unity. This finding clashes with common sense though, and we would need further studies to understand it.

Odds are calculated by dividing cell frequencies within a single row or column.

The *odds ratio* can now be calculated. This is the ratio of the odds of 'Short sleep' if you do not drink tea (1.9) to the odds of short sleep if you do drink tea (0.76), i.e. $^{1.9}/_{0.76} = 2.5$. It seems that subjects in the study who do not drink tea are 2.5 times as likely to suffer insomnia than those who do drink tea. Alternatively, those who do drink tea are only 0.4 times (i.e. $^{0.76}/_{1.9}$) as likely to suffer insomnia as those who do not.

Howell (1997, p. 159) gives a compelling example of the use of odds ratios. In a landmark study investigating the benefits of small daily doses of aspirin on reducing heart attacks in men, 22 000 physicians were administered either aspirin or a placebo, and the incidence of heart attacks in this groups was recorded. The data from the study are given in Table 19.8.

*The **odds ratio** is calculated by dividing the odds for one column by the odds for another column, or the odds for one row by the odds for another row.*

Table 19.8 Data for study investigating the efficacy of aspirin

	Heart attack	No heart attack	TOTAL
Aspirin	104	10 933	11 037
Placebo	189	10 845	11 034
TOTAL	293	21 778	22 071

The odds of having a heart attack given that you were in the aspirin group = 104/10 933 = 0.0095. The odds of having a heart attack if you were in the placebo group = 189/10 845 = 0.0174. Neither of these odds look like very great risks. But when you calculate the odds ratio, 0.0174/0.0095 = 1.83, it appears that a person in the control (placebo) group is 1.83 times more likely to have a heart attack than is a person in the aspirin group. This finding was considered so convincing that the researchers – who had intended to collect a great deal more data than this – immediately stopped the study on the basis that it would be unethical to treat one group as a placebo group, given the demonstrated efficacy of aspirin in reducing the incidence of heart attacks.

Activity 19.6

Two groups of 50 eye-witnesses to a crime are shown two police line-ups either containing the perpetrator of the crime, or an innocent suspect, standing with a number of foils.

	Identifies target	Identifies foils or 'no decision'
Perpetrator absent	25	75
Perpetrator present	50	50

The number of eye-witness who identify the 'target' (perpetrator or innocent suspect) is recorded and tabulated above, or who identify a foil. Use the odds ratio to determine the risk of identifying an innocent suspect in a police line-up relative to making a correct identification of a guilty suspect.

Isolating sources of association in $r \times c$ tables

*A significant χ^2 does not tell us **where** significant differences are located, and we need to investigate our data further to find these (in an analogous manner to multiple comparisons in ANOVA).*

A significant χ^2 for an $r \times c$ contingency table indicates that the variables forming the table are **not** independent. But this result does not tell us whether the lack of independence occurs throughout the table or only in a specific section. We may wish to know which parts of a table are responsible for a deviation from independence for the same reason that ANOVA researchers may wish to discover where, amongst three or more groups, the significant difference lies.

A number of different ways for isolating the parts of the contingency table responsible for the departure from independence have been proposed, including a method for splitting *(partitioning)* a large table into smaller 2 × 2 tables (see Siegel & Castellan, 1988). The method we will present here is called *the analysis of residuals* and was devised by Haberman (1973).

A *residual* in a contingency table is the deviation of the observed from the expected frequency. Because the size of a deviation is related to the size of the sample (see the discussion of measures of association), we *standardise* the residuals by dividing by the root of the expected frequency. In symbols, the standardised residual for each cell is:

$$e = \frac{O - E}{\sqrt{E}}$$

Equation 19.6

where: *e* is the standardised residual of the cell
       O is the observed count in the cell
       E is the expected count in the cell

Haberman (1973) shows that these *standardised residuals* can be further adjusted to give them a very desirable property, assuming that the variables forming the contingency table are independent. These *adjusted residuals*, called *d*, are approximately normally distributed with a mean of zero and a standard deviation of one. Recall from earlier work on the normal distribution and *z*-scores that the normal curve can be standardised with a mean of zero and a standard deviation of one. The areas under the standardised curve have been calculated. This means that the size of an adjusted residual can be directly interpreted in a probabilistic way using a table of areas under the standardised normal curve. From earlier work using the standardized normal curve, you will know that if the adjusted residual is 1.96 or greater (or, alternatively, less than –1.96), its associated probability is less than 0.05. Hence we can conclude that any adjusted residual of this magnitude is significant (i.e. likely to occur by chance less than 1 in 20 times). Similarly, if the adjusted residual is 2.58 or greater (or, alternatively, –2.58 or less), it would occur by chance less than 1 in 100 times, so we can conclude that if the adjusted residual exceeds this value, it is significant at the 1% level.

The adjusted residuals *d*, are defined as follows:

$$d = \frac{e}{\sqrt{\left(1 - \frac{n_{row}}{n_{total}}\right)\left(1 - \frac{n_{col}}{n_{total}}\right)}}$$

Equation 19.7

Clearly, adjusted residuals can be time-consuming to calculate! Fortunately, SPSS® will calculate these for you if you select the appropriate options in the dialog boxes, or you can do them quite easily on a spreadsheet.

We apply the analysis of residuals to our tea-drinking and insomnia example. The calculations are shown in Table 19.9 on the next page.

Side notes:

*A **residual** in a contingency table is the deviation of the observed from the expected frequency.*

*A **standardised** residual (e) is a residual corrected for (expected) cell size.*

*An **adjusted residual** (d) is a residual adjusted to have a (approximate) standard normal distribution.*

Interpret adjusted residuals in the same way as z-scores.

From the analysis of residuals, it seems that moderate tea-drinkers are significantly more likely to be long sleepers than expected (adjusted residual = 2.87 > z_{crit} = 1.96), whilst tea abstainers have significantly fewer long sleepers than expected (adjusted residual = -2.92 < z_{crit} = -1.96). The adjusted residuals do not reach significance for heavy tea-drinkers.

Table 19.9 Calculation of standardised and adjusted residuals for the data of Table 19.4

	Heavy tea-drinkers	Moderate tea-drinkers	Tea abstainers	TOTAL
Short sleepers	28	32	40	100
Long sleepers	27	52	21	100
TOTAL	55	84	61	200

	Standardised residuals (e)		
Short sleepers	0.0953	-1.543	1.72
Long sleepers	-0.0953	1.543	-1.72

	Adjusted residuals (d)		
Short sleepers	0.158	-2.865	2.918
Long sleepers	-0.158	2.865	-2.918

Assumptions of the χ^2 test

Assumptions of χ^2
1. (Rule of thumb)
Expected frequencies
should be greater
than 5 in at least
80% of the cells in
the table.
2. Observations
summarised by the
frequency counts
must be independent.

There are two assumptions that must be satisfied if a χ^2 test is to be used appropriately.

The first is that the number of subjects *expected* in each cell must reach a certain minimum. (*Note:* the assumption concerns the smallest *expected* frequencies and not the smallest *observed* frequencies.) Consequently, if there are many categories involved in the classification, larger samples will be necessary. A rule of thumb that is frequently used is that the expected frequency should be no less than 5 in at least 80% of the cells, but for a more detailed exposition see Wickens (1989) or Everitt (1992). If a problem in meeting these conditions arises, then it is usual to try overcoming it by combining categories, as we did in Table 19.7.

A second assumption of the test is that all the items or people involved in the test are independent of each other. In practice in the social sciences, the assumption of independence is usually reduced to two points:

1. Each observation comes from a different subject.
2. No subject should be omitted from the table.

Neither of these points should be applied mindlessly – for example, sometimes, even though each observation comes from a different subject, the subjects are still linked (perhaps they filled in their questionnaire together, or perhaps they are identical twins!). The second point is intended to prevent systematic bias of the sample. One should include not only subjects who gave a positive response, but also subjects who failed to respond.

Box 19.1

The χ^2 test and SPSS®

SPSS® offers two ways of entering frequency data for analysis by means of χ^2. Paradoxically, this is easier if you have the raw data, i.e. the individual data points recording the categorical variables, rather than the frequency counts. To analyse the data, you select the 'Analyze' menu, the 'Descriptive Statistics' submenu, and then the 'Crosstabs' command (see Figure 19.1). This will produce an SPSS® variable selection dialog box, which you should be familiar with if you have used SPSS® at all. To produce residuals, significance tests and effect sizes, choose 'Options', and select accordingly (Figure 19.1). The output produced by SPSS® for the 'tea-drinker' data is shown in Figure 19.2 on the next page.

However, if you have a ready-made table (i.e. you already know the frequencies for the cells of the contingency table), you will have to use the 'Data Weighting' command. In our tea-drinking example, the table can be entered as shown in Table 19.11 on the next page.

Here you enter the code for the rows in the first column, then the code for the columns in the second column, and then the frequencies in the third column. You will now have to use the 'Data' menu and the 'Weight Cases' command. You will weight the cases by var00003 (the cell frequencies).

Notice how the combination of the var00001 and var00002 uniquely identifies each cell of the table. The first column contains the code for long and short sleepers, and the second column contains the code for the quantity of tea consumed. The third column contains the frequencies to be found in each cell of the table. Notice that SPSS® requires that you enter 'codes' for each of the categorical variables. You cannot enter the names of the categories directly, though you can have them inserted in the print-out by using the 'Labels' command. Be sure to make a note of what your codes mean so that you can interpret your data correctly when you review your work at a later date.

SPSS® can be used to conduct tabular and χ^2 analyses on either:
1. the raw scores, or
2. the cell frequencies.

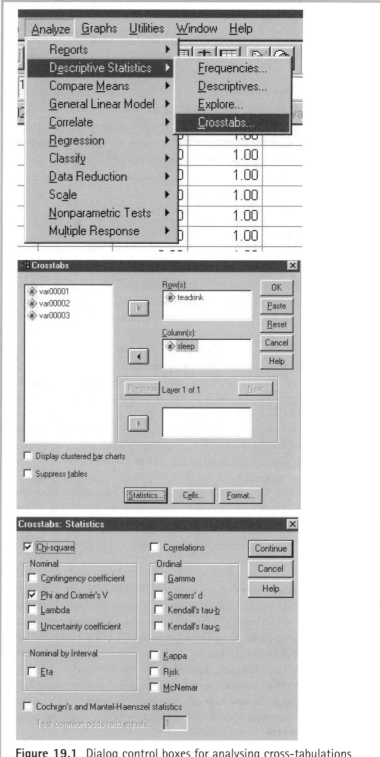

Figure 19.1 Dialog control boxes for analysing cross-tabulations (contingency tables) in SPSS®

Table 19.10 Data set-up for conducting a χ^2 analysis of a contingency table in SPSS®

	Var00001	Var00002	Var00003	Var00004
1	1	1	28	
2	1	2	32	
3	1	3	40	
4	2	1	27	
5	2	2	52	
6	2	3	21	

CHI-SQUARE TESTS

	Value	df	Asymp. Sig (2-sided)
Pearson Chi-Square	10.698[a]	2	.005
Likelihood Ratio	10.844	2	.004
Linear-by-Linear Association	2.783	1	.095
N of Valid Cases	200		

SYMMETRIC MEASURES

		Value	Approx. Sig.
Nominal by Nominal	Phi	.231	.005
	Cramer's V	.231	.005
N of Valid Cases		200	

TEADRINK * SLEEP Crosstabulation

			SLEEP		Total
			1.00	2.00	
TEADRINK	1.00	Count	28	27	55
		Residual	.5	−.5	
		Std. Residual	.1	−.1	
		Adjusted Residual	.2	−.2	
	2.00	Count	32	52	55
		Residual	−10.0	10.0	
		Std. Residual	−1.5	1.5	
		Adjusted Residual	−2.9	2.9	
	3.00	Count	40	21	61
		Residual	9.5	−9.5	
		Std. Residual	1.7	−1.7	
		Adjusted Residual	2.9	−2.9	
Total		Count	100	100	200

Figure 19.2 Output of crosstabs command in SPSS® for 'tea-drinker' data

Box 19.2

Using a spreadsheet for tabular analysis

The calculations in a tabular analysis are usually quite easy, but laborious. A spreadsheet program can help with the laborious part of the calculations, and we show how this can be done with Microsoft Excel, for the data in Figure 19.1.

The best way to do it in Excel is to create a layout almost identical to what you would probably do on a piece of paper. You then insert built-in arithmetic formulas in the appropriate places, as shown in Figure 19.3, where formulas have been entered for the marginal sums, the expected frequencies, the χ^2 statistic, two measures of effect size, and the decomposition of the table into residuals. What is especially helpful is the ability to use built-in distribution formulas for χ^2, and for the adjusted residuals (which are approximate standard normal deviates), since this gives accurate probability calculations.

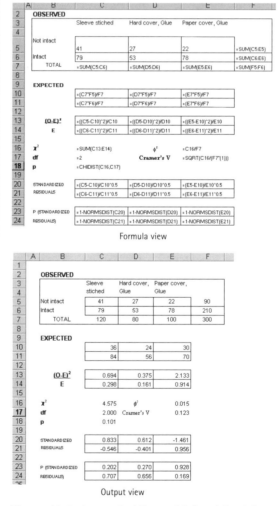

Figure 19.3 Layout in Microsoft® Excel for doing tabular analysis

Worked example

What are the psychological consequences of traumatic events? One answer is that it depends on the nature of the trauma. Gelman *et al.* (2001) investigated a large sample of students at the student health service of a South African university, and collected data on any traumatic events they may or may not have experienced. She also diagnostically assessed each student for the presence or absence of a condition known as 'post-traumatic stress disorder' (PTSD), using criteria set down in the *Diagnostic and Statistical Manual of the American Psychiatric Association*. Cross-tabulations for the relationship between two different types of trauma and the presence/absence of PTSD are shown in Table 19.11.

Table 19.11 The relationship between trauma and PTSD

		Sexual assault					Car accident	
		Y	N				Y	N
PTSD	Y	24	90		PTSD	Y	17	95
	N	31	370			N	40	361

Calculations for these tables using a spreadsheet layout are shown in Figure 19.4. It is clear from these calculations (verify this for yourself) that there is a significant relationship between sexual assault and the presence of PTSD, but this is not true for the relationship between having a car accident and the presence of PTSD.

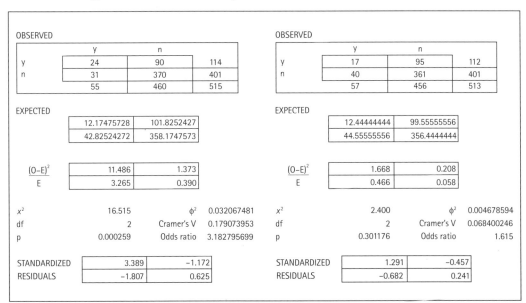

Figure 19.4 Excel analysis of the data in Table 19.11

In terms of the odds ratio, if a student had been sexually assaulted, it was 3.18 times more likely that he or she would develop PTSD than if he or she had not been sexually assaulted. On the other hand, if a student had had a car accident, it was only 1.6 times more likely that he or she would develop PTSD than if he or she had not had a car accident. Inspection of the standardized residuals in the case of the significant cross-tabulation shows that the cell with the greatest departure from chance expectation is that recording the number of respondents who had been sexually assaulted, and who had developed PTSD.

Summary

1. In tabular analysis, we use classifications that are exhaustive and mutually exclusive. Classifications are a form of measurement (nominal measurement), but they constitute qualitative rather than quantitative data.

2. When data are classified with respect to two or more qualitative variables, the data form what is known as a contingency table. The number in each of the cells of the table is a frequency, or a count. We refer to the table as an $r \times c$ table, where r = the number of rows, and c = the number of columns (e.g. a 3×2 table).

3. A statistical significance test that is appropriate for the analysis of counts is the χ^2 test, typically used to test the *association* between two or more categorical variables or dimensions against a null hypothesis of *no association*.

4. The key concept in the χ^2 test is that of expected frequency. This value is what we would expect in each cell if only chance variation were operating across the categories of interest, and the category frequencies were equal in the population. To calculate χ^2, the differences between the observed frequencies and the expected frequencies are squared, divided by the expected value, and summed.

5. The size of a calculated χ^2 cannot serve as a measure of effect size since it is directly proportional to sample size. Three common measures of effect size in χ^2 analysis are the mean square contingency coefficient (ϕ^2), Cramer's V (ϕ), and the odds ratio (2×2 tables only).

6. A significant χ^2 for an $r \times c$ contingency table indicates that the variables forming the table are **not** independent, but does not tell us whether the lack of independence occurs throughout the table or only in a specific section. One useful way of isolating the parts of the contingency table responsible for the departure from independence is the analysis of residuals, in which the

differences between expected and observed frequencies are transformed to standard normal deviates, and significant values are identified.

7. Some important assumptions of χ^2 analysis are: expected frequencies should be greater than 5 in at least 80% of the cells in the table and observations summarised by the frequency counts must be independent.

Exercises

1. In the second grade, children were classified as showing or not showing attention deficit disorder (ADD) behaviour. When these same children reached the ninth grade, it was noted which of them were enrolled in a remedial English programme. The data are shown below. Is attention deficit disorder behaviour during elementary school associated with enrolment in a remedial English class in high school? If you find a significant association, calculate Cramer's V and the odds ratio to determine the strength of the association.

	Remedial English	Non–remedial English	TOTAL
Normal	24	189	213
ADD	17	76	93
TOTAL	41	265	306

2. Darley and Latané (1968) asked subjects to participate in a discussion carried on over an intercom. Aside from the experimenter to whom they were speaking, subjects thought that there were 0, 1, or 4 other people (bystanders) also listening over intercoms. Halfway through the discussion, the experimenter feigned serious illness and asked for help. Darley and Latané noted how often the subject sought help for the experimenter as a function of the number of supposed bystanders. The data are presented below. What could Darley and Latané conclude from the results? What is the strength of any significant finding? Can you isolate the source of any significant association in this table?

		Sought assistance		
		Yes	No	TOTAL
Number of	0	13	3	16
bystanders	1	17	10	27
	4	4	10	14
TOTAL		34	23	57

3. Of 107 married couples, 11 of the women compared to 33 of the men said that they fell in love with their partners at first sight.
   a) What test would you use to determine whether this difference was significant?
   b) What are the degrees of freedom?
   c) Would you use a one- or two-tailed probability level to evaluate the significance of this value?
   d) What is the probability value of the test?
   e) Do significantly more men than women fall in love with their future spouses at first sight?

4. We asked a group of 50 subjects whether they liked watching rugby. We then made them watch a game, and then asked them again whether they liked watching rugby. We recorded the data as shown alongside: Would χ^2 calculated on such a table be appropriate? Why or why not?

	Pro	Against	TOTAL
Before	29	21	50
After	41	9	50
TOTAL	70	30	100

5. Briefly outline the assumptions of the chi-square test.

6. Make up an example of a contingency table where the classification is not exhaustive. Make up another example where the classification is not mutually exclusive.

TUTORIAL 20

Distribution-free tests

Lance Lachenicht

> After studying this tutorial, you should be able to:
> - Understand the advantages and disadvantages of distribution-free statistical tests.
> - Calculate the sign test and the Wilcoxon matched pairs tests for related samples.
> - Calculate the Mann-Whitney U-test for unrelated samples.
> - Calculate the Kruskal-Wallis and Friedman tests for three or more samples.

*Statistical tests that require assumptions about parameters or their estimation are known as **parametric tests**.*

Most of the inferential statistical tests you have learned so far in this course require you to estimate one or more population *parameters.* Further, you are often required to make assumptions concerning the *shape of the distribution* of the population. For example, the *t*-test uses the sample variance s^2 as an estimate of the population variance (σ^2) and also requires the assumption that the population from which the sample was drawn is normal (or at least symmetrical). Tests such as the *t*-test that require either assumptions about parameters or their estimation are known as *parametric* tests.

There is, however, a class of tests that do not rely on parameter estimation and/or distributional assumptions. Such tests are known as *non-parametric* or *distribution-free* tests. It is usually the case that if a test is non-parametric it is also distribution-free, so the two names are used interchangeably. In fact, it is the distribution-free characteristic of non-parametric tests that make them most valuable to us. Sometimes the assumption of normality or symmetry

*Statistical tests that do not rely on parameter estimation and/or distributional assumptions are known as **non-parametric or distribution-free tests**.*

is so badly violated that the use of parametric tests seems unacceptable. In such circumstances, we will turn to distribution-free tests.

All statistical tests need to estimate probabilities, and if distribution-free tests do not use the well-understood characteristics of the normal curve, how do they estimate probabilities? Most distribution-free tests use either the characteristics of ranked data or they use randomisation procedures to calculate probabilities. Tests based on ranking usually require you to assign ranks to your original numerical scores. It is unusual for a researcher to collect data in the form of ranks in the first place.

The advantages and disadvantages of distribution–free tests

There is a long-standing argument between advocates of parametric tests and distribution-free tests, and we can certainly not settle this argument here. Siegel and Castellan (1988) is a good source for arguments in favour of using distribution-free tests. Generally, however, parametric tests and procedures have been developed more than distribution-free tests. There is a much smaller range of procedures and much less flexibility when using distribution-free procedures.

Further, parametric tests have been shown to be relatively robust to violations of their assumptions (i.e. they continue to perform reliably even when their assumptions do not hold). However, there are undoubtedly occasions when they should not be used, and we have no alternative but to use distribution-free tests. Conditions that cause parametric tests to fail include not only violations of assumptions such as the symmetry of the population distribution, but also the presence of *outliers* (i.e. extreme and unusual values) in the dataset. On the whole, distribution-free tests are much more robust than parametric tests are to both kinds of violations. This makes distribution-free tests and procedures ideal for the exploratory analysis of data.

On the whole, distribution-free tests are much more robust than are parametric tests.

Another argument often advanced in favour of parametric tests is that they tend to be more powerful than distribution-free tests (i.e. they will require smaller samples to obtain significant results when there is a real difference or relationship). This, however, turns out to be true mainly if the distributional assumptions of the parametric procedures are correct. Howell (1997, p. 646) notes that it is possible to construct perfectly reasonable datasets where 'distribution-free tests may have greater power than the corresponding parametric tests'. When the distributional assumptions of parametric tests fail altogether, distribution-free tests are much more powerful than parametric tests.

> How, practically, would you go about testing to see whether a non-parametric test might be better to apply to a particular dataset than a parametric test?
>
> *(Hint: think of the kinds of graphical displays you could construct, and what they would tell you about the data, as well as suitable descriptive statistics.)*

Activity 20.1

Reasons for learning about distribution-free tests include their widespread use in social science and medical literature (you may often come across them in reading the literature), as well as their relative simplicity of calculation (an advantage that has lost some force since statistical computer packages became available). With respect to simplicity of calculation on a computer, Howell (1997, p. 646) points out that 'for an experimenter who has just invested six months in collecting her data, a difference of five minutes in computation time hardly justifies using a less desirable test'. With respect to hand calculation, distribution-free tests are simple to calculate only with small datasets. Ranking a very large amount of data by hand is extremely cumbersome and laborious.

A difficulty of rank-based distribution-free tests arises from the fact that data are gathered using a restricted range of scores. This often results in the same score value appearing many times in a particular dataset. When the same value appears more than once in a dataset, a *tied* rank has to be assigned to that value. Many tied values in a dataset will make rank-based tests cumbersome to calculate and will also cause them to lose accuracy.

To summarise, it seems that distribution-free tests are most useful with small datasets and in circumstances where the assumptions of the parametric test are severely violated or where there are outliers and extreme scores in the dataset making robust procedures desirable.

Distribution-free tests are most useful with small datasets, and when parametric assumptions are severely violated.

Theory of ranks

The operation of ranking involves ordering the dataset from smallest to largest, and assigning a rank of 1 to the smallest, 2 to the second smallest, 3 to the third smallest, etc. until all the scores have been ranked. Ranks are commonly used in distribution-free tests because the theory of ranked data has been much studied in the same way as the theory of normally distributed scores has been much studied. The properties of ranked distributions are the same no matter what the original data looked like. Ranking ten IQ scores will produce the same distribution properties as ranking ten race times, or ten scores of self-esteem – i.e. they will all receive the ranks 1, 2, 3, 4, 5, 6, 7, 8, 9, and 10. Therefore it is comparatively easy for the statistician to estimate what the distribution of ranks would be if the null hypothesis were true – the exact numerical value of the scores will have no impact on the ranks, though the statistician will have to repeat her/his probability calculations for different sample sizes.

A cornucopia of tests

A glance through Siegel & Castellan (1988) will show that there are many distribution-free tests. However, many of them are interchangeable (i.e. they effectively test the same null hypothesis). Further, many are rather obscure and specialised. We will concentrate only on the better known and more widely used procedures in this tutorial. You have already been introduced to some distribution-free procedures in earlier tutorials, including Spearman's correlation coefficient for ranked data, and χ^2 for frequency data. In this tutorial we will examine some distribution-free tests that are really alternatives for parametric procedures covered in earlier tutorials. For example, we will consider distribution-free replacements for the *t*-test.

Related samples: The sign test

Related samples occur when the same group of people is measured more than once, such as in 'before and after' research designs. For example, to see whether a good movie lifts mood, we measure the mood of a group of people before seeing a movie and then again after they have seen the movie. Classically, the two measurements (before and after) are then subtracted from one another, and the differences between them are tested against the null hypothesis that the mean difference is zero.

*The **sign test** tests whether two related samples have the same median.*

Just as the related samples *t*-test considers the difference between two related samples, so does the *sign test*. However, the sign test does **not** consider the size of the differences – it only considers the **sign** of the differences. In other words, this test discards a great deal of information about the inherent size of the differences between the two samples. The sign test is really testing whether the two samples have a median difference of zero.

Begin your analysis *(Step 1)* by deleting any case with identical scores for both variables. Identical scores in the two variables are ignored in the sign test. Now *(Step 2)* subtract the second group of scores from the first group. It is important to remember to include the **sign** of the difference (+ or –). Table 20.1 illustrates the process. In the table we compare a group of chronic-pain patients on the number of pain-free hours after treatment with hypnosis as opposed to treatment with acupuncture (data adapted from Sprent, 1981, p. 119).

Activity 20.2

Which of the following sets of data pairs do you think would be most affected by the 'loss of information' inherent in the way the sign test is constructed?

a)

| 4 | 4 | 7 | 6 | 8 | 5 | 4 |
| 5 | 3 | 9 | 2 | 4 | 5 | 5 |

b)

| 9 | 6 | 4 | 8 | 3 | 6 | 8 |
| 1 | 7 | 5 | 1 | 5 | 1 | 9 |

c)

| 2 | 8 | 6 | 4 | 7 | 8 | 1 |
| 9 | 1 | 6 | 6 | 5 | 2 | 6 |

Table 20.1 Pain-free hours for chronic-pain patients under two treatments

Patient:	A	B	C	D	E	F	G	H	I	J
Hypnosis:	11.7	12.1	13.3	15.1	15.9	15.3	11.9	16.2	15.1	13.6
Acupuncture:	10.9	11.9	13.4	15.4	14.8	14.8	12.3	15.0	14.2	13.1
Difference:	0.8	0.2	−0.1	−0.3	1.1	0.5	−0.4	1.2	0.9	0.5
Sign of diff.:	+	+	−	−	+	+	−	+	+	+

Having calculated the sign of the differences, your next step (*Step 3*) is to count the *number* of difference scores that are positively signed and the number of scores that are negatively signed. (Recall that zero differences are ignored in the sign test.) For the above data there are 7 positively signed differences and 3 negatively signed differences.

Now (*Step 4*) take as your score whichever is the smaller number – either the number of positive signs or the number of negative signs. In our case, 3 is the smaller number (the number of negative signs). You can look up the significance of this number in Table 8 in Appendix 1 (*Step 5*). From the table, with ten pairs of scores, we see that we need values of 0 or 1 for the smaller of the sign sums for significance at the 0.05 level – i.e. we cannot reject the null hypothesis that there is no difference between the two treatments for chronic pain.

The sign test is not a powerful test, but it can be applied in practically any circumstance in which the expected population distribution under the null hypothesis is 50% of one outcome and 50% of another outcome. This means that the sign test can always be used to test for a departure from an expected 50:50 outcome.

Related samples: The Wilcoxon matched pairs test

The *Wilcoxon matched pairs test* (also known as the Wilcoxon signed ranks test) is similar to the sign test except that when we have obtained the difference scores between the two samples we must rank-order the differences, ignoring the sign of the difference.

*The **Wilcoxon matched pairs test** tests whether two related samples have the same median.*

To begin, difference scores are calculated *(Step 1)* and ranked *(Step 2)*, ignoring the sign of the difference. When there are tied values, the mean of the ranks that would have been assigned if it were possible to separate the scores is given. For example, in the pain data, which is repeated in Table 20.2, two differences of 0.5 are to be found. These two differences should be assigned the ranks of 5 and 6, but because they are tied, they are both assigned the mean rank of 5.5.

Table 20.2 Pain-free hours for chronic-pain patients under two treatments

Patient:	A	B	C	D	E	F	G	H	I	J
Hypnosis:	11.7	12.1	13.3	15.1	15.9	15.3	11.9	16.2	15.1	13.6
Acupuncture:	10.9	11.9	13.4	15.4	14.8	14.8	12.3	15.0	14.2	13.1
Difference:	0.8	0.2	−0.1	−0.3	1.1	0.5	−0.4	1.2	0.9	0.5
Rank:	7 +	2 +	1 −	3 −	9 +	5.5 +	4 −	10 +	8 +	5.5 +

Having ranked the differences, we now *(Step 3)* re-attach the sign of the differences (the signs follow the differences in Table 20.2). Next *(Step 4)*, the sum of the positive ranks is calculated and the sum of the negative ranks is also calculated. For the example given in Table 20.2, the calculations are:

S^+ = sum of positive ranks: $7 + 2 + 5.5 + 9 + 10 + 8 + 5.5 = 47$
S^- = sum of negative ranks: $1 + 3 + 4 = 8$

Activity 20.3

Calculate the sums of positive ranks and negative ranks for each of the datasets in Activity 20.2, as you would do for a Wilcoxon matched pairs test. Do you think the Wilcoxon test suffers from the 'loss of information' problem to the same extent as the sign test? Support your answer by completing the sign and Wilcoxon tests for each of the data pairs.

We now *(Step 5)* have to decide which is the smaller of the two sums of ranks. In this case it is the sum of the negative ranks (S^-), namely 8. The smaller of the two values is normally designated T. It is now possible *(Step 6)* to find the significance of the value of T (the smaller of the two sums of ranks) from Appendix 1. The table is designed in terms of the number of pairs of scores used, in this case 10. We look up 10 in the table, and see that a T of 8 or less is significant at the 0.05 level. Our T-value is 8, so we have a significant difference between the two treatments at the 0.05 level. This is a different result from the one we obtained using the sign test, a demonstration of the greater power of the Wilcoxon matched pairs test, which uses more of the information in the scores than does the sign test.

The Wilcoxon matched pairs test is more powerful than the sign test.

Unrelated samples: The Mann–Whitney U-test

Perhaps the most common distribution-free test for differences between unrelated samples is the *Mann-Whitney U-test*. This test is also known as the Wilcoxon rank sum test. This test is used for research designs similar to those for which the independent samples *t*-test is used. This means that it can be used whenever you have two groups of scores that are independent of each other (e.g. different samples of people).

*The **Mann-Whitney U-test** tests whether two independent samples have the same median.*

Consider an example. Suppose a traditional healer claims that a particular herb will reduce the absorption of alcohol into the bloodstream. To test this claim, 11 men are asked to drink three glasses of beer each. Five of the 11 men are randomly selected and dosed with the herb. After 30 minutes, a blood sample is taken from each of the men. The blood alcohol level (measured in mg/100 ml) of the 11 men is given in Table 20.3. Is there sufficient evidence to conclude that the herb influences the level of alcohol in the bloodstream?

Table 20.3 Blood alcohol after three glasses of beer (mg/100 ml)

Given herb	79	85	105	93	100	
Not given herb	99	102	107	117	110	108

Our first step *(Step 1)* is to rank all the scores from *both* groups of participants from the smallest to the largest (see Table 20.4). Tied scores are given average ranks. The scores for the larger group should be entered into the first column. If both groups are the same size, then it does not matter which group is entered into the first column. In this case the larger group has 6 scores and the smaller group has 5 scores.

Table 20.4 Calculating the Mann-Whitney U-test

Not given herb (x_1) (use this column for larger group)	Rankings	Given herb (x_2)	Rankings
99	4	79	1
102	6	85	2
107	8	105	7
117	11	93	3
110	10	100	5
108	9		
	$R_1 = \Sigma r = 48$		

The next step (*Step 2*) is to sum the ranks for the larger group of scores (see Table 20.4). In this case, the sum of the ranks of the larger group of scores, R_1, is 48. Next (*Step 3*) R_1 and its sample size n_1 ($n_1 = 6$) together with the sample size of group 2 ($n_2 = 5$) are entered into the formula (see Equation 20.1), which returns the U-statistic.

Equation 20.1

$$U = (n_1 \times n_2) + \frac{n_1 \times (n_1 + 1)}{2} - R_1$$

Applying this formula to our data:

$$U = (n_1 \times n_2) + \frac{n_1 \times (n_1 + 1)}{2} - R_1 = (6 \times 5) + \frac{6 \times (6 + 1)}{2} - 48$$

$$= 30 + \frac{42}{2} - 48 = 3$$

It is possible to calculate two values of U depending on which sample size you used in the above formulas. Check that you have obtained the lesser of the two possible U values by applying this transformation:

$$U' = n_1 n_2 - U$$

If U' is less than U, then use U' when using the tables to determine significance.

Having obtained U, we must (*Step 4*) determine its significance by consulting Appendix 1. Using the table for the unequal samples Mann-Witney U-test requires you to find the n_a value in the column headings and the n_b value in the row headings. The table gives *maximum* ranges of values for U that are significant. The calculated value of U must be *less than* or *equal to* these tabled values, or *greater than or equal to* the table values to be significant. The table reveals that for sample sizes of 6 and 5, a calculated U of 3 equals the tabled value of 3 for the 5% (right diagonal of the table) two-tailed (lower table) test and so is significant at the 5% level. In other words, we can reject the null hypotheses of no difference between the two groups of beer drinkers in blood alcohol levels and conclude that the herb did prevent the absorption of alcohol.

Activity 20.4

If you have already studied the independent samples *t*-test (see Tutorial 9), and know how to use it, run the test on the data of Table 20.4. Does the result differ from that obtained when running the Mann-Whitney test? If so, why the difference?

Three or more groups of scores: Kruskal–Wallis test for unrelated samples

There are distribution-free tests that can test the difference between three or more groups in much the same way as ANOVA does in parametric statistical procedures. The Kruskal-Wallis test is an extension of the Mann-Whitney U-test for three or more independent samples, and the Friedman test is an extension of the Wilcoxon test for three or more related samples. In both cases, these tests depend upon the same ranking procedures as their simpler two-sample versions. We will briefly work through the calculation procedure, but these tests can be performed by most statistical packages, including SPSS®.

*The **Kruskal-Wallis** test is an omnibus test, analogous to ANOVA, for the equality of independent population medians.*

The Kruskal-Wallis test is an omnibus test for the equality of independent population medians. Consider the following problem. We randomly select pages from a work by each of three writers, from editions having the same typeface and page size. The number of sentences per page is counted, and set out in Table 20.5. We use the Kruskal-Wallis to test whether the median number of sentences per page is the same for all three writers. We would like to know whether the number of sentences per page is the same for the three writers of detective fiction.

Table 20.5 Sentences per page for three detective writers

Homme Aside:	13	27	26	22	26		
Roman Noir:	43	35	47	32	31	37	
Penny Dreadful:	33	27	33	26	44	33	54

To perform the Kruskal-Wallis, we rank all the scores without regard to group membership and then calculate the sum of the ranks for each group. R will denote the sums. If the null hypothesis is true then we would expect the Rs to be roughly the same except for any differences due to sample size. A measure of the extent to which the Rs do differ is given by Equation 20.2.

$$H = \frac{12}{n(n + 1)} \sum \frac{R^2}{n_i} - 3 (N + 1)$$

Equation 20.2

where: k = the number of groups
n = the number of observations in the group
R = the sum of the ranks in the group
N = the total sample size

H is evaluated like chi-square at $k - 1$ df (i.e. use the χ^2 tables).

Applying this method to the detective writers data at hand, we get the workings shown in Table 20.6.

Table 20.6 Workings for comparing sentences per page with the Kruskal-Wallis test

Homme Aside		Roman Noir		Penny Dreadful	
Sentences	Rank	Sentences	Rank	Sentences	Rank
13	1	43	15	33	11
27	6.5	35	13	27	6.5
26	4	47	17	33	11
22	2	32	9	26	4
26	4	31	8	44	16
		37	14	33	11
				54	18
Σ	17.5		76		77.5

The Rs are thus 17.5, 76, and 77.5, while the n's are 5, 6, and 7 respectively. $k = 3$, since there are three groups, and N = 18.

$$H = \frac{12}{18(18 + 1)} \times 1881.952 - 3(19)$$

$$= 66.033 - 57$$

$$= 9.033$$

$$df = 3 - 1$$
$$= 2$$

The critical value of chi-square at 2 df for $\alpha = 0.05$ is 5.99 (see the χ^2 tables), which H exceeds. Thus we can reject the null hypothesis and conclude that the three detective writers do not write the same number of sentences per page.

Three or more groups of scores: Friedman's rank test for related samples

Friedman's rank test is an omnibus test, analogous to repeated measures ANOVA, for the equality of related population medians.

The Friedman test for k correlated samples is an analogue of one-way repeated measures analysis of variance. It is used for the analysis of within-subjects designs where more than two conditions are being compared. This test was developed by Milton Friedman, the famous economist and Nobel laureate.

Suppose we want to test the hypothesis that the performance of university students is related to how close they sit to the front of the lecture hall. The experimenter obtains ten student participants. Each student is randomly assigned to sit in the front, the middle, or at the back of the lecture hall for a period of three weeks, after which a test is written. The same student then takes up another one of the three positions in the lecture hall, and another test is written.

Eventually each student has three test results associated with three different positions in the lecture hall. Hypothetical data for this study are presented in Table 20.7. The ranking of the raw scores within each subject's set of three scores is shown in brackets. The ranks are summed, and totals appear below each column.

Table 20.7 Test results associated with different seating positions in a lecture theatre

Student	Seating position		
	Front	Middle	Back
1	60 (1)	70 (3)	63 (2)
2	41 (1)	66 (3)	59 (2)
3	52 (2)	57 (3)	49 (1)
4	58 (3)	50 (1)	56 (2)
5	60 (1)	70 (3)	63 (2)
6	50 (1)	58 (3)	54 (2)
7	72 (1)	73 (2)	75 (3)
8	49 (2)	54 (3)	42 (1)
9	51 (1)	63 (2)	68 (3)
10	39 (1)	48 (2)	54 (3)
$R = \Sigma r$	14	25	21

If the null hypothesis is true, we would expect the rankings to be distributed randomly for each student (i.e. sitting in the front, the middle, or at the back will make no difference to a student's performance). So, if the null hypothesis is true, the sum of the rankings in each seating position (column) would be roughly the same. However, if seating position does make a difference, then there should be large differences in the sum of the rankings for each column.

We rank the three test scores for each student and then sum the rankings for the different seating positions. The variability of the rankings is then assessed by means of Equation 20.3:

$$\chi_F^2 = \frac{12}{Nk(k+1)} \ \Sigma \ R^2 - 3N(k+1)$$

Equation 20.3

where: R = the sum of the ranks for each condition
N = the total number of subjects (students)
k = the number of conditions

The value of χ_F^2 (Friedman's 'chi-square') can be evaluated just like a normal chi-square value at a df of $k - 1$.

The data for our student seating position study can be evaluated as follows:

$$\chi_F^2 = \frac{12}{10 \times 3 \times 4} \times (14^2 + 25^2 + 21^2) - 3(10)(4) = 126.2 - 120 = 6.2$$

$$df = 3 - 1 = 2$$

The critical value of chi-square at 2 df for $\alpha = 0.05$ is 5.99. Since 6.2 is larger than this value, we can conclude that the students' performance does vary with seating position (i.e. we can reject the null hypothesis).

Siegel & Castellan (1988) explore some procedures for performing multiple comparisons between the conditions in a Friedman's analysis of variance by ranks. We will not report these here, but suggest that you explore them when the need arises.

Activity 20.5

If you have studied repeated measure tests (e.g. related samples *t*-tests, or repeated measures ANOVA), you will know that repeated measures tests are often more powerful than independent group tests. With this in mind, conduct a Kruskal-Wallis test on the data in Table 20.3, and decide whether this appears to be the case for non-parametric procedures.

Worked example

As you may know, the Cape Flats is an area in Cape Town comprising several suburbs, including Manenberg, Lavender Hill, and Mitchells Plain. Crime statistics over a number of years show that it is one of the most violent areas in the world. For example, it has a higher murder rate (over 90 per 100 000 population per annum) than any of the countries listed in Interpol statistics for the period 1994–1996. It should clearly be a national goal to address this problem. One NGO (COPES, a part of the New World Foundation) has developed a violence-reduction programme, which aims to reduce violence levels in schools through a programmatic intervention. In one part of the programme, school classes in the early grades are randomly assigned to one of four interventions:

1. a control condition
2. an intervention aimed at improving numeracy and literacy skills (N),
3. an intervention aimed at improving the said skills, plus improving classroom management skills of teachers in the school (NC),
4. an intervention consisting of (1) + (2), as well as an additional intervention aimed at teaching children positive, confrontation-mediating social skills (NCS) (see Carolissen *et al.*, 2001).

One measure taken periodically is a rating of children's aggressiveness towards each other. Each child is asked to name the three most aggressive children in the class, and the three most friendly. A tabulation is then constructed for each child in the class showing how many children identify the child in question as being amongst the three most aggressive. Data is given in Table 20.8 for each of the four conditions. The question is whether the conditions show any systematic difference.

Table 20.8 Data for each of four conditions in a violence-reduction programme

NCS	2	1	0	2	1	11	3	2	1	2	2
NC	2	13	2	1	4	0	0	2	1		
N	1	2	17	3	4	1	2	14	2	1	0
Control	12	18	4	3	14	2	1	3	13	5	

Note: Entries are the number of raters who list the child among the three most aggressive

Solution

Mere visual inspection of the data should convince you that the distributions are highly asymmetrical. A small number of children get very high scores, but most children receive very low scores. We decide to construct boxplots for each condition, using SPSS® (see Figure 20.1). The data setup and dialog boxes for constructing the boxplots are shown in Figure 20.2

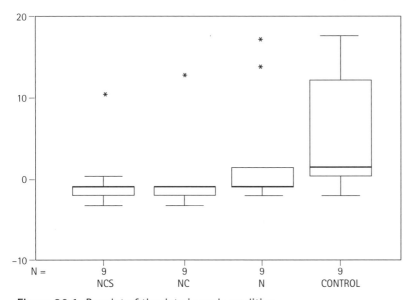

Figure 20.1 Boxplot of the data in each condition

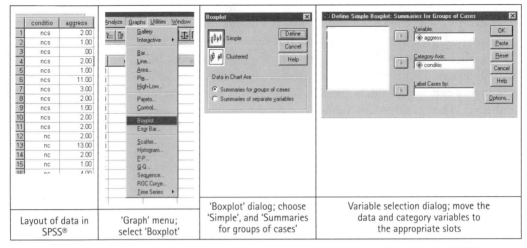

Figure 20.2 Data layout, menus, and dialog boxes for creating boxplots of the data in SPSS®

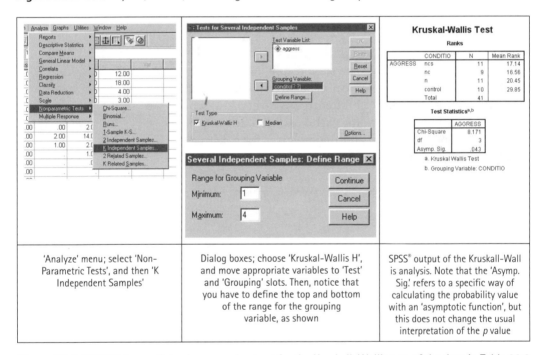

Figure 20.3 SPSS® Menus, dialog boxes, and output for the Kruskall–Wallis test of the data in Table 20.8

As you can see from the boxplots (Figure 20.1), each of the conditions shows a highly asymmetrical pattern, and the presence of outliers is suggested in each. The 'outliers', however, are clearly acceptable data points, and we cannot simply exclude them. Although we could explore the data further, producing frequency distributions and descriptive measures, it seems fairly clear from a visual inspection and the graphical display that we should consider using non-parametric statistics here. Since we want to compare four groups simultaneously, the preferred test is the Kruskal-Wallis test. We use SPSS® to conduct the test, although it is easy enough to do by hand (with a calculator), or on a spreadsheet. The steps required to conduct the test, as well as the output, are shown in Figure 20.3. The significant result (the calculated p value is smaller than 0.05) tells us that the experimental conditions did indeed differ. From the table of ranks, it is clear that the mean rank decreases according to the condition; in particular, the 'NCS' and 'NC' conditions appear to have the lowest average rating of aggressiveness.

Summary

1. Statistical tests that require assumptions about parameters or their estimation are known as parametric tests. These assumptions are occasionally unreasonable, and then we use non-parametric (or distribution-free) tests, which do not rely on parameter estimation and/or distributional assumptions. On the whole, distribution-free tests are much more robust than are parametric tests, but parametric tests tend to be more powerful than distribution-free tests.

2. All statistical tests involve the calculation of probabilities, and so need suitable probability models. Parametric tests use probability distributions (e.g. the normal distribution), whereas non-parametric tests tend to use the theoretical distribution of ranks as a probability model.

3. The sign test for matched samples is designed to test the equivalence of two medians in a repeated measures, or related samples, design. It is a non-parametric alternative to the repeated measures t-test, but it considers only the sign of the difference scores, and not the size.

4. The Wilcoxon matched pairs test is similar to the sign test except that it takes the size of the difference scores into account, and not merely the sign.

5. The Mann-Whitney U-test is used for research designs similar to those for which the independent samples t-test is used, i.e. when we want to test for a difference between two independent groups.

6. There are distribution-free tests that can test the difference between three or more groups in much the same way as ANOVA does in parametric statistical procedures. The Kruskal-Wallis test is an extension of the Mann-Whitney U-test for three or more independent samples, and the Friedman is an extension of the Wilcoxon test for three or more related samples.

Exercises

1. An employer is testing 16 applicants for a job, one at a time. Each has to perform a series of tests and the employer awards an overall points score to each. As each applicant may discuss the tests with later applicants before the latter are tested, it is suggested that applicants tested later may have an unfair advantage. Do the test scores below support this assertion? Use an appropriate distribution-free test.

42	89	79	77	83	81	74	49	75	72	68	64	71	55	69	72

2. A parapsychologist asks nine subjects who each claim psychic powers to use these to induce carelessness in customers visiting a china shop. Subjects are to induce an increase in the breakage rate due to customer accidents while the customers examine stock. Each subject is asked to 'will' customers to break items on a specified but different morning (the test day). The numbers of breakages per 500 customers entering the shop on each test day is compared with the number of breakages per 500 customers entering the shop on the same day of the previous week (the control day), when no such attempt to produce breakages had been made. The results (numbers of items broken per 500 customers) for the nine subjects are shown in the table below. Analyse these results using a distribution-free method to determine whether or not they provide acceptable evidence that a paranormal phenomenon occurred.

Subject:	1	2	3	4	5	6	7	8	9
Test day:	3.5	4.5	2.0	5.6	4.8	6.9	7.1	16.1	3.4
Control day:	1	4.7	3.4	4.8	5.1	2.2	2.1	2.3	1

3. To compare two different keyboard layouts on a pocket calculator, a company divided 21 staff volunteers randomly into a group of ten (A) and a group of 11 (B). Each group was asked to carry out the same set of calculations, group A using the first type of keyboard, and group B the second. Individuals were assessed on the total times in minutes taken to complete the calculations. These are given in the table below. Use an appropriate test to determine whether one layout is preferable to another.

Group A:	21	20	15	27	20	21	29	26	26	34	
Group B:	26	26	34	26	43	25	37	32	29	33	35

4. A sergeant-major orders 36 soldiers to parade tallest on the right, shortest on the left, numbered 1 (tallest) to 36 (shortest). Each soldier is then asked whether he/she smokes or drinks, and the rank numbers of soldiers in the various categories are given below. Is there evidence of an association between height and drinking and smoking habits? (*Hint: test whether there is an effect for height between the four groups.*)

Drinker and smoker:	3	8	11	13	14	19	21	22	26	27	28	31	33	35
Smoker, non-drinker:	2	12	25	32	34									
Drinker, non-smoker:	1	7	15	20	23	24	30	36						
Non-smoker, non-drinker:	4	5	6	9	10	16	17	18	29					

5. A social worker running a home for delinquent children wishes to show that it is successful in reducing delinquency. Twelve adolescents who have been declared delinquent are selected for the investigation. The number of days of truancy during the month prior to placement in the home is measured. Similarly, the number of days of truancy during the month they live in the home, and the number of days of truancy during the month after they leave the home are recorded. What do you conclude?

Adolescent:	1	2	3	4	5	6	7	8	9	10	11	12
Before:	10	12	12	19	5	13	20	8	12	10	8	18
During:	5	8	13	10	10	8	16	4	14	3	3	16
After:	8	7	10	12	8	7	12	5	9	5	3	2

Meta-analysis

Colin Tredoux

> After studying this tutorial, you should be able to:
> - Explain what is meant by the term 'meta-analysis'.
> - Present the arguments typically made against narrative literature review methods.
> - Outline the steps of the Schmidt-Hunter model of meta-analysis.
> - Conduct a meta-analysis of correlational studies.
> - Conduct a meta-analysis of simple experimental studies.

Most theories of human knowledge recognise the cumulation of information as a vital goal. If we take a Popperian approach, we can view the process of cumulation as one that proceeds by disconfirming incorrect views – in which we approach the 'truth' by accumulating knowledge about what is false (see Popper, 1959; Hacking, 1981). Alternately, we can take a Kuhnian perspective, and view the process as one in which we make substantial gains by overthrowing dominant paradigms, which are essentially collections of knowledge (see Kuhn, 1962, 1970; Hacking, 1981). The views are numerous; what they have in common is the notion that the process of cumulation is fundamental to the enquiry after knowledge.

The process of cumulation is fundamental to the enquiry after knowledge.

In the social sciences, the process of cumulation assumes an exaggerated importance. In the physical sciences it is common to await a theory that will solve a theoretical or factual problem (and it is not unusual for *one* theory to solve a tremendous number of problems), but in the social sciences, this is rarely the case. Here we are usually faced with situations in which there are literally hundreds of relevant studies. These studies characteristically disagree with each other in a number of respects, with no prospect of a definitive study on the horizon to resolve the disagreements.

Activity 21.1

> Choose a well-researched topic from your discipline (e.g. differences in suicide rates across demographic categories). Using library and other information sources available to you, do a quick search for published literature on the topic. How many studies have you identified from this cursory search?

Take the case of psychotherapy outcome studies (Smith & Glass, 1977). If you look at recent reviews of the literature, you will find that they refer to over 400 studies. Simply reading the studies will take you over six months, never mind the task of drawing conclusions about who is right and who is wrong! This is not an exceptional state of affairs: in virtually any area in the social sciences, you will find a hundred relevant studies.

In many areas of research and study in the social sciences there are literally hundreds of studies.

Characteristic responses to the problem

The response from researchers to the problems posed by integration of research findings across studies usually takes one of two forms. In the first place, the researcher may provide a narrative review of all the studies that constitute an entire research area. When the research area is large, which may mean that more than 100 studies are involved, the review is often as intimidating as the research area itself. The review is a pedestrian exercise, '[with] … verbal synopses of studies … strung out in dizzying lists' (Glass, 1976, p. 4). In the second instance, which is frequently seen in social science journals, researchers limit their review to a subset of studies in the area, the rest being rejected as methodologically flawed. A manageable amount of information is selected from the body of published research and presented in the review, and the rest is simply swept aside.

Both of these methods appear unacceptable. The first provides little more than a re-description of the research to be reviewed, and the second wastes most of the available information, drawing *a priori* conclusions about matters that should really be settled empirically.

This dissatisfaction with traditional forms of review is widespread, particularly among quantitative researchers, who have developed a family of alternative methods, which are quantitative in nature. Although quantitative review methods have been used since the 1950s (Hunter *et al.*, 1982), it is only in recent years that a

Three types of literature review:
1. narrative review
2. key-study review
3. quantitative review (meta-analysis)

Key approaches to meta-analyses:
1. Hunter, Schmidt & Jackson, 1982
2. Glass, 1976
3. Rosenthal, 1984

fully-fledged statistical theory of quantitative review has emerged. Glass (1976), one of the architects of the theory, has dubbed quantitative review meta-analysis. However, it should be noted that there are several forms or versions of *analysis*, and practitioners disagree about statistically acceptable techniques. In this tutorial, the most advisable route to take seems to adopt the more conservative approaches in the literature. Consequently, the form of meta-analysis outlined here is that pioneered by Hunter *et al.* (1982), known as the Schmidt-Hunter model, which advises against the use of inferential methods in quantitative review. However, we can use the descriptive techniques suggested by Hunter *et al.* in a manner that enables us to make quasi-inferential conclusions. If you are interested to learn about other forms of meta-analysis, you will find the treatments by Glass *et al.* (1981) and Rosenthal (1984) instructive.

The Schmidt–Hunter model of meta–analysis

Meta-analysis is:
'… the quantitative cumulation and analysis of descriptive statistics across studies' (Hunter et al., 1982)

The Schmidt-Hunter model offers a definition of meta-analysis as '… the quantitative cumulation and analysis of descriptive statistics across studies' (Hunter *et al.*, 1982, p. 137). It is possible to cumulate any of a number of descriptive statistics across studies, but for most purposes we will want to cumulate either *correlations* or *effect* sizes, since most quantitative studies in the social sciences will express their outcomes as one or the other.

For example, we may be interested in the relationship between authoritarianism and racial prejudice, as many sociologists and psychologists in South Africa have been. This relationship is typically quantified as a correlation coefficient, and it shows considerable variation across studies. Thus, Orpen (1973) finds $r = 0.19$, whereas Duckitt (1991) finds $r = 0.63$.

Alternatively, we may be interested in the effect that misleading information has on memory of an event, a research question pioneered by Elizabeth Loftus (Loftus, 1974, 1975, 1983). In this paradigm of research, participants are given information (e.g. a film), randomised into control and experimental groups, misled (differentially across experimental and control groups) for some aspect of the information, and then tested for their recollection of the event. There are over 70 studies on this question, and although many find an effect for misinformation, the effect sizes vary considerably. Thus, Sheehan and Tilden (1984) report $d = 0.01$, but Christiaansen and Ochalek (1983) report $d = 1.87$.

To the extent that correlations or effect sizes vary across studies, the Schmidt-Hunter model proposes that they exhibit the influence of (1) *artefactual error*, and (2) *moderator variables*.

By artefactual error we mean that the variation in effect sizes is due to sources that do not have anything to do with real underlying differences (e.g. the effectiveness of a treatment), but have to do with the way the data was collected, and the measuring instruments used. Imagine that two studies investigated the effectiveness of a drug treatment for paranoia. If study A collected data using 100 19-year-old female undergraduate college students from Pleasantville, and study B collected data using a sample of male and female prisoners ranging in age from 18 to 70, they might well find very different effect sizes, and this may be due to the sample and sampling method, rather than the effectiveness of the treatment. When the variation is due to extraneous factors of this kind, we say that it is an *artefact* of the study method or design.

The effect size d is equal to the difference between the means divided by the standard deviation (see Tutorial 13).

To the extent that correlations or effect sizes vary across studies, they exhibit
1. ***artefactual error**, and/or*
2. ***substantive variation***

Activity 21.3

Classify each of the following sources of variation as 'artefactual' or 'substantive':
a) different interview techniques
b) different attitude questionnaires
c) different countries in which studies were conducted
d) size of the samples used
e) the stability of a common measuring instrument.

The Schmidt-Hunter model proposes that there are three major sources of artefactual variation, which should be removed, or corrected, when we do meta-analysis.
1. *Sampling error.* The notion of a random sample is central to statistical theory, but is just a fiction in practice. How would we draw a random sample of all human beings? This task is close to impossible, and in practical research situations in the social sciences sampling is highly haphazard. Samples are drawn from quite distinct populations, the size of samples drawn is often quite small, and the method of drawing the samples relies less on random selection than voluntarism. This means that sampling error is likely to exert a substantial influence on the variation in effect sizes, and we should try to correct for it, where possible.
2. *Measurement error.* Most measuring instruments in the social sciences are imprecise, and can also vary substantially in terms of their scale reliability. In the latter case, 'reliability' refers to the replicability of observations using the instrument in question,

*Artefactual sources of variation in study statistics are: **sampling error**, **measurement error**, and **restriction of range**.*

and even instruments considered to have high reliability can yield scores that fluctuate considerably. Thus, if you measure your weight on a bathroom scale now, and again in 30 minutes, the fluctuation should be very small, but this is not the case for all measuring instruments – many questionnaires, attitude scales, and other social science instruments can show considerable fluctuation. Where measurement error is known to be present, it should be corrected for in the meta-analysis.

3. *Restriction of range.* This important concept was discussed in Tutorial 11, and we refer you back to it if you do not remember what it refers to. Simply put, if the selection process in some studies has reduced the range of observed variation on the dependent measure, relative to the population variation on the same measure, we can expect effect sizes or correlations in those studies to be reduced when compared to other studies. This source of variation is again artefactual, and we should correct for it in the meta-analysis, if we can.

In addition to artefactual error, there are also many *substantive sources of the variation* in effect sizes between studies. A different method may have been used, or different measures of the dependent variable administered to participants, among their possible differences. A key goal of meta-analysis is to find or provide evidence of such substantive forms of variation. We do this by coding potentially substantive sources of variation as moderator variables.

Meta-analysis derives its usefulness from its ability to statistically correct effect sizes for the types of error listed above, and its ability to identify theoretically substantive sources of variation.

The Schmidt-Hunter model of meta-analysis can be represented as a set of steps, as in the flow chart in Figure 21.1 on the next page.

1. Collection of the population of studies

The point of a meta-analysis is to summarise the entire set of studies on a particular topic. However, the topic needs to be defined carefully, or it will not be possible to conduct a meta-analysis. If we decide to review the population of psychotherapy studies, for instance, we will find many that are not amenable to quantitative summary, e.g. Freud's case-studies. We must define the exact topic explicitly: thus, 'studies that evaluate psychotherapy outcome quantitatively, and that use some form of statistical experimental design' will be more suitable for meta-analysis than 'studies that evaluate psychotherapy'.

List five research areas for which a meta-analysis is unlikely to be appropriate.

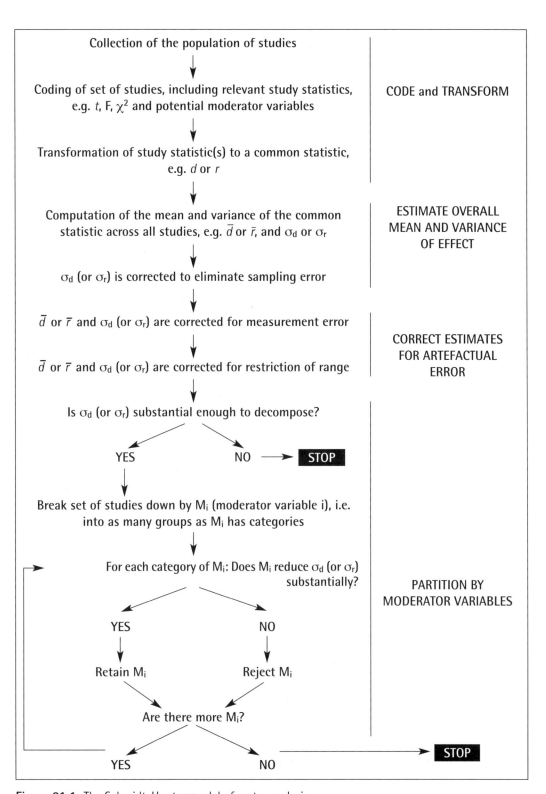

Figure 21.1 The Schmidt-Hunter model of meta-analysis

How do we go about collecting a *population* of studies? This task presents formidable problems, and is probably not attainable in practice. Although there are many information sources available to modern researchers that will allow the quick accumulation of published studies (see Kaniki, 1999 for an overview), many studies are not published, particularly when the findings are negative, or at odds with prevailing opinion within a discipline (see Garcia, 1981, for a remarkable example). Often studies are rejected by journal reviewers, and remain confined to a file drawer.

It is important to collect as many unpublished studies as possible for a meta-analysis.

The file drawer problem

*The **file drawer problem** refers to the failure to publish disconfirmatory findings and the consequent relegation of the study to a 'file drawer'.*

It is well known in many scientific disciplines that disconfirmatory findings are less likely to be published than confirmatory findings (Rosenthal & Rosnow, 1991). This may be due to editorial intervention in the scientific journals, or self-censorship on the part of researchers. Whatever the reason, it is clear that many research findings are not published, and the majority of these are findings of no correlation or no effect. This is known as the *file drawer problem* (unpublished disconfirmatory studies end up in 'file drawers' rather than journals).

This poses an obvious problem for meta-analytic procedures, since the published literature on a particular topic will contain a preponderance of confirmatory findings, and averaged correlations or effect sizes will be biased upwards.

We can evaluate the sensitivity of a meta-analysis by working out how many disconfirmatory findings of d = 0 it would take to obtain $\bar{d}$ = 0.

There are a couple of strategies we can consider using to lessen the extent of this problem. In the first instance, researchers should make an active effort to obtain as many unpublished studies as possible and include them in the meta-analysis. This is difficult to do, but a simple request to researchers in a particular field for copies of unpublished papers will help. A second strategy is to consider how 'resistant' a particular meta-analytic statistic is to disconfirmatory findings. For example, if $\bar{d}$ = 0.9, on the basis of 50 studies and a total of 5 000 subjects, we can work out how many findings of $d = 0$ would be needed to reduce the figure of 0.9 to 0, or to 0.45, or indeed to any alternative estimate. If it is clear that a very large number of disconfirmatory findings would be needed, it is reasonable to conclude that it is unlikely that undiscovered studies substantially bias the estimates arrived at in the meta-analysis.

2. Coding the set of studies

Each study in a meta-analysis is 'coded' for potential moderator variables.

Once the entire set of studies has been collected, each study should be 'coded' – i.e. the variables that are of interest to the meta-analysis are noted, and data for each are collected from all studies in the set. Typically, we will collect descriptive statistics from each study (e.g.

s, n, etc.), and information about variables that may be useful in the search for moderator variables (e.g. measures used, type of experimental design, country the study was conducted in, etc.).

3. Transforming to a common statistic

Studies that investigate particular topics often use different statistical tests, even though their research designs may be very similar (see Tutorial 22 for a discussion of this). Thus, one study might use a *t*-test to explore an intervention effect, and another an F-test. These different test statistics must be transformed to a common statistic in order to conduct a meta-analysis. There are a number of transformations available to us, and a number of potential common statistics. For most purposes, though, we decide whether the topic being investigated is that of a hypothesised *relationship*, or that of a hypothesised *difference* between means. In the former case, we transform to *r* (the correlation coefficient), and in the latter to *d* (Cohen's *d*).

Test statistics may differ across studies in the set, and must be transformed to a common statistic.

In the case of *r*, studies usually report this statistic directly, but where they do not, we can use specific formulas for the transformation. For example, to transform *t* into *r*, we use the formula:

$$r = \sqrt{\frac{t^2}{t^2 + (n_1 + n_2 - 2)}}$$

In the case of *d*, we can usually calculate this from the sample means and standard deviations. The formula for *d* is:

$$d = \frac{\bar{x}_e - \bar{x}_c}{s_p}$$

Equation 21.1

where: $\bar{x}_e$ = the mean of the experimental group
$\bar{x}_c$ = the mean of the control group
s_p = the pooled standard deviation of the experimental and control groups

Notice that Equation 21.1 reflects the difference between two groups. Where a study has a more complex design, multiple *d*s will need to be calculated. Thus, in a three-group design, you will calculate a *d* for the difference between groups 1 and 2, a *d* for the difference between groups 1 and 3, and a *d* for the difference between groups 2 and 3. For details on how to calculate the pooled standard deviation(s), see Tutorial 9.

*The most widely used **common statistics** are r (the correlation coefficient), and d (effect size, in standard deviation units).*

It is common practice in journal review to require that these details are reported in published studies, but where authors have not reported them, you will need to request the details.

4. The computation of the mean value and variance of the statistic across studies

The first step in a meta-analysis is to calculate the mean statistic across all studies. However, we will need to weight each component statistic (e.g. each study d) by the sample size of the study – we want to give more weight to studies that had larger sample sizes, since statistic estimates improve when based on larger sample sizes. The formulas for calculating the mean r and d are shown as:

Equation 21.2

$$\bar{r} = \frac{\Sigma\, n_i r_i}{\Sigma\, n_i} \qquad \bar{d} = \frac{\Sigma\, n_i d_i}{\Sigma\, n_i}$$

where: n is the number of data pairs
If a particular d is derived from a comparison with unequal sample sizes, the harmonic mean of the two ns should be used (see Tutorial 13).

In Tutorial 11 you were warned against simply averaging correlation coefficients, and here we are simply averaging them! It is possible to apply a Fisher transformation to each r in the study set, and this is probably a better way to do it from a technical point of view, but many authors do not agree that averaging correlation coefficients is fraught with dangers, as Tutorial 11 suggested, and do not apply the correction.

Activity 21.5

Why do you think the formulas for cumulating effect size weight each individual effect size by the size of the sample it was collected from?

We also need to calculate the average variance of the study statistic across studies. Again, we weight each statistic by its associated sample size, as shown in Equation 21.3

Equation 21.3

$$\sigma^2_r = \frac{\Sigma\, n_i (r_i - \bar{r})^2}{\Sigma\, n_i} \qquad \sigma^2_d = \frac{\Sigma\, n_i (d_i - \bar{d})^2}{\Sigma\, n_i}$$

The mean statistic may be a good estimate of the mean population value across studies, but the variance of the statistic across studies will invariably be greatly inflated by several sources of artefactual error (see the discussion on this earlier in the chapter).

5. Correcting for sampling error

The first correction we make is for sampling error. We use the formulas set out in Equation 21.4

Equation 21.4

$$est.\sigma^2_d = \sigma^2_d - \frac{4\,(1 + \frac{d^2}{8})k}{N}$$

where: k = the number of studies in the set
N = the total sample size (over all studies)
est σ^2 = the estimated population variance

The estimate of the variance of the common statistic across studies is thus adjusted, and will be reduced to the extent that k and N are large (i.e. to the extent that there are a greater number of studies in the set, and therefore a greater number of subjects).

6. Correcting for measurement error and restriction of range

Two common problems in many research designs are the presence of measurement error, and restriction of range. Ideally, we should correct the variance of the common study statistic for both. We rarely have data in the social sciences to effect the latter (and it is not typical for social science research to suffer from the problem). In the former case, we frequently do have data that bear on measurement reliability, and we can make some corrections. However, many authors dispute the validity of these corrections, and they can become quite complex. We will not provide details here – as an advanced exercise you may wish to consult Hunter *et al.* (1982).

7. Searching for moderator variables

When we have finished making corrections to the estimates of the variance of the study statistic(s) across studies, we examine the size of this corrected variance, e.g. $est.\sigma_d^2$. If it is clear that the variance is non-negligible, then we argue that there are real differences between studies – that there are substantive differences over and above differences introduced by artefact. We then use the information we collected about the studies to try to find the source of the differences – e.g. the type of experimental design used, the country in which the data were collected, etc. We call each potential source of variation a *moderator variable*, and we use these to split the studies into subsets. Meta-analysis is applied to each subset separately. If moderator variables are operative in the studies reviewed, then large differences between subset means should appear, with corresponding reduction in within-subset variation across studies.

If the corrected variance of the common statistic is substantial, we conclude that there are real differences between studies.

Rank the following sets of effect sizes according to the amount of variation in them. In which would it be most profitable to look for substantive sources of variation? Is there any way of definitively telling this?

a)	1.3	0.4	0.01	0.9	0.23
b)	0.3	0.24	0.4	0.35	0.29
c)	0.9	0.9	0.9	0.9	0.9

Activity 21.6

For example, say we have a collection of 20 studies, ten of which derive from the USA, and ten from South Africa. The studies measure the effectiveness of Z therapy (which induces catharsis by tickling patients' feet with emu feathers). We calculate $\bar{d} = 0.4$, and $\sigma_d^2 = 0.3$. Clearly, this value of σ_d^2 suggests that effect size varies a lot across studies. However, we do not know whether this variation is due to real study differences, or to artefactual error. Once we correct for artefactual error, we find $\sigma_d^2 = 0.1$. Although this may not seem a high value, it does suggest that there is still variation in effect size across studies, even after correction for artefactual error. We then break the set of studies down into two sets, namely those conducted in the USA and those conducted in South Africa. We now re-do the meta-analysis for each subset, separately. We find for the USA set, $\bar{d} = 0.7$, and $\sigma_d^2 = 0.05$, and for the SA set, $\bar{d} = 0.1$, and $\sigma_d^2 = 0.1$. Clearly, there is a massive difference between effect sizes collected in the USA and SA. However, the variation in effect size *within subsets* is still quite large, and we will want to (1) correct the estimates for artefactual error, and (2) explore the two study subsets for additional characteristics that might explain/reduce this variation. The goal should be to reduce the observed variance in effect sizes within subsets to zero.

Perhaps the best way to demonstrate the Schmidt-Hunter model of meta-analysis is through worked examples. Two are provided below.

Worked example 1 (correlations)

Earlier we referred to the interest in South Africa in the relationship between authoritarianism and racial prejudice. The original work, however, was published by Adorno *et al.* (1950), who popularised the so-called authoritarian personality theory. According to this theory, racial prejudice is associated with a particular personality style. This personality style is marked by a rigid adherence to conventional values, the idealisation of figures of authority, and the intolerance of ambiguity – a closed mind, so to speak. There have been many criticisms of this theory – and empirical tests of the theory in countries in which prejudice is institutionalised have proved to be disconfirmatory. This, of course, is why South African researchers have been interested in the theory. In his 1991 review of the research, John Duckitt identified a total of 11 studies, and 25 correlation coefficients indexing the relationship between authoritarianism and racial prejudice. To these we should add all published studies in the period from 1991 to the present, and we should make a concerted attempt to find as many unpublished studies as possible. A good way to do this is to (1) search the local literature databases for postgraduate theses, and (2) contact all authors who have published studies (e.g. Orpen, Duckitt), to see whether they have or know of additional, unpublished studies.

Since this is merely an example, we will not add any studies to the list, but will expediently assume that this is the population of studies. The studies are summarised in Table 21.1. We can use meta-analysis to ask certain questions regarding this set of studies. We may want to ask, for instance, whether the difference in size between the coefficients reported by Duckitt (1991) and Orpen (1973) is a 'real difference' (e.g. the use of different attitude scales), or merely artefactual error (e.g. sampling error). This is an important question, since Duckitt (1991) claims that most of the scales used in South African research on the authoritarian personality have poor psychometric properties.

An analysis of the set of studies, using the Schmidt-Hunter model, is reported below.

Table 21.1 South African studies of the authoritarianism-racism relation (until 1991)

Study	Sample	Measure of prejudice	r
Colman & Lambley, 1970	60 English students	Anti-African scale 1	0.23
Colman & Lambley, 1970	60 English students	Anti-African scale 2	0.33
Heaven, 1983	106 residents of Bloemfontein	Social Distance	0.27
Heaven, 1983	106 residents of Bloemfontein	Anti-Black	0.39
Heaven & Rajab, 1980	91 residents of Bloemfontein	Anti-Black	0.38
Lambley, 1973	190 English	Ethnocentrism scale	0.38
Lambley & Gilbert, 1970	106 English students	Social Distance	0.32
Lambley & Gilbert, 1970	106 English students	Social Distance	0.43
Orpen, 1971	88 English	Anti-African	0.20
Orpen, 1971	88 English	Social Distance	0.19
Orpen, 1973a	90 English	Social Distance	0.29
Orpen, 1973b	81 Rhodesian students	Anti-African	0.22
Orpen, 1973b	81 Rhodesian students	Social Distance 1	0.19
Orpen, 1973b	81 Rhodesian students	Social Distance 1	0.26
Orpen, 1973b	81 Rhodesian students	Social Distance 1	0.11
Orpen, 1973b	81 Rhodesian students	Social Distance 1	0.24
Orpen & Tsapogas, 1972	131 English scholars	Anti-African 1	0.15
Orpen & Tsapogas, 1972	131 English scholars	Anti-African 2	0.11
Orpen & Tsapogas, 1972	131 English scholars	Social Distance	0.05
Orpen & Van der Schyff, 1972	58 apprentices	Anti-African	0.33
Orpen & Van der Schyff, 1972	98 students	Anti-African	0.20
Ray, 1980	100 residents of Johannesburg	Anti-Black	0.59
Duckitt, 1990a	217 Pietermaritzburg students	Subtle Racism	0.69
Duckitt, 1990a	217 Pietermaritzburg students	Anti-Black Attitudes	0.53
Duckitt, 1990a	217 Pietermaritzburg students	Social Distance	0.56
Duckitt, 1990a	217 Pietermaritzburg students	Modif. Soc. Distance	0.63
Duckitt, 1990b	303 Wits students	Subtle Racism	0.63
Duckitt, 1990b	303 Wits students	Modif. Soc. Distance	0.65
Duckitt, 1990b	303 Wits students	Inter-racial Behaviour	0.36

Following the 8-point Schmidt-Hunter model, an inspection of Table 21.1 shows that we have completed steps 1 and 2. In addition, step 3 is not required, since all studies report r. It should be pointed out that although we have identified a fair amount of published research in the area, it is not clear that this is an exhaustive list of published research. We should try to satisfy ourselves that this is the case. Furthermore, we have not identified any relevant unpublished studies, and it is highly likely that there are many of these, especially since studies that produce disconfirming evidence are more likely to remain unpublished (see Rosenthal & Rosnow, 1991).

Step 4 requires us to calculate the mean value of the correlation across studies, along with the variance of this value across studies. Thus,

$$\bar{r} = \left(\frac{60 \times 0.23}{3922} + \frac{60 \times 0.33}{3922} + \dots + \frac{303 \times 0.36}{3922}\right) = 0.41$$

$$\sigma_r^2 = \left(\frac{60 \times (0.23 - 0.41)^2}{3922} + \frac{60 \times (0.33 - 0.41)^2}{3922} + \dots + \frac{303 \times (0.36 - 0.41)^2}{3922}\right) = 0.0375$$

In other words, the average correlation coefficient between authoritarianism and prejudice, across studies, is 0.41, and the variance of this coefficient is 0.0375. This estimate of the variance may appear small on inspection, but it is not: if we convert it to a standard deviation, for example, the value becomes 0.194 (remember $\sigma = \sqrt{\sigma^2}$). If we construct an interval around the mean estimated coefficient of two standard deviations (0.41 ± 0.38), we get (0.03; 0.79). (Remember from normal distribution theory that approximately 95% of the normal distribution is contained within two standard deviations of the mean.) In other words, the observed correlations in South Africa between authoritarianism and racial prejudice vary considerably. We should try to correct the variance estimate for artefactual error, and see whether there is any room after that for partitioning by moderator variables.

First, we correct for sampling error:

$$est.\sigma_r^2 = 0.0375 - \frac{(1 - 0.41^2)^2 29}{3922} = 0.0375 - \frac{20.07}{3922} = 0.0324$$

We should at this point correct for measurement error and for restriction of range. However, since it is an example, and we do not have the estimates of measurement error, we will assume that we have effected as much correction as we can for artefactual error, and it is clear that a lot of variation in effect size remains, even after correction. (In practice we would definitely make a concerted effort to find estimates of measurement error for authoritarianism and prejudice measures.)

We move to step 7 of the model. It is clear that there is a considerable amount of variance around the mean estimate of the correlation coefficient, so we need to look for moderator variables. We have already coded the studies for some details, but in a more detailed meta-analysis we would want to include additional information about the studies. The most fruitful code to explore for present purposes is probably the type of measure of racial prejudice used in the studies, as Duckitt (1991) has argued that many of them have poor psychometric properties. We therefore repeat steps 3 to 6 of the Schmidt-Hunter model for each distinct type of test, excluding two studies that used unique prejudice measures. The results are reported in Table 21.2.

Table 21.2 Measures of race prejudice used in South African studies of the authoritarianism-racism relationship

Prejudice measure	$\bar{r}$	$est.\ \sigma^2$	k	n
Anti–African	0.20	0.00	8	707
Anti–Black	0.49	0.002	4	514
Modified Social Distance	0.64	0.00	2	520
Social Distance	0.29	0.02	11	1 168
Subtle Racism	0.66	0.00	2	520

It appears from Table 21.2 that the correlation between authoritarianism and racial prejudice depends on the scale used to measure racial prejudice. The correlation is highest when measured with the Subtle Racism and Modified Social Distance scales, and lowest when measured with the Anti-African and Social Distance scales. The corrected variance around the estimated mean correlation suggests that the variation in correlations from studies using the Social Distance scale should be investigated further. We can do this by coding those studies for additional characteristics, and re-running the meta-analysis for sub-groups of studies. The corrected variance for studies using the Anti-Black scale is small enough, on the other hand, for us to accept the mean correlation and not investigate any further.

Worked example 2 (effect sizes)

Witnesses to crimes are often exposed to information regarding the event some time after it has taken place. There is an obvious and important question here, namely what effect this information has on the original memory of the event. Applied cognitive psychologists have investigated this question for some 25 years with a variety of laboratory experiments. These *postevent information experiments* show that information acquired after an event may influence witness reports of the event. Where the information is *consistent* with what originally happened, witness reports are usually more accurate than they would have been in the absence of this information, and where the information is *inconsistent* with what originally happened, the reports are usually less accurate. However, there is considerable controversy in the literature, and findings often differ quite dramatically. A review that delineates the clear and unambiguous findings in the literature is of some value. Tredoux (1989) attempted such a review, and reported a meta-analysis. The details follow below.

Identification of Studies

A literature search of journals that report studies in English and that are abstracted in *Psychological Abstracts* and the *Social Sciences Citation Index* was conducted. Studies reporting experiments in which postevent information was a stated concern were selected for analysis. Of these studies, those that reported differences between experimental and control groups in terms of proportions were selected for the meta-analysis. Altogether 70 experiments were selected for meta-analysis, from some 25 studies. (An experiment is defined here as an experimental-control comparison.)

An estimate of the effect of the experimental manipulation on the proportions of experimental and control groups correctly completing the required task was calculated using probit transformations of the difference between the two groups – i.e. by differencing the standard normal deviates corresponding to the proportions observed in the experimental and control groups (Glass *et al.*, 1981, p. 138).

$$d = z_e - z_c$$

where: z_e and z_c = the standard normal deviates (z-scores) for the experimental and control groups

Note that this way of indexing an effect is typically used when the measured variable is a *proportion*. In the postevent information experiments, the outcome measure is normally the proportion of items or details remembered correctly, and the difference between the proportions remembered correctly by the experimental and control group is the key measure of the experiment.

The meta-analysis was conducted in a stepwise manner, breaking down sets of studies according to residual variance remaining after the meta-analysis at the previous level. Unfortunately, only correction for sampling error could be made, as the psychometric properties of the measures used in postevent information studies are not well enough documented to permit correction for measurement error, or for restriction of range.

A total of 2 041 subjects was used in the 70 experiments. The mean effect ($\bar{d}$) across studies was 0.581, and the variance of the observed effects was 0.299. After correction for sampling error (which was 0.116), the variance was 0.183. This 'unexplained variance' is high, and means that the differences in effect sizes between studies are likely to be due to real differences in the properties of the studies.

Accordingly, studies were coded to permit inspection of differences between studies. Studies were coded on a total of 13 properties, but for present purposes it is useful to note only the following codes:

1. *The type of information manipulation* – neutral (i.e. unrelated) vs inconsistent, consistent vs neutral, or consistent vs inconsistent. The key idea in a postevent-information (PEI) experiment is that research participants first witness some event, and are then given information that attempts to mislead them for the original event information (e.g. they could be told that the man they say committed the crime was bearded, when he was in fact clean-shaven). A second group of participants is either used as a no-treatment control (e.g. they are given neutral or irrelevant information), or as a booster-control (e.g. they are re-presented with the original information). Alternatively, the experimental group can be treated as a booster-experimental group (i.e. they are re-presented with the original information), and compared to a no-treatment control group.

2. *Whether the experimental design used a paradigmatic or revised experimental design.* On the final test, in which participants are tested for their memory of the original information, pairs of items are presented to participants, and they have to choose the correct option. Traditionally (or paradigmatically), an item from the original event is paired with a corresponding misleading item, e.g. participants are asked to declare whether the perpetrator had a beard or was clean-shaven. However, it is also possible to pair the original information with new (but feasible) information, rather than with the misleading information. Thus, if witnesses see a man wielding a screwdriver as a weapon, we could try to mislead the participants to believe that the weapon was a knife, but at test time we need not pair 'screwdriver' and 'knife', but could instead pair 'screwdriver' and 'chisel', for example. The difference is fundamental, and the subject of a substantial controversy (see McCloskey & Zaragoza, 1985).

3. *The type of questioning method on the final test* – hypnosis-assisted, verbal questioning, or strictly paradigmatic, i.e. as in the original studies reported by Loftus. How you attempt to elicit information from a witnesses is important, and may affect whether a witness gives misleading testimony. In the so-called *strictly paradigmatic* studies, the test is always a multiple-choice type pairing

of items, and participants have to choose the correct option. In other studies, the final test may elicit information by hypnosis interview, or by verbal questioning.

The meta-analysis then proceeded in a hierarchical fashion. In the first step, the total set of studies was split into three subsets, namely whether the postevent information was consistent, inconsistent, or neutral with respect to the original information. As can clearly be seen from Figure 21.2, the 'Consistent' and 'Neutral' manipulations each boost performance relative to the 'Inconsistent' (misled) manipulation, with the 'Consistent' manipulation boosting performance over that of the 'Neutral' group. In the case of both the 'Consistent' and 'Neutral' manipulations, the variance in effect sizes is quite small, and analysis ceased. In the case of the 'Inconsistent' (or 'misled') manipulation, the variation in effect size is quite large, though, even after correction for sampling error.

In the second step, the 'Inconsistent' studies were split into subsets of studies that either used the 'Paradigmatic' or 'Revised'

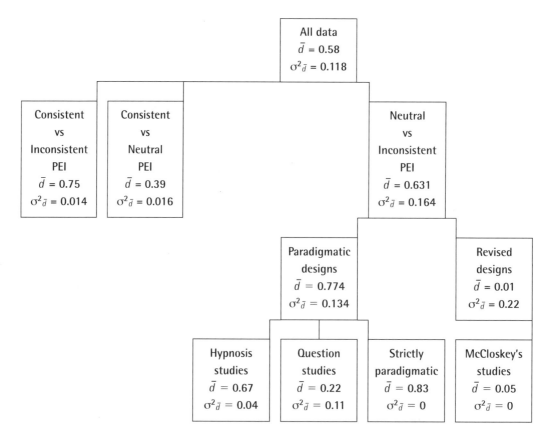

Figure 21.2 Meta-analytic categorisation of literature on the postevent information effect (until 1987)

versions of the experimental procedure. Here, after meta-analysis is again applied, it is clear that the two types of design yield very different effect sizes, but it is also clear that both subsets of studies must be explored further, as the residual variance in effect size is still large (0.134 and 0.22).

In the third step, the 'paradigmatic' and 'revised' subsets are themselves split up into subsets. In the case of the 'paradigmatic designs', the subsets are created on the basis of the type of information-eliciting method used in the final test. In the case of the revised designs, the subset had become so small that it only made sense to group a set of six experiments reported by McCloskey & Zaragoza (1985), and to omit the rest. A meta-analysis of each of the four subsets created at this level of the hierarchy showed that the 'strictly paradimatic' designs produced an average effect size of 0.83, with no or negligible residual variance. Similarly, the experiments reported by McCloskey and Zaragoza produced a mean effect size of 0.05, with no residual variance in effect size. The other two subsets clearly require further exploration, as their residual variance is relatively large, but we will not consider any analysis deeper than this level of the hierarchy.

We can summarise the literature, and say that there seems to be little doubt that the type of information presented at the second stage of postevent information experiments has a strong effect on the memory performance of witnesses. Where consistent information is presented, memory is improved relative to controls given neutral information, or to participants given misleading information. These effect sizes differ, which leads one to the conclusion that the effect of misleading information is linear (or at least monotonic): as postevent information changes from misleading to neutral, and finally to consistent, the corresponding memory performance increases at each stage. More than this, it seems that the type of final test used and the method of eliciting information in the test both strongly affect memory performance. The differential size of the effects is very striking: strictly paradigmatic designs produce effects that are 0.78 larger than the revised designs of McCloskey and Zaragoza. This is a considerable difference.

Box 21.1

Software for meta–analysis

The calculations for the Schmidt-Hunter model of meta-analysis are comparatively straightforward, and there is no real need for sophisticated software. You will find spreadsheet programs particularly useful, though, since their tabular layout and easy sorting procedures are particularly well suited for Schmidt-Hunter meta-analysis. For other models of meta-analysis, it is useful to consider software options. At the time of writing, none of the major statistical packages (SAS®, SPSS®, Statistica®) offer explicit support, but there are a number of specialised software packages. Here is a listing of some of these, with Internet details.

EPIMETA   http://www.cdc.gov/epo/dpram/epimeta/epimeta.htm A meta-analysis package with an emphasis on applications in epidemiology

METAWIN   http://www.metawinsoft.com A meta-analysis package that allows you to specify different underlying statistical assumptions

DSTAT   email: orders@leahq.mhs.compuserve.co An early and simple implementation of the Schmidt-Hunter model of meta-analysis

ABMA   email: orders@leahq.mhs.compuserve.co A revised and more sophisticated version of DSTAT

Conclusion

Proponents of meta-analysis have certainly made a strong case for quantitative research review, and there is little doubt that meta-analysis is becoming a favoured form of review in quantitative research areas. This is not to say that meta-analysis is without critics, though. As early as 1984, Hans Eysenck objected to the underlying ideas, and re-named meta-analysis 'mega-silliness'. His objections (and those of other commentators) centred on the way in which good quality studies are aggregated with relatively weak studies (and given the same weight as them). For a long time, researchers in the social sciences have stressed the point of carefully evaluating study methodology, and have developed a formidable literature (see, for example, Campbell, 1988), but this is simply overlooked by meta-analysts. A number of other criticisms are often made, including that the goal of obtaining every study on a particular problem is not feasible – given the file drawer phenomenon. We will leave you to review this literature, and make up your own mind about the feasibility of the enterprise. There is no doubt, though, that the point of departure for meta-analysis – that narrative review methods are unsuited to the task of dealing with large bodies of quantitative research – is convincing, and many social scientists have been won over to the meta-analytic way of deciding research questions.

Summary

1. Meta-analysis is the name given to a family of approaches that attempt the quantitative review of research literature. We have focused only on the Schmidt-Hunter model in this tutorial.

2. The key idea underlying meta-analysis is that differences in findings produced by different studies are due to both substantive differences between the studies, and artefactual differences. The key goal of meta-analysis is to partition the variance (in the 'common statistic') into sources that are artefactual and sources that are substantive.

3. There are four major steps in the Schmidt-Hunter model:
   a) *Code and transform.* We identify and collect the population of studies on a particular topic, including as many unpublished studies as possible. Studies are then coded for potential moderator variables. A 'common statistic' is chosen, and each study's finding is transformed to this statistic.
   b) *Estimate overall mean and variance.* We find the weighted mean and variance of the common statistic.
   c) *Correct estimates for artefactual error.* We reduce the variance of the common statistic by the amounts attributable to sampling error, measurement error, and restriction of range.
   d) *Partition by moderator variables.* We follow a hierarchical heuristic, applying meta-analysis to progressively deeper subsets of studies, formed according to moderator variables.

Exercises

1. The table below contains data for a set of studies which have examined the relation between marital communication and marital satisfaction (the column labelled 'r' has entries of correlation coefficients). A number of other variables are included, since they may moderate or mediate the correlation in question. Examine the data, and provide a narrative review of this set of studies. Then conduct a meta-analysis of the set of studies. Do the conclusions of the meta-analysis agree with the conclusions drawn in your narrative review?

Study	n	r	Gender	Class	Race	Language	Married with ANC
1	19	0.52	m	2	w	African	Y
2	30	0.45	m	1	w	African	N
3	58	0.3	m	1	w	African	Y
4	20	0.36	m	1	w	African	N
5	25	0.26	m	1	w	English	Y
6	26	0.53	f	2	b	English	Y
7	62	0.45	f	2	w	English	N
8	58	0.33	m	2	w	English	N
9	71	0.18	f	2	w	Afrikaans	N

Study	n	r	Gender	Class	Race	Language	Married with ANC
10	19	−0.02	m	1	b	Afrikaans	Y
11	25	0.56	m	2	c	English	Y
12	22	0.55	f	1	b	English	N
13	46	0.41	f	1	w	African	Y
14	69	0.44	f	2	w	English	N
15	30	0.22	m	2	w	African	Y
16	72	0.32	m	2	c	African	N
17	60	0.44	f	2	c	African	N
18	23	0.5	f	1	w	African	Y
19	55	0.32	m	1	w	African	
20	19	0.19	f	1	b	Afrikaans	N
21	23	0.14	m	1	b	Afrikaans	Y
22	44	−0.1	m	1	w	Afrikaans	N
23	20	0.46	f	1	b	English	N
24	59	0.43	f	2	w	African	N
25	28	0.54	f	1	w	African	Y
26	28	0.09	f	2	w	Afrikaans	N
27	69	0.31	f	2	w	African	N
28	29	0.1	m	1	w	Afrikaans	N
29	67	0.34	m	2	w	African	N
30	26	0.31	f	1	c	English	Y

Note: ANC = ante-nuptial contract

2. Consider the data in the table below, which is taken from a meta-analysis reported by Darlington *et al.* (1980).

Darlington *et al.* examined the short-, medium-, and long-term impact of pre-school programmes on competence of school-children in low-income areas. The key outcome variable was the proportion of pupils who failed to meet the requirements for admission to a higher grade. Conduct a meta-analysis, and decide whether the accumulated data show any support for the programme intervention.

Study	n	Experimental proportion	Control proportion
1	82	0.38	0.61
2	55	0.32	0.47
3	221	0.55	0.76
4	123	0.61	0.83
5	69	0.50	0.54
6	127	0.56	0.78
7	125	0.89	0.79

TUTORIAL

22

Statistical reasoning

Ingrid Palmary and Kevin Durrheim

At the end of this tutorial, you should be able to:
- Select appropriate statistical tests to analyse different types of data.
- Understand the difference between brash and stuffy approaches to data analysis.
- Provide a reasoned defence of your statistical choices.

A data set can often be analysed with different procedures, sometimes leading to different conclusions.

So far, each tutorial in this book has focused on a single statistical procedure, considering when the procedure is appropriate and showing how to calculate the statistics. In real-life statistical analysis, however, as well as in examinations, the most difficult task is selecting the appropriate statistical procedure. With some experience and practice, the mechanics of doing statistical analysis – especially with a computer – are relatively straightforward. The difficulty, when faced with a dataset, is deciding on the appropriate statistical procedure to employ. In this chapter we consider some basic rules-of-thumb for selecting appropriate statistical procedures. This is done in two stages. First, a decision-making tree is presented which provides a set of rules for selecting appropriate statistical procedures. Next, we argue that the decision-making tree is only of limited value because it is often the case that different approaches can be used to make sense of data, sometimes leading to different conclusions. The main theme of this chapter is that doing statistical analysis is an exercise in careful decision-making and principled argument.

The aim of statistical analysis is to identify patterns in a matrix of raw data.

By now you should recognise that a mass of numbers arranged in a data matrix is the basic raw material used in statistical information processing. The aim of statistical analysis is to find meaning in the seemingly chaotic arrangement of numbers. Consider the data matrix in Figure 22.1, which contains the scores of 23 subjects on 12 variables. The original study from which the dataset was taken sought to examine whether there was a relationship between conservatism, racism, and matric results among learners from three different schools in the Eastern Cape. The original data matrix was made up of the responses of 107 subjects on 56 variables. If the numbers in rows and columns in this small matrix appear a confusing and meaningless jumble, you can imagine the complexity and apparent chaos of the original dataset, and other large datasets that consist of thousands of subjects and hundreds of variables.

To detect meaning in a data matrix, describe the variables and determine associations between variables.

The magic of statistical analysis lies in its power to detect meaning and order in this apparent complexity and chaos. This is done principally by describing the distributions of the variables and identifying patterns of covariance – that is, relationships – between variables. With the numerical processing power of inexpensive

S	Gender	Age	School	C1	C2	C3	Csum	A1	A1r	A2	A3	Asum	Matric
1	1	18	3	0	1	1	2	5	1	1	1	3	71
2	1	18	3	1	0	0	1	2	4	3	3	10	69
3	1	19	3	3	4	4	11	1	5	2	3	10	32
4	0	18	2	1	0	2	3	6	0	2	1	3	59
5	0	25	1	4	3	2	9	3	3	4	6	13	45
6	0	18	2	1	0	2	3	6	0	0	0	0	68
7	1	30	2	3	2	4	9	6	0	1	2	3	41
8	1	18	1	0	1	3	4	4	2	2	3	7	59
9	1	17	3	2	3	4	9	3	3	3	3	9	41
10	0	27	3	0	0	0	0	0	6	6	6	18	84
11	1	18	1	0	1	1	2	2	4	1	3	8	65
12	0	25	1	0	0	1	1	0	6	4	6	16	58
13	0	18	2	3	2	4	9	6	0	1	3	4	37
14	1	23	2	3	2	4	9	3	3	2	3	8	42
15	0	19	2	0	2	2	4	4	2	0	0	2	55
16	1	18	3	2	0	2	4	0	6	3	3	12	59
17	1	18	3	1	2	2	5	4	2	3	1	6	68
18	1	18	1	0	2	4	6	5	1	3	0	4	52
19	0	19	1	2	3	2	7	6	0	0	3	3	53
20	0	18	3	3	2	3	8	0	6	4	5	15	39
21	0	21	2	0	0	0	0	0	6	5	3	14	77
22	0	42	1	0	3	2	5	1	5	1	1	7	56
23	1	20	3	0	0	0	0	2	4	3	2	9	32

Asum = a composite of items A1–A3, measuring authoritarianism; Csum = a composite of items C1–C3, a measure of conservatism.

Figure 22.1 Data matrix from study investigating the relation between conservatism, authoritarianism, and matric results

technology, it has also become relatively easy to do statistical analysis. The mechanics of pulling down windows and generating statistical output are not at all complicated. The art is in knowing which windows to pull down, which analyses to perform, and how to skillfully interpret the output. Analysing statistics is like doing detective work, where 'the investigator must solve an interesting case, similar to the "whodunnit" of a traditional murder mystery, except that it is a "howcummit" – how come the data fall in a particular pattern' (Abelson, 1995, p. 14). In making sense of data matrices such as that in Figure 22.1, the analyst is doing more than crunching numbers on a computer. The work of statistical analysis is guided continually by reasoned decision-making, while striving for accuracy, economy, and elegance of analysis.

Rules for making statistical decisions

Getting a feel for the data

The first step in data analysis, after the dataset has been constructed and properly cleaned, is to get a feel for the data. The analyst can only make reasoned decisions about which statistical procedures to use after she or he has a clear picture of the type and nature of the variables in the dataset. This initial scanning of the data involves three operations.

After collecting data:
1. *create a data matrix, and*
2. *clean the data by identifying data entry errors.*

Defining variable type
Each variable should be examined to determine its scale or level of measurement (see Tutorial 1). Is the variable discrete (categorical) or continuous? Is the variable measured on a nominal, ordinal, interval, or ratio scale of measurement? The type of variable that we are working with has an impact

Refer to Figure 22.1. Identify the scale of measurement of each variable, and decide whether each variable is discrete or continuous.

Activity 22.1

on the kind of descriptive and inferential statistics we can perform with the variable. Procedures such as frequency counts and bar charts are used to describe discrete variables, whereas means, standard deviations, and histograms are used to describe interval and ratio data. Similarly, the variable type will determine whether we employ parametric or non-parametric inferential tests.

The scale of measurement of a variable determines the kind of descriptive and inferential statistics that can be conducted with the variable.

Describing the variables
Once we know the type of variables we are working with, we are well placed to gain a greater familiarity with the data by describing each variable. The most useful descriptive statistics to generate for *continuous* and *interval variables* are means, standard deviations,

Describe variables by commenting on the shape, central tendency and variability of the distributions.

ranges, and graphical displays (e.g. boxplots, or histograms). These will give you an idea of how the sample scored on a variable (e.g. high or low mean, within a wide or narrow range of scores), whether the distribution of scores is skewed or symmetrical, and whether there are any significant outliers. This information is useful later in deciding whether the assumptions of inferential tests have been met. *Categorical* or *discrete variables* are described by means of frequency tables and bar charts to determine the number or proportion of subjects in each category. Frequency tables should be studied to determine whether any categories are very small, or whether the sample is roughly equally distributed across the categories.

Activity 22.2

Refer to Figure 22.1. Describe each of the variables in the dataset. Are there any interesting features of the data that you should bear in mind when doing inferential statistics and when interpreting the output? Refer to the discussion in Tutorials 2–4.

Computing scale scores
At this early stage in the analysis, summed scale scores should be computed. Responses to items that make up measurement scales should be reverse scored where necessary, item analysis should be conducted, and then the items summed to form composite variables. Composite scores for the three item measures of conservatism and authoritarianism have been calculated for the data in Figure 22.1. Once sound composite measures have been constructed, we should define the type and nature of each variable by identifying its measurement scale and generating descriptive statistics. (For a discussion of these issues, see Tutorial 12)

Activity 22.3

Refer to Figure 22.1. Were any of the items for conservatism and authoritarianism reverse scored? Conduct item analyses on the conservatism and authoritarianism items. Do you think the scales have been properly calculated? Define the measurement scale of each variable, and generate descriptive statistics for each variable.

Only once the researcher has developed a close feel for the data should inferential statistics be undertaken. A keen sense of the type of data we are working with is essential for making informed decisions about the type of statistical procedures to employ, and will guide the interpretation of the results.

Selecting the appropriate inferential test

The second stage of data analysis involves selecting and conducting appropriate inferential procedures. Although it is possible that different procedures can be used to analyse the same data, as will be shown later, a set of rules should guide our decision-making at this stage. These rules are set out in Figure 22.2.

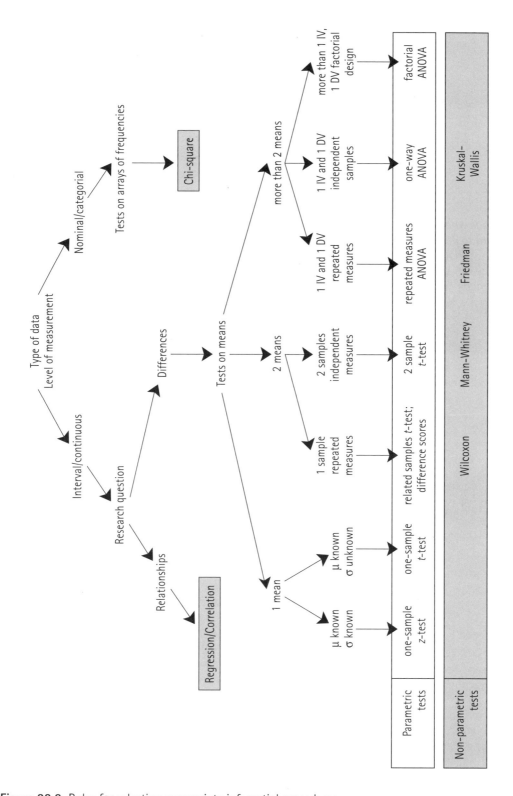

Figure 22.2 Rules for selecting appropriate inferential procedures

Type of data

The first decision to make is whether we are working with categorical, interval, or continuous data. If we have categorical variables, an appropriate test of association is chi-square. If we want to determine whether gender and school are independent in the data in Figure 22.1, we would cross-tabulate these two variables, and determine whether the χ^2 statistic is significant. On the other hand, for continuous and interval variables, we need to make further decisions before selecting the appropriate inferential procedure.

Type of research question

Decide whether you want to investigate relationships between scores, or group differences.

Research questions may be broadly divided into two kinds: we may either be looking for relationships between variables, or for differences between means. If the data consists of two or more continuous variables, such as conservatism, authoritarianism, and matric results (see Figure 22.1), correlation and regression analysis is appropriate. Correlations are used to determine whether two variables are related, while regression is used to determine whether predictor variables are related to dependent variables. If, on the other hand, our independent variables are categorical and our dependent variable is continuous, the aim of the analysis is to determine whether the subjects in the different categories have different mean scores on the dependent variable. In this situation, there are a number of procedures available, depending on the number of means.

To analyse the relationship between conservatism, authoritarianism, and matric results in Figure 22.1, first generate a correlation matrix to determine the bivariate associations between the variables, and then perform a multiple regression analysis to determine the regression of matric results on conservatism and authoritarianism. Evaluate whether the regression is satisfactory (i.e. examine its strength, and significance).

One mean

The number of means being compared and the relationship between the means (dependent or independent scores) determine which inferential test should be used.

In some situations, the aim of the analysis is to determine whether an obtained mean differs from some criterion. For example, we may want to know whether the mean matric result for our sample differs significantly from the mean matric result for the whole country. In these cases we use either the one-sample *z*- or *t*-test. If we have the *population standard deviation,* the *z*-test is appropriate, but if we only have the sample standard deviation, and have to use this as an estimate of the population standard deviation, the *t*-test is appropriate (see Tutorials 7 and 9).

Two means

If we want to determine whether two means differ significantly from each other, the appropriate test is determined by the nature of the *relationship between the two means.* If the means are independent – i.e. they are derived from different samples – an independent samples *t*-test is used for parametric data, and the Mann-Whitney test is used for non-parametric data. If the means are related – i.e. if both means come from the same subject – a related samples *t*-test is used for parametric data, and a Wilcoxon test is used for non-parametric data.

*Only by **practice** will you learn the appropriate use of the different statistical tests.*

Multiple means

Here too, the kind of test to use is determined by the nature of the *relationship between the samples.* For dependent or related samples, repeated measures ANOVA is used for parametric data, and the Friedman test is used for non-parametric data. If the samples are independent, the appropriate test is determined by the number of independent variables. If we have one independent variable, one-way ANOVA is used to analyse parametric data, and the Kruskal-Wallis test is used to analyse non-parametric data. If there are multiple independent variables, factorial ANOVA is used for parametric data and series of one-way Kruskal-Wallis tests are used to analyse non-parametric data.

> Refer to Figure 22.1. Conduct a series of statistical analyses to determine whether there is an association between:
> a) gender and matric results
> b) gender and C1
> c) school and authoritarianism
> d) school and A2
> e) school, gender and A3
> f) school, gender and matric results
> g) matric results for this sample, and the national mean of 48%.
>
> Try to do each analysis in more than one way.

Activity 22.5

It is of the utmost importance that you know how to use the decision-making tree presented in Figure 22.2. It is no use merely learning the tree by heart. You need to practise using the tree until the decision-making process becomes second nature. In this regard, you will find the exercises at the end of the tutorial invaluable.

Defending statistical decisions

While the rules discussed above are *necessary* for selecting appropriate statistical procedures, they are not *sufficient*. Statistical analysis

Statistical analysis should produce economical, information rich, elegant results.

is not simply a rule-following activity. Creativity is required to produce economical, information-rich, and elegant results. The reason for this is that there is often more than one way of analysing a particular set of variables. Different procedures will sometimes yield the same results, but will sometimes yield different results. The skill of analysis lies in selecting procedures that best answer the research question at hand, and then defending these selections in a written report of the analysis.

Variability in outcome and procedure

The problem with the decision tree reported in Figure 22.2 is that it gives the impression that there is only one correct way of analysing data. One of the most basic distinctions in the tree is between statistics that can be used for analysing relationships and statistics that can be used to test for differences between means. The distinction between these two forms of analysis does not stand up to close scrutiny. If group means – e.g. male and female – differ on a variable – e.g. Matric results – it is obvious that there is a relationship between the variables Gender and Matric results: the data are so patterned that an individual's score on one variable is related to his or her score on the other.

You must always defend your statistical decisions in your research report.

Correlation Coefficients

	MATRIC
GENDER	−.1691
	(23)
	P = .440

t-tests for Independent Samples of SEX

Variances	t-value	df	2-Tail Sig	SE of Diff	CI for Diff
Equal	.79	21	.440	6.079	(−7.861, 17.422)
Unequal	.79	20.79	.441	6.081	(−7.875, 17.435)

Figure 22.3 SPSS® output for equivalent tests on the data of Figure 22.1

The SPSS® output in Figure 22.3 shows that correlation analysis and the t-test can yield the same results. Both analyses were performed to test whether the Gender and Matric results were related. As you can see, the two analyses are equivalent. The p-values are precisely the same ($p = 0.440$), and thus lead equally to the same conclusion not to reject the null hypothesis.

If two different procedures lead to the same results, on what basis can we select one above the other? It all depends on the nature of your research question, on the reasons why you are doing the analysis, and on the other analyses that you are conducting. If the main purpose of the analysis is to scan a number of variables for association, correlation analysis would be sufficient. Correlation analysis is more economical than analysis by *t*-test. You can scan a large correlation matrix in a matter of seconds and have an idea of the strength and nature of association between variables. It is often useful therefore to use correlation analysis in early or exploratory analyses of large datasets. On the other hand, if gender differences are a central concern of the research, a *t*-test would be more appropriate, because it tests group mean differences.

In situations where there is more than one way of analysing data, the appropriate statistical procedure will depend on the nature of the research question.

Different procedures can be legitimately used for the same analysis, and yield different results. Figure 22.4 reports the results of two different ways of investigating the relationship between the variables, School and Authoritarianism (Asum). First, a one-way ANOVA was used to determine whether there was a significant effect. The results indicate that there is no significant effect at the $\alpha = 0.05$ level of significance. Normally we would terminate the

ANALYSIS OF VARIANCE

Source of Variation	Sum of Squares	DF	Mean Square	F	Sig of F
Main Effects	114.159	2	57.079	2.693	.092
SCHOOL	114.159	2	57.079	2.693	.092
Explained	114.159	2	57.079	2.693	.092
Residual	423.841	20	21.192		
Total	538.000	22	24.455		

t-tests for Independent Samples of SCHOOL

Variances	t-value	df	2-Tail Sig	SE of Diff	CI for Diff
Equal	1.37	12	.197	2.508	(−2.037, 8.894)
Unequal	1.37	12.00	.197	2.508	(−2.037, 8.894)

t-tests for Independent Samples of SCHOOL

Variances	t-value	df	2-Tail Sig	SE of Diff	CI for Diff
Equal	−.84	14	.413	2.298	(−6.864, 2.991)
Unequal	−.84	12.72	.418	2.312	(−6.942, 3.069)

t-tests for Independent Samples of SCHOOL

Variances	t-value	df	2-Tail Sig	SE of Diff	CI for Diff
Equal	−2.33	14	.035	2.303	(−10.305, −.425)
Unequal	−2.31	12.68	.038	2.319	(−10.388, −.342)

Figure 22.4 SPSS® output for ANOVA and *t*-test analysis

analysis here, and not reject the null hypothesis. Conducting a series of t-tests would increase the familywise error rate, and increase the probability of making a Type I error. Next, Figure 22.4 reports the results of three t-tests. Although the omnibus F-test was not significant, note that the third test, for differences between School 2 and 3 is significant at $\alpha = 0.05$. In this instance we would reject the null hypothesis and conclude that there is a difference between the authoritarianism (Asum) scores of subjects from School 1 and School 2.

Applying different statistical procedures to the same data can produce consistent or inconsistent results.

Using different analytic procedures on exactly the same data, we arrive at two different conclusions. Which is the best? Once again, it depends on your research question. If you have a general interest in the relationship between school and authoritarianism, it would be best to conduct an ANOVA. This would protect against increased familywise error rate and provide conclusions we can have confidence in. However, as we have seen, this may hide small differences between groups. If you especially want to look for differences between School 2 and School 3 – perhaps you suspect differences because School 2 is an elite urban school while School 3 is an impoverished rural school – it would be perfectly legitimate to conduct this single t-test to confirm your suspicions, as long as you conduct only this test, and not the overall ANOVA, or the other two t-tests. This is what is called a *planned comparison*.

The main purpose of statistical analysis is to reveal interesting patterns in a dataset in the most economical and information-rich way. We should not be constrained by a rigid set of rules, but should adapt the type of analysis we use to the purpose of the analysis. Of course, it is of the utmost importance that we do not use incorrect procedures, which produce false or misleading results. If you do use a non-standard type of analysis, it is very important to explain why the procedure has been used, and argue why it is appropriate.

Activity 22.6

Use SPSS® to re-run the analyses reported in Figure 22.3 and Figure 22.4. (Use the data in Figure 22.1)

Defensible reasoned argument

In selecting one statistical procedure over another, the researcher has some influence over the findings that do or do not emerge from a study. Statistical analysis therefore involves reasoned decision-making. The researcher must choose tests wisely, give reasons why certain tests were selected in favour of others, and interpret the results in a way that makes sense to others working in the area.

According to Abelson (1995) there are two opposing approaches to statistical analysis: the *brash* approach and the *stuffy* approach.

Researchers adopt a brash approach when they employ analytic strategies that increase the likelihood of rejecting the null hypothesis. For example, instead of conducting an F-test, a brash researcher would conduct a number of *t*-tests, with increased familywise error rate increasing the probability of falsely rejecting at least one null hypothesis. In contrast to the brash approach, the stuffy approach involves an overly conservative approach to analysis, employing procedures that decrease the likelihood of falsely rejecting the null hypothesis. For example, a stuffy researcher would refuse to use *t*-tests to examine differences between theoretically interesting groups when the F-test is not significant. This could lead the researcher to conclude that there are no significant group differences, when there may in fact be differences between the means of select groups. The brash approach thus makes liberal use of data, rejecting the null hypothesis on the basis of relatively weak evidence in the data, whereas the stuffy approach is conservative, only rejecting the null hypothesis in the light of very strong evidence. Box 22.3 summarises Abelson's rules for brashness and stuffiness.

The researcher has influence on the actual findings that do or do not emerge from a study – either by the statistical procedures employed or the interpretation of the results.

Box 22.1

Abelson's rules for brashness and stuffiness

Rules for brashness
1. Use a one-tailed test.
2. When there is more than one test procedure available, use the one producing the significant result(s).
3. Either include or exclude outliers from your data, depending on which works better.
4. Use the 'hocus-focus' trick, i.e. when several outcomes are tested simultaneously, focus on the one(s) with the best *p*-value(s).
5. State the actual *p*-value but talk around it.

Rules for stuffiness
1. Never use one-tailed tests.
2. Only use a single, predetermined analysis for any dataset.
3. Never exclude outliers.
4. Avoid special focus on any particular result, especially if it is favourable.
5. Stick strictly to a fixed significance level, for example, 0.05, and make no distinctions between outcomes that nearly beat it (e.g. $p < 0.06$) and those far from significance.

Consider Abelson's rules for brashness and stuffiness. For each rule, explain why the brash approach provides a liberal test of the null hypothesis, and the stuffy approach provides a conservative test of the null hypothesis.

Activity 22.7

Abelson recommends that researchers should strive for a middle ground between approaches that are brash (overly liberal use of the data) or stuffy (overly conservative use of the data). Instead of adopting either one or the other approach, statistical procedures should be used flexibly, i.e. in a manner that allows the researcher to detect theoretically important significant differences if they exist, but does not force the data to reveal 'significant effects' that are chance events. If researchers adopt this flexible approach, Abelson suggests that their decision-making should be guided by defensible reasoned argument (see Box 22.2). It is fine to employ procedures that lean either towards brashness or stuffiness, as long as you can provide good reasons for your choices. Most often, these reasons depend on your research question – on what you are trying to find. If you have a specific theoretical interest in the differences between two group means, you can justify selecting the *t*-test over the F-test. If you anticipate the way in which the means differ, you can justify using a one-tailed test. However, if you are merely 'scoping' a large dataset, looking for patterns of difference, you would need to use relatively conservative, stuffy rules, to produce results that will be believable. Statistical analyses that are believable contain high-quality evidence with sizeable, well articulated, and general effects.

Box 22.2

Rules for a defensible reasoned argument
1. Decide on one-tailed, two-tailed, or lopsided tests.
2. Decide on which test to apply to the data.
3. Choose between different calculation formulas.
4. Determine your error rate.
5. Present your findings in an interesting way.

---

1. Decide on one-tailed, two-tailed, or lopsided tests

Suppose we use a *t*-test to determine whether learners from rural schools perform less well in matric final examinations than learners from urban schools. We find that $p = 0.055$. Should we reject the null hypothesis or not? It depends on whether you are using a one- or two-tailed test. A two-tailed test with $\alpha = 0.10$ will have a critical region with $p = 0.05$ in each tail, leading to the conclusion not to reject the null hypothesis. In contrast, we would reject the null hypothesis if we used a one-tailed test with alpha set at 0.10, with $p = 0.10$ in one tail (see Tutorial 8). In this situation it would be liberal (brash) to reject the null hypothesis and conservative (stuffy) not to. Which approach we follow depends on what we already know before conducting the analysis. We would be justified in using a liberal approach if there was (1) a strong theoretical argument or (2) previous statistical evidence that the results of the study were likely to fall only in that tail of the curve. For example, there is much evidence that indicates that learners from rural schools obtain lower matric results than learners from urban schools; and this observation is supported by theory: that rural schools are poorly resourced, and have higher student:teacher ratios than urban schools. In cases such as this, we can justify adopting a liberal approach to the data. In contrast, if we do not have firm expectations about the outcome of a statistical test, it would be better to adopt a more conservative approach, using two-tailed tests, and only rejecting the null hypothesis if the evidence for this is strong.

The tailedness of the test is determined by what we already know about the effect – i.e. from the literature.

The problem that immediately presents is 'What happens if the results fall into the "wrong" tail'? What if we find that the rural school sample has a higher mean matric score than our urban school sample? If we were to make this discovery after using a one-tailed test with α = 0.05, and then switch to a two-tailed test, we would then have a 5% region of rejection in one tail and a 2.5% region of rejection in the other tail. In sum, then, our significance level would be increased to α = 0.075. A compromise would be to use what is known as a *lopsided test*. This would involve having a rejection region of 5% in the expected tail and a very small 0.5% in the wrong tail (see Figure 22.5). This means that we would reject the null hypothesis in the 'wrong' tail only in the light of very strong evidence. The overall probability of rejecting a true null hypothesis is 0.055, which is defensibly close to our accepted two-tailed region of rejection (i.e. 0.05).

Very strong evidence and a conservative or stuffy approach is needed to support unexpected findings.

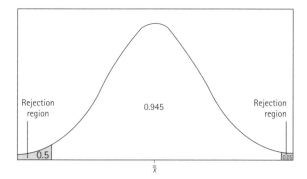

Figure 22.5 Examples of a setup for a 'lopsided' significance test

2. Decide on which test to apply to the data

Often more than one test can be applied to the same data. How do we choose which test is appropriate, given that there is seldom a 'right' test? To simply choose the one that leads to a significant result would be tempting, but brash. The decision-making tree in Figure 22.2 should guide test selection, but there are two other considerations:

a) *Expectations.* Our research questions are informed by theory and/or previous empirical research. If you have strong expectations about the outcome of an analysis – e.g. which means will differ, and the direction of the differences – a more liberal approach is appropriate. Because of the strong expectations, we would need less strong evidence from the data to convince other researchers that our conclusions are sound. For example, in the analysis reported in Figure 22.4, we would be justified in using the more liberal *t*-test only if we have specific expectations about the difference between these two groups.

b) *Properties of the data.* Numerous properties of the data influence test selection. Parametric tests are most powerful, but they can lead to incorrect conclusions if applied to data that do not satisfy certain assumptions. For example, there has been much debate about whether a lack of normality should lead one to use the non-parametric equivalent of the independent samples *t*-test. The Mann-Whitney test uses ranks rather than the original problematically distributed scores, but is has less power than the *t*-test. Since the *t*-test is quite robust to threats to normality, we may choose to use this more powerful parametric statistic. However, in situations where data is very skewed, the Mann-Whitney would be preferred.

The more confident you are about the outcome of the analysis, the more brash you can be. Of course, you need to give good empirical or theoretical reasons for your confidence.

3. Choose between different calculation formulas

Several tests exist as a set of variants which can be used for similar purposes. For example, there are many variants of multiple comparison tests. Some of these procedures (e.g. Tukey's HSD) are more conservative than others (e.g. Fisher's LSD). Choosing between different calculation formulas is similar to choosing between different tests. The appropriate test depends on the *expectations* we have about the outcome of the test *before* we do the analysis. If we have strong theoretical and empirical grounds for expecting particular group means to differ, we may use more liberal calculation formulas that increase the likelihood of rejecting the null hypothesis. However, if we have no prior expectations about the nature of group mean differences, we would select more conservative tests.

4. Determine your error rate

Adopt a conservative approach when conducting numerous test – e.g. when you are 'scoping' your data.

The increased Type I error rate produced by conducting multiple inferential tests is one of the biggest problems facing data analysts. If enough tests are conducted, we are bound to find a 'statistically significant' pattern that is in fact just a random outcome. If we conduct 100 inferential tests all with $\alpha = 0.05$, we expect five tests to be significant even where there are no significant relationships or differences between variables. Where we are conducting numerous inferential tests, it may be wise to adopt a more conservative approach, setting the alpha level slightly lower. On the other hand, we would not want to adopt an overly conservative approach that could lead us to miss something genuinely significant in the data. We must strive for a middle path, adjusting our error rate, at the start of the data analysis, to the number of tests we expect to conduct. If you are conducting multiple inferential tests, you could adopt a more conservative approach by setting your alpha level at 0.01. Whatever you decide, always report exact p-values (provided by SPSS®), as this allows the reader to judge your conclusions for themselves.

5. Interesting and credible presentation

Writing up the results of the analysis is an integral part of doing statistics. Here too the researcher has an influence on what does and does not look significant in the data. The brash approach would be to interpret only the statistics that are significant, and support your expectations. We could use what Abelson calls the hocus-focus trick by focusing only on particular significant findings and making marginal findings seem significant. For example, a result that is not significant at 0.05 may be reported as 'being significant at the 0.07 level', or 'being marginally significant ($p = 0.07$)'. This liberal approach would be very interesting but somewhat misleading. A conservative approach might report all significant p-values with equal weighting but not examine the effect sizes associated with the significant findings. While this would not be misleading, it would also not be very interesting. There is an art to finding a meaningful pattern of associations in the dataset, and then making this the central theme of the write-up. The researcher emphasises especially interesting and important findings, while also presenting findings that are non-significant and/or disconfirming. This will ensure that the presentation is both interesting and credible.

Always report exact p-values and effect sizes.

Sometimes it makes no difference which alternative test or formula you use, what the error rate is, or how you report your results. Sometimes, however, it can make a huge difference. Where it does, the credibility of your statistical argument will depend on reasoned decisions that you make. Where choices between alternatives do exist, we can adopt either a conservative or liberal approach. The advice is simple. Be your own toughest critic. Know your data and be alert to any factors that make the above decisions necessary. Above all, when writing up the results of the analysis, clearly state your rationale for any decisions that you have made.

When reporting your statistical analyses, first provide a statement and a defence of the procedures used.

Conclusion

One of the most difficult aspects of doing statistics is selecting the appropriate statistical procedures to make sense of the data. This is partly a problem of rational decision-making. Certain tests can only be used if certain specified conditions hold. If you use the incorrect test, your conclusions will be wrong. The decision tree in Figure 22.2 will assist you in selecting the correct test. However, there is more to selecting appropriate statistical procedures than using the decision tree. Often multiple methods can be used to analyse the same data. Sometimes these lead to similar conclusions, but sometimes they do not. In these situations we should follow Abelson's advice. We should avoid committing to either a brash or a stuffy approach, and rather make flexible use of approaches that best suit our data, whether they be conservative or liberal.

Worked example

The South African October Household Survey uses a nationally representative sample of all South Africans to gain social statistics. Figure 22.6 provides a sample of 20 cases and ten variables from the survey. We are presented with the data and asked to analyse it. You will need to attempt an analysis of this dataset before reading the following commentary.

Before conducting inferential statistics, the variables must be defined and described. Region, gender, race, and language group

Subject	Region	Gender	Race	Lang	Age	Yrs educ	Mother educ	Income	% income
1	2	1	1	1	61	12	8	97	12
2	2	2	1	2	32	20	20	220	19
3	1	1	0	2	35	20	16	130	4
4	2	9	2	2	26	20	20	350	18
5	2	2	1	4	25	12	6	78	5
6	1	2	0	7	59	10	8	65	22
7	1	1	1	7	46	10	8	115	0
8	2	2	0	7	99	16	5	160	1
9	2	2	2	7	57	10	6	140	0
10	2	2	1	1	64	14	8	180	7
11	1	2	1	6	72	9	12	55	3
12	2	1	0	2	67	12	8	13	8
13	1	2	0	1	33	15	11	180	10
14	1	2	2	2	23	14	12	97	13
15	2	2	2	7	33	12	12	50	3
16	2	1	2	6	59	12	8	12	0
17	1	2	0	4	60	14	6	97	2
18	1	1	2	6	77	9	0	82	8
19	2	2	0	12	52	14	8	145	11
20	1	1	3	5	55	7	98	48	9

Region: urban (1) rural (2); Gender: female (1) male (2); Race: black (0) white (1) coloured (2) Indian (3); Yrs educ = years of education; Mother educ = mother's years of education; Income = annual household income (in R1 000s); % income = percentage of income spent on information (e.g. TV licence, newspapers, books, etc.)

Figure 22.6 Sample data matrix for the October Household Survey

are nominal variables, while the remainder are scale (interval or ratio) variables. Can you see why? The only ambiguous variable is % income. Although percentages have properties of a ratio scale of measurement, the data that we have are skewed, and it might be better to treat % income as an ordinal variable, ranking the sample from lowest to highest in terms of the amount spent on information.

A scan of the boxplots indicates something amiss with the data for mother's education. There is an outlier in the data, and it appears as though there is a data entry error for Subject 20. Frequency tables also indicate a problem for the variable Gender. Can you spot it? When there are errors in the dataset, you should return to the raw data to find the correct entry, or delete the incorrect entry from the data matrix, treating it as missing. The frequency table for Race shows that there was only one Indian person in the sample. We would thus only compare the means of the black, white, and coloured samples in later inferential analyses. Similarly, a number of the categories for the variable Language have low frequencies, and these would need to be excluded from inferential analysis involving this variable.

The next step in our descriptive analysis is to conduct bivariate descriptive analyses. These will help us get an overall picture of how the variables are related to each other. This exercise is often called *scoping* the data. Since we are running a number of inferential tests, we will set $\alpha = 0.01$ for this exercise, thereby reducing the familywise error rate. Three sets of bivariate analyses are used. Cross-tabulations and chi-square analyses are used to determine associations between the nominal variables; correlation coefficients are generated for the scale and ordinal variables; and a series of one-way ANOVAs are used to identify associations between the scale and the nominal variables.

The analyses suggest that although none of the nominal variables are related to each other, the scale variables are. This is useful to know, since it suggests that, if we use these scale variables as independent variables, we will have problems with multicollinearity. The correlation analysis indicates that Income is positively related to Education ($r = 0.714$, $p < 0.0001$) and mother's education ($r = 0.547$, $p = 0.015$). In addition, Mother's education is negatively correlated with Age ($r = -0.63$, $p = 0.004$), and positively correlated with Education ($r = 0.727$, $p < 0.0001$). The outcomes of the one-way ANOVAs indicate that there are no significant relationships between the scale and nominal variables.

Once the descriptive analyses are complete, you should reach a decision about appropriate inferential analyses. Ideally, this decision should be based on theoretical grounds, reflected in your research question. The researchers want to know what variables predict

Income, and thus we know that Income should be the dependent variable in a multivariate analysis. Since we have determined that Income is a continuous variable, and that it is associated only with other continuous variables (Education and Mother's education) we would use multiple regression analysis to build a predictive model. If income were significantly associated with the nominal variables, factorial ANOVA would perhaps have been more appropriate. If income were associated with both continuous and nominal variables, we would first have to convert the continuous variables into categorical variables (e.g. quartiles) and then run a factorial ANOVA.

Create an SPSS® dataset from the October Household Survey data reported in Figure 22.6.
a) Define each of the variables.
b) Compute appropriate descriptive statistics for each of the variables. What conclusions do you reach? Are there any outliers? What is the shape of each distribution? What kind of inferential tests will you use to analyse the data?
c) Conduct inferential tests on the data and report the outcome of the analysis. What research questions were you examining?

Summary

1. Statistical decision-making involves a dual process of rule-following and defensible reasoned argument.

2. Use descriptive statistics to 'scope' or get a feel the data before selecting the appropriate inferential test.

3. To decide which statistical procedure to use, a) determine the level of measurement of your variables, b) determine whether the research question is about relationships or differences, and c) if the research question concerns group differences, determine how many means and variables are to be investigated.

4. Since it is possible to analyse the same data in different ways, sometimes producing different conclusions, it is necessary to adopt a flexible approach to analysis and to defend the choices you make.

Exercises

For each of the following research problems, decide which statistical procedure is most appropriate for analysis of the data. Justify your decision. Once you have decided which procedure is most appropriate, conduct the analysis.

1. An M.A. clinical psychology student is conducting a research project on favoured theoretical models among practising clinical psychologists in Cape Town. The student collects data for 167 clinical psychologists (each psychologist indicates his or her favoured theoretical model), which she reports as follows:

   Freudian: 71; Kleinian: 36; Jungian: 42; Rogerian: 18

   Is there any evidence to suggest that some theoretical models are favoured over others?

2. A researcher suspects that 'rapid smoking', a behavioural therapy devised as a reduction aid for smokers, has no greater effect than a placebo treatment would have. The researcher places an advertisement in a newspaper, through which he recruits 19 subjects, all of whom smoke. He randomly assigns the 19 subjects to the experimental (rapid smoking) and control (placebo) groups (10 in the experimental group, 9 in the control group). The subjects undergo a period of treatment, and the researcher compares the groups in terms of number of cigarettes smoked daily. The results are as follows:

   Experimental: 11, 21, 7, 19, 34, 20, 6, 15, 4, 10

   Control: 39, 28, 43, 47, 38, 31, 30, 27, 40

   Is the researcher's contention supported by this data? Make a point of analysing the data in as many different ways as you can.

3. In Milgram's famous experiment on obedience (Milgram, 1974), one of the critical variables was the proximity of the subject to the victim. Four proximity conditions are reported below, and the maximum voltage administered by each of ten subjects is reported within the cells (in units of 10):

1	2	3	4
45, 38, 26, 34.5, 25, 30, 40, 39, 29, 45	35, 41, 30, 35, 29, 30, 34.5, 38,	20, 16, 31, 39, 29, 31, 30, 29, 10, 23, 3	23, 32, 18 12, 19, 25 17, 20, 25 25

   1 = no contact at all with victim; 2 = baseline condition; 3 = in same room as victim; 4 = has to force victim's hand onto electric plate to deliver shock

   Does obedience vary as a function of proximity?

Section 2

Mathematics and Software Support

TUTORIAL
23

Basic work with numbers

Colin Tredoux

> After studying this tutorial, you should be able to:
> - Carry out the basic arithmetic operations in the correct order.
> - Do simple computations involving negative numbers.
> - Simplify and carry out arithmetic on common fractions.
> - Perform operations on decimal numbers, including conversions to fractions.
> - Define and use the terms frequency, proportion, percentage, and ratio.
> - Carry out calculations involving exponents.

Do you need this chapter?

Some social science students have a long-standing aversion to numbers and any activity with the dreaded word mathematics in it! In an earlier chapter we tried to persuade you that anyone can do the mathematics we require in social science statistics courses. However, some of you have long decided that mathematics is poison, and may have given up the subject relatively early in your schooling. On the other hand, some of you may be quite adept at mathematics, even if you do not have an abiding interest in the discipline.

In order to determine whether you need to work through this tutorial, we ask that you complete the test below. If you give correct answers to fewer than 16 of the 20 questions, we recommend that you work through the tutorial (the answers are at the end of the tutorial). You can use a calculator.

Self-test 23.1

1. $12 \times 32 = ?$
2. $390/15 = ?$
3. $-3 + 4 = ?$
4. $2 - 7 = ?$
5. $-2 \times 3 = ?$
6. $-15/-3 = ?$
7. $\frac{1}{2} + \frac{1}{4} = ?$
8. $\frac{1}{2} \times \frac{1}{4} = ?$
9. $0.6 + 1.3 = ?$
10. $4 \times 0.5 = ?$
11. Express $\frac{2}{10}$ in decimal form.
12. If 3 people in 400 are hemophiliacs, what proportion is this?
13. If 0.3 of the population have blue eyes, how many people in a group of 500 will have blue eyes?
14. Express 0.001 as a percentage.
15. If I score 20% for a test where the total mark was 80, how many marks did I score?
16. If a university spends R3 000 000 on employing science lecturers, and R1 500 000 on employing social science lecturers, what is the ratio of money spent employing these two kinds of lecturers?
17. $9^2 = ?$
18. $3^2 + 4^2 = ?$
19. $\sqrt{16} = ?$
20. $81^{1/4} = ?$

Number systems

Mathematicians recognise a great many *number systems*. For most purposes in statistics, we deal with what may simply be called the *counting numbers* (0, 1, 2, 3, 4 …). These are also commonly known as *integers* or *whole numbers*. When we need to, we will make use of number systems that recognise *negative numbers* (−1, −2, …) and *real numbers* (e.g. $\frac{1}{2}$, 0.1). It is not necessary for us to deal with formal or abstract properties of these systems, since the concern in this section is merely that you brush up some of your arithmetic and algebraic skills.

Elementary operations

The most fundamental or elementary procedures or operations in mathematics are addition, subtraction, multiplication, and division. These operations are represented by symbols we call *operators*. Addition is represented by a plus sign (+), subtraction by a minus sign (−), multiplication by three signs (×, ., *), and division by two signs (/, ÷).

Addition

*The order in which we **add** numbers is not important. Thus, 3 + 4 = 7, and 4 + 3 = 7.*

You should already know how to add single digit numbers, without using a calculator. Consider the following sum:

$$4 + 5 = 9$$

We say that 9 is the *sum* of 4 and 5; in other words, the number 9 results when we add 4 and 5. But note that $5 + 4 = 9$, or more generally:

$$3 + 1 = 4 \quad 1 + 3 = 4 \quad 3 + 8 = 11 \quad 8 + 3 = 11$$
$$2 + 7 = 9 \quad 7 + 2 = 9 \quad 5 + 1 = 6 \quad 1 + 5 = 6$$

The order in which we add numbers is thus unimportant. For example, if we are faced with the expression $4 + 3 + 9 = 16$, then we can re-express this as any of the following:

$$3 + 4 + 9 = 16, \quad \text{or} \quad 9 + 3 + 4 = 16, \quad \text{or} \quad 9 + 4 + 3 = 16$$

In order to break longer sums up, we can use brackets to make the task a bit easier to follow. Thus, $3 + 4 + 9 = 16$ can be written as $(3 + 4) + 9 = 7 + 9 = 16$. The idea is to complete the section in brackets first, and then move on.

Subtraction

*The order in which we **subtract** numbers is important. Thus, 4 − 3 = 1, but 3 − 4 = −1.*

You should also be very familiar with subtraction as an operation. Instead of referring to the outcome of the operation as a sum, we now refer to it as a *difference*. Thus, $6 − 2 = 4$ can be expressed as 'the difference between 6 and 2 is 4'.

Unlike addition, *the order in which we subtract is very important*. Consider that $5 − 3 = 2$, but $3 − 5 = −2$ (2 and −2 are **not** the same number).

When we are faced with long expressions involving subtraction, it is useful to use brackets to simplify the task, thus $10 − 2 − 3 = 5$ can be written as $(10 − 2) − 3 = 8 − 3 = 5$.

Multiplication

You will doubtless already know how to multiply numbers (even if you cannot remember the 17 × table!). When two numbers are multiplied, the result is referred to as the *product*. The order in which numbers are multiplied is unimportant, at least when the expression contains only multiplication. Thus, 6 × 4 = 24, and 4 × 6 = 24.

As with addition and subtraction, it is useful to break long multiplication sums up with brackets, e.g. 5 × 6 × 2 = (5 × 6) × 2 = 30 × 2 = 60.

Note that an additional way of indicating multiplication is to place terms next to each other, in brackets. Thus (4)(3) = 4 × 3 = 12; or (3 + 2)(5 + 1) = 5 × 6 = 30.

*The order in which we **multiply** numbers is not important. Thus, 3 × 4 = 12 and 4 × 3 = 12.*

Division

When we divide, the result is referred to as the *quotient*. The order in which numbers are divided is important. So, 12 ÷ 3 = 4, but 3 ÷ 12 = 0.25.

As with multiplication, it is useful to break long division sums up with brackets, e.g. 50 ÷ 5 ÷ 2 = (50 ÷ 5) ÷ 2 = 10 ÷ 2 = 5.

*The order in which we **divide** numbers is important. Thus, 12 ÷ 3 = 4, but 3 ÷ 12 = 0.25.*

Expressions involving different operations

You will often be faced with arithmetic calculations involving multiple, different operations. For example, 5 + 4 × 3 − 6 ÷ 2. These expressions are best done by using brackets to simplify matters. However, this simplification must be done according to rules of priority regarding the sequence of arithmetic operations. These rules are nicely summarised by the mnemonic BoDMAS (Brackets first, then Division, then Multiplication, then Addition, then Subtraction). Let us apply it to a complicated expression (note that the values in bold were computed in the previous step):

Rules of priority in doing arithmetic:
BoDMAS
Brackets, then Division, then Multiplication, then Addition, then Subtraction.

$$5 + 6 \times (3 + 2) \times 7 - 8 \div 2$$

Step 1:	Work out bracketed section.	5 + 6 × **5** × 7 − 8 ÷ 2
Step 2:	Work out division.	5 + 6 × 5 × 7 − **4**
Step 3:	Work out first multiplication.	5 + **30** × 7 − 4
Step 4:	Work out second multiplication.	5 + **210** − 4
Step 5:	Work out addition.	**215** − 4
Step 6:	Work out subtraction.	**211**

You may find it useful to place brackets around the part of the expression that you work on in each step. Thus, for step 2 above, do this in two parts:

1. Bracket the part of the expression you are working on:
   $5 + 6 \times 5 \times 7 - (8 \div 2)$
2. Do the calculation within the brackets, and replace the brackets and bracket contents with the results of that calculation:
   $5 + 6 \times 5 \times 7 - \mathbf{4}$

It is also useful to know that we can expand expressions inside brackets when multiplication is involved. Thus, $4 \times (3 + 5) = (4 \times 3) + (4 \times 5) = 12 + 20 = 32$. What we have done here is to multiply 4 by each of the numbers inside the brackets.

Exercise 23.1

Answers for all exercises in this tutorial are provided at the end.

1. Determine which of the following expressions are *true*:
   a) $10 (6 + 5) = 60 + 50$ b) $5 (6 + 5) = 35$
   c) $10 (50 + 1) = 500 + 1$ d) $(7/7) (8/4)/2 = 1$
   e) $10 (10 + 10) 10 = 2\,000$ f) $100 \times 6 + 7 \times 4 = 28 + 100 \times 6$
2. Evaluate the following expressions:
   a) $7 (7 + 7/7)$ b) $(7 \times 5 + 3)/(9 \times 2 + 1)$
   c) $12 \times 7 \div 3 - 6 \times 1 \div 6$ d) $(4 + 3) (5 + 2)$

Negative numbers

Although we intuitively think of the counting numbers as starting at 0 and increasing by steps of 1, there is considerable value also in allowing the counting numbers to move in the opposite direction, i.e. to values less than zero. Banks in particular find this is a useful concept – think about the concept of an overdraft. If you have no money in the bank, and then borrow R500 to pay a student loan, how much money have you got? You have R500 less than nothing, which is represented by –R500.

Imagine a *number line*, extending from an infinite negative number to an infinite positive number:

Now, addition can be thought of as moving to the right: $3 + 2$ is the same as starting at 3 and moving two places to the right:

In the same way, we can think of subtraction as moving to the left.

Consider the expression 2 − 3:

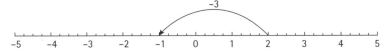

Note that we have ended up to the left of 0. In order to give this expression any meaning, we have to allow numbers to the left of 0 to exist.

There are certain rules we have to follow when we perform operations using negative numbers.

Addition and subtraction with negative numbers

We have said that we can think of addition as moving to the right on the number line, and subtraction as moving to the left on the number line. This is easy to see when we add positive numbers to negative numbers. For example, the number line below shows the operation −2 + 3 = 1:

Adding a negative number to a positive number is equivalent to subtracting a positive number from a positive number, e.g. 3 + (−2) = 3 − 2 = 1.

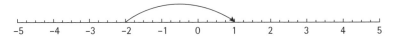

Addition of negative numbers to positive numbers is a bit more difficult, but becomes easier when you understand the multiplication rules for negative numbers. For the moment we will ask you to take it on faith that **adding** *a negative number to a positive number is equivalent to subtracting a positive number from a positive number.* Thus, 3 + (−2) = 3 − 2 = 1. Similarly,

Subtracting negative numbers from positive numbers is equivalent to adding positive numbers to positive numbers. Thus, 3 − (−2) = 3 + 2.

$$3 + (-1) = 3 - 1 = 2 \quad 1 + (-3) = 1 - 3 = -2 \quad 11 + (-20) = -9$$

When we subtract negative numbers from positive or negative numbers, things are a little more complex, but will be easier to grasp when you know the multiplication rules for negative numbers. *Subtracting negative numbers from positive numbers is equivalent to adding positive numbers to positive numbers.* Thus, 3 − (−2) = 3 + 2. The negative signs 'cancel' each other, and produce a positive sign. Similarly:

$$3 - (-1) = 3 + 1 = 4 \quad -5 - (-3) = -5 + 3 = -2 \quad 11 - (-20) = 11 + 20 = 32$$

Multiplication and division with negative numbers

It is easiest to learn how to multiply negative numbers by following rote rules. There are only two rules that need to be learned.

Rule 1 The product of a negative and positive number is a negative number, regardless of which of the multiplying numbers are positive or negative, e.g. −2 × 3 = −6, and 2 × −3 = −6.

Rules for multiplication and division with negative numbers:

- *The product of a negative and a positive number is a negative number.*
- *The product of two negative*

Rule 2 The product of two negative numbers is a positive number, e.g. $-2 \times -3 = 6$.

Similar rules can be specified for division:

Rule 3 The result of dividing either a negative number by a positive number, or a positive number by a negative number, is a negative number, e.g. $-4 \div 2 = -2$, $4 \div -2 = -2$.

Rule 4 The quotient of two negative numbers is a positive number, e.g. $-4 \div -2 = 2$.

Exercise 23.2

numbers is a positive number.

- *The result of dividing either a negative number by a positive number, or a positive number by a negative number, is a negative number.*
- *The quotient of two negative numbers is a positive number.*

1. Evaluate the following expressions:
   a) $36 + (-6)$ b) $13 - 6$
   c) $(-3) + (-4)$ d) $-8 + 1$
   e) $17 - (-4) - 2$ f) $7 + (-1) - (-4) + 2$
2. Evaluate the following expressions:
   a) $-4 \times 3 \times 2$ b) $(-4)(-5)(4)$
   c) $(-6)(-3) \div 3 \times 3$ d) $(-6)(3) + 6 \times 4 + (-2)(-3)$
   e) $(-6)(4) - (-1)(-3)$ f) -1×-1

Fractions

You will surely remember having encountered fractions in your early school years – even if the memories are not entirely pleasant! It is particularly easy to forget the simplifying procedures, and you may find the reminders that follow quite useful.

Fractions are often thought of as 'parts of whole numbers' or 'numbers in between whole numbers'. Look at the number line below, and think of the number the arrow points to. It is neither 2 nor 3, but a number in between these numbers:

We write fractions in what is known as *divisional notation*:

$$\frac{1}{2} \quad \frac{3}{4} \quad \frac{5}{8} \quad \frac{9}{5} \quad \frac{13}{14} \quad \frac{7}{8}$$

We refer to the number 'at the top' as the *numerator* and the number 'at the bottom' as the *denominator*:

$$\frac{\text{numerator}}{\text{denominator}}$$

The denominator tells us how many parts there are in total, and the numerator tells us how many parts of the total we are considering at this point. For example, the fraction $\frac{1}{4}$ might mean that we have cut a cake into four slices, and that each person is given one of these slices.

Likewise, we can cut the line between 0 and 1 into 4, and $^1/_4$ represents one of these devisions.

Addition and subtraction with fractions

The rules for adding and subtracting fractions differ markedly from those for multiplying and dividing fractions, and it is easy to forget or overlook this.

    When we add or subtract fractions, we need to find a *common denominator* before we can proceed. For example, if we wish to evaluate $\frac{1}{2} + \frac{1}{4}$, we have to change them so that the denominators are the same – that is, the denominator value for both fractions should be the same, but the overall value of each fraction should not change. We do this by taking advantage of the fact that fractions can be expressed in different, but equivalent forms. For example, the fraction $\frac{1}{2}$ is equivalent to the fraction $\frac{2}{4}$. (Do you need convincing of this? If we cut the same cake into 2 or 4 pieces, would you have more cake if you had 1 of the 2 pieces, or if you had 2 of the 4 pieces?)

    The simplest way to find a common denominator is to multiply each fraction in the sum (top and bottom) by the denominator of every other fraction in the sum. Thus, for the sum $\frac{1}{2} + \frac{1}{4}$, we get

$\frac{1}{2} \times \frac{4}{4} = \frac{4}{8}$ as a transformed version of the first fraction in the sum,

and $\frac{1}{4} \times \frac{2}{2} = \frac{2}{8}$ as the transformed version of the second fraction. We add the fractions by adding the numerators, and keeping the denominators constant, thus:

$$\frac{1}{2} + \frac{1}{4} = \frac{4}{8} + \frac{2}{8} = \frac{6}{8}$$

Subtraction of fractions follows exactly the same procedure, except that we subtract numerators rather than adding them. For example:

$$\frac{1}{2} - \frac{1}{4} = \frac{4}{8} - \frac{2}{8} = \frac{2}{8}$$

It is usual to transform fractions to their simplest form. This means that we prefer to write $\frac{2}{4}$ as $\frac{1}{2}$. (We saw above that these fractions are equivalent numbers.) This can be achieved by dividing the top and bottom terms by a *common factor* (i.e. a number that divides exactly into both top and bottom). For example, in the answer to the addition problem $\frac{1}{2} + \frac{1}{4}$, we wrote $\frac{6}{8}$, but this can be simplified. Notice that 2 divides into both top and bottom, and the fraction can be simplified:

$$\frac{6 \div 2}{8 \div 2} = \frac{3}{4}$$

We need to develop a rule about how to change the fraction while keeping its value constant:

*To find a **common denominator**, multiply the denominators in the sum by each other (e.g. for the sum $\frac{1}{2} + \frac{1}{4}$, multiply 2 and 4 to get the common denominator 8.*

*Find a **common factor** to simplify fractions.*

When simplifying fractions, whatever you divide the numerator by, you must also divide the denominator by (e.g. to simplify $\frac{2}{4}$, divide top and bottom by 2 to get $\frac{1}{2}$).

Rule 5 When simplifying fractions, whatever you divide the numerator by, also divide the denominator by.

Exercise 23.3

1. Evaluate the following expressions:

   a) $\frac{2}{3} + \frac{1}{4}$ b) $\frac{1}{8} + \frac{3}{4}$

   c) $\frac{1}{9} + \frac{1}{8} + \frac{1}{7}$ d) $\frac{1}{3} - \frac{1}{4}$

   e) $-\frac{1}{2} + \frac{1}{4}$ f) $\frac{7}{2} - \frac{1}{4}$

2. Simplify the following fractions:

   a) $\frac{4}{6}$ b) $\frac{8}{56}$

   c) $\frac{9}{33}$ d) $\frac{9}{36}$

Multiplication and division with fractions

Fractions are multiplied by multiplying the numerators by each other and the denominators by each other.

Contrary to what you might expect, multiplication and division are actually easier for fractions than they are for whole numbers! There is only one complexity, in the case of division.

Fractions are multiplied by multiplying the numerators by each other, and the denominators by each other. Thus:

$$\frac{1}{2} \times \frac{2}{3} = \frac{1 \times 2}{2 \times 3} = \frac{2}{6} = \frac{1}{3}$$

Fraction multiplication frequently produces answers that need simplification, and it is often beneficial to simplify by *cancelling* while multiplying. An example will make this clear:

$$\frac{\cancel{2}}{3} \times \frac{1}{\cancel{2}} = \frac{1}{3}$$

Notice how the 2 on the top is cancelled by the 2 on the bottom. To explain why this is allowable, the sum can be re-written as $\frac{2}{1} \times \frac{1}{3} \times \frac{1}{1} \times \frac{1}{2} = \frac{1}{3}$, which is equivalent to $\frac{2}{2} \times \frac{1}{3} = \frac{1}{3}$. As $\frac{2}{2}$ is simply the number 1, we can ignore multiplication by $\frac{2}{2}$ (i.e. 1), since it does not affect the answer.

Fractions are divided by inverting the fraction you are dividing by, and multiplying the inverted fraction by the remaining, non-inverted fraction.

Fractions are divided in two steps. First we *invert* the fraction we are dividing ('stand it on its head'), and then we multiply the resulting fractions in the sum. To invert a fraction, we simply replace the numerator with the denominator, and the denominator with the numerator. Thus, to invert $\frac{1}{2}$, we write $\frac{2}{1}$. An example should make the process clear:

$$\frac{1}{2} \div \frac{1}{4} = \frac{1}{2} \times \frac{4}{1} = \frac{4}{2} = 2$$

An easy way to conceptualise this is to ask how many quarters there are in a half, and the answer would be 2.

Exercise 23.4

1. Evaluate the following expressions:

   a) $\frac{3}{4} \times \frac{1}{16}$

   b) $\frac{5}{11} \times \frac{11}{5}$

   c) $\dfrac{(\frac{8}{9} \times \frac{3}{11})}{\frac{24}{99}}$

   d) $\frac{5}{11} \div \frac{11}{5}$

   e) $(\frac{5}{10} + \frac{1}{5}) \times \frac{3}{4}$

   f) $(\frac{5}{10} + \frac{1}{5}) \div \frac{3}{4}$

Decimal numbers

A common way of expressing fractions (i.e. numbers that are 'in-between' whole numbers) is as *decimal numbers*. It is more common, for example, to write 0.1 than $\frac{1}{10}$.

Decimal numbers can be broken down into components, i.e.

The easiest way to think of decimal numbers is as transformed versions of common fractions, where the transformation expresses the common fraction in terms of a denominator that is a multiple of ten. Instead of $\frac{1}{10}$ we write 0.1, and instead of $\frac{23}{100}$ we write 0.23, etc. (The decimal point separates a number into a whole number part and a fractional part.) Thus, 2321.93 is 2 thousands + 3 hundreds + 2 tens + 1 unit + 9 tenths + 3 hundredths, or 2000 + 300 + 20 + 10 + 9 + 0.9 + 0.03.

13.26

Fractional part
Decimal point
Whole number part

Addition and subtraction with decimals

Addition and subtraction in the case of decimals is no different from addition and subtraction with whole numbers, except that decimal places must be strictly lined up. A few examples:

2321.93	57.25	918.23	8918.48
+ 47.21	+ 12.90	− 4.06	− 345.12
2369.14	70.15	914.17	8573.36

Multiplication and division with decimals

If you follow a very simple rule, you should have no difficulties multiplying decimals – and arriving at the right answer!

To multiply two decimal numbers, multiply the numbers as if they had no decimal places, and then insert as many decimal places in your answer as there were in total in the original numbers.

Rule 6   To multiply decimal numbers, multiply the numbers as if they had no decimal places, and then insert as many decimal places in your answer as there were in total in the original numbers.

For example, if you are asked to multiply 1.3 by 1.3, you multiply 13 by 13 = 169, and then add two decimal places (since each number had one decimal place) = 1.69. Further examples:

a) $4.7 \times 6.1 = 47 \times 61 = 2867$. Add two decimal places = 28.67

b) $1.23 \times 2.45 = 30135$. Add four decimal places = 3.0135

c) $19.01 \times 14.2 = 269942$. Add three decimal places = 269.942

Although it is a salubrious thing to do these calculations mentally, or on paper, most of us prefer to use a calculator nowadays! If you use a calculator, there will also be no need to use the rule above, since calculators allow you to enter decimal numbers directly.

In the case of division with decimal numbers, there is no need to compute sums manually or mentally if you have a calculator, and we will not demonstrate manual ways of dividing with decimal numbers here.

Converting from fractions to decimals, and from decimals to fractions

In statistical calculations, we frequently need to convert from common fractions to decimal numbers. The easiest way of doing this is to divide – especially if you have a calculator at hand. This is because common fractions are expressed in division notation: $1/4$ *means 'divide 1 by 4'.* Examples:

a) $\frac{9}{36} = 9 \div 36 = 0.25$

b) $\frac{6}{8} = 6 \div 8 = 0.75$

c) $\frac{1}{2} = 1 \div 2 = 0.5$

To convert a decimal number to a fraction, take the fractional component of the decimal number as the numerator, and for the denominator take the number 1 and add as many 0s to it as there are digits in the numerator.

To convert from decimal numbers to common fractions, on the other hand, takes some manual – but uncomplicated – work. Remember from the discussion above that a decimal number can be thought of as fraction with a denominator that is some multiple or power of 10. Thus:

$$0.2 = \frac{2}{10} \qquad 0.87 = \frac{87}{100} \qquad 0.147 = \frac{147}{1000} \qquad 0.9843 = \frac{9843}{10000}$$

You can confirm that these are correct by dividing numerator by denominator. A simple rule for converting decimal numbers to fractions can be derived from these examples.

Rule 7 To convert decimal numbers to fractions, take the fractional component of the decimal number (e.g. for 0.23 take 23) as the numerator, and for the denominator take the number 1 and add as many 0s to it as there are digits in the numerator (e.g. for the numerator 23 add 00 to 1).

For the number 0.23, the numerator will be 23, and the denominator 100, so the fractional form is $\frac{23}{100}$.

Exercise 23.5

1. Evaluate the following expressions:
   a) 0.23 + 0.08
   b) 0.456 − 0.1901
   c) 0.57 × 0.43
   d) 0.34 × (0.45 + 0.12)
   e) 0.4 ÷ 0.5
   f) 0.67 ÷ (0.104 + 0.34)

2. Convert to decimal numbers:
   a) $\frac{1}{47}$
   b) $\frac{3}{7}$
   c) $\frac{4}{3}$
   d) $\frac{437}{1000}$

3. Convert to common fractions:
   a) 0.08
   b) 0.456
   c) 0.5712
   d) 0.005

Frequencies, proportions, percentages and ratios

The notion of *frequency* or *frequencies* plays an important role in statistics, particularly in descriptive methods. Similarly, the notion of a *proportion* is vital if we are to understand probability theory and its use in inferential methods. It is important to master these concepts, and the related concepts introduced in this section, if you are to succeed at statistical analysis.

In many forms of research, we collect units of information. For example, we may ask passers-by in a shopping mall whom they intend to vote for in the national election. We could then count the 'votes' each political party got, and compare the parties. Or we might scrutinise the files of a public hospital and count the number of people who presented with physical trauma sustained in a domestic environment. In each of these cases, we would use the word *frequency* to represent the total number of instances of the event we are interested in. For example, if 120 people vote for the ANC, we say that the frequency (or *frequency count*) in that category is 120.

By itself the frequency of an instance rarely tells us all that we need to know. We need comparative information to make the frequency meaningful. For example, if we also knew that the total frequency of voters in our shopping mall study was 200, then we would be in a better position to make sense of the frequency count of 120 who voted for the ANC. A common way of transforming a frequency, then, is to express it as a *proportion* of the total frequency count. This is achieved by dividing the frequency of the instance by the total frequency.

*A **proportion** is created by dividing how often or numerous something is by the total number of things in the population it is drawn from.*

$$\text{proportion} = \frac{\text{frequency of the instance}}{\text{total frequency count}}, \text{e.g. } 0.6 = \frac{120}{200}$$

To convert a proportion to a percentage, multiply the proportion by 100.

Proportions are themselves often converted to *percentages* to make their meaning still clearer. This is done by multiplying the proportion by 100, and expressing the resulting sum as 'percentage' or '%'. This gives a rate per 100 units. For example, we discover in the second of our research projects listed above, that 120 000 people have been admitted to the public hospital in the past year, and that 3 560 of these presented with domestic abuse. The proportion of people presenting for domestic abuse is thus $\frac{3560}{120\,000} = 0.03$. If we express this as a percentage, we get $0.03 \times 100 = 3\%$. In other words, of every 100 people admitted to the hospital in the previous year, three presented with trauma from domestic abuse. The conversion from proportion to percentage is thus:

$$\text{percentage (\%)} = \text{proportion} \times 100$$

The converse of this calculation, namely to derive a frequency from a proportion or percentage, is also useful. Thus, if we read that 21% of people in South Africa are HIV-positive, and we also know that there is a total population of 43 million people in South Africa, then we can convert this percentage into a frequency, using:

$$\text{frequency} = \text{proportion} \times \text{total frequency}$$

For the HIV calculation:

$$\text{frequency} = 0.21 \times 43\,000\,000 = 9\,030\,000$$

Another *numerical index* that is frequently used to assist interpretation is the ratio of one frequency to another. Here the comparative value is not the total frequency, but the frequency of instances in another category. Let us imagine that we find from our hospital study that 3 000 of the 3 560 people presenting with domestic abuse are female. One way of expressing this in an interpretable manner is to express the presenting rate among females in relation to males. The usual way of doing this is as a *ratio*. For example, we divide the number of presenting females by the number of presenting males:

$$\frac{3000}{560} = 5.357$$

In other words, for every male who presents, there are 5.357 females who present (or we can say that the ratio is 1 : 5.357).

1. Irma Pogg-en-poel conducts a survey in 'The Edge' rave club in Johannesburg. She records the location of body piercings for each person in the nightclub (assume that each 'pierced' person has one piercing only). Her results are shown in the *frequency distribution* below:

   Eyebrow 8; nose 13; ear 48; nipple 6; navel 23; genital 2.

   a) Calculate the ratio of genital piercings to ear piercings.
   b) What percentage of people have eyebrow piercings?
   c) What proportion of people have navel piercings?
   d) For every person who has a pierced nipple, how many people have a pierced nose?

2. If a student spends 43% of her time sleeping, how many hours are left in the day for other activities?

3. If a certain university spends 18% of its funds on remuneration for management, and its total budget was R450 000 000, how much was management paid?

Powers, exponents, roots

Mathematics is to a large extent concerned with *notation* and ways of simplifying operations and calculations. For example, when we write the common fraction $\frac{1}{2}$, we mean 1 divided by 2. Simplification by notation becomes exceptionally useful when we apply it to complicated and repetitive operations. Consider the following multiplication problem: $5 \times 5 \times 5 \times 5 \times 5 \times 5 \times 5 \times 5$. Completing this calculation manually is almost as laborious as writing it!

When we wish to simplify problems involving multiplication, we use what are called *powers*. For example, 5×5 can be written as 5^2 ('the square of 5', or '5 squared'). In general, the power (2 in this example) expresses number of times the base (5 in this example) is multiplied by itself. Thus:

$5 \times 5 = 5^2 = 25$ (the second power of 5, or 5 to the power of 2)
$5 \times 5 \times 5 = 5^3 = 125$ (the third power of 5, or 5 to the power of 3)
$5 \times 5 \times 5 \times 5 = 5^4 = 625$ (the fourth power of 5, or 5 to the power of 4)

There are some useful properties relating to the addition, subtraction, multiplication, and division of powers, but since these are rarely required in elementary statistical work we will not detail them here. However, it is worth knowing the following two special powers:

1. *The power '1'.* Any number raised to the power '1' is merely itself.

Thus, $5^1 = 5$, $9^1 = 9$, etc. By extension, any number that does not have its power declared is implicitly raised to the power 1 (e.g. when we write 5×3, we could equally write $5^1 \times 3^1$).

2. *The power '0'.* Any number raised to the power '0' is *unity*, in other words, the number 1. Thus $5^0 = 1$, $3^0 = 1$, etc.

A concept closely related to that of a *power* is the *root*. We have seen that the number 25 can be written as 5^2, but we can also express this fact as $\sqrt{25} = 5$. What we mean is that the number which when multiplied by itself gives 25 is 5, and we use the *square root* sign $\sqrt{\ }$ to symbolise this property. Just as there are third, fourth, and larger powers, so there are cubed, quartic, and smaller roots. For example:

$$\sqrt[2]{25} = 5, \text{ the square root (although it is customary not to show the 2)}$$

$$\sqrt[3]{125} = 5, \text{ the cube root}$$
$$\sqrt[4]{625} = 5, \text{ the quartic root}$$

Finding the values of expressions that raise numbers to the powers, or that take roots, is best done by electronic calculator or computer. Most calculators have an exponent button that looks much like the following: $\boxed{x^{\wedge}y}$

To find the value of 5^3, for example, press 5, then press the exponent button, and then press 3.

Powers and roots are collectively known as *exponents*, and it is possible to express roots in the same superscripted way in which powers are expressed. In general, a root is transformed to an exponent by raising the number-to-be-rooted by a fractional exponent, where the numerator of the fraction is always 1, and the denominator is the number corresponding to the 'dimension' of the root. Thus:

$$\sqrt{5} = 5^{\frac{1}{2}} \qquad \sqrt[3]{81} = 81^{\frac{1}{3}}$$

Exercise 23.7

1. Evaluate the following expressions (use a calculator!):
   a) 9^2
   b) 9^4
   c) $9^2 - 9$
   d) $9^{\frac{1}{2}}$
   e) $\sqrt{54}$
   f) $\sqrt{81} - 9^2$
   g) $5*\sqrt{9}$
   h) $(10 - 8)^2$
2. Transform the following expressions or numbers to use exponents:
   a) 7×7
   b) $(6 \times 6 \times 6) - (3 \times 3 \times 3)$
   c) 81
   d) 625

How much do you think you have improved? Test yourself with the following test, which is a 'parallel form' of that at the beginning of the chapter. If you score more than 16 out of 20, you can expect to cope with the kind of mathematical material in this book. If not, we suggest that you work through this tutorial again, doing lots more examples, which can be downloaded from the webpage on the CD.

1. $12 \times 8 = ?$
2. $225/5 = ?$
3. $2 + (-4) = ?$
4. $-2 - 8 = ?$
5. $-4 \times -2 = ?$
6. $6/-2 = ?$
7. $\frac{1}{2} - \frac{1}{8} = ?$
8. $\frac{1}{3} \times \frac{1}{2} = ?$
9. $1.7 - 0.2 = ?$
10. $0.25 \times 0.5 = ?$
11. Express $\left(\frac{8}{20}\right)$ in decimal form.
12. If in a light-bulb factory 2 out of every 160 bulbs fail, what proportion is this?
13. If 0.01 of the population suffers from schizophrenia, how many students in a class of 300 will succumb to the disease?
14. Express 0.125 as a percentage.
15. If 80% of Psychology students are women, how many women will there be in a class of 600?
16. If on average a student spends R500 on textbooks, and R3 000 on beer, what is the book to beer expense ratio?
17. $6^2 = ?$
18. $2^3 + 5^0 = ?$
19. $\sqrt{169} = ?$
20. $81^{\frac{1}{4}} = ?$

Answers to Self-test 23.1

1. 384
2. 26
3. 1
4. −5
5. −6
6. 5
7. $\frac{3}{4}$
8. $\frac{1}{8}$
9. 1.9
10. 2

Answers to Self-test 23.2

1. 96
2. 45
3. −2
4. −10
5. 8
6. −3
7. $\frac{3}{8}$
8. $\frac{1}{6}$
9. 1.5
10. 0.125

Answers to Self-test 23.1

11. 0.2
12. 0.0075
13. 150
14. 0.1%
15. 16
16. 2:1
17. 81
18. 25
19. 4
20. 3

Answers to Self-test 23.2

11. 0.4
12. 0.0125
13. 3
14. 12.5%
15. 480
16. 1:6
17. 36
18. 9
19. 13
20. 3

Answers to exercises

Exercise 23.1
1. a) true, b) false, c) false, d) true, e) true, f) true
2. a) 56, b) 2, c) 27, d) 49

Exercise 23.2
1. a) 30, b) 7, c) –7, d) –7, e) 19, f) 12
2. a) –24, b) 80, c) 18, d) 12, e) –27, f) 1

Exercise 23.3
1. a) $^{11}/_{12}$, b) $^{7}/_{8}$, c) $^{191}/_{504}$, d) $^{1}/_{12}$, e) $-^{1}/_{4}$, f) $^{13}/_{4}$
2. a) $^{2}/_{3}$, b) $^{1}/_{7}$, c) $^{3}/_{11}$, d) $^{1}/_{4}$

Exercise 23.4
1. a) $^{3}/_{64}$, b) 1, c) 1, d) $^{25}/_{121}$, e) $^{21}/_{40}$, f) $^{14}/_{15}$

Exercise 23.5
1. a) 0.31, b) 0.2659, c) 0.2451, d) 0.1938, e) 0.8, f) 1.509
2. a) 0.021, b) 0.428571, c) 1.333, d) 0.437
3. a) $^{2}/_{25}$, b) $^{57}/_{125}$, c) $^{357}/_{625}$, d) $^{1}/_{200}$

Exercise 23.6
1. a) 1:24, b) 8%, c) 0.23, d) $^{13}/_{6}$, or 2.17
2. 13.68 hours
3. R81 000 000

Exercise 23.7
1. a) 81, b) 6561, c) 72, d) 3, e) 7.35, f) –72, g) 15, h) 4
2. a) 7^2, b) $6^3 - 3^3$, c) 9^2, d) 5^4

24

Equations, substitution, and summation

Colin Tredoux

After studying this tutorial, you should be able to:
- Identify constants and variables in descriptions of problems.
- Solve equations with one unknown term.
- Evaluate summation expressions, given problem data.

Do you need this tutorial?

As we indicated in the previous tutorial, many students do not have sufficient mathematical preparation for statistics courses. It may be a good idea for you to work through the material in the present tutorial, but it might also be of little value to you. If you decided that you needed to work through the previous tutorial, then you will probably need to work through this one too. If you decided that you did not need to work through that material, and are uncertain about whether you need to work through the present tutorial, we ask that you complete the test that follows. If you give correct answers to fewer than 12 of the 15 questions, we recommend that you work through the tutorial (the answers are at the end of the tutorial). You may use calculators.

Solve the following equations for x:

1. $x + 3 = 4$
2. $x + 3 = 2$
3. $-x + 2 = 1$
4. $x + y - 2 = 8$
5. $x/2 + 7 = -43$
6. $z = (x - \mu)/\sigma$

Evaluate the following expressions for $x = \{4, 3, 2\}$, $k = 5$, $y = \{8, 1, 2\}$:

7. Σx
8. Σx^2
9. $\Sigma(x - y)$
10. Σk
11. Σkxy
12. $(\Sigma x)^2$
13. $\Sigma y^2 - (\Sigma x)^2$
14. $\Sigma(y - 1)$
15. $\Sigma x/n$

Some basic terms

*Quantities that do not change are called **constants** (e.g. the speed of light).*

In statistics, we frequently deal with *variables, constants, equations,* and *coefficients*. It is useful to have some idea of what these terms mean before we outline operations and procedures typically applied to them.

It is very handy to use a symbol, letter, or some other means to refer to an object. Imagine how difficult it would be to talk about the country South Africa if a name did not exist for it! Mathematicians exploit this function of language to the fullest. The radius of a circle, the speed of light, specific gravity, the operations of addition, exponentiation, etc. are all assigned letters or symbols that denote them. This is done in several ways.

1. Numbers or values that do not change (within a particular context) are called *constants*. There are many well-known examples in the physical world that satisfy this condition, e.g. c, the speed of light ($\approx$300 000 km/s in a vacuum), used in Einstein's famous formula, $E = mc^2$.

__Variables__ are entities that can exhibit change in their quantity (e.g. height, across a sample of children).

2. Objects or entities that show change in their quantity are called *variables* and are referred to by symbols or letters. Thus, x might refer to the Full Scale Intelligence Quotient as measured in a group of children – 'x' would have many different values across the children. Similarly, we could use y to refer to height, in a sample of 100 people.

3. Symbols are often combined in a kind of 'sentence form' (e.g. $F = \frac{9}{5} + 32$). This form of sentence is known as an *equation*, since the left-hand side of the statement equates (i.e. is equal) to the right-hand side of the statement:

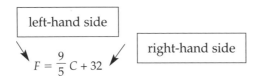

left-hand side

right-hand side

$$F = \frac{9}{5}C + 32$$

4. Equations are usually formed from combinations of variables, constants, and the basic arithmetic operations (addition, subtraction, multiplication, and division). We refer to a value in the equation by which another value is to be multiplied as a *coefficient* of the other value. Thus, in the example above, $\frac{9}{5}$ is the coefficient of C.

As a general rule, whatever you do to one side of an equation, you must do to the other side. If you remove an added value from one side of the equation by subtracting it, you must subtract the same value from the other side. If you remove a value that one side is being divided by, by multiplying by that same value, then you must multiply the other side by the same value too. Simply, what this amounts to is the *shortcut rule that you can remove a value from one side of the equation, across the equals sign, but that you must do the opposite mathematical operation with that value once it is inserted into the other side of the equation.*

Equations

Equations are put to a number of typical uses in mathematics. In the first place, they can be used to translate from one scale of measurement to another. Thus, the equation $F = \frac{9}{5}C + 32$ translates from degrees Celsius to degrees Fahrenheit (both are scales of measurement for temperature). For example, we can *substitute* 40 for $C°$ in the equation, and complete the calculations:

$$F° = \frac{9}{5}C° + 32 = \frac{9}{5} \times 40 + 32 = 72 + 32 = 104$$

Another typical use is to express problems in the form of an equation, so that solutions can be found for one or more of the variables in the equation. This often has great practical value. Imagine that you are doing the family shopping at your local supermarket, and you only have R12 left. You want as many toilet rolls as you can get for your R12. Each toilet roll costs 75c. In order to solve this problem, we notice that we can write the following statement (in mathematical notation):

Equations consist of two parts – a *left-hand side*, and a *right-hand side*, connected by an equals sign. The sides are different but equivalent ways of expressing the same property or characteristic.

Another formula that translates from one scale into another: miles*1.60943 = kilometres

total price = (price per unit) × (number of units)

We start by substituting known values into the equation. Thus, 'total price' = R12, and the 'price per unit' = R0.75. With a little bit of algebraic manipulation, we can rewrite the statement as:

R12 ÷ R0.75 = number of units

The answer to this is 16 units, or toilet rolls.

Solving equations

*The usual way to solve an equation for an unknown (e.g. **x**) is to use arithmetic operations to 'isolate' **x** until it is alone on the left- or right-hand side of the equation.*

The second use of equations, as outlined in the example above, is the most important for our purposes. The point is to find the value of an unknown element in the equation, when all the other elements are known. In other words, what value, when substituted for the unknown element or variable, 'satisfies' the equation – i.e. makes it true? If our equation is

$$3 + x = 5$$

then only the value 2 will substitute for x so that the statement is true.

Most of the work in solving equations is finding out how to manipulate the equation so that we can determine the value of the unknown element (here 'x'). The fundamental insight is that *any operation carried out on both sides of an equation does not affect its truth-value*. To see this, examine the following statements. The first is obviously true. Now convince yourself that the rest are also true, and notice that all we have done in each case is to apply the same operation to each side of the equation:

*When attempting to isolate **x** in an equation, arithmetic operations carried out on one side of the equation must also be carried out on the other side.*

$$x = x$$
$$3x = 3x$$
$$x - 3 = x - 3$$
$$x + 3 = x + 3$$
$$x/3 = x/3$$

Let us take an earlier example to solve:

$$3 + x = 5$$

In the example above, we can subtract 3 from both the left-hand and right-hand sides of the equation and be confident that we have not corrupted the equation. Thus,

$$3 + x - 3 = 5 - 3$$
$$(3 - 3) + x = 2$$
$$x = 2$$

Note that we could have applied the shortcut rule here by simply taking + 3 accross the equals sign and making + –3.

A strategy that works very well is to isolate x on one side of the equation. This can be a little tricky, but should pose no real problem if you remember to 1) apply the rules of precedence regarding arithmetic operations, and 2) perform one simplification at a time.

Let us do a slightly more complex example. Solve for C in the equation below, given that $F° = 120°$.

$$F = \frac{9}{5} C + 32$$

Step 1: Replace F with 120:

$$120 = \frac{9}{5} C + 32$$

Step 2: Eliminate all the constants. Since the equation is adding 32 on the RHS (right-hand side), subtract 32 from **both** sides of the equation:

$$120 - 32 = \frac{9}{5} C + 32 - 32$$

$$88 = \frac{9}{5} C$$

Step 3: Since the equation is multiplying the unknown (C) by $\frac{9}{5}$, divide both sides by $\frac{9}{5}$:

$$88 \div \frac{9}{5} = \frac{9}{5} C \div \frac{9}{5}$$

$$88 \times \frac{5}{9} = \frac{9}{5} C \times \frac{5}{9}$$

$$48.889 = C$$

> **Shortcut rule:** whatever you do to one side of an equation, you must do to the other side. If you remove an added value from one side of the equation by subtracting it, you must subtract the same value from the other side. If you remove a value that one side is being divided by, by multiplying by that value, you must multiply the other side by the same value.

In principle, it is not necessary to know the *value* of any of the elements of the equation, if we accept that the goal is to express a particular unknown in terms of the other elements of the equation. For example, we can write the equation for converting from Celsius to Fahrenheit in terms of Celsius rather than Fahrenheit, as initially presented in this chapter.

$$F = \frac{9}{5} C + 32$$

$$F - 32 = \frac{9}{5} C$$

$$(F - 32) \frac{5}{9} = C$$

1. Substitute:
   a) Given the equation $y = 2x + 7$, calculate y for: i) $x = 1$, ii) $x = -3.5$, iii) $x = \frac{-2}{8}$
   b) Given the equation $y = 4x - 4$, calculate y for: i) $x = 0$, ii) $x = -2$, iii) $x = \frac{2}{3}$
   c) Given the equation $y = x^3 - 1$, calculate y for: i) $x = -1$, ii) $x = 2$, iii) $x = 0$

2. What is the coefficient of x?
   a) $y = 3x + 2$
   b) $y = 4x^2 + 2x + 1$
   c) $y = (3 + 5)x + 2$
   d) $12 \times 4x$

3. Solve for x:
   a) $y = 2x + 7$
   b) $y = 3 - 6x$
   c) $y + 3 = x - 2$
   d) $y = \frac{x}{2} + 8$
   e) $y = 2x + k$, given that k is a constant
   f) $2y = 2x + k$, given that k is a constant
   g) $y = ax + b$, given that both a and b are constants

Summary

Of all the mathematical skills you require for statistics, the ability to read and work with *summation operators* is perhaps the most important. You may have observed how much effort is made in mathematics to find simplifying notation. We saw in the previous tutorial how efficiently this is achieved for multiplication by using exponents.

In the social sciences, we typically use abbreviated summation notation, e.g. Σx rather than $\sum_{i=1}^{n} x_i$

In statistics, we are frequently faced with large datasets, and we are required to conduct fairly laborious, repetitive calculations involving addition. For this reason, we use notation that greatly simplifies our work, making it more readable and efficient. To express addition, we use the Greek letter Σ (capital sigma). For example, to add the numbers $\{3, 1, 5\}$, we use the notation:

$$\sum_{i=1}^{n} x_i$$

Some explanation is required here! We read this as: 'the sum of x, from the first value of x to the nth value of x'.

$$\sum_{i=1}^{n} x_i = x_{i=1} + x_{i=2} + x_{i=3} = 3 + 1 + 5 = 9$$

'i' is thus called an *index variable*, since it indexes the variable x. n refers to the last value of x in the given set. The notation can be varied in many ways. For example:

$$\sum_{i=2}^{3} x_i$$

Scientific calculators have many built-in functions that make summation calculations easy (e.g. Σx, Σx^2.)

This notation means that you should add the second and third values in the set for the variable x.

In practice, you will usually add the entire set, and for that reason it is common in social science statistics texts to omit the superscripts and subscripts. We will follow this simplification here. In other words, when we mean $\sum_{i=1}^{n} x_i$, we will merely write Σx.

Summation notation can be used to denote more complex operations than just adding a set of first-power numbers. We can add squares, differences, and indeed any result of an arithmetic operation. This is demonstrated below for the datasets $x = \{5, 7, 3, 1\}$, and $y = \{4, 2, 1, 6\}$

Squares: $\Sigma x^2 = 5^2 + 7^2 + 3^2 + 1^2 = 25 + 49 + 9 + 1 = 84$
Differences: $\Sigma(x - y) = (5 - 4) + (7 - 2) + (3 - 1) + (1 - 6) = 1 + 5 + 2 - 5 = 3$
Cross products: $\Sigma xy = (5 \times 4) + (7 \times 2) + (3 \times 1) + (1 \times 6) = 20 + 14 + 3 + 6 = 43$

Arithmetic operations can also be applied to the outcomes of expressions involving summation. Assuming the same datasets as above:

$$(\Sigma x)^2 = (5 + 7 + 3 + 1)^2 = (16)^2 = 256$$
$$(\Sigma x - (\Sigma \tfrac{x}{n}))^2 = [(5 + 7 + 3 + 1) - (5/4 + 7/4 + 3/4 + 1/4)]^2 = (16 - 4)^2 = 144$$

There are a number of rules that make manual summation operations much easier. In the example just above, we divided each x in the term $(\Sigma \frac{x}{n})$ by n, but a rule tells us that $(\Sigma \frac{x}{n})$ is equivalent to $\frac{(\Sigma x)}{n}$. There are a number of these rules, but we will not detail them here, since it is all much more easily done on your calculator! Most reasonable quality calculators have summation functions, and for the price of three movie tickets you will be able to purchase one. Several tutorials in this book (e.g. Tutorials 3 and 4) explain how to use calculators for statistical calculations, and we suggest that you work through the sections dealing with summation (see especially Box 3.1).

A couple of rules that are important, and that your calculator will not be able to solve for you, concern how to work with constants in summation notation. Consider the following expressions, where $x = \{7, 3, 9\}$ and $k = 6$:

$$\Sigma x = 7 + 3 + 9 = 19$$
$$\Sigma k = k + k + k = 6 + 6 + 6 = 18 = 3 \times 6 = nk$$
$$\Sigma kx = (6 \times 7) + (6 \times 3) + (6 \times 9) = 42 + 18 + 54 = 114 = 6 \times 19 = k\Sigma x$$

*Rules for using con-
stants in summation
terms:*
- $\Sigma k = nk$
- $\Sigma kx = k\Sigma x$

In other words:

1. When you sum a constant, you simply multiply it by the number of data points in the set it is associated with. In the example above, we multiplied the constant, 6, by the number of items in the data set, 3, to get 18 as our result. The rule can be stated as $\Sigma k = nk$.

2. When you sum a multiple of a constant, you multiply the *sum* of the variable by the constant, i.e. the constant moves to the front of the summation sign. The rule can be stated as $\Sigma kx = k\Sigma x$.

The best way to get on top of summation calculations is to do as many practice calculations and exercises as possible.

Examples

Calculate a) to j), where $k = 4$, $x = \{2, 4, 6, 8, 3\}$ and $y = \{-3, 5, 3, 6, 4\}$:
a) Σx b) Σy c) Σx^2 d) Σy^2 e) Σxy f) $(\Sigma x)^2$ g) $(\Sigma y)^2$ h) $\Sigma x\Sigma y$
i) Σkx^2 j) $\Sigma k\Sigma x^2$

a) $\Sigma x = 2 + 4 + 6 + 8 + 3 = 23$
b) $\Sigma y = -3 + 5 + 3 + 6 + 4 = 15$
c) $\Sigma x^2 = 2^2 + 4^2 + 6^2 + 8^2 + 3^2 = 4 + 16 + 36 + 64 + 9 = 129$
d) $\Sigma y^2 = -3^2 + 5^2 + 3^2 + 6^2 + 4^2 = 9 + 25 + 9 + 36 + 16 = 95$
e) $\Sigma xy = (2 \times -3) + (4 \times 5) + (6 \times 3) + (8 \times 6) + (3 \times 4)$
    $= -6 + 20 + 18 + 48 + 12 = 92$
f) $(\Sigma x)^2 = 23^2 = 529$
g) $(\Sigma y)^2 = 15^2 = 225$
h) $\Sigma x\Sigma y = 23 \times 15 = 345$
i) $\Sigma kx^2 = k\Sigma x^2 = 4 \times 129 = 516$
j) $\Sigma k\Sigma x^2 = nk\Sigma x^2 = 20 \times 129 = 2\ 580$

Exercise 24.2

1. For all 3 of the following datasets, calculate a) to i) below (use calculators):
   a) $x = 4.2, 3.5, 6.7, 8.6$ $y = 3.5, 2.3, 7.8, 8.5$
   b) $x = 12, 19, 16, 18, 35$ $y = 19, 13, 23, 18, 11$
   c) $x = 102, 121, 231, 143, 119$ $y = 112, 98, 231, 119, 103$

   a) Σx b) Σx^2 c) $(\Sigma x)^2$ d) Σy e) Σy^2 f) $(\Sigma y)^2$ g) Σxy
   h) $\Sigma x^2 - (\Sigma x)^2$ i) $\frac{(\Sigma y^2 - (\Sigma y)^2)}{n - 1}$ j) $\Sigma x\Sigma y$

2. For the datasets x, y and z, below, calculate a) to i)

x	2	6	4	5	5	1
y	3	6	5	2	2	1
z	4	2	8	1	2	7

a) Σx b) Σz c) Σy^2 d) $(\Sigma x)^2$ e) Σxy f) $\frac{\Sigma xy}{2}$

g) $\Sigma(x-4)(y-3)$ h) $(\Sigma z^2 x)/\Sigma y$ i) $\sum\limits_{i=1}^{2} y_i$

Solve the following equations for x:

1. $x - 1 = 4$
2. $-x + 4 = 2$
3. $x \div 2 = 1$
4. $x + 2x - y = 8$
5. $x^2/2 + 7 = 43$
6. $z = (x + \mu)/\sigma$

Evaluate the following expressions for $x = \{5, 1, 2\}$, $k = 5$, $y = \{9, 7, 2\}$:

7. $\Sigma x/n$
8. $\Sigma(x^2)$
9. $\Sigma(x - y)^2$
10. Σnk
11. Σxy
12. $(\Sigma x)^2$
13. $\Sigma x^2 - (\Sigma x)^2$
14. $\Sigma(y - k)$
15. $\Sigma x^2/n$

Solutions to Self-test 24.1

1. $x = 1$
2. $x = -1$
3. $x = 1$
4. $x = 10 - y$
5. $x = -100$
6. $x = z\sigma + \mu$
7. 9
8. 29
9. -2
10. 15
11. 195
12. 81
13. -12
14. 8
15. 3

Solutions to Self-test 24.2

1. $x = 5$
2. $x = 2$
3. $x = 2$
4. $x = \frac{(8 + y)}{2}$
5. $x = \sqrt{72}$
6. $x = z\sigma - \mu$
7. 2.7
8. 30
9. 52
10. 45
11. 56
12. 64
13. -34
14. 3
15. 10

Solutions to exercises

Exercise 24.1

1. a) i) 9   ii) 0   iii) 6.5

    b) i) −4   ii) −12   iii) $-\frac{4}{3}$

    c) i) −2   ii) 7   iii) −1

2. a) 3
    b) 2
    c) 8
    d) 48

3. a) $x = (y - 7)/2$
    b) $x = (3 - y)/6$
    c) $x = y + 5$
    d) $x = 2y - 16$
    e) $x = (y - k)/2$
    f) $x = (2y - k)/2$
    g) $x = (y - b)/a$

Exercise 24.2

1. 1st dataset
    a) 23
    b) 148.74
    c) 529
    d) 22.1
    e) 150.63
    f) 488.41
    g) 148.11
    h) −380.26
    i) −112.59
    j) 508.3

    2nd dataset
    a) 100
    b) 2 310
    c) 10 000
    d) 84
    e) 1 504
    f) 7 056
    g) 1 552
    h) −7 690
    i) −1 388
    j) 8 400

3rd dataset
a) 716
b) 113 016
c) 512 656
d) 663
e) 100 279
f) 439 569
g) 105 917
h) −399 640
i) −84 822.5
j) 474 708

2. a) 23
b) 24
c) 79
d) 529
e) 83
f) 41.5
g) 10

Reading and understanding graphs

Lance Lachenicht

After studying this tutorial, you should be able to:
- Understand and interpret simple line graphs.
- Understand and interpret simple category plots.
- Draw simple line graphs.
- Draw simple category plots.

*A **graph** is a way of making numerical information **visual**, so that patterns and relationships can be clearly seen.*

Social science research makes extensive use of graphs and charts. Graphs are intended to make things easier for you. A good graph reveals things that might otherwise be obscure or difficult to understand. A *graph* is a way of making numerical information *visual*, so that patterns and relationships can be clearly seen.

About graphs

A man you may have heard about in other contexts, called René Descartes (b. 1596), invented graphical illustration while lying in bed recovering from an illness. Lying on his back, feeling bored, Descartes kept his mind occupied by studying a crack spreading across the ceiling (see Figure 25.1).

The thought occurred to him that to find any point or small spot on the ceiling, we need two measurements. One measurement is not enough, but two measurements will exactly locate any point on the ceiling. Thus, a particular point could be exactly three metres from the edge of the ceiling near your feet, and two metres from the left-hand ceiling edge.

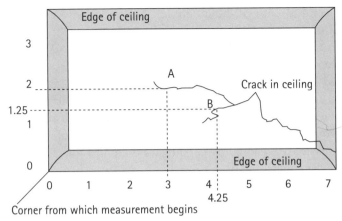

Points A and B are located by means of two measurements

Figure 25.1 Locating a point on the crack in Descartes' ceiling

It is quite simple: you start by taking those two edges of the ceiling as your base or '0' lines. Then, from any point on the ceiling you can obtain a pair of numbers that exactly locate the point (each number being a measurement from one of the two edges or base lines). Figure 25.1 illustrates this for two different points on Descartes' ceiling.

However, Descartes was more interested in the fact that we can start from pairs of numbers and place them as points in space. Given any pair of numbers, we can locate them as a unique point on a surface (such as a ceiling, or a sheet of paper) if we have base lines on the surface from which to plot the point. Even more interesting for Descartes was the fact that if you have a series of many pairs of numbers linked together by some rule, they will form a line. (A line, for our purposes, is just an accumulation of many points.) The characteristics of the line – whether it runs up or down, whether it slopes forward or backwards, whether it is curved or straight, etc. – show the kind of rule that links the pairs of numbers. We will examine this in more detail after giving some examples.

The (x,y) pairs Descartes used as the basis for describing his ceiling are often referred to as Cartesian co-ordinates.

Activity 25.1

Do you think we could extend Descartes' co-ordinate system to describe three-dimensional objects (we would then have x, y, and z axes)? Do you think we could extend the co-ordinate system beyond that? Can you think of uses for a multi-dimensional co-ordinate system?

Example 1: Study and leisure hours

You decide to plan your day. There are only 24 hours in it. A little self-observation and consultation of your lecture timetable show that 14 hours of each day will be spent sleeping, having meals, and attending lectures. Only 10 hours are left to divide between study and leisure activities.

There are many ways in which you could divide your 10 hours – at one extreme you could spend all 10 at leisure and none at study. That would be unsatisfactory, because you might not pass your exams. You could also spend all 10 hours studying. That too would be unsatisfactory, because you would become bored with studying and you would lack exercise. Between these extreme choices there are many possible divisions. We set out 7 of them in Table 25.1

It is possible to represent the data in Table 25.1 as pairs of data points, i.e. (0, 10), (2, 8) ... (10, 0), rather than in tabular format.

Table 25.1 Seven combinations of leisure and study time

	A	B	C	D	E	F	G
Leisure hours:	10	8	7	6	4.5	2.5	0
Study hours:	0	2	3	4	5.5	7.5	10
TOTAL	10	10	10	10	10	10	10

Here we have two lists of numbers. One set gives the possible leisure hours and the other the possible study hours. However, these sets of numbers are dependent on each other. Each leisure time number is paired with a study time number. If we only have 10 free hours, then spending 10 hours at recreation means that it is impossible to study at all. However, spending 4 of the 10 hours studying means that there can only be 6 hours left for recreation. Similarly, spending 25% of your 10 hours (i.e. $2\frac{1}{2}$ hours) at leisure means that you must have $7\frac{1}{2}$ hours in which to study. The link between the two sets of numbers is therefore quite simple: together they must add up to 10.

The study time/leisure time example reveals the kind of situation that graphs illustrate: a series of pairs of numbers linked together by some rule. The graph based upon these pairs of numbers appears in Figure 25.2. In the figure, the vertical line (|) at the left, and the horizontal line (——) at the bottom correspond to the two edges of Descartes' ceiling. Each is divided into a numbered scale, and the meaning of the numbers is given by the labels, 'Hours of study time' (horizontally) and 'Hours of leisure time' (vertically). The slanting line with points marked A through G is the actual graph illustrating the relationship between study time and leisure time.

*The **horizontal** or x-axis is placed at the bottom of the graph. The **vertical** or y-axis is placed at the left of the graph.*

The horizontal line is the *horizontal axis*, sometimes called the *x-axis*. The horizontal axis is just a useful line for measuring distances in the horizontal dimension. In the study time/leisure time example, one member of each number pair must stand for a certain number of study hours. In the figure, the study time number has been given to the horizontal dimension of the graph. The horizontal axis provides a

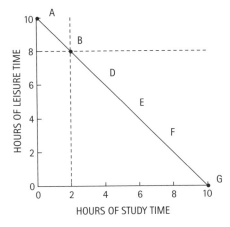

Figure 25.2 Graph of the data in Table 25.1

scale for dividing this dimension into numbers between 0 and 10, with 0 at the extreme left and 10 at the extreme right.

The horizontal or *x*-axis is placed at the bottom of the graph as a matter of custom and convenience. You can think of it as a kind of sliding line that could be moved vertically up or down the diagram – much as you would move a ruler up or down the page, always keeping it completely horizontal. For example, look at the 2 mark on the *x*-axis. Above it is a broken line extending up to point B. Any point on this broken line stands for 2 study hours, because it is 2 measuring units away from the left-hand edge. If the horizontal axis were to be moved upwards, the 2-mark on that axis would touch every point on the broken line up to and beyond B, and it would only touch points on this line.

Activity 25.2

Drawing a few graphs is helpful in learning about them. On a piece of paper, redraw Figure 25.2.
1. Label your axis lines.
2. Pick a scale for each axis – i.e. choose how much distance on the axis you are going to use to represent one hour.
3. Record as many pairs of numbers as you please (e.g. 1 and 9 hours, 30 minutes and 9.5 hours, etc.) on the graph.

Your plotted points should lie along a line comparable to AG in Figure 25.2. After you are satisfied that this is true, draw in the line that represents all the possible points you could mark if you had the time and patience. You cannot possibly find any 'add-up-to-10' combination that does not fall on the line. The beauty of the line AG, however, is not simply that it includes all the points that satisfy the linking rule (adding up to 10), but that it includes *only* those points. In other words, the line has no point that does not meet the linking rule that determines the two sets of numbers you are graphing.

Similarly, the vertical line at the left of the graph is the *y*-axis or the vertical axis. It is a measuring line that could be moved from the left to the right across the diagram measuring amounts of leisure time. Thus any point on the broken horizontal line running from the *y*-axis through B, stands for 8 hours of leisure time.

Given the two axes, their position at the bottom and at the left of the graph is convenient because they perform a service for each other. In Figure 25.2, the vertical axis is primarily the measuring line for leisure time, but because of its position it is also the zero line for study time. Any point that falls on this line represents no time spent studying. Similarly, any point on the horizontal axis represents 0 leisure hours.

*The lower left-hand corner at which the two axes meet is called the **origin**.*

The lower left-hand corner at which the two axes meet is called the *origin*. It signifies 0 leisure hours and 0 study hours. (*Note:* Not all graphs have a double zero origin.)

Example 2: The relation between word length and recognition latency

One concept/tool that cognitive scientists use to explore the mind is 'mental chronometry' (a 'chronometer' is a very precise clock). This involves an attempt to determine how long different tasks take. From the length of time required for each mental process, researchers can work out the complexity and nature of the task. Suppose you decided to study the effect of word length (measured in letters) on the time needed for a research participant to push a button. Pushing the button would show that the research participant had recognised and understood the word (the subject's 'recognition latency' for the words, in technical jargon). You would expect that the longer words would take longer to recognise than the shorter words (the clocks needed to measure such a relationship would have to be very precise).

Suppose that you present a group of ten research participants with six sets of five words. In this task the first set of words is three letters long, the second set is four letters long, the third set is five letters long, etc. until the sixth set of words that are eight letters long. The words are presented on a computer screen in a random order (i.e. no particular order at all), and the researcher requires that participants push a button as soon as they recognise the word. In each case the computer measures the delay between presentation of the word and the participant pushing the button, showing that her or she had recognised the word. The computer then calculates an average 'response latency' score for each of the six sets of words of different lengths. Table 25.2 sets out these average scores. Try to sketch this graph before looking at the solution, shown in Figure 25.3.

Table 25.2 Response latencies for words of different
           lengths

Word length (letters):	3	4	5	6	7	8
Word recognition latency (msec.):		510	540	565	585	610	630

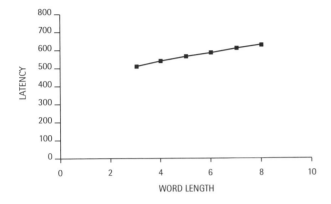

Figure 25.3 Graph of the data in Table 25.2

Example 3: A preference curve

A special type of curve is found whenever preferences are dealt with.
Consider the relationship between a person's enjoyment of a bath and
the temperature of the bath water. In psychology, we often refer to a
person's enjoyment or lack of enjoyment as the person's *hedonic tone*.
(*Hedonic* means 'of pleasure'.) Suppose we measured hedonic tone on
a five-point scale with zero (0) being the point of indifference – the
person finds the bath water neither unpleasant nor pleasant. A very
pleasant experience is assigned the number 1, and an extremely pleasurable experience (maximum enjoyment) is assigned the number 2.
On the other hand, an unpleasant experience (very little enjoyment) is
given the number –1, and an extremely unpleasant experience is given
the number –2. The hedonic scale then ranges from –2 to 2 and would
look something like: –2 –1 0 +1 +2.

Table 25.3 The enjoyment of baths at different
           temperatures

Temperature (C°):	0	10	20	30	40	50	60	70	80	90
Hedonic tone:	–2	–1	–.5	0	1	2	1.8	.5	–.5	–2

Suppose we run an experiment where we ask participants to get into baths where the water has different temperatures. Sometimes the participants want to jump out the baths almost immediately, at other times they want to linger (perhaps the length of time they linger in the bath could be used as an alternative measure of hedonic tone?). Each participant takes ten baths, each bath at a different set temperature. After each bath, the participant is asked to rate how pleasurable the bath was in terms of the five-point hedonic tone rating scale. Table 25.3 sets out the average scores for 20 subjects. Try to sketch the graph before looking at the solution in Figure 25.4

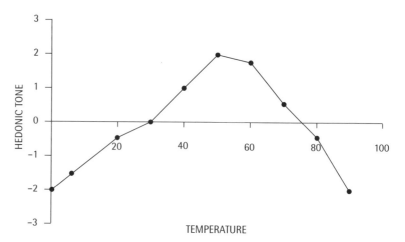

Figure 25.4 Graph of the data in Table 25.3

The direction of the line

*If the line points downwards (from left to right), it has a **negative** (or **inverse**) slope.*
*If the line points upwards (from left to right), it has a **positive** slope.*

In the 'study time vs leisure time' graph, the line slopes downwards from left to right, but in the 'response latency vs word length' graph, the line slopes upwards from left to right. The downward slope of the study/leisure graph illustrates the trade-off between study time and leisure time – more study time has the consequence that you will have less leisure time. In terms of the graph, if you are to stay on the line, you must inevitably follow the downward movement of the line – and this means that you have to give up some leisure time to have more study time. The increase in one member of the number pair is associated with a decrease in the other member of the pair.

*If the slope of the line is constant, it is a straight line, and is said to be **linear**.*
*If the slope of the line is not constant, it is a curved line, and is said to be **non-linear**.*

We are now trying to describe the graph line in terms of what happens to it as we start following the line at the left and move towards the right. Think of the line as the path traced by a point that moves towards the right, always satisfying the requirements of the linking rule as it does so.

In the study/leisure example, an increase of one hour in study time means a decrease of one hour in leisure time. Graphically, this means a straight line falling constantly to the right. We describe such graphs as depicting *inverse* relationships.

In the 'response latency for words of different lengths' graph, the line does not slope downwards but upwards. Increasing the length of the word increases the length of time that a person needs to respond to the word. There is a *positive* relationship between the pairs of numbers: an increase in one number of the pair leads to an increase in the other number of the pair. Can you work out whether the increase is (roughly) constant for all pairs of numbers?

In the 'bath water preference' curve, there is initially an increasing relationship between both numbers of the pair (the line initially slopes upwards like the 'word length latency' graph), but the curve seems to reach a peak and then slope downwards like the study/ leisure graph.

Figure 25.5 contains six different graphs. In each of these graphs x signifies the amount being measured horizontally, and y the amount being measured vertically. Each graph depicts a different direction and/or curvature of the line. Graphs (a), (d), and (c) have a *negative* slope (on average), whereas (e) and (f) have a *positive* slope (on average). Graphs (a), (b), (d), and (e) are *straight-line* graphs (i.e. with a *constant slope*), whereas (c) and (f) are *non-linear* graphs (i.e. with a slope that changes at different x,y locations).

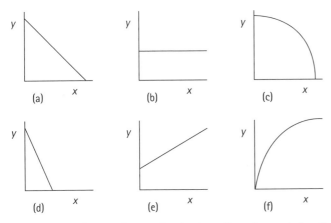

Figure 25.5 Six graphs, varying in slope, linearity, and direction

Points to remember

1. When you encounter a graph, always establish what is being measured on the horizontal axis and what is being measured on the vertical axis.
2. The line on the graph always measures some form of relationship between two items or variables. Behind the line are two sets of numbers linked together, pair by pair.

3. Notice which way the line runs. If it rises to the right, it means that as one number in each pair of numbers increases, the other number increases too. If the line falls as it moves to the right, then the paired numbers change inversely. As one goes up the other goes down.
4. If the pairs of numbers are related by a constant amount, the graph will depict a straight line. But if the pairs of numbers are related by varying amounts (increasing, decreasing, etc.), then the graph will depict a curved line.

When graphs are used to show relationships between variables, knowing the exact pairs of numbers behind the graph is often not very important. Of greater importance may be such questions as: Is the line rising or falling from left to right? Is the line straight or curved?

Graphing numbers by categories

When we considered the relation between leisure and study time, we were considering the relation between two sets of numbers (those representing leisure hours, and those representing study hours). It sometimes happens that we have to consider the relation between a set of numbers and a set of categories. Suppose you had the class test results for five students. Their results could be tabulated as in Table 25.4. Here the categories we are concerned with refer to different students, and the numbers we are concerned with are the percentage marks they obtained in their test. A student does not sound

Table 25.4 Class test results for five students

	Dumisani	Peter	Sandra	Kajal	Precious
Test %:	80	60	67	70	64

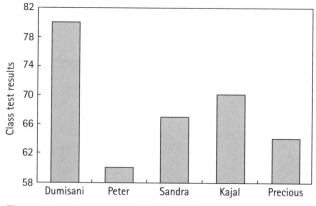

Figure 25.6 Bar graph of data in Table 25.4

like a category but of course it is possible to think of each student as a set containing only one member. Instead of students, we could have been presenting the average percentage marks for whole classes. Although the link in the above table is between students (non-numeric) and numbers (percentage marks), it is still possible to present this information graphically. Each number will be paired with a category, and the categories will be assigned an arbitrary amount of space on the graph. (See Figure 25.6.)

Graphing numbers by categories is very important in many social science studies. Consider a study of memory in four-year-old and eight-year-old children. Each child in the study is instructed to remember a list of 12 words. After being presented with the words, the children are asked to wait five minutes, and then the experimenter comes back and asks the child to repeat the words she or he remembers. The number of words the child remembers is the child's 'memory score'. Suppose, after one such study, the experimenter obtains the results in Table 25.5. These can be represented by either a line graph or a bar graph. (See Figure 25.7.)

Table 25.5 Uninstructed memory for words in children

Age (years):	four	eight
Number of words remembered:	3	7.5

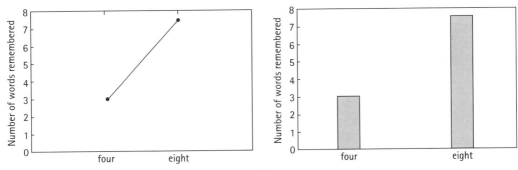

Figure 25.7 Bar graph and line graph of data in Table 25.5

Suppose a subsequent researcher discovers this finding (which seems to be that older children remember more words than younger children). This researcher believes that there is no deficit of memory in young children. Instead, he thinks that perhaps the young children are merely ignorant of the limits of their own memory, and in not realising that they will forget the words, they do not rehearse them. So he speculates that if the younger children are instructed in some techniques to enhance memory, they will perform as well as, or nearly as well as, the older children. The researcher decides that it will be easy to instruct the children in the use of rehearsal – they will be told to repeat the words over and over to themselves until the researcher returns and asks them what words they remember. Naturally, the researcher believes that it will be important to assess whether rehearsal helps the older children as well as the younger children.

So this is what the researcher does. He has two conditions in his experiment: an 'uninstructed condition' where neither of the two groups of children are told how to remember the words, and a 'rehearsal condition' in which both the four-year-old and eight-year-old groups of children are told to remember the words by saying them over and over until the experimenter comes back and asks them what they remember.

In this *two-condition study*, the researcher obtains the results in Table 25.6.

Table 25.6 Instructed and uninstructed memory in children

	Uninstructed		Rehearsal instruction	
Age (years)	four	eight	four	eight
No. of words remembered	2.5	8	8	9.5

Activity 25.3

Try to construct a line graph of the test results of Table 25.6. What would you do if the table had 100 names in it?

These findings can be drawn using one graph with two lines on it (each line depicting a different condition of the experiment). See Figure 25.8.

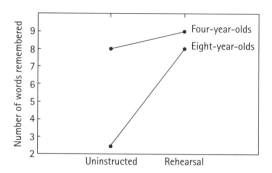

Figure 25.8 Categorised line graph of data in Table 25.6

Figure 25.9 shows four graphs depicting possible outcomes of 'two-condition' experiments carried out upon two categories of subjects. In each case the dependent variable score (number of words remembered) is shown as y in the graphs, the two age-group categories (four and eight years) are assigned to the x-axis, and the two conditions are labelled R and U (Rehearsal and Uninstructed).

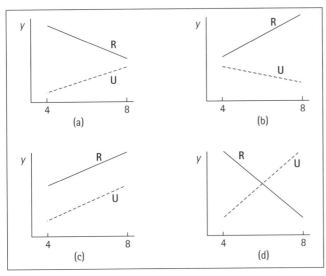

Figure 25.9 Four graphs, depicting possible outcomes of two–condition experiments

Activity 25.4

Try to interpret each of the patterns in Figure 25.9. What are the results of the study in each case?

Exercises

1. Fill in the missing numbers. In Figure 25.2, point **D** stands for _____ leisure hours and for _____ study hours.

2. Fill in the missing word. Take any point inside the triangle formed by the two axes and the line AG in Figure 25.2 (i.e. below and to the left of AG). The pair of measurements for any such point must together total _____ than 10.

3. Plot a graph depicting the relationship between response latency and length of words using the data in Table 25.2. Notice that it is not sensible to attempt to start the graph from zero milliseconds! Notice also in this graph that you do not know the linking rule that relates the points to one another – part of the point of the research is to discover whether there is such a linking rule.

4. Which of the six diagrams in Figure 25.5 illustrates an inverse relation (positive change in one and a negative change in the other) between x and y?

5. In which of the diagrams in Figure 25.5 is y's response to a change in x zero?

6. In which of the diagrams in Figure 25.5 do you find a positive relation (i.e. a positive change in x is accompanied by a positive change in y) rather than an inverse relation between x and y?

7. Imagine that graph (d) in Figure 25.9 depicts the outcome of the instructed and uninstructed memory research with four- and eight-year-old children. Explain what the results depicted in the graph would mean for the experiment.

8. The following table reports the average price of gold on the London bullion market for five consecutive years. Draw a line graph and bar graph of the data. When should you have invested in gold to make the most profit in the period in question? When should you have sold the gold in order to make the most profit?

1990	1991	1992	1993	1994
$265	$255	$275	$295	$290

9. Blood pressure is measured as two variables – *systolic blood pressure* and *diastolic blood pressure*. Below is a table reporting average systolic and diastolic measures for cardiac risk patients who have undergone three different treatment regimens. Draw a graph of the data, including both blood pressure readings on the same graph.

	Bypass	Stent	Transplant
Systolic	90	110	150
Diastolic	50	75	120

Statistical tables

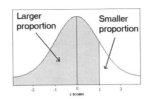
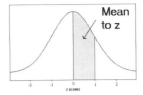

Table A1.1: z-table – the standard normal distribution

z	Smaller p	Larger p	Mean to z	z	Smaller p	Larger p	Mean to z	z	Smaller p	Larger p	Mean to z
0	0.50000	0.50000	0.00000	0.65	0.25785	0.74215	0.24215	1.3	0.09680	0.90320	0.40320
0.01	0.49601	0.50399	0.00399	0.66	0.25463	0.74537	0.24537	1.31	0.09510	0.90490	0.40490
0.02	0.49202	0.50798	0.00798	0.67	0.25143	0.74857	0.24857	1.32	0.09342	0.90658	0.40658
0.03	0.48803	0.51197	0.01197	0.68	0.24825	0.75175	0.25175	1.33	0.09176	0.90824	0.40824
0.04	0.48405	0.51595	0.01595	0.69	0.24510	0.75490	0.25490	1.34	0.09012	0.90988	0.40988
0.05	0.48006	0.51994	0.01994	0.7	0.24196	0.75804	0.25804	1.35	0.08851	0.91149	0.41149
0.06	0.47608	0.52392	0.02392	0.71	0.23885	0.76115	0.26115	1.36	0.08692	0.91308	0.41308
0.07	0.47210	0.52790	0.02790	0.72	0.23576	0.76424	0.26424	1.37	0.08534	0.91466	0.41466
0.08	0.46812	0.53188	0.03188	0.73	0.23270	0.76730	0.26730	1.38	0.08379	0.91621	0.41621
0.09	0.46414	0.53586	0.03586	0.74	0.22965	0.77035	0.27035	1.39	0.08226	0.91774	0.41774
0.1	0.46017	0.53983	0.03983	0.75	0.22663	0.77337	0.27337	1.4	0.08076	0.91924	0.41924
0.11	0.45620	0.54380	0.04380	0.76	0.22363	0.77637	0.27637	1.41	0.07927	0.92073	0.42073
0.12	0.45224	0.54776	0.04776	0.77	0.22065	0.77935	0.27935	1.42	0.07780	0.92220	0.42220
0.13	0.44828	0.55172	0.05172	0.78	0.21770	0.78230	0.28230	1.43	0.07636	0.92364	0.42364
0.14	0.44433	0.55567	0.05567	0.79	0.21476	0.78524	0.28524	1.44	0.07493	0.92507	0.42507
0.15	0.44038	0.55962	0.05962	0.8	0.21186	0.78814	0.28814	1.45	0.07353	0.92647	0.42647
0.16	0.43644	0.56356	0.06356	0.81	0.20897	0.79103	0.29103	1.46	0.07215	0.92785	0.42785
0.17	0.43251	0.56749	0.06749	0.82	0.20611	0.79389	0.29389	1.47	0.07078	0.92922	0.42922
0.18	0.42858	0.57142	0.07142	0.83	0.20327	0.79673	0.29673	1.48	0.06944	0.93056	0.43056
0.19	0.42465	0.57535	0.07535	0.84	0.20045	0.79955	0.29955	1.49	0.06811	0.93189	0.43189
0.2	0.42074	0.57926	0.07926	0.85	0.19766	0.80234	0.30234	1.5	0.06681	0.93319	0.43319
0.21	0.41683	0.58317	0.08317	0.86	0.19489	0.80511	0.30511	1.51	0.06552	0.93448	0.43448
0.22	0.41294	0.58706	0.08706	0.87	0.19215	0.80785	0.30785	1.52	0.06426	0.93574	0.43574
0.23	0.40905	0.59095	0.09095	0.88	0.18943	0.81057	0.31057	1.53	0.06301	0.93699	0.43699
0.24	0.40517	0.59483	0.09483	0.89	0.18673	0.81327	0.31327	1.54	0.06178	0.93822	0.43822
0.25	0.40129	0.59871	0.09871	0.9	0.18406	0.81594	0.31594	1.55	0.06057	0.93943	0.43943
0.26	0.39743	0.60257	0.10257	0.91	0.18141	0.81859	0.31859	1.56	0.05938	0.94062	0.44062
0.27	0.39358	0.60642	0.10642	0.92	0.17879	0.82121	0.32121	1.57	0.05821	0.94179	0.44179
0.28	0.38974	0.61026	0.11026	0.93	0.17619	0.82381	0.32381	1.58	0.05705	0.94295	0.44295
0.29	0.38591	0.61409	0.11409	0.94	0.17361	0.82639	0.32639	1.59	0.05592	0.94408	0.44408
0.3	0.38209	0.61791	0.11791	0.95	0.17106	0.82894	0.32894	1.6	0.05480	0.94520	0.44520
0.31	0.37828	0.62172	0.12172	0.96	0.16853	0.83147	0.33147	1.61	0.05370	0.94630	0.44630
0.32	0.37448	0.62552	0.12552	0.97	0.16602	0.83398	0.33398	1.62	0.05262	0.94738	0.44738
0.33	0.37070	0.62930	0.12930	0.98	0.16354	0.83646	0.33646	1.63	0.05155	0.94845	0.44845
0.34	0.36693	0.63307	0.13307	0.99	0.16109	0.83891	0.33891	1.64	0.05050	0.94950	0.44950
0.35	0.36317	0.63683	0.13683	1	0.15866	0.84134	0.34134	1.65	0.04947	0.95053	0.45053
0.36	0.35942	0.64058	0.14058	1.01	0.15625	0.84375	0.34375	1.66	0.04846	0.95154	0.45154
0.37	0.35569	0.64431	0.14431	1.02	0.15386	0.84614	0.34614	1.67	0.04746	0.95254	0.45254
0.38	0.35197	0.64803	0.14803	1.03	0.15151	0.84849	0.34849	1.68	0.04648	0.95352	0.45352
0.39	0.34827	0.65173	0.15173	1.04	0.14917	0.85083	0.35083	1.69	0.04551	0.95449	0.45449
0.4	0.34458	0.65542	0.15542	1.05	0.14686	0.85314	0.35314	1.7	0.04457	0.95543	0.45543
0.41	0.34090	0.65910	0.15910	1.06	0.14457	0.85543	0.35543	1.71	0.04363	0.95637	0.45637
0.42	0.33724	0.66276	0.16276	1.07	0.14231	0.85769	0.35769	1.72	0.04272	0.95728	0.45728
0.43	0.33360	0.66640	0.16640	1.08	0.14007	0.85993	0.35993	1.73	0.04182	0.95818	0.45818
0.44	0.32997	0.67003	0.17003	1.09	0.13786	0.86214	0.36214	1.74	0.04093	0.95907	0.45907
0.45	0.32636	0.67364	0.17364	1.1	0.13567	0.86433	0.36433	1.75	0.04006	0.95994	0.45994
0.46	0.32276	0.67724	0.17724	1.11	0.13350	0.86650	0.36650	1.76	0.03920	0.96080	0.46080
0.47	0.31918	0.68082	0.18082	1.12	0.13136	0.86864	0.36864	1.77	0.03836	0.96164	0.46164
0.48	0.31561	0.68439	0.18439	1.13	0.12924	0.87076	0.37076	1.78	0.03754	0.96246	0.46246
0.49	0.31207	0.68793	0.18793	1.14	0.12714	0.87286	0.37286	1.79	0.03673	0.96327	0.46327
0.5	0.30854	0.69146	0.19146	1.15	0.12507	0.87493	0.37493	1.8	0.03593	0.96407	0.46407
0.51	0.30503	0.69497	0.19497	1.16	0.12302	0.87698	0.37698	1.81	0.03515	0.96485	0.46485
0.52	0.30153	0.69847	0.19847	1.17	0.12100	0.87900	0.37900	1.82	0.03438	0.96562	0.46562
0.53	0.29806	0.70194	0.20194	1.18	0.11900	0.88100	0.38100	1.83	0.03362	0.96638	0.46638
0.54	0.29460	0.70540	0.20540	1.19	0.11702	0.88298	0.38298	1.84	0.03288	0.96712	0.46712
0.55	0.29116	0.70884	0.20884	1.2	0.11507	0.88493	0.38493	1.85	0.03216	0.96784	0.46784
0.56	0.28774	0.71226	0.21226	1.21	0.11314	0.88686	0.38686	1.86	0.03144	0.96856	0.46856
0.57	0.28434	0.71566	0.21566	1.22	0.11123	0.88877	0.38877	1.87	0.03074	0.96926	0.46926
0.58	0.28096	0.71904	0.21904	1.23	0.10935	0.89065	0.39065	1.88	0.03005	0.96995	0.46995
0.59	0.27760	0.72240	0.22240	1.24	0.10749	0.89251	0.39251	1.89	0.02938	0.97062	0.47062
0.6	0.27425	0.72575	0.22575	1.25	0.10565	0.89435	0.39435	1.9	0.02872	0.97128	0.47128
0.61	0.27093	0.72907	0.22907	1.26	0.10383	0.89617	0.39617	1.91	0.02807	0.97193	0.47193
0.62	0.26763	0.73237	0.23237	1.27	0.10204	0.89796	0.39796	1.92	0.02743	0.97257	0.47257
0.63	0.26435	0.73565	0.23565	1.28	0.10027	0.89973	0.39973	1.93	0.02680	0.97320	0.47320
0.64	0.26109	0.73891	0.23891	1.29	0.09853	0.90147	0.40147	1.94	0.02619	0.97381	0.47381

z	Smaller p	Larger p	Mean to z	z	Smaller p	Larger p	Mean to z	z	Smaller p	Larger p	Mean to z
1.95	0.02559	0.97441	0.47441	2.6	0.00466	0.99534	0.49534	3.3	0.00048	0.99952	0.49952
1.96	0.02500	0.97500	0.47500	2.61	0.00453	0.99547	0.49547	3.4	0.00034	0.99966	0.49966
1.97	0.02442	0.97558	0.47558	2.62	0.00440	0.99560	0.49560	3.5	0.00023	0.99977	0.49977
1.98	0.02385	0.97615	0.47615	2.63	0.00427	0.99573	0.49573	3.6	0.00016	0.99984	0.49984
1.99	0.02330	0.97670	0.47670	2.64	0.00415	0.99585	0.49585	3.7	0.00011	0.99989	0.49989
2	0.02275	0.97725	0.47725	2.65	0.00402	0.99598	0.49598	3.8	0.00007	0.99993	0.49993
2.01	0.02222	0.97778	0.47778	2.66	0.00391	0.99609	0.49609	3.9	0.00005	0.99995	0.49995
2.02	0.02169	0.97831	0.47831	2.67	0.00379	0.99621	0.49621	4	0.00003	0.99997	0.49997
2.03	0.02118	0.97882	0.47882	2.68	0.00368	0.99632	0.49632	4.1	0.00002	0.99998	0.49998
2.04	0.02068	0.97932	0.47932	2.69	0.00357	0.99643	0.49643	4.2	0.00001	0.99999	0.49999
2.05	0.02018	0.97982	0.47982	2.7	0.00347	0.99653	0.49653				
2.06	0.01970	0.98030	0.48030	2.71	0.00336	0.99664	0.49664				
2.07	0.01923	0.98077	0.48077	2.72	0.00326	0.99674	0.49674				
2.08	0.01876	0.98124	0.48124	2.73	0.00317	0.99683	0.49683				
2.09	0.01831	0.98169	0.48169	2.74	0.00307	0.99693	0.49693				
2.1	0.01786	0.98214	0.48214	2.75	0.00298	0.99702	0.49702				
2.11	0.01743	0.98257	0.48257	2.76	0.00289	0.99711	0.49711				
2.12	0.01700	0.98300	0.48300	2.77	0.00280	0.99720	0.49720				
2.13	0.01659	0.98341	0.48341	2.78	0.00272	0.99728	0.49728				
2.14	0.01618	0.98382	0.48382	2.79	0.00264	0.99736	0.49736				
2.15	0.01578	0.98422	0.48422	2.8	0.00256	0.99744	0.49744				
2.16	0.01539	0.98461	0.48461	2.81	0.00248	0.99752	0.49752				
2.17	0.01500	0.98500	0.48500	2.82	0.00240	0.99760	0.49760				
2.18	0.01463	0.98537	0.48537	2.83	0.00233	0.99767	0.49767				
2.19	0.01426	0.98574	0.48574	2.84	0.00226	0.99774	0.49774				
2.2	0.01390	0.98610	0.48610	2.85	0.00219	0.99781	0.49781				
2.21	0.01355	0.98645	0.48645	2.86	0.00212	0.99788	0.49788				
2.22	0.01321	0.98679	0.48679	2.87	0.00205	0.99795	0.49795				
2.23	0.01287	0.98713	0.48713	2.88	0.00199	0.99801	0.49801				
2.24	0.01255	0.98745	0.48745	2.89	0.00193	0.99807	0.49807				
2.25	0.01222	0.98778	0.48778	2.9	0.00187	0.99813	0.49813				
2.26	0.01191	0.98809	0.48809	2.91	0.00181	0.99819	0.49819				
2.27	0.01160	0.98840	0.48840	2.92	0.00175	0.99825	0.49825				
2.28	0.01130	0.98870	0.48870	2.93	0.00169	0.99831	0.49831				
2.29	0.01101	0.98899	0.48899	2.94	0.00164	0.99836	0.49836				
2.3	0.01072	0.98928	0.48928	2.95	0.00159	0.99841	0.49841				
2.31	0.01044	0.98956	0.48956	2.96	0.00154	0.99846	0.49846				
2.32	0.01017	0.98983	0.48983	2.97	0.00149	0.99851	0.49851				
2.33	0.00990	0.99010	0.49010	2.98	0.00144	0.99856	0.49856				
2.34	0.00964	0.99036	0.49036	2.99	0.00139	0.99861	0.49861				
2.35	0.00939	0.99061	0.49061	3	0.00135	0.99865	0.49865				
2.36	0.00914	0.99086	0.49086	3.01	0.00131	0.99869	0.49869				
2.37	0.00889	0.99111	0.49111	3.02	0.00126	0.99874	0.49874				
2.38	0.00866	0.99134	0.49134	3.03	0.00122	0.99878	0.49878				
2.39	0.00842	0.99158	0.49158	3.04	0.00118	0.99882	0.49882				
2.4	0.00820	0.99180	0.49180	3.05	0.00114	0.99886	0.49886				
2.41	0.00798	0.99202	0.49202	3.06	0.00111	0.99889	0.49889				
2.42	0.00776	0.99224	0.49224	3.07	0.00107	0.99893	0.49893				
2.43	0.00755	0.99245	0.49245	3.08	0.00104	0.99896	0.49896				
2.44	0.00734	0.99266	0.49266	3.09	0.00100	0.99900	0.49900				
2.45	0.00714	0.99286	0.49286	3.1	0.00097	0.99903	0.49903				
2.46	0.00695	0.99305	0.49305	3.11	0.00094	0.99906	0.49906				
2.47	0.00676	0.99324	0.49324	3.12	0.00090	0.99910	0.49910				
.48	0.00657	0.99343	0.49343	3.13	0.00087	0.99913	0.49913				
2.49	0.00639	0.99361	0.49361	3.14	0.00084	0.99916	0.49916				
2.5	0.00621	0.99379	0.49379	3.15	0.00082	0.99918	0.49918				
2.51	0.00604	0.99396	0.49396	3.16	0.00079	0.99921	0.49921				
2.52	0.00587	0.99413	0.49413	3.17	0.00076	0.99924	0.49924				
2.53	0.00570	0.99430	0.49430	3.18	0.00074	0.99926	0.49926				
2.54	0.00554	0.99446	0.49446	3.19	0.00071	0.99929	0.49929				
2.55	0.00539	0.99461	0.49461	3.2	0.00069	0.99931	0.49931				
2.56	0.00523	0.99477	0.49477	3.21	0.00066	0.99934	0.49934				
2.57	0.00508	0.99492	0.49492	3.22	0.00064	0.99936	0.49936				
2.58	0.00494	0.99506	0.49506	3.23	0.00062	0.99938	0.49938				
2.59	0.00480	0.99520	0.49520	3.24	0.00060	0.99940	0.49940				

All values calculated by the authors of this text.

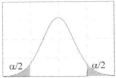

Table A1.2: *t*-table – values of the *t* distribution for varying degrees of freedom (df) and α

α for two-tailed test	0.001	0.01	0.02	0.05	0.1	0.2	0.3
α for one-tailed test	0.0005	0.005	0.01	0.025	0.05	0.1	0.15

DEGREES OF FREEDOM (df)							
1	636.5776	63.6559	31.8210	12.7062	6.3137	3.0777	1.9626
2	31.5998	9.9250	6.9645	4.3027	2.9200	1.8856	1.3862
3	12.9244	5.8408	4.5407	3.1824	2.3534	1.6377	1.2498
4	8.6101	4.6041	3.7469	2.7765	2.1318	1.5332	1.1896
5	6.8685	4.0321	3.3649	2.5706	2.0150	1.4759	1.1558
6	5.9587	3.7074	3.1427	2.4469	1.9432	1.4398	1.1342
7	5.4081	3.4995	2.9979	2.3646	1.8946	1.4149	1.1192
8	5.0414	3.3554	2.8965	2.3060	1.8595	1.3968	1.1081
9	4.7809	3.2498	2.8214	2.2622	1.8331	1.3830	1.0997
10	4.5868	3.1693	2.7638	2.2281	1.8125	1.3722	1.0931
11	4.4369	3.1058	2.7181	2.2010	1.7959	1.3634	1.0877
12	4.3178	3.0545	2.6810	2.1788	1.7823	1.3562	1.0832
13	4.2209	3.0123	2.6503	2.1604	1.7709	1.3502	1.0795
14	4.1403	2.9768	2.6245	2.1448	1.7613	1.3450	1.0763
15	4.0728	2.9467	2.6025	2.1315	1.7531	1.3406	1.0735
16	4.0149	2.9208	2.5835	2.1199	1.7459	1.3368	1.0711
17	3.9651	2.8982	2.5669	2.1098	1.7396	1.3334	1.0690
18	3.9217	2.8784	2.5524	2.1009	1.7341	1.3304	1.0672
19	3.8833	2.8609	2.5395	2.0930	1.7291	1.3277	1.0655
20	3.8496	2.8453	2.5280	2.0860	1.7247	1.3253	1.0640
21	3.8193	2.8314	2.5176	2.0796	1.7207	1.3232	1.0627
22	3.7922	2.8188	2.5083	2.0739	1.7171	1.3212	1.0614
23	3.7676	2.8073	2.4999	2.0687	1.7139	1.3195	1.0603
24	3.7454	2.7970	2.4922	2.0639	1.7109	1.3178	1.0593
25	3.7251	2.7874	2.4851	2.0595	1.7081	1.3163	1.0584
26	3.7067	2.7787	2.4786	2.0555	1.7056	1.3150	1.0575
27	3.6895	2.7707	2.4727	2.0518	1.7033	1.3137	1.0567
28	3.6739	2.7633	2.4671	2.0484	1.7011	1.3125	1.0560
29	3.6595	2.7564	2.4620	2.0452	1.6991	1.3114	1.0553
30	3.6460	2.7500	2.4573	2.0423	1.6973	1.3104	1.0547
31	3.6335	2.7440	2.4528	2.0395	1.6955	1.3095	1.0541
32	3.6218	2.7385	2.4487	2.0369	1.6939	1.3086	1.0535
33	3.6109	2.7333	2.4448	2.0345	1.6924	1.3077	1.0530
34	3.6007	2.7284	2.4411	2.0322	1.6909	1.3070	1.0525
35	3.5911	2.7238	2.4377	2.0301	1.6896	1.3062	1.0520
36	3.5821	2.7195	2.4345	2.0281	1.6883	1.3055	1.0516
37	3.5737	2.7154	2.4314	2.0262	1.6871	1.3049	1.0512
38	3.5657	2.7116	2.4286	2.0244	1.6860	1.3042	1.0508
39	3.5581	2.7079	2.4258	2.0227	1.6849	1.3036	1.0504
40	3.5510	2.7045	2.4233	2.0211	1.6839	1.3031	1.0500
45	3.5203	2.6896	2.4121	2.0141	1.6794	1.3007	1.0485
50	3.4960	2.6778	2.4033	2.0086	1.6759	1.2987	1.0473
55	3.4765	2.6682	2.3961	2.0040	1.6730	1.2971	1.0463
60	3.4602	2.6603	2.3901	2.0003	1.6706	1.2958	1.0455
100	3.3905	2.6259	2.3642	1.9840	1.6602	1.2901	1.0418
1000	3.3002	2.5807	2.3301	1.9623	1.6464	1.2824	1.0370

All values calculated by the authors of this text

Table A1.3: Power – calculating power (1 - β) from a known delta (δ)

δ	Alpha (α) for a two-tailed test	
	0.05	0.01
1.00	0.17	0.06
1.10	0.20	0.07
1.20	0.22	0.08
1.30	0.26	0.10
1.40	0.29	0.12
1.50	0.32	0.14
1.60	0.36	0.17
1.70	0.40	0.19
1.80	0.44	0.22
1.90	0.48	0.25
2.00	0.52	0.28
2.10	0.56	0.32
2.20	0.60	0.35
2.30	0.63	0.39
2.40	0.67	0.43
2.50	0.71	0.47
2.60	0.74	0.51
2.70	0.77	0.55
2.80	0.80	0.59
2.90	0.83	0.63
3.00	0.85	0.66
3.10	0.87	0.70
3.20	0.89	0.73
3.30	0.91	0.77
3.40	0.93	0.80
3.50	0.94	0.82
3.60	0.95	0.85
3.70	0.96	0.87
3.80	0.97	0.89
3.90	0.97	0.91
4.00	0.98	0.92
4.10	0.98	0.94
4.20	0.99	0.95
4.30	0.99	0.96
4.40	0.99	0.97
4.50	0.99	0.97
4.60	–	0.98
4.70	–	0.98
4.80	–	0.99
4.90	–	0.99
5.00	–	0.99

From: Howell, D.C. (1995). *Fundamental Statistics for the Behavioural Sciences.* Duxbury: N.J.

NUMBERS, HYPOTHESES, AND CONCLUSIONS

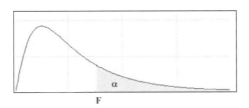

Table A1.4: Table of the F-distribution: $\alpha = 0.05$

Numerator degrees of freedom (df)

	1	2	3	4	5	6	7	8	9	10	15	20	25	30	40	50	100
1	161.45	199.50	215.71	224.58	230.16	233.99	236.77	238.88	240.54	241.88	245.95	248.02	249.26	250.10	251.14	251.77	253.04
2	18.51	19.00	19.16	19.25	19.30	19.33	19.35	19.37	19.38	19.40	19.43	19.45	19.46	19.46	19.47	19.48	19.49
3	10.13	9.55	9.28	9.12	9.01	8.94	8.89	8.85	8.81	8.79	8.70	8.66	8.63	8.62	8.59	8.58	8.55
4	7.71	6.94	6.59	6.39	6.26	6.16	6.09	6.04	6.00	5.96	5.86	5.80	5.77	5.75	5.72	5.70	5.66
5	6.61	5.79	5.41	5.19	5.05	4.95	4.88	4.82	4.77	4.74	4.62	4.56	4.52	4.50	4.46	4.44	4.41
6	5.99	5.14	4.76	4.53	4.39	4.28	4.21	4.15	4.10	4.06	3.94	3.87	3.83	3.81	3.77	3.75	3.71
7	5.59	4.74	4.35	4.12	3.97	3.87	3.79	3.73	3.68	3.64	3.51	3.44	3.40	3.38	3.34	3.32	3.27
8	5.32	4.46	4.07	3.84	3.69	3.58	3.50	3.44	3.39	3.35	3.22	3.15	3.11	3.08	3.04	3.02	2.97
9	5.12	4.26	3.86	3.63	3.48	3.37	3.29	3.23	3.18	3.14	3.01	2.94	2.89	2.86	2.83	2.80	2.76
10	4.96	4.10	3.71	3.48	3.33	3.22	3.14	3.07	3.02	2.98	2.85	2.77	2.73	2.70	2.66	2.64	2.59
11	4.84	3.98	3.59	3.36	3.20	3.09	3.01	2.95	2.90	2.85	2.72	2.65	2.60	2.57	2.53	2.51	2.46
12	4.75	3.89	3.49	3.26	3.11	3.00	2.91	2.85	2.80	2.75	2.62	2.54	2.50	2.47	2.43	2.40	2.35
13	4.67	3.81	3.41	3.18	3.03	2.92	2.83	2.77	2.71	2.67	2.53	2.46	2.41	2.38	2.34	2.31	2.26
14	4.60	3.74	3.34	3.11	2.96	2.85	2.76	2.70	2.65	2.60	2.46	2.39	2.34	2.31	2.27	2.24	2.19
15	4.54	3.68	3.29	3.06	2.90	2.79	2.71	2.64	2.59	2.54	2.40	2.33	2.28	2.25	2.20	2.18	2.12
16	4.49	3.63	3.24	3.01	2.85	2.74	2.66	2.59	2.54	2.49	2.35	2.28	2.23	2.19	2.15	2.12	2.07
17	4.45	3.59	3.20	2.96	2.81	2.70	2.61	2.55	2.49	2.45	2.31	2.23	2.18	2.15	2.10	2.08	2.02
18	4.41	3.55	3.16	2.93	2.77	2.66	2.58	2.51	2.46	2.41	2.27	2.19	2.14	2.11	2.06	2.04	1.98
19	4.38	3.52	3.13	2.90	2.74	2.63	2.54	2.48	2.42	2.38	2.23	2.16	2.11	2.07	2.03	2.00	1.94
20	4.35	3.49	3.10	2.87	2.71	2.60	2.51	2.45	2.39	2.35	2.20	2.12	2.07	2.04	1.99	1.97	1.91
21	4.32	3.47	3.07	2.84	2.68	2.57	2.49	2.42	2.37	2.32	2.18	2.10	2.05	2.01	1.96	1.94	1.88
22	4.30	3.44	3.05	2.82	2.66	2.55	2.46	2.40	2.34	2.30	2.15	2.07	2.02	1.98	1.94	1.91	1.85
23	4.28	3.42	3.03	2.80	2.64	2.53	2.44	2.37	2.32	2.27	2.13	2.05	2.00	1.96	1.91	1.88	1.82
24	4.26	3.40	3.01	2.78	2.62	2.51	2.42	2.36	2.30	2.25	2.11	2.03	1.97	1.94	1.89	1.86	1.80
25	4.24	3.39	2.99	2.76	2.60	2.49	2.40	2.34	2.28	2.24	2.09	2.01	1.96	1.92	1.87	1.84	1.78
26	4.23	3.37	2.98	2.74	2.59	2.47	2.39	2.32	2.27	2.22	2.07	1.99	1.94	1.90	1.85	1.82	1.76
27	4.21	3.35	2.96	2.73	2.57	2.46	2.37	2.31	2.25	2.20	2.06	1.97	1.92	1.88	1.84	1.81	1.74
28	4.20	3.34	2.95	2.71	2.56	2.45	2.36	2.29	2.24	2.19	2.04	1.96	1.91	1.87	1.82	1.79	1.73
29	4.18	3.33	2.93	2.70	2.55	2.43	2.35	2.28	2.22	2.18	2.03	1.94	1.89	1.85	1.81	1.77	1.71
30	4.17	3.32	2.92	2.69	2.53	2.42	2.33	2.27	2.21	2.16	2.01	1.93	1.88	1.84	1.79	1.76	1.70
35	4.12	3.27	2.87	2.64	2.49	2.37	2.29	2.22	2.16	2.11	1.96	1.88	1.82	1.79	1.74	1.70	1.63
40	4.08	3.23	2.84	2.61	2.45	2.34	2.25	2.18	2.12	2.08	1.92	1.84	1.78	1.74	1.69	1.66	1.59
45	4.06	3.20	2.81	2.58	2.42	2.31	2.22	2.15	2.10	2.05	1.89	1.81	1.75	1.71	1.66	1.63	1.55
50	4.03	3.18	2.79	2.56	2.40	2.29	2.20	2.13	2.07	2.03	1.87	1.78	1.73	1.69	1.63	1.60	1.52
60	4.00	3.15	2.76	2.53	2.37	2.25	2.17	2.10	2.04	1.99	1.84	1.75	1.69	1.65	1.59	1.56	1.48
70	3.98	3.13	2.74	2.50	2.35	2.23	2.14	2.07	2.02	1.97	1.81	1.72	1.66	1.62	1.57	1.53	1.45
80	3.96	3.11	2.72	2.49	2.33	2.21	2.13	2.06	2.00	1.95	1.79	1.70	1.64	1.60	1.54	1.51	1.43
90	3.95	3.10	2.71	2.47	2.32	2.20	2.11	2.04	1.99	1.94	1.78	1.69	1.63	1.59	1.53	1.49	1.41
100	3.94	3.09	2.70	2.46	2.31	2.19	2.10	2.03	1.97	1.93	1.77	1.68	1.62	1.57	1.52	1.48	1.39
200	3.89	3.04	2.65	2.42	2.26	2.14	2.06	1.98	1.93	1.88	1.72	1.62	1.56	1.52	1.46	1.41	1.32
300	3.87	3.03	2.63	2.40	2.24	2.13	2.04	1.97	1.91	1.86	1.70	1.61	1.54	1.50	1.43	1.39	1.30
400	3.86	3.02	2.63	2.39	2.24	2.12	2.03	1.96	1.90	1.85	1.69	1.60	1.53	1.49	1.42	1.38	1.28
500	3.86	3.01	2.62	2.39	2.23	2.12	2.03	1.96	1.90	1.85	1.69	1.59	1.53	1.48	1.42	1.38	1.28
1000	3.85	3.00	2.61	2.38	2.22	2.11	2.02	1.95	1.89	1.84	1.68	1.58	1.52	1.47	1.41	1.36	1.26
10000	3.84	3.00	2.61	2.37	2.21	2.10	2.01	1.94	1.88	1.83	1.67	1.57	1.51	1.46	1.40	1.35	1.25

Denominator degrees of freedom (df)

All values calculated by the authors of this text

Table A1.5: Table of the F-distribution: $\alpha = 0.01$

Numerator degrees of freedom (df)

	1	2	3	4	5	6	7	8	9	10	15	20	25	30	40	50	100
1	4052.2	4999.3	5403.5	5624.3	5763.96	5858.95	5928.3	5980.95	6022.4	6055.9	6156.97	6208.66	6239.86	6260.4	6286.4	6302.3	6333.9
2	98.50	99.00	99.16	99.25	99.30	99.33	99.36	99.38	99.39	99.40	99.43	99.45	99.46	99.47	99.48	99.48	99.49
3	34.12	30.82	29.46	28.71	28.24	27.91	27.67	27.49	27.34	27.23	26.87	26.69	26.58	26.50	26.41	26.35	26.24
4	21.20	18.00	16.69	15.98	15.52	15.21	14.98	14.80	14.66	14.55	14.20	14.02	13.91	13.84	13.75	13.69	13.58
5	16.26	13.27	12.06	11.39	10.97	10.67	10.46	10.29	10.16	10.05	9.72	9.55	9.45	9.38	9.29	9.24	9.13
6	13.75	10.92	9.78	9.15	8.75	8.47	8.26	8.10	7.98	7.87	7.56	7.40	7.30	7.23	7.14	7.09	6.99
7	12.25	9.55	8.45	7.85	7.46	7.19	6.99	6.84	6.72	6.62	6.31	6.16	6.06	5.99	5.91	5.86	5.75
8	11.26	8.65	7.59	7.01	6.63	6.37	6.18	6.03	5.91	5.81	5.52	5.36	5.26	5.20	5.12	5.07	4.96
9	10.56	8.02	6.99	6.42	6.06	5.80	5.61	5.47	5.35	5.26	4.96	4.81	4.71	4.65	4.57	4.52	4.41
10	10.04	7.56	6.55	5.99	5.64	5.39	5.20	5.06	4.94	4.85	4.56	4.41	4.31	4.25	4.17	4.12	4.01
11	9.65	7.21	6.22	5.67	5.32	5.07	4.89	4.74	4.63	4.54	4.25	4.10	4.01	3.94	3.86	3.81	3.71
12	9.33	6.93	5.95	5.41	5.06	4.82	4.64	4.50	4.39	4.30	4.01	3.86	3.76	3.70	3.62	3.57	3.47
13	9.07	6.70	5.74	5.21	4.86	4.62	4.44	4.30	4.19	4.10	3.82	3.66	3.57	3.51	3.43	3.38	3.27
14	8.86	6.51	5.56	5.04	4.69	4.46	4.28	4.14	4.03	3.94	3.66	3.51	3.41	3.35	3.27	3.22	3.11
15	8.68	6.36	5.42	4.89	4.56	4.32	4.14	4.00	3.89	3.80	3.52	3.37	3.28	3.21	3.13	3.08	2.98
16	8.53	6.23	5.29	4.77	4.44	4.20	4.03	3.89	3.78	3.69	3.41	3.26	3.16	3.10	3.02	2.97	2.86
17	8.40	6.11	5.19	4.67	4.34	4.10	3.93	3.79	3.68	3.59	3.31	3.16	3.07	3.00	2.92	2.87	2.76
18	8.29	6.01	5.09	4.58	4.25	4.01	3.84	3.71	3.60	3.51	3.23	3.08	2.98	2.92	2.84	2.78	2.68
19	8.18	5.93	5.01	4.50	4.17	3.94	3.77	3.63	3.52	3.43	3.15	3.00	2.91	2.84	2.76	2.71	2.60
20	8.10	5.85	4.94	4.43	4.10	3.87	3.70	3.56	3.46	3.37	3.09	2.94	2.84	2.78	2.69	2.64	2.54
21	8.02	5.78	4.87	4.37	4.04	3.81	3.64	3.51	3.40	3.31	3.03	2.88	2.79	2.72	2.64	2.58	2.48
22	7.95	5.72	4.82	4.31	3.99	3.76	3.59	3.45	3.35	3.26	2.98	2.83	2.73	2.67	2.58	2.53	2.42
23	7.88	5.66	4.76	4.26	3.94	3.71	3.54	3.41	3.30	3.21	2.93	2.78	2.69	2.62	2.54	2.48	2.37
24	7.82	5.61	4.72	4.22	3.90	3.67	3.50	3.36	3.26	3.17	2.89	2.74	2.64	2.58	2.49	2.44	2.33
25	7.77	5.57	4.68	4.18	3.85	3.63	3.46	3.32	3.22	3.13	2.85	2.70	2.60	2.54	2.45	2.40	2.29
26	7.72	5.53	4.64	4.14	3.82	3.59	3.42	3.29	3.18	3.09	2.81	2.66	2.57	2.50	2.42	2.36	2.25
27	7.68	5.49	4.60	4.11	3.78	3.56	3.39	3.26	3.15	3.06	2.78	2.63	2.54	2.47	2.38	2.33	2.22
28	7.64	5.45	4.57	4.07	3.75	3.53	3.36	3.23	3.12	3.03	2.75	2.60	2.51	2.44	2.35	2.30	2.19
29	7.60	5.42	4.54	4.04	3.73	3.50	3.33	3.20	3.09	3.00	2.73	2.57	2.48	2.41	2.33	2.27	2.16
30	7.56	5.39	4.51	4.02	3.70	3.47	3.30	3.17	3.07	2.98	2.70	2.55	2.45	2.39	2.30	2.25	2.13
35	7.42	5.27	4.40	3.91	3.59	3.37	3.20	3.07	2.96	2.88	2.60	2.44	2.35	2.28	2.19	2.14	2.02
40	7.31	5.18	4.31	3.83	3.51	3.29	3.12	2.99	2.89	2.80	2.52	2.37	2.27	2.20	2.11	2.06	1.94
45	7.23	5.11	4.25	3.77	3.45	3.23	3.07	2.94	2.83	2.74	2.46	2.31	2.21	2.14	2.05	2.00	1.88
50	7.17	5.06	4.20	3.72	3.41	3.19	3.02	2.89	2.78	2.70	2.42	2.27	2.17	2.10	2.01	1.95	1.82
60	7.08	4.98	4.13	3.65	3.34	3.12	2.95	2.82	2.72	2.63	2.35	2.20	2.10	2.03	1.94	1.88	1.75
70	7.01	4.92	4.07	3.60	3.29	3.07	2.91	2.78	2.67	2.59	2.31	2.15	2.05	1.98	1.89	1.83	1.70
80	6.96	4.88	4.04	3.56	3.26	3.04	2.87	2.74	2.64	2.55	2.27	2.12	2.01	1.94	1.85	1.79	1.65
90	6.93	4.85	4.01	3.53	3.23	3.01	2.84	2.72	2.61	2.52	2.24	2.09	1.99	1.92	1.82	1.76	1.62
100	6.90	4.82	3.98	3.51	3.21	2.99	2.82	2.69	2.59	2.50	2.22	2.07	1.97	1.89	1.80	1.74	1.60
200	6.76	4.71	3.88	3.41	3.11	2.89	2.73	2.60	2.50	2.41	2.13	1.97	1.87	1.79	1.69	1.63	1.48
300	6.72	4.68	3.85	3.38	3.08	2.86	2.70	2.57	2.47	2.38	2.10	1.94	1.84	1.76	1.66	1.59	1.44
400	6.70	4.66	3.83	3.37	3.06	2.85	2.68	2.56	2.45	2.37	2.08	1.92	1.82	1.75	1.64	1.58	1.42
500	6.69	4.65	3.82	3.36	3.05	2.84	2.68	2.55	2.44	2.36	2.07	1.92	1.81	1.74	1.63	1.57	1.41
10^2	6.66	4.63	3.80	3.34	3.04	2.82	2.66	2.53	2.43	2.34	2.06	1.90	1.79	1.72	1.61	1.54	1.38
10^3	6.64	4.61	3.78	3.32	3.02	2.80	2.64	2.51	2.41	2.32	2.04	1.88	1.77	1.70	1.59	1.53	1.36

Denominator degrees of freedom (df)

All values calculated by the authors of this text

NUMBERS, HYPOTHESES, AND CONCLUSIONS

Table A1.6: Values of Tukey's Studentised Range Statistic (Q)

Degrees of freedom within groups (degrees of freedom in denominator of F-ratio)	α	k = number of means being compared										
		2	3	4	5	6	7	8	9	10	11	12
1	0.05	18	27	32.8	37.1	40.4	43.1	45.4	47.4	49.1	50.6	52
	0.01	90	135	164	186	202	216	227	237	246	253	260
2	0.05	6.09	8.3	9.8	10.9	11.7	12.4	13	13.5	14	14.4	14.7
	0.01	14	19	22.3	24.7	26.6	28.2	29.5	30.7	31.7	32.6	33.4
3	0.05	4.5	5.91	6.82	7.5	8.04	8.48	8.85	9.18	9.46	9.72	9.95
	0.01	8.26	10.6	12.2	13.3	14.2	15	15.6	16.2	16.7	17.1	17.5
4	0.05	3.93	5.04	5.76	6.29	6.71	7.05	7.35	7.6	7.83	8.03	8.21
	0.01	6.51	8.12	9.17	9.96	10.6	11.1	11.5	11.9	12.3	12.6	12.8
5	0.05	3.64	4.6	5.22	5.67	6.03	6.33	6.58	6.8	6.99	7.17	7.32
	0.01	5.7	6.97	7.8	8.42	8.91	9.32	9.67	9.97	10.2	10.5	10.7
6	0.05	3.46	4.34	4.9	5.31	5.63	5.89	6.12	6.32	6.49	6.65	6.79
	0.01	5.24	6.33	7.03	7.56	7.97	8.32	8.61	8.87	9.1	9.3	9.49
7	0.05	3.34	4.16	4.69	5.66	5.36	5.61	5.82	6	6.16	6.3	6.43
	0.01	4.95	5.92	6.54	7.01	7.37	7.68	7.94	8.17	8.37	8.55	8.71
8	0.05	3.26	4.04	4.53	4.89	5.17	5.4	5.6	5.77	5.92	6.05	6.18
	0.01	4.74	5.63	6.2	6.63	6.96	7.24	7.47	7.68	7.87	8.03	8.18
9	0.05	3.2	3.95	4.42	4.76	5.02	5.24	5.43	5.6	5.74	5.87	5.98
	0.01	4.6	5.43	5.96	6.35	6.66	6.91	7.13	7.32	7.49	7.65	7.78
10	0.05	3.15	3.88	4.33	4.65	4.91	5.12	5.3	5.46	5.6	5.72	5.83
	0.01	4.48	5.27	5.77	6.14	6.43	6.67	6.87	7.05	7.21	7.36	7.48
11	0.05	3.11	3.82	4.26	4.57	4.82	5.03	5.2	5.35	5.49	5.61	5.71
	0.01	4.39	5.14	5.62	5.97	6.25	6.48	6.67	6.84	6.99	7.13	7.26
12	0.05	3.08	3.77	4.2	4.51	4.75	4.95	5.12	5.27	5.4	5.51	5.62
	0.01	4.32	5.04	5.5	5.84	6.1	6.32	6.51	6.67	6.81	6.94	7.06
13	0.05	3.06	3.73	4.15	4.45	4.69	4.88	5.05	5.19	5.32	5.43	5.53
	0.01	4.26	4.96	5.4	5.73	5.98	6.19	6.37	6.53	6.67	6.79	6.9
14	0.05	3.03	3.7	4.11	4.41	4.64	4.83	4.99	5.13	5.25	5.36	5.46
	0.01	4.21	4.89	5.32	5.63	5.88	6.08	6.26	6.41	6.54	6.66	6.77
16	0.05	3	3.65	4.05	4.33	4.56	4.74	4.9	5.03	5.15	5.26	5.35
	0.01	4.13	4.78	5.19	5.49	5.72	5.92	6.08	6.22	6.35	6.46	6.56
18	0.05	2.97	3.61	4	4.28	4.49	4.67	4.82	4.96	5.07	5.17	5.27
	0.01	4.07	4.7	5.09	5.38	5.6	5.79	5.94	6.08	6.2	6.31	6.41
20	0.05	2.95	3.58	3.96	4.23	4.45	4.62	4.77	4.9	5.01	5.11	5.2
	0.01	4.02	4.64	5.02	5.29	5.51	5.69	5.84	5.97	6.09	6.19	6.29
24	0.05	2.92	3.53	3.9	4.17	4.37	4.54	4.68	4.81	4.92	5.01	5.1
	0.01	3.96	4.54	4.91	5.17	5.37	5.54	5.69	5.81	5.92	6.02	6.11
30	0.05	2.89	3.49	3.84	4.1	4.3	4.46	4.6	4.72	4.83	4.92	5
	0.01	3.89	4.45	4.8	5.05	5.24	5.4	5.54	5.56	5.76	5.85	5.93
40	0.05	2.86	3.44	3.79	4.04	4.23	4.39	4.52	4.63	4.74	4.82	4.91
	0.01	3.82	4.37	4.7	4.93	5.11	5.27	5.39	5.5	5.6	5.69	5.77
60	0.05	2.83	3.4	3.74	3.98	4.16	4.31	4.44	4.55	4.65	4.73	4.81
	0.01	3.76	4.28	4.6	4.82	4.99	5.13	5.25	5.36	5.45	5.53	5.6
120	0.05	2.8	3.36	3.69	3.92	4.1	4.24	4.36	4.48	4.56	4.64	4.72
	0.01	3.7	4.2	4.5	4.71	4.87	5.01	5.12	5.21	5.3	5.38	5.44
∞	0.05	2.77	3.31	3.63	3.86	4.03	4.17	4.29	4.39	4.47	4.55	4.62
	0.01	3.64	4.12	4.4	4.6	4.76	4.88	4.99	5.08	5.16	5.23	5.29

From B. J. Winer (1962). *Statistical Principles in Experimental Design.* New York: McGraw-Hill

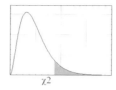

χ^2

Table A1.7: Values of the χ^2 distribution for varying degrees of freedom (df) and α

df	\(\alpha\) 0.0005	0.001	0.005	0.01	0.025	0.05	0.1	0.15	0.2	0.25	0.3
1	12.1153	10.8274	7.8794	6.6349	5.0239	3.8415	2.7055	2.0722	1.6424	1.3233	1.0742
2	15.2014	13.8150	10.5965	9.2104	7.3778	5.9915	4.6052	3.7942	3.2189	2.7726	2.4079
3	17.7311	16.2660	12.8381	11.3449	9.3484	7.8147	6.2514	5.3170	4.6416	4.1083	3.6649
4	19.9977	18.4662	14.8602	13.2767	11.1433	9.4877	7.7794	6.7449	5.9886	5.3853	4.8784
5	22.1057	20.5147	16.7496	15.0863	12.8325	11.0705	9.2363	8.1152	7.2893	6.6257	6.0644
6	24.1016	22.4575	18.5475	16.8119	14.4494	12.5916	10.6446	9.4461	8.5581	7.8408	7.2311
7	26.0179	24.3213	20.2777	18.4753	16.0128	14.0671	12.0170	10.7479	9.8032	9.0371	8.3834
8	27.8674	26.1239	21.9549	20.0902	17.5345	15.5073	13.3616	12.0271	11.0301	10.2189	9.5245
9	29.6669	27.8767	23.5893	21.6660	19.0228	16.9190	14.6837	13.2880	12.2421	11.3887	10.6564
10	31.4195	29.5879	25.1881	23.2093	20.4832	18.3070	15.9872	14.5339	13.4420	12.5489	11.7807
11	33.1382	31.2635	26.7569	24.7250	21.9200	19.6752	17.2750	15.7671	14.6314	13.7007	12.8987
12	34.8211	32.9092	28.2997	26.2170	23.3367	21.0261	18.5493	16.9893	15.8120	14.8454	14.0111
13	36.4768	34.5274	29.8193	27.6882	24.7356	22.3620	19.8119	18.2020	16.9848	15.9839	15.1187
14	38.1085	36.1239	31.3194	29.1412	26.1189	23.6848	21.0641	19.4062	18.1508	17.1169	16.2221
15	39.7173	37.6978	32.8015	30.5780	27.4884	24.9958	22.3071	20.6030	19.3107	18.2451	17.3217
16	41.3077	39.2518	34.2671	31.9999	28.8453	26.2962	23.5418	21.7931	20.4651	19.3689	18.4179
17	42.8808	40.7911	35.7184	33.4087	30.1910	27.5871	24.7690	22.9770	21.6146	20.4887	19.5110
18	44.4337	42.3119	37.1564	34.8052	31.5264	28.8693	25.9894	24.1555	22.7595	21.6049	20.6014
19	45.9738	43.8194	38.5821	36.1908	32.8523	30.1435	27.2036	25.3289	23.9004	22.7178	21.6891
20	47.4977	45.3142	39.9969	37.5663	34.1696	31.4104	28.4120	26.4976	25.0375	23.8277	22.7745
21	49.0096	46.7963	41.4009	38.9322	35.4789	32.6706	29.6151	27.6620	26.1711	24.9348	23.8578
22	50.5105	48.2676	42.7957	40.2894	36.7807	33.9245	30.8133	28.8224	27.3015	26.0393	24.9390
23	51.9995	49.7276	44.1814	41.6383	38.0756	35.1725	32.0069	29.9792	28.4288	27.1413	26.0184
24	53.4776	51.1790	45.5584	42.9798	39.3641	36.4150	33.1962	31.1325	29.5533	28.2412	27.0960
25	54.9475	52.6187	46.9280	44.3140	40.6465	37.6525	34.3816	32.2825	30.6752	29.3388	28.1719
26	56.4068	54.0511	48.2898	45.6416	41.9231	38.8851	35.5632	33.4295	31.7946	30.4346	29.2463
27	57.8556	55.4751	49.6450	46.9628	43.1945	40.1133	36.7412	34.5736	32.9117	31.5284	30.3193
28	59.2990	56.8918	50.9936	48.2782	44.4608	41.3372	37.9159	35.7150	34.0266	32.6205	31.3909
29	60.7342	58.3006	52.3355	49.5878	45.7223	42.5569	39.0875	36.8538	35.1394	33.7109	32.4612
30	62.1600	59.7022	53.6719	50.8922	46.9792	43.7730	40.2560	37.9902	36.2502	34.7997	33.5302
31	63.5813	61.0980	55.0025	52.1914	48.2319	44.9853	41.4217	39.1244	37.3591	35.8871	34.5981
32	64.9935	62.4873	56.3280	53.4857	49.4804	46.1942	42.5847	40.2563	38.4663	36.9730	35.6649
33	66.4013	63.8694	57.6483	54.7754	50.7251	47.3999	43.7452	41.3861	39.5718	38.0575	36.7307
34	67.8042	65.2471	58.9637	56.0609	51.9660	48.6024	44.9032	42.5140	40.6756	39.1408	37.7954
35	69.1975	66.6192	60.2746	57.3420	53.2033	49.8018	46.0588	43.6399	41.7780	40.2228	38.8591
36	70.5882	67.9850	61.5811	58.6192	54.4373	50.9985	47.2122	44.7641	42.8788	41.3036	39.9220
37	71.9713	69.3476	62.8832	59.8926	55.6680	52.1923	48.3634	45.8864	43.9782	42.3833	40.9839
38	73.3500	70.7039	64.1812	61.1620	56.8955	53.3835	49.5126	47.0072	45.0763	43.4619	42.0450
39	74.7237	72.0550	65.4753	62.4281	58.1201	54.5722	50.6598	48.1263	46.1730	44.5395	43.1053
40	76.0963	73.4029	66.7660	63.6908	59.3417	55.7585	51.8050	49.2438	47.2685	45.6160	44.1649
45	82.8734	80.0776	73.1660	69.9569	65.4101	61.6562	57.5053	54.8105	52.7288	50.9849	49.4517
50	89.5597	86.6603	79.4898	76.1538	71.4202	67.5048	63.1671	60.3460	58.1638	56.3336	54.7228
55	96.1607	93.1671	85.7491	82.2920	77.3804	73.3115	68.7962	65.8550	63.5772	61.6650	59.9804
60	102.6971	99.6078	91.9518	88.3794	83.2977	79.0820	74.3970	71.3411	68.9721	66.9815	65.2265
100	153.1638	149.4488	140.1697	135.8069	129.5613	124.3421	118.4980	114.6588	111.6667	109.1412	106.9058
1000	1153.7344	1143.9196	1118.9475	1106.9690	1089.5307	1074.6794	1057.7240	1046.3849	1037.8381	1030.1157	1023.2140

Degrees of freedom

All values calculated by the authors of this text

NUMBERS, HYPOTHESES, AND CONCLUSIONS

Table A1.8: Two-tailed 5% significance values for the sign test giving values for the smaller of the two sums

NOTE: The value must be in the listed ranges for the sample result to be significant at the 5% level.

Number of pairs of scores (ignoring ties)	Significant at 5% if in these ranges
6–8	0 only
9–11	0 to 1
12–14	0 to 2
15–16	0 to 3
17–19	0 to 4
20–22	0 to 5
23–24	0 to 6
25–27	0 to 7
28–29	0 to 8
0–32	0 to 9
33–34	0 to 10
35–36	0 to 11
37–39	0 to 12
40–41	0 to 13
42–43	0 to 14
44–46	0 to 15
47–48	0 to 16
49–50	0 to 17

Table A1.9: Wilcoxon matched pairs – two-tailed 5% significance values for the Wilcoxon matched pairs test giving values of T (the smaller of the two signed rank sums)

Number of pairs of scores (ignoring any tied pairs)	Significant at 5% if in these ranges
6	0 only
7	0 to 2
8	0 to 4
9	0 to 6
10	0 to 8
11	0 to 11
12	0 to 14
13	0 to 17
14	0 to 21
15	0 to 25
16	0 to 30
17	0 to 35
18	0 to 40
19	0 to 46
20	0 to 52
21	0 to 59
22	0 to 66
23	0 to 73
24	0 to 81
25	0 to 89

Table A10: Critical Values of the Mann-Whitney U for a Directional Test at .05 or a Nondirectional Test at .10

n_B \ n_A	1	2	3	4	5	6	7	8	9	10	11	12	13	14	15	16	17	18	19	20
1	--	--	--	--	--	--	--	--	--	--	--	--	--	--	--	--	--	--	0/19	0/20
2	--	--	--	--	0/10	0/12	0/14	1/15	1/17	1/19	1/21	2/22	2/24	2/26	3/27	3/29	3/31	4/32	4/34	4/36
3	--	--	0/9	0/12	1/14	2/16	2/19	3/21	3/24	4/26	5/28	5/31	6/33	7/35	7/38	8/40	9/42	9/45	10/47	11/49
4	--	--	0/12	1/15	2/18	3/21	4/24	5/27	6/30	7/33	8/36	9/39	10/42	11/45	12/48	14/50	15/53	16/56	17/59	18/62
5	--	0/10	1/14	2/18	4/21	5/25	6/29	8/32	9/36	11/39	12/43	13/47	15/50	16/54	18/57	19/61	20/65	22/68	23/72	25/75
6	--	0/12	2/16	3/21	5/25	7/29	8/34	10/38	12/42	14/46	16/50	17/55	19/59	21/63	23/67	25/71	26/76	28/80	30/84	32/88
7	--	0/14	2/19	4/24	6/29	8/34	11/38	13/43	15/48	17/53	19/58	21/63	24/67	26/72	28/77	30/82	33/86	35/91	37/96	39/101
8	--	1/15	3/21	56/27	8/32	10/38	13/43	15/49	18/54	20/60	23/65	26/70	28/76	31/81	33/87	36/92	39/97	41/103	44/108	47/113
9	--	1/17	3/24	6/30	9/36	12/42	15/48	18/54	21/60	24/66	27/72	30/78	33/84	36/90	39/96	42/102	45/108	48/114	51/120	54/126
10	--	1/19	4/26	7/33	11/39	14/46	17/53	20/60	24/66	27/73	31/78	34/75	37/82	41/88	44/106	48/112	51/119	55/125	58/132	62/138
11	--	1/21	5/28	8/36	12/43	16/50	19/58	23/65	27/72	31/79	34/87	38/94	42/101	46/108	50/115	54/122	57/130	61/137	65/144	69/151
12	--	2/22	5/31	9/39	13/47	17/55	21/63	26/70	30/78	34/86	38/94	42/102	47/109	51/117	55/125	60/132	64/140	68/148	72/156	77/163
13	--	2/24	6/33	10/42	15/50	19/59	24/67	28/76	33/84	37/93	42/101	47/109	51/118	56/126	61/134	65/143	70/151	75/159	80/167	84/176
14	--	2/26	7/35	11/45	16/54	21/63	26/72	31/81	36/90	41/99	46/108	51/117	56/126	61/135	66/144	71/153	77/161	82/170	87/179	92/188
15	--	3/27	7/38	12/48	18/57	23/67	28/77	33/87	39/96	44/106	50/115	55/125	61/134	66/144	72/153	77/163	83/172	88/182	94/191	100/200
16	--	3/29	8/40	14/50	19/61	25/71	30/82	36/92	42/102	48/112	54/122	60/132	65/143	71/153	77/163	83/173	89/183	95/193	101/203	107/213
17	--	3/31	9/42	15/53	20/65	26/76	33/86	39/97	45/108	51/119	57/130	64/140	70/151	77/161	83/172	89/183	96/193	102/204	109/214	115/225
18	--	4/32	9/45	16/56	22/68	28/80	35/91	41/103	48/114	55/123	61/137	68/148	75/159	82/170	88/182	95/193	102/204	109/215	116/226	123/237
19	0/19	4/34	10/47	17/59	23/72	30/84	37/96	44/108	51/120	58/132	65/144	72/156	80/167	87/179	94/191	101/203	109/214	116/226	123/238	130/250
20	0/20	4/36	11/49	18/62	25/75	32/88	39/101	47/113	54/126	62/138	69/151	77/163	84/176	92/188	100/200	107/213	115/225	123/237	130/250	138/262

(Dashes in the body of the table indicate that no decision is possible at the stated level of significance.)

If the observed value of U falls between (but not including) the two values presented in the table for n_A and n_B, do not reject H_0. Otherwise, reject H_0.

Table A11: Critical Values of the Mann–Whitney U for a Directional Test at .025 or a Nondirectional Test at .05

n_B \ n_A	1	2	3	4	5	6	7	8	9	10	11	12	13	14	15	16	17	18	19	20
1	--	--	--	--	--	--	--	--	--	--	--	--	--	--	--	--	--	--	--	--
2	--	--	--	--	--	--	--	0/16	0/18	0/20	0/22	1/23	1/25	1/27	1/29	1/31	2/32	2/34	2/36	2/38
3	--	--	--	--	0/15	1/17	1/20	2/22	2/25	3/27	3/30	4/32	4/35	5/37	5/40	6/42	6/45	7/47	7/50	8/52
4	--	--	--	0/16	1/19	2/22	3/25	4/28	4/32	5/35	6/38	7/41	8/44	9/47	10/50	11/53	11/57	12/60	13/63	13/67
5	--	--	0/15	1/19	2/23	3/27	5/30	6/34	7/38	8/42	9/46	11/49	12/53	13/57	14/61	15/65	17/68	18/72	19/76	20/80
6	--	--	1/17	2/22	3/27	5/31	6/36	8/40	10/44	11/49	13/53	14/58	16/62	17/67	19/71	21/75	22/80	24/84	25/89	27/93
7	--	--	1/20	3/25	5/30	6/36	8/41	10/46	12/51	14/56	16/61	18/66	20/71	22/76	24/81	26/86	28/91	30/96	32/101	34/106
8	--	0/16	2/22	4/28	6/34	8/40	10/46	13/51	15/57	17/63	19/69	22/74	24/80	26/86	29/91	31/97	34/102	36/108	38/111	41/119
9	--	0/18	2/25	4/32	7/38	10/44	12/51	15/57	17/64	20/70	23/76	26/82	28/89	31/95	34/101	37/107	39/114	42/120	45/126	48/132
10	--	0/20	3/27	5/35	8/42	11/49	14/56	17/63	20/70	23/77	26/84	29/91	33/97	36/104	39/111	42/118	45/125	48/132	52/138	55/145
11	--	0/22	3/30	6/38	9/46	13/53	16/61	19/69	23/76	26/84	30/91	33/99	37/106	40/114	44/121	47/129	51/136	55/143	58/151	62/158
12	--	1/23	4/32	7/41	11/49	14/58	18/66	22/74	26/82	29/91	33/99	37/107	41/115	45/123	49/131	53/139	57/147	61/155	65/163	69/171
13	--	1/25	4/35	8/44	12/53	16/62	20/71	24/80	28/89	33/97	37/106	41/115	45/124	50/132	54/141	59/149	63/158	67/167	72/175	76/184
14	--	1/27	5/37	9/47	13/51	17/67	22/76	26/86	31/95	36/104	40/114	45/123	50/132	55/141	59/151	64/160	67/171	74/178	78/188	83/197
15	--	1/29	5/40	10/50	14/61	19/71	24/81	29/91	34/101	39/111	474/121	49/131	54/141	59/151	64/161	70/170	75/180	80/190	85/200	90/210
16	--	1/31	6/42	11/53	15/65	21/75	26/86	31/97	37/107	42/118	47/129	53/139	59/149	64/160	70/170	75/181	81/191	86/202	92/212	98/222
17	--	2/32	6/45	11/57	17/68	22/80	28/91	34/102	39/114	45/125	51/136	57/147	63/158	67/171	75/180	81/191	87/202	93/213	99/224	105/235
18	--	2/34	7/47	12/60	18/72	24/84	30/96	36/108	42/120	48/132	55/143	61/155	67/167	74/178	80/190	86/202	93/213	99/225	106/236	112/248
19	--	2/36	7/50	13/63	19/76	25/89	32/101	38/114	45/126	52/138	58/151	65/163	72/175	78/188	85/200	92/212	99/224	106/236	113/248	119/261
20	--	2/38	8/52	13/67	20/80	27/93	34/106	41/119	48/132	55/145	62/158	69/171	76/184	83/197	90/210	98/222	105/235	112/248	119/261	127/273

(Dashes in the body of the table indicate that no decision is possible at the stated level of significance.)

Source: From Mann, H. B., and Whitney, D. R., "On a Test of Whether One of Two Random Variables Is Stochastically Larger Than the Other," *Annals of Mathematical Statistics* 18 (1947): 50–60, and Auble, D., "Extended Tables for the Mann-Whitney Statistic," *Bulletin of the Institute of Education Research at Indiana University*, vol. 1, no. 2 (1953), as used in Runyon and Haber, *Fundamentals of Behavioral Statistic*, 3rd ed., Addison-Wesley, Reading, Mass., 1976. Reprinted by permission.

APPENDIX

2

Starting with SPSS®

Kevin Durrheim

At the end of this tutorial, you should be able to:
- Start SPSS® and make a shortcut to SPSS® on your desktop.
- Understand and use three different kinds of windows available on SPSS®.
- Create, import, and save a data file.
- Transform and manipulate data entered into SPSS®.
- Be able to work with output from SPSS®.
- Have an overview of the variety of procedures available in SPSS®.

If you are using SPSS® on a computer network (LAN), you will need to register with the computer administrators of your institution.

If you are reading this material and you are not sitting in front of a computer (with SPSS®), you are wasting your time.

SPSS® is an acronym for Statistical Package for the Social Sciences. It is a powerful data management and statistical analysis program that has been specifically designed for applications in the social sciences. The Windows version is easy to learn and use, and newer versions of the package (from version 8 onward) offer not only a number of specialised statistical applications for social scientists, but also good quality graphical output.

This chapter provides a brief introduction to SPSS®, taking the reader on a basic step-by-step tour of the program. You are encouraged to spend time playing with the program, trying out different procedures, as you gradually become comfortable in the SPSS® environment. Specific applications of the program are considered in more detail in the relevant tutorials in this book. SPSS® has an online help menu that you should consult if you get stuck.

496   NUMBERS, HYPOTHESES AND CONCLUSIONS

Starting SPSS®

Starting SPSS® from the 'Program' group

Click the 'Start' button at the bottom left of the desktop window; select 'Programs', and then select 'SPSS® for Windows'.

Setting up an SPSS® shortcut

A shortcut will allow you to access SPSS® easily from your desktop. To set up a shortcut:

1. Right click any blank area of your desktop window. Select the option 'New' and then select 'Shortcut'. A 'Create Shortcut' dialog box will appear.
2. Type in the command line – 'C:\Program Files\SPSS®\Spsswin. exe' – or browse if Spsswin.exe is in a different directory.
3. A SPSS® shortcut should appear on your desktop. By double clicking on the icon, you open SPSS®.

The SPSS® environment

SPSS® has three different main windows: a Data Editor window, an Output Viewer window, and a Syntax window. You will need to know how to use some functions of all three windows, and to switch between them. This is the SPSS® environment.

1. The Data Editor window

When you open SPSS®, the Data Editor window appears on the screen (see Figure A2.1). The window contains a spreadsheet consisting of a matrix of rows and columns. This is the context in which to enter and edit data, and do various transformations of the data. Data can either

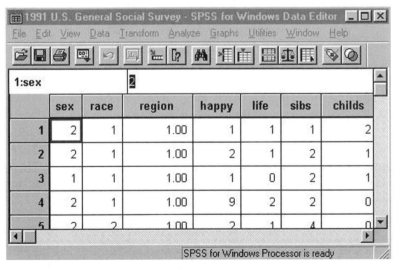

Figure A2.1 SPSS® Data Editor window

To move around the Data Editor, use the arrow keys. To enter data, highlight a cell of the matrix, type in the data entry, and press the 'Enter' key.

be entered directly into SPSS®, or imported from a spreadsheet (e.g. Excel), and then saved as an SPSS® data file.

Above the data matrix are a set of pull-down menus – 'File', 'Edit', 'View', etc. – that allow you to perform various operations such as saving and editing files, manipulating and transforming data, performing statistical analysis and producing graphical displays. Just below the set of pull-down menus is a toolbar that provides shortcuts for some key operations.

2. The 'Output Viewer' window

The results of an analysis are given in the 'Output Viewer' window (see Figure A2.2). The window opens automatically once you have run SPSS® commands. A new 'Data Editor' window can be opened by selecting the options 'New' and 'Data' on the 'File' menu. Data files can be saved and opened in the usual way – i.e. by options on the 'File' menu. 'Output Viewer' window files have a .spo extension. The window on the left of the SPSS® 'Output Viewer' provides an

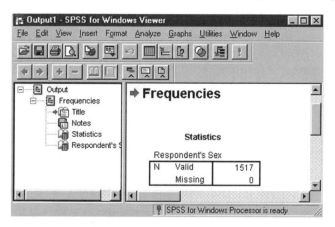

Figure A2.2 SPSS® 'Output Viewer' window

historical record of the analyses you have conducted. It helps you to navigate through the output. The 'Output History' window in Figure A2.2 shows that the SPSS® 'Frequencies' procedure was conducted, and that frequency statistics were generated as well as a bar chart.

The window on the right provides the actual output.[1] In Figure A2.2, frequency statistics are reported in this output window. There are two kinds of objects in an output file: tables and charts. These objects can be highlighted, cut, copied, and deleted; and you can move about both windows by means of the arrow keys.

SPSS® provides two kinds of output: tables and charts.

---

1 The 'Output Viewer' windows for earlier versions of SPSS® are a little different. They do not have an 'Output History' window, and the output in the right window is formatted differently.

NUMBERS, HYPOTHESES AND CONCLUSIONS

3. The 'Syntax Editor' window

Before SPSS® adopted the Windows environment, statistical commands were written out in SPSS® syntax. The 'Syntax Editor' window in Figure A2.3 illustrates the syntax for the 'Frequencies' command. 'Syntax Editor' provides a powerful but rather cumbersome way of issuing SPSS® commands, and it has been replaced by the use of menus, dialog boxes, and windows. Nevertheless, there are some procedures that can only be performed by writing syntax files. If you need to use such a procedure, you should consult an SPSS® reference manual.

You can switch between windows either by pulling down the 'Window' menu, or by selecting the file on the 'Start' bar at the bottom of your desktop.

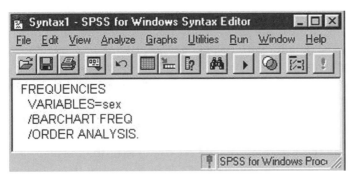

Figure A2.3 SPSS® 'Syntax Editor' window

Activity A2.1

Open one of the sample files that are provided by SPSS®.

1. Pull down the 'File' menu and select 'Open' (or use the 'Open file' icon on the left of the toolbar).
2. In the SPSS® directory you will find a number of sample SPSS® data files (which all have a .sav extension). Double click on any one of these files (e.g. 1991 U.S. General Social Survey.sav). Data will now appear in rows and columns in the data matrix.

How many subjects and variables are in the dataset? Do you recognise which are nominal or interval variables?

Now try running some descriptive statistics.

3. Pull down the 'Analyze' menu, select the 'Summarize' option and then select 'Frequencies'.
4. On the 'Frequencies' window, select two nominal variables by highlighting them in the display box, and then clicking the arrow to shift them into the variables box. Click the 'OK' button to run the analysis.

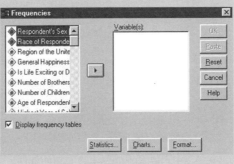

Setting up an SPSS® data file

Creating a data file is the first step in every analysis. The data must be arranged in a format that the statistical software can recognise and work with. SPSS® gives you the option of creating a new data file with the SPSS® data editor, or of importing a data file from some other spreadsheet format. Once the spreadsheet has been set up, the data can be transformed in useful ways, and the file can be saved as an SPSS® data file.

Using the SPSS® 'Data Editor'

*Always **enter data** in the form of one column for each variable and one row for each respondent.*

The SPSS® 'Data Editor' is used in much the same way as any spreadsheet. Data (scores) are entered in cells, along rows, and down columns. The data for each respondent are entered in a single row, and the columns contain data for different variables.

To **move about** the 'Data Editor', use the mouse and the scroll bars or the arrow keys. To **enter data** simply position the cursor on the cell into which you want to enter a score, and type in the score. When you move to the next cell the score will be entered.

After entering the data, name each variable and define its scale of measurement.

To **name the variables**, double click on one of the cells labelled 'var' at the top of the columns of a new spreadsheet. A 'Define Variable' dialog box will open (see Figure A2.4). In this dialog box you can name the variable by typing in the variable name in the box provided. The dialog box also allows you to **define the scale of measurement** on which the variable is measured: nominal, ordinal, or scale (interval or ratio).

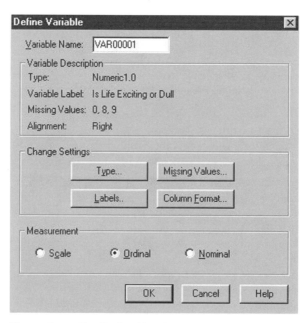

Figure A2.4 The 'Define Variable' dialog box

Note that the variable is named and described in the dialog box, and that you are provided with options for changing the variable settings. The default settings for 'Missing Values' and the 'Column Format' options do not normally need to be changed, but it is often useful to change the 'Type' and 'Labels' settings.

1. *'Type'.* Variables can be defined as a number of different types. For our purposes, the default 'Numeric' type is used most often. Numeric variables should contain only numeric data. If your data includes letters, the variable should be defined as a string variable. Be careful not to define numeric data as string variables or you will not be able to perform any statistical operations on them.

2. *'Labels'.* The 'Define Labels' dialog box (see Figure A2.5) allows you to specify variable and value labels. The 'Variable Label' is simply another longer and more descriptive name for your variable. Variable names cannot be longer than eight characters, so you can define your variable more fully here. Thus, the variable name '%income' may be described here as '% household income spent on information (e.g. books, magazines, TV licence)'. In addition to describing the variable, we can also describe numeric data here. SPSS® supports a double notation, where each score (in the 'Data Editor' window) can simultaneously have a numeric and a text value. These text values are called 'Value Labels'. For example, if you used the code 1 to represent female respondents and 2 to represent males, you can here apply the 'Value Labels' 'female' and 'male' to the values 1 and 2 respectively. These value labels will appear in your output (instead of raw codes), making it easier to interpret.

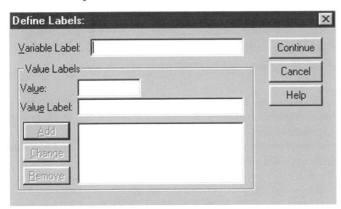

Figure A2.5 The Define Labels dialog box

To set the value labels
1. Open the 'Define Labels' dialog box by double clicking on the variable name.
2. In the space provided in the dialog box, enter the numeric 'Value' and the text 'Value Label'. Click 'Add'.
3. Once all value labels have been specified in this manner, click 'Continue'.

Specifying variable and value labels is essential for communicating the meaning of the data to others and to yourself, when you have to redo analysis at a later stage.

a) Create a small dataset that contains the variables 'Subject' and 'Gender'. Label the subjects 1, 2, 3, 4. Subjects 1 and 2 are female (code 1) and subjects 3 and 4 are male (code 2).
b) Open the 'Define Variable' window to name the two variables and to check that they are defined as numeric variables. For the variable Gender, (a) enter the variable label 'Gender of subjects', and (b) specify the value labels 'female' and 'male' for the values 1 and 2.
c) Define the scale of measurement of each variable.

Importing data

Importing data from another spreadsheet format into SPSS® is as easy as opening a file. It is important, though, that the data should be in a recognised format such as Excel or DBase. If the data is in another format, it is best to save the file first in Excel format before importing it.

Box A2.2

Entering data in Excel so that it is 'SPSS® ready'
Some limitations of SPSS® are worth bearing in mind when entering data into Excel, since this will affect data importation.
a) SPSS® does not support variable names longer than eight characters, and does not support variable names entered over more than one row. Enter variable names only in the first row of the Excel worksheet, and make sure that none are longer than eight characters.
b) Make sure that all the data in the Excel worksheet are in 'value format'. Where you have variables defined as formulas, convert these so that they are fixed values. (Use the 'Copy' and 'Paste Special Values' commands off the 'Edit' menu.)
c) If you have missing data, do not enter symbols or values to denote these. Rather leave the cell blank. All blank cells will be read into SPSS® as missing data.

Cut-and-paste provides an easy way to import or export data into or from SPSS®. Variables and cells of a spreadsheet may be moved between applications such as SPSS®, Excel, and MS Word simply by blocking (selecting) the variables or cells, copying them (use the Ctrl-C key), and then pasting them (use the Ctrl-V key) in the other application.

To import a file
1. Pull down the 'File' menu and select the 'Open' option. An 'Open File' dialog box will appear. Specify the type of file you want to open by selecting from the range in the 'Files of Type' list.
2. Select the correct directory and file, and click the 'Open' button. An 'Open File Options' dialog box will open.
3. Indicate whether you want to 'Read variable names'. If your external spreadsheet has variable names specified, tick the appropriate box and click 'OK'. The external spreadsheet will be imported into SPSS®. It will appear in the 'Data Editor' dialog box with variable names at the top of the columns.

Saving data

Data is precious, and should be saved on a reliable computer and backed up. The data file can be saved in SPSS® format or it can be exported in a different format.

1. *Saving a file in SPSS® format.* Once you have created an SPSS® data file, the file should be saved in SPSS® format (i.e. with a .sav extension). This is done by selecting the 'Save' option on the 'File' menu. You will be prompted to provide a directory and file name.
2. *Saving a file in other formats.* To save your data file in another format (e.g. Excel, DBase), select the 'Save As' option on the 'File' menu. The 'Save Data As' dialog box allows you to select the required output format.

Transforming data with SPSS®

It is often the case that the original dataset needs to be modified in various ways before you can proceed with data analysis. For example, items may need to be reverse-scored or summed to form scale scores. SPSS® provides two menus that allow you to work with datasets that are saved in the SPSS® 'Data Editor' (see Figure A2.6).

The 'Transform' menu enables you to perform a number of useful data transformations, including ranking the cases in a particular order and generating random numbers. The 'Data' menu enables you to sort and re-order cases, to select specific cases for analysis, and to weight cases. We only consider more frequently used options of these two menus here. It is recommended that you experiment with the other options, with the aid of the SPSS® 'Help' menu.

*Data transformations are **not** automatically entered into the data editor. You must instruct SPSS® to **run pending transformations**.*

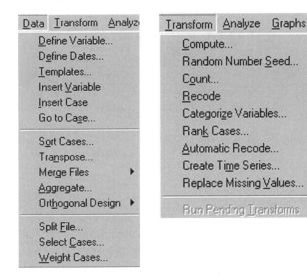

Figure A2.6 The 'Data' and 'Transform' menus

Compute

This option allows you to compute data values according to specified mathematical formulas. For example, you can sum and multiply different variables, or transform the values according to other mathematical operations (e.g. logarithmic, square). The 'Compute' option is often used at the beginning of an analysis, to reverse score variables and to construct summed scale scores.

To compute
1. Select the 'Compute' option on the 'Transform' menu.
2. Complete the 'Compute Variable' dialog box (see Figure A2.7).
   a) Insert the 'Target Variable', which is the name of the new variable you want the transformed data to be saved into in the 'Data Editor' window.
   b) Complete the 'Numeric Expression'. For example, if you want to sum variables VAR1 and VAR2, you would write 'VAR1 + VAR2' or 'SUM(Var1, Var2)'; or if you wanted to subtract the value of 1 from VAR1, you would write 'VAR1 – 1'.
3. Click the 'OK' button and the new transformed variable will be calculated and stored in memory.
4. To insert the 'Pending Transformations', open the 'Transform' menu and click the 'Run Pending Transformations' option. The newly computed variable will automatically be inserted into the data file.

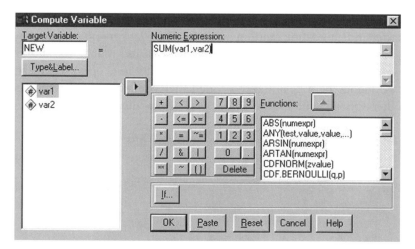

Figure A2.7 The 'Compute Variable' dialog box

Recode

This option allows you to recode the values of a variable, either 'Recode into Same Variables' or 'Recode into Different Variables'. Recoding into the same variable will write the transformed data into the original variable and thereby change your original data. Recoding into a different variable will create a new variable with the transformed data. The 'Recode' option is often used to change the scores of nominal data – e.g. change all 1 values to 3 – or to create categories (e.g. quartiles) from continuous data.

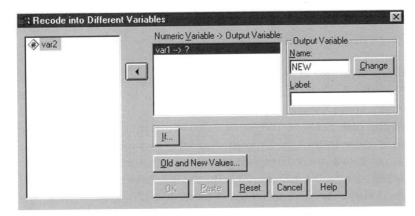

Figure A2.8 Recode dialog box

To recode
1. Select the 'Recode' option on the 'Transform' menu, and indicate whether you want to code into the same variable or a different variable.
2. Complete the 'Recode' dialog box (see Figure A2.8).
   a) Select the variable you want to recode, and name your new output variable. Click 'Change' and the recode statement will be inserted in the dialog box.
   b) You can recode either by selecting 'Old and New Values' or by selecting the 'If' option and specifying an expression. A dialog box will appear, which should be completed to run the procedure.
3. The 'Old and New Values' dialog box allows you to indicate each value or range of values that you want to recode.
   a) Specify the old value or range.
   b) Specify the new value.
   c) Click the 'Add' button. Once you have specified all values to be recoded, click 'Continue', and then click 'OK' on the 'Recode' dialog box.
4. To insert the newly recoded variable into the data file, open the 'Transform' menu and click the 'Run Pending Transformations' option. The new variable will automatically be inserted into data file.

Once you have made any changes to your data, remember to save the data file before exiting SPSS®.

Select cases

This option provides several methods for selecting a subgroup of cases. When a statistical procedure is to be conducted with only a subsample of cases, this subsample should first be selected for analysis. Most often this subsample will be chosen if a **condition is satisfied**. This option allows you to specify the conditions under which a case is included in the dataset. To select cases from a nominal variable, specify the categories to be included (e.g. Gender = 1). To select cases from a continuous variable, specify the range of cases to be included (e.g. Age > 40). Before running the 'Select Cases' procedure, make sure that unselected cases are filtered and not deleted.

Weight Cases

Recall that the rule for data entry states that the spreadsheet should contain one variable per column and one subject per row. This rule needs to be bent in order to analyse cross-tabulations where the data consists of cell frequencies (see Figure A2.9). When these data are entered onto a spreadsheet, we end up with one cell per row instead of one case per row. Weighting cases is a means of instructing the data editor to treat the frequency variable as a cell frequency rather than a case score. What this does is to treat the data as though there are 65 cases in the first cell, 25 in the second, 25 in the third, and 12 in the fourth. The new weighted data set has 127 cases, whereas the original cross-tabulation has only four rows of cells frequencies. If your data is in the form of a cross-tabulation, you need to weight the cases before running procedures such as chi-square analysis.

<table>
<tr><td colspan="2" rowspan="2"></td><td colspan="2">Church attendance</td></tr>
<tr><td>Yes</td><td>No</td></tr>
<tr><td rowspan="2">Age</td><td>Old</td><td>65</td><td>25</td></tr>
<tr><td>Young</td><td>25</td><td>12</td></tr>
</table>

	age	church	frequency
1	1.00	1.00	65.00
2	1.00	2.00	25.00
3	2.00	1.00	25.00
4	2.00	2.00	12.00

Figure A2.9 Weighting cases

To weight cases
1. On the 'Data' menu select the 'Weight Cases' option.
2. Weight cases by the frequency variable, and run the procedure.

Activity A2.3

Experiment with the options on the 'Data' and 'Transform' menus. Open one of the SPSS® sample data files (e.g. 1991 U.S. General Social Survey.sav) and do the following:
a) Change any continuous variable into a dichotomous variable using the 'Recode' command.
b) Compute a new variable that is the sum of any two original variables.
c) For any nominal variable (e.g. Gender), select only cases coded '1'.

Conducting statistical analyses with SPSS®

The SPSS® 'Analyze' menu offers a wide range of statistical procedures, only some of which will be covered in this book. SPSS® will run any procedure that is specified correctly. It is up to the researcher to determine which procedures are appropriate to any set of data, and to specify these procedures correctly. The discussion here aims to provide a brief overview of the statistical procedures available, and to introduce the novice to a few basic SPSS® procedures. More detailed discussion of select procedures is provided in relevant tutorials throughout the book.

Descriptive Statistics

This provides options to generate summary statistics, frequency tables, and graphical displays for continuous and categorical data. These functions are especially useful for generating univariate descriptive statistics and cross-tabulations. The following functions are offered:

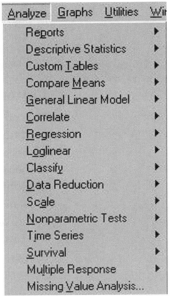

Figure A2.10 The 'Analyze' menu

- *'Frequencies'* provides descriptive statistics (e.g. measures of dispersion and central tendency) and graphical displays (e.g. bar charts, pie charts). This option is especially useful for 'getting a feel' of categorical data.
- *'Descriptives'* generates descriptive statistics (e.g. percentile values, and measures of dispersion, central tendency, and skewness). This option is also useful for 'getting a feel' of continuous data.
- *'Explore'* produces summary statistics and graphical displays (e.g. stem-and-leaf displays and histograms), either for all of your cases or separately for groups of cases. It is particularly useful for data screening, identifying outliers, and testing assumptions on the sample as a whole and on subgroups.
- *'Crosstabs'* creates two-way and multiway tables, and provides a number of tests of association for two-way tables (including chi-square tests). It is useful for conducting simple descriptive and inferential analyses of categorical data, and for generating clustered bar charts.

The procedures for running each of these four types of descriptive statistics on SPSS® are straightforward and very similar.

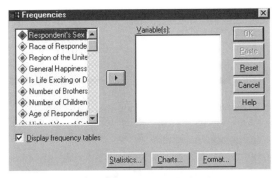

Figure A2.11 The 'Frequencies' dialog box

Running descriptive procedures

1. Select the kind of procedure you wish to run. For nominal data use 'Frequencies' or 'Crosstabs'; and use 'Descriptives' and 'Explore' for interval and ratio (i.e. scale) variables.

2. Although the dialog box for each operation differs slightly, you can specify all four procedures by the following steps:
   a) Select the variables to be described.
   b) Browse the statistics and chart options, and select the output you require (see Figure A2.11).

Custom Tables

This provides options to produce different kinds of tables, containing both frequencies and summary statistics.

- *'Basic Tables'* produces tables displaying cross-tabulations between two or more categorical variables. It is used to generate publication-quality tables of descriptive statistics (e.g. means, standard deviations) for scale variables, among subgroups that are defined in terms of one or more categorical variables.
- *'General Tables'* provides summary statistics of frequencies, counts, percentages, etc. in the cells defined by one or more categorical variables.
- *'Multiple Response Tables'* produces basic univariate and multi variate frequency tables and cross-tabulations, similar to 'Basic Tables', but in which one or more of the variables is a repeated measure. It is useful for generating descriptive data for repeated measures data.
- *'Tables of Frequencies'* produces multiway tables of frequencies and/or percentages.

Producing custom tables

1. Select the kind of procedure you wish to run. For nominal data use 'General Tables' or 'Tables of Frequencies'; for scale variable summary statistics in subgroups use 'Basic Tables; and for repeated measures data use 'Multiple Response Tables'.
2. Although the dialog box for each operation differs slightly, you can specify all four procedures by the following steps:
   a) Specify the variables to be described, arranging them in table rows and columns.
   b) Browse the 'Statistics' options, and select the output you require (see Figure A2.12).

Activity A2.4

Open one of the SPSS® sample data files (e.g. 1991 U.S. General Social Survey.sav) and do the following:
a) Conduct descriptive analyses of any two nominal and any two scale variables.
b) Cross-tabulate two categorical variables.
c) Produce a table of summary statistics for one scale variable by all categories of a second categorical variable.
d) For any nominal variable (e.g. Gender), select only cases coded 1
e) Produce a summary table of frequencies for the intersection of two categorical variables (only for Gender = 1).

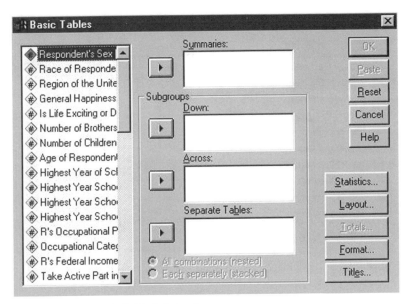

Figure A2.12 'Basic Tables' dialog box

Compare means

This offers procedures to compute inferential statistics for the difference between means. Each procedure also allows you to specify options to generate descriptive statistics, contrasts, and charts.

- *'Means'* calculates subgroup means and other univariate statistics for dependent variables within categories of one or more independent variables. It also allows you to compute one-way ANOVA, eta-square, and tests for linearity.
- *'One-Sample T Test'* tests whether the mean of a single variable differs from a specified value.
- *'Independent-Samples T Test'* tests for differences between the means for two independent groups of cases.
- *'Paired-Samples T Test'* computes a within-subjects or repeated measures *t*-test, by comparing the means of two variables (e.g. pre-test and post-test scores) for a single group.
- *'One-Way ANOVA'* computes one-way analysis of variance as well as post hoc tests, mean plots, and homogeneity of variance tests.

Comparing means
1. On the 'Analyze' menu, select the kind of procedure you want to run.
2. The dialog boxes for all the **compare means** options are similar to the box for the **independent samples t-test** (see Figure A2.13).
   a) Specify the DV (test variable) and the IV (grouping variable).
   b) Use the 'Define groups' key to specify the levels (i.e. the indicator values for each group) of the IV.
   c) Click 'ok' to run the procedure.

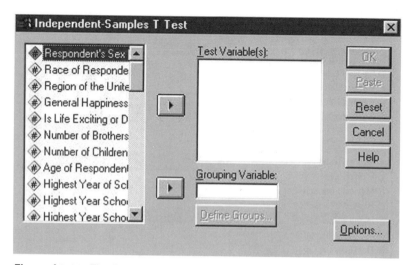

Figure A2.13 The 'Independent-Samples T Test' dialog box

General Linear Model (GLM)

This option on the 'Analyze' menu offers procedures for computing one-way, factorial, and repeated measures ANOVA. GLM output includes both regression analysis and analysis of variance output, and you can specify options to generate descriptive statistics, contrasts, and charts.

Detailed instructions for running GLM procedures are provided in Tutorials 15 and 16.

- '*Univariate*' tests the effects of IVs on the means of various groupings of a single dependent variable. It is used to analyse one-way and factorial designs (independent samples).
- '*Repeated Measures*' tests the effects of multiple independent variables on related measures. It is used when the DV comprise multiple scores by each subject on the same measure.

Correlate

This analysis option offers three different ways of computing the strength and direction of association between variables. Only the 'Bivariate Correlations' option is relevant to this course. 'Bivariate Correlations' allows you to compute correlation matrices for a list of variables.

Correlating variables

1. Select the 'Bivariate Correlations' option.
2. In the dialog box (Figure A2.14), select the variables you wish to correlate, indicate the kind of correlation coefficient you require, decide whether you require one- or two-tailed tests, and run the procedure by clicking 'OK'.

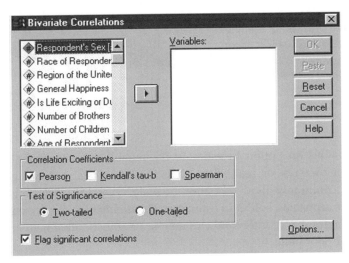

Figure A2.14 The 'Bivariate Correlations' dialog box

Regression

This offers a number of options to investigate linear and non-linear relations between variables. It is used to construct predictive models of a criterion (DV) from combinations of predictor variables (IVs). Only the 'Linear Regression' option is relevant to this course. It provides estimates of the coefficients of the linear equation (of IVs) that best predicts the DV.

Regressing variables
1. Select the 'Linear Regression' option, and complete the dialog box (Figure A2.15) as follows:
2. a) Select the dependent variable you want to predict.
   b) Select independent variables.
   c) If you have more than one IV, indicate the method by which the IVs will be entered into the regression model (e.g. stepwise, forward).
   d) Specify additional statistics and plots.
   e) Run the procedure by clicking 'OK'.

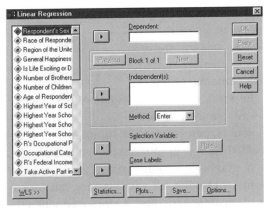

Figure A2.15 Linear regression dialog box

Open one of the SPSS® sample data files (e.g. 1991 U.S. General Social Survey.sav) and do the following:
a) Correlate a set of five continuous variables.
b) Correlate a set of ordinal variables.
c) Correlate a set of dichotomous variables.

Scale

SPSS® provides an option to estimate the reliability of items that make up a measure or scale. The 'Reliability Analysis' procedure calculates commonly used measures of scale reliability, including Cronbach's alpha and split-half estimates. The dialog box allows you to specify a number of inter-item and item-scale statistics that help in identifying poor items.

Non-parametric tests

This is used for calculating non-parametric tests of measures of association (goodness-of-fit tests) and differences (rank tests) between two or more groups. Options include the chi-square test, the Mann-Whitney test, Kruskal-Wallis test, the Wilcoxon signed rank test, and the Friedman test.

Generating graphical displays with SPSS®

If a graph does not turn out as you expected, try re-specifying it.

The SPSS® 'Graphs' menu provides a number of options to produce publication quality graphs. These options generate charts that illustrate patterns and associations for all kinds of data. The 'Gallery' option contains thumbnail images of each of the charts, and you can select a graphical procedure from there. The 'Interactive' option opens interactive dialog boxes that can help guide you through the chart construction. Once a graph option has been selected, a series of dialog boxes will open to guide you. You are strongly advised to use the help menus to find examples that illustrate the different options.

Figure A2.15 Graphs

• *Bar* creates simple, clustered, or stacked bar charts to represent summaries for groups of cases (e.g. counts, percentages) or summaries of separate variables (e.g. means). Simple graphs are univariate, whereas clustered and stacked graphs are multivariate. 'Summaries of groups of cases' is employed when all variables are categorical, whereas 'Summaries of separate variables' is employed when the bars represent properties of a distribution of an ordinal or scale variable.

- *Line* creates single or multiple line charts, to represent summaries for groups of cases or summaries of separate variables.
- *Boxplot* creates simple and clustered boxplots to represent the distributions of scores.
- *Scatter* creates two- and three-dimensional scatterplots representing the association between variables (for one or more groups of cases).
- *Histogram* creates a histogram showing the frequency distribution of a single numeric variable.

Creating charts

The dialog boxes for the different graphs are very similar to each other, and all are very helpful. The 'Bar chart' option is used to illustrate how you go about setting up a chart.

1. Select the kind of chart required (i.e. 'Bar').
2. Complete the first dialog box (Figure A2.16).
   a) Select the 'Simple' option for univariate charts, and select 'Clustered' or 'Stacked' for multivariate charts.
   b) If the data in charts are descriptive statistics of a scale or ordinal variable, select 'Summaries of separate variables'; if the data in the charts are the summary statistic of a categorical variable (e.g. frequency, percentage) then select 'Summaries for groups of cases'.
   c) Click 'Define'.
3. Complete the second dialog box. Figure A2.17 provides a dialog box for a clustered bar chart.
   a) Select a variable to be represented in the category axis (i.e. *x*-axis) and define the clusters by means of a second categorical variable.
   b) Select the option that you want the bars to represent.
4. Select 'Titles' and 'Options' as desired, and click 'OK' to run the procedure.

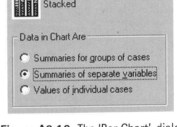

Figure A2.16 The 'Bar Chart'-dialog

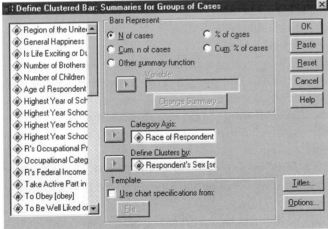

Figure A2.17 The 'Clustered Bar' chart dialog box

Open one of the SPSS® sample data files (e.g. 1991 U.S. General Social Survey.sav) and do the following:

a) Using variables of your choice, create a clustered bar chart to summarise groups of cases.

b) Using variables of your choice, create a clustered line chart to summarise separate variables.

c) Construct a histogram and a boxplot for any two scale variables.

d) Construct a scatterplot to illustrate an association between variables.

e) Correlate these two variables.

e) Save the output.

Working with SPSS® output

Print SPSS® output either by clicking the print icon on the toolbar of the 'Output Viewer' window, or by selecting the 'Print' command on the 'File' menu of the 'Output Viewer' window.

Once you have run an SPSS® procedure, the output is saved automatically into an 'Output Viewer' window (see Figure A2.2). On the left is the output history window; on the right is the actual output. You can either edit the output in SPSS® to tailor tables and graphs to specific publishing requirements, or you can save the output in different formats, to be edited later in other Windows applications.

The SPSS® output window is comprised of 'objects' that are saved in SPSS® format. There are two kinds of objects – tables and charts. These objects have different virtual structure and are edited and saved in different ways.

Editing output

1. *Selecting bits of output to edit.* To edit, cut, copy, delete or save output, the output must first be selected. To select a piece of output, click on the output you want to select in the 'Output History' window. The selected output will appear in the right-hand output window. It is also possible to select a piece of output by scrolling down the output window and then clicking on the graph or table you want to select.

2. *Editing tables.* Once you have selected a table, double click on the table in the right-hand output window. You will now be able to edit the table. Left click on the table, and a menu of editing options will appear. The following options are particularly helpful:
   - *'Toolbar'* enables you to edit the font, justification, and table content.
   - *'Pivoting Trays'* enables you to change the format of tables (e.g. making rows columns and vice versa) simply by dragging icons.

3. *Editing graphs.* Once you have selected an SPSS® chart, double click on the chart in the right-hand output window. This will automatically open an 'SPSS® Chart Editor' window (see Figure A2.18).

The 'Chart' menu gives you a wide range of editing options. You can also edit particular parts of the chart (e.g. the legend, title) by double clicking on these in the chart window. Once you have completed editing your chart, close the 'Chart Editor' window.

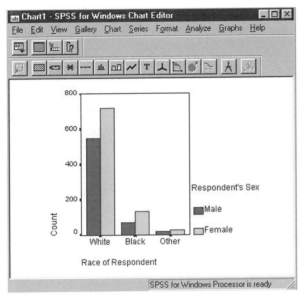

Figure A2.18 The 'Chart Editor' window

Saving output

1. *Saving the output file*
   - *SPSS® format.* To save your output as an SPSS® viewer (.spo) file, open the 'File' menu on the SPSS® 'Output' window and select 'Save' or 'Save As'. You will be able to open this file again in SPSS® for further editing, but you will not be able to open the file in another program.
   - *Exporting a file.* To save your output in an external format, open the 'File' menu on the SPSS® 'Output' window and select 'Export'. An 'Export' window will open that allows you to save your output in various ways (Figure A2.19). Charts are saved as images in JPEG or other graphic formats. Tables are saved as text files. It is also possible to save both tables and charts in HTML format. You can choose to save either the whole file or selected objects in the 'Output Viewer' window. Once you have selected what you want to export, named the export file and specified the export format, click 'OK' and the file will be saved in an external format. HTML files can be viewed in a web browser, text files can be viewed in a word processor, and graphic files can be viewed in a graphics editor such as Paint.

To open Paint (if you have it installed on your computer), select the 'Programs' option on your start bar (to open the start bar, click 'Start' on the bottom left-hand corner), select 'Accessories', and then select 'Paint'.

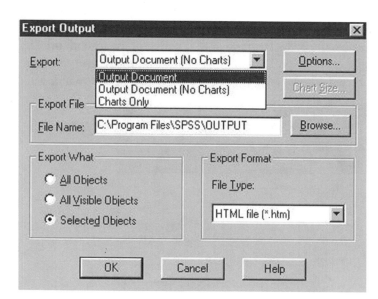

Figure A2.19 The 'Export Output' dialog box

2. *Saving objects.* In addition to saving whole files and parts of files, there are a number of different ways of saving selected tables and charts.
   - *Selecting (edited) output objects.* Find the item to be saved by scrolling down either the 'Output History' or 'Output' windows. Select an object by clicking on it in either window.
   - *Using the 'Export Output' dialog box.* Once the object is selected, follow the steps for 'Exporting a file' (see above). In the dialog box make sure that the 'Selected Objects' option is selected, and that you have indicated whether you are saving a table or a chart. The exported object will be saved as an external file.
   - *Copying and pasting objects.* It is cumbersome to save each selected object in a unique file. It is far more efficient to copy an object and then simply paste it into a word processor. In this way you will be able to transfer select tables and charts into your final written report. There are two ways of copying objects. The best way is to select the object, then left-click on the object. On the pop-up menu, select the 'Copy Object' option. Once the object has been copied into memory, open your word processor, and paste the object. Both tables and graphs can be copied in this way. The other way of copying and pasting is to use keyboard shortcuts. Select the output, copy it with the Crtl-C shortcut, open the word processor and paste the object with the Ctrl-V shortcut. It is often a good idea to save text and tables in a non-scalable font such as Courier (9pt) to keep the formatting.

Always write up the results of your analysis in a professional manner. Construct a report by copying tables and charts from SPSS® output into a word processor, and then adding your written analysis.

NUMBERS, HYPOTHESES AND CONCLUSIONS

Activity A2.7

Open the SPSS® output file that you saved in Activity A2.6. Do the following:
a) Select the bar chart; open the chart editor; change the title, the 'Legend' and the 'Axis' title, and add a footnote.
b) Select the correlation matrix, and edit the table by making the column headings bold.
c) Copy the edited bar chart and table into a word processor, and save the file.
d) Export the entire file as an HTML file and open it in your web browser.

Summary

1. SPSS® is a powerful statistical processing package for social scientists. It can be used to transform and manipulate data, to do statistical analysis, and to produce graphs.

2. The SPSS® environment is comprised of three windows: the 'Data Editor' window, the 'Output Viewer' window, and the 'Syntax Editor' window. You should know how to open, save, and export these windows, to navigate about them, and to use the available functions of each window.

3. Transform and manipulate data in the SPSS® 'Data Editor' by using options on the 'Data' and 'Transform' menus. These options allow you to order your dataset by defining variables and value labels, and to do preliminary operations on your data, such as reverse scoring and creating summed scale scores.

4. Generate statistical analysis by using the procedures on the 'Analyze' menu. It is important that you apply the correct procedure to the data at hand, and that you specify the operation correctly.

5. Produce SPSS® charts by selecting from the options on the 'Graphs' menu. Make sure that you select the correct graph to illustrate the data you have, and then play around with different options until you are satisfied that you have the best graph.

6. Produce professional reports by copying select SPSS® output objects into a word processor and then adding your written analysis.

Exercises

1. a) Create a new data file called Orgstress. (Use the 'New' option on the 'File' menu.)
   b) Enter the following data in the spreadsheet editor:

Subject	Sex	Age	Stress1	Stress2
Sizwe	Male	45	13	18
Susan	Female	30	22	21
Achmat	Male	34	23	19
Megan	Female	46	9	7
Liziwe	Female	32	26	20
Bulelwa	Female	21	14	5
Johan	Male	59	13	29
Charl	Male	24	11	7

   c) Now change the 'Stress1' value for Susan to 8.
   d) Use the mouse and navigation keys to familiarise yourself with moving around the SPSS® spreadsheet window.
   e) Insert a new variable. *(On the 'Data' menu, select 'Insert variable'.)*
   f) Make the new variable equal to the sum of 'Stress1' and 'Stress2'.
   g) Create a new variable which is the product of 'Age' and 'Stress1'.
   h) Select only the male subjects, and compute their mean age.

2. a) Export the SPSS® data file Orgstress (created above) to an Excel file format.
   b) Import the Excel file you have just saved, making sure to import the first row as variable names.
   c) Check whether each variable is a string or numeric variable.
   d) Change all variables, excluding 'Subject', into numeric variables.
   e) Give all variables a variable label, and give all categorical variables value labels.

3. a) Open the file Orgstress.
   b) Produce a frequency distribution for the variable 'Age'.
   c) Edit the frequency table as follows:
      i) Make the row and column headings bold.
      ii) Give the table a new title.
   d) Produce a histogram for the variable 'Age'.

e) Edit the graph as follows:
   i)   Increase the font size of the title.
   ii) Change the spacing between the bars.
   iii) Give the graph an outer frame.
   iv) Change the legend font. (Play around and experiment with different options on the 'Chart Editor' dialog box.)
f) Copy the frequency table and the histogram as objects and insert them into a word processor.
g) Save the SPSS® output file as Orgstress.spo and exit SPSS®.
h) Re-start SPSS® and call up the file Orgstress.spo.

4. a) Open the file Orgstress.sav. Make sure that a word processor is running in the background.
   b) Produce boxplots for 'Age', 'Stress1', and 'Stress2'.
   c) Produce clustered bar charts of mean scores on 'Stress1' and 'Stress2' for males and females.
   d) Produce a table of summary statistics for male and female scores on 'Age', 'Stress1', and 'Stress2'.
   e) Edit all tables and graphs by giving them suitable titles.
   f) Export the file by saving it in HTML format. Open the file in a web browser.

5. a) Open the file Orgstress.sav.
   b) Correlate 'Stress1', 'Stress2', and 'Age'.
   c) Conduct t-tests to determine whether males and females score differently on 'Stress1', 'Stress2', and 'Age'.
   d) Produce a professional report of the analysis by saving each of the tables produced in (b) and (c) into a word processor, and writing up commentary on the procedure and outcome of each analysis.

References

Abelson, R. P. (1995). *Statistics as Principled Argument*. Hillsdale: Lawrence Erlbaum.

Adorno, T. Frenkel-Brunswick, E., Levinson, D.J. & Sanford, R. (1950). *The Authoritarian Personality*. New York: Harper.

Bakan, D. (1966). The test of significance in psychological research. *Psychological Bulletin, 66*, 423–37.

Baron, L. & Strauss, M. A. (1989). *Four Theories of Rape in American Society: A State-level Analysis*. New Haven: Yale University Press.

Bennett, D. (1998). *Randomness*. Cambridge, Mass.: Harvard University Press.

Berk, K. N. & Carey, P. (1998). *Data Analysis with Microsoft Excel*. Duxbury Press.

Blakley, B. A., Quinones, M. A., Crawford, M. S. & Jago, I. A. (1994). The validity of isometric strength tests. *Personnel Psychology, 47*, 247–74.

Burger, J. M. (1981). Motivational biases in the attribution of responsibility for an accident: A meta-analysis of the defensive attribution hypothesis. *Psychological Bulletin, 90*, 496–512.

Butterworth, B. (1999). *How Every Brain is Hard-wired for Math*. New York: Free Press.

Campbell, D. T. (1988). *Methodology and Epistemology for Social Science: Selected Papers*. Chicago: University of Chicago Press.

Carolissen, R., Jacobs, E. & van der Riet, J. (2001). *Report on pilot violence prevention project*, July 1999-2000. Unpublished report prepared by the Community Psychological Empowerment Project. Cape Town.

Christiaansen, R. E. & Ochalek, K. (1983). Editing misleading information from memory: Evidence for the coexistence of original and postevent information. *Memory and Cognition, 11*, 467–75.

Cliff, N. (1996). *Ordinal Methods for Behavioral Data Analysis*. Mahwah: Lawrence Erlbaum.

Cohen, J. & Cohen, P. (1975). *Applied Multiple Regression/Correlation analysis for the Behavioral Sciences*. Hillsdale: Lawrence Erlbaum.

Cohen, J. (1962). The statistical power of abnormal-social psychological research: A review. *Journal of Abnormal and Social Psychology, 65*, 145–53.

Cohen, J. (1988). *Statistical Power Analyses for the Behavioral Sciences* (2nd edn). New York: Academic Press.

Danziger, K. (2000). Making social psychology experimental. *Journal of the History of the Behavioral Sciences, 36*, 329–47.

Darley, J. M. & Latane, B. (1968). When will people help in a crisis? *Psychology Today, 2* (7), 54–7, 70–1.

Darlington, R. B., Royce, J. M., Snipper, A. S., Murray, H. W. & Lazar, I. (1980). Preschool programs and later school competence of children from low-income families. *Science, 208*, 202–4.

Doob, A. N. & Kirshenbaum, H. M. (1973). Bias in police lineups – partial remembering. *Journal of Police Science and Administration, 1*, 287–93.

Draper, N. & Smith, H. (1981). *Applied Regression Analysis*. New York: John Wiley.

Duckitt, J. (1988). The prediction of violence. *South African Journal of Psychology, 18*(1), 10–16.

Duckitt, J. (1991). Prejudice and racism. In D. Foster & J. Louw-Potgieter (eds). *Social Psychology in South Africa*, Johannesburg: Lexicon.

Ekman, P., Levenson, R. W. & Friesen, W. V. (1983). Autonomic nervous system activity distinguishes among emotions. *Science, 221*, 1208–10.

Ellis, N. C., & Hennelly, R. A. (1980). A bilingual word-length effect: Implications for intelligence testing and the relative ease of mental calculation in Welsh and English. *British Journal of Psychology, 71*, 43–51.

Everitt, B. S. (1992). *The analysis of Contingency Tables* (2nd edn). London: Chapman & Hall.

Eysenck, H. (1984). Meta-analysis: An abuse of research integration. *Journal of Special Education, 18*, 41–59.

Fisher, R. A. (1937). *The Design of Experiments.* Edinburgh: Oliver & Boyd.

Garcia, J. (1981). Tilting at the paper mills of academe. *American Psychologist, 36*, 149–58.

Gardner, M. (1978). *Aha: Insight.* New York: Scientific American Books.

Gelman, T., Swartz, L., Tredoux, C. & Strauss, R. (2001). Minor psychiatric morbidity in students attending a South African University Health Service. *Journal of Clinical Psychology in Medical Settings, 8*, 131–6.

Glass, G. (1976). Primary, secondary and meta-analysis of research. *Education Researcher, 5*, 3–8.

Glass, G. V., McGaw, B. & Smith, M. (1981). *Meta-analysis in Social Research.* Beverley Hills: Sage.

Gonzalez, R. (1994). The statistics ritual in psychological research. *Psychological Science, 5*, 321–8.

Goodman, L. A. & Kruskal, W. H. (1954). Measures of association for cross-classifications. *Journal of the American Statistical Association, 49*, 732–64.

Haberman, S. J. (1973). The analysis of residuals in cross-classified tables. *Biometrica, 25*, 489–504.

Hacking, I. (1981). *Scientific Revolutions.* Oxford: Oxford University Press.

Hays, W. L. (1994). *Statistics* (5th edn). New York: Harcourt Brace.

Herman, E. S. & Chomsky, N. (1988). *Manufacturing Consent.* New York: Pantheon Books.

Hoosain, R. (1997). Language and thought. In H. S. R. Kao & D. Sinha (eds), *Asian Perspectives on Psychology.* New Delhi: Sage.

Hornstein, G. (1988). Quantifying psychological phenomena: Debates, dilemmas, and implications. In J. G. Morawski (ed.), *The rise of Experimentation in American Psychology.* New Haven: Yale University Press.

Howell, D. (1997). *Statistical Methods for Psychology* (4th edn). Belmont: Duxbury Press.

Hunter, J. E. & Schmidt, F. L. (1990). *Methods of Meta-analysis: Correcting Error and Bias in Research Findings.* Newbury Park: Sage.

Hunter, J. E., Schmidt, F. L. & Jackson, G. B. (1982). *Meta-analysis: Cumulating Research Findings across Studies.* Beverley Hills: Sage.

Kaniki, A. (1999). Doing an information search. In M. Terre Blanche & K. Durrheim (eds), *Research in Practice: Applied Methods for the Social Sciences.* Cape Town: UCT Press.

Kraemer, H. C. & Thiemann, S. (1987). *How Many Subjects? Statistical Power Analysis in Research.* Newbury Park: Sage.

Kuhn, L., Coutsoudis, A., Meddows-Taylor, S., Mngqundaniso, N., Trabattoni, D., Clerici, M., Shearer, G., Tiemessen, C. & Gray, G. (2000). *HIV-specific T-helper cell responses in infants of HIV-infected mothers exposed or not to anti-retroviral treatment.* Paper presented at XIII International AIDS Conference, Durban, July.

Kuhn, T.S. (1962). *The Structure of Scientific Revolutions.* Chicago: Chicago University Press.

Loftus, E. F. (1974). Reconstructing memory: The incredible eyewitness. *Psychology Today*, August, 116–19.

Loftus, E. F. (1975). Leading questions and the eyewitness report. *Cognitive Psychology, 7*, 585–9.

Loftus, E. F. (1983). Misfortunes of memory. *Philosophical Transactions of the Royal Society of London, B, 302*, 413–21.

Mangxolo, M. (2000). Military deployment and stress: An empirical survey in the SANDF's operational military personnel of the Western Cape. Unpublished masters thesis, University of Cape Town.

McCloskey, M., & Zaragoza, M. (1985). Misleading post-event information and memory for events: Arguments and evidence against memory impairment hypotheses. *Journal of Experimental Psychology: General, 114*, 1–16.

Neuman, W. L. (1997). *Social Research Methods: Qualitative and Quantitative*

Approaches (3rd edn). Boston: Allyn and Bacon.

Orpen, C. (1973). Sociocultural and personality factors in personality: The case of white South Africa. *South African Journal of Psychology, 3,* 91–6.

Orpen, C. (1975). Authoritarianism revisited: A critical examination of 'expressive' theories of prejudice. In S. Morse & C. Orpen (eds), *Contemporary South Africa: Social Psychological Perspectives.* Cape Town: Juta.

Pedhazur, E. J. (1982). *Multiple regression in Behavioral Research* (2nd edn). New York: Holt, Rinehart, & Winston.

Piele, D. (1990). *Introductory Statistics with Spreadsheets.* Addison-Wesley.

Popper, K. R. (1959). *The Logic of Scientific Discovery.* London: Hutchinson.

Rosenthal, R. (1984). *Meta-analytic Methods for Social Research.* Beverly Hills: Sage.

Rosenthal, R. & Rosnow, R. L. (1985). *Contrast Analysis: Focused Comparisons in the Analysis of Variance.* New York: Cambridge University Press.

Rosenthal, R. & Rosnow, R. L. (1991). *Essentials of Behavioral Research: Methods and Data Analysis.* New York: McGraw-Hill.

Schuckit, M. A. (1985). Ethanol-induced changes in body sway in men at high alcoholism risk. *Archives of General Psychiatry, 42,* 375–9.

Sheehahn, P. W. & Tilden, J. (1984). Real and simulated occurences of memory distortion in hypnosis. *Journal of Abnormal Psychology, 93,* 47–57.

Siegel, S. & Castellan, N. J. (1988). *Nonparametric statistics for the Behavioral Sciences* (2nd edn). New York: McGraw-Hill.

Smith, M. & Glass, G. (1977). Meta-analysis of psychotherapy outcome studies. *American Psychologist, 32,* 752–60.

Sprent, P. (1981). *Quick Statistics: An Introduction to Non-parametric Methods.* Harmondsworth: Penguin.

Sprent, P. (1989). *Applied Nonparametric Statistical Methods* (2nd edn). London: Chapman-Hall.

Sprinthall, R. C. (1987). *Basic statistical analysis* (2nd edn). Reading, Mass: Addison-Wesley.

Stephan, W. G., & Rosenfield, D. (1978). The effects of desegregation on race relations and self-esteem. *Journal of Educational Psychology, 70,* 670–9.

Stewart, I. (1998). Repealing the law of averages. *Scientific American, 278,* 87–8.

Sturges, H. (1926). The choice of a class-interval. *Journal of the American Statistical Association, 21,* 65–6.

Tabachnick, B. G. & Fidell, L. S. (1989). *Using Multivariate Statistics.* New York: Harper & Row.

Taylor, J. G. (1958). Experimental design: A cloak for intellectual sterility. *British Journal of Psychology, 49,* 106–16.

Thorndike, E. & Lorge, I. (1944). *The Teacher's Word Book of 30,000 Words.* New York: Columbia University Teacher's College Press.

Tredoux, C. G. (1998). Statistical interference on measures of lineup fairness. *Law and Human Behaviour, 22,* 217–37.

Tredoux, C. G. (1989). *Post-event Information and the Impairment of Eyewitness Memory: A Methodological Examination.* Unpublished masters thesis, University of Cape Town.

Tukey, J. W. (1977). *Exploratory Data Analysis.* Reading, Mass.: Addison-Wesley.

Tyson, G. & Turnbull, O. (1990). Ambient temperature and the occurrence of collective violence: A South African replication. *South African Journal of Psychology, 20,* 159–62.

Wickens, T. D. (1989). *Multiway Contingency Table Analysis for the Social Sciences.* Hillsdale: Lawrence Erlbaum.

Winer, B. J. (1971). *Statistical Principles in Experimental Design.* New York: McGraw-Hill.

Index

Entries in **bold type** refer to margin text and definitions. Entries in *italics* refer to illustrative material.

box-and-whisker plot 62–64
boxplot 62–64, *63*, *282*, *296*, *297*
    drawing **64**; interpretation **64**
brash approach to statistical analysis
    432–433

C
calculation formulas, choosing between
    436
calculator, using 42, 49, 58–60
cardinal numbers 196, *196*, *197*
casewise deletion 153
cause and effect 190
cell mean plots 301, *305*, 327, **327**
Central Limit Theorem 9, 113–114, **113**,
    115, 117, 118, 127, 142–143, 145, 258
central tendency 40–51, 52, 65
chance, games of, probability and 72–74
chart, bar 21–22, **21**, 27
chi-square test 364–384
class interval 23, 24, **23**, *23*–*24*, 47
    midpoint 27
classical measurement theory 211
classifications 365
    additional 365; dichotomous 365;
    exhaustive 365, **365**; multiple 365;
    mutually exclusive 365, **365**
coding
    responses 208; the set of studies
    408–409
coefficient
    alpha 213–214; of correlation, rank
    186, **186**; of determination 191; mean
    square contingency 371; multiple
    correlation 346–347; Pearson's
    correlation 183, **183**; product-moment
    correlation 183–185, **183**; of rank
    correlation, Spearman's 186, **186**;
    slope **167**; of variation **61**, *61*
coefficients 462, 463
    regression 163, 342–348; regression,
    calculating 164–167; standardised
    regression 346
Cohen's conventions 239–240
common
    denominator 451, **451**; factor 451, **451**;
    statistics **409**
comparison, planned 432
comparisons
    multiple 274–276; pairwise 324
complex null hypotheses 324

compound symmetry 329, 331, **331**
concurrent validity 217, **217**
confidence
    intervals 120–122, **120**, *121*, 238, **238**;
    limits 120–122, **120**
conjunctions, probability law of **75**
consistency, internal 213–214
constants 9–13, **10**, 462, **462**
construct
    measuring 201–202, validity 218
constructing norms 222
content validity 217
contingency
    coefficient, mean square 371; tables
    365–366, **366**, *366*
continuous
    data 27; measures **10**; scales 10;
    variables 19; variables/measures 10
convergent validity 218
    criterion-groups 218; discriminant
    218
correction, Bonferroni **329**
correlation 171–172, **171**, 181–200
    cannot be directly compared 191–192;
    coefficient of 186, **186**; coefficients
    not averaged 191; and linear rela-
    tions 191; misleading 192–193;
    partial 344–346; perfect negative *172*;
    perfect non-linear *172*; perfect
    positive *172*; rank 186–187; semi-
    partial 345; sensitive to restrictions
    in range of variables 193–195;
    Spearman's coefficient of rank 186,
    186; weak negative *172*; zero *172*;
    zero-order 349–351
correlation coefficient
    Pearson's 183, **183**; product-moment
    183–185, **183**
count, frequency 455
counting numbers 445
counts 364, 366
covariance 424
Cramers' V 372
criterion 162, **162**
    variables 13
criterion-groups validity 218
critical
    effect size 238, **238**, 246; value 135,
    135
Cronbach's coefficient alpha 213, 219,
    225

crosstabulation 366, *366*
cross-validation 355, **355**
crude range 54, **54**, 65
cumulative
    frequency 25, **25**, 34; indices 26; per-
    centage frequency 25–26, **26**, 31, 34
curve
    bell-shaped 83, 143; preference
    477–478
cut-off points *121, 122*

D
D 152–153, **153**
data 28, 52
    continuous 27; deciding on test to
    apply to 435–436; design, multivariate
    317, **317**; displaying 18–39; entry
    errors **43**; getting a feel for 425–426;
    graphing 161–162; grouped 44;
    inspection of descriptive 349–351;
    matrix *424*; paired 160–162;
    properties of 436; qualitative 365;
    quantitative 365; raw 18; sample
    61–62; type of 428
data, nominal 21, **21**, 22, 47
    assumptions about 146–147; discrete
    22; interval 22; ordinal 22; ratio 22
    bimodal 46; unimodal 46
de Moivre, Abraham 83, 84
deciles 102
decimal numbers 453–455
    addition and subtraction with 453;
    multiplication and division with
    453–454
decomposition of variance 312–314
defensible reasoned argument 432–437
    rules for 434
degrees of freedom (df) 150, 153, 257,*487*
    error 274, group 274
deletion, casewise 153
delta 240, **240**
denominator 450
    common 451, **451**
dependent variables 13, **13**
depression 315, *315*, 316, *316*, 341
Descartes, René 472, 473, *473*
descriptive data, inspection of 349–351
design
    multivariate data 317, **317**; two-way
    factorial 290
designs

balanced 276, **277**; factorial 290, **290**;
fully repeated 320–325, **320**; mixed
320, **320**, **321**, 326–329; reasons for
using factorial 291–292
determination, coefficient of 191
deviation
    average 56–57, **57**, 66; calculating
    average *56*; population standard 428;
    standard 52, 60–61, **61**, 66
dichotomous classifications 365
directional alternative hypothesis 129,
    129
discontinuity 21
discrete
    data 22; distribution 83; measures **10**;
    variables 19; variables/measures 10
discriminant validity 218
discrimination, item 220
disjunctions, probability of **76**
disordinal interactions 304
displaying data 18–39
displays
    graphical 19; tabular 19
distribution
    asymmetrical *30*; bimodal 29; bino-
    mial 79–83; discrete 83; frequency
    19–20, **19**, 21, 22, 27, 28–31, 90,*101,*
    103, 111; kurtosis 29, *30*; negatively
    skewed 29; normal 83–85, *84*, 108,
    110, 113; peakedness 29, *30*; popula-
    tion *114*; positively skewed 29; sam-
    pling *111*, 112, *114*, 114–122, *116, 118,*
    119, 132, 133; sampling, of the mean
    108–126, **108**, **113**, 127; shape of 19,
    385; standard normal 90–107, *95, 96,*
    98, 99, *101, 103*, 114–122, *116,*
    485–486; standard normal, χ^2 *492*;
    symmetrical 29; unimodal 29;
distribution-free tests 283, 385–401, **387**
    advantages and disadvantages 386–387
distributions, skewed 46
    bimodal 47; unimodal 47
distributions, theoretical 70–89
division 447
    with decimals 453–454; with fractions
    452–453; with negative numbers
    449–450
divisional notation 450
domain, defining 202–203
drawing inferences **109**
dyslexic children 151

Gauss, Carl 84
generalisability theory 211
GPOWER 248, *249*
graph, bar 54
graphical displays 19
    representations 21
graphing paired data 161–162
graphs 472–484, **472**
Greenhouse Geisser 330
group degrees of freedom 274
grouped
    data 44; frequency distribution
    22–26, **22**
Guilford, informal interpretations of the
    magnitude of *r* 184

H
harmonic mean 243, **243**
heterogeneity of variance 150–151
hierarchical multiple regression 354
histogram 27–28, **27**
    class test marks *28*
homogeneity of variance, assumption of
    147–147
Honestly Significantly Difference test
    (HSD) 275, 280, 300
horizontal axis 21, 27, 474, **474**
hypothesis
    alternative 129, **129**, 130, 131,
    233, 234, 253; complex null 324;
    directional alternative 129, **129**,
    130; non-directional 129, **129**;
    null 128, **128**, 129, 130, 131, 132,
    134, 146, 231, 232, *233*, 253;
    testing 127–141, **128**; testing
    statistical 230
hypothetical population 15

I
independence, assumption of 147
independent
    event 74, **74**; samples *t*-test 149–152,
    149; variables 13, **13**
index
    item-difficulty 219, **219**; numerical
    456; variable 10, 467
indices
    of range 65; of variation 65–67
individual score 110
inferences 109
    drawing **109**

inferential
    statistics 42; test, selecting the
    appropriate 426–429
integers 445
interaction 292, 293
    plots 327, **327**
interactions
    disordinal 304; ordinal 304; types of
    304–306
intercept 163
internal consistency 213
interpolations 168, **168**
    linear 97–98
interquartile range 54, **55**, 65
interval
    class 23, 24, *23*, *23–24*; class midpoint
    27; data 22; variables 12
intervals, confidence 120–122, **120**, *121*
inverse relationship 479
investigation, empirical 128
isolating sources of association 374–376
item
    analysis 218–220; discrimination 220;
    facilitation 219–220
item-difficulty index 219, **219**

J
James, William 2–3
judges, expert 217

K
Kendall, Maurice 73
Kolmogorov, 72, 73
Kruskal-Wallis test 392–394, **393**, 429
Kuhnian perspective 402

L
least-squares line 164
level
    alpha 231, 232; significance 132, **132**,
    133, 231, 245
levels 290
Levenes' test 297, *297*
Likert scale 204–205
limit
    apparent, 24; real lower 24, **24**, 27;
    real upper 24, **24**, 27
limits
    confidence 120–122, **120**; probable, 120
line
    best fitting 162–167; least-squares
    164; regression 163, 171

representations
    graphical 21; tabular 21
research
    question, type of 428; prior 239
residual 355, 375, **375**
    adjusted 375, **375**, *376*; analysing 374;
    standardised 375, **375**, *376*
response
    scaling 203–206; variables 13
responses, coding 208
restriction of range 193–195, 406, 411
reverse scoring 208–209
revised experimental design 417
risk 64
RLL 32, 34
robust measure 185, **185**
roots 457–458
RUL 31, 32

S
sample 13–15, **14**, 224
    data, estimating population
    parameters 61–62; mean 41, *111*, 130;
    random 109, 111; size 235, 246;
    symbol for 47
sample size 235, 246
    factors that influence choice of
    245–246; unequal 153
sampling
    means 110–113; with replacement 75
sampling distribution *111*, 112, *114*,
    114–122, *116*, *118*, *119*, *132*, *133*
    of the mean 108–126, **108**, **113**, 127
sampling error 405
    correcting for 410–411
scale
    items, development of 223–224; of
    measurement 11, 425; scores,
    computing 426
scale, rating 204–205
    Likert 204–205; scores, summing
    206–210; semantic-difference 205
scales, construction of 201–229
scaling, response 203–206; alter-
    native-choice 203–204; multiple-
    choice 204
scatter 171–172
scatterplots 161, 164, 168, *172*, 182, *183*,
    193, **351**, *358*, 359
Schmidt-Hunter model of meta-analysis
    404–420, *407*

score 115
    individual 110; model 293, **293**; or
    test, evaluating 210–221
scores 18, 112
    calculating 225–226; computing scale
    426; distribution of 19; frequency of
    19; number of 20; 'raw' 22; standard
    221; summing 209–210; summing
    scale 206–210
scoring, reverse 208–209
semi-partial correlation 345
sensitivity analysis 165
sequential F-test 351–352
serial test 73
shape of the distribution 385
sign test 388–389, **388**
significance
    level 132, **132**, 133, 231, 245; testing of
    r 195–196; two-tailed *493*
simple
    effect analysis 301; effects 302, **302**,
    304, 324
skewed distributions 46
skewness of frequency distribution 28,
    29
slope 163
    coefficient **167**; linear **478**; negative
    478, 479, *479*; non-linear **478**, 479, *479*;
    positive **478**, 479, *479*
Spearman, Charles 186
Spearman's coefficient of rank correla-
    tion 186, **186**, 191
split-half reliability 213
spreadsheet 49–50, 85, 104–105, 119,
    155–157, 188–189
    electronic 81; regression analysis
    with 175–178
SPSS 156–157, 177–178, 188–189,
    214–215, 248, 430, *431*, 496–519
    ANOVA table produced by *319*;
    compute 503–504; correlate 510;
    custom tables 508–509; data, import-
    ing 502; data, saving 502–503; data,
    transforming 503–506; Data Editor
    500–502; Data Editor Window
    497–498; data file, setting up 500–503;
    descriptive statistics 507–508; factorial
    ANOVA, running 294–296; General
    Linear Model 510; graphical displays
    512–514; means, comparing 509; non-
    parametric tests 512; one-way

ANOVA, doing 276–281; one-way repeated measures ANOVA with 317–320; output, editing 514–515; output, saving 515–517; output, working with 514–517; Output Viewer window 498; recode 504–505; regression 511; simple effects, computing with 303; scale 512; select cases 505; statistical analyses 506–512; two-way ANOVA, computing 308; Syntax Editor window 499; weight cases 506; χ² test and 377–380, *378, 379, 380*

squares
     mean 257; sums of 257
standard
     deviation 52, 60–61, **61**, 66; deviation, population 428; error 117–120, **117**, 143, 145, **145**; error of estimate 168–170, **169**, 346–347, **347**; normal distribution 90–107, **92**, *92, 95, 96,* 98, 99, *101, 103,* 114–122, *116, 485–486*; scores 221
standardisation and norms 221–226
standardised
     regression coefficients 346; residuals 375, **375**, *376*
stanines 221, 222
statistic
     mean, calculating 410; transforming to a common 409
statistical
     analysis, approaches to 432–433; decisions, defending 429–432; decisions, rules for making 425–429; hypothesis testing 230; interference **14**; power 230–251; reasoning 423–441; tests, error and 231–239; world 98–103
statistics 13–15
     common **409**; inferential 42
stepwise
     algorithms **349**; multiple regression 352–353; regression 349
studies, coding 408–409
stuffy approach to statistical analysis 432–433
substitution 461–471
subtraction 446
     with decimals 453; with fractions 451–452; with negative numbers 449

success 73
     probability of 75
summary 19
summation 461–471
     operators 466
summing
     scale scores 206–210; scores 209–210
sums of squares (SS) 257
symmetrical
     bimodal distribution 29, *29*; unimodal distribution 29, *29*
symmetry, compound 329, 331, **331**
systematic variance 257, **258**, 259, **259**

T
T scores 221
t-table *487*
t-test 10, 142–159, **143**, 253, 255, 256, 257, 311
     common concepts 144–147; equation 144–145; independent samples 149–152, **149**; interpreting a significant result 145–146; one-sample 147–149; power calculations for the matched sample 244–245; power calculations for one-sample 240–241; power calculations for two-sample 241–243, 243–244; repeated measures 152–155, **152**; subtypes 147–155; using spreadsheets 155–157
t, transforming *r* to 195–196
table
     frequency distribution 22, 27; nominal data 27
tables
     contingency 365–366, *366*; two-dimensional 366
tabular displays 19
     representations 21
tendency, central 40–51, 52, 65
test
     evaluating a score or 210–221; Friedman's rank 394–396, **394**; Honestly Significantly Difference (HSD) 275; Kruskal-Wallis 392–394, **393**; lopsided 434–435; Mann-Whitney U- 391–392, **391**; one-tailed *132, 133,* 434–435; selecting the appropriate inferential 426–419, *427*; sign 388–389, **388**; two-tailed 133, *133,*

X

x-axis 21, 92, 474, **474**, 475
x-scores 92, 110
  converting to z-scores 100–102;
  converting z-scores to 102–103
x-values 92, 115, 116

Y

y-axis 21, 22, **474**

Z

z calculations, using spreadsheets 104–105
z formula **100**, 115, 122

z-scores 92, 93, **93**, *93*, 95, 96, 97, 100,
  101, 110, 115, 116, 118, 121, 236
  converting x-scores to 100–102;
  converting to x-scores 102–103;
  and t-test transformation 144; using
  tables of 93–98
z-tables 93, *93*, 94, *94*, 95, *96*, 110, 121
z-test 127–141, **131**, 147, 148, 257
z-values 92
zero
  correlation *172*; value, true 12
zero-order correlations 349–351